NECROLOGY

OF

ALUMNI OF HARVARD COLLEGE,

1851–52 TO 1862–63.

By JOSEPH PALMER,

Of the Class of 1820.

BOSTON:
PRINTED BY JOHN WILSON AND SON,
15, Water Street.
1864.

NOTE BY THE COMMITTEE OF PUBLICATION.

The advantage of having in a compact and accessible form the obituary notices contained in this volume is so obvious, that no apology for their republication is needed. It has been often suggested, but was brought about directly by a communication from a member of the class of 1811, written in Europe, to a friend in Boston, a little more than a year ago, urging that it should be undertaken at once, sketching a plan of operations, and promising a handsome subscription. This communication resulted in a meeting of friends of the undertaking, and in the choice of a committee of publication, who issued the following circular, drawn up, at their request, by Hon. Edward Everett: —

TO THE ALUMNI OF HARVARD COLLEGE.

It is well known to the Alumni that an annual necrology of those who have died in the course of the year has, for the last thirteen years, regularly appeared in the *Boston Daily Advertiser* on the morning of Commencement-Day. This necrology has, from the first, been prepared by Dr. Joseph Palmer of the class of 1820. Originally consisting of a very brief notice, it has gradually swelled to ample dimensions, embracing all the known facts of any public interest in the life and career of the individuals commemorated. This work has been executed by Dr. Palmer with great diligence, fidelity, and good judgment. From his connection with a daily newspaper, he has derived early notice of the deaths as they have occurred; and he has then resorted to the most authentic sources, and especially to the class-books, since those records began to be kept, for all further accessible information. It may be said without exaggeration, so successfully has Dr. Palmer's work been performed, that no paper in the course of the year is read with greater interest, by every graduate of Harvard, than the *Boston Daily Advertiser* which appears on Commencement-Day. Nor is the interest of these articles likely to be confined to the present time. As they will unquestionably be the means of preserving from oblivion many facts which would otherwise perish, they will, for the classes to which they pertain, form the basis of any future *Athenæ Cantabrigienses.* The favor with which Dr. Palmer's necrologies have been received is not confined to the alumni of Harvard. They are scarcely less valuable to all who study American biography, and have served as a model for similar necrologies in the other New-England colleges.

These articles, including that of the present year, fill above one hundred columns of the *Daily Advertiser*, and would make an octavo volume of about four hundred pages. They are far too valuable not to be collected in a permanent form, and it is manifestly a question of time alone when that shall be done.

Thus far the preparation of them has been, on the part of Dr. Palmer, purely a labor of love. It has involved the employment of much time; the consultation of many journals, tracts, and larger volumes; continual reference to surviving friends; and a voluminous correspondence. All this has been gratuitous, and that on the part of an individual whose stated occupation might seem sufficient to fill a busy day. It is manifestly neither just nor honorable to the body of the Alumni, that this great amount of labor should continue without compensation. With this impression it has been proposed by some personal friends of Dr. Palmer, to take charge of the publication of his necrologies in a handsome volume for his benefit.

To secure him from the possibility of loss, it has been deemed expedient, with Dr. Palmer's permission, that the copyright of the work should be held by a committee by whom the net proceeds shall be applied for his benefit. . . . As the volume will be of common interest to all the sons of Harvard, it is confidently expected that it will be so generally subscribed for as to yield a handsome compensation for the labor and care bestowed upon the work by its worthy compiler.

Messrs. WILLIAM BRIGHAM of the class of 1829, NATHANIEL B. SHURTLEFF of the class of 1831, and HENRY G. DENNY of the class of 1852, will act as a committee of publication; and communications on the subject and subscriptions may be addressed to them at Boston.

JOSIAH QUINCY.
EDWARD EVERETT.
JARED SPARKS.
JAMES WALKER.
THOMAS HILL.
SAMUEL SWETT.
ROBERT C. WINTHROP.
WILLIAM BRIGHAM.
NATHANIEL B. SHURTLEFF.
C. WILLIAM LORING.
HENRY G. DENNY.

CAMBRIDGE, July 15th, 1863.

The enormous labor required by such a compilation as this must be evident to all; while few but those who have been engaged in similar works can appreciate the impossibility of perfect, or even approximate, accuracy of detail in items so various, and coming, in many cases, from such remote and uncertain sources. Many errors and omissions, resulting in part from the circumstances under which the necrology has from time to time appeared, have been corrected by the compiler; but it is much to be regretted that but few, comparatively, of the friends of deceased alumni, have taken the opportunity offered them by the public notice given a year ago, and lately repeated, to correct or add to the obituaries.

The Committee have given much time to the arrangements for the publication of this work, in order that all sums received from its sale, after paying the actual cost of paper, printing, and binding, may go for the benefit of its compiler; and they trust that the considerations set forth in their circular are such as will secure a speedy sale of the limited edition that has been issued.

For the Committee of Publication,

HENRY G. DENNY.

Boston, July 20th, 1864.

PREFACE.

The suggestion of preparing a necrology of alumni of Harvard College was made by Hon. Edward Everett to the compiler of these notices in the year 1851. He began the work the next succeeding year, and has since, at the request of the Executive Committee of the Association of the Alumni, published it annually in the "Boston Daily Advertiser" on Commencement-Day. He acknowledges his obligations to Mr. John Langdon Sibley, the accomplished librarian of Harvard College, for the use he has been permitted to make of the notes and memoranda of the alumni, collected by him during his long connection with the college. The compiler intended to rewrite the earlier notices, as they were meagre and imperfect; but he was unable to do it, by reason of having partially lost his eyesight. They are therefore republished nearly as they appeared in the "Advertiser." It is to be regretted that the necrology was not begun a century earlier; for then much valuable information would have been preserved which is now irrecoverably lost. The compiler hopes, that, when he shall have passed away (which, in the course of nature, will occur at no distant period), the necrology will be continued by more able hands.

NECROLOGY.

1851–52.

1785. — Dr. SAMUEL EMERSON died in Kennebunk, Me., 7 August, 1851, aged 86 years and 11 months. He was born in Hollis, N.H., 6 September, 1765. He served in the war of the Revolution, in the regiment of Col. Prescott, and was quartered at Cambridge at the time of the battle of Bunker Hill.

1785. — THEODORE LINCOLN died at Dennysville, Me., 15 June, 1852, aged 89. He was a son of Gen. Benjamin Lincoln, of Hingham, where he was born 30 December, 1763; was one of the earliest settlers of the town of Dennysville, and was Judge of the Court of Common Pleas and Sessions for the County of Washington.

1788. — HENRY PHELPS died at Gloucester, 18 February, 1852, aged 86. He was born in Salem, 10 November, 1765. His father was a shipmaster sailing from that town, from which, about the commencement of the Revolutionary War, he removed to Beverly. He was lost at sea on his homeward passage from France in 1786. He was spoken by a vessel when sixty days out, being short of provisions and water, with his vessel disabled and leaky. On board of the ship that spoke him, he sent a letter for his wife, in a sealed bottle attached to a line, written in a strain of complete despondency as to his chance of reaching home. From the contents of this letter, it is supposed that the vessel must have foundered not long after it was written. His son Henry was then in college. He had to contend with the congenital difficulties of a club foot and an imperfectly developed right arm and hand; but, not allowing them to discourage him, soon after leaving college he commenced the study of medicine with Dr. Joshua Plummer, of Salem, quite a distinguished physician, formerly of Gloucester, who established him in business as an apothecary and physician in Gloucester, in 1790. He acquired some practice as a physician, but soon abandoned that branch of his business. Being a man of lively temperament and companionable qualities, his shop was the resort of the most respectable and influential men of the town. He was for some time postmaster in Gloucester, and also for many years the principal acting magistrate in the town.

1790. — Dr. WILLIAM INGALLS died in Wrentham, 9 September, 1851, aged 82. He was born in Newburyport, 3 May, 1769, and was for many years an eminent physician in Boston.

1792. — NATHANIEL CHANDLER, of Lancaster, died at the Insane Hospital in Worcester, 4 June, 1852, aged 78. He was born in Petersham, 6 October, 1773.

1792. — Rev. JOHN SNELLING POPKIN died in Cambridge, 2 March, 1852, aged 80. He was born in Boston, 19 June, 1771. Ordained pastor of the Federal-street Church in Boston, 10 July, 1799. Dismissed 28 November, 1802. Installed pastor of the First Church in Newbury, 19 September, 1804. Dismissed 5 October, 1815, having accepted the appointment of professor of the Greek language in Harvard College. This office he held till 1826, when he was appointed Eliot Professor of Greek literature. He resigned his professorship in 1833, but continued to reside in Cambridge during the remainder of his life. He was a member of the Massachusetts Historical Society, and of the American Academy.

1793. — JOSEPH STOWERS died at North Chelsea, 31 August, 1851, aged 77 years and 10 months. He was born in Chelsea, 10 November, 1773. He was justice of the peace, town-clerk, town-treasurer, selectman, representative; and, in fact, made himself "generally useful" to the people of his native place.

1794. — WILLIAM CROSBY died at Belfast, Me., 31 March, 1852, aged 81. He was born in Billerica, Mass., 3 June, 1770. Soon after he left college, he entered as a student-at-law in the office of William Gordon, Esq., of Amherst, N.H., and in due time finished his legal studies with Judge Dana, of Groton, Mass. In January, 1802, he went to Belfast, and settled as a practising lawyer. He was one of the pioneer band of professional adventurers, who, at that early day, dared to penetrate this new region, and locate themselves east of the Kennebec River; a tract of country then, as now, comprising much the largest portion of the now State of Maine. There were at that period less than a dozen framed houses in the village, with a few log cabins; some Indian-built wigwams, and not more than three hundred inhabitants in the whole town. Thus by his enterprise he became an early citizen of that undefined space called "Down East," and was the associate and the first legal adviser of the founders of that beautiful town.

1795. — OLIVER CROSBY died at Atkinson, Me., 29 July, 1851, aged 82. He was born in Billerica, Mass., 17 March, 1769; and settled as a lawyer in Dover, N.H., in 1798. He subsequently removed to Maine. For several years before his death, he had discontinued the practice of his profession.

1795. — JOSIAH STURGES died in New York, 22 February, 1852, aged 78. He was son of Jonathan Sturges, of Fairfield, Conn., Judge of the Supreme Court of Connecticut, and was born 10 September, 1773. He was a merchant in New York, and was at one time wealthy, but lost his property during the war of 1812.

1796. — Rev. NATHAN TILTON died at Scarborough, Me., 4 October, 1851, aged 79. He was born in East Kingston, N.H., 2 July, 1772; was ordained pastor of the church in Scarborough, 10 December, 1800; and resigned his pastoral charge, 12 December, 1827.

1798. — THOMAS COLE died at Salem, 24 June, 1852, aged 72. He was born in Marlborough, Mass., 29 December, 1779. He was preceptor of the Aurean Academy, at Amherst, N.H., afterwards teacher of the Ladies' High School at Salem; a Fellow of the American Academy.

1798. — Rev. ABRAHAM RANDALL died at Stow, 3 March, 1852, aged 80. He was born in Stow, 25 October, 1771; was fitted for college at Westford Academy, under the tuition of the late Levi Hedge, LL.D. During a part of his collegiate course, he was room-mate with the late Judge Story. He was ordained at Manchester, 2 September, 1802; dismissed September, 1808, and returned to Stow.

1798. — Dr. ROBERT THAXTER died in Dorchester, 10 February, 1852, aged 75. He was son of Dr. Thomas Thaxter, of Hingham; and was born in that town, 21 October, 1776. He commenced his professional practice in Hingham in 1802. In 1809 he established himself in Dorchester, and for more than thirty years was not kept from his professional business a single day by illness.

1799. — Rev. WILLIAM FROTHINGHAM died at Belfast, Me., 24 June, 1852, aged 77. He was born in Cambridge, 14 March, 1777. Ordained pastor of the Third Church in Lynn, 26 September, 1804; dismissed 7 May, 1817; installed at Belfast, 21 July, 1819.

1800. — BENJAMIN MARSTON WATSON died at Newton, 31 August, 1851, aged 71. He was born in Marblehead, 11 January, 1780. He studied law with the late Chief Justice Parsons; but soon left the profession, and went into mercantile business in Boston. He was also president of the Mercantile Marine Insurance Company.

1801. — SAMUEL MATHER CROCKER died at Milford, 9 March, 1852, aged 69. He was a lawyer by profession, and practised successively in the towns of Douglass, Uxbridge, Fitchburg, and Milford.

1804. — JOSEPH E. SPRAGUE died at Salem, 22 February, 1852, aged 69. He was the eldest son of Dr. William Stearns, and was born in Salem, 9 September, 1782. Soon after he graduated, he took the name of Sprague, to which family his mother belonged. He was a member of the Essex bar, and for many years was an active politician of the Jefferson school. Under the administration of Jefferson, he was for a time one of the United-States marshals. In October, 1811, he was appointed clerk of the courts for Essex County, and continued in the office about nine months. In 1815, under the presidency of Madison, he was appointed postmaster of Salem, and retained the office until the accession of Gen. Jackson to the presidency in 1829. Previous to this time he had served several years as representative from Salem in the General Court, as a senator from Essex, and as an executive councillor. In September, 1830, he was appointed high sheriff of the county, succeeding his father-in-law, Bailey Bartlett, whose resignation of the office in the month preceding had been accepted, to take effect on the 14th of September. On the 15th, Mr. Sprague's nomination was unanimously confirmed by the Council; and he remained in the office until his commission expired, about nine months before his death, when another person was appointed in his place. Mr. Sprague died of apoplexy; and it may be mentioned as a singular coincidence, that his grandfather, whose name he assumed, died in the same way, in the same room, at nearly the same age, in the same month, February, 1808.

1804. — Dr. JOHN STARR died at Northwood, N.H., 8 September, 1851, aged 67. He was son of Dr. Ebenezer Starr, of Dunstable, N.H., where he was born 3 December, 1783; studied medicine with Dr. Matthias Spalding, of Amherst, N.H., and commenced practice in Peterborough, N.H., where he remained three years, excepting a brief absence, during the war of 1812, as a surgeon of the Second Regiment of the New-Hampshire Detached Militia, commanded by Col. John Steele, of Peterborough. From Peterborough, Dr. Starr removed to Northwood, where he continued in practice thirty-eight years. He was a gentleman of the old school. His political principles were of the Federal stamp. He was constant at town-meeting, casting his vote for none but just men, whether upon regular tickets or not.

1805. — WARD CHIPMAN died at St. John, N.B., 26 November, 1851, aged 65. He was son of Hon. Ward Chipman, (H.C. 1770), and was born in St. John, N.B., 10 July, 1787. He was appointed one of the justices of the Supreme Court of Judicature, 17 March, 1825; and was elected to the office of chief justice of the same tribunal, 29 September, 1834. He resigned January, 1851.

1805. — Rev. JOHN WHITE died at Dedham, 1 February, 1852, aged 64. He was son of Deacon John White, of Concord; and was born in that town, 2 December, 1787. He was ordained pastor of the Third Parish in Dedham, 20 April, 1814.

1806. — THOMAS PRINCE BEAL died at Kingston, 16 July, 1852, aged 66 years and 5 months. He was a native of Kingston, and was born 12 February, 1786. He was formerly a member of the Senate of Massachusetts, and an eminent counsellor-at-law.

1808. — BENJAMIN RAND died in Boston, 26 April, 1852, aged 67. He was born in Weston, 18 April, 1785, and was one of the most distinguished members of the Suffolk bar.

1810. — Rev. JOSEPH HAVEN died at Amherst, Mass., 15 October, 1851, aged 65. He was son of Noah Haven, and was born at Holden, 19 June, 1786; ordained at Dennis, 27 July, 1814; dismissed 12 May, 1826, on account of his health, and removed to Amherst to superintend the collegiate education of his son. On the 8th of June, 1836, his health having been partially restored, he was installed pastor of the Orthodox Church in Billerica, and continued in this service five years; at the close of which period, on account of returning and increasing bodily infirmities, he felt constrained to relinquish the labors of a settled minister for ever.

1810. — Dr. JOHN MANNING died at Rockport, 7 February, 1852, aged 62 years and 6 months. He was born in Gloucester, Mass., 12 October, 1789; and was son of the late Dr. Manning of that town.

1811. — WALTER BAKER, of Dorchester, died in Boston, 7 May, 1852, aged 59. He was son of Dr. James Baker, (H.C. 1760), and was born in Dorchester, 28 June, 1792. He was well known as an extensive chocolate manufacturer, in which business he acquired an ample fortune.

1813. — Dr. JOHN BROWN died at Lancaster, Erie County, N.Y., 27 February, 1852, aged 60. He was son of Samuel Brown of Concord, Mass., where he was born 10 January,

1792. He studied medicine, but relinquished the profession, and settled as a merchant in the vicinity of Buffalo, N.Y.

1814. — EPHRAIM MAY CUNNINGHAM died in Washington City, 26 May, 1852, aged 60. He was son of William Cunningham, of Boston, and was born in Fitchburg, Mass., 4 February, 1792. He was a lawyer by profession, and practised successively in Ashburnham, Lunenburg, and Sterling. He was afterwards an officer in the Boston Custom House, and finally was employed as a clerk at Washington. He obtained considerable notoriety by publishing, in the year 1823, what is known in political circles as the "Cunningham Correspondence."

1814. — AARON PRESCOTT died at Randolph, 24 November, 1851, aged 64. He was son of Deacon John Prescott, and was born in Westford, Mass., 19 November, 1787; was preceptor of Framingham Academy, one year after he graduated; then studied law, and settled in Randolph, where he practised his profession with success during the remainder of his life. He represented that town once or twice in the Legislature.

1816. — Rev. WILLIAM WARE died at Cambridge, 19 February, 1852, aged 54. He was son of Rev. Henry Ware, D.D. (H.C. 1785), and was born at Hingham, 3 August, 1797. He was ordained pastor of the Unitarian Church in New York, 18 December, 1821; dismissed 19 September, 1836. Installed at West Cambridge, December, 1843; dismissed 1845.

1819. — WALTER ROGERS JOHNSON died in Washington City, 26 April, 1852, aged 57. His death was occasioned by inhaling noxious gas while performing some chemical experiments in the laboratory of the Smithsonian Institute. He was born in Leominster, Mass., 21 June, 1794; was for many years preceptor of an academy in Germantown, Penn.; afterwards Professor of Chemistry in the Medical College at Philadelphia, and subsequently of the Smithsonian Institute at Washington. He was one of the persons employed by the city of Boston, previous to the construction of the water-works, to examine Long and Spot Ponds, and ascertain which was the best source for obtaining a supply of water for the city.

1822. — Joseph Green Cole died at Paris, Me., 12 November, 1851, aged 52. He was son of Capt. Abraham Cole, of Lincoln, Mass., and was born in that town in 1799. After studying law with Hon. Levi Lincoln, of Worcester, he settled in Paris. He successively held the offices of clerk of the House of Representatives, representative to the Legislature, register of probate, clerk of the courts, and judge of the Western District Court.

1825. — Dr. Augustus Sidney Doane died at the quarantine station, Staten Island, New-York Harbor, 27 January, 1852, aged 44. He was son of the late Samuel B. Doane, of Boston; was born 2 April, 1808; settled in New York as a medical practitioner, and for several years had been employed as the quarantine physician of that port.

1827. — Rev. William Matticks Rogers died at Dorchester, 11 August, 1851, aged 45. He was born on the Island of Alderney, England, 10 September, 1806; was ordained at Townsend, 16 February, 1831; dismissed 2 July, 1835. Installed pastor of the Winter-street Church, Boston, 6 August, 1835. His original name was Samuel Matticks Ellen Kittle.

1828. — William Sawyer was instantly killed on the Fitchburg Railroad in West Cambridge, near the Waverly Depot, 24 May, 1852. He was 45 years of age. He had been a practising lawyer in Charlestown; but, a short time previous to his death, had removed to Waltham.

1830. — Franklin Sawyer died at Cambridgeport, 18 November, 1851, aged 51. He was born in Cambridge, 18 June, 1810. He was a lawyer by profession, but for several years was connected with the newspaper press. He was for a time editor of the "Crescent" in New Orleans; and, for about two years previous to his death, was one of the editors of the "Watchman and Reflector," in Boston. He was representative of Cambridge to the Legislature in 1851; and, at the time of his decease, was a member of the Common Council of the city of Cambridge.

1834. — William Smith Cruft died in Paris, France, 16 July, 1851, aged 36. He was son of Edward Cruft, of

Boston; was born 17 February, 1815; and was a merchant in New York, of the firm of Newbold and Cruft.

1845. — George Washington Brown died at Charlestown, 7 December, 1851, aged 29. He was a native of Charlestown; born 12 May, 1822, and had established himself as a lawyer in Boston.

1845. — Dr. Paul Lewis Nichols died at Kingston, 28 April, 1852, aged 29. He was a native of Kingston; was born 24 May, 1823, and had settled as a physician in Roxbury.

1846.—John Adams Hastings died at Erie, Penn., 16 October, 1851, aged 27. He was son of Jonathan Hastings, of Brighton; and was born in that town, 16 July, 1824. He was preceptor of an academy in Erie at the time of his death.

1847.— George Edward Waters died at Henrietta, N.Y., 23 July, 1851, aged 23; born in Boston, 17 September, 1828. His death was occasioned by his being thrown from a carriage. He was son of the late Isaac Waters, of Boston.

1851. — Arnold Welles Brown was killed on the Boston and Worcester Railroad, at Newton Lower Falls, 21 January, 1852, aged 25. He was son of Dr. John Ball Brown, and was born in Boston, 19 January, 1827. He was very desirous of having a collegiate education, and entered the Boston Latin School for the purpose of pursuing his preparatory studies. But, while in the school, his father lost all his property by a fire which destroyed a large laundry and two dwelling-houses belonging to him. His hopes of going to college were therefore destroyed, and he was placed in a wholesale dry-goods store in Boston, where he remained a few months, when the firm was dissolved, and he was thrown out of employment. He was afterwards put into a dry-goods store in Dover, N.H., where he remained but a short time. Being still desirous of going to college, he went to work on a farm, hoping to earn money enough to get a liberal education; but, as he was unacquainted with farming, his father determined to send him to sea as the best way to earn money to pay his collegiate expenses. He went to New Bedford, and was shipped on board a whaling vessel, and made a long voyage. After his return, he entered college; and, with the money he made in his whaling voyage, he succeeded in going through college. After graduating, he made a tour as colporter; and in the fall of 1851 he entered the Theological Seminary at Andover, where he remained until the following January; when, about three o'clock in the afternoon of the 21st, as he was passing along the viaduct on the railroad at Newton Lower Falls, he was caught between the cars and the railing of the bridge, and thrown from the latter by the passing train, which struck him down, and instantly deprived him of life.

1852–53.

1787. — Hon. SAMUEL PUTNAM, of Boston, died at Somerville, 3 July, 1853, aged 85. He was son of Gideon Putnam, and was born at Danvers, 13 April, 1768; commenced the practice of law in Salem about the year 1790; was senator for Essex in 1808 and 1809, representative from Salem in 1812, and again senator in 1813 and 1814. On the death of Chief Justice Sewall, in 1814, he was appointed, by Gov. Strong, Judge of the Supreme Court.

1790. — Rev. MICAH STONE died in Brookfield, 20 September, 1852, aged 82. He was son of Rev. Eliab Stone, of Reading (H.C. 1758), and was born in that town, 22 September, 1770; ordained pastor of the Second Church in Brookfield, 11 March, 1801.

1791. — EZEKIEL HERSEY DERBY died in Salem, 31 October, 1852, aged 80. He was son of Hasket Derby, of Salem, where he was born 1 November, 1772; was early in life a merchant, but for the last thirty-five years was a conspicuous and active agriculturist.

1793. — Rev. CHARLES COFFIN, D.D., died in Greenville, Tenn., 3 June, 1853, aged 77. He was born in Newburyport, 15 August, 1775, and was successively president of Greenville and Knoxville Colleges in Tennessee.

1793. — Dr. CHARLES WILLIAMS WINSHIP died in Roxbury, 27 August, 1852, aged 78. He was son of Dr. Amos Winship (H.C. 1771), and was born in Boston, 22 June, 1774, and was considered a skilful physician. He practised successively in the western country, in Havana, Cuba, in Boston and Roxbury.

1794. — Hon. CHARLES HUMPHREY ATHERTON died in Amherst, N.H., 8 January, 1853, aged 79. He was son of

Hon. Joshua Atherton (H.C. 1762), and was born in Amherst, 14 August, 1773; read law with his father, and with Hon. William Gordon, of Amherst (H.C. 1779); was admitted to the bar, and opened an office in Amherst in 1797; appointed register of probate for Hillsborough County in 1798; representative to Congress from 1815 to 1817; represented his native town in the State Legislature in 1823, 1838, and 1839.

1794. — Rev. David Kendall died in Augusta, Oneida County, N.Y., 19 February, 1853, aged 85. He was born in Athol, Mass., 20 March, 1768; ordained at Hubbardston, 20 October, 1802; dismissed April, 1809, and removed to Augusta, N.Y., where he was installed over the Congregational Society in that town, and where he spent the remainder of his life. For several years before his death, he was unable to perform his clerical duties, on account of a paralytic affection.

1795. — Capt. Josiah Bartlett died in Newburyport, 24 February, 1853, aged 77. He was a native of Newburyport, and was born 15 September, 1775. After leaving college, he went to sea several years as supercargo, and subsequently as master. During the war of 1812, he sailed from Bourdeaux as commander and principal owner of the ship "Volant," with a very valuable cargo, bound for Boston. When he had nearly reached his port of destination, he was captured by a British cruiser, and carried to Halifax, and subsequently to England. He resided in England and France till the close of the war, when he returned to Newburyport, and resided there the remainder of his life, employed principally as a teacher, particularly of the French language, of which he had acquired a knowledge during his residence in Europe.

1795. — Thomas Beale Wales died in Boston, 15 June, 1853, aged 77. He was son of Dr. Ephraim Wales, of Randolph (H.C. 1768), where he was born 1 January, 1776. He was a highly respected and eminently successful merchant in Boston.

1796. — George Wingate died in Stratham, N.H., 12 September, 1852, aged 75. He was son of Hon. Paine Wingate (H.C. 1759), and was born in Stratham, 14 May, 1778.

He did not study a profession, but devoted himself to agriculture.

1798. — Nathaniel Lord died in Ipswich, 16 October, 1852, aged 72. He was son of Isaac Lord, of Ipswich, where he was born 25 September, 1780. For several years after leaving college, he was employed as a teacher. He was subsequently associated with the late Daniel Noyes, register of probate; upon whose decease he was appointed his successor by Gov. Strong, in May, 1815, and held the office till he was removed by Gov. Boutwell in June, 1851.

1799. — Daniel Adams died in Medfield, 2 September, 1852, aged 73. He was son of Rev. Daniel Adams, of Watertown (H.C. 1774), where he was born 26 March, 1779. He fitted for college with Rev. Dr. Prentiss, of Medfield (H.C. 1766). On leaving college, he was appointed preceptor of Bristol Academy, where he continued one year; after which he studied divinity a year with Rev. Dr. Bancroft of Worcester (H.C. 1778), when his fondness for the law led him to the office of Benjamin Whitman, Esq. of Hanover, Mass., where he completed his studies. He then opened an office in Medfield, where he settled. He also had for a time an office in Hopkinton. With the exception of having once represented Medfield in the Legislature, he was never in public life.

1801. — William Bartlett died in Newburyport, 28 December, 1852, aged 70. He was son of William Bartlett, of Newburyport, where he was born 23 July, 1782, and was a merchant in his native place.

1802. — Isaac Gates died in Harvard, 9 November, 1852, aged 74; found dead in his bed. He was born (supposed) in Charlestown, 7 May, 1777; was a lawyer successively in Concord, N.H., Brunswick, Me., Lynn, Mass., and Harvard.

1802. — Henry Gardner Rice died in Boston, 26 March, 1853, aged 69. He was son of Dr. Tilly Rice, of Brookfield, where he was born 18 February, 1784; was a merchant in Boston.

1803. — John Farrar died in Cambridge, 8 May, 1853, aged 73. He was son of Deacon Samuel Farrar, of Lincoln, and was born 1 July, 1779. He was appointed tutor in Greek in 1805; and, in 1807, was chosen Hollis Professor of Mathematics and Natural Philosophy in Harvard College; which latter office he held till June, 1831, when he resigned on account of ill health.

1804. — Rev. OLIVER BROWN died at Haddam, Conn., while on a journey from Lyme to Middletown, 9 February, 1853, aged 76. He was born in Charlestown, 13 January, 1777; was for some years chaplain of the State Prison; was installed at Kingston, R.I., 19 December, 1821, dismissed April, 1835; moved to Bozrahville, Conn.; was afterwards settled as pastor of the Congregational Society at Grass Hill, Lyme, Conn.

1804. — SETH LOW died in Brooklyn, N.Y., 19 June, 1853, aged 71 years and 10 months. He was born in the West Parish of Gloucester, Mass., 19 March, 1782; moved to Brooklyn about the year 1827, where he resided during the remainder of his life, and was one of the most influential and useful citizens of that community. He was a prominent merchant in New York; and his prosperity furnished him with the ability to give when needed, and his ripe judgment always made his donations discreet. At the time of his death, he was president of the Board of Supervisors, and also of the Association for the Relief of the Poor.

1806. — JOHN BOIES THOMAS died in Plymouth, 2 December, 1852, aged 65. He was born in Plymouth, Mass., 28 July, 1787. He commenced and pursued the practice of law in Plymouth till he received the appointment of clerk of the judicial courts for Plymouth County; which office he held for a period of about thirty-eight years, when he resigned on account of ill health. He filled numerous municipal offices for many years; was seventeen years president of the Old-Colony Bank; was a member of the Convention to revise the Constitution in 1820; and was elector of President and Vice-President in 1840.

1806. — Dr. TIMOTHY WELLINGTON died in West Cambridge, 6 May, 1853, aged 71. He was son of Timothy

Wellington, of Lexington; where he was born 8 October, 1781. After completing his professional studies, he settled in West Cambridge as a physician, where he resided till his death, always engaged in the active and arduous duties of an extensive and successful practice.

1807. — Abiel Jaques died in Worcester, 7 October, 1852, aged 72. He was son of Samuel Jaques, and was born in Worcester, 7 March, 1780. He was teacher in Salem, Watertown, Newton, Brooklyn (Conn.), Palmyra (N.Y.), and Uxbridge (Mass.); then settled, as a farmer, in Worcester.

1807. — Rev. Francis Parkman died in Boston, 12 November, 1852, aged 64. He was son of Samuel Parkman, and was born in Boston, 4 June, 1778; ordained at the New North Church in Boston, 8 December, 1813; resigned 1 February, 1849.

1808. — Henry Codman died in Roxbury, 4 May, 1853, aged 63. He was a lawyer in Boston; he was born in Portland, 1 October, 1789.

1808. — John Farwell died in Tyngsborough, 19 November, 1852, aged 66. He was born in Tyngsborough, 2 October, 1785. He studied law with Hon. Asahel Stearns (H.C. 1797); settled as a lawyer in Tyngsborough, and became a member of the Middlesex bar. He succeeded to his father's landed estate in Tyngsborough, and the greater part of his life was successfully devoted to agricultural pursuits.

1809. — Major David S. Townsend died in Boston, 28 January, 1853, aged 62. He was son of Dr. David Townsend (H.C. 1770), and was born in Boston, 19 April, 1790. Soon after he graduated, he entered a merchant's counting-room, where he continued till the commencement of the war of 1812, when he entered the army as lieutenant and adjutant in the ninth regiment of infantry, commanded by Col. Tuttle. During a skirmish on the banks of the St. Lawrence, he received a wound, from a musket-ball, through the leg, below the knee; in consequence of which, his leg was amputated. Soon after the close of the war, he received the appointment of paymaster, which office he held till his death.

1810. — Dr. BENJAMIN DIXON BARTLETT died in Cambridge, 7 February, 1853, aged 63. He was son of Samuel Bartlett, of Concord; and was born 17 September, 1789; commenced practice as a physician in that town in 1813; removed to Bath, Me., in 1816, and subsequently to Cambridge.

1811. — HENRY HOLTON FULLER, of Boston, died at Concord, 15 September, 1852, aged 62. He was son of Rev. Timothy Fuller, of Princeton (H.C. 1760), where he was born 1 July, 1790. He was a distinguished lawyer in Boston.

1812. — Dr. ABEL LAWRENCE PEIRSON, of Salem, was killed on the New-York and New-Haven Railroad, at Norwalk, Conn., 6 May, 1853, on his return from New York, where he had been to attend a medical convention. He was son of Samuel Peirson, of Biddeford, Me., where he was born 25 November, 1794; commenced practice as a physician in Maine; removed to Salem in 1819, and has been for many years considered one of the most eminent of the profession in Essex County.

1813. — Dr. CHARLES AUGUSTUS CHEEVER, of Portsmouth, N.H., died in Saugus, 22 September, 1852, aged 58. He was born in Lynn, 1 December, 1793; was for many years a highly respectable physician in Portsmouth; came to Boston some months before his death on account of ill health, and entered the Massachusetts General Hospital to be under the charge of the physicians of that establishment; but after remaining some time, his disease being considered incurable, he left, and went to Saugus, where he owned an estate, and died soon after he arrived there.

1814. — Dr. NATHANIEL BREWER, of Boston, died in Pepperell, 17 May, 1853, aged 57. He was born in Northfield, Mass., 23 July, 1795; and was a druggist of the firm of Brewers, Stevens, and Cushing, of Boston.

1814. — ARTHUR MIDDLETON, of South Carolina, died in Naples, Italy, 9 June, 1853, aged 57. He was son of Hon. Henry Middleton, who was for many years American minister at St. Petersburg, and grandson of Hon. Arthur Middleton, one of the signers of the Declaration of Independence. He was born in South Carolina, 28 October, 1795; was, for eight years, secretary to the American Legation in Spain; married the Countess Benivoglio, of Rome, who survives him, with two children. He had resided in Naples with his family for three years previous to his death.

1815 — JOHN DALL died in Boston, 7 August, 1852, aged 56. He was son of William Dall, and was born in Boston, 22 February, 1797; was for many years teller, first in the New-England, and afterwards in the State Bank. He became insane some years before his death, and was for a considerable time in the McLean Asylum at Somerville.

1815. — JOHN SPRAGUE WHITWELL died at College Hill, Cincinnati, 30 January, 1853, aged 57. He was born in Brunswick, Me., 17 September, 1795; was for a time a teacher; afterwards a merchant; and at the time of his death was Professor of Ancient and Modern Languages, and Belles Lettres, in Farmer's College, Cincinnati.

1816. — Dr. GEORGE BAKER died in Chelsea, 25 December, 1852, aged 56. He was son of Eliphalet Baker, of Dedham, where he was born 9 July, 1796; was a physician in Lancaster, next a druggist in Cambridge, afterwards resumed his profession in Chelsea.

1817. — RICHARD FARWELL died in Marlborough, 20 February, 1853, aged 63. He was born at Fitchburg, 23 July, 1789, but removed with the family, when quite young, to Harvard. He studied law, was admitted to the bar, and went to the West, — believed to Dubuque, Iowa; but subsequently returned to Massachusetts, and established himself at Marlborough, where he resided the remainder of his life.

1818. — Dr. RALPH EMMS ELLIOTT, of South Carolina, died in New York, 5 June, 1853, aged 55. He was born in Beaufort, S.C., 15 July, 1797; studied medicine with Dr. Hosack, of New York, but did not practise his profession. He was an extensive planter in South Carolina, but resided during the winter seasons in Savannah, Ga.

1819. — Hon. ALFRED DWIGHT FOSTER died in Worcester, 10 August, 1852, aged 52. He was son of Hon. Dwight

Foster, of Brookfield (B.U. 1774), where he was born 26 July, 1800; settled as a lawyer in Worcester; was representative, senator, and councillor in the state legislature.

1820.—Rev. WILLIAM GRAGG died in Groton, 19 November, 1852, aged 66. He was son of Thomas Gragg, of Groton, where he was born 17 September, 1786; ordained at Windham, Me., 15 October, 1828; after a few years was dismissed, and removed to Carlisle, Mass., thence to Bedford, and finally returned to his native place, Groton, where he passed the remainder of his life. His wife died 29 November, having survived him but ten days.

1820.—Hon. CHARLES PAINE, of Northfield, Vt., died in the village of Waco, Texas, 6 July, 1853, aged 54. He had gone to that part of the country for the purpose of exploring a southern route for the proposed Pacific Railroad; and it was while in Texas that he contracted the disease common to the climate, which caused his death. He was son of Hon. Elijah Paine, of Williamstown, Vt. (H.C. 1781), where he was born 15 April, 1799. After leaving college, he went to Northfield to take charge of his father's factory in that town. He became a manufacturer from necessity, and continued the business until the burning of his factory in March, 1848,—a period of nearly twenty-five years. By his influence and energy, the charter of the Vermont Central Railroad was obtained, and he was the first president of that corporation. The Vermont and Canada Railroad, the Champlain and St. Lawrence Railroad, and the Ogdensburg Railroad, were largely indebted to him for their construction. In the year 1841, he was elected governor of Vermont; which office he held two years, when he declined being a candidate for re-election.

1821.—HENRY BULFINCH died at Nahant, 28 January, 1853, aged 55. He was born in Lynn, 6 June, 1797; studied divinity, and preached occasionally, but, most of his time, was engaged as a teacher.

1824.—JOHN THOMAS PHILIP DUMONT died in Hallowell, Me., 6 October, 1852, aged 50. He was a lawyer in Hallowell, and an ardent politician of the whig school.

1824. — JOHN GREENOUGH died in Paris, France, 16 November, 1852, aged 51. He was son of David Greenough, and was born in Boston, 19 November, 1801; was an artist by profession.

1825. — HORATIO GREENOUGH died at the McLean Asylum, Somerville, 18 December, 1852, aged 47. He was son of David Greenough, and was born in Boston, 6 September, 1805. He was an eminent sculptor, and resided many years in Italy, pursuing his profession there with great success.

1825. — HIRAM MANLEY died in St. Mark's, Fla., 9 July, 1853, aged 51. He was son of David Manley, and was born in Easton, Mass., 11 June, 1802. He settled as a lawyer in Tallahassee, where he resided about ten years, when he removed to St. Mark's. At the time of his death, he was judge of one of the courts in Florida.

1825. — SEARS COOK WALKER died at the house of his brother, Judge Timothy Walker, in Cincinnati, 30 January, 1853, aged 47. He was born in Wilmington, Mass., 28 March, 1805; taught a private school in Philadelphia several years; was for a considerable period actuary of the Pennsylvania Life-Insurance Company; a short time attached to the National Observatory; and, for several years preceding his death, one of the assistants of the Coast Survey. He was a distinguished member of the American Academy, and one of the most eminent mathematicians and astronomers in the country.

1826. — ROBERT RANTOUL, Jun., died in Washington, D.C., 7 August, 1852, aged 47. He was son of Robert Rantoul, and was born in Beverly, 13 August, 1805; admitted to the bar in 1828; in 1833 became a resident of Gloucester, which town he represented in the state legislature several years. In 1843 he was appointed collector of Boston; but his appointment was not confirmed by the Senate, and he held the office but one year. In 1845 he was appointed United-States attorney for Suffolk District, which office he held till 1849. In 1851 he was chosen United-States senator, to fill, for a few days only, the unexpired term of Mr. Webster; and, the same year, was chosen representative in Congress from Essex District, which office he held at the time of his death.

1828. — Thomas Philander Ryder died in the Lunatic Hospital, at South Boston, 21 November, 1852, aged 47. He was son of Thomas Ryder, and was born in Hallowell, Me., 19 August, 1806. He taught school in Dedham for some time; was afterwards a temperance lecturer, and for several years was a constable in Boston.

1829. — Ezra Weston died in Duxbury, 6 September, 1852, aged 43. He was son of Ezra Weston, and was born in Duxbury, 23 December, 1809. He was a lawyer in Boston, and for a few years held the office of city-marshal.

1830. — Isaac Appleton Jewett died in Keene, N.H., 14 January, 1853, aged 44. He was born in Burlington, Vt.; settled as a lawyer, first in Cincinnati, and afterwards in New Orleans. For several years latterly, he resided principally at the North, and was engaged in other business. He had travelled extensively, and published two volumes entitled "Passages in Foreign Travel." He also wrote a series of letters from the West Indies, which were published in the "Christian Register" about three years before his death.

1831. — Henry Frederick Friese died in Baltimore County, Md., about seven miles from the city, 24 May, 1853, aged 42. He was son of Philip R. J. and Julia G. Friese, of Baltimore, where he was born 16 November, 1810. He was fitted for college at the Round-Hill School at Northampton, Mass., under the charge of Messrs. Joseph G. Cogswell and George Bancroft. By profession he was a lawyer, and practised in his native city, where for a time he held a justice's commission.

1831. — Frederick Furber died at the Lunatic Hospital, South Boston, 1 July, 1853, aged 42. He was son of Thomas Furber and Elizabeth Green (Foster) Furber, of Boston; and was born 22 January, 1811. He was distinguished for his mathematical attainments; and, after graduating, qualified himself for the profession of a civil engineer. He was insane for twenty years; the last thirteen of which he passed at South Boston, where he latterly beguiled the tedium of confinement by draughting plans for similar institutions.

1832. — William Prescott Gibbs died in Lexington, 27 July, 1852, aged 39. He committed suicide by drowning himself in a pond near his house. He was the eldest son of William Gibbs, of Salem; where he was born 5 August, 1812. He was a lawyer by profession.

1833. — Rev. Joseph Harrington died in San Francisco, 2 November, 1852, aged 39. He was son of Joseph Harrington, of Roxbury (Y.C. 1803), and was born 21 February, 1813; ordained in Boston as an evangelist, 27 September, 1840; installed at Hartford, Conn., 23 April, 1846; was dismissed; went to San Francisco to take charge of the Unitarian society in that place, and died of fever a few weeks after his arrival there.

1835. — Allen Crocker Spooner died in Boston, 28 June, 1853, aged 39. He was born in Plymouth, 9 March, 1814; was a lawyer in Boston.

1835. — John Hunt Welch died in Dorchester, 9 September, 1852. He was son of John Welch, and was born in Pennington, N.J., 17 November, 1814. He studied law, but left the profession; went into mercantile business, and was for a time of the firm of Heard and Welch in Boston.

1836. — Daniel Cook died at East Boston, 1 June, 1853, aged 35. He was son of Nathan Cook, and was born in Salem, 4 January, 1815. After graduating, he went to the South, and kept school several years in Mississippi and vicinity. For the last ten years, or thereabouts, of his life, he resided mostly in Salem, and subsequently in East Boston, as a machinist.

1837. — Manlius Stimson Clark died in Boston, 28 April, 1853, aged 36. He was son of Rev. Pitt Clark, of Norton (H.C. 1790), where he was born 17 October, 1816; was a highly respected lawyer in Boston.

1837. — William Davis, of Plymouth, died in Boston, 19 February, 1853, aged 34. He was son of Nathaniel Morton Davis (H.C. 1804), and was born in Plymouth, 12 May, 1818; was a lawyer in Plymouth, and, at the time of his death, vice-president of the Pilgrim Society.

1843. — Francis Whitney Bigelow died in San Francisco, 11 July, 1853, aged 29. He was son of Tyler Bigelow of

Watertown (H.C. 1801), where he was born 4 June, 1824. He was a lawyer by profession.

1843. — Washington Very died in Salem, 28 April, 1853, aged 37. He was son of Jones Very, of Salem, and was born in that place, 12 November, 1815. For some time before he entered college, he was a clerk in one of the Salem banks. After he graduated, he studied divinity at the Theological School in Cambridge. He preached one year, and subsequently was teacher of a private school in Salem.

1844. — Francis Willard Sayles was killed on the New-York and New-Haven Railroad, at Norwalk, 6 May, 1853, as he was on his return from a journey to the South. He was son of Willard Sayles, and was born in Boston, 30 September, 1823. Was a merchant, of the firm of Sayles, Merriam, and Brewer, in Boston.

1846. — James Morris died at Staten Island, N.Y., 28 January, 1853, aged 27. He was born in the city of New York, 19 March, 1825; and was, by profession, a civil engineer.

1847. — Dr. James Bemis Adams died of yellow fever at Curaçoa, West Indies, 16 January, 1853, aged 28. He was son of William Henry Adams, and was born at Lyons, Wayne County, N.Y., 12 January, 1825. He studied medicine, and received the degree of M.D. at the New-York Medical School in 1851.

1847. — Mark Sibley Adams died in San Francisco, 19 February, 1853, aged 25. He was son of William Henry Adams, and was born at Lyons, Wayne County, N.Y., 10 April, 1827.

1849. — James Pierce, of Brookline, died at sea of consumption, 29 May, 1853, on board ship "Parliament," on the passage from Liverpool to Boston. He was son of James Pierce, and was born in Dorchester, 20 November, 1825.

1849. — Augustus Warren Whipple was scalded to death, 4 September, 1852, at Saugerties, N.Y., on board the steamboat "Reindeer," in consequence of the bursting of the boiler. He had just completed his studies at the Theological School at Cambridge.

1852. — Alfred Wellington Cooke died at Weston, Mass., 3 August, 1852, aged 22 years. He was the son of Josiah Wellington and Sarah (Hancock) Cooke, and was born in Cambridge, Mass., 25 August, 1830. He began his preparatory course for college at the Cambridge High School, where he remained till the last two years, which he spent at the classical school of Edmund Burke Whitman (H.C. 1838), in the same city. During his last school vacation, before entering college, he suffered an attack of bleeding at the lungs, from which, in a few days, he appeared to entirely recover; but though after that his health seemed to be good till the last year of his college-life, yet the seeds of disease were probably lurking in his system, and he gradually sank under confirmed pulmonary consumption. By class-day he had become so ill, that he was unable to take part in its exercises. During his whole college-course, he was an earnest, faithful student, and performed his scholastic duties with untiring perseverance. In spite of his failing health, he continued to labor, till, from bodily weakness, he could no longer attend the recitations. Never was a more worthy example of scholarly devotion shown than was displayed by him in feebly going to and from his college-exercises, after all could see that the hand of death was already upon him. His energy, though quiet, was indomitable; and, if a resolute will could ever avert the approach of mortality, his would have done so.

From his earliest years, he was impressed with the need of a religious life; and, at the age of twelve, he made a profession of his faith, and united with the First Baptist Church of Cambridge (of which Rev. Joseph White Parker was then the pastor), 24 March, 1842. When very young, he had displayed great talents for music and painting. He played with much ability upon the piano and the organ; and his first and untaught efforts with the pencil showed a hand by no means unskilful. He was extremely persevering, and never idle. When not engaged upon his college-studies, he was always busy with his brush or pencil, or playing upon some instrument of music. Careful in his choice of friends, and invariably preferring merit to numbers, he was faithfully devoted to those he had. They who knew him best thought most highly of him, and warmly appreciated both his talents and his unassuming virtues. It was ever his earnest desire to visit Italy, for the purpose of perfecting himself in the arts he loved so well. He would often exclaim, with true artistic fervor, "I shall certainly see Italy before I die!" but Providence had ordained that he should look upon a fairer land than that.

Only a few days before his death, he received an appointment, at a liberal salary, as teacher of music in a Southern academy. He had applied for this in the hope that rest from mental exertion and a year's residence in a warmer climate might restore his failing health; but, when the letter announcing his engagement reached him, he was too weak to answer it. Reserved and gentle in his manners, ever fearful of obtruding himself upon the society of others, cordial and kind towards all, his short life flowed on peacefully into the ocean of eternity. With his promising talents and abundant sources of enjoyment, he had much to live for; and it is matter for deep sorrow, that a youth so bright was so early clouded by the approach of death.

1853–54.

1784. — THOMAS GREENLEAF died in Quincy, 5 January, 1854, aged 86. He was son of John Greenleaf, and was born in Boston, 15 May, 1767. He was for many years an apothecary in Boston: his shop was No. 62, Cornhill, now Washington Street.

1786. — Rev. EBENEZER HILL died in Mason, N.H., 27 May, 1854, aged 88. He was son of Samuel Hill, and was born in Cambridge, 29 January, 1766; was ordained at Mason, 3 November, 1796.

1787. — Dr. NATHANIEL SHEPHERD PRENTISS died in West Cambridge, 5 November, 1853, aged 87. He was son of Nathaniel Prentiss, saddler, of Cambridge, and his wife Mercy (Pierce), and was born in the old tavern building near Porter's hotel, in Cambridge, 7 August, 1766. He studied medicine with Dr. Israel Atherton, of Lancaster (H.C. 1762); and settled in Marlborough, where he remained twelve or thirteen years. He then removed to Roxbury, where he had charge of the Latin School eight years, and fitted many distinguished men for college; he also practised medicine in Roxbury, and was town-clerk over thirty years. On leaving Roxbury, in 1850, he presented to the Roxbury Athenæum a set of valuable books. For the last few years of his life, he resided with his son-in-law, the Rev. Mr. Banvard, in West Cambridge.

1789. — Rev. AARON GREEN died in South Andover, 23 December, 1853, aged 89. He was born in Malden, 2 January, 1765; was ordained as pastor of the First Church in his native town, 30 September, 1795; resigned 8 August, 1827, and soon afterwards removed to Andover, where he passed the remainder of his days.

1789. — Hon. NAHUM MITCHELL, of East Bridgewater, died suddenly in Plymouth, 1 August, 1853, aged 84. He was son of Cushing Mitchell, and was born in Bridgewater, 12 February, 1769. He was a lawyer by profession; was for many years chief justice of the Old County Circuit Court of Plymouth; was representative in Congress at a most important period of our history; was representative and councillor in our state legislature; was for several years librarian of the Massachusetts Historical Society; and published a valuable history of his native town.

1790. — Hon. SAMUEL CHANDLER CRAFTS died in Craftsbury, Vt., 19 November, 1853, aged 85. He was son of Col. Ebenezer Crafts (Y.C. 1759), and was born in Woodstock, Conn., 6 October, 1768, where his father then resided; but the family soon after removed to Sturbridge, Mass., and Samuel C. was fitted for college at Leicester Academy, of which his father was one of the principal founders and patrons. Soon after leaving college, he moved with the family to Craftsbury, where his father died in 1810, and where he ever after resided. In 1792, he was appointed clerk of the town; which office he held, by yearly re-elections, for thirty-seven successive years. In 1796, he was chosen member of the legislature; and, the two following years, was elected clerk of the same. He was again elected to the legislature in 1800, 1801, 1803, and 1805. From 1800 to 1810, he held the office of first assistant judge of the County Circuit Court; and, after that time to 1816, was chief judge. In 1816, he was elected a representative in Congress, and was continued a member for eight years. In 1828, he was chosen governor of the state, and was re-elected in 1829 and 1830. In 1842, he was appointed, by the executive of the state, to a seat in the Senate of the United States, in place of Judge Prentiss, who had resigned; and, at the following meeting of the legislature, he was chosen for the remainder of the period for which Judge Prentiss had been elected. From that time to his death, he retained no important public office, exept that of justice of the peace for the town.

1796. — FRANCIS DANA died in Cambridgeport, 28 December, 1853, aged 76. He was son of Hon. Francis Dana (H.C. 1762), and was born in Cambridge, 14 May, 1777. He was a merchant by profession; and he passed several years, after he entered into business, in Russia, Germany, India, South America, and the western regions of our own country. In the latter part of his life, he represented his native town in the state legislature.

1797. — Hon. DANIEL ABBOT died in Nashua, N. H., 3 December, 1853, aged 76. He was son of Timothy Abbot of Andover, and was born in that town, 25 February, 1777. He studied law with Parker Noyes of Salisbury, N. H. (D. C. 1796), where he was a fellow-student with Daniel Webster. In 1802, he commenced the practice of law in Londonderry, N. H., but moved to Dunstable the same year. He represented the town in the legislature many years, and was once a member of the senate. He was president of the Nashua Manufacturing Company for several years of its early existence; president of the Nashua Bank many years; president of the Nashua and Lowell Railroad Company for fourteen years after its incorporation; president of the Wilton Railroad from its organization till within a short time before his death; and, for a long period, president of the Hillsborough-County bar.

1797. — Rev. FREEMAN PARKER died in Wiscasset, Me., 24 April, 1854, aged 78. He was born in Barnstable, 13 July, 1776; ordained at Dresden, Me., 2 September, 1801, and was minister there about twenty-five years; when he resigned his pastoral charge, and removed to Wiscasset. On the fiftieth anniversary of his ordination, he went to Dresden, and preached an occasional sermon to his former congregation. This was the last discourse he ever delivered. He was blind for upwards of forty years before his death.

1798. — JOHN ABBOT died in Westford, 30 April, 1854, aged 77. He was born in Westford, 27 January, 1777; and was a lawyer in his native town.

1799. — BARTHOLOMEW BROWN died in Boston, 14 April, 1854, aged 81. He was son of John Brown, and was born in Danvers, 8 September, 1772; was a lawyer in Sterling from

1803 to 1809, when he removed to East Bridgewater, where he continued in practice of his profession till about ten years before his death, when he removed to Boston. He possessed great talent for music; and, in connection with the late Judge Mitchell, he edited, for about twenty years, the "Bridgewater Collection of Church Music," in which book may be found many pieces of his composition. He wrote the calendars in Thomas's "Old Farmer's Almanac" for fifty-nine years successively.

1800. — Rev. JOSHUA BATES died in Dudley, 14 January, 1854, aged 77. He was born in Cohasset, 20 March, 1776; was ordained at Dedham as colleague-pastor of the First Church with the Rev. Jason Haven (H.C. 1754), 16 March, 1803; resigned 10 February, 1818, and, the following month, was inaugurated president of Middleborough College, Vt.; which office he held till 1843, when he resigned, and was installed the same year as pastor of the Congregational Church in Dudley, where he remained till his death.

1800. — Dr. JOHN DWIGHT died in Roxbury (Jamaica Plain), 5 August, 1853, aged 78. He was born in Shirley, 22 December, 1773; studied medicine with Dr. John Jeffries, of Boston (H.C. 1763); practised his profession in Boston till 1844, when he joined the "Community" in West Roxbury, where he remained about four years, continuing the practice of his profession among them. He then removed to Jamaica Plain, where he passed the remainder of his life.

1801. — JOSIAH ADAMS died in Framingham, 9 February, 1854, aged 72. He was son of Rev. Moses Adams, of Acton (H.C. 1771), and was born in that town, 3 November, 1781. He was a lawyer in Framingham.

1804. — ANDREWS NORTON, of Cambridge, died in Newport, R.I., 18 September, 1853, aged 66. He was son of Samuel Norton, of Hingham; and was born in that town, 31 December, 1786. In 1801, he entered college a year in advance, and was the youngest in his class. After graduating, he studied divinity, but was never ordained. In 1813, he was appointed librarian, which office he held till 1821. He was also, in 1813, appointed Dexter Lecturer. In 1819, when the Theological

School was organized, he was elected Professor of Sacred Literature, which office he resigned in 1830. In 1833–4, in connection with Charles Folsom, Esq., he edited "The Select Journal of Foreign Periodical Literature," which closed with the fourth volume. The elaborate theological works of Professor Norton are well known.

1806. — JAMES DAY died in Paxton, Mass., 16 December, 1853, aged 74. He was born in Paxton, 14 December, 1779. After leaving college, he studied law, but soon relinquished the profession, and devoted himself to teaching in his native town and the vicinity.

1806. — ABRAHAM MOORE died in Boston, 30 January, 1854, aged 69. He was born in Bolton, Mass., 5 January, 1785; studied law with Hon. Timothy Bigelow (H.C. 1786); and settled as a lawyer in Groton in 1809, where he resided till 1815, when he removed to Boston.

1807. — Rev. JOSHUA CHANDLER died at the Massachusetts General Hospital, in Boston, 31 May, 1854, aged 67. He was son of Major Abiel Chandler, of Andover, where he was born 15 May, 1787; was ordained at Swanzey, N.H., 20 January, 1819; dismissed 26 November, 1822; installed in Orange, 27 November, 1822; dismissed 31 October, 1827; installed in Bedford, 20 January, 1836; dismissed and installed in Pembroke, 9 February, 1842; dismissed, and removed to Boston, where he spent the remainder of his days.

1807. — Rev. PHINEAS FISH died in Cotuit (Barnstable), 16 June, 1854, aged 69. He was born in Sandwich, 30 January, 1785; was ordained at Marshpee, 18 September, 1812; and, for more than forty years, was a devoted and faithful missionary to the Indian tribe at that place.

1807. — WILLIAM COFFIN HARRIS died in Portsmouth, N.H., 22 November, 1853, aged 65. He was seized with an apoplectic fit in his school-room, fell on the floor, and died within ten minutes afterwards. He was son of Abiel Harris, of Portsmouth, where he was born 17 March, 1788. He had been a teacher in Newington and Portsmouth between thirty and forty years; and, for faithfulness, energy, and thoroughness in this capacity, was greatly distinguished and highly esteemed.

1807. — Hon. JAMES CUSHING MERRILL died in Boston, 4 October, 1853, aged 69. He was son of Rev. Giles Merrill (H.C. 1759), and was born in Haverhill, 27 September, 1784. He was a lawyer in Boston; and, for many years, was one of the judges of the Police Court.

1808. — JOSEPH BOLLES MANNING, of Rockport, died suddenly in Ipswich, 22 May, 1854, aged 67. He was born in Gloucester (now Rockport), 5 March, 1787; was for several years a lawyer in Ipswich; and afterwards removed to Gloucester.

1810. — Hon. JAMES GORE KING died in New York, 4 October, 1853, aged 62. He was the third son of Hon. Rufus King (H.C. 1777), and was born in New York, 8 May, 1791. He went with the family to England, on the appointment of his father, in 1796, as minister from the United States to the court of St. James. He was placed at school near London for some time; and was afterwards sent to Paris, where he also attended school. He returned to the United States in the year 1805, and was fitted for college by the Rev. Dr. Gardiner, of Boston. After graduating, he commenced the study of law with Peter van Schaick, Esq., of Kinderhook; and completed his studies at Litchfield under the instruction of Judges Reeve and Goold. He afterwards turned his attention to commerce, and formed a commission-house in New York, which he soon after transferred to Liverpool. In 1823, he returned to New York, and became a partner in the banking-house of Prime, Ward, and King; and subsequently, on its dissolution, was the head of the house of James G. King and Sons.

1810. — Dr. RUFUS KITTREDGE died in Portsmouth, N.H., 21 February, 1854, aged 64. He was son of Dr. Benjamin Kittredge, of Tewksbury, Mass., where he was born 28 June, 1789. His father, who died at the age of 81, had eight sons and three daughters. All the sons reached manhood, and were all physicians. Dr. Rufus was the last of the brothers. He had been a resident of Portsmouth since 1817; had an extensive practice in his profession, and enjoyed the confidence of the public.

1810. — Dr. THOMAS GARDNER MOWER died in New York, 7 December, 1853, aged 63. He was son of Thomas Mower, and was born in Leicester, 18 February, 1790, but removed with the family, at an early age, to Worcester. He studied medicine with Dr. Thomas Babbitt, of Brookfield (H.C. 1784). He was appointed surgeon's mate in the Ninth Regiment of United States Infantry, 2 December, 1812, and immediately joined his regiment in winter-quarters at Burlington, Vt. On the 30th of June, 1814, he was promoted to the surgeoncy of his regiment, and continued on the New-York frontier till the close of the war, February, 1815. The war being ended, he was one of the regimental-surgeons, out of about forty, that were selected for the peace establishment. After nine or ten years' service on the frontier, the last two on the Upper Missouri, he was placed on special duty in the harbor of New York, and charged with the various duties pertaining to the station. Here, with occasional absences on duty, he was continued till the time of his death.

1811. — Dr. JOSEPH WHEELWRIGHT died in Heathsville, Northumberland County, Va., 24 August, 1853, aged 61. He was born in Newburyport, 29 December, 1791. He established himself as a physician in Virginia, and for nearly forty years was actively engaged there in the practice of his profession. His loss was deeply felt by a large circle of friends.

1812. — JAMES FOSTER GOULD died in Canton, Miss., 14 February, 1854, aged 61. He was born in a part of Dorchester which is now South Boston, 24 November, 1791; was a teacher, first in Baltimore, and afterwards at the South.

1813. — EDWARD HINKLEY died in Baltimore, 28 June, 1854, aged 63. He was born in Barnstable, Mass., 26 August, 1790. He was a lawyer by profession, and for many years had been a prominent member of the Baltimore bar.

1814. — Hon. ELIJAH PAINE died in New York, 7 October, 1853, aged 57. He was son of Hon. Elijah Paine, of Williamstown, Vt. (H.C. 1781), where he was born 10 April, 1796; studied law with Judge Cady, of Montgomery County, N.Y., and settled in New-York City as a lawyer about the year 1823. In 1849, he was elected one of the justices of the Superior Court, and discharged the duties of his office as long as his health would permit. His term would not have expired till 1 January, 1857.

1816.—Rev. WILLIAM DANIELS WISWALL died in Roxbury, 30 November, 1853, aged 66. He was son of Timothy and Diadama Wiswall, and was born in Milford, 23 October, 1787. His name, originally, was Lot Wiswall. He was ordained at Ellsworth, Me., 5 July, 1837; dismissed 5 July, 1839. He was never settled over any other society, but preached occasionally in various places.

1817.—GEORGE STORER BULFINCH died in Boston, 7 October, 1853, aged 54. He was son of Charles Bulfinch (H.C. 1781), and was born in Boston, 23 January, 1799; was a lawyer in Boston, and for some time librarian of the Boston Library.

1818.—THOMAS COOK WHITTREDGE died suddenly of apoplexy, in Salem, 26 January, 1854, aged 54. He was son of Capt. Thomas Whittredge, of Salem, where he was born 28 May, 1799. He adopted the maritime profession, and was, for some time, master of a merchant-ship; but, several years before his death, he retired from active life.

1820.—Rev. ALEXANDER YOUNG died in Boston, 16 March, 1854, aged 53. He was son of Alexander Young, and was born in Boston, 22 September, 1800; was ordained pastor of the New South Church, in Boston, 19 January, 1825.

1822.—Hon. CHARLES GORDON ATHERTON, of Nashua, N.H., died at the Manchester House, in Manchester, N.H., 15 November, 1853, aged 49. He died of paralysis, with which he was attacked in the court-house, in Manchester, while engaged in professional business. He was son of Hon. Charles Humphrey Atherton (H.C. 1794), and was born in Amherst, N.H., 4 July, 1804; studied law with his father; was admitted to practice in 1825, and soon afterwards opened an office in Nashua Village, then called Dunstable. He was elected to the state legislature in 1830, and in 1831 he was chosen clerk to the Senate. He was again chosen representative in 1833–6; and was Speaker of the House during three of those years. He was elected representative in Congress in 1837, 1839, and 1841; was elected senator in 1842, and took his seat in the Senate in March, 1843. His term expired in 1849; and he was again elected to that place in 1852, and took his seat in March, 1853.

1822. — JOHN THOMPSON died in Centre Harbor, N.H., 21 January, 1854, aged 52. His house was destroyed by fire; and while endeavoring to save an article of furniture which he highly prized, it being a present from his mother, he perished in the flames. He was son of Benjamin Thompson of Durham, N.H., where he was born 2 December, 1801. He was a practising lawyer in Centre Harbor.

1826. — Rev. NATHANIEL PHIPPEN KNAPP died in Mobile, Ala., 17 February, 1854, aged 46. He was son of Capt. Joseph J. Knapp, of Salem, where he was born 25 June, 1807. He was for a time a lawyer in Marblehead, but subsequently relinquished the profession; studied divinity, and became an Episcopal minister; was ordained priest at Jamaica, N.Y., 15 March, 1837. In 1838, he was instituted rector of Christ Church, in Montgomery, Ala.; and afterwards removed to Mobile.

1827. — THOMAS KEMPER DAVIS died in Boston, 13 October, 1853, aged 45. He was son of Isaac P Davis, and was born in Boston, 20 June, 1808. He graduated with the highest honors of his class. He studied law with Hon. Daniel Webster; was admitted to the bar in 1830, and opened an office in Boston; but, for several years before his death, was an inmate of the McLean Asylum at Somerville.

1828. — CHARLES TRACY MURDOCH died in Cambridge, 25 November, 1853, aged 44. He was son of John Murdoch; and was born in Havana, Island of Cuba, 5 January, 1809. He was a lawyer by profession; had an office in Boston, but resided in Cambridge.

1830. — JAMES BENJAMIN, of Boston, died in Springfield,

Mass., 28 August, 1853, aged 42. He was son of Ashur Benjamin, and was born in Boston, 23 April, 1811. He was fitted for college partly at Exeter Academy, and partly at the Boston Latin School. He was a lawyer in Boston.

1830. — JOSEPH BARNEY WILLIAMS died in Baltimore, Md., 30 August, 1853, aged 43. He was son of Nathaniel Williams (H.C. 1801), and was born in Baltimore, 16 October, 1810. He was fitted for college at the Round-Hill School, Northampton, and entered the sophomore class in 1827. He was a lawyer by profession; and, for many years previous to his death, was notary-public and commissioner.

1834. — DRAUSIN BALTAZAR LABRANCHE died at his residence in the parish of St. Charles, Louisiana, 25 August, 1853, aged 38. He was born in that place, 12 April, 1815, and was by profession a lawyer.

1837. — EDWARD PINKNEY WILLIAMS died in New Orleans, 18 November, 1853, aged 34. He was born in Baltimore, 9 June, 1819; and was a merchant in New Orleans.

1838. — JONAS WHITE THAXTER died in Watertown, 1 March, 1854, aged 34. He was son of Hon. Levi Thaxter, and was born in Watertown, 27 February, 1820. He studied medicine for a time, but did not pursue the profession.

1842. — FRANCIS HENRY APPLETON, of Boston, died at the McLean Asylum in Somerville, 28 May, 1854, aged 30. He was son of Hon. William Appleton, and was born in Boston, 11 September, 1823.

1843. — Dr. JOHN GARDNER LADD, of Brooklyn, N.Y., died at Saratoga Springs, 19 August, 1853, aged 33. He was son of John H. Ladd, of Savannah; and was born in Alexandria, D. C., 4 July, 1820. He was a physician in Brooklyn.

1845. — GORHAM BARTLETT, of Concord, died at the McLean Asylum in Somerville, 17 June, 1854, aged 28. He was son of Dr. Josiah Bartlett (H.C. 1816), and was born in Concord, 22 January, 1826. He commenced the study of divinity at the Theological School at Cambridge, but relinquished it on account of his health.

1845. — NICHOLAS LAFAYETTE MARR died in Tuscaloosa, Ala., 17 April, 1854, aged 29. He was born in Tuscaloosa, 2 August, 1824, and was a planter by occupation.

1848. — EDWARD IRVING BIGELOW died in Cairo, Egypt, 9 April, 1854, aged 26. He was son of Tyler Bigelow, of Watertown (H.C. 1801), where he was born 1 June, 1827. He was a lawyer by profession.

1848. — HENRY WHITCOMB HOLMAN died in Carrollton, La., 1 October, 1853, aged 29. He was son of Hon. Amory Holman, of Bolton, Mass., where he was born 8 October, 1824. He taught school in Jackson, Miss., in 1849–50; afterwards studied law in New Orleans, and established himself as a lawyer in that city.

1849. — GEORGE WASHINGTON COGSWELL died in Le Roy, N.Y., 22 April, 1854, aged 23. He was born in Peterborough, N.H., 1 July, 1830, and was a student-at-law.

1852. — GORHAM THOMAS died in Cambridge, 16 August, 1853, aged 21. He was son of Dr. Alexander Thomas (H.C. 1822), and was born in Boston, 8 September, 1831. He was a student of medicine.

1853. — EDWARD JARVIS TENNEY was washed overboard from steamship "San Francisco," 25 December, 1853. He had taken passage in that ill-fated vessel for Valparaiso, South America, where he intended to establish himself in mercantile business. He was son of John Tenney, of Methuen, where he was born 20 September, 1833; and was consequently twenty years of age at the time he was lost.

1854–55.

1791.—Hon. THOMAS RICE died in Winslow, Me., 24 August, 1854, aged 86. He was son of Dr. Thomas Rice (H.C. 1756), and was born in Pownalborough (now Wiscasset), 30 March, 1768. He studied law with Hon. Timothy Bigelow of Groton (H.C. 1786). After completing his studies, he went to Winslow on horseback, carrying in his saddle-bags his clothes, and a few law-books which constituted his whole library. He commenced the practice of law in that town in 1795, where he soon gained a lucrative business, and became successful as an advocate. In 1814, he was representative to the Massachusetts legislature; in 1817, he was elected representative to Congress, where he continued two terms. With the exception of two years, when he resided in Augusta, he continued to live in Winslow till his death. He was naturally of a cheerful and social temperament; and had quite a taste for gardening, which he indulged to the last. He relinquished the practice of law about twenty years before he died.

1792.—Hon. JOHN LOCKE died in Boston, 29 March, 1855, aged 91. He was son of Jonathan and Mary (Haven) Locke, and was born in Hopkinton, Mass., 14 February, 1764. In 1769, he, with his father's family, removed to Framingham; whence, in June, 1770, they removed to Fitzwilliam, N.H., then called Monadnock No. 2, and lived in a log-house. In May or June, 1772, he removed with the family to Ashby, Mass. He worked on a farm till twenty-two years of age, when he went to Phillips Academy in Andover, where he continued till he entered Dartmouth College, in the second quarter of the sophomore year. He left Dartmouth, and entered Harvard in the beginning of the junior year. In November, 1793, he entered the law-office of the late Hon. Timothy Bigelow of Groton (H.C. 1786). In September, 1796, he was admitted to the bar in Middlesex County, and opened an office in Ashby. He was elected representative to the Legislature in 1804, 1805, 1813, and 1823. In 1820, he was a member of the Convention for revising the Constitution of Massachusetts. From 1823 to 1829, he was representative in Congress from the Worcester North District. In 1830, he was chosen senator from Middlesex to the Massachusetts Legislature. In 1831, he was a member of the Executive Council. In 1837, he removed to Lowell to reside with his son, John Goodwin Locke; with whom, in 1849, he removed to Boston, where he passed the remainder of his days.

1792.—Dr. Hector Orr died in East Bridgewater, 29 April, 1855, aged 85. He was son of Col. Robert Orr, and was born in East Bridgewater, 24 March, 1770. He settled as a physician in his native town, where he passed his life; and, besides having held offices of honor and trust, he was distinguished as a skilful physician and a man of cultivated intellect.

1793.—Thomas Wigglesworth died in Boston, 27 April, 1855, aged 79. He was son of Rev. Edward Wigglesworth, of Cambridge (H.C. 1749), and grandson of Rev. Edward Wigglesworth, of Cambridge (H.C. 1710); both Hollis Professors of Divinity in Harvard College. He was born in Concord, Mass., 2 November, 1775. At the time of his birth, his father's family were residing temporarily in Concord, to which place the students and teachers of the college had removed a short time before, in consequence of the occupancy of Cambridge and the university buildings by the American forces collected to besiege the British army, who were then in possession of Boston. Mr. Wigglesworth, immediately after graduating, commenced the study of law at Salisbury, N.H., near the residence of the family of the late Daniel Webster, whom he remembered very well as a boy. In a few months, he discontinued his legal studies, and went to Newburyport, where he entered the counting-room of Messrs. Searle and Tyler. At the age of twenty-one, he came to Boston, and soon formed a copartnership with William Sawyer, Esq. (H.C. 1788), who survived him for a few years. They carried on business together for several years. Mr. Wigglesworth early engaged in the Russia and India trade, and continued in the latter to the end of his life, having accumulated a large fortune. He was connected, as a director, with several of our financial institutions, and was respected for his industry, integrity, and capacity for business; but he was retiring in his habits, and never served in any state or city office, except for a short time on the school-committee.

1795. — SAMUEL ADAMS DORR died in Boston, 25 February, 1855, aged 79. He was son of Ebenezer Dorr, of Boston, and was born in Medfield, Mass. (where his parents resided during the siege of Boston), 1 July, 1775. He studied law with Gov. James Sullivan, but relinquished the profession; engaged in commercial pursuits; went abroad, and passed many years of his life in foreign countries.

1796. — Rev. LEONARD WOODS died in Andover, Mass., 24 August, 1854, aged 80. He was son of Samuel and Abigail Woods, and was born in Princeton, Mass., 19 June, 1774. He commenced the study of Latin with the parish minister of Princeton; and, after three years, he entered as freshman in 1792, having received but three months' regular instruction, which he obtained at Leicester Academy, under the tuition of Ebenezer Adams (D.C. 1791, afterwards professor in Dartmouth College), and graduated with the highest honors of his class. For eight months after he left college, he was engaged as a teacher in Medford. He united with Rev. Dr. Osgood's church in Medford in 1797. In the autumn of the same year, he studied theology three months with Rev. Dr. Charles Backus, at Somers, Conn. (Y.C. 1769). The following winter he continued his studies at home. In the spring of 1798, he was licensed to preach, and was ordained pastor of the Fourth Church in Newbury, 5 December, 1798. He was dismissed 26 May, 1808; was inaugurated Professor of Theology in the Institution at Andover, 20 September, 1808; and continued to give instruction till 1846, when his active connection with the seminary ceased. After that time, he was engaged in revising and giving to the world his lectures and other writings, in an edition of five volumes; and in preparing a history of the seminary, which was nearly or quite completed at the time of his death.

1797. — Dr. HENRY GARDNER died in Charlestown, Mass., 22 August, 1854, aged 81. He was born in Charlestown, 13 September, 1772; and settled as a physician in his native town, where he passed his life.

1800. — Hon. LEONARD JARVIS died in Surry, Me., 18 September, 1854, aged 62. He was born in Cambridge, Mass., 19 October, 1781. Immediately after leaving college, he entered the counting-room of the late David Greene and Son, where he acquired a knowledge of commerce, and habits of business, which entitle him to an honorable name among the merchants of Boston. He became subsequently connected with mercantile operations, in the prosecution of which he spent several years abroad, chiefly in France and South America. On his return home, he settled in Maine, where he filled various important positions; being at one time collector of Eastport, afterwards sheriff of Hancock County. In the year 1831-33, he represented his district in the Congress of the United States. He was a prominent politician in the Democratic party. Under the administration of President Van Buren, he was appointed navy agent for the port of Boston. From this post he was removed by the administration of Gen. Harrison; and soon afterwards returned to Maine, where he spent the closing years of his life in the pursuits of agriculture and literature.

1802. — Rev. JAMES FLINT died in Salem, 4 March, 1855, aged 73. He was born in Reading, 10 December, 1781. After leaving college, he spent a few years in teaching; then studied divinity with the Rev. Joshua Bates, D.D., of Dedham (H.C. 1800). On finishing his studies, he received a call from the First Church and Society in East Bridgewater, Mass.; which he accepted, and was ordained 29 October, 1806. Possessing a fine taste for horticulture, he improved it by embellishing the grounds about his house, and made it one of the most attractive places of residence in the county. Here, too, he cultivated his love for classical literature by superintending the education of students who were committed to his care by the college government. He occasionally wrote poetry, and contributed largely to the literary journals of the day.

At his own request, his connection with the church in East Bridgewater was dissolved 6 April, 1821; when he was invited by the East Church and Society in Salem to supply their pulpit, then vacant by the death of the Rev. Dr. William Bentley (H.C. 1777). After officiating a few sabbaths, he received an invitation for a permanent settlement, which he accepted, and was installed 20 September, 1821; and continued to be the sole pastor till the installation of his colleague, the Rev. Dexter Clapp, 17 December, 1851. His ready humor, lively sympathy, and rare conversational powers, peculiarly fitted him for discharging parochial duties; and in these he was eminently successful.

1803. — Hon. Josiah Butler died in Deerfield, N.H., 29 October, 1854, aged 74. He was son of Nehemiah and Lydia (Wood) Butler, and was born in Pelham, N.H., 4 December, 1779. At the age of 14, he was sent to the academy in Londonderry, N.H., and subsequently to Atkinson Academy, where he completed his preparation for college under the instruction of William Merchant Richardson (H.C. 1797). Immediately after leaving college, he entered, as a student-at-law, the office of Hon. Clifton Claggett, of Amherst, N.H., where he remained a short time, and then went to Virginia, where he resided in 1804, 1805, and 1806; taught an academy; pursued his law studies in the offices of Gov. Cabot and Jacob Kinney, Esq., and was admitted to practice in that State. In 1807, he returned to New Hampshire, and practised law in his native town about two years, during which time he represented the town in the State Legislature. In 1809, he removed to Deerfield, where he resided during the remainder of his life. In 1810, he was appointed high sheriff of the county of Rockingham, and continued in that office nearly four years. In 1815 and 1816, he was elected a representative of Deerfield; and, in 1816, he held the office of clerk of the Court of Common Pleas. In 1816, 1817, he was nominated and elected a representative to Congress; and, by successive elections, continued in Congress six years. In 1825, he was appointed associate justice of the Court of Common Pleas; and continued in that office till 1833, when the court was abolished. He then returned to the practice of law, which he continued a few years; and was subsequently engaged in agriculture. A few years since, he was appointed postmaster at South Deerfield, which office he held at the time of his decease.

1803. — Rev. JACOB COGGIN died in Tewksbury, Mass., 12 December, 1854, aged 72. He was son of Jacob Coggin, of Woburn (H.C. 1763), and was born in that town, 5 September, 1782. He studied theology with his pastor, the Rev. Joseph Chickering (H.C. 1799), then of Woburn. In April, 1806, he received an invitation to take the pastoral charge of the church and society in Tewksbury, and was ordained on the 22nd of October of the same year. He continued his ministry till 1847, when the Rev. Mr. Tolman was settled as a colleague with him. After that time, he was twice a representative to the legislature; in 1852, was chosen one of the Presidential electors; and, in 1853, was a delegate to the Convention for revising the Constitution of the State. Upon the establishment of the state alms-house in Tewksbury, he was appointed by Gov. Clifford one of the inspectors, and was chaplain of it till the time of his decease. He was one of the pioneers in the temperance cause, and served as agent for it in all the towns around him. Three sabbaths before his death, he preached his last sermon from the fourteenth verse of the ninety-second psalm, "They shall bring forth fruit in old age." Two of his sons have been educated for the ministry: one died in the ministry, at West Hampton.

1804. — Dr. JOHN MERRILL died in Portland, Me., 7 June, 1855, aged 73. He was son of Thomas Merrill, by his fourth wife; and was born in Conway, N.H., 2 March, 1782. He was highly respected as a skilful physician and good citizen.

1808. — Col. JOHN BLISS died in St. Augustine, Fla., 22 November, 1854, aged 66. He was born in Haverhill, N.H.,

26 April, 1788. After leaving college, he entered the United-States army. He was appointed first lieutenant in the Eleventh Regiment of Infantry, 12 March, 1812; and made captain in May, 1813. He distinguished himself, and was wounded in the battle of Niagara Falls, 25 July, 1814. When the army was re-organized, in May, 1815, he was retained in the Sixth Regiment of Infantry. From April, 1813, to January, 1819, he was instructor in infantry tactics, and commandant of cadets at West Point. For "ten years' faithful service," he was made brevet-major, 13 May, 1823. He was commissioned major of the First Regiment of Infantry, 15 July, 1830; and commanded his regiment in person at the battle of the Bad-Axe. He was promoted to be a lieutenant-colonel of the Sixth Infantry, 30 September, 1836; and resigned 6 September, 1837. For several years subsequent to his resignation, he resided in Buffalo, N.Y.

1809. — Hon. WILLIAM PLUMER died in Epping, N.H., 18 September, 1854, aged 65. He was the oldest son of Gov. William Plumer, of Epping, where he was born 9 February, 1789. He studied law with his father, but did not pursue the profession. He was repeatedly elected a member of both branches of the New-Hampshire legislature, and was also a member of the New-Hampshire Constitutional Convention of 1850. From 1819 to 1825, he was a representative in Congress; where, in 1820, he opposed the Missouri Compromise, on the ground that Congress thus superseded its powers, and legislated slavery where it did not exist. He commenced his public career as a member of the Democratic party: but, in 1828, he became a Whig; and ever after that time he adhered to that party. He possessed quite a literary and historical turn of mind, and published two small volumes of poems. He collected a large library, particularly valuable for the works it contained on America and American history.

1810. — RUFUS BACON died in Taburg, Oneida County, N.Y., 6 November, 1854, aged 70. He was born in Plymouth, Mass., 13 February, 1792. He settled as a lawyer in Freetown, Mass.; and about the year 1827 removed to Taburg, where he resided during the remainder of his life.

1810. — Stephen Fales died in Cincinnati, Ohio, 3 September, 1854, aged 64. He was born in Boston, 3 May, 1790. In the autumn of 1810, he was appointed tutor in Latin and Greek at Bowdoin College, where he remained two years. He afterwards read law in the office of Jeremiah Mason (Y.C., 1788), of New Hampshire; was admitted to the bar in Portsmouth; and, in 1819, removed to Cincinnati, where he became a partner with Francis Arthur Blake (H.C., 1814), a distinguished lawyer, since deceased. In 1821, he removed to Dayton, Ohio, where he practised law about ten years, when he returned to Cincinnati. He was elected to the senate of Ohio while he resided in Dayton, and served with great honor to himself, and advantage to his constituents. He was a good classical scholar; and, to the latest period of his life, read the New Testament in the original Greek, as his constant exercise. He often carried that volume in his pocket, and perused it in private. He left behind him many pleasant memories, many delightful evidences that one lived and died who keenly felt for his race, and loved the image of God in his fellow-man.

1810. — Col. Benjamin Faneuil Hunt died in New-York City, 5 December, 1854, aged 62. He was son of William Hunt, of Watertown, Mass., where he was born 29 February, 1792. His mother, a woman of high spirit, the second wife of William Hunt, was Jane, daughter of George Bethune, of Brighton, whose wife was Mary Faneuil, a descendant of one of the Huguenot families, who fled from France at the revocation of the Edict of Nantes. Faneuil Hall was named for her grandfather's brother. Col. Hunt's father died in 1804. As young Hunt manifested aptitude for study, and a determined purpose of obtaining a liberal education, his widowed mother made provision for meeting the expenses. Immediately after he left college, as all his brothers had died of consumption, and as his health was very delicate, he adopted the advice of his physician to quit the New-England climate, and went to Charleston, S.C., where he arrived 1 November, 1810. He entered as a student the law-office of the late Keating Lewis Simons, at that time one of the most distinguished ornaments of the legal profession in Charleston. After two years' study, he was admitted to the bar in Charleston, at a period when it was crowded with eminent practitioners. Gifted with high intellectual powers, and a ready and powerful rhetoric, he at once took his place in the front rank of the profession; and, as a jury lawyer, was perhaps never surpassed at that bar. His practice was extensive and successful, and his professional triumphs generally, and especially in defence of criminals in capital cases, were multiplied and signal. His ability and eloquence as an advocate soon gave him prominence in the field of politics, and he frequently served in the state legislature as a representative from Charleston, and was always regarded as one of the ablest and most influential debaters on the floor of the House. Although a Northern man, his sympathies were mainly with the South. He was chairman of the Committee on Federal Relations; and his reports on the tariff, the tenure of the presidential office, and the distribution of the sales of public lands, have been received as text-books of the state-rights democracy. On the declaration of war in 1812, he was active in the organization of a military company, which was drafted, during the war, into the service of the United States. He successively rose through the intermediate military grades; and, about the year 1818, was made colonel of the Sixteenth Regiment, in which capacity he served about twenty years. About a year before his death, he removed from Charleston to the city of New York.

1811. — Robert Hawkins Osgood died in New York, 27 February, 1855, aged 64. He was son of Capt. John Osgood, of Salem, where he was born 14 June, 1790. After leaving college, he entered upon the study of the law in his native town, but did not pursue the profession. With his brother John, he entered into business as a wholesale clothing merchant in Baltimore. Here he was one of the most self-sacrificing and active men in founding the society over which President Sparks and Dr. Burnap were afterwards settled. Subsequently, he and his partner engaged in the wholesale clothing business in New York. Having relinquished this occupation, he became a partner in the house of Harnden and Co., and resided, as European agent for the firm, during a few years, in Liverpool, Eng. The last years of his life were spent in New York. He was noted for his excellent sense, even temper, social accomplishments, and kind heart.

1812. — HENRY PETER COBURN died of cholera in Indianapolis, Ind., 22 July, 1854, aged 64. He was son of Peter and Elizabeth (Poor) Coburn, and was born in Dracut, Mass., 12 March, 1790. The Coburns (originally Colburns) came to America at an early period, and were among the first settlers on the Merrimack: the family emigrated from Scotland. The Poors are also an old family in Dracut. The paternal and maternal grandfathers of the subject of this memoir were both in the battle of Bunker Hill. His father was a farmer, — as had been all his ancestors in America, — and he was brought up on a farm. At the age of sixteen, he began his preparation for college; telling his parents, brothers, and sisters, that he would take, in the form of an education, his portion of his father's estate. He did so, and graduated with distinction. He studied law at Ipswich, Mass.; and, in the year 1815, emigrated to the West. During the session of the Constitutional Convention, at the organization of the state government of Indiana, in June, 1816, he went to Corydon, Ind., then the capital of the state. There he located himself, and began the practice of the law. He continued to practise until the year 1840. In 1818, he was appointed clerk of the Supreme Court of the state, and continued in office till November, 1852. In 1825, when the state capital was permanently located at Indianapolis, he removed to that place, and there resided during the remainder of his life. His name, originally, was Peter Coburn; but, after he removed to the West, he prefixed Henry to his given name Peter. As a man, he was quiet, plain, honest, straightforward, and decided. He had no ambition for notoriety, public honor, or public favor. He retired from popular turmoils, and shrank from contention. He took little or no part in politics, except as a voter, though he was a firm and unwavering Whig. His character as a lawyer was fair; as a counsellor, he was considered excellent; as an advocate, he never shone. He was called the "honest lawyer." He was a member of the Presbyterian Church; he was an ardent friend of education and temperance; his efforts to promote intelligence and to forward literary enterprises were constant, and in some degree successful. The Indiana Historical Society, the Indiana Law-Library, the Marion-County Library, and the free schools of Indianapolis, owe much to his constant efforts; and were partly, for years, under his management. Although he made less public display than almost any one, he did more for the moral and educational interests of the city of his adoption than any man in it. He was truly one of those to whom the Saviour promised an open reward for secret good.

1812. — Rev. JONATHAN MAYHEW WAINWRIGHT died in New-York City, 21 September, 1854, aged 61. He was son of Henry Wainwright, and his wife Elizabeth Mayhew, daughter of Rev. Jonathan Mayhew, D.D., of Boston; and was born in Liverpool, Eng. (during the temporary residence of his parents there), 24 February, 1793. His father was an English merchant, who removed to this country shortly after the war, and became a naturalized citizen of the United States. Dr. Wainwright's boyhood was spent in England, at school; and, on the return of his parents to this country, he fitted for college at Sandwich Academy, under the instruction of Elisha Clap (H.C. 1797). After he graduated, he was for two years instructor in rhetoric and oratory in Harvard College. In 1816, he was ordained a deacon in the Protestant Episcopal Church, and was soon after placed in charge of Christ Church, Hartford, where he remained three years. In 1819, he was called, as an assistant minister of Trinity Church, New York, to fill the vacancy occasioned by the election of Rev. Dr. Brownell as Bishop of Connecticut. A few months afterwards, he became rector of Grace Church, in New York. Here he remained until 1834; when, upon a very urgent call, he accepted the rectorship of Trinity Church, Boston, where he resided three years. On the 25th of March, 1837, he returned to New York, as an assistant minister, once more, of Trinity Church, and retained this connection during the remainder of his life. Meanwhile, however, he had been of distinguished service to the church in many other capacities. He succeeded Bishop Henry U. Onderdonk as secretary of the Board of Trustees of the General Theological Seminary in 1828; in which capacity his zeal and activity were of great and lasting service until his removal to Boston in 1834. He was for many years a manager of the Bible, Prayer-book, and Tract Society. He was secretary of the House of Bishops from the year 1838 until he took his seat as a member of that house; and it was in his capacity as secretary that he went to England, in the summer of 1852, bearing the resolutions of the American bishops responsive to the invitation to attend the closing services of the third semi-centennial jubilee of the venerable Society for the Propagation of the Gospel in Foreign Parts. But the crowning energies of his long and laborious life were devoted to the episcopate, to which he was elected as provisional bishop by the Diocesan Convention of 1852, and consecrated on the 10th of November following. Anxious to serve faithfully that diocese which had called him to preside over it, he refused to moderate his episcopal labors by any consideration of his own health. This enormous diocese is too heavy a burden for even the most vigorous man in the flower of his age; and the determination to do what no man of his years could reasonably expect to perform hurried him to the grave. His last Sunday's duty was at Haverstraw (on 27 August), where full and somewhat exciting services were held; he preaching both morning and afternoon to crowded congregations, with a confirmation of thirteen persons, and an appropriate address besides. During his brief episcopate of one year, ten months, and eleven days, he went through a far greater amount of episcopal labor than was ever before crowded into the same space of time by any American bishop. He paid for his brilliant pre-eminence with his life.

1813.—Dr. ZABDIEL BOYLSTON ADAMS died in Boston, 25 January, 1855, aged 62. He was born in Roxbury, Mass., 19 February, 1793. He was long known as one of the most skilful and successful practitioners in Boston; and he was greatly endeared to the many families who availed themselves of his professional services, as well as to the community at large.

1815. — ELISHA FULLER died suddenly of disease of the heart, in Worcester, 18 March, 1855, aged 60. He was son of Rev. Timothy Fuller (H.C. 1760), and was born in Princeton, Mass., 28 October, 1794. Immediately after he was graduated, he commenced the study of divinity, and completed his studies at the Theological School in Cambridge in 1818, when he was licensed to preach. For three years, he officiated in various pulpits, but finally relinquished the profession, and in July, 1821, he began the study of law. In May, 1823, he settled as a lawyer in Concord, Mass. In May, 1831, he removed from Concord to Lowell; and, in the spring of 1844, from Lowell to Worcester, where he remained diligently practising his profession till death suddenly called him away. At the time of his decease, he held the office of Associate Judge of the Police Court in Worcester. His interest in the university, which gave to him his education, was large and unintermitted. Its history, as it was unfolded, was his study. It was a subject of gratulation with him, that, from the period of his matriculation, no Commencement-Day had come that did not find him a visitor at Cambridge, if it were only for an hour, to manifest, by his presence, his interest in his Alma Mater.

1816. — JOHN AMORY DEBLOIS died in Columbus, Ga., 30 May, 1855, aged 57. He was son of Stephen Deblois, and was born in Boston, 20 July, 1797. After leaving college, he engaged in mercantile business in New Orleans. He afterwards removed to Columbus, where he formed a copartnership under the firm of Hall and Deblois; and where, for eighteen years, he was one of the most prominent merchants of that place, possessing strict integrity, gentle and courteous manners.

1816. — Rev. WILLIAM POOLE KENDRICK died in Bristol, Kendall County, Ill., 5 November, 1854, aged 64. He was born in Hollis, N.H., 27 January, 1790. At the early age of eleven years, he became seriously impressed, and resolved, by the aid of divine grace, to devote the best of his life to the eternal welfare of his fellow-man. In accordance with this resolution, he fitted for college; and, after graduation, studied his profession at the Theological Seminary in Andover. He remained some time at the East, ministering to destitute churches; after which, he removed to the state of New York, acting as home missionary for nearly thirty years at Shelby, Parma Centre, and other places. In 1846, he repaired to Illinois, and there ended his days.

1817.—FREDERICK HOBBS died in Bangor, Me., 10 October, 1854, aged 57. He was son of Isaac Hobbs, of Weston, Mass., where he was born 28 February, 1797. On his maternal side, he was a lineal descendant from the celebrated Rev. John Cotton, the minister of the First Church in Boston. As such a descendant, he was entitled to, and received, certain benefits from Harvard College, while a student there, growing out of bequests to the institution from the Cotton family. After graduating, he read law in the office of Daniel Webster, in Boston; and, in 1820, went to Eastport, Me., where he opened an office. He soon entered upon an extensive practice, and gained a high position at the bar of Washington County. He filled various municipal offices in Eastport, and represented the town one year in the legislature. He was once nominated by the whig party as their candidate for representative to Congress in the Eastern Congressional District, and received the united vote of that party; but, as it was then in a minority in the district, he failed of an election. In 1836, he removed to Bangor, where he successfully continued the practice of the law; having, up to the time of his sickness, more business in the United-States Court than any practitioner east of the Kennebec. Although devoted to his profession, he found time for other employments, and always took a lively interest in municipal affairs; and, as an alderman, his services in the city council were laborious and efficient. He was for some time president of the Musical Association in Bangor, and freely lent his aid to this branch of education. He was a great friend to horticulture; was among the few who first started the Bangor Horticultural Society, and was for some time its president. In the cause of schools, lyceums, and temperance, he was an earnest advocate, and contributed his full share for their general advancement. He was a good and useful citizen; of stern integrity, of strict honesty, and highly exemplary in all his habits. In February, 1849, while engaged in an important case before the Supreme Court of Massachusetts, in Boston, he was suddenly attacked with blindness and dizziness, which for some time incapacitated him for labor. Rallying, however, from this attack, he continued his business until February, 1852, when he was struck down with severe paralysis as he was finishing a written argument to be delivered before the United-States Court at Washington. He was a Christian. Many years ago, he embraced the Unitarian faith; and, through all his after-life, his thoughts and actions appeared to have been regulated from conscientious motives. He was sincerely attached to his church, and sought in all proper ways to advance the spread of its doctrines. A present of a rich silver communion-service, which he made to the church where he worshipped in Bangor, after he was taken sick, showed that the effect of his illness tended to draw his affections still closer to the best object of his wishes.

1817. — Caleb Reed died in Boston, 14 October, 1854, aged 57. He was son of Rev. John Reed, D.D., of West Bridgewater, where he was born 22 April, 1797. His mother was Hannah Sampson. He studied law with his brother, Hon. John Reed (B.U. 1803), in Yarmouth, Mass.; with whom he continued in practice until 1828. In that year he removed to Boston, and entered into business with Cyrus Alger and Co., in a foundry which is now known as the South-Boston Iron Company, of which he was treasurer. In 1821, he published in 18mo a small work entitled "The General Principles of English Grammar." For more than twenty years of his life, he was editor of the "New-Jerusalem Magazine," and a liberal contributor to its pages. He was a very efficient member of the Swedenborgian Society.

1818. — Dr. Jesse Chickering died at Jamaica Plain, West Roxbury, 29 May, 1855, aged 57. He was born in Dover, Mass., 31 August, 1797. After graduating, he entered the Theological School at Cambridge; completed his studies at that institution in 1821, and preached for several years; but was never settled over any society. He then relinquished the profession, and commenced the study of medicine. He completed his studies and received his medical degree in 1833. He practised in Boston for ten years; but, his studious habits not agreeing with the active life of a physician, he retired from the service, and devoted himself to statistics, for which he had great partiality. His elaborate work on the "Population of Massachusetts from 1765 to 1840" was published in 1846. His valuable book on "Immigration into the United States" appeared in 1848. His reports on the "Census of Boston" were printed in 1851. He also contributed many valuable articles to magazines and other periodicals. He rendered essential service to the Senate committee that arranged the details of the last United-States census. He was for several years a confidential correspondent of Daniel Webster, John Davis, and other leading statesmen. A few weeks before his death, he was engaged in writing a long communication to the celebrated Marshall Hall, of London, who had misunderstood his article in De Bow's Review for August, 1853. Dr. Hall, in his work on slavery, alluded to the article as "an admirable paper;" but the author found his English friend had mistaken his views, and therefore prepared an elaborate letter in reply. His last published work was a "Letter addressed to the President of the United States on Slavery, considered in relation to the Constitutional Principles of Government in Great Britain and in the United States." It was issued from the press a few weeks before his death, and will rank its author among the profound thinkers and writers on the slavery-question. He was an intelligent, upright, and conscientious man. Few persons could be in his society without receiving instruction, as his mind was active and his habits were communicative.

1818. — Rev. James Delap Farnsworth died in Bridgewater, 12 November, 1854, aged 61. He was born in Groton, Mass., 11 September, 1793; was ordained at Orford, N.H., 1 January, 1823; dismissed 9 April, 1832; installed at Paxton, Mass., 30 April, 1835; dismissed 1840; installed at North

Chelsea; dismissed 1853; installed at Bridgewater, 1 September, 1853. In 1853, he was chaplain to the Massachusetts Senate.

1819. — JOHN HARLESTON CORBETT died in Charleston, S.C., 11 May, 1855, aged 56. He was son of Thomas and Elizabeth (Harleston) Corbett, and was born in Charleston, 16 February, 1799. He studied the profession of law; but lost his eyesight in 1826, and was blind to the day of his death. He enjoyed life, however, very highly; was fond of society; and kept himself well informed in all the great topics of the day, and felt an interest in all its leading movements. He was of a gay and elastic temperament. Still his misfortune necessarily threw him much into the shade, and he was rarely seen in public or general society.

1819. — Hon. SAMUEL BAKER WALCOTT, of Salem, died at the Massachusetts General Hospital in Boston, 4 December, 1854, aged 59. He was born in Bolton, Mass., 7 March, 1795. His given name originally was Jesse, which he had changed to Samuel Baker by legislative enactment. He received a portion of his academic education at Andover. In 1821, he was appointed tutor in Greek at Harvard College; which position he occupied about one year, having previously labored with much success as a school-teacher in Salem. He subsequently studied law in the office of Hon. Daniel Webster, and secured the esteem and confidence of his distinguished teacher, which never abated during life, and which afterwards placed the pupil in the position of guardian and guide of the son of that statesman whose whole time and care were claimed by his country. After his admission to the bar, he opened an office in Boston, but soon removed to Salem. After a brief residence in Salem, he removed to Hopkinton, where he pursued his profession with success. His public life began in this town; and no man, who frequented the halls of our legislature for more than twelve years prior to 1845, can have forgotten the calm and proper presence of the member from Hopkinton, the senator from Middlesex, or can have failed to mark the attentive hearing he always received from whatsoever assembly he addressed. No representive, no senator, ever served his town and county better than he, during many years of public life. His scholarship was excellent, his manners unostentatious; his conduct, in whatever he undertook, prudent and discreet; in public, a reliable man; in private, dignified, exemplary, and conscientiously kind and attentive.

1819. — BENJAMIN WHEATLAND died in Salem, 28 December, 1854, aged 53. He was son of Capt. Richard Wheatland, of Salem, where he was born 27 May, 1801. After graduating, he studied law, but did not pursue the profession. He engaged in the service of the New Market (N.H.) Manufacturing Company at the commencement of its career, and continued with it to the time of his death; a faithful, intelligent, upright, and honorable agent in the various stations he filled.

1822. — LUTHER BARKER LINCOLN died in Deerfield, Mass., 11 May, 1855, aged 53. He was son of Luther Lincoln, of Westford, Mass., where he was born 3 April, 1802. At an early age, he lost his mother; and, from that time, he knew little of a home till he formed one for himself. His father, who was a sea-captain, was absent most of the time, and he was kept at school. At one time, his father possessed considerable property, but lost it during the youth of his son; who was thus left, at an early age, to struggle hard for means to complete the course of study on which he had entered. He was fitted for college at Westford Academy. In college he took a respectable rank as a scholar, and was faithful and conscientious in the performance of every exercise. On leaving college, he went to Sandwich, and had charge of the academy in that place for several years. From Sandwich he removed to Hingham, and was associated with Dr. Willard in a private school in that place. In 1835, he became the principal of the academy in Deerfield; which office he filled with much acceptance till 1844, when he resigned his situation there, and accepted one in the Derby Academy at Hingham, where he remained till 1848, when he returned to Deerfield. The last seven years of his life were devoted to teaching, for the most part in a private school; a part of the time in Deerfield, and a part of the time in Greenfield. His last situation in this capacity was in the Greenfield High School. The last four months previous to his death were spent in arduous labors as representative in the legislature, to which office he was chosen with a unanimity rarely witnessed in these days. It will thus be seen that teaching was the chosen occupation to which he devoted more than thirty years of his life. It was an occupation which he loved, and to which he gave himself with all the ardor of his soul. He had a rare taste for his work: he commanded the respect of the young to a degree seldom equalled. It may be truly said of him, that he led a pure and blameless life.

1823. — Thomas Wilson Dorr died in Providence, R.I., 27 December, 1854, aged 49. He was son of Sullivan and Lydia (Allen) Dorr, and was born in Providence, 5 November, 1805. He commenced his education at the free school and the Latin Grammar School in Providence; and completed his studies, preparatory to entering college, at Phillips Academy, in Exeter, N.H. He graduated as the second scholar of his class. He attended the law lectures, and was under the instruction of Chancellor Kent in New York in 1824–25; and after passing some time in the office of John Whipple, in Providence, was admitted to the bar in 1827. He did not pursue the practice of his profession, but early turned his attention to political life, and the more congenial studies of scholastic lore. He devoted much attention to matters of public utility and general improvement. He was a trustee and treasurer of the Providence Historical Society at the time of the troubles in 1842. He gave long and zealous attention to the subject of education in the free schools; was president of the committee in 1842; introduced, and carried through the committee, the plan of a high school, which was finally adopted by the city government, and resulted in the present improved system of education.

He commenced political life in 1834. Early in that year, he attended the Freeholders' Convention, designed to bring about an extension of suffrage, and establish a republican constitution. In April of the same year, he was elected representative from the city of Providence; and was re-elected semi-annually till August, 1837. In June, 1836, he drew up a report of the investigation of the banks, and a draft of the Bank Act, which was adopted. In 1839, he was nominated as a candidate for representative to Congress, but was defeated. While a member of the Assembly, he exerted himself to obtain an extension of suffrage; he also attempted to procure the call of a convention, without success. He took an active interest in the movement which was organized in 1840 for obtaining a written constitution, securing an extension of suffrage, &c.; and was a prominent member of the convention resulting from this movement, holden in 1841, and which framed and submitted to the people a constitution, the original draft of which is in his handwriting.

He was tried upon the charge of treason at the term of the Supreme Court at Newport, in June, 1844; was convicted, and sentenced on the 25th of June to imprisonment for "life at hard labor in separate confinement." At the May term of the General Assembly holden in 1845, an act was passed, providing for his liberation on conditions which he refused. At the June session following, he was unconditionally liberated, without being restored to the rights of citizenship. The time of his continuance in prison was just one year. He was elected a delegate to the Baltimore National Democratic Conventions in 1848 and 1852, but was unable to attend either of them. The General Assembly, at their June session in 1851, restored him to all the rights and privileges of citizenship, without condition. At the January session in 1853, an act was passed annulling the sentence passed upon him by the Supreme Court. During his last illness, he connected himself with the Episcopal Church. The Democratic State Convention, holden in March last, voted to erect a monument to his memory, and appointed a committee to carry the same into effect.

1826. — Dr. GEORGE FRANKLIN TURNER died at Corpus Christi, Texas, 17 October, 1854, aged 47. He was son of Robert Turner, and was born in Boston, 22 April, 1807. After leaving college, he studied medicine in the army hospital with the late Dr. B. Turner, with a view of entering the army. His commission as assistant-surgeon was dated 23 July, 1833; previous to which time, he had practised medicine for a short period in Indiana. His commission of surgeon was of date 1 January, 1840. He was stationed at Mackinaw in 1834; when he married Mary, the eldest daughter of the late Robert Stuart, Esq., of Detroit, Mich. He afterwards served in Florida during the Seminole War; and was subsequently stationed at Fort Snelling, at the Falls of St. Anthony, on the Mississippi, until the Mexican War, when he was ordered to Mexico, where he served as medical surveyor. Afterwards, in California and Texas, he continued to render the services of his profession, which, from the time of his entering the service until the end of his life, were uninterrupted, and often as arduous as they were faithful and able.

1827. — MARSHALL TUFTS died in Lexington, Mass., 18 May, 1855, aged 52. He was son of Thomas and Rebecca (Adams) Tufts, and was born in Lexington, Mass., 26 September, 1802. In the winter of 1826, he taught a school in Woburn, Mass. After graduating, he entered as a student in the Theological School at Cambridge, but left after a short period. In 1828, he commenced his theological studies with the Rev. Abiel Holmes, D.D. (Y.C. 1783), of Cambridge. After completing his studies, he preached for some years, but was never ordained.

1828. — Dr. JOHN APPLETON SWETT died in New-York City, 18 September, 1854, aged 45. He was son of John and Alice (Appleton) Swett, and was born in Boston, 3 December, 1808. He commenced practice as a physician, in Boston; but a few years afterwards removed to the city of New York, where he resided till his death. He was one of the brightest lights of the profession in that city. For many years, he was recognized as an authority of the first standing, especially upon diseases of the chest; on which subject a volume of his, published a year or two since, has become a valuable text-book. His private practice was extensive: but he was much more largely known through his connection with the New-York City Hospital; to fill one of the most responsible offices in which, he was elected in the year 1842. His minute pathological examinations, and their comparison with the diseases illustrated thereby in the living, made him one of the most instructive lecturers that walked the wards of that famous charity; and his clinical classes were always large. He held too, at his death, an important professorship in the medical department of the University (the Fourteenth-street School). In that institution, he lectured with great success on the Institutes and Practice of Medicine.

1829. — Elbridge Gerry Austin died at Nahant, 25 July, 1854, aged 43. He was son of Hon. James T. Austin (H.C. 1802), and was born in Boston, 4 October, 1810. He studied law, and opened an office in Boston, where he practised several years. About four years before his death, he removed to San Francisco; where he opened an office, and soon obtained an extensive practice. A few weeks before his decease, he came to Boston on a visit to his relatives; and, on his passage across the Isthmus, contracted the seeds of disease which terminated his life.

1831. — Caleb Fletcher Abbott died in Toledo, Ohio, 24 April, 1855. He was son of Caleb and Mercy (Fletcher) Abbott, and was born in Chelmsford, 8 September, 1811. He studied law at Lowell and at the Law School in Cambridge; and, in 1836, removed to Toledo, where he attained a high rank in his profession, and held many important offices. He was formerly mayor of the city, and prosecuting-attorney for that judicial district. He was a ripe scholar, possessed of fine literary and scientific acquirements. As a speaker, he had but few equals as a logical and eloquent debater, and held a front rank among the members of the bar. He was a warm friend, and possessed elements of character which entitled him to the admiration and respect of his fellow-citizens.

1831. — Francis Lowell Dutton died in Brookline, Mass., 15 December, 1854, aged 42. He was son of Hon. Warren Dutton (Y.C. 1797) and Elizabeth Cabot Lowell, and was born in Boston, 21 June, 1812. He studied law in Boston, but did not long pursue the profession.

1832. — William O'Hara Robinson died in Pittsburg, Pa., 6 February, 1855, aged 41. He was second son of Gen.

William Robinson, and was born in Alleghany, Pa., 7 October, 1813. He was a lawyer in Pittsburg.

1833. — Dr. CHARLES HENRY PEIRCE died in Cambridge, Mass., 16 June, 1855, aged 41. He was son of Benjamin Peirce, of Salem, Mass. (H.C. 1801), where he was born 28 January, 1814. He studied medicine, and established himself as a physician in Salem; but subsequently removed to Cambridge. For a few years, he held the office of special examiner of drugs in the Boston custom-house.

1834. — Rev. GEORGE HENRY HASTINGS died in Chattanooga, Tenn., 2 September, 1854. He was the oldest son of Joseph Stacy Hastings, and was born in Boston, 17 June, 1814. He was for several years chaplain in the American legation at Rome, Italy; and held the place until he was compelled to relinquish it in consequence of the rapid progress of pulmonary disease. During his residence at Rome, he was a regular correspondent of the "New-York Commercial Advertiser;" and continued to write for it after his return, and during his travels through the Southern States.

1834. — Dr. SAMUEL PARKMAN died in Boston, 15 December, 1854, aged 38. He was son of Samuel Parkman (H.C. 1810), and was born in Boston, 21 June, 1816. He studied medicine and established himself as a physician in Boston, where he rapidly gained an extensive practice; and bade fair to take the highest rank among the numerous members of the profession in the city, when he was suddenly cut off in the prime of life. A few days before his death, he had been elected a member of the School Committee.

1836. — FREDERICK WILLIAM GALE, of Worcester, Mass., was lost at sea in the steamship "Arctic" on his passage from Liverpool for New York, 27 September, 1854. The "Arctic" left Liverpool 20 September; and on the 27th, off Newfoundland, was run into by another steamer, and sunk. He was born in Northborough, Mass., 22 June, 1815. He was a practising lawyer in Worcester.

1838. — CHARLES HENRY HARTSHORN died in Cincinnati, Ohio, 2 May, 1855, aged 35. He was son of Caleb Hartshorn;

and was born in Boston, 4 December, 1819. He studied no profession, but was employed as a clerk in various mercantile houses in New York, Boston, New Orleans, and Cincinnati.

1842.—WILLIAM GRINNELL CROSS died in New Bedford, Mass., 29 October, 1854, aged 37. He was son of Capt. Latham and Deborah (Snell) Cross, and was born in New Bedford, 6 November, 1816. His father was born in Fairhaven, 5 November, 1774. His mother was born 4 January, 1779; and died 15 July, 1853, aged 74. In 1789, his father learned the trade of a hatter in New Bedford, which he pursued until 1795, when he abandoned it, and went a whaling voyage on the coast of Brazil. He soon became master of a vessel, first of a coaster, which he built in 1802, and ran to New York; but subsequently was commander of a merchant-ship, and went to Liverpool; at which port he was at the time of the declaration of war in 1812. After peace, he resumed the whaling business, which he continued with success until 1828, when he retired with an ample competence.

The subject of this notice, at the age of nine years, was attacked with a severe affection of the right thigh-bone, which confined him to the house until nearly seventeen years of age; and resulted in exfoliation and shortening of the bone, and rendered him a cripple for life. He then entered the High School in New Bedford, which he attended about a year; when he entered the counting-room of William T. Russell, afterwards collector of New Bedford, where he continued two years. He then determined to obtain a collegiate education, and pursued his preparatory studies under the instruction of Dr. Julius Stewart Mayhew, of New Bedford. After leaving college, he studied law under the instruction of Hon. Thomas Dawes Eliot; when, on being admitted to the bar, he opened an office in New Bedford, but abandoned the profession within a year. He married (1st), in January, 1846, Rebecca C. Wady, daughter of Humphrey Wady. She died without issue, 20 February, 1847, in her 24th year; and he married (2d), 19 January, 1851, Ruth Almy Weaver, daughter of John Weaver, and had two children (daughters), the elder of whom survives him. His second wife died 13 May, 1857, at the age of 31. Mr. Cross pursued no business after relinquishing his profession, as his health continued feeble. The later years of his life were cheered, amid so much affliction, by devotion to choice literature and by the kind offices of numerous friends. His integrity of character was unimpeached, and his society was sought by his religious associates.

1843. — Eliphalet Birchard died in Lebanon, Conn., 20 September, 1854, aged 39. He was born in Lebanon, 21 January, 1815. After graduation, he entered the Theological Seminary in Andover, and completed his studies there in 1846. Though invited by several churches to settle as pastor, he was prevented by imperfect health from accepting any of these invitations; but he was a faithful and acceptable preacher, and will long be remembered with gratitude by many who were richly blessed by his labors.

1846. — William Thaddeus Harris died in Cambridge, Mass., 19 October, 1854, aged 28. He was son of Dr. Thaddeus William Harris (H.C. 1815), and was born in Milton, Mass., 26 January, 1826. He removed with his father's family to Cambridge when five years old. He began to fit for college in September, 1840, at the Hopkins Classical School in Cambridge, then first established by Mr. John B. Henck (H.C. 1840); and completed his preparatory studies under Mr. Edmund B. Whitman (H.C. 1838). A physical infirmity, a congenital weakness of the spine, followed by its permanent curvature, debarred him from the usual pleasures of those of his own age; and he was obliged to have recourse to books, which, in process of time, became his meat and drink, his only solace, his only amusement. While in college, in his junior year, he printed a collection of "Epitaphs from the Old Burying-ground in Cambridge." This collection was made mostly during his boyhood, while attending the town-school. He finished it, and added the notes, while in college; and the book was published in May, 1845. Immediately after graduation, he entered the Law School at Cambridge; and was admitted to the bar on the 1st of December, 1853. His acquaintance with early New-England history was thorough and extensive. He projected several historical performances, which, had he lived, would have been of great value: one was a "Continuation of Prince's Chronology." To what extent he went with it, is not known; but what he did was so well done, that Mr. Prince, it is believed, could not have wished it better done had he been here with all his former ability to appreciate such a work.

1846. — NATHANIEL GILMAN PERRY died at sea, on board ship "William Tell," on the passage from Havre to New York, 2 June, 1855, aged 28. He was son of Dr. William Perry (H.C. 1811), of Exeter, N.H.; where he was born 28 October, 1826. He inherited a feeble constitution; and, at the age of seven, lost one of his eyes by an arrow in the hands of another boy. He was fitted for college in Phillips Exeter Academy, and entered the freshman class in August, 1842. He was taken with raising blood while in college, which recurred frequently, on exertion of the arms, for three or four years. On leaving college in 1846, he commenced reading law with Gilman Marston, Esq., of Exeter; and entered the Law School in Cambridge in 1847, where he remained a year. In the spring of 1849, he accompanied Capt. John C. Long, as his clerk, in the United-States steam-frigate "Mississippi," to the Mediterranean. He returned home in November, 1851, and was admitted to the Rockingham bar. In March, 1852, he was chosen to represent the town of Exeter in the legislature, and again in 1853. His health now became so feeble, that he was unable to engage fully in the labors of his profession; and, thinking himself benefited by being at sea, he was reluctantly induced, in the following October, to accept Capt. Long's invitation to go again with him to the Mediterranean, in the United-States steamer "Saranac." For a time, his health seemed to improve; but, in the autumn of 1854, he became so unwell as to find it expedient to leave the ship for a time, and remain in Nice. The latter part of the winter, and the first of the spring, he spent in Florence. In April, he visited Tunis and Naples; but became so feeble, that he was compelled to leave for home under the care of a benevolent gentleman and his wife, who volunteered the responsible and arduous undertaking.

They left Leghorn the 3d of May, and went to Paris by way of Marseilles. Here he joined a brother, who had previously been with him in Florence, and now, finding him so ill, prepared to accompany him home. They sailed from Havre the 24th of May; and, on the 2d of June, he died in the arms of his brother, a firm believer in the mercy of God through the merits of his Son.

1850. — Oscar Fitzalan Parker died in St. Louis, Mo., 5 August, 1854, aged 26. He was son of Peter Parker, and and was born in Schroeppel, Oswego County, N.Y., 19 February, 1828. He was a young man of pure life, sterling integrity, and marked abilities. He was a member of the legal profession, and had recently established himself in St. Louis, with the intention of making that his place of residence. A meeting of the St. Louis bar was held on the day of his death, at which resolutions were passed in warm eulogy of the deceased, who, though but recently attached to that bar, had already made himself beloved and respected by his associates.

1851. — William Coombs Wheelwright was lost at sea, 9 September, 1854, aged 25. He was son of Ebenezer and Sarah (Boddily) Wheelwright, and was born in Portsmouth, N.H., 13 December, 1829. His grandparents, on his father's side, were Ebenezer Wheelwright (born in Gloucester), and Anne (born at Newburyport), daughter of William Coombs. On his maternal line, his grandfather, John Boddily, was born in England, probably in 1760. His grandmother, Sarah (Tuckmell) Boddily, was born in Bristol, Eng., or, at least, came from that place. When the subject of this notice was four years old, he moved with his father's family to Boston, where, and at Roxbury and at Salem, he lived till he entered college in 1847. His childhood was marked with fearlessness and self-reliance, fondness for the sea, a taste for the mechanic arts, correct deportment, and benevolence. From a defect in his vision, he was never able clearly to discern objects about him; and consequently, being quite liable to accidents, he received several slight injuries. Although his inclination for a liberal education was not strong, he began to fit for college, in

1841, at the Boston Latin School; where, with the exception of ten months at the Salem Latin School, he continued till the last two years before entering college, when he was at the Roxbury Latin School. During the first year of his college-course, he was parietal freshman; and, in his second year, monitor at the lectures and declamations. In the junior year, he was absent nearly two months, and seriously threatened with consumption. While an undergraduate, his love of adventure was strengthened by his reading; which, besides poetry, — to which he was much attached, — consisted principally of travels and voyages, particularly of the narrations of various arctic exploring expeditions. The state of his eyesight, however, interfered with his literary pursuits. His strong memory, enabling him to repeat long poems, — particularly of Walter Scott, — and his activity in the college playgrounds, relieved many an hour which otherwise might have been unemployed. After graduating, he was engaged for a short time in teaching at Raynham: but the trouble in his eyesight continuing, and his passion for a sea-life increasing, he went on board one of his father's vessels, as a common sailor, to the West Indies; and he was so much pleased and benefited, that he abandoned all thoughts of studying a profession. After another voyage to the West Indies, he went to the Sandwich Islands. While there, he was deeply impressed with the importance of personal religion, occasioned by the sabbath worship of the islanders. He had never witnessed the gospel in New England as he saw it manifested in the conduct of these converted heathen. He described their religious worship as more impressive than could be imagined; being marked by a degree of solemnity, sincerity, and reverence, such as he had never seen. Subsequently, he went on a voyage to Havre, in France, where he attended the Bethel worship; and on his return to New York, and thence home, it was manifest that an important change had taken place in his character. His mind was solemn and thoughtful. His evening hours were spent in solitude, reading the Scriptures, and prayer. He became much concerned for the welfare of seamen, collected money for tracts, and employed his efforts in various ways for their good; and, in his conversation with his friends, it was evident that he was deeply concerned to fulfil the duties of life, and always to be prepared for death. His eyesight continuing to improve, he took the post of first officer on board the brig "Horace Greeley," of Philadelphia. He made a voyage to Cuba and back; thence proceeded to Charleston, S.C.; and thence to Georgetown, in the same State. The brig was there loaded for Philadelphia; and, sailing on the 5th of September, encountered a hurricane on the eighth and ninth of the same month, in which the brig, on the last day named, was upset, and all on board perished. Two other vessels sailed the same day from Georgetown, bound north; and both vessels, with all their crews, were lost.

He cherished a love for literature; and, in all his voyages, he made some of his old Latin classics his companions. The rough men among whom he was thrown felt the refining influences of his education, and at once and cheerfully acknowledged his superiority. His benevolence and sympathy created bonds of strong attachment between him and his friends. He had no sunshine of his own which did not gladden the hearts of others, and he counted no blessing he possessed complete till it was largely shared by his friends and others. He loved much, and was greatly beloved, and left a void in the hearts of his parents and in the circle of his friends which can never be filled. He kept a journal, on the title-page of which was the following memorandum: "Should God in his providence see fit to take my life during this voyage, I wish this book to be kept strictly private, and sent to my friends in Newburyport, Mass."

1854. — Henry Cobb, of Barnstable, died suddenly, of inflammation of the bowels, at Tazewell, Tenn., 5 January, 1855, aged 21 years and 11 months. He was son of Enoch T. and Abiah Cobb, and was born in Barnstable, Mass., 5 February, 1833. He had studied and qualified himself for civil engineering; and, seeking a more southern climate for the benefit of his precarious health, he joined an engineer corps in Tennessee, in November, 1854, and was actively engaged with them in surveying for and locating a railroad through that state, when, after about a week's confinement, he died. He was remarkable for his studious and correct habits; and though compelled by a pulmonary attack to leave college, and, by the advice of physicians, to travel in Europe, passing several months of his junior year in Italy, he kept his place in his class, and graduated with the usual honors.

1854. — NICHOLAS GILMAN died in Exeter, N.H., 31 October, 1854, aged 20. He was son of Capt. Nathaniel Gilman, and was born in Exeter, 8 May, 1834; was fitted for college at Phillips Academy, Exeter, and entered the sophomore class in 1851. He was distinguished for his scholarship, courtesy of manners, singular sweetness of disposition, and correct morals.

1855-56.

1782. — Hon. JOHN WELLES died in Boston, 25 September, 1855, aged 90. He was son of Arnold Welles (H.C. 1745), and was born in Boston, 14 October, 1764; was fitted for college by Rev. Daniel Shute, D.D., of Hingham (H.C. 1743), where he had among his fellow-students Capt. James Sever, of Kingston, Mass. (H.C. 1781), and Col. Thomas H. Perkins, of Boston. He was the youngest in his class; having graduated before he had completed his eighteenth year. Soon after leaving college, he entered into mercantile business with his father. About the year 1802, he formed a copartnership with his cousin Samuel Welles (H.C. 1796), under the firm of John and Samuel Welles. This partnership was dissolved in 1815; and his partner proceeded to Paris, where he became connected with the celebrated banking-house of Welles and Co. Mr. Welles soon afterwards took into partnership his kinsman, Benjamin Welles of Boston, under the style of John and Benjamin Welles. This firm continued until a recent period, when the infirmities of age compelled the senior partner to retire, having accumulated an ample fortune. He was one of the few survivors who were claimants for French spoliations prior to 1800. He was several times elected a representative, and also a senator, in our state legislature. He was a member of the executive council under the administration of Gov. Strong. When the city charter was granted in 1822, he was elected a member of the first common council; and, the following year, was re-elected, when he was chosen president of that branch of the city government. He was one of the earliest promoters of agricultural societies; was for several years an active member of the Massachusetts Agricultural Society; and was associated with the late Hon. John Lowell in editing an agricultural journal. He owned a valuable farm in Natick, Mass., on which, for many years, he passed the summer season, devoting himself to agricultural pursuits. This farm has been in possession of the Welles family ever since the days of the old Apostle Eliot, the translator of the Bible into the Indian language. In politics, Mr. Welles was ever a firm and consistent federalist of the Washington school. In all his business transactions, he was characterized as a merchant of strict integrity and upright conduct. In the last two triennial catalogues of the college which were issued before his death, his name stood as the senior surviving alumnus. He outlived all his classmates many years.

1783. — Asa Andrews died in Ipswich, Mass., 13 January, 1856, aged 93. He was son of Robert Andrews, and was born in that part of Shrewsbury which is now within the limits of Boylston, 11 May, 1762. His father was a native of Boxford. His mother — who was a Bradstreet, a native of Topsfield — was a descendant of Gov. Simon Bradstreet. Since the death of the Hon. John Welles, Mr. Andrews has been the oldest surviving graduate of Harvard; and, at the time of his death, was the oldest man in Ipswich. He studied law with Hon. Caleb Strong, of Northampton (H.C. 1764). After completing his legal studies, he opened an office in Ipswich, where he resided during the remainder of his long life. In 1794, he was appointed, by Washington, collector of the port and district of Ipswich; which office he held until 1829, when he was removed by Jackson. At the time of his removal, a balance was claimed as due from him to the government; but on a trial before Judge Story, in the Circuit Court at Boston, the jury found that there was due *to* him from the government about two thousand dollars. This was not paid him until about a year before his death; when, by an appropriation made by Congress, he received the balance which had been due to him more than a quarter of a century. He was a man of distinguished ability. He filled many offices of honor and trust, and enjoyed the entire confidence of his fellow-citizens.

1785. — Rev. Thaddeus Fiske died in Charlestown, Mass., 14 November, 1855, aged 93. He was son of Jonathan and

Abigail Fiske; was born in Weston, Mass., 22 June, 1762; and was, at the time of his death, the oldest clergyman in Massachusetts. He was ordained pastor of the church in West Cambridge, 23 April, 1788; and resigned his pastoral charge, 23 April, 1828, on the completion of the fortieth year of his ministry. It is remarkable that he lived to see five clergymen successively ordained over the society where he had faithfully labored for forty years, three of whom passed off the stage before him: viz., Rev. David Damon, who died 25 June, 1843, aged 55; Rev. William Ware, who died 19 February, 1852, aged 54; and Rev. James Francis Brown, who died 13 June, 1853, aged 32. In the year 1821, the degree of D.D. was conferred upon Dr. Fiske by Columbia College, New York. A few months before his death, he removed from West Cambridge to Charlestown to reside with a relative in the latter place, where he passed the few remaining days of his life.

1787. — Hon. WILLIAM CRANCH died in Washington, D.C., 1 September, 1855, aged 86. He was son of Richard and Mary (Smith) Cranch, and was born in Weymouth, Mass., 17 July, 1769. His mother was sister of the wife of President John Adams. He was prepared for college under the instruction of Rev. John Shaw, of Haverhill (H.C. 1772); and entered the freshman class, six months in advance, in February, 1784. He studied law with Hon. Thomas Dawes, of Boston (H.C. 1777); and in July, 1790, was admitted to practice in the Court of Common Pleas in this State. He opened an office in Braintree, near Quincy; but, one year afterwards, removed to Haverhill. For three years he attended the courts in Essex County, Mass., and Rockingham County, N.H.; and was admitted to practice in the Massachusetts Supreme Judicial Court in July, 1793. In September, 1794, he was employed as the land-agent of the firm of Morris, Nicholson, and Greenleaf, in the city of Washington; to which place he removed in October of that year, and there resided during the remainder of his life. In April, 1795, he was married to Nancy Greenleaf, daughter of Hon. William Greenleaf, with whom he lived nearly fifty years; she having died in Washington, 16 September, 1843. In 1800, he was appointed one of the commissioners of the city of Washington, which office he resigned in 1801; when he was appointed, by President Adams, junior assistant-judge of the United-States Circuit Court of the District of Columbia, under the act of Congress of 27 February, 1801: the late Gov. Thomas Johnson, of Maryland, having been appointed chief judge; and Mr. James Marshall, brother of the late Chief Justice Marshall, having been appointed elder assistant-judge. Mr. Adams consented to give this appointment to his nephew, only upon the earnest personal appeal of Chief-Justice Marshall, after a public petition to the same end; as he was apprehensive, that, in the dispensation of office, the public might charge upon him that system of nepotism which has since become so common at the seat of government; and hence his reluctance to elevate one whom he loved next to his own son. Gov. Johnson refused to accept the office; and President Jefferson appointed William Kitty, Esq., chief judge. Mr. Marshall resigned in 1803; and Nicholas Fitzhugh, Esq., of Virginia, was appointed in his place. In 1805, Mr. Kitty having been appointed chancellor of Maryland, Judge Cranch was appointed by President Jefferson to the office of chief-justice; and, by virtue of that office, he was sole judge of the District Court of the United States for the District of Columbia, which has the same jurisdiction as the other district courts of the United States. He published nine volumes of cases in the Supreme Court of the United States; a memoir of the life, character, and writings of President John Adams, read before the Columbian Institute, 16 March, 1837; and an address upon the subject of temperance in 1831, a small pamphlet. He was a member of the American Academy of Arts and Sciences, and of the American Antiquarian Society. In 1829, he received the honorary degree of Doctor of Laws from Harvard College. For fifty years and more, he was looked up to in Washington, Alexandria, Georgetown, and in the neighborhood, as the chief citizen of the district. By his kindness and benevolence to the poor, by his uniform courtesy to all men, by his life-long industry and patience in labor, by his love of letters, by his fidelity to every private and public trust reposed in him, he won a love and respect which were felt by every man, and even every child, who knew him. His life, too, was eminently a religious one; and as he lived, so he died, in the fullest hope of a blessed immortality.

1787. — Dr. WALTER HUNNEWELL died in Watertown, Mass., 19 October, 1855, aged 86. He was born in Cambridge, 10 August, 1769; studied medicine with Dr. Marshall Spring, of Watertown (H.C. 1762); and settled in Watertown, where he passed the whole of his professional life, and was highly respected as a good citizen and a skilful physician.

1793.—Hon. CHARLES JACKSON died in Boston, 13 December, 1855, aged 80. He was the eldest son of Hon. Jonathan Jackson, of Newburyport (H.C. 1761), — one of the most prominent men of this state during the revolutionary era; being a member of the Continental Congress in 1780; marshal of the district of Massachusetts, under Washington; treasurer of the commonwealth for five years, and of Harvard College at the time of his death; — and grandson of Edward Jackson (H.C. 1726), a distinguished merchant of Boston. He was born in Newburyport, 31 May, 1775; was fitted for college under the instruction of Nicholas Pike, of Newburyport (H.C. 1766), and at Dummer Academy. He graduated with the highest honors of his class. He pursued the study of law in Newburyport, under the instruction of Hon. Theophilus Parsons (H.C. 1769); was admitted to practice in the county of Essex in 1796; immediately entered upon the practice of his profession in his native town, and rose rapidly to eminence. In 1803, he removed to Boston, and soon attained the highest rank at the bar, where James Sullivan, John Lowell, Christopher Gore, Rufus Amory, Harrison Gray Otis, Samuel Dexter, William Sullivan, and other distinguished men, were his associates and competitors; and, in partnership with Hon. Samuel Hubbard, (Y.C. 1802), acquired probably the most lucrative practice ever before known in Massachusetts. In 1813, he was appointed by Gov. Strong to the office of judge of the Supreme Court, to fill the vacancy occasioned by the death of Hon. Theodore

Sedgwick (Y.C. 1765); which appointment, he, after much hesitation, accepted, impelled by a high sense of duty, and by the urgency of the chief-justice and his other professional friends of his peculiar fitness for that high station. He discharged its duties with eminent fidelity until the year 1823; when he was compelled by declining health to resign his seat, to the universal regret of the bar and the people of the state. Immediately on his retirement, for the purposes of relaxation and recovery, he went to Europe; and, while in England, received great attention from the jurists and statesmen of the times. In 1820, he was a very influential member of the convention for revising the constitution of the state. In 1832, Gov. Lincoln, acting under a resolve of the legislature, appointed three commissioners to revise the General Statutes of the commonwealth; and Judge Jackson was placed at the head of this important trust. His associates were Hon. Asahel Stearns (H.C. 1797), and John Hooker Ashmun (H.C. 1818). Mr. Ashmun died soon afterwards, and Hon. John Pickering (H.C. 1796) was appointed in his place. Before his elevation to the bench of the Supreme Court, he was elected, in 1808, in 1809, and in 1812, a representative to the General Court. After his resignation, he was selected for the performance of various important trusts; among which was that of a member of the corporation of Harvard College, which he filled from 1825 to 1834. In politics, he clung with the ardor and tenacity of settled principle to the ancient faith of the old Essex platform, of which his master, Parsons, so admirably sketched the outlines in his famous "Resolutions," and from which so many of the noblest men, whom this country has ever counted among its jewels, have so often uttered the words of warning and wisdom and encouragement and patriotism, in the roughest times the country has ever seen. In religion, he was a Christian believer in faith and practice, without ostentatious profession, but with earnest and never-shrinking fidelity to the great principles which his faith inculcates. He had long looked upon his work as done upon earth, and was awaiting in calmness and serene composure the summons which was at last kindly sent, translating him from this to a higher world, so gently and free from suffering, that it seemed little else than falling asleep.

1795. — HENRY GASSETT died in Boston, 15 August, 1855, aged 81. He was son of Henry and Persis (Howe) Gassett, and was born in Northborough, Mass., 1 February, 1774. He was of French extraction, and the name was, originally, Gachet. About the year 1700, two Frenchmen, brothers, Huguenots, named Henri and David Gachet, emigrated from Rochelle, France, and landed in Boston. David married a Miss White, and settled in Raynham, Mass.: Henri married Miss Sarah Hoskins, and settled at Taunton, Mass. The descendants of the two have Anglicized the name in different ways: those of the elder brother writing it Gassett; and those of the younger, Gushee. Most of them reside in Massachusetts, in Bristol County, where the descendants of both are numerous; and but few, if any of them, live out of New England. They do not, however, retain the name of their progenitors to a very great extent, owing to the large proportion of females in the families. The subject of this notice was a descendant in the third generation from Henri the Huguenot. He was fitted for college at Leicester Academy. On graduating, he began teaching school, which he continued some twelve or eighteen months: but, finding it not a very profitable business, he relinquished it, and engaged in trade, first in the country, and afterwards in Boston, in a small, cautious way; till, about the year 1804, he became the head of the extensive dry-goods importing house of Gassett, Upham, and Co.; and on the 18th of April, 1805, he sailed for Liverpool, being the first of three visits he made to England. He continued doing a large and profitable business for more than forty years; and retired about eleven years before his death, having accumulated an ample fortune. He married, 17 February, 1812, Lucy Wood, of Northborough; by whom he had nine children, five of whom survive him. Three of his sons are graduates at Harvard College; namely, Henry in 1834, Edward in 1843, and Francis in 1847. There is in the possession of the family a letter from the mother — then a widow — of the two emigrants, Henri and David, dated "A la Rochelle, le 1r de mars, 1711," and directed thus: "La présente, qu'il donne à Maître Henri Gachet, charpentier de navire, à Boston." Mr. Gassett was one of the most distinguished of the old anti-masonic party, and by his pen and wealth contributed liberally to its aid. He was an intimate personal friend of John Quincy Adams, for whose talents and character he had the most unbounded respect.

1795.—Hon. BENJAMIN GORHAM died in Boston, 27 September, 1855, aged 80. He was son of Hon. Nathaniel Gorham, and was born in Charlestown, Mass., 13 February, 1775. Nathaniel Gorham, a member and president of the Continental Congress, was the father of a numerous family, among whom was the late Mrs. Peter C. Brooks, and a son, who became one of the pioneers of Western New York, and died a few years since at Canandaigua. Benjamin, who was a younger son, soon after graduating, entered the office of the Hon. Theophilus Parsons, in Newburyport, as a student of law, where he pursued and completed his legal studies. He then opened an office in Boston, where he permanently resided. He rose rapidly to eminence in his profession, and soon became one of the leading members of the Boston bar. He was a familiar associate of the famous circle in which were comprised Prescott, Jackson, Parsons, Gore, Dexter, Sullivan, Cabot, Ames, Otis, Parker, and Lowell. From 1820 to 1823, he represented Suffolk District in the United-States Congress. He was succeeded by Hon. Daniel Webster, who held the office until 1827, when he was chosen senator; and Mr. Gorham was again elected representative from Suffolk, which office he filled with honor to himself and the entire satisfaction of his constituents until 1831, when, his term having expired, he declined a re-election. When in Congress, although not a frequent speaker, he was always listened to with marked attention, as he possessed a mind of great logical acuteness, and his speeches commanded the respect even of his political opponents. The great questions which fell within these periods, under the administration of Mr. Adams and Gen. Jackson, were those of internal improvements, the revenue-tariff, and the bank of the United States. No one understood them better than Mr. Gorham. He discussed them on several occasions with eminent ability; and no student of the history of our legislation on these subjects should fail to consult the reports of his arguments. His speech, in 1828, on the occupation of Oregon, is another monument of his enlightened and prudent statesmanship. In 1833, after repeated fruitless attempts of his party to choose another candidate, he was reluctantly persuaded to accept a third election; and served in the third Congress, under the administration of Jackson; of the proceedings of which body, his speech on the removal of the deposits from the United-States Bank, in February, 1834, was a prominent feature. After his retirement from Congress, he never accepted office, except for a short time as a member of one or both branches of the state legislature. Being at ease in point of fortune, the remainder of his life was passed in the company of his books and his friends. He was of a singularly sociable nature: he loved to talk, and talked admirably well. His equanimity was imperturbable, and his cheerfulness seldom clouded. In the closer relations of life, he was singularly favored. By his first marriage, he became connected with the family of Judge Lowell; and by his second, with that of John Coffin Jones. Left a widower for many years, death had been made familiar to his mind. He had often expressed a desire that it might be sudden; and the gentle messenger that summoned him fulfilled his wish.

1795.—Dr. EBENEZER LAWRENCE died in Pepperell, Mass., 14 June, 1856, aged 86. He was son of Ephraim and Anna (Fisk) Lawrence, and was born in Pepperell, 9 January, 1770. He pursued his medical studies under the instruction of Gov. John Brooks, of Medford; and settled as a physician in Hampton, N.H., where he acquired an extensive practice, which he continued with eminent success for fifty-one years. Unlike most of his contemporaries in the medical profession, he administered to his patients but very little medicine; relying rather upon the *vis medicatrix naturæ* to effect a cure. He married, in 1800, Abigail Leavitt, daughter of Col. Thomas Leavitt, of Hampton; and had a large family of children. His wife and four children, two sons and two daughters, survive him. He was highly esteemed and respected by the citizens among whom he so long resided, and who intrusted to him many offices of importance and responsibility. He was repeatedly elected a selectman, and several times represented the town in the New-Hampshire legislature. About five years before his death, he returned to his native town, where he resided in the family of one of his sons during the remainder of his life. He died full of years, universally respected; and will long be remembered as the "beloved physician."

1795. — Rev. Silas Warren died in Jackson, Waldo County, Me., 7 January, 1856, aged 88. He was son of John and Mary (Myrick) Warren, and was born in Weston, Mass., 11 May, 1767. For several years after leaving college, he was engaged in the instruction of youth. He was ordained at Jackson, 16 September, 1812. He was a liberal divine of the old school; and after a peaceful ministry of about ten years, in consequence of some dissatisfaction with the liberality of his opinions, felt by a portion of his people, his pastoral relation to the church in Jackson was dissolved. He continued to reside in the town, and spent the remainder of his days, until overtaken by the infirmity of age, in teaching, and in cultivating a farm. He possessed a naturally vigorous constitution, and retained his faculties of body and mind to such a degree as enabled him to enjoy life to almost the close of its period of eighty-eight years. A cheerful and happy temperament made him peculiarly acceptable in his favorite occupation of instruction, and sustained him under the privations of straitened circumstances. His appearance in the pulpit was calm, dignified, and grave; and his manners, in private intercourse, affable and polite. He had long looked forward to death as a happy release, and at last sank quietly away as in sleep. It was the natural, peaceful close of a venerable old age.

1797. — Leonard Jarvis died in Baltimore, Md., 16 November, 1855, aged 76. He was son of Nathaniel Jarvis, and was born in Cambridge, Mass., 7 January, 1779. For ten years after leaving college, he followed maritime pursuits, and was master of an indiaman, making successful voyages. He then quitted this sphere to enter upon mercantile life, and formed a partnership with Mr. Asaph Stone; their place of business being first at No. 9, Union Street, and afterwards at the corner of Court and Washington streets, Boston; which firm continued for six years. During the war of 1812, Mr Jarvis disposed of his interest in the business, and resided in Cambridge until the close of the war, when he removed to Baltimore for the benefit of a milder climate. Here he was highly successful in business, and became wealthy. He married, in 1806 or 1807, Mary Cogswell, of Littleton. They had no child. He was a gentleman without ostentation or display, and remarkable for his generosity towards young men in the mercantile profession. By his will, he devised the Melange edifice in Baltimore, known as the "Jarvis Building," and occupied by the "Baltimore Patriot," one half to Harvard College, and the other half to the Baltimore Humane Impartial Society, the House of Refuge, the Aged-Women's Home, and the Baltimore Orphan Asylum. These devises do not, however, take effect until the decease of his widow, to whom nearly the whole of the income of his estate is given during her life. The estate is estimated at not less than twenty thousand dollars a year, and is increasing.

1797. — JOSEPH TILTON died in Exeter, N.H., 27 March, 1856, aged 81. He was born in East Kingston, N.H., 10 August, 1774; and was fitted for college at Exeter Academy. On leaving college, he returned to Exeter, where he studied law with Hon. Jeremiah Smith (Rutg. C. 1780), who had that year removed from Peterborough to Exeter. He was admitted to the bar in 1801; and immediately afterwards opened an office in Wakefield, N.H., where he practised four or five years; when he removed to Rochester, N.H., where he remained two or three years; and, in the summer of 1809, went to Exeter, and there passed the remainder of his life. He acquired an extensive and respectable practice, which he continued for forty-five years, when he retired from the active duties of his profession. It is a sufficient proof of his professional success, that he gained a prominent position at a bar where Webster,

Mason, Smith, Sullivan, Woodbury, Bartlett, Cutts, and Haven were his contemporaries and competitors. He was held in high estimation by his fellow-citizens, as was indicated, among other things, by their electing him to represent the town of Exeter, in the New-Hampshire legislature, nine successive years, — from 1815 to 1823 inclusive. He was a director in the old Exeter Bank, for many years, until it closed. In 1806, he married Nancy Folsom, of Exeter. She died in 1837. In his professional and social relations, his good-humor was as unfailing as his integrity was undoubted. He appeared to regard his profession as his post of duty, in which he was to do his part in guarding and advancing the interests of society. He passed through life in the enjoyment of the respect of his brethren of the bar, and the confidence of the community. He lived to a good old age, and his memory will be long cherished by those who knew him.

1797. — Dr. JOHN COLLINS WARREN died in Boston, 4 May, 1856, aged 77. He was the eldest of ten children of Dr. John and Abigail (Collins) Warren.; and was born in Boston, 1 August, 1778. His father, Dr. John Warren (H.C. 1771), was born in Roxbury, Mass,, 27 July, 1753; studied medicine with his brother, Gen. Joseph Warren; and acquired a reputation as a physician and surgeon no less extensive than that to which his distinguished son afterwards attained. His mother was the daughter of John Collins, who was governor of Rhode Island from 1786 to 1789, a patriot of the Revolution, and a delegate to Congress in 1789. He died at Newport, R.I., March, 1795, at the age of 78 years. His uncle, Gen. Joseph Warren (H.C. 1759), was born in Roxbury, 11 June, 1741; and was a physician in Boston. He fell a martyr to the cause of freedom in the battle of Bunker Hill.

Dr. Warren was a pupil at the Public Latin School in Boston when the first Franklin medals were distributed; and was a successful competitor for one of them, an honor of which he was justly proud. After going through a course of medical studies under the instruction of his father, he went to Europe, where he passed several years studying in the hospitals of London and

Paris. While in London, he enjoyed the friendship and instruction of Sir Astley Cooper. On his return, he established himself as a physician in Boston, and soon rose to the highest rank in his profession. In 1806, he was appointed assistant-professor of anatomy and surgery in Harvard College; and on the death of his father, which took place 4 April, 1815, he succeeded him to the full professorship in that chair, and was inaugurated 1 November of that year. The duties of this office he discharged with signal ability and success for a period of thirty-two years. In 1847, he tendered his resignation, which was accepted so far as to relieve him from the active duties of the professorship; but he was retained as emeritus-professor until his death. He was elected president of the Massachusetts Medical Society, 7 June, 1832; which office he held until 25 May, 1836, when, at the annual meeting of the society, he declined a re-election. He was a member of the American Academy of Arts and Sciences, of the American Philosophical Society, of the Philadelphia Academy of Natural Sciences, of the Academy of Naples, and the Medical Society of Florence; a corresponding member of the Royal Academy of Medicine of Paris, and an honorary member of the Medico-Chirurgical Society of London. He was, at the time of his death, president of the Boston Society of Natural History. He was one of the original members of the Boston Light Infantry; and was third sergeant on the first parade ever made by that corps, in 1798. After his retirement from the active duties of his professorship, he devoted much of his time to the study of the natural sciences. His museum of specimens in comparative anatomy, osteology and paleontology, was one of the most valuable private collections in the world; and he had probably the most perfect skeleton of the *mastodon giganteus* of North America known to be in existence. He was, in conjunction with his friend and contemporary, Dr. James Jackson, mainly instrumental in originating the Massachusetts General Hospital and McLean Asylum, by issuing, in August, 1810, a circular to the public on the need of such an institution; and afterwards rendered valuable service in arranging and perfecting its organization. He was, for nearly thirty-six years (from 6 April, 1817, to February, 1853), at first the sole, and subsequently the principal, acting surgeon, in daily attendance upon its wards; and by his eminent talents, knowledge, and practical skill, as well as by his fidelity, energy, and untiring devotion in behalf of its interests, largely contributed to make it what it now is, — an honor to the city and to the commonwealth. He married, first, 17 November, 1803, Susan Powell, daughter of Hon. Jonathan Mason, by whom he had seven children, six of whom survive him. His wife died 3 June, 1841; and he married, second, 17 October, 1843, Anna Winthrop, daughter of Hon. Thomas L. Winthrop, by whom he had no issue. She died 17 December, 1850. He contributed a large number of valuable papers in the Massachusetts Medical Society's publications. A few years since, he prepared and published, at his own expense, and for gratuitous distribution to public institutions and scientific persons, his great work on the *mastodon* of this country; and, a few weeks before his death, he issued a second and enlarged edition, which is offered for sale at a price which will barely meet the cost of publication. In 1854, he published, in a splendid quarto volume, a "Genealogy of Warren." He died full of years and honors; and, by his death, science lost one of its most ardent and devoted laborers.

1798. — Hon. Samuel Phillips Prescott Fay died in Cambridge, Mass., 18 May, 1856, aged 78. He was son of Jonathan Fay, and was born in Concord, Mass., 10 January, 1778. He was the orator, who, by the appointment of his classmates, addressed them in Latin, according to the usage of that time, before the faculty, at the close of the college-studies of the class, and at the time of their separation until the recurrence of the annual commencement. On leaving college, he began the study of law: but soon afterwards he received a captain's commission in the American army, raised in consequence of French hostilities; and joined the forces under the command of Gen. Hamilton, stationed at Oxford, Mass., in 1798–9. His military career, however, was not of long duration. After the successful issue of the second mission of envoys sent to France by President Adams, the army was disbanded, and young Fay resumed the study of the law. Having completed his course of legal studies, and been admitted to the bar, he opened an office in Cambridge, where he soon acquired a high reputation as a successful lawyer. He was early and happily married, and enjoyed, in an uncommon degree, the blessings of domestic life; and, when the partner of his comforts and cares was taken from him, he was not left in entire domestic solitude, but was cared for and solaced by dutiful and affectionate children. In his professional business, he was faithful and exact, and possessed the utmost confidence of his clients. Without seeking for political distinction, he took a reasonable degree of interest in politics, which was demonstrated by his pen, and by his acceptance of the office of representative of the town. He was a member of the governor's council in 1818 and 1819, and of the Convention for revising the Constitution of Massachusetts in 1820. On the 1st of May, 1821, he was appointed judge of probate for Middlesex County; the duties of which office he discharged with singular fidelity and promptness for nearly thirty-five years, until the latter part of March, 1856, when he was compelled to resign it on account of the feeble state of his health. He was elected a member of the Board of Overseers of Harvard College in 1824, which office he held until the new organization of the board in 1852. In all his civil, social, and official relations, his uprightness and urbanity will be among the cherished memories of a host of survivors.

1798.—Hon. Ralph Hill French died in Manchester, N.H., 31 October, 1855, aged 79. He was born in Marblehead, Mass., 31 January, 1776. He studied law with Hon. William Gordon, of Amherst, N.H. (H.C. 1779); and opened an office in Marblehead, in which town, and in Salem, he practised law more than twenty years, during which time he held many offices of trust and importance. In 1819, he was elected a senator in the Massachusetts legislature from Essex District. He was chosen register of deeds for Essex County, and held the office twenty years, until he was compelled to resign it on account of the impaired state of his health. Three years before his death, he removed to Manchester, where he spent the remainder of his days. He married a sister of Hon. Charles Humphrey Atherton, of Amherst, N.H. (H.C. 1794). He was highly respected by the bar, and by the people of Essex County, among whom he passed the greater portion of his life.

1799. — Hon. EBENEZER CLAP died in Bath, Me., 28 January, 1856, aged 77. He was born in Mansfield, Mass., 21 January, 1779. His father was a respectable farmer of that town. When a boy, he had an unaccountable presentiment that he was born to greater things than he saw awaited him should he remain and labor with his father on a farm: so he betook himself to study, for the purpose of acquiring a liberal education. Soon after graduating, he began the study of law under Hon. Seth Padelford, of Taunton (Y.C. 1770); and finished his legal studies under the instruction of Hon. Benjamin Whitman, of Pembroke (B.U. 1788). He was admitted to the bar at Taunton in 1803, and immediately opened an office in Nantucket; but removed the same year to Bath, where he resided during the remainder of his life. During that long period, he held many important positions among his fellow-citizens; at the bar, in the legistature of Massachusetts, on the bench, as judge of the Court of Sessions, and fourteen years judge of the Municipal Court in Bath. In 1812, he married Sarah Winslow, of Marshfield, Mass., daughter of Dr. Isaac Winslow, and a descendant, in a direct line, from Gov. Winslow. They had no children. Judge Clap was an honest lawyer. In disposition he was modest, mild, and humane; in integrity he was above reproach.

1800. — Hon. TIMOTHY BOUTELLE died in Waterville, Me., 12 November, 1855, aged 77. He was son of Col. Timothy and Rachel (Lincoln) Boutelle, and was born in Leominster, Mass., 10 November, 1778. After leaving college, he became an assistant preceptor in Leicester Academy, where he remained one year. He began the study of law, in his native town, with Hon. Abijah Bigelow (D.C. 1795); and completed his studies in the office of Edward Gray, Esq., of Boston (H.C. 1792). Soon after his admission to the bar, he established himself in

Waterville, and made that place his home until the close of his life. He soon acquired a good practice in the counties of Kennebec and Somerset, to which his attention was principally limited. For many years, he devoted himself mainly to the regular duties of his profession, without being much allured by the honors and emoluments of political life. With the exception of acting as elector of President and Vice-President in 1816, he was not much in public life until after the separation of Maine from Massachusetts, when he subsequently served at least a dozen years as senator and representative in the legislature of Maine. He was a warm friend of the cause of education, and took a deep interest in Waterville College, of which he was, at the time of his death, one of the trustees, and from which he received, in 1839, the honorary degree of Doctor of Laws. During the latter years of his life, having in a great measure withdrawn from the active duties of his profession, he gave much of his time and labor to the promotion of railroads and the means of internal improvement. Active, energetic, and public-spirited, he was ever ready to engage in any enterprise, which, in his judgment, would tend to promote the best interests of the public; and, in all situations of influence and trust, he enjoyed, in a high degree, the confidence of those associated with him. He closed a long, active, and useful life with a reputation for sound judgment, public spirit, and kindness of heart, which might well afford the richest consolation to those who loved and respected him.

1802. — John Mico Gannett, of Walpole, Mass., died suddenly in Boston, 25 July, 1855, aged 71. He was son of Caleb and Katharine (Wendell) Gannett; and was born in Cambridge, Mass., 15 March, 1784. His father, Rev. Caleb Gannett (H. C. 1763), was born in Bridgewater, Mass., 22 August, 1745; was ordained in Hingham, Mass., 12 October, 1767, as minister at Amherst and Cumberland, N.S.; where he remained until 1771, when he returned to Massachusetts. He was tutor in Harvard College from 1773 to 1780; a member of the corporation from 1778 to 1780; and steward from 1779 till his death, which took place 25 April, 1818.

His mother was daughter of John Mico Wendell, whose wife was Katharine, daughter of William Brattle. Mr. Gannett was fitted for college at Phillips Academy, Andover, Mass. Immediately after he graduated, he began to study law in the office of Hon. William Stedman, of Lancaster, Mass. (H.C. 1784); but soon went to Plymouth, Mass., and entered the office of Judge Joshua Thomas (H.C. 1772), with whom he studied two years. He was admitted to the bar, in Boston, before he was twenty-one years old. He was married, 30 June, 1805, in Hartford, Conn., to Mary Woodbridge Wyllys, daughter of Gen. Samuel Wyllys (Y.C. 1758). He opened an office in Northfield, Mass., where he remained about two years. While there, he was chosen major-general of the militia. Early in the year 1807, he was prevailed on by his father-in-law, who was secretary of the state of Connecticut, and between seventy and eighty years of age, to move to Hartford. Here he practised law, became a prominent politician of the old federal school, was a representative to the General Court, a senator, and a member of the council. About 1823, his health became impaired so much as to prevent him in a great measure from pursuing his profession. His wife died 25 April, 1825. This produced a a great effect on his spirits, and he spent two or three years in Cambridge and Boston. In 1828, his health having improved, he moved to Walpole, Mass., with the view of leading a quiet country life. Here he declined entering extensively into the practice of law; but, as he held a commission of justice of the peace, he rendered various services, mostly gratuitous, to his friends and neighbors. He was married a second time, 3 April, 1837, to Hannah, daughter of William Kingsbury, a farmer in Walpole. She died in April, 1839. He was a member of the school committee of Walpole during his residence there. He devoted much of his time to literature, and published many articles in the newspapers. "He was a fine specimen of a gentleman of the old school, courteous, genial, of great integrity, of fine tastes, varied attainments, and of high culture." His death, which was caused by disease of the heart, took place while he was on a temporary visit to Boston.

1806. — CHARLES HAYWARD died in Boston, 18 December, 1855, aged 68. He was son of Dr. Lemuel Hayward (H.C. 1768), and was born in Boston, 18 August, 1787. His father was a surgeon in the Revolutionary army; was afterwards for many years an eminent physician in Boston, where he died 20 March, 1821, aged 72. Mr. Hayward, after leaving college, engaged in mercantile business, but relinquished it; and, for the last thirty-five years, was well known as a notary public. He was highly respected as a quiet, unobtrusive, upright, worthy citizen.

1808. — NAHUM HOUGHTON GROCE died in Westford, Mass., 14 March, 1856, aged 74. He was born in Sterling, Mass., 8 December, 1781. He was, for fourteen years, preceptor of Westford Academy. The subsequent part of his life he devoted to agricultural pursuits.

1812. — GEORGE PHILLIPS PARKER died in New-York City, 19 January, 1856, aged 62. He was son of John Parker, of Boston; where he was born 2 March, 1793. His name originally was George Parker; but, some years after leaving college, he took the intermediate name of Phillips. He entered his father's counting-room, where he remained a short time; after which he went to Europe, where he travelled several years. For some years before his death, he was actively engaged in the temperance cause, and contributed liberally from his ample means to promote its objects.

1814. — GORHAM BROOKS died in Medford, Mass., 11 September, 1855, aged 60. He was son of Hon. Peter C. Brooks, and was born in Boston, 10 February, 1795. He was prepared for college at Phillips Academy, Andover, Mass. After reading law one year in the office of Hon. Lewis Strong at Northampton (H.C. 1803), he made a voyage to Calcutta, not in the way of business, but for amusement and to see the world. In 1833, he engaged in mercantile business in Baltimore as one of the firm of William E. Mayhew and Co. Possessing an ample fortune, he retired after a few years, and returned to Massachusetts, where he subsequently resided, passing the winters in Boston, and the summers at his country seat in Medford; devoting himself to agriculture and gardening, for which he had great taste and fondness. He married the only daughter of Resin D. Shepherd, Esq., of New Orleans. Being of a modest, retiring disposition, he did not seek distinction, and was never in public life, except that he one year represented the town of Medford in the state legislature. Distinguished by spotless integrity, he added lustre to a family name already honored in the history of the commonwealth for its bravery in the field, and its unsurpassed success in active business.

1814. — Ezekiel Hildreth died in Wheeling, Va., 15 March, 1856, aged 71. He was born in Westford, Mass., 18 July, 1784, and was fitted for college at Westford Academy. On leaving college, he entered upon the business of teaching. He taught in Washington City, D.C.; Wheeling, Va.; Zanesville, O.; Louisville, Ky.; Newmarket, Va.; and Decatur, Tenn.; in all, forty-two years. He published a grammatical work, entitled "Logopolis, or City of Words;" also a "Key to Knowledge;" an "Essay on the Mortality of the Soul;" and an "Address on Education," delivered before the Educational Convention of Virginia, held at Clarksburg, Va., in 1836. He also left a number of unpublished manuscripts on various subjects, translations from the Septuagint, &c. He married, in June, 1818, Sally, daughter of Jonathan Zane; had three sons and four daughters, of whom all the sons and one daughter survive him. His wife died in July, 1854. For the last eight years of his life, particularly, his mind was in an unbalanced state. The particular form of mental disturbance appeared to be an alternation of melancholia and hypochondriasis. His reasoning powers, so far from being obtunded, were, at times, remarkably acute. Difficult mathematical problems proposed to him he would work out. Incorrect quotations from Greek and Latin authors, purposely made to him, he would promptly correct. There was a sullen and dogged idea with him that he could not "get along," that is, provide for his family, although the family had not only provided for themselves, but for him. For the last eight or nine years, the family were very comfortably situated, without necessity for labor of any kind. Mr. Hildreth's oldest son, who is an eminent physician in Wheeling, supplied his father's place in the family, when the latter, from mental malady, was no longer able to preside over the household; and watched over him in his last hours with true filial affection.

1815. — ANDREW CUNNINGHAM DAVISON, of Boston, died in Lexington, Mass., 27 January, 1856, aged 66. He was son of Henry and Mary Davison, and was born in Boston, 5 June, 1789. After graduating, he began the study of law in the office of Hon. George Blake, in Boston (H.C. 1789). From March, 1818, to November, 1828, he was assistant teacher in the Adams School in Boston. For many years previous to his death, his health did not permit him to engage in any active pursuit; and, for the last few months of his life, his mental and physical powers were so much impaired, that his friends removed him to Lexington, where he was tenderly watched and cared for until death came to his and their relief.

1815. — Dr. THADDEUS WILLIAM HARRIS died in Cambridge, Mass., 16 January, 1856, aged 60. He was son of Rev. Thaddeus Mason Harris, D.D. (H.C. 1787); and was born in Dorchester, Mass., 12 November, 1795. On leaving college, he chose the medical profession; and, after completing his studies, he established himself for medical practice in Milton, in connection with the eminent physician Dr. Amos Holbrook, whose advanced years (although he lived a score of years longer) already demanded some relief. As a physician, he acquired a solid reputation for learning, fidelity, and skill: but his little confidence in himself, and a growing taste for natural sciences, led him to desire some mode of life more consistent with its leisurely cultivation; and in 1831, on the decease of Benjamin Pierce, the librarian of Harvard College, he was chosen as his successor. This office he accepted, and held until his decease, discharging its duties with great assiduity and fidelity. In the study of nature, he possessed those rare powers of observation, discrimination, and analysis, which, united to a hearty love of the pursuit, make a naturalist of the highest order. He was a learned botanist: but the department of natural history to which he was especially devoted was the study of the insect tribes; and he was recognized, by common consent of European naturalists, as the first entomologist in the world. His "Treatise on some of the Insects of New England which are Injurious to Vegetation," first published in 1841 under a commission from the commonwealth, is a permanent contribution to science, of the highest value. He felt a strong interest in our New-England antiquities, and the fruits of his occasional investigations in that sphere often enabled him to give valuable information to more systematic inquirers. He was a member of the Boston Society of Natural History, the American Academy of Arts and Sciences, and of the Massachusetts Historical Society. He lived a pure, useful life, and died as a Christian dieth, leaving behind him a good name.

1816. — John James Devereux died in Salem, Mass., 16 March, 1856, aged 59. He was son of Capt. James and Sarah (Crowninshield) Devereux, and was born in Salem, Mass., 12 June, 1796. His father was born in Waterford, Ireland, May, 1766; and emigrated, when quite young, to Salem, where he married, 12 September, 1792, Sarah, daughter of John Crowninshield and Mary Ives, both natives of Salem. His mother was born in 1768, and died 13 March, 1815. Mr. Devereux, the subject of this notice, when in the eighth year of his age, entered the private school of Robert Rogers (H.C. 1802) in Salem, where he remained about two years, when he was transferred to the Branch School, established by an association of gentlemen, and under the direction of Benjamin Tappan (H.C. 1805). Mr. Tappan was succeeded in the school by Abiel Chandler and Samuel Adams (both H.C. 1806), by whom young Devereux was fitted for college. He entered in 1812, and remained with his class till 1815, when he left college to become a merchant. He did not receive his degree of Bachelor of Arts until 1849, and the following year he received his degree of Master. He pursued the mercantile profession until 1829, when he relinquished it, and began the study of law under the instruction of Hon. David Cummins, of Salem (D.C. 1806). Upon his admission to the bar, he opened an office in Boston, where he remained a few years, and then removed to New York, and, three years afterwards, to Philadelphia, where he practised nearly twenty years, and attained an honorable rank among the learned members of that distinguished bar. Being endowed with the rare combination of great versatility of mind, elegant manners, a facility of speech seldom equalled, and generous impulses, he was a welcome visitor at every social circle that was graced by his presence. Possessing all the advantages that ample wealth could bestow, he travelled extensively in various quarters of the globe, and circulated in the most polished society of Europe. He visited nearly every part of the European continent, and most of the islands of the Eastern Archipelago; having, at one time, actually travelled the Island of Java from one extremity to another. He was never married. He was polished without affectation, learned without pedantry, and, with all his accomplishments, easily recognizable as a gentleman and a scholar; cheerful as to his future destiny, sinking to rest with that serenity which results from a heart at peace with itself, and with a world to which it bids an everlasting adieu.

1816. — George Frederick Farley died in Groton, Mass., 8 November, 1855, aged 62. He was son of Benjamin and Lucy (Fletcher) Farley, of Brookline, N.H.; and was born in Dunstable, Mass., 5 April, 1793; his mother, at the time of his birth, being on a visit at her father's house. He was prepared for college at Westford Academy; and, on leaving college, began the study of law with his brother, Benjamin Marcus Farley (H.C. 1804), in Brookline, N.H,; afterwards, for a time, studied with Luther Lawrence, of Groton (H.C. 1801), but completed his studies with his aforementioned brother. He was admitted to the bar in New Hampshire in 1820, and opened an office in New Ipswich, N.H., where he practised until 1831 or 1832, when he removed to Groton, Mass., where he resided during the remainder of his life. For the last two or three years previous to his death, he had an office in Boston. He was one of the most eminent and successful lawyers in Middlesex County.

1817. — Rev. Asa Cummings died at sea, on board the steamship "George Law," on the passage from Panama to New York, 5 June, 1856, aged 65. He was son of Deacon Asa Cummings, and was born in Andover (now North Andover), Mass., 29 September, 1790. His immediate ancestors lived to advanced ages. His grandfather died in 1794, aged 102 years. His father was born in Topsfield, Mass., September, 1759; and died in Albany, Me., 22 February, 1845, aged 85. The family removed to Albany in 1798, where the subject of this notice resided until 1811; when he left home, and entered Phillips Academy in Andover, where he was prepared for college. After graduating, he taught school a few months in Danvers, Mass. He joined the junior class in the Andover Theological Seminary, 6 December, 1817, where he remained about two years, when his health failed, and he feared he should be obliged to give up his intention of entering the ministry. Under the advice of physicians, he left the seminary, and went a journey; and finally became connected with Bowdoin College as a tutor in 1819-20. His health improved, and he accepted a call from the First Church and Society in North Yarmouth, Me., and was ordained 14 February, 1821. His pastoral life, however, was brief; for, after a few years, the difficulty which occasioned the suspension of his studies at Andover returned, and he was compelled to give up preaching; but, at the desire of his people, he retained his pastoral office until his successor's ordination, 17 February, 1830, when he was released from his charge, with high testimonials as to his ability and Christian character both from the church and the ecclesiastical council. On the 18th of August, 1826, he undertook the editorship of the "Christian Mirror," a religious paper published in Portland; and on the 31st of July, 1845, he became sole proprietor of it, and continued to edit it until the close of the year 1855, when he transferred it into other hands. He was a man of vigorous intellect, and devoted all his energies to the advancement of the cause to which the "Mirror" was originally consecrated. Amidst all the conflicts of party strife, he kept on the even tenor of his way with a zeal and steadfastness worthy of his Christian calling. His editorial labors, however, yielded him but a meagre support during the long years of toil; but unexpectedly, a few months before his death, he became possessed of an abundant competence of worldly goods. From 1825 to 1848, he was an efficient member of the Board of Trustees of the Maine Missionary Society. He was also a member of the American Board, and was ever a warm friend of missions at home and abroad. He was deeply interested in the cause of education, and rendered long and valuable services in connection with the college at New Brunswick and the academy at North Yarmouth. In 1847, the honorary degree of Doctor of Divinity was conferred upon him by Bowdoin College. In February, 1856, it being known that he was about to make a voyage to Panama to visit a daughter who resides there, a large number of the most respectable people of Portland, irrespective of political or religious opinions, united in tendering to him a testimonial of appreciation of his moral worth, and his editorial services of nearly thirty years, by an entertainment at Lancaster Hall, in Portland, on the evening of the 29th of February. This invitation, however, he was obliged to decline, on account of the brief time allowed for preparation for his proposed journey. He left New York in the steamship on the 5th of March, arrived safely at Panama, and enjoyed the new scenes and the re-union with his children very much; and it was hoped he might return with re-invigorated health. But, during his stay at Panama, he was taken ill; and his physicians deciding that there was no hope of his recovery in remaining there, and that the sea air might possibly revive him, he was conveyed on board the steamship which left Aspinwall on the 4th of June for New York; but he rapidly sank, and died on the second night out. On the following morning, after a short funeral-service by the Rev. J. Sessions, of Albany, N.Y., his body was committed to the deep. He was greatly beloved and respected by the community in which he lived: his life was one of great activity and usefulness; and it might be truly said of him, that he was "an Israelite indeed, in whom there was no guile."

1817.—Dr. Edward Augustus Holyoke died in Syracuse, N.Y., 17 December, 1855, aged 59. His name, originally, was Edward Augustus Holyoke Turner; but, in 1820 or 1821, he assumed the name of his maternal grandfather, Dr. Edward Augustus Holyoke, of Salem. He was son of William and Judith (Holyoke) Turner, and was born in Boston, 12 July, 1796. He studied medicine under the instruction of Dr. James Jackson, of Boston (H.C. 1796). On completing his medical studies, he established himself as a physician in Salem, Mass.; where he continued until 1840, when he removed to Framingham, Mass. Here he resided two years; at the end of which time he returned to Salem, and there resided until the spring of 1853, when he removed to Syracuse, where he remained until his death. He married Maria Osgood, daughter of Dr. George Osgood, of Andover, Mass. His widow and six children survive him. He was greatly respected for his estimable character and professional skill.

1817. — Paul Willard died in Charlestown, Mass., 18 March, 1856, aged 60. He was son of Paul and Martha (Haskell) Willard, and was born in Lancaster, Mass., 4 August, 1795. His maternal grandfather, Col. Henry Haskell, was an officer in the Revolutionary army. Mr. Willard was fitted for college at Westford Academy. Soon after he graduated, he began the study of law in the office of Hon. Calvin Willard in Worcester. Having completed his studies, he was admitted to the bar in 1821, and opened an office in Charlestown, where he resided, and continued in the practice of his profession, until the day of his death. In September, 1822, he was appointed postmaster of Charlestown, which office he held for seven years. In 1823, he was elected clerk of the state senate, and was re-elected for seven successive years. He held a highly respectable rank at the Middlesex bar, and had an extensive and lucrative practice. He enjoyed the full confidence of his fellow-citizens, as was shown by his being repeatedly elected chairman of the board of selectmen, and of the school-committee, of Charlestown, before the organization of the city government. He was either cashier or president of the Charlestown Bank the whole time of its existence; and, at the time of his death, he held the office of magistrate under the truant-act, to which he was elected by the city council. He was of an exceedingly sociable and affable temperament, and his house was the home of hospitality. He was a worthy and honored citizen.

1821. — George Barrell Moody died in Bangor, Me., 6 July, 1856, aged 53. He was son of Joseph and Maria (Barrell) Moody, and was born in Kennebunk, Me., 17 July, 1802. He was fitted for college at the academy in Gorham, Me. Immediately after leaving college, he began the study of law under the instruction of Hon. William Sullivan, of Boston (H.C. 1792). Having completed his legal studies, and been admitted to the bar, he opened an office in Kennebunk; but soon afterwards removed to Gardiner, and thence to Brewer, in which places he remained but a few months. He then went to Oldtown, where he continued several years; and finally removed to Bangor, where he practised law for nearly thirty years. He acquired a high reputation as a sound, thorough, rather than a brilliant lawyer; and was especially distinguished for dignity and courtesy of manners, as well as integrity of character, which made him esteemed by all his professional brethren and by his fellow-citizens, so far as his naturally quiet and reserved habits admitted general acquaintance. On the next day subsequent to his decease, at a meeting of the Penobscot bar, Hon. Edward Kent, who was his classmate and roommate, announced his death, accompanying the announcement with some eloquent and highly appropriate remarks, in which he spoke of his guileless and confiding nature, his simplicity, his high sense of honor, his refined and polished manners, his domestic virtues, which always rendered his house attractive to its inmates and his friends. He concluded by offering a series of resolutions, expressing a high appreciation of his character as a correct, capable, and honorable lawyer, an upright man, a useful citizen, a refined and accomplished gentleman. Chief-Justice Tenney responded in just and touching terms, in which he bore testimony to the worth and virtues of the deceased, and concluded by ordering the clerk to place the resolutions upon the records. Mr. Moody married Mary, daughter of Mr. John Barker, of Bangor, and had four children (one son and three daughters), all of whom, with their mother, survive him.

1824. — GEORGE THOMAS SANDERS died in Salem, Mass., 1 May, 1856, aged 51. He was son of Thomas and Elizabeth Sanders, and was born in Salem, 30 October, 1804. He was descended from Thomas Sanders, one of the first settlers of Cape Ann. His great-grandfather commanded the sloop-of-war "Massachusetts" at the capture of Louisburg in 1745. His grandfather, Thomas Sanders (H.C. 1748), was for several years a counsellor under the provincial government. Mr. Sanders did not study a profession. After he graduated, he spent a few years in travelling on the Eastern continent. When abroad, and particularly in Italy, he acquired a love for the music of the opera, which afforded him the greatest pleasure through life. After his return, he was married to Marianne, daughter of Samuel Browne; a very estimable lady, who survives him. His two sons are all that remain to perpetuate the name. He lived in the old mansion-house of his wife's family, with hospitality, but without ostentation. He will be long remembered for his kind and benevolent disposition, his integrity and truthfulness.

1826. — Hon. TIMOTHY WALKER died in Cincinnati, O., 15 January, 1856, aged 53. He was born in Wilmington, Mass., 1 December, 1802. His father was a farmer, and died when this son was nine years old; leaving a widow to rear up six children. Through his paternal grandmother, a Miss Brewster, he was directly descended from William Brewster, who came over in the "Mayflower." The patrimony left was small, and the sons had to labor on the farm for their support. Young Walker continued to work on the farm until he was sixteen years old, when his friends reluctantly consented to his earnest desire to obtain a collegiate education; and he began his studies with a clergyman in a neighboring town, and completed his preparation for college at Mr. Putnam's academy, in North Andover. He graduated with the highest honors of his class. He supported himself, while in college, by school-keeping, and by translating, in his junior year, from the French, for Prof. Farrar, Biot's "Course of Natural Philosophy." During the three years succeeding his graduation, he was employed as a teacher of mathematics in the Round-Hill School at Northampton. In October, 1829, he entered the Law School at Cambridge, where he remained until July of the next year; when he concluded to emigrate to the West, and arrived at Cincinnati on the 6th of the following month. Here he completed his studies in the office of Messrs. Storer and Fox, who were among the leaders of the Cincinnati bar. He opened an office by himself; but soon afterwards entered into partnership with Edward King (since deceased) and Salmon P. Chase, then governor of Ohio. This firm was dissolved in 1835; and he formed a copartnership with John C. Wright, well known as a distinguished member of Congress, and judge of the Supreme Court of Ohio. In 1833, he, together with Judge Wright, established a law-school in Cincinnati. Two years afterwards, this school was united with the Cincinnati College, with, at first, three professors; but, after a short time, it fell under the exclusive charge of Mr. Walker. In the winter of 1837–8, he delivered a course of ten or twelve lectures, upon commercial law, before the Young Men's Mercantile-Library Association. In March, 1842, he accepted an executive appointment to the place of president-judge of the Hamilton-County Common Pleas, until the next legislature should fill the vacancy. In his short term of office, he despatched cases with such rapidity, that the court-docket was soon materially diminished. In 1844, finding his business again increasing, he resigned his professorship which he had held in the law-school from its foundation, and took in John Kebler as a junior partner. From that time he was a lawyer in full practice, confining himself chiefly to cases interesting from their intricacy or from the amount of property involved, and editing the "Western Law Journal." He declined a judgeship of the Superior Court which was proffered to him by the governor of Ohio. The comments and explanations which he gave to the students upon their text-books, while professor of the law school, were subsequently developed into formal lectures, and published in a volume under the title of "Introduction of American Law." In 1854, the honorary degree of Doctor of Laws was conferred upon him by Harvard College. By his death, the Cincinnati bar lost one of its brightest ornaments, and the profession one of its most profound and learned jurists.

1832. — LEWIS JOSEPH GLOVER, of Boston, died in Pepperell, Mass., 24 June, 1856, aged 49. He was a twin-child (the other being a daughter) of Ezra and Eunice Glover, and was born in Dorchester, Mass., 26, February, 1807; but was brought up in Quincy, the family having removed into that town during his infancy. He began to fit for college at Lexington Academy, where he remained a year, when that school was broken up, and he was sent to Milton Academy, where he completed his preparatory studies. On leaving college, he began the study of medicine in Boston, under the instruction of Dr. James Jackson (H.C. 1796); and received his medical diploma at the end of three years, when he began the practice of his profession in Boston. He was quite successful, and was rapidly attaining a high rank as a physician, until, about two years before his death, he had a slight attack of paralysis, which was followed by mental alienation. This continued, with occasional lucid intervals, until death came to his relief.

1832. — WILLIAM RICHARDSON died in Dorchester, Mass., 6 June, 1856, aged 42. In a fit of temporary insanity, he committed suicide by drowning himself in Neponset River. He was son of Asa and Elizabeth (Bird) Richardson, and was born in Boston, 2 December, 1813. His father was a native of Billerica. His mother was a native of Dorchester, but removed to Walpole, Mass., about 1804. He was fitted for college at the Boston Latin School, and graduated with high honors. On the 1st of October, 1832, he was appointed usher in the reading-department of the Mayhew School in Boston, where he remained one year. In September, 1833, he began the study of divinity in the theological school at Cambridge, but relinquished it at the end of six months; and on the 20th of March, 1834, he began the study of law in the office of Hon. Jeremiah

Mason, of Boston (Y.C. 1788). Having completed his legal studies, he was admitted to the bar in April, 1837; and, on the 6th of the same month, opened an office in Boston. He soon attained to a high rank in his profession, and gained an extensive and lucrative business. He was married in Walpole, Mass., 30 June, 1836, to Almira Kingsbury, daughter of Hon. Daniel Kingsbury of that place, but had no children. As a pleader he was not conspicuous, but as a counsellor he was considered as one of the safest and most able of his age in Boston. Mr. Mason, with whom he studied, often spoke in strong terms of his high intellectual powers and of his great legal attainments. He was distinguished for perfect integrity, for faithfulness to his clients, and for the moderation of his charges for his services. He was largely intrusted with the settlement of estates, and was president of the Dorchester Savings Bank. He was in affluent pecuniary circumstances, and happy in his domestic relations; was highly esteemed by his acquaintances as well as by his professional brethren; of an exceedingly affable and social disposition, but of a somewhat nervous temperament; and it was supposed that anxiety, caused by the overwhelming care and responsibility of duties intrusted to his charge by his rapidly increasing professional business, induced a temporary aberration of mind, which led him to commit the act of self-destruction.

1832. — ARCHER ROPES died in Baltimore, Md., 2 October, 1855, aged 46. He was son of William and Rachel (Archer) Ropes, and was born in Salem, Mass., 10 December, 1808. For several years previous to his preparing to enter college, he was an apprentice in the apothecary store of Benjamin F. Browne in Salem. He was fitted for college at the Salem Latin School, then under the charge of Theodore Eames (Y.C. 1809). His name, originally, was Jonathan Archer Ropes; but, the year of his graduation, he dropped the name of Jonathan, and was styled Archer Ropes. After going through a course of legal studies, he removed to Baltimore, and in 1835 began the practice of law in that place, where he continued until his death. He was married in Baltimore, 13 January, 1852, to M. Emilie W. Tucker, but had no children. He was, for several years, commander of the Maryland Cadets, at that time regarded as one of the best disciplined companies in the country; was a colonel of Maryland militia; a past grand-master of the order of Odd Fellows; a Mason; and, under the municipal term of Mayor Jerome, was the city-counsellor of Baltimore. He was a man of great kindness of heart and of considerable intellectual ability.

1832. — Rev. GEORGE FREDERICK SIMMONS died in Concord, Mass., 5 September, 1855, aged 41. He was son of Hon. William Simmons (H.C. 1804), and was born in Boston, 24 March, 1814. He was fitted for college at the Latin School in Boston. Immediately after leaving college, he went as a tutor in a private family to Europe, and travelled through Italy and Greece, where he had the opportunity of cultivating those tastes for art, and for foreign languages and literature, which in him were always strong. On returning, he studied theology at the Divinity School in Cambridge. He was ordained as an evangelist, in the Federal-street church in Boston, 9 October, 1838, and immediately proceeded to Mobile, and there began his ministry, which went on prosperously and acceptably until the 17th of August, 1840, when he preached a sermon in which he alluded to the peculiar institutions of the South in a manner which gave great offence to the people in Mobile; and, it being feared that personal violence might be offered to him, he was concealed on board a vessel in the bay, bound to Boston, and returned to his native city. On the 27th of October, 1841, he was installed at Waltham as associate pastor with Rev. Samuel Ripley, whose daughter, Mary Emerson Ripley, he married 17 October, 1845; who now survives him, the mother of four orphaned children. Here he labored a few years with encouraging results: but his views with regard to the slavery question, which he occasionally expressed in the pulpit, created dissatisfaction among some of his parishioners, which resulted in his leaving the place; and, in 1843, he went to Germany for the purpose of theological study, where he remained two years. Here he enjoyed the instructions of Tholuck and Neander, and returned with some peculiarities of opinion, but with no less of faith, and a marked increase of scholarship. On the 9th of February, 1848, he was installed at Springfield as the immediate successor of Rev. William B. O. Peabody (H.C. 1816), who had deceased the previous year. In this new and attractive field, his labors were abundantly rewarded until 1851, when his antislavery zeal broke out anew; and, as he had little disposition and less power to conciliate those who differed from him, he was compelled to resign his post, to bring back peace to the parish. From Springfield he went to Albany; and, in the prime of life and the maturity of his mind, he was devoting himself unremittingly to his ministry, and reaping, even then, a high reward, when symptoms of consumption manifested themselves in his system, and obliged him to retire for a short period to the home of his mother in Concord, where soon, in middle age, the invalid pastor exchanged earthly hope for heavenly fruition.

1836. — Rev. JAMES CHISHOLM died of yellow fever in Portsmouth, Va., 15 September, 1855, aged 39. He was son of William and Martha (Vincent) Chisholm, and was born in Salem, Mass., 30 September, 1815. His father, William Chisholm, was born, 24 September, 1772, in Inverness-shire, near the city of Inverness, Scotland. His mother, Martha Vincent, was born at Salem, Mass., 22 September, 1774. Mr. Chisholm was prepared for college at the Salem Latin Grammar School. Immediately after graduating, he went to the South to take the associate charge of an academy at Charlestown, Jefferson County, Va. A year afterwards, he went to Washington, D.C., where he taught a private classical school a year and a half. In the mean time, he became a candidate for orders in the Episcopal church, and left Washington to enter the theological seminary near Alexandria, Fairfax County, Va. He was ordained to deacon's orders in October, 1840. His first ministerial labors were over a colored congregation in Albemarle County, Va., consisting of the servants on the estate of Hon. William C. Rives and other gentlemen of that neighborhood, who were desirous that all under their care should enjoy the best privileges of the gospel in meetings of their own. In this office he had an opportunity to observe the depth and fervency of religious feeling which characterizes the African race. In the spring of 1842, he was admitted to priest's orders, and was settled over three congregations, — viz., Trinity Church, at Martinsburg; Mount-Zion Church, at Hedgeville; and Calvary Church, at Back Creek. To the first two of these congregations he preached on alternate Sundays, and occasionally at Calvary Church, which was built through his instrumentality. These churches were so far apart, that it made a circuit of twenty-seven miles to visit them. From this scene of his arduous labors, he was called, in 1850, to Portsmouth, Va., where he was instituted rector of St. John's Church. This was a new church, and in a feeble condition, numbering scarcely twenty communicants; but it flourished under his ministry, and is now in a vigorous state. Here he continued until his death. On the 10th of August, 1847, he was married to Jane Byrd Page, daughter of John White Page, and great-grand-daughter of Carter Braxton, one of the signers of the Declaration of Independence. She died in February, 1855, leaving two children, one of whom deceased but a few days before his father. During the prevalence of the epidemic in Norfolk and Portsmouth in September last, he felt it his duty to remain at his post. With a fidelity and courage worthy of his sacred profession, he met the terrible dangers of the scene, and continued to the last, ministering consolation and hope to the mourning and the dying. He left an only son, about seven years old, whose pride it may be, in future years, to look back upon the well-spent life and glorious death of his father. As a proof of the estimation in which Mr. Chisholm was held by the denomination to which he belonged, we may state, that, at the annual convention of the Protestant Episcopal Church in Virginia, held at Fredericksburg, in May last, on the recommendation of Bishop Meade, in his annual report, it was voted that the sum of one hundred and fifty dollars be appropriated, from the fund of the society for the relief of widows and orphans of deceased clergymen, annually, until otherwise ordered, for the support and education of the son of the deceased, although the latter was not a member of the society, and therefore his son

was not entitled to any thing from its funds. An interesting memoir of Mr. Chisholm, by Rev. David H. Conrad, of Martinsburg, Va., was published about three months since, and a third edition of the book is now in press. It has received the highest commendation from the Rev. Dr. Tyng, of New York, and the Rev. Prof. Huntington, of Cambridge.

1838.—Dr. HENRY WARE WALES died in Paris, France, 8 June, 1856, aged 37. He was son of Thomas B. (H.C. 1795) and Ann (Beale) Wales, and was born in Boston, 11 December, 1818. He was fitted for college, in Boston, at the private school of Mr. Daniel Greenleaf Ingraham (H.C. 1809). Immediately after graduating, he began the study of medicine under the instruction of Dr. John C. Warren (H.C. 1797); and received his medical degree in 1841. He then went to Paris to pursue his professional studies further at the medical schools in that city; but after studying a few months, finding that the medical profession was not congenial to his tastes, he abandoned it, and devoted himself to the study of philology and the acquisition of languages, for which he had great fondness. These studies he pursued with great ardor and success. He soon acquired a thorough knowledge of French, Italian, and German, and was able to converse fluently in either of them. He also made himself master of the modern Greek; and, under the celebrated professors and teachers in Prussia, he pursued the study of Sanscrit and of other oriental languages. After an absence of eight years, he returned to his native city. He did not, however, remain long at home, as his predilections were for a foreign residence. On this, his second visit to Europe, he extended his travels to far eastern regions, visiting Egypt and other oriental places of note. This tour extended through a period of three years, when he again returned to Boston. Here he remained until October, 1854, when he started on his third visit to Europe. Before his departure, his health began to fail; and, some time after his arrival in Europe, he was seized with an affection of one of his knees. He passed the last winter in Rome, but shut up in his house, suffering sickness and pain. In the spring, he was carried to Paris, where he submitted to amputation of his limb; but this could not save him. He gradually sank, and breathed his last in a foreign land, comforted, however, by the presence of friends and the attentions of a devoted brother. His life was consecrated to literature, which he pursued with untiring ardor. He had collected a large library of rare and valuable works, with which he delighted to pass his time; the temptations and frivolities of great foreign cities offering no allurements for him. He pursued the even tenor of his way, leading a quiet, blameless life; and, when the hour of his departure arrived, he calmly resigned his spirit into the hands of Him who gave it.

1846. — Benjamin Newhall died in Milwaukie, Wis., 30 March, 1856, aged 29. He was son of Benjamin Franklin and Dorothy (Jewett) Newhall, and was born in Lynn, Mass., 7 March, 1827. His father was born in Lynn, 29 April, 1802. His mother was born in Stanstead, Can., in 1807. He removed with his father's family to Saugus, Mass., when nine years old. At thirteen, he was placed at the Lynn Academy, where he was fitted for college by Mr. Jacob Batchelder (D.C. 1830), whom he mentions in his autobiography, in the "class-book," as a man of the greatest worth and intelligence. On graduating, he entered the Law School in Cambridge, and remained three years; receiving in course the degree of LL.B. in 1849. He then returned to Saugus, where he resided until June, 1851. In May of this year, he changed his name to Benjamin Newhall; it having been originally Benjamin Franklin Newhall. On leaving Saugus, he went to Brooklyn, N.Y., where he passed about eight months. In June, 1852, he removed to Milwaukie, and entered the office of Messrs. Emmons and Van Dyke for the further prosecution of his legal studies. Being shortly afterwards admitted to the bar, he began practising in December, 1852, in partnership with A. C. May, Esq. Although, at the time of his death, he had been but four years in practice, he had attained an enviable position as a sound and well-read lawyer. He had conducted several very important suits to a successful issue, and his business was rapidly increasing. He chiefly excelled in equity- and admiralty-law. At a meeting of the Milwaukie bar, held the day after his decease, resolutions of a highly eulogistic character were passed, in which a tribute was paid to his courteous demeanor, and manly, elevated principles, which had won the good-will of all; to his industry, energy, and marked ability, which had given sure promise of a successful and distinguished career in his profession. A committee was appointed "to make suitable arrangements for forwarding his remains to his friends in Massachusetts, and to invite a clergyman to deliver a funeral discourse before the members of the bar." His remains were interred at Saugus, 9 April, 1856. When in college, he attained an excellent rank as a scholar; and, throughout his short life, he bore a high character for honor and integrity. He was of an open, frank temperament, a firm friend, and of a most generous, self-sacrificing disposition. He always evinced the greatest interest in old college associations; and the favorable effects of the collegiate course upon his hopes, desires, and principles, he has himself recorded.

1850. — BENJAMIN PAYSON WILLIAMS died in West Roxbury, Mass., 17 May, 1856, aged 29. He was son of Major Benjamin Payson and Margaret (Childs) Williams, and was born in Roxbury (now West Roxbury), 6 February, 1827. After going through a course of legal studies, he was admitted to the Suffolk bar; opened an office in Boston, and had already attained a highly respectable rank in his profession. He took an active part in politics, his opinions being those of the old-line democracy. He was endeared to all his associates by his open and generous disposition, his rare social qualities, and his genial and affectionate nature. Of an unusually strong and powerful frame, he was foremost in athletic sports, into which he entered with great zest. In the various literary and social clubs which make so prominent a feature in college-life, he was particularly conspicuous; his ready wit, his overflowing humor, and his lively and poetic fancy, making him one of the most valued members.

1851. — PETER SMITH BYERS died in Andover, Mass., 19 March, 1856, aged 27. He was son of James and Mary (Smith) Byers, and was born at Brechin, in Forfarshire, Scotland, 12 September, 1828. He emigrated with his father's family to Andover, Mass., in 1836. His father was sent for to take charge of the shoe-thread manufactory of Smith, Dove, and Co., the first establishment of the kind in the United States, in which the subject of this notice worked two years. In 1844, he entered Phillips Academy for the purpose of being fitted for college. In the winter of 1846–7, he taught school in Andover, and entered the freshman class of Harvard College in 1847. In his sophomore year, he taught school in Holliston; in his junior, in Andover; and, in his senior, in Boxford. He graduated with high honor, being the third scholar in a class of sixty-three members. In the following autumn, he was engaged as an assistant teacher in the Greek and Latin school where he had prepared for college. There he continued for two years, discharging the duties of the station with great credit to himself, and acknowledged usefulness to the pupils. During most of this time, he was a devoted teacher in the Sunday school of the Episcopal Church in Andover; and frequently, in the desk, assisted the rector in reading the service, — an acceptable duty, which was congenial with his tastes, and in accordance with the ultimate object of his pursuits. In the spring of 1853, he was elected principal of the Abbot Female Seminary in Andover; a position, however, which he did not long occupy, as he was appointed to the like office in the High School of Providence, R.I. There he continued but a single term, since his declining health induced him to listen to overtures tendered by the trustees of the Punchard Free School in Andover, who, in choosing him its first principal, showed the exalted estimation in which they held him and his attainments by offering him a salary till their building should be erected, that he might, by relieving himself of all anxiety, have the opportunity of regaining his strength. But his health continued to fail, and he fell a martyr to nine years of ceaseless application and unyielding toil in the pursuit of knowledge.

1851. — Edmond Franklin Raymond died in Cambridge, Mass., 12 October, 1855, aged 24. He was the eldest son of Hon. Zebina L. and Rhoda Clark (Hildreth) Raymond, and was born in Shutesbury, Mass., 31 July, 1831. When about two years old, he removed with his parents to Boston, where, and in the vicinity, they have since lived. He was fitted for college at the Hopkins Classical School in Cambridge, under the charge of Mr. Edmund Burke Whitman (H.C. 1838). In October of the sophomore year, in consequence of ill health, he was obliged to go to Havana, where he spent the winter. In his junior year, he taught school in Sherborn; and, in his senior year, he taught at Taunton, but his health compelled him to leave at the end of seven weeks. He studied law, and began the practice of his profession in Greenfield, Mass., with flattering prospects of distinction; but his health failed, and he returned to his father's house, in Cambridge, about a week before his death. His early decease is deeply lamented by his family circle, and the many friends to whom his amiable disposition had endeared him.

1853. — John Daves died in Beaufort, Cartaret County, N.C., 1 October, 1855, aged 23. He was the eldest son of John Pugh and Elizabeth (Graham) Daves, and was born in Newbern, N.C., 24 December, 1831. His father was son of John Daves, a major in the Revolutionary war, and grandson of John Daves, who came from Wales. His mother was a third wife, and was the daughter of Edward Graham, a lawyer, born at Newbern, whose father came from Scotland. Mr. Daves studied at the academy at Newbern, N.C., until about fifteen years of age, when he went to Scuppernong, N.C., where he spent a year in the family of his cousin, Josiah Collins, Esq., under the charge of a private tutor. In 1848, he entered the freshman class at St. James's College, Md., where he remained one year. In 1849, he entered the freshman class at Harvard College. At the end of the first term of the junior year, he left college on account of his health, and returned at the end of the junior year, and passed the examinations with his classmates, but was unable to join the class afterwards. He was, however, able to return for his degree, which was granted to him, notwithstanding his absence, and to join his class in their parting ceremonies. After receiving his degree, he studied law, privately, one year at Scuppernong, when his failing health compelled him to abandon it. Possessed of a manly, upright, and frank nature, and endowed with brilliant conversational powers, — the natural fruit of a gifted and cultivated mind, — he was greatly beloved by his classmates and his numerous friends.

1856 – 57.

1786. — Rev. Henry Lincoln died in Nantucket, Mass., 28 May, 1857, aged 91. He was son of William and Mary (Otis) Lincoln, and was born in Hingham, Mass., 3 November, 1765. His mother was daughter of Dr. Ephraim Otis, who was born in Scituate, Mass., in 1708, and was a physician in that town. Mr. Lincoln was fitted for college, partly at the grammar school in Hingham, under the instruction of Eleazer James (H.C. 1778), and partly by Dr. Joshua Barker (H.C. 1772), of Hingham. After leaving college, he studied divinity with Rev. William Shaw (H.C. 1762), of Marshfield, Mass. He was ordained pastor of the Congregational church in Falmouth, Mass., 3 February, 1790; and continued his labors with great fidelity, and to the entire acceptance of his people, until 26 November, 1823, when, at his own request, his pastoral connection was dissolved, and he removed to Nantucket, where he resided, during the remainder of his life, in the family of his son-in-law, Dr. Elisha P. Fearing (B.U. 1807). He married, 26 April, 1790, Susannah Crocker, daughter of Timothy Crocker, of Falmouth, and had, by her, seven children, four sons and three daughters, of whom six survive him. One son was drowned in 1798, at the age of five years and seven months. His wife died 29 July, 1819, aged 51. He was, at the time of his death, with one exception, the oldest clergyman in this state; his classmate, Rev. Jacob Norton, of Billerica, afterwards the oldest surviving graduate of Harvard College), being his senior by nearly two years. Mr. Lincoln was a gentleman of the old school, of fine personal appearance, always remarkably neat in his dress, of an affable and social disposition, and, above all, a sincere Christian. For a few years before his death, his eyes were dimmed, so that he was unable to read; but his mental faculties were unclouded to the last. He was a highly popular preacher, a fine speaker; and his sermons were characterized by sound, practical, good sense. Having finished the work which was given him to do, with a serenity of mind seldom witnessed, he calmly waited his summons, and gently passed away, like the twilight of a long summer's day, into that solemn darkness which mortal eye cannot pierce, but which, to him, doubtless is lighted up by the radiance of a never-ending noon.

1786. — Dr. Joseph Loring died in Lisbon, Portugal, about 1 March, 1857, aged 88. He was son of Caleb and Sarah (Bradford) Loring, and was born in Boston, 11 August, 1768. After leaving college, he studied medicine under the instruction of Dr. Samuel Danforth (H.C. 1758), of Boston. Having completed his medical education, he was employed as surgeon on board the ship "Massachusetts," on a voyage to Batavia and Canton. This ship was built in 1789 for Messrs. Shaw and Randall, and was the largest merchant-ship in the United States. Her commander was Capt. Job Prince, brother of James Prince, formerly United-States marshal for Massachusetts, The ship sailed from Boston, 28 March, 1790; and, after a brief stay at Batavia, arrived at Macao 30 September following. Soon after her arrival, she was sold to the Danish Company for $65,000, and Dr. Loring returned to Boston. He then went to France, and settled as a physician in Paris. After remaining there a few years, he relinquished the practice of his profession, and went to Lisbon, where he established himself as a merchant, and where he resided during the remainder of his life, never having afterwards revisited the United States. He married a Portuguese lady of great personal beauty, and possessing a large fortune. His mercantile transactions proved, after a time, unsuccessful, and the property fell a sacrifice to unfortunate speculations. He left several children.

1792. — Jacob Wyeth died in Cambridge, Mass., 14 January, 1857, aged 92. He was son of Ebenezer Wyeth, and was born in Cambridge, Mass., 29 April, 1764. He worked at brick-making, which was his father's occupation, until he was twenty-three or twenty-four years old, when he concluded to obtain a liberal education; and after six months only, devoted to the preparatory studies, he was admitted to the freshman class. Although so imperfectly prepared, he maintained a respectable rank as a scholar, and graduated with distinction. Soon after leaving college, he went to Hamburg to transact some business for Andrew Craigie, Esq., either in Hamburg or England. On his return, he brought home some European goods, which he had purchased on his own account. These goods he disposed of at a large profit, and soon afterwards married Betsey Jarvis, daughter of Nathaniel Jarvis, of Cambridge. He then entered into partnership with Phineas Stone (who married his wife's sister); and they established themselves in Littleton, Mass., as country traders. In this business they were unsuccessful, became insolvent, and Mr. Wyeth was left without a dollar. He returned to Cambridge, and his father gave him a deed of the land on which the Fresh-Pond Hotel now stands. He made a contract with Walter and Moore, and they erected for him the hotel entirely on credit; he giving them a mortgage on the property as security. In eighteen months after he opened the house, he paid the contractors every dollar he owed them; having made it all in this brief period in keeping the public house. He continued in the hotel business until he accumulated a handsome fortune, when he retired, but resided in the house until death closed his long life.

1795. — Samuel Jackson Prescott died in Brookline, Mass., 7 February, 1857, aged 83. He was son of Dr. Oliver (H.C. 1750) and Lydia (Baldwin) Prescott, and was born in Groton, Mass., 15 March, 1773. He was fitted for college at Phillips Academy in Andover. After graduating, he studied law in the office of Hon. William Prescott (H.C. 1783), and was admitted to the bar; but soon left the profession on account of being affected with deafness, and engaged in mercantile business; having formed a copartnership with Aaron P. Cleveland, under the style of Prescott and Cleveland. In this pursuit he was unsuccessful, owing to the embargo of 1807, the non-intercourse, and the war with Great Britain which ensued. He then became a magistrate, and for more than twenty years was a notary-public for Suffolk county. He married Margaret Hiller, daughter of Joseph Hiller, Esq., by whom he had five children, — two sons and three daughters; of whom the sons only survive him. He was a man of strong powers of mind, and held a high rank in his class as a scholar. He had a taste for genealogical and statistical investigations: he compiled the index for the triennial catalogue of Harvard College, which was first published in the triennial in 1830. Later in life, to his physical infirmity of deafness was added that of blindness. His intellectual faculties, too, became clouded; and he passed his closing years at the residence of one of his sons in Brookline, where he was kindly cared for with all the attention which filial affection could bestow.

1797. — Hon. Nathaniel Paine Denny died in Barre, Mass., 23 August, 1856, aged 85. He was son of Col. Samuel Denny, of Leicester, Mass., a distinguished patriot of the Revolution, whose father was one of the four original proprietors of that town, where the subject of this notice was born 22 July, 1771. His academical education was acquired at Leicester Academy. After graduating, he studied law with Hon. Nathaniel Paine, of Worcester (H.C. 1775); and, about the beginning of the present century, he opened an office in Leicester, where he practised law for a period of nearly forty years. His name, originally, was Thomas Denny, which he changed to Nathaniel Paine Denny, on account of there being another Thomas Denny in the town. He became widely known as a thoroughly-read lawyer. He was a man of strong mind; and, as a citizen and lawyer, he was distinguished for his sound judgment, and a strict and impartial adherence to justice. He enjoyed in an eminent degree the confidence and esteem of his fellow-citizens; having represented the town of Leicester in the state legislature successively from 1804 to 1809, in 1812, 1826, 1829, 1834, and 1841. He was elected senator for Worcester District in 1824 and 1825; was a county-commissioner; and, for several years, president of the Leicester Bank. In all these stations, he discharged his duties in such a manner as to win the respect and confidence of his fellow-citizens. His modesty forbade his seeking public distinctions; and the honors conferred upon him were voluntary on the part of his friends, and the result of the unwavering confidence which they placed in his integrity. In private life he was social and hospitable, and his numerous acquaintances will long remember his house on Mount Pleasant as the home of hospitality. In October, 1798, he married Sally Swan, a native of Leicester, who was equally distinguished for her humble piety, intellectual refinement, and personal charms. He had ten children, of whom five are now living. His wife died at Leicester in 1843, aged 71 years. In 1845, he married Mary, daughter of the late Daniel Denny, of Worcester; and removed to Norwich, Conn., where he resided about eleven years. In June, 1856, he returned to his native state to pass the few remaining days of his life with his eldest son, Hon. Edward Denny, of Barre: and they proved to be few indeed; for in two months he passed peacefully from this to the other world. With the exception of the last few years of his life, he was in constant and active intercourse with his fellow-citizens in their various pursuits; and whatever relation he sustained towards them, or in whatever position placed, his motto was always, "Be just, and fear not."

1797. — Joseph Hurd died in Malden, Mass., 19 March, 1857, aged 78. He was the eldest son of Joseph Hurd, late of Portsmouth, N.H., formerly an eminent merchant in Charlestown and Boston; and was born in Concord or Lincoln (during the temporary removal of the family from their home in Charlestown at the time of the Revolutionary war), 27 July, 1778. While in college, he was remarkable for his habitual courtesy and kindness, and for his upright and exemplary conduct. He held a distinguished rank in his class, and graduated with high honor. On leaving college, he adopted the mercantile profession, and was known and respected for his intelligence and commercial knowledge in his own country, and also in England, where he formed important connections in business, and where he passed several years of his mercantile life. An eminent member of the Essex bar — a classmate of Mr. Hurd — gives the following sketch of his subsequent life: "Soon after the disastrous war of 1812 broke out, he retired from the troubled affairs of commerce, and purchased a farm in Stoneham, beautifully situated on the borders of Spot Pond. Here he derived the chief enjoyment of his subsequent life from the indulgence of his rural taste and his philosophical ingenuity. Science and taste happily co-operated in the various improvements which he introduced upon his extensive grounds; but he soon became deeply interested in various scientific experiments in regard to heat, and the best mode of constructing stoves, the results of which have inured to the public benefit through others employed in his service, and who availed themselves of his discoveries. He had little thought of profit to himself beyond the gratification he found in thus endeavoring to promote the general good. He also turned his attention to the manufacture of maple and beet sugar; and also, with more important success, to the refining of sugar, for which he obtained a patent, as well as much celebrity. The following brief sentence in a letter from France, found among his papers, asking for a description of his patent, and highly complimenting him upon it, gives the best idea of the discovery that we can at this moment present: 'You took, in 1844, a patent, in your country, for a new system to purify and cleanse sugar by means of the centrifuge force.' This patent, without his seeking, inured largely to his profit, and immensely to the profit of those who were so fortunate as to purchase it. In his will, he bequeathed the sum of five thousand dollars to each of the states of Maine, New Hampshire, Vermont, and Massachusetts, the income to be applied yearly in giving prizes to promote and encourage the manufacture and refining of sugar."

In the early period of Mr. Hurd's residence at his beautiful retreat in Stoneham, his friends were often attracted to visit him, and were always received with the kindest hospitality. Ladies were cordially welcomed among his visitors. Happy would it have been had he chosen some one to share his fortunes, and bless him in his retirement. Left to his own solitary resources, he became so absorbed in his studies and experiments as to impair his health, and finally to obscure his intellect. During his later years, he divided his time between Stoneham and Malden; boarding at the latter place in a worthy family, where he found every accommodation suited to his simple habits. He retained, through life, the simplicity of childhood, with the firmness of the philosopher. He was as independent in his own opinions as he was deferential to others. In respect to his deeper feelings, he had great reserve. An unspotted life was his only religious profession. Throughout his lingering illness he manifested the resignation of a "Christian; and in peace and serenity his spirit ascended to God, who gave it."

1798. — Rev. JONATHAN FRENCH died in North Hampton, N.H., 13 December, 1856, aged 78. He was son of Rev. Jonathan French (H.C. 1771), and was born in Andover, Mass., 16 August, 1768. He was ordained at North Hampton, 18 November, 1801; formally resigned the active duties of his pastorate, 18 November, 1851; and actually resigned them at the ordination of his colleague, Rev. John Dinsmore, 18 November, 1852. He was for many years one of the most active, influential, and highly esteemed clergymen in the Piscataqua Association of Congregational Ministers. He was known and had preached in all their congregations, had been called to advise in their churches, and had many friends in all their parishes. He was one of the finest specimens of ministerial character. Evangelical, sincere, earnest, devoted, he was the good preacher, the wise counsellor, the sympathizing pastor, the obliging ministerial brother, the ready helper of all good enterprises. He was a diligent student until he reached the age of threescore years and ten. He was a reliable historian, and left behind him manuscripts of great value. Above all, he was a good husband, loving and beloved; a good father, honored, and worthy of honor; a good neighbor and friend, welcoming every worthy guest to his board, and in turn welcomed by worthy households everywhere. In 1851, the honorary degree of Doctor of Divinity was conferred upon him by Dartmouth College. He delivered a half-century discourse four years before his death, from the text, "Behold, I die; but God shall be with you." He "came to his grave in a full age," after a useful and honored life.

1798. — Hon. SIDNEY WILLARD died in Cambridge, Mass., 6 December, 1856, aged 76. He was son of Rev. Joseph Willard (H.C. 1765), formerly minister in Beverly, Mass., and subsequently, for nearly a quarter of a century, president of Harvard College; and was born in Beverly, 19 September, 1780. Immediately after leaving college, he began the study of theology under the instruction of the Hollis Professor of Divinity. In April, 1800, the office of librarian became vacant by the death of Samuel Shapleigh (H.C. 1789), and Mr. Willard was elected as his successor. This office he held five years. In the mean time, having completed his theological studies, he was licensed as a preacher. He preached in various places in this state, as well as in Maine and Vermont; and was invited to settle as a minister in Wiscasset, Me., and in Burlington, Vt.; but he declined both invitations. In December, 1806, he was chosen Hancock Professor of Hebrew and other Oriental Languages in Harvard College, and was inaugurated in February of the following year. This office he held until 1831, discharging its duties with great fidelity and ability. While connected with the college, he was interested in several literary publications, and contributed valuable articles to the "Monthly Anthology" and "Christian Examiner." He was a member, with many other distinguished men, of the Anthology Society, to which the Boston Athenæum is so deeply indebted. He contributed many valuable articles for the "North-American Review;" and, about two years before his death, he published his "Memories of Youth and Manhood," in many points a valuable work. His learning was varied and extensive, his style of writing clear and plain, his views sound and practical. Accustomed to the best society for moral worth, social position, and intellectual power, he appreciated and enjoyed the advantages he possessed. In his manners he was easy, polite, and urbane. He was firm in his principles, and amiable in disposition. His feelings were tender and refined; and he was remarkably honest, sincere, and truthful. Filial reverence and piety marked his character, and he was esteemed by all who knew him. Nearly his whole life was passed in Cambridge; and he filled various offices, always acceptably. He was mayor of Cambridge in 1848, 1849, and 1850; was several times elected a representative to the state legislature; and was a member of the executive council. He was the last relic of the officers of the college government during the first quarter of the present century.

1802. — Hon. SAMUEL HOAR died in Concord, Mass., 2 November, 1856, aged 78. He was son of Hon. Samuel Hoar, and was born in Lincoln, Mass., 18 May, 1778. After leaving college, he spent two years as a private tutor in the state of Virginia; and it was while he was on his return to Massachusetts, and during a temporary stay in the city of New York, that the fatal and memorable duel between Hamilton and Burr deprived the country of one of its most honored and illustrious statesmen. Arriving home, Mr. Hoar entered, as a student of law, in the office of the Hon. Artemus Ward, of Charlestown, (H.C. 1783), afterwards, and for many years, the learned chief-justice of the Court of Common Pleas. He was admitted to the bar in September, 1805; and, the same month, opened an office in Concord, where he soon attained a high rank; and for forty years he was one of the most eminent and successful practitioners in the county of Middlesex. The last few years of his life were withdrawn from that activity of legal service, to which, from early manhood to late maturity, he had devoted his energies; and the people of Middlesex were deprived of the forensic talents and experience of the veteran leader, who, for more than a generation, had been engaged in most of the important cases tried at their bar. To the neighboring bars of Worcester, Essex, and Suffolk, he had been no stranger; nor was his voluntary surrender of the excitements of the more public and conspicuous positions of his honorable profession unnoticed or unregretted by them. He was associated with Mr. Webster in the celebrated case of the Commonwealth against Crowninshield and the brothers Knapp, convicted of the murder of Capt. White, in Salem, in 1830. He was repeatedly honored by being elected to offices of honor, trust, and importance. He was a member of the convention for revising the constitution of the state in 1820; was elected a senator, in the state legislature, in 1825 and 1833; was a member of the executive council in 1845 and 1846. He was a representative from Middlesex in the twenty-fourth Congress of the United States in 1836-7. He was also a representative in our state legislature in 1850. In 1844, he was appointed by Gov. Briggs, in accordance with a resolve passed by the legislature of Massachusetts, a commissioner to proceed to Charleston, S.C., to test, in the Court of the United States, the constitutionality of an act passed by the legislature of South Carolina on the 20th of December, 1825, legalizing the imprisonment of colored persons who should enter their boundaries: but on his arrival at Charleston, and making known the object of his visit, such was the excitement against him, on account of his mission's being deemed by the people of the place an unwarrantable interference with their state rights, that he was obliged to leave the city forthwith, to escape threatened personal violence; and he returned to Massachusetts without fulfilling the object of his appointment.

The most agreeable characteristic of his latter years was the interest with which he pursued every movement of benevolence or education. He always possessed a liberal and charitable spirit; but his retirement from the bar afforded leisure for a more extensive indulgence and cultivation of such affections. From the institution of the sunday-school of his church, until the Sunday of his death, he officiated either as teacher or superintendent. He was a member of the Massachusetts Peace Society and of the American Bible Society, and was an invariable participant in all charitable organizations. His private charities also were incessant, ample, and intelligent. He was a member of the American Academy of Arts and Sciences, and of the Massachusetts Historical Society. At the time of his death, he was one of the Board of Overseers of Harvard College; and the college, in 1838, conferred upon him the honorary degree of Doctor of Laws. In 1812, he was married to Miss Sarah Sherman, youngest daughter of the celebrated Roger Sherman, of Connecticut. They had five children; viz., Elizabeth, Sarah

Sherman, Ebenezer Rockwood, Edward Sherman, and George Frisbie. The sons were graduates of Harvard College in 1835, 1844, and 1846, respectively.

Mr. Hoar was a man of deep religious principles: he was a sincere and devout Christian. He will be remembered and regretted longer than many men of more brilliant lives and more conspicuous history, by the bar, of which he was an ornament; by the social circle of friendship, where affections always cluster around one so sincere and earnest as he; by the community where he dwelt, and which he aimed to serve; and by the commonwealth, of which he was a wise and faithful son.

1802. — ELIAS UPTON died in Bucksport, Me., 16 June, 1857, aged 85. He was born in Reading, Mass., 16 February, 1772. He devoted a great portion of his life to the instruction of youth in various places. He was, for eleven years, preceptor of the Bluehill (Me.) Academy. He afterwards removed to Bucksport, where he engaged in trade, and kept a store in that place for many years, and there finally closed his long life.

1803. — Dr. THOMAS IVERS PARKER died in Boston, 10 December, 1856, aged 72. He was son of Rev. Samuel Parker, D.D. (H.C. 1764), and was born in Boston, 29 March, 1784. He was fitted for college at the Public Latin School in Boston. On leaving college, he chose the medical profession, and pursued his studies under the instruction of Dr. James Jackson (H.C. 1796). Having been admitted to practice, he established himself as a physician in the city of New York, where he remained several years. He then returned to Boston, where he resumed the practice of his profession, and where he resided during the remainder of his life. For ten or twelve years, he held the office of county-physician for Suffolk. He was never married.

1806. — Rev. ISAAC HURD, of Exeter, N.H., died suddenly, at the residence of his son, in South Reading, Mass., 4 October, 1856, aged 70. He was son of Joseph Hurd, and was born in Charlestown, Mass., 7 December, 1785. On leaving college, he began the study of theology under the instruction of Rev. David Osgood, D.D., of Medford, Mass.,

(H.C. 1771). He afterwards went to Europe, and completed his studies at Divinity Hall in Edinburgh. He preached his first sermon in London. On his return he received several invitations to settle; and finally accepted one given him by the Unitarian society in Lynn, Mass., and was ordained 15 September, 1813. He was dismissed, at his own request, 22 May, 1816. A few months afterwards, he was invited to settle over the Second Society in Exeter, of the same liberal denomination; to whom he had rendered himself so acceptable, that although he frankly avowed he had changed his theological views, and declared his belief in the Trinitarian doctrine, yet they persisted in the call, and he was installed pastor of that church, 11 September, 1817. Notwithstanding a conscientious difference of opinion on certain important points, he continued to enjoy, undiminished, their cordial respect and affection. After a ministry of thirty years, Rev. Samuel Dering Dexter (H.C. 1843) was ordained, 2 December, 1847, colleague-pastor. Mr. Dexter died in Roxbury, Mass., 20 April, 1850; and Rev. Asa D. Mann was settled as a colleague, 19 November, 1851. In Mr. Hurd the society found a single-hearted devotedness to his Divine Master as his guide, and to the Scriptures as the source and illustration of Christian truth, together with solid learning, true taste, ardent piety, and exemplary fidelity in all his ministerial and social relations. He was a chaste, correct writer, and, to the extent of his vocal powers, a good speaker. He was affable in his manners, and given to hospitality. In 1854, the honorary degree of Doctor of Divinity was conferred upon him by Dartmouth College. He married, 16 March, 1819, Mrs. Elizabeth Emery, of Exeter, whose maiden name was Folsom; by whom he had two sons, one of whom died in early childhood. The other son, Francis Parkman Hurd, graduated at Harvard College in 1839, and is a physician in Exeter.

1808. — Rev. James Johnson died in St. Johnsbury, Vt., 31 October, 1856, aged 77. He was born in that part of Lynn which is now within the boundaries of Lynnfield, Mass., 12 July, 1779. He studied theology in Cambridge under the tuition of Rev. Henry Ware, D.D. (H. C. 1785), and was licensed to preach in 1810. He was ordained pastor of the Presbyterian church in Potsdam, N.Y., 11 March, 1812; the ordination-sermon being preached by Rev. Amos Pettengill, of Champlain, N.Y. (H.C. 1805). In 1817, he was dismissed from his charge at Potsdam; and, in October of the same year, was installed pastor of the Congregational church in Williston, Vt. While settled at Williston, he preached at St. Alban's the only sermon of his that found its way to the press. It was preached at the anniversary meeting of free-masons, on the festival of St. John the Baptist, 24 June, 1826, from the text, "Every house is builded by some man; but he that built all things is God" (Heb. iii. 4). On the 28th of February, 1827, his pastoral connection was transferred to the Second Congregational Church in St. Johnsbury, Vt., where he ministered until 3 May, 1838; when his relation to that church was dissolved, and he was installed, February, 1839, at Irasburg, Vt., where he labored till the autumn of 1849, when, at the age of seventy, he was dismissed, and passed the remainder of his days at the Centre Village, in St. Johnsbury, preaching occasionally, as opportunity offered, without pastoral relation. He was an industrious, faithful, and successful preacher of the word of life. His discourses evinced a most affectionate regard for the welfare of his hearers, and the simplicity of his manner was as touching as his love was sincere. To him more than to any other man is to be attributed a great reformation in the moral condition of St. Johnsbury. He found his parish full of pestilent doctrines and evil practices; and he gave himself no rest until he had extirpated heresy, root and branch, and trained the people to a high standard of morality. He "set his face like a flint" against all *isms*. Two revivals of more than ordinary interest occurred during his ministry in St. Johnsbury; one of which, in 1831, resulted in the addition of more than sixty to the church. The whole number added to the church during his eleven years' connection with it was one hundred and seventy. The closing years of his life were devoted mainly to the care of his faithful wife, who was for many years a confirmed invalid. She died only eleven days before him; and when, at length, she was released from her sufferings, there seemed no more for him to do on earth, and he hastened to rejoin her above.

1808. — Dr. Samuel Scollay died in Smithfield, Jefferson County, Va., 11 January, 1857, aged 74. He was son of Grover and Rebecca Scollay, and was born in Ashburnham, Mass., 21 January, 1782. His personal character and history furnish a beautiful instance of persevering industry and stern integrity, united to high mental accomplishments, a heart of the noblest impulses, and the keenest sensibility. He began life with no advantages, except those which a good name and a faithful training of his parents conferred. Having to make the money to pay for his education, it was several years beyond the usual period of entering upon college-life that he was matriculated as a member of an advanced class. While his classmates were enjoying the recreations of vacation and the endearments of home, he was exerting himself to provide for the next term of study by teaching school. Thus, one term after another, did he succeed in partially anticipating the expenses of his education. At college he was distinguished no less by his excellence in scholarship among his fellow-students, than for his perseverance and fidelity, during the vacation, as a public teacher. In 1810, he went to Virginia; settled in the vicinity of Charlestown, Jefferson County; and taught school in the family of Mr. Henry Turner. His school soon attracted the members of other families, and became very large. For three years, he thus labored to free himself from the encumbrance of debts contracted in acquiring his education, and also to enable him to qualify himself for a profession. He at the same time prepared himself to enter upon the course of study at the Jefferson Medical College in Philadelphia, where he graduated as one of the first in his class. He began the practice of medicine in Jefferson County at the age of thirty; soon became highly distinguished in his profession, not less eminent in his humble sphere than some of his contemporaries at college in the exalted position they have attained in the nation's councils. By perseverance and industry, for nearly half a century, he was enabled to bring up and educate a large family of children, and become one of the most affluent citizens in that part of the state. His first wife was Miss Harriot Lowndes, a grand-daughter of the late Gov. Lloyd, of Maryland, and first cousin of the late Francis S. Key. His second wife was Miss Sarah Page Nelson, grand-daughter of the late Gen. Thomas Nelson. His remains repose in the graveyard of the beautiful Episcopal church in the village of Smithfield, which his liberality largely contributed to build.

1809.—Hon. FRANCIS CALLEY GRAY died in Boston, Mass., 29 December, 1856, aged 66. He was son of Hon. William Gray, well known as an enterprising and wealthy merchant; and was born in Salem, Mass., 19 September, 1790. After leaving college, he went through a course of legal studies in the office of Hon. William Prescott, of Boston (H.C. 1783), and was admitted to the bar; but he did not pursue the profession for any considerable time. Possessing ample wealth, he became a man of letters, and devoted his powerful and well-cultivated mind to the pursuits of literature. He was private secretary of Hon. John Quincy Adams, when the latter was minister in Russia. He was one of the most brilliant and accomplished writers of his time, and was an early contributor to the "North-American Review." He was the author of a valuable paper, entitled "Remarks on the Early Laws of Massachusetts Bay, with the Code adopted in 1641, and called 'The Body of Liberties,'" which is replete with important historical information. This paper was published in the eighth volume of the third series of the Collections of the Massachusetts Historical Society. In August, 1816, he delivered the oration before the Phi Beta Kappa Society of Harvard College, which was published in the "North-American Review" for September of that year; and in August, 1840, he delivered the annual poem before the same society, which was highly commended in the "North-American" for January, 1841. In 1848, he published a pamphlet entitled "Prison-Discipline in America," in which he made a powerful argument against the separate system of imprisonment, or solitary confinement of prisoners. This pamphlet was noticed, in strong terms of commendation, in an able article in the "Christian Examiner" for March, 1848. On the 4th of July, 1818, he delivered the oration, before the town authorities of Boston, on the anniversary of the Declaration of Independence. This oration takes rank among the ablest productions which that occasion has brought forth. He had a decided taste for antiquarian and historical researches. On the 29th of January, 1818, he was elected a member of the Massachusetts Historical Society, and he edited several volumes of its published Collections. He was elected to many offices of honor and trust. He was a member of the American Academy of Arts and Sciences, and its corresponding secretary; was president of the Boston Athenæum; a trustee of the State Lunatic Hospital at Worcester, on its establishment; a trustee of the Massachusetts General Hospital in Boston; and a fellow of Harvard College from 1826 to 1836. In 1822, he was elected a representative from Boston to the state legislature; and was re-elected in 1823, 1824, and 1836. He was chosen senator from Suffolk in 1825, 1826, 1828, 1829, 1831, and 1843; and was elected one of the executive council in 1839. He was vice-president of the Prison-Discipline Society; and was, for several years, chairman of the Board of Directors of the state prison at Charlestown. In all these several stations, he discharged his duties with eminent ability. In 1841, the honorary degree of Doctor of Laws was conferred upon him by Harvard College. He died a bachelor.

1810. — Rufus Bradford Allyn died in Belfast, Me., 25 January, 1857, aged 63. He was son of Rev. John Allyn, D.D., of Duxbury, Mass. (H.C. 1785), and Abigail (Bradford) Allyn; was born in that town, 27 March, 1793; and was the seventh in descent from Gov. Bradford, of Plymouth Colony. He studied law in the office of Hon. William Sullivan, of Boston (H.C. 1792); and, having been admitted to the bar, he removed, 28 July, 1815, to Belfast, Me., where he opened an office, and there he resided during the remainder of his life. He soon acquired an extensive and lucrative practice, and became one of the leaders of the bar in Waldo County. Some of the wealthy men of Boston were proprietors of large tracts of land in the vicinity of Belfast; and at the solicitation of Mr. Sullivan, himself one of the proprietors, Mr. Allyn accepted an agency for the sale of these lands, such an agency not interfering, but being connected, with the practice of his profession. He continued in this agency for more than twenty years, when it was terminated by his purchase of the remaining interest of the proprietors. He was a scholar of rare attainments, of profound learning, and great refinement of taste. As a lawyer, he had hardly his superior in the country. He was thoroughly versed in the authorities, and of memory so retentive and remarkable as to be able to make a brief upon any given question, referring with accuracy to volume and page without taking the books from their cases; and yet he was by no means exclusively what is called a book-lawyer. He was master of the great principles of jurisprudence; and, with a mind of great logical acuteness as well as comprehensiveness, he applied those principles with wonderful readiness and discrimination. He was a man of great promptness in business, faithful to his clients, and of unbending integrity, but of great eccentricity of character,—reserved to the very borders of misanthropy; an hereditary temperament, which oftentimes endured very great depression, and which tended to obscure his faith, and obliterate the faintest trace of ambition or desire to be known or noticed by his fellow-men. He shunned distinction, and every thing like notoriety he avoided with disgust. He might at one time have removed to Boston, and become the partner of Daniel Webster; but he preferred a life of absolute seclusion. Towards the close of his life, those gloomy doubts superinduced by his melancholy temperament, which had at times obscured his religious faith, were dispelled; and he often prayed, "Lord, I believe: help thou mine unbelief." He was ever a zealous advocate of the principles of liberal Christianity maintained by his father; and retained his respect for the institutions of religion, to which he gave his personal countenance and support. Late in life, he married Rebecca P., the eldest daughter of his friend Samuel Upton, formerly of Boston; and he, perhaps, was the only person not connected by family ties towards whom he had any feeling deserving the name of friendship. Mr. Upton resided in Belfast for some years prior to his removal to Washington, where he died in 1840. His friendship, which was *the* sunny spot in Mr. Allyn's early life, was strengthened by the family tie which united them after Mr. Upton's removal to Washington, and was only dissolved by death; and now, in firmer, purer, and better bonds, and brighter realms, the friends are re-united. His widow and five children survive him in independent circumstances.

1810. — FREDERICK KINLOCH died in Charleston, S.C., 7 August, 1856, aged 66. He was son of Francis and Martha (Rutledge) Kinloch, and was born in Charleston, 17 February, 1790. He began his preparatory studies under the Rev. Dr. Buist; and at the age of 12 he left Charleston, when his father took him to Geneva, in Switzerland, where he remained four years under the instruction of the celebrated Prof. Prevost. He returned with the family to Charleston in 1806; and, that year, entered college. For some time after he graduated, he followed the business of planting; but he was an ardent lover of learning, and he took great delight in acquiring knowledge in all useful arts and sciences, and imparting his information for the benefit of others. He was a thorough French scholar; was also familiar with the Italian and Spanish languages. Amiable in private life, self-sacrificing for the benefit of others, he was without an enemy, and was beloved by all who knew him. Perseverance and punctuality were marked qualities in his character; a sincere friend, but vindictive when angry, sarcastic when offended, yet, if opportunity offered, ready to forget and forgive. Such was Mr. Kinloch. He died at the house of a friend, where he had resided for the last thirty-one years of his life; and, by his own request, he was buried in Magnolia Cemetery.

1812. — CHARLES BROWNE died in Boston, 21 July, 1856, aged 63. He was son of Moses (H.C. 1768) and Mary Browne, and was born in Beverly, Mass., 24 May, 1793. He studied law three years in the office of Hon. Nathan Dane, of Beverly (H.C. 1778); but did not enter upon the practice of the profession, but became a partner in the extensive publishing firm of Hilliard, Gray, and Co., of Boston, where he continued for many years. He was for nearly ten years a director in the New-England Mutual Life-Insurance Company, in which he took great interest; and his labors in the management of its affairs contributed essentially to its success. He was also, for a long period, one of the most active members of the Boston-Library Society, and through life was much interested in historical and genealogical researches. Modest and unobtrusive in his manners, he never sought notoriety, but chose rather to do his duty as a good citizen and a Christian, and to be known by his works. He was in truth a just and good man; one who contributed much to the happiness and dignity of human life; one who was never weary in well-doing, and sought no other reward than the consciouness of a life well spent. He married, 14 December, 1825, Elizabeth Isabella, daughter of Bryant P. Tilden, Esq., of Boston; and had two sons and one daughter, who, with his wife, survive him.

1812. — Leonard Jackson died in West Newton, Mass., 1 April, 1857, aged 65. He was son of Major Daniel and Lucy (Remington) Jackson, and was born in Newton, 26 July, 1791. His father was an officer in the Revolutionary war, and was in the battles of Concord, Bunker Hill, Germantown, and Monmouth. After leaving college, Mr. Jackson studied theology, and preached for a few years, but was never ordained. The subsequent portion of his life was devoted to agricultural pursuits in his native town.

1812. — George Thacher died in Westford, Mass., 12 June, 1857, aged 66. He was son of Hon. George (H.C. 1776) and Sarah (Savage) Thacher, and was born in Biddeford, Me., 7 September, 1790. He was partly fitted for college by Joseph Adams (H.C. 1805), who was private tutor in his father's family; and completed his preparatory studies at Gorham Academy, under the instruction of Rev. Reuben Nason (H.C. 1802). He studied law with Hon. Cyrus King, of Saco; and began practice in that place in 1815, where he continued until 1835. For five years, he was senior partner in law-business with the late Gov. Fairfield. For several years, he was register of probate of York County. In 1835, he left Saco for Monroe, where he remained until 1841, when he was appointed, by Pres. Tyler, collector of Belfast, and removed to that place. After the expiration of his commission, he returned to Monroe, where he resumed business; and continued there until 1853, when he removed to Westford, Mass. He married, 20 January, 1818, his cousin, Lucy Bigelow, daughter of Amos Bigelow, of Weston, Mass. By this marriage he had six children, four of whom survived him. This happy connection was severed by her death at Belfast in September, 1843. He married again, 14 June, 1847, to Lucy, daughter of Dr. Amos Bancroft (H.C. 1791), of Groton, Mass., who survived him. Mr. Thacher was a gentleman of most pleasing address, and distinguished for his generous qualities. He had a deep sense of the importance of truth and justice, and discharged every trust and every duty with conscientious integrity. Believing the truth and importance of the Christian religion, he was a firm supporter of public worship, a communicant and constant attendant on the ordinances of the gospel.

1812.—Dr. Ezekiel Thaxter died in Abington, Mass., 11 October, 1856, aged 69. He was son of Dr. Gridley and Sarah (Lincoln) Thaxter, and was born in Abington, 22 July, 1787. His mother was daughter of Gen. Benjamin Lincoln, of Hingham, the revolutionary hero. He was fitted for college at Hingham Academy, under the tuition of James Day (H.C. 1806). After completing his collegiate course, he studied medicine under the instruction of Dr. John C. Warren, of Boston (H.C. 1797); and, having received his medical diploma in 1815, immediately began practice with his father in Abington. He was quite successful in his profession, and acquired the fullest confidence of his patients. As his father advanced in age, he gradually withdrew from practice; and, for some time before his death (which took place February, 1845, at the age of 89), he gave it up entirely, and his son, the subject of this notice, was the only physician in the town, which is quite large, and embraces four considerable villages, three of them from one and a half to two and a half miles from the doctor's residence. Notwithstanding this, so popular was he, that no physician was able to establish himself even in the remote parts of the town while Dr. Thaxter retained his health. Now there are seven physicians on the territory which he occupied. For the last two or three years, he was able to ride very little, having suffered from paralysis, which in a great measure disabled one side of his body; and his death occurred from a repetition of the shock. As he resided all his life in Abington, he became one of its fathers; and always occupied a large place in the community, being highly esteemed and honored by his fellow-townsmen. In 1821, he was chosen town-clerk; and held the office, by successive annual re-elections, until 1832. He married Diantha Brown, daughter of Samuel Brown, of Abington; and left four children, two sons and two daughters, all residing in that town. His wife died a few years since. He was a man of strong social attachments, and loved to live in the bosom of his family, and in the society of his near relatives and intimate friends. He was a kind and affectionate father, a worthy and estimable citizen.

1814. — Francis Dallas Quash died in Charleston, S.C., 17 February, 1857, aged 63. He was born in Charleston, 19 December, 1793. When in college, he was distinguished by his strength of memory, his finished recitations, and his graceful elocution. He graduated with high honors. Many will remember the animated and graceful manner in which he pronounced the Latin salutatory oration in August, 1814, and the valedictory oration in August, 1817, when he took his degree of master of arts. The latter was afterwards published. After leaving college, he studied law with Judge Samuel Prioleau, but did not enter upon its practice. Inheriting a plantation, his time for several years was devoted to its care. During eighteen years, he was a member of the legislature of his native state; and, for some time previous to his decease, he held a responsible office in the custom-house in Charleston. He married, 6 January, 1819, Emma J. Doughty, by whom he had six children, of whom one son and two daughters survived him.

1815. — Henry Felt Baker, of Cincinnati, died suddenly, of congestion of the brain, in Portsmouth, O., 20 February,

1857, aged 59. His name, originally, was Henry Felt; but his father having died, and his mother marrying Joseph Baker, he took the surname of his step-father. He was the only child of Henry Felt, and was born in Salem, Mass., 6 November, 1797. He was fitted for college, in Salem, under the instruction of Josiah Willard Gibbs (Y. C. 1809). Immediately after graduating, he entered the counting-room of Baker and Hodges, of Boston, for the purpose of acquiring a mercantile education. Here he remained several years, when the firm was dissolved, Mr. Hodges retiring; and a new copartnership was formed, under the style of Joseph Baker and Son. This firm was, after a few years' continuance, dissolved; and the subject of this notice went to London, where he established himself as a merchant. He remained there a little more than two years, and returned to Boston in the autumn of 1841. Soon afterwards, he went to New Orleans, with a view of establishing himself in that city; but, not succeeding according to his wishes, he returned to Boston, and became one of the most active and efficient persons in establishing steam flour-mills in East Boston. He was subsequently treasurer of the Flour-Mills Company. It was at this period that he exhibited his scientific tastes; and he was led to studies and investigations, that resulted, in 1846, in the patent of an invention, and the issue of an illustrative pamphlet entitled "Improvement in Steam-boiler Furnaces." The value of this improvement, whatever the strength of confidence with which he regarded it, he was willing that its own intrinsic merits and practical experience should determine. A year or two afterwards he went to Cincinnati, where he was employed as a clerk in a bank, and where he passed the remainder of his life. In 1853 and 1854, he published, in two parts, a work on "Banks and Banking in the United States;" which, to men of business, is of intrinsic and durable value. In August, 1856, he began writing a series of articles, which were published in the "Banker's Magazine," in New York, illustrative of the specific interests to which that periodical is dedicated. These evidences of a public nature establish the conclusion, that, even amid the active and sensitive habits of mercantile life, he did not suffer his mind to be alienated from that love of science and letters to which it had been early devoted. He was not an inattentive observer of the course of public affairs; and he will be remembered by many of his contemporaries in Boston as always in sympathy with principles of high honor and of a large and generous patriotism. The interests of private virtue and social improvement found in him a friend and benefactor. He was an early associate and patron of the Young Men's Mercantile-Library Association in Boston, and always watched its success with the interest of one who had, in some measure, been instrumental in its establishment. In 1828, he was elected commander of the Boston Independent Company of Cadets; a post that has ever been connected with high and noble bearing in the activities of life. He was a gentleman of polished manners; and, possessing rare colloquial faculties, his acquaintance was much courted in fashionable society. He was often called upon to preside at military dinners and on other festive occasions, which he did with a grace seldom equalled. He married, 21 November, 1822, Caroline, daughter of Capt. John Boit, of Jamaica Plain, Roxbury, Mass.; and had two children, — a son and a daughter, — who, with their mother, survive him. His son graduated at Harvard College in 1848. Of his domestic virtues and religious aspirations, of his firmness in trial, his fortitude in disappointment, his trust in God, and his hope in his Saviour, it is given to those who were united with him in the loved and loving experiences of home to cherish memories into which it were not fitting for the present writer to enter. After a life of activity, varied, as most lives are, by alternate elevations and depressions, he passed away; and his grave is found in the quiet and beautiful Spring-Grove Cemetery, in the queen-city of the West, Cincinnati.

1818. — William Augustus Carson died at Sullivan's Island, near Charleston, S.C., 17 August, 1856, aged 55. He was son of James and Eliza (Neyle) Carson, and was born in Charleston, 27 November, 1800. His father was a native of Camden, S.C., and was a merchant in Charleston. His mother was a native of Exeter, Eng. Mr. Carson was prepared for college, in Charleston, by an Irishman of the name of Moriarty, who was a distinguished scholar. After leaving college, he studied medicine, but never practised; being entirely occupied with his business as a planter. This, however, did not exclude the study of chemistry, botany, astronomy, and mechanics; for all which he had a strong inclination. He married Miss Caroline Petigru, the accomplished and interesting daughter of the Hon. James Louis Petigru, the special friend of Daniel Webster, and the head of the Charleston bar. He had two sons, — William and James Petigru, — who survive him, as does also his widow. Mr. Carson always preserved the liveliest recollection of his college life and college friends, and frequently spoke of revisiting those scenes dear to his youth; but his devotion to his business as a planter, and intendant of Sullivan's Island, always prevented him from putting this wish into execution.

1818. — CHARLES WILLIAM CUTTER died in Chatfield, Minn. Ter., 6 August, 1856, aged 57. He was born in Portsmouth, N.H., 11 June, 1799. He studied law in the office of Hon. Jeremiah Mason (Y.C. 1788); and, having been admitted to the bar, he entered upon the practice of the law in Portsmouth. For several years he was a contributor to the "Portsmouth Journal." He afterwards entered upon the political field; and, espousing the whig cause, was a writer of much spirit. For a year or two, he became a resident of Dover, N.H.; where, about 1823, he established the "Dover Republican." From July, 1825, to January, 1830, he was an associate editor of the "Portsmouth Journal." As a writer and public speaker he was always well received, and enjoyed a confidence which was rewarded by the honors and emoluments of office. He was aide to Levi Woodbury when the latter was governor of New Hampshire, and also aide to Major-Gen. Upham for several years. He several times represented Portsmouth in the New-Hampshire legislature, held the offices of clerk of the United-States District and Circuit Courts in New Hampshire, naval storekeeper and navy-agent. With the heads of the national government, enjoying the personal friendship of Daniel Webster, he at times possessed an influence from which others have derived advantage. But, although in a degree successful in his course, he expressed deep regrets that he ever left his profession to enter the race in the political arena. To a young man who wished his influence at Washington for an office, he said, "I would caution every young man to follow any honest calling rather than rely for support on any public office." Well informed in the literature of the day, interested in all that relates to state historical researches, the promoter of the interest of literary institutions, the ready public speaker, whether on the political platform, at the forensic club, or the desk at the lyceum, he was ever listened to with attention and interest, and cheered with enthusiasm. Though his aim might be high personal position, he was ever noble and generous-hearted to all; and, in filial affection, none could be more devoted. He was never married.

1818. — Dr. JOSHUA HENSHAW HAYWARD died in Boston, 2 December, 1856, aged 59. He was the youngest son of Dr. Lemuel Hayward (H.C. 1768), and was born in Boston, 6 February, 1797. He was fitted for college in Boston by the celebrated Ebenezer Pemberton, and graduated with high honors. On leaving college, he chose the medical profession; and, having completed the regular course of studies, was admitted to the degree of M.D. in 1821. He then went to Europe for the purpose of more thoroughly qualifying himself for the practice of his profession. He remained in Europe three years, and embarked at Havre for New York on board the packet-ship "Cadmus," Capt. Allyn, in the summer of 1824; being a fellow-passenger with Lafayette, when he visited the United States as the nation's guest. He opened an office in Boston, and pursued the practice of his profession a few years; when he relinquished it, and became a partner in the house of Fletcher and Hayward, wholesale druggists. Possessing a taste for the fine arts, he, a few years afterwards, devoted himself to portrait-painting, which he followed for some time with good success. In 1849, he was appointed a weigher in the Boston custom-house; which office he held until his death. He was a gentleman widely known, and universally respected; of an amiable disposition, modest and unobtrusive in manners, and unblemished moral character. He married a daughter of the Hon. John McLean, of Ohio, judge of the Supreme Court of the United States. Her early and sudden death, after a few years of happy union, made a deep impression upon him, which was never effaced. She left two children, — a son and a daughter; both of whom survived their father.

1819. — Hon. STEPHEN CLARENDON PHILLIPS, of Salem, Mass., was lost by the burning of the steamboat "Montreal," in the river St. Lawrence, on the passage from Quebec to Montreal, 26 June, 1857. He was the only child of Capt. Stephen Phillips, an active and enterprising shipmaster and merchant; and was born in Salem, 4 November, 1801. He graduated with high honors at the early age of 18. After leaving college, he began the study of law; but soon relinquished it, and entered upon his father's business as a merchant, in which he engaged with great energy and success. While yet quite young, he was called into the public service. In 1824, he was elected a representative for Salem to the state legislature; which office he held, by successive re-elections, until 1830, when he was chosen to the senate, where he remained two years; and, in 1832 and 1833, he was again a member of the house of representatives. In 1834, he was elected a representative in Congress from the Essex South District to fill the vacancy occasioned by the resignation of Hon. Rufus Choate; and continued to occupy that post until the autumn of 1838, when he resigned, and was succeeded by Hon. Leverett Saltonstall. On the 5th December, 1838, he was elected mayor of Salem; and remained in office until March, 1842, when he voluntarily retired, giving the whole of his three years' salary, amounting to twenty-four hundred dollars, for the benefit of the public schools of Salem. In 1840, he was one of the presidential-electors for Massachusetts. He was a member of the Board of Education of Massachusetts from 1843 to 1852, and a trustee of the State Lunatic Hospital from 1844 to 1850. Of positions of less prominence, which he filled with honor, were those of president of the Salem Young-Men's Temperance Society, organized 15 February, 1832; trustee and president of the Bible Society of Salem and vicinity; president of the Salem

Moral Society; one of the managers of the Salem Dispensary, and vice-president of the Salem Savings-Bank. In 1848, he left the whig party, and engaged actively in the free-soil movement, in the success of which his sympathies were thoroughly enlisted. He was the candidate of that party for governor of Massachusetts in that and the following year, but failed of an election. From that time he withdrew from political life. In private life he was a man of genial disposition, a devoted husband and fond parent; as a man of business he was prompt and energetic; as a Christian he was above reproach. He was a member of the Barton-square Unitarian Church, where he was a constant attendant for thirty-six years. He was eminently a friend of youth, and contributed largely to the support of the sunday-school. Through his munificence a chapel was built; and the church and society, in his death, lost a valued friend and member. He married, first, Jane Appleton, daughter of Willard Peele, of Salem (H. C. 1792): she dying, he married, 3 September, 1838, Margaret M., sister of his former wife. The fruits of these marriages are ten children, — six sons and four daughters. Three of his sons, Stephen Henry, George William, and Charles Appleton, are graduates of Harvard College in 1842, 1847, and 1860, respectively.

1820. — Rev. William Lawrence Stearns died in Chicopee, Mass., 28 May, 1857, aged 63. He was son of Rev. Charles (H.C. 1773) and Susanna (Cowdry) Stearns, and was born in Lincoln, Mass., 30 October, 1793. His twin-brother, Daniel Munroe Stearns, graduated at Brown University in 1822. He was fitted for college by his father. After graduating, he studied divinity under his father's instruction, and was licensed to preach in 1823. He was ordained pastor of the Unitarian church in Stoughton, Mass., 21 November, 1827. His pastoral relation with this society was dissolved 30 March, 1831. He was installed at Rowe, Mass., 30 January, 1833; where he labored as a diligent and faithful pastor until 31 December, 1849, when he was dismissed, and, 1 January, 1850, was settled over the Unitarian church in Pembroke, Mass. He continued his labors in this place until a few months before his death, when ill health compelled him to resign his pastoral charge; and he removed to Chicopee, where he resided in the family of his son until death closed his earthly career. He was married, 5 June, 1828, to Mary Monroe, daughter of Isaac and Grace (Bigelow) Monroe, of Lincoln; and had four children, three sons and one daughter, of whom the daughter and one son died before their father. Mr. Stearns was emphatically a good man, an honest, worthy Christian. He never aimed at eminence or sought popularity, but pursued the even tenor of his way, laboring diligently in the vocation to which he was called, and no doubt made his calling and election sure. His religious sentiments, and his views of the course a minister of the gospel ought to pursue, are well expressed in the following extract of a letter written by him about five years before his death: "I have good reason to believe my ministerial services have been as profitable, in a moral and religious point of view, as those of my brethren who have had larger salaries and obtained notoriety. All kinds and degrees of transcendentalism and Germanism I have detested, and held on in the good old ways of evangelical preaching, for which I have somewhat lost caste, and been considered a little old-fashioned; but I have the consolation to think I have in no way been accessory to infidelity, come-outism, and the other abominations in which the times abound. I wish we had in our denomination fewer of what are called smart preachers, and more of those who teach for doctrine the commands of God, and the simplicity of the truth by Jesus Christ."

1822. — Samuel Manning died in Baltimore, Md., 16 May, 1857, aged 54. He was son of Dr. Samuel (H.C. 1797) and Lucy (Cogswell) Manning, and was born in Westford, Mass., 6 July, 1802; but, from the age of eight years until he entered college, had his home in Lancaster, Mass., and was fitted for admission at Lancaster Academy under the instruction of Pres. Jared Sparks (H. C. 1815); but on account of his youth, being then only fifteen years of age, he remained one year longer at the academy under Mr. Sparks's successor, George Barrell Emerson (H.C. 1817), and entered in 1818. In his freshman year, he taught a school in Lancaster; and, in the winter of his senior year, in Leominster. He was captain of the college company; and, at that time, Capt. Shaw, of the United-States navy, was under suspension. It was intimated to the company that it would be agreeable to Capt. Shaw to see them. Manning asked Pres. Kirkland's permission. The president inquired whether they intended to visit Capt. Shaw as an officer, or as a private citizen. Manning replied, "As a private citizen." The company went, and saluted Shaw as had always been the custom of saluting their hosts. This gave great offence to the officers of the court-martial, among whom was Com. Hull; and, shortly afterwards, Hull published a communication in a newspaper, asking to what literary institution they were indebted for the insult they had received. The consequence was, Manning was deprived of a part he was to have performed at Commencement. It was his intention, through college, to study medicine with his father; and, accordingly, he attended the medical lectures in Boston the first winter after he graduated. But his father died 11 October, 1822; and he relinquished the plan of pursuing the medical profession. In 1823, he went to Maryland, and taught a school of twenty or thirty scholars in Baltimore County, about eight miles from the city of Baltimore, for two years. During the winter of 1825–6, he studied Spanish under Cubi y Soler; and, the following spring, went to Mexico, about eighty miles from the city, to Timascaltapec, as agent for a silver-mining company. In the summer of 1827, he sailed from Vera Cruz in a schooner for Philadelphia, and the voyage occupied sixty-five days. They were twenty days becalmed in the Gulf. The vessel had neither quadrant nor compass; and, for twenty days, all on board were reduced to an allowance of one biscuit and one pint of water each a day. The vessel, too, was leaky; and all were obliged to take their turns at the pumps fifteen minutes successively, until they got into Tampa Bay. He lost his hat soon after leaving Vera Cruz, and had only a paper one, which he made to keep off the heat of the tropical climate. In the spring of 1829, he returned to Baltimore, and on the 10th of June, the same year, was married to

Miss Susan Shepard, of Baltimore; and they passed the summer at Cambridge, Mass. In October, he, with his wife, went to Mexico, and returned the following spring. A few months afterwards, he settled as a lawyer in Baltimore, having attended to the study of law at such intervals as he had after first going to that city. He was quite successful in the profession, and continued in practice until the spring of 1838, when he removed to a farm a few miles from Palmyra in Missouri. The first ground broken on his farm was to bury one of his five children. He intended to practise law; but he lost his law-books on the way out. The Ohio was low, and he had the promise that his books should go by the next boat; but the last he heard of them was that the boxes on which his name was marked were seen floating in the river. Then he lost several hundred dollars' worth of fencing by prairie fire, and other misfortunes followed. Subsequently he lived for a time at St. Louis, where he was still unsuccessful. About 1843, he returned to Baltimore, where he remained until his death. For some time, he was in the office of the Baltimore and Ohio Railroad Company; and afterwards in the coal and iron business, as one of the firm of Manning, Stimpson, and Co. Latterly he was in the hardware business with his brother Joseph, at the Avalon Iron-works. For the last year, he felt that he had a heart disease, and often said that he should die suddenly. About four weeks before his death, he was taken with hemorrhage from the stomach, which confined him for several days. He recovered, and went daily to the iron-works. On the 15th of May, on the way to the cars, on his return, he was taken with fainting, which was immediately followed by paralysis; and he died about one o'clock on the following morning. He was a gentleman of fine personal appearance, great suavity of manner, and of unblemished integrity.

1823. — Rev. William Parsons Lunt, of Quincy, Mass., died at Akabah, a town in Arabia Petræa, 21 March, 1857, aged 51. He left Boston on the 31st December last to make the tour of Europe, intending to return in July following; and was on a journey to visit some of the spots memorable in sacred history, with the intention of proceeding to Jerusalem. He was attacked, while in the desert, with an illness which seemed to be a sharp seizure of rheumatism; and it was with some difficulty that he could reach Akabah. Here his disorder increased in violence; assumed a more distinct febrile type: delirium supervened, and death closed the scene. His last moments were soothed by the kindness and attention of two English gentlemen — one of them a clergyman — with whom he had for some time been travelling; and one of his own countrymen, — Rev. Mr. Dowdney, of New York, — who was at Akabah, performed the last sacred office to his remains. He was son of Henry and Mary (Greene) Lunt, and was born in Newburyport, 21 April, 1805. He was fitted for college at Milton Academy, and graduated with high honors. On leaving college, it was his intention to have pursued the profession of law; and accordingly he entered, as a student, the office of Charles Pelham Curtis (H.C. 1811), of Boston. After studying one year, he changed his mind, relinquished the study of law, and entered the Theological School at Cambridge for the purpose of studying for the ministry. After completing his studies, he was invited to take the pastoral charge of the Second Unitarian Church (now the Church of the Messiah) in the city of New York. This invitation he accepted, and was accordingly ordained 19 June, 1828. His pastoral relation with that church was dissolved 19 November, 1833; and he was installed over the Unitarian church in Quincy, 3 June, 1835, where he faithfully labored until his death, — a period of nearly twenty-two years. He married, 14 May, 1829, Ellen Hobart, daughter of Barnabas Hedge (H.C. 1783), of Plymouth, Mass., and had seven children, — four daughters and two sons, — of whom six, with their mother, survived him: one child died in infancy. Dr. Lunt was one of the most popular and eloquent divines of the day, and was greatly beloved by the society among whom he had labored so long. His writings, both in prose and poetry, display a singularly pure taste and classic refinement, and have been much admired. Quiet, unobtrusive, and refined in his manners, he sought rather to do good than to court popularity. He was a learned and accurate historian, and was a member of the Massachusetts Historical Society. In 1850, the honorary degree of doctor of divinity was conferred upon him by Harvard College.

1823. — Dr. JOHN MARSH, of Contra Costa, Cal., was murdered about two miles from Martinez, Cal., by two Spaniards, named Jose Antonio Olivas and Felipe Morena, on the evening of 24 September, 1856. He was son of John and Mary (Brown) Marsh, and was born in that part of Danvers, Mass., which is comprised within the limits of South Danvers, 5 June, 1799. His great-grandfather's name was Ezekiel. He died the same year that John was born. The paternal estate was given by will to John's father. It has been in the Marsh family for more than one hundred years. The subject of this notice was fitted for college at the academy in Lancaster, Mass. When a boy, he was more remarkable for active exercises than for abstruse studies. The groves and the brooks around will bear testimony to his adroitness in capturing their tenants. No fox, squirrel, or muskrat, could live in peace where John wandered. Shortly after he graduated, he went to the Western country, where he secured employment as Indian agent at one of the government stations on the Upper Mississippi. While in this region, he began the study of medicine with a physician who died before the regular course was completed, and he did not finish the usual term. He then removed across the country to California, where he established himself as a physician. His personal appearance was commanding; his adroitness as a manager by no means wanting. He had the good fortune to obtain from the Mexican Government a grant of land on and about Monte Diablo, and settled thereon in the business of rearing cattle; and his herds became as numerous as those of the patriarch of old. When the gold fever began to rage, Dr. Marsh's lands began to advance in worth, and it is not now easy to estimate their value. The title to a large part of his claim was confirmed to him since the United States came in possession of the territory. On all hands, it is admitted that his possessions are large and valuable. He was married in California, in June, 1851, to Miss Abba Tuck, of Chelmsford, Mass., who went thence to seek her fortune as an instructress. She died before the doctor, leaving one daughter, four years old, as his only legal heir. Dr. Marsh had four brothers and two sisters. The standing of the family has ever been that of substantial, respectable farmers. His father survived him, a vigorous old gentleman of the age of eighty years. He had one brother who graduated at Yale, and was educated for the ministry, but died young.

The following additional particulars of Dr. Marsh's life and character are extracted from a letter written by a gentleman formerly of Salem, but who has for some years past been a resident of California. It is dated San Francisco, Dec. 11, 1856.

"He [Dr. Marsh] had seen much of life; was a keen observer of men and things; had much general information; read much, and was very ready and willing to communicate of his knowledge to others. He was a very thorough Spanish and French scholar, speaking and writing both languages with great fluency and correctness. In his residence for several years in the Western states as an Indian agent, he obtained a more perfect knowledge of the habits, manners, and dialects of the various Indian tribes than any other person, I suspect, except Mr. Schoolcraft. His mind was a sound and logical one, capable of thoroughly discussing and fully comprehending most subjects. His good judgment, together with his resolute and adventurous spirit, would, I think, have made him distinguished as a soldier. I am not aware that he saw more service than while in command of a company of rangers in the Black-Hawk war, under Gen. Atkinson. All his qualities of mind, and experiences of life, made him a most entertaining and instructive companion. His long residence in California, and his intimate knowledge of the history of the country in early times, induced Mr. Larkin and other pioneers in the settlement of the state often to urge him to write an account of the most important portions of its history. For such a work he was eminently qualified; but his own affairs had too many claims upon his time and thoughts to allow him to do so. He came to this state in 1836, and spent six months after his arrival in exploring the state, to select a location. The one upon which he finally decided is situated beyond the coast range of mountains, and at the foot of Monte Diablo, a high mountain across the bay, and in full view from San Francisco. At the time he came here, land had not much value; and he purchased the estate of Signor Norriéga, a native of California, for almost a nominal sum. There are about fifty thousand acres of land included in the estate. Much of it is excellent for cultivation; but he has devoted himself to the business of cattle-raising, gradually increasing his stock, till he had, at the time of his death, some four or five thousand head. He lived for many years in an adobe house, which he built with the assistance of Indians hired for the purpose. He was twice plundered in early times by gangs of thieves, to which his almost solitary mode of life exposed him. When the gold-fever broke out in this state, all the persons in his employment left him, and went to the mines. He went there likewise, and was tolerably successful; but fell sick in a short time, and returned to his rancho. The growth of San Francisco and other cities and towns has of late greatly increased the value of his property, as it has opened a market for cattle, which of course, in early times, did not exist. He had just completed a beautiful house, and was making arrangements for that comfort and enjoyment which he had for many years denied himself. But he was not permitted to carry out his plans, and to spend the evening of his life in ease and enjoyment, as he had contemplated. He was doomed to death by felon hands at the very time when all life's projects seemed to be accomplished, and the burden and heat of the day was to be succeeded by rest and enjoyment. Truly the ways of Providence are inscrutable!"

The writer of the above extract states previously that he had received a letter from the doctor the day but one before his death, requesting him to go with the bearer of the note to give evidence against some cattle-thieves, who had committed many depredations on his property. The doctor intended to visit San Francisco on the day of his assassination. He started about noon in his buggy for Martinez, about twenty miles from his residence, where he would take water conveyance to San Francisco; and about dark, when two miles from Martinez, he was met by the two wretches, who, it is supposed, threw a lasso over him, and then dirked him. He never could be induced to go armed, although so exposed to peril in consequence of plunderers of his timber and cattle, against whom he had instituted legal proceedings. The two murderers, however, were not among this class of persons. They were men who had been in his employ, and who knew his habits. It is conjectured that they knew of his having four hundred dollars about his person, which, together with the gold watch, were taken. Dr. Marsh retained a warm attachment for his friends, and was intending to visit his native town the following spring.

1825. — Dr. JOHN GOODHUE TREADWELL died in Salem, Mass., 6 August, 1856, aged 51. He was son of Dr. John Dexter Treadwell (H.C. 1788) and Dorothy (Goodhue) Treadwell; was born in Salem, 1 August, 1805; and was fitted for college at the Latin School in Salem. He held a high rank as a scholar in his class, and graduated with distinguished honors. Immediately after graduation, he began the study of medicine under the instruction of Dr. William Johnson Walker, of Charlestown (H.C. 1810). He attended two courses of medical lectures in Boston, one in New York, and spent one season in a dissecting-room in Baltimore. Having completed his medical studies, he received the degree of M.D. in 1828. In August, 1829, he went to London; in the spring of 1830, to Dublin; and the following summer to Paris, at the time of the revolution, the scenes of which he saw. Thence he went again to London, and returned home in November, 1830. He then established himself as a physician in Salem, when he rose rapidly to distinction, and in a few years stood at the head of the medical profession in his native city. When thus in the full tide of a successful and lucrative practice, in November, 1839, he made a post-mortem examination of a child which had died of scarlet fever; and, through a slight sore on one of his fingers, the virus became infused into his system, which affected him severely, although he continued his practice until March, 1841, when he was obliged to give up, and did nothing for two or three years. He subsequently, however, so far recovered, that he was consulted at home, and occasionally visited some of his patients. His father died 6 June, 1833, at the age of 65; and he lived with his mother, who survived him. He was never married. He was somewhat eccentric, but was enthusiastically fond of his profession, ignored almost every thing but that, and read scarcely any work that did not pertain to it. By his will he made several valuable public bequests. The principal one, amounting to nearly fifty thousand dollars, was to Harvard College, for the establishment of a free course of medical lectures. The property appropriated for this purpose was given to the college after the decease of his mother, who was then about eighty years of age. The principal conditions of this bequest are, that the money is to be appropriated to the establishment of professorships of anatomy and physiology. The candidates for these offices are to be examined, before appointment, by a commission of experienced men, after the custom of the French university. If the income of the funds appropriated should not be sufficient for the support of the professors, then they are to be allowed to lecture before private classes, but not to the Lowell Institute or to public lyceums. His valuable library, containing all the latest medical European publications, was left to the college under certain conditions. In case the college authorities should not accede to the conditions of the will, the whole amount, after the death of his mother, goes to the Massachusetts General Hospital, without conditions. A valuable theological library he bequeathed to the Barton-square Church, in Salem, for the use of the pastor. A fine farm of seventy acres, situated in Topsfield, Mass., he left to the Essex Agricultural Society, for the purposes of an experimental farm.

1828. — HENRY SWASEY McKEAN died in Boston, 17 May, 1857, aged 47. He was son of Rev. Joseph (H.C. 1794) and Amy (Swasey) McKean, and was born in Boston, 9 February, 1810. He was fitted for college at the Latin School in Boston, and graduated with high honors. In the winter of his senior year, he kept school at Nine-acre Corner, in Concord, Mass. Immediately after graduating, he was employed as assistant in the private school of Charles Winston Greene (H.C.

1802), at Jamaica Plain; but was taken sick a few weeks afterwards, and left. He next taught a school a short time in Cambridge. In January, 1830, he entered the Law School in Cambridge, where he remained about six months; when, on the 18th of August the same year, he was appointed tutor in Latin in Harvard College; which office he held until August, 1835, when he resigned, and began the study of engineering under Loammi Baldwin (H.C. 1800), of Charlestown, and continued in this profession, with some intervals, during the remainder of his life. For this occupation he had peculiar qualifications, as he was an excellent mathematician, and was thoroughly versed in the theoretical part of the profession. He had an accurate eye, was an excellent draughtsman, and performed with great neatness all the mechanical work which his duties required. During part of 1842, he was engaged in instruction in Georgia, and in 1845–6 in New Jersey. From July, 1842, until May, 1845, he was librarian of the Mercantile-Library Association in the city of New York, during which time he made the catalogue of the library. From July, 1846, to October, 1848, he was employed as assistant engineer of the second division of the Boston Water-works, residing at Newton Lower Falls; his friend Mr. Chesborough being the official chief. Here he labored with great assiduity and skill, and earned the praise and confidence of those who were intrusted with the supervision and responsibility of that enterprise. Two of the works constructed under his immediate charge — a bridge across the river Charles, and an embankment over which the aqueduct is carried, and under which the county road goes — have been mentioned as works reflecting great credit on his skill and science. He continued in the service of the city so long as Mr. Chesborough was chief engineer; and, upon that gentleman's removal from the city, Mr. McKean resigned his place, and opened an office as engineer on his own account. At the time of his death he was meditating a change of occupation, and proposing to engage in some literary employment. He married, 3 November, 1851, Anna H. Hosmer, of Camden, Me., and had one child. His life was eminently pure, honorable, and faithful. He had excellent capacities, trained by thorough and careful preparation; and yet his success in life was not commensurate with his gifts and accomplishments. No man was less zealous to set forth his own claims, or more inclined to recognize the claims of others. His health was not robust. His temperament was sensitive, and inclined to melancholy, which affected him to such a degree, as to induce, occasionally, mental alienation, in a paroxysm of which he ended his life with his own hand. He was a man of warm domestic and social affections; and in his relations of friend, son, brother, husband, and father, he tasted the purest joys of which the heart is capable. He was often tried, alike by external disappointments and by struggles with his own peculiar temperament; but he never lost his sense of the paternal relations of God, and never murmured at any dispensation of his providence.

1830. — Hon. THOMAS HOPKINSON died in Cambridge, Mass., 17 November, 1856, aged 52. He was son of Theophilus and Susanna (Allen) Hopkinson, and was born in New Sharon, Me., 25 August, 1804. He was fitted for college at the academy in Farmington, Me., and graduated with the highest honors of his class. After leaving college, he studied law under the instruction of Hon. Luther Lawrence (H.C. 1801); and, on being admitted to the bar, became his partner, and began to practise in Lowell. He was married, 1 November, 1836, to Corinna Aldrich Prentiss, daughter of Hon. John and Diantha (Aldrich) Prentiss, of Keene, N.H.; with whom he lived in uninterrupted harmony and happiness for twenty years. In his profession, he soon rose to an eminent rank; and was extensively known as an able lawyer and safe counsellor. He was elected a representative from Lowell to the state legislature in 1838 and 1845; and, in 1846, he was chosen senator from Middlesex District. He was chairman of the committee on railroads at a time when the situation was one of great importance. In 1848, he was appointed judge of the Court of Common Pleas; but resigned his seat on the bench the following year, having been elected president of the Boston and Worcester Railroad Corporation. When he entered upon the duties of his office as president, he removed to Boston, where he lived until the autumn of 1855; when he removed to Cambridge, and there resided until his death. He was a member of the convention called in 1853 for revising the constitution of the state. In the discharge of his duties, he was conscientious, judicious, and indefatigable; and entered into the various details so minutely, that the labor and anxiety, in connection, perhaps, with organic tendencies to disease, seriously impaired his health. In May, 1856, he went to Europe; travelled in England, Scotland, France, Germany, Holland, the upper part of Italy; and spent some time in Switzerland. On his return, he was not able to resume his duties, but rapidly sank away, until death terminated his severe sufferings.

1831. — Rev. Nathaniel Tucker Bent died in Worcester, Mass., 4 November, 1856, aged 46. He was son of Josiah and Susannah Bent, and was born in Milton, Mass., 30 July, 1810. He began his preparatory studies for admission to college under the instruction of his brother, Rev. Josiah Bent, of Weymouth (H.C. 1822), and completed them at Phillips Academy in Andover. He held a distinguished rank in college, and graduated with high honors. After leaving college, he began the study of divinity at the Episcopal Theological Seminary in New York; and finished his studies, under the instruction of Bishop Alexander Viets Griswold, at Salem. He was ordained as deacon at Salem, and was afterwards instituted as rector over the following churches: viz., Grace Church, in New Bedford, where he remained five years; St. John's, in Charlestown, two years; St. Thomas's, in Taunton, five years; St. John's, in Bangor, Me., two and a half years; All Saints', in Worcester, two and a half years; and Grace Church, again, in New Bedford, a few months. He retired from the ministry in 1853, and removed to Worcester, where he taught a private school for young ladies, which he continued until his death. He married, 18 June, 1834, Catharine E. D. Metcalf, eldest daughter of Col. Eliab W. Metcalf, of Cambridge; and had four children by birth, and one by adoption; three of whom, including the adopted one, are now living. Mr. Bent was a man of rare abilities, and, when engaged in the active duties of the ministry, was very popular and efficient as rector. Much might be said truly in praise of his fidelity to all the details of parochial duty, the interest he took in promoting musical taste in its sacred department, his zeal in missionary enterprises, and the genial flow which he manifested in social life. Not a few of his former parishioners and friends will long cherish a most kindly remembrance of him as a beloved and respected pastor.

The mortality of the class of 1831, of which Rev. Mr. Bent was a member, was very great during the first twenty years after graduation; twenty-four of the sixty-five members of the class having died before the systematic publication of the obituary notices commenced in the year 1852. The following list comprises a brief notice of these twenty-four: William Austin, jun., a school-teacher, son of Hon. William and Charlotte (Williams) Austin, born in Charlestown, 15 September, 1811; died of typhus fever, in Groton, 8 January, 1835; never married. Rufus Bigelow, son of Tyler and Clarissa (Bigelow) Bigelow, born in Watertown, 3 June, 1809; died of consumption, in Watertown, 6 July, 1832; never married. Robert Adams Coker, a school-teacher, son of John and Hannah (Adams) Coker, born in Newbury, 19 March, 1807; died of consumption, in West Newbury, 30 March, 1833; unmarried. George Clinton Coombs, a lawyer, born in 1810; died of consumption, in New Bedford, 16 March, 1835; unmarried. Edward Cruft, jun., a lawyer, son of Edward and Elizabeth (Storer) Cruft, born in Boston, 7 May, 1811; died of hemorrhage from the lungs, at St. Louis, Mo., 23 April, 1846; unmarried. Jeremiah George Fitch, a lawyer, son of Jeremiah and Mary (Rand) Fitch, born in Boston, 19 February, 1810; died of dropsy at Orono, Me., 25 February, 1845; unmarried. John Giles, jun., a lawyer, son of John and Mary (Adams) Giles, born in Townsend, 3 March, 1806; died of consumption, at Townsend, 14 June, 1838; unmarried. William Cabot Gorham, a merchant, son of Hon. Benjamin and Susan (Lowell) Gorham, born in Boston, in the year 1814; died of typhus fever, in Boston, 18 April, 1843; unmarried. Robert Habersham, jun., a student of law, son of Robert Habersham, of Savannah, Ga.; died of typhus fever, at Savannah, 30 August, 1832, aged twenty years; unmarried. Charles George Clinton Hale, son of Moses and Mary Hale, born in Winchenden, August, 1812; died of consumption, in New York, 6 May, 1832; unmarried. John George McKean, a lawyer, son of Rev. Prof. Joseph and Amy (Swasey) McKean, born in Cambridge, 1 December, 1811; died of spinal disease, in Cambridge, 31 January, 1851; unmarried. Benjamin Franklin Parker, a physician, son of Samuel and Eusebia Parker, born in Roxbury, 21 November, 1810; died of consumption, in Roxbury, 27 February, 1844; unmarried. John Peters, a merchant, son of John and Charlotte (Langdon) Peters, of Boston; died in Brooklyn, N.Y., 17 July, 1846; unmarried. Francis James Russell, a merchant, son of Nathaniel and Martha (Le Baron) Russell, born in Plymouth, 11 September, 1811; died in Plymouth, of typhus fever, 6 September, 1833; unmarried. Francis Henry Silsbee, who studied law, and subsequently became a bank-officer, son of Zachariah F. and Sarah (Boardman) Silsbee, born in Salem, 6 September, 1811; died of marasmus, in Salem, 19 November, 1848; unmarried. William Hammatt Simmons, a teacher of elocution, and law-student, son of Judge William and Priscilla (Hammatt) Simmons, born in Boston, 11 May, 1812; married at Roxbury, 24 June, 1840, Josephine Matilda Fellowes, daughter of Nathaniel and Aglaie (de Chambellan) Fellowes; died of fever, in Boston, 10 August, 1841. Henry Cheever Simonds, a lawyer, son of Shepherd and Joanna Thayer (Gool) Simonds, born in Boston, 3 June, 1810; died in Charlestown, of disease of the brain, 3 April, 1840; unmarried. Charles Henry Tilghman, a planter, son of William G. Tilghman, of Talbot County, Md.; died in Talbot County, Md., 18 September, 1842; unmarried. Abner Bennett Wheeler, a physician, son of Abner and Mary (Swift) Wheeler, born in Framingham, 2 February, 1812; married at Boston, 26 October, 1836, Caroline Harris Sumner; died at Somerville, of disease of the brain, 8 December, 1847. Alexander Whitney, a school-teacher, son of Nathaniel Ruggles and Sally (Stone) Whitney, born in Watertown, 12 March, 1810; died of consumption, in East Cambridge, 13 May, 1842; unmarried. Samuel Wigglesworth, a physician, son of Thomas and Jane (Norton) Wigglesworth, born in Boston, 16 December, 1811; married at Boston, 7 December, 1841, Louisa G. Davenport, daughter of Isaac and Mary Davenport; died of disease of the spine, 7 April, 1847, at Boston. Frederick Wright, a lawyer, son of Theodore and Mary (Dickinson) Wright, born in Northampton, 6 July, 1811; married at Willoughby, O., 10 November, 1841, Helen Irene Wilson, daughter of Samuel Wilson; died in Manhattan, O., 10 April, 1846. Hartley Hezekiah Wright, a lawyer, son of Hezekiah and Charlotte (Sewall) Wright, born in Boston, 22 December, 1812; died in Boston, 8 March, 1840; unmarried.

1833. — FREDERICK PARKER died in Lowell, Mass., 29 January, 1857, aged 43. He was son of Joseph and Olive (Bailey) Parker, and was born in Carlisle, Mass., 2 September, 1813. He was fitted for college in the adjoining towns. After graduating, he taught school in Gloucester and Billerica, Mass., and in Hallowell, Me. In the autumn of 1838, he began the study of law with Hon. Samuel Wells, of Hallowell. In September, 1839, he entered the Law School at Cambridge, where he completed his legal studies, and received the degree of LL.B. in 1841. He then established himself in Lowell. After spending a short time in the office of Joel Adams, Esq., of that city (H.C. 1805), he was admitted to the bar. In October, 1844, he married Harriet M. Kimball. In 1845, he experienced a long and severe illness, the effects of which never left him; and, from that time forward, he was forced to struggle with ill health. In the same year he was chosen one of the school committee, and held that office during four successive years. The cause of education always interested him; and, during his term of office, he suggested several important changes in the arrangements of the Lowell schools. In 1849, he was instrumental in forming the Howard Fire-Insurance Company, of which, for several years, he was secretary and treasurer. In 1852, he opened a book and print store in Lowell, and, soon afterwards, another in Boston. The former was soon closed, and he devoted his energies to the latter. In this employment he manifested great taste and enterprise. In the summer of 1856, his health failed; and he gave up his interest in his business in Boston, and retired to Lowell. In the autumn of that year, he had repeated attacks of hemorrhages, and died of consumption. He kept up his literary tastes in a greater degree than is usual with men of business. In character he was grave and earnest. He encountered reverses; but maintained, through them all, unsullied integrity. No misfortune had power to diminish the energy of his spirit, or to mar his Christian temper.

1834. — Dr. WILLIAM PUTNAM RICHARDSON died in Kendall, Ill., 27 March, 1857, aged 41. He was son of Capt. William P. and Deborah (Lang) Richardson, and was born in Salem, Mass., 15 August, 1815. He was fitted for college at the Latin School in Salem. He studied medicine with Dr. Abel Lawrence Peirson, of Salem (H.C. 1812); and in 1837 received the degree of M.D., when he entered upon the practice of his profession in Salem, where he continued until 1846, when he removed to Kendall. There he was chiefly engaged in horticultural and agricultural pursuits, for which his fine tastes, and love of natural history, peculiarly fitted him. While in Salem, he was an active and useful citizen, interested in whatever tended to elevate and improve the community. He was a valuable member of the school-committee, and a pattern and coworker in various public institutions. He was unmarried.

1837. — GALES SEATON died in Washington, D.C., 9 February, 1857, aged 39. He was son of William W. Seaton, and was born in Washington, 27 July, 1817. He passed through his preparatory studies for admission into Harvard College under the instruction of the faculty of Georgetown College. On graduating, he selected the law as his profession; and repaired to the University of Virginia, where he prosecuted his legal studies with assiduity and success. He was admitted to the bar, but was not long in discovering that he had given his nights and his days to the study of that, as a science, which his mental habitudes and literary tastes rendered distasteful as a pursuit; and, abandoning the profession of the law, he became the proprietor and editor of the Raleigh (N.C.) "Register," in which station he continued several years. He afterwards went to Europe, where he resided some time. While there, he was intrusted by the administration of President Taylor with a confidential commission, which he discharged in a manner highly creditable to himself, and satisfactory to the Secretary of State, — the late John M. Clayton. Of polished manners and commanding presence, without fear and without reproach, shrinking instinctively from all that was base in act or indecorous in thought and word, he was, in all respects, a true gentleman. In every relation of life, he was remarkable for a singular combination of modesty and self-reliance. To the inevitable ills of life he opposed the firmness of manhood with the submission enjoined by Christianity; and, amid the consolations and hopes of the latter, his mortal life slowly and calmly ebbed away, until the waiting spirit dropped the tabernacle of the flesh to take on the robes of immortality.

1838. — CHARLES DELANO BOWMAN died in Oxford, Mass., 19 January, 1857, aged 40. He was the youngest son of Joseph and Sally (Penniman) Bowman, and was born in New Braintree, Mass., 12 December, 1816. He pursued his preparatory studies at Leicester Academy, and entered Amherst College, where he remained one year, and then entered Harvard. After leaving college, he went to Georgia, where he was instructor in private schools and families, about three years, at Richmond Factory, Richmond County, at Athens, and at Augusta. In 1842, he entered the office of Hon. Emory Washburn (W.C. 1817), at Worcester, Mass., as a student-at-law. In March, 1845, he was admitted to the bar; and began practice in Oxford, 22 April, 1845, where he continued to reside until his decease. He had, considering his experience, a good knowledge of law; was a man of more than ordinary promise, and of considerable literary taste. He had a valuable legal and miscellaneous library. The legal part he gave to the Worcester-County Lawyers' Literary Association, and the other part to some literary institution in Worcester.

He married, 24 November, 1846, Almira Louise Jones,

daughter of Elnathan and Almira (Jencks) Jones, of Enfield, Mass.

1838.—William Abijah White died in Milwaukie, Wis., 10 October, 1856, aged 38. He was son of Abijah and Anne Maria (Howard) White, and was born in Watertown, Mass., 2 September, 1818. He was fitted for college at the school of Rev. Samuel Ripley (H.C. 1804), of Waltham, Mass. Having chosen the profession of law, he, immediately after graduating, entered the Law School in Cambridge, where he pursued his professional studies for a year, and completed them in the office of Messrs. Charles P. and Benjamin R. Curtis (H.C. 1811 and 1829) in Boston. He never, however, devoted himself to the practice of his profession; but, becoming very much interested in the antislavery and temperance movements, he devoted much of his time to lecturing on these subjects, and, in 1843, spent several months in travelling through Ohio and Indiana, holding antislavery meetings in company with Frederick Douglass and George Bradburn. In the course of this tour, their meetings were frequently broken up by mobs; and both White and Douglass were, on one occasion, severely wounded by stones. After his return, he took a farm in Watertown, which he cultivated until his father's death in 1845; for two or three years after which, he was engaged in settling his estate. He then engaged in manufacturing, and for some time edited a temperance newspaper in Boston. In 1853, he removed to Madison, Wis. The circumstances of his death were peculiar. On the 7th of October, 1856, he went from Madison to Milwaukie for the purpose of attending the state fair. On the evening of the 8th, he went to Chicago by steamboat, and returned to Milwaukie on the evening of the 9th. On the morning of the 10th, he left the hotel, intending to return in a few hours, and was recognized by a person on the street shortly afterwards. From that time, nothing was seen or heard of him, although every exertion was made to find him, until the first day of May following, when his body was found near the Lake Shore, above North Point, in Milwaukie. It was so much decayed, that it was identified only by the clothing, watch, and a peculiar watch-key. By what means he came to his death, remains a mystery. He married first, 7 May, 1846, Harriet T. Sturgis, daughter of Nathaniel R. Sturgis, of Boston: she died 18 March, 1850. On the 15th of May, 1855, he married Ada A. Butterfield, daughter of Justin Butterfield, of Chicago, Ill. His children were, by his first wife, William Howard White, born 21 February, 1847; Amy, born 25 September, 1848: by his second wife, Justin Sydney, born 19 April, 1856; died 5 February, 1857. Mr. White possessed fine natural abilities. He was a fluent and impressive speaker, and wrote with ease and pungency. He had a keen wit and a strong sense of humor, which frequently did him good service in the hot debates in which he was engaged as an antislavery and temperance orator. He was incapable of a mean or selfish act; and his first and only rule of action was to do what was right, without regard to whether it was expedient. As an eminently brave, sincere, and honest man, who earnestly sought to do his duty, and to benefit his fellow-men at the cost of much personal sacrifice to himself, he will long be remembered with affection and respect by an unusually extensive circle of friends and acquaintances.

1842. — Dr. Henry Whiting died in Lowell, Mass., 23 June, 1857, aged 35. He was son of Capt. Phineas and Sarah (Coburn) Whiting, and was born in that part of Chelmsford which is now Lowell, 19 February, 1822. He was prepared for college partly in Lowell; partly in Boston, under the instruction of Mr. Tilly Brown Hayward (H.C. 1820); and partly in Derry, N.H. He studied medicine with Dr. Gilman Kimball, of Lowell; Dr. Marshall S. Perry, of Boston; at Jefferson College, Penn.; and at the Harvard Medical School. He received the degree of M.D. at Jefferson College in 1845, and immediately afterwards went to Paris, where he passed one year in completing his professional studies; and, in the succeeding year, travelled over various portions of the continent. On his return, he began practice in the city of Lowell. He held a good rank among the profession; was of a frank, noble disposition; and was popular with all classes. He was never married. During the last two years of his life, he was confined to the house by sickness; did not see any person except his nearest relatives; and, after this long and painful confinement, gladly welcomed death as a relief from his sufferings.

1843. — CHARLES FREDERICK ADAMS died in Boston, 30 December, 1856, aged 32. He was son of Charles Frederick and Caroline Hesselrigge (Walter) Adams; was born in Boston, 3 February, 1824; and was fitted for college at the Boston Latin School. On leaving college, he entered the Law School at Cambridge, where he remained one year; and completed his legal studies in the office of Charles Greely Loring, of Boston (H.C. 1812). Having been admitted to the bar, he opened an office in Boston. The profession, however, being crowded, afforded but little encouragement for one of so modest and retiring habits as Mr. Adams; and he, after a few years, determined to seek a new field for practice, and, in 1849, sailed for California, via Cape Horn; but, on the passage, he was attacked with pleurisy-fever, and arrived at the end of his long voyage in a feeble state of health. After remaining a few weeks in San Francisco, by the advice of friends he proceeded to the Sandwich Islands; but, on his arrival there, he found the accommodations for invalids very scanty and undesirable, and he shortly afterwards sailed for China. But this voyage was of little benefit to him; and he returned home after an absence of about thirteen months, and resumed the practice of his profession in Boston. His health, however, was never fully restored; and that insidious disease, consumption, closed his mortal career while in the prime of life. Exemplary in all the duties of private life, he showed a diligence, exactness, and fidelity in his profession, which, had his life been prolonged, would have insured success, and the confidence and esteem of the community. He had a taste for archæological and genealogical studies. An interesting paper, entitled "Notices of the Walter Family," furnished by him, was published in the "Historical and Genealogical Register" for July, 1854. He died full of Christian hope and resignation, leaving many devoted friends to mourn his early death.

1844. — ROBERT LEMMON died at Patuxent, Md., 24 December, 1856, aged 31. He was son of Richard and S. A. Lemmon, and was born in Baltimore, 25 September, 1825. After leaving college, he studied law in the office of the late Judge Glenn, and practised his profession in Baltimore until 1848; when he relinquished it to pursue the business of an iron-master at the Patuxent Furnaces in Anne Arundel County, Md. He married, in the autumn of 1854, Fannie C., daughter of Henry A. Hall, of West River, Md. They had two children, — sons, — who, with their mother, survived him.

1848. — JOHN EDSON died in New-York City, 29 April, 1857, aged 29. He was born in Quincy, Mass., 27 June, 1827. While very young, he removed with his father's family to Bridgewater, where he was fitted for college. In September, 1844, he was admitted to the freshman class in Trinity College, Hartford. There he remained not quite five months; and in February, 1845, entered Columbia College, in the city of New York. He was in this institution one year and a half, until the close of the sophomore year; and in August, 1846, he was admitted into the junior class at Cambridge. After graduating in 1848, he spent the remainder of that year and the following year in Troy, N.Y., in the study of engineering. He then went to the city of New York, where he studied architecture; and afterwards established himself there as an architect, which profession he pursued until his death.

1849. — Rev. JULIUS WALKER STUART died in Beaufort, S.C., 30 October, 1856, aged 28. He was born in Beaufort, 30 September, 1828. After graduating, he went through a course of theological studies, preparatory to becoming an Episcopal clergyman; and was ordained in Beaufort, as assistant-pastor to the Rev. Mr. Pinckney, of Grace Church, in Charleston, S.C.: but his labors in his sacred calling were destined to be short. He left Charleston on a visit to Beaufort; and, a few days after his arrival there, he was taken with yellow fever, of which he died, after an illness of seven days. The editor of the "Charleston Mercury," who was his classmate, in announcing his death, says, "He had just begun a career in the ministry of the Episcopal church, which opened the highest prospects of future usefulness. Knowing him from his early boyhood, we can say that we have never known a human being more thoroughly blameless. Nor were his virtues of the negative sort; he was earnest, conscientious, firm in his convictions, and courageous in their maintenance and defence: but all his manly qualities were pervaded with a gentleness and unselfishness that never allowed them to give offence; and we do not believe, that, in the whole course of his life, he ever made an enemy, or has left a solitary spark of human unkindness to be extinguished on his grave."

1850. — William Lowell Stone died in Cambridge, Mass., 9 January, 1857, aged 27. He was son of William Fiske and Harriet (Brigham) Stone, and was born 24 June, 1829, during the temporary residence of his mother at Westborough, Mass., while his parents were inhabitants of East Cambridge. He was prepared for college at the High School in East Cambridge, under Justin Allen Jacobs (H.C. 1839). He maintained, during the whole of his academic career, the same conscientious industry, and steady excellence of deportment, which distinguished him in his earlier years at home and at school; and graduated with the esteem of his instructors, and an honorable rank in his class. During the latter part of his college course, symptoms of failing health began to show themselves, and it was with difficulty that he performed his commencement part. For nearly two years after he graduated, he was employed in the office of the register of deeds in Middlesex county. In the mean time, by the advice of his friends, he concluded to study law, not with a view to practice in the profession, but to enable him to pursue successfully, at the offices in East Cambridge, the business of examining land titles, — a business well suited to his quiet tastes and habits. Accordingly, he entered the Law School at Cambridge, where he took his degree in 1854. By this time, his health was so much impaired, that he abandoned his purpose; and, confined mostly to his father's house, he experienced great mental depression and physical suffering, until he was relieved by death. He was a young man of great purity and delicacy of mind; of unspotted integrity and truthfulness; of conscientious fidelity to the studies he pursued, and the work, whatever it might be, that he undertook: but he was one of those who are ill fitted for the rough conflicts of life, or for making their way to worldly distinction and worldly success. He had a morbid sensitiveness of temperament, an extreme humility and self-distrust, a constitutional shyness and reserve, that shrank from all publicity, and sometimes made him unjust to himself. His abilities and merits could be known only by the few who had opportunity to pass beyond the barrier of his natural reserve, and to see the sterling excellence behind.

1852. — JOHN SYLVESTER GARDINER died in Boston, 25 July, 1856, aged 25. He was son of William Howard Gardiner (H.C. 1816) and Caroline (Perkins) Gardiner, and was born in Boston, 5 October, 1833. After finishing his collegiate course, he went to Europe, where he passed a year or two. After his return, before he had fixed upon any profession, he was suddenly cut down in the bloom of life, and his earthly career terminated by the inscrutable decree of an all-wise Providence.

1852. — Dr. JAMES SENECA HILL died in Sacramento, Cal., 21 April, 1857, aged 32. He was son of George Washington and Sallie (Albee) Hill, and was born in Pawtucket, Mass., 3 March, 1825. His father, who was the son of Samuel (commonly called Judge) Hill, was a native of Smithfield, R.I., and died about 1832. When about five years of age, he moved with his father (who was in feeble health) to his grandfather's in Smithfield. After his father's death, he, with his mother, went to Willimantic, Conn.; his uncle being appointed his guardian. Soon afterwards, he went to school at Windham, Conn., and lived with James Wilson. There he remained three or four years, occasionally residing a while at Willimantic. Being then eleven or twelve years old, he went to Willimantic, residing with his uncle; assisting him occasionally on his farm in summer, but most of the time attending school. About 1837, he went to Holliston Academy, then under the charge of Rev. Gardner Rice. About two years and a half afterwards, he went to the Colchester (Conn.) Academy one winter, where his mother then lived. He then went to Chaplin, Conn., to learn the trade of a carpenter. After working at the trade two years, he went to Northampton, Mass., whither his mother and guardian had removed. The following year, he built a small house for his mother. He afterwards built several small houses, having two or more hired men under him; always, after the first winter, attending the academy at Easthampton. He also built four barns; and, in 1846, assisted his elder brother, George A. Hill, in building the wood-work to a stone dam. Working very hard on the dam, worn down and fatigued, it occurred to him, one day, to go to college; and, about the 1st of December, he entered Williston Seminary at Easthampton, where he was fitted, and entered the freshman class at Amherst College in 1848, and took the first prize there, as a speaker, in 1850. He remained in Amherst three years; and, in the autumn of 1851, he left, and entered the senior class at Harvard College. He taught school, in his junior year, at East Douglass, and at Duxbury in his senior year. After graduating, he studied medicine at the Boylston Medical School in Boston; and received his degree of M.D., 18 July, 1855. Shortly afterwards, he was appointed physician to the state almshouse in Tewksbury, where he remained a year and a half; when he concluded to go to California, and left New York for that place on the 21st of January last. During his stay in Tewksbury, he had some twenty-five hundred patients under his charge, and performed many difficult surgical operations with great success. By his uniform kindness and gentlemanly bearing, he endeared himself to all. By nature, as well as by early education, he was eminently qualified to be a surgeon of the highest order; and there is no doubt in the minds of those who knew him, that such would have been the case had his life been spared. While at Tewksbury, many a poor creature had cause to bless him, not only for his medical and surgical skill, but also for his ingenious contrivances to alleviate their misery; such as easy-chairs for those unable to walk; padded crutches for the lame. Being no respecter of persons, he treated the poor and unfortunate, whatever their color or country, with the same kind care and attention bestowed upon the more favored ones. He was a man of rare genius, and could make almost any thing, however complicated, to which he turned his attention. Life-saving articles he was considerably interested in; being the inventor of a life-boat, and also of a safety-lamp. He sometimes wrote poetry; and a few of his compositions were set to music, and arranged for the piano-forte. His poetical writings, while in Amherst College, gave him a high rank among his fellow-students. Early in April, after his arrival in California, he was taken sick of typhoid fever at the residence of his brother in Sacramento; and, after an illness of two weeks, he died. Thus, at the early age of thirty-two, when a new field of enterprise was open before him, with flattering prospects of success, he was cut off, far from the land of his birth, deeply lamented by his relatives and by his classmates, to whom he had endeared himself by his amiable disposition, his social habits, and his unblemished moral character.

1852. — Edward Horatio Neal died at Newton Lower Falls, Mass., 24 August, 1856, aged 23. He was son of Benjamin and Eunice (Daniell) Neal, and was born at Newton, 23 October, 1832. He was fitted for college at the private school of Mr. William Hathorne Brooks, of Boston (H.C. 1827); going from Newton Falls, and returning daily in the cars, from February, 1846, till he entered college, at the beginning of the sophomore year, in 1849. He soon became a prominent and valued member of his class. While an undergraduate, he was not ambitious, but he was conscientious and diligent; and it is a remarkable fact, that, during his whole collegiate course, he was not absent from one recitation. After graduation, he studied law at the Law School in Cambridge, where he received the degree of LL.B. in 1854. After leaving the Law School early in that year, he pursued his studies with his brother, George Benjamin Neal, of Charlestown (H.C. 1846). He was distinguished from childhood for moral worth; and, while a resident in Charlestown, connected himself with the Episcopal church in that place. In the autumn of 1854, in consequence of ill health, he travelled in the Southern States, visiting New Orleans, Savannah, Charleston, and other places, and returned the following summer; after which he resided at Newton Lower Falls until his death.

1852. — George Walter Norris died in Mobile, Ala., 21 January, 1857, aged 25. He was son of Shepherd Haynes Norris, then of Boston, but now a resident of Milwaukie, Wis.; was born in Boston, 21 November, 1831; pursued his studies, preparatory to his admission into college, at the Boston Latin School. Immediately after graduating, he went to New York, and pursued the study of law one year in the office of John Cleveland, an eminent attorney of that city; another year in the office of N. F. Waring, counsellor to the corporation of the city of Brooklyn; and there he began the practice of his profession. Soon afterwards, however, he opened an office, with William Henry Waring (H.C. 1852), in the city of New York. In October, 1855, he was seized with hemorrhage of the lungs, an hereditary disease; and, from that time, fell away rapidly in consumption. In the summer of 1856, he removed to Milwaukie to reside, in hopes that a change of climate might save him; but his physicians soon discovered that his case was hopeless, and, as soon as cold weather came, sent him to Mobile, where he died. He possessed a mind of quick conception, and with talents which, had his life been spared to a more mature age, would have enabled him to take an elevated rank in his profession. Of a mild, amiable, and social disposition, he was greatly beloved by his classmates and friends; and his premature death is deeply deplored by his relatives and the community in which he was known.

1853. — William Henry Whittemore died in Cambridge, Mass., 9 February, 1857, aged 23. He was son of Thomas Jefferson and Susanna Frances (Boardman) Whittemore; was born in Boston, 10 October, 1833; and moved with his father's family to Cambridge in July, 1837. In 1842, he entered the Hopkins Classical School in Cambridge, under Edmund Burke Whitman (H.C. 1838); and remained there seven years, until he entered the freshman class in 1849. In August, 1851, he was on board the steamer "Governor" when she struck a rock near Owl's Head in Maine, and the lives of the passengers were imperilled. Part of the winter vacation of 1851–2 he spent in Washington. In his senior year, his eyesight began to fail; and, instead of studying a profession as he had proposed, he made arrangements to engage in mercantile business. His sight not improving, in the September after graduating, he sailed for Rio Janeiro, and returned in March of the following year. In the summer of 1854, he had an attack of hemorrhage, which was followed by two or three others about a year afterwards. A cough followed; and he finally died, at the residence of his father, greatly lamented by his class-mates, relatives, and friends.

1855. — WARREN BROOKS died in Townsend, Mass., 4 February, 1857, aged 25. He was son of Samuel and Sarah (Campbell) Brooks, and was born in Townsend, 15 February, 1831. He worked on his father's farm until 1850; but, having always had a desire to obtain a liberal education, in May of that year he entered the academy of New Ipswich, N.H., to prepare for college. After staying there two terms, he left New Ipswich in the autumn, and entered Meriden Academy in Connecticut, where he remained six months, and then entered Yale College. He remained at Yale two years; when, having, as he states in the class-book, a desire to study the modern languages, he left New Haven, and entered the junior class at Harvard in 1853. While at Yale, he gained a prize, during the freshman year, for Greek composition. He supported himself almost entirely, while in college, by teaching school in the winter vacations; working on a farm and at the coopering business in the summer. In the September following his graduation, he entered the Theological Seminary at Andover: but his health failing, obliged him, in 1856, to relinquish his studies; and, leaving the seminary, he returned to his home in Townsend. He himself supposed that the consumption of which he died was induced by an attack of typhoid fever in August, 1856; but his physicians thought it might be traced further back. He was even told, while studying at Cambridge, that his lungs were diseased; but his desire to complete his theological studies made him disregard medical advice. His strength failed so gradually, that he was not aware of his near approach to death until a few hours before his departure. His whole scholastic career was embarrassed by pecuniary troubles. While few, perhaps, of his classmates knew much of his personal history or his pecuniary difficulties, no one could help respecting him as an honest, independent man, who met his duties resolutely, and did his best to be faithful to them. His whole bearing showed a man of fine principle, and would have commanded the confidence even of a stranger.

1857–58.

1786. — Rev. JACOB NORTON died in Billerica, Mass., 17 January, 1858, aged 93. He was son of Samuel Norton, and was born in Abington, Mass., 12 February, 1764. He was prepared for college partly at Hingham Academy, and partly by Rev. James Briggs, of Cummington, Mass. (Y.C. 1775). He held a high rank as a scholar in his class, and graduated with distinction. At the time of his death, he was the oldest surviving graduate of Harvard College. After passing a brief time in the study of divinity under the instruction of Rev. Perez Fobes, of Raynham (H.C. 1762), he was ordained over the Congregational church in Weymouth, Mass., 10 October, 1787; where he continued his pastoral labors until 4 July, 1824, when he resigned his charge, and a few years afterwards removed to Billerica, where he resided during the remainder of his long life. He was much esteemed as a preacher, and was particularly known as a polemical writer. The following are his principal publications: —

1. Sermon preached in Weymouth, and in several other places in the vicinity, illustrating the Duty of Impenitent Sinners. 8vo. Boston, 1803. 2. The Will of God respecting the Salvation of all Men; illustrated. A Sermon at Weymouth, 18 December, 1808. 8vo. Boston, 1809. 3. Remarks on an Address from the Berean Society of Universalists in Boston to the Congregation of the First Church in Weymouth, in Answer to a Sermon delivered there 18 December, 1808, &c. 8vo. Boston, 1809. 4. Sermon before the Massachusetts Missionary Society, May 29, 1810. 8vo. Boston, 1810. 5. Discourse at Weymouth, 3 February, 1811, on the Death of his Wife. 8vo. Boston, 1811. 6. Seasonable and Candid Thoughts on Human Creeds, or Articles of Faith, as Religious Tests, connected with an Humble Attempt to ascertain the true Character of Jesus

Christ, &c., by an Orthodox Clergyman of Massachusetts. 8vo. Boston, 1813. [Published anonymously.] 7. Things set in a Proper Light; in Answer to a Letter from T. A. to a Friend, by an Orthodox Clergyman of Massachusetts. 8vo. Boston, 1814. [Published anonymously.] 8. Things as they are; or, Trinitarianism Developed; in Answer to a Letter of the Rev. Daniel Thomas, of Abington; with Strictures on the Sentiments of the late Rev. Dr. Hopkins. 8vo. Boston, 1815. 9. The same. Second Part. In Reply to a Letter written in February, 1815, to the Rev. Jacob Norton, by Daniel Thomas. 8vo. Boston, 1815. 10. "A Short and Easy Method" with a late Writer, arrogating to himself the Title of "Orthodox Clergyman," in a Letter to a young Gentleman just entered on a Course of Theological Studies, with a View to the Christian Ministry. By an Aged Clergyman of Massachusetts. 8vo. Boston, 1815. 11. Sermon at the Interment of Hon. Cotton Tufts. 8vo. Boston, 1816. 12. A Candid and Conciliatory Review of the late Correspondence of the Rev. Dr. Worcester with the Rev. W. E. Channing on the Subject of Unitarianism. By a Serious Inquirer. 8vo. Boston, 1817. [Published anonymously.] 13. An Humble Attempt to ascertain the Scripture Doctrine of the Father, Son, and Holy Spirit. In Three Discourses. To which is added "The Awakener," delivered in the Months of January and February, 1819, before the First Religious Society in Weymouth. 8vo. Boston, 1819. 14. Dispassionate Thoughts on the Subjects and Mode of Christian Baptism. 8vo. Boston, 1821. 15. The Duty of Religious Toleration, Mutual Sympathy, and Fellowship, among different Denominations, exhibited in a Sermon delivered in the South Meeting-house in Weymouth, 8 November, 1821, on a peculiarly interesting and important Occasion. 8vo. Boston, 1822. 16. Valedictory Discourse delivered before the First Religious Society in Weymouth, in Two Parts, on the morning and afternoon of Lord's Day, July 4, 1824. 8vo. Boston, 1824. 17. "Dialogue between a Minister and a Parishioner on the Trinity," begun in the "Boston Observer" in 1835, and continued for several months in that paper and the "Christian Register."

Mr. Norton married, 11 February, 1789, Elizabeth Cranch, the eldest daughter of Hon. Richard Cranch, of Braintree (now Quincy); sister of the late Judge William Cranch (H.C. 1787), of Washington, D.C.; and niece of the wife of President John Adams; by whom he had five sons and three daughters. His wife died 25 January, 1811, aged 46. He was married again, by Rev. Henry Cumings, D.D., 7 May, 1813, to Hannah Bowers, daughter of Josiah Bowers, of Billerica. She died 26 March, 1842, aged 76 years. He left two daughters, eleven grandchildren, and eleven great-grandchildren. He outlived five sons and one daughter. Two of his sons, Richard Cranch Norton and William Smith Norton, graduated at Harvard College in 1808 and 1812 respectively. He retained his mental and physical powers to a remarkable degree until past the age of ninety. For the last year or two of his life, he spent most of his time during the day reading, without glasses, which he never used, with the exception of a short time, and then laid them aside as useless.

1791.—Hon. CHARLES PORTER PHELPS died in Hadley, Mass., 22 December, 1857, aged 85. He was son of Charles and Elizabeth (Porter) Phelps, and was born in Hadley, 8 August, 1772. His name, originally, was Moses Porter Phelps; which was changed by act of the legislature, 15 February, 1796. He was fitted for college by Rev. Joseph Lyman, D.D., of Hatfield, Mass. (Y.C. 1767), and graduated with high honors; the salutatory oration in Latin having been assigned to him at Commencement. Having selected the profession of the law, he pursued his legal studies under the instruction of Hon. Theophilus Parsons, of Newburyport (H.C. 1769). On his admission to the bar in 1795, he established himself in Boston, where he resided twenty-two years, and attained a high rank in his profession. In 1816, he was chosen a representative from Boston to the state legislature. In 1816 and 1817, he was commander of the celebrated company of cavalry, well remembered by the elder portion of this community as the Hussars; being the immediate successor in command to the Hon. Josiah Quincy. This company was probably the most splendid one that ever existed in this state. Every member of it was required to own the horse upon which he appeared in parade; and the expense of equipment to each man, including his horse, was not less than fifteen hundred dollars. The company paraded for the last time on the occasion of the visit of

President Monroe to Boston in June, 1817; and was soon afterwards disbanded. In 1816, Mr. Phelps was appointed cashier of the Massachusetts Bank in Boston. This office he resigned the following year, when he returned to his native place, Hadley, where he passed the remainder of his long life, beloved and respected by the community, who manifested their regard for him by repeatedly electing him to offices of honor and trust. He represented the town of Hadley in the state legislature in 1821, 1822, 1823, 1825, 1830, and 1832; and, in 1828, he was elected senator from the district of Hampshire. There were two religious societies in Hadley, and it sometimes happened that they could not agree upon a candidate for representative. When this was the case, so popular was Mr. Phelps, that they would compromise the matter by electing him. When, therefore, the legislature assembled, and Mr. Phelps appeared as the representative from Hadley, it was at once said that there had been a quarrel between the societies about the choice of a person to represent the town. Mr. Phelps married, in January, 1800, Sarah Davenport Parsons, daughter of Moses Parsons, of Haverhill, Mass. (H.C. 1765). She died October, 1817; and he married, November, 1820, Charlotte Parsons, daughter of Hon. Theophilus Parsons. His second wife died in July, 1830. In 1833, he married, for his third wife, Mrs. Elizabeth C. Judkins, who survived him. He had fourteen children, of whom ten survived him.

1792. — Henderson Inches died in Boston, 9 September, 1857, aged 83. He was son of Henderson and Elizabeth (Brimmer) Inches, and was born in Boston, 7 February, 1774. He was fitted for college at Andover Academy. Soon after graduating, he entered the counting-house of Hon. Thomas Russell, of Boston, where he received his mercantile education; and, on the termination of his apprenticeship, he began business in Boston, at No. 47, Long Wharf, where he remained several years. After the death of Mr. Russell, he purchased Russell's (now known as Russia) Wharf; whither he removed, and where he retained an office until his decease. He married, September, 1802, Miss Susan Brimmer, daughter of Martin Brimmer,

Esq., of Boston. They had ten children, of whom seven are now living. Mrs. Inches died 21 September, 1823, aged 40 years. Mr. Inches was long and favorably known as an honorable and upright merchant. He was, in every sense, a gentleman: intelligent, affable, of a genial, social disposition, he was a welcome guest wherever he went; beloved at home as a kind husband and affectionate father, and respected by the community as an estimable and valued citizen.

1796. — Rev. LUTHER WRIGHT died in Woburn, Mass., 21 June, 1858, aged 88. He was son of Samuel and Rachel Wright, and was born in Acton, Mass., 19 April, 1770. As he was afflicted with severe lameness in 1781, which became permanent, and rendered him incapable of manual labor, he was designed for college by his parents, as well as by his own inclination. He pursued his preparatory studies partly at New Ipswich, N.H., under the instruction of John Hubbard (D.C. 1785), the preceptor of the academy in that town, and partly under the tuition of Rev. Moses Adams, of Acton (H.C. 1771). After leaving college, he taught school five months in Watertown, and three months in Cambridge, near the college, studying divinity at the same time; and, a few months after relinquishing those schools, he placed himself under the instruction of Rev. David Tappan (H.C. 1771), professor of theology in Harvard College. He was licensed to preach by the Marlborough Association, April, 1797. The first society to which he preached as a candidate for settlement was at Medway, where he was ordained 13 June, 1798; and over which he continued his pastoral labors for nearly eighteen years, on a salary of eighty pounds per annum, and the use of a wood-lot from which he obtained his wood. By frequent and kind presents from his people, and by taking into his family lads and youth from Boston, and other towns in this and other states, to board, and fit for college, and to study English branches, he was enabled to supply the deficiency of his salary, and to accumulate something for his support in the decline of life. In September, 1815, he asked and received a dismission from his church and society. He immediately began preaching as a candidate for re-settlement, and received invitations to settle in Dunstable, and the upper parish in Beverly, Mass.; in Raymond, N.H.; and Barrington, R.I. At the last-named place, he accepted the call, and was installed as their pastor, 17 January, 1817, over a feeble church and parish, and on feeble support. As the society was small, its means for competent support scanty, and unhappy divisions existed in the church and society, he expected his mission would be short; and so it proved. After a residence of about four and a half years, he requested a dismission. His request was granted, 5 July, 1821. In May, 1825, he was installed over the church in Tiverton, R.I., where he continued until 24 May, 1828, when he was dismissed; and, his health being feeble, he felt it his duty not to resettle again in the ministry. He, however, continued to preach in different places, — about six months in Dartmouth, Mass.; three years in Carver; one year in Billerica; seven months in South Weymouth; several weeks in Plymouth, Middleborough, and Lynnfield; besides occasionally in a few other places for short periods. About eight years before his death, he relinquished his clerical labors entirely, and resided in Woburn. His only publications were (1) A Sermon, occasioned by the Death of Capt. Cyrus Bullard, preached 25 May, 1806. 8vo. Dedham, April, 1807. (2) A Sermon delivered at Medway, 4 November, 1813, on the Close of a Century since the Incorporation of the Town. 8vo. Dedham, 1814. He married, 23 December, 1799, Anna Bridge, second daughter of Rev. Josiah Bridge (H.C. 1758), of East Sudbury, now Wayland; but had no children. His wife survived him. By prudence and good management he accumulated considerable property, which he bequeathed, after the death of his widow, to the Congregational Board of Publication, the Massachusetts Home-Missionary Society, the American Missionary Association, and the New-England Female Medical College.

1797. — Hon. James Richardson died in Dedham, Mass., 7 June, 1858, aged 86. He was son of James and Hannah (Clapp) Richardson, and was born in Medfield, Mass., 6 October, 1771. He was fitted for college by Rev. Thomas Prentiss, D.D., of Medfield (H.C. 1766). He held a high rank in his class as a scholar, and graduated with distinction. He pursued his professional studies with the Hon. Fisher Ames, of Dedham (H.C. 1774); was admitted to the bar in the autumn of 1800; and began the practice of the law in Dedham, where he continued it until within a few years of his decease. He was for some time a law-partner with Mr. Ames, and was ever a great favorite of that eminent statesman. He attained to a high rank as a lawyer; and, for many years, was one of the leading members of the bar in Norfolk county. His connection with Mr. Ames was dissolved, by the death of the latter, the 4th of July, 1808. He was but little in public life; for, being in political principles an ultra-federalist, a majority of the voters of the town, as well as of the county, in which he resided, were of opposite politics. These principles he retained through life, although he acted with new parties as new times demanded. He was elected a senator in the state legislature in 1813; was a member of the convention, in 1820, for revising the state constitution; and was a member of the executive-council in 1834 and 1835. He was also a master-in-chancery, and a trial-justice, in connection with his professional practice. He was much interested in measures designed for public improvement, such as the construction of turnpikes and the establishment of manufactures. He was at one time a considerable owner in manufactories, although he never abandoned the practice of his profession. He was one of the projectors of the Dedham Bank, and was president of the Norfolk Mutual Fire-Insurance Company from 1833 until April, 1857. He delivered a poem before the Phi Beta Kappa Society, at Cambridge; a Fourth-of-July oration, at Dedham, in 1808, being the day of the death of Fisher Ames, to which event the oration contains an allusion; and an address before the Norfolk bar, at their request, in 1837, upon the profession and practice of the law. All these were printed. As a lawyer, he had a clear and discriminating judgment, and an ample knowledge of legal principles derived from the very fountains of jurisprudence. He was president of the Norfolk bar, and held that position at the time of his death. He was a man of fine sensibilities, fond of letters, especially of the classics and of early English poetry; of elevated views of life and character, especially as applicable to his own profession. He married, December, 1813, Sarah Elizabeth, daughter of Samuel Richards, of Dedham; by whom he had three children, two sons and one daughter. One son died in infancy in 1820. His other children survive him. The son graduated at Harvard College in 1837. His wife died October, 1820. His peculiarly tender attachment to her prevented his ever forming a second marriage connection, although his children were young. Indeed, for many years after her death, the very mention of her name affected him even to tears.

1798. — Dr. ANDREW CROSWELL died in Mercer, Me., 4 June, 1858, aged 80. He was son of Andrew and Sarah (Palmer) Croswell, and was born in Plymouth, Mass., 9 April, 1778. When in college, he was remarked for his amiable disposition, and, withal, for his diffidence and retired habits; and he seldom mingled in the pastimes of his classmates. He studied medicine under the instruction of Dr. Zaccheus Bartlett, of Plymouth (H.C. 1789). On completing his professional studies, he settled as a physician in the town of Fayette, Me.; and subsequently removed to Mercer, which was afterwards his permanent residence. He acquired an extensive practice; and, by his skill and success, he gained the entire confidence not only of the people of the town in which he resided, but of all the neighboring towns; and was frequently called to go long distances for consultation in critical cases. He was a man of the kindest feelings; and to the indigent he was ever prompt to render his best services, without expectation of reward other than the consciousness of having relieved, as far as was in his power, the sufferings of a fellow-being. He was justly entitled to the appellation the apostle bestowed upon St. Luke; namely, "the beloved physician."

He married Susan Church, of Farmington, and had six children, — four sons and two daughters. His widow, and all his children, excepting one daughter, survived him. He was a kind and affectionate husband and father, greatly beloved by his family, and respected by all his acquaintances.

1798. — Dr. Henry Gardner died in Boston, 19 June, 1858, aged 78. He was son of Henry and Hannah (Clap) Gardner, and was born in the old Province-House, in Boston, 2 August, 1779. His father, Henry Gardner (H. C. 1750), was born in Stow, Mass., 14 November, 1731. He was a member of the Middlesex Convention in 1774; also of the Provincial Congress, which met 7 October, 1774, and in February and May, 1775. He was judge of the Court of Common Pleas for Middlesex. In December, 1774, he was chosen first state treasurer; when he removed to Boston, and occupied the Province-House, where were vaults for the safe keeping of the provincial revenues. He held this office until his death. He was a member of the American Academy of Arts and Sciences, and had the character of a learned man. He was a sincere patriot, and rendered very important service to the province by his diligence and fidelity. He died 8 October, 1782, aged 50. Dr. Gardner's grandfather, Rev. John Gardner (H.C. 1715), was born in Charlestown, Mass., 22 July, 1695; was ordained pastor of the Congregational church in Stow, 26 November, 1718; and died 10 January, 1775, aged 79. Dr. Gardner was fitted for college in Andover, Mass. He studied medicine with Dr. John Warren, of Boston, (H.C. 1771), who, at the death of Dr. Gardner's father, had been appointed his guardian; and received his first medical degree in 1801, but never practised. According to the laws of primogeniture then existing, he, being the eldest son, inherited a double portion of his father's estate; and he was thus placed above the necessity of engaging in any stated business. He employed himself in the care of his property, which increased under his judicious management. He resided many years in Dorchester, Mass., where he was highly esteemed by the people of that ancient town, who elected him a representative to the legislature in 1822, 1823, and 1824. He was chosen a senator from Norfolk District in 1825, 1826, and 1827. He was also, in 1820, a member from Dorchester of the convention for revising the constitution of the state. He was, for a number of years, one of the trustees of the State Lunatic-Hospital at Worcester.

Of late years, he declined all public offices, preferring the quiet of private life. He was a gentleman of strict integrity, and was highly respected in the community. He married, first, 17 May, 1803, Joanna Bird Everett, daughter of Rev. Moses Everett, of Dorchester (H.C. 1771) : she died 7 February, 1807, leaving one daughter, who is now the wife of Daniel Denny, Esq., of Boston. He married, second, 20 March, 1810, Clarissa Holbrook, daughter of Dr. Amos Holbrook, of Milton, Mass. ; by whom he had three children, — two daughters and a son ; of whom only the son, Hon. Henry Joseph Gardner, late governor of Massachusetts, is living. His second wife survived him.

1799. — Hon. Joseph Dane died in Kennebunk, Me., 1 May, 1858, aged 79. He was son of John and Jemima (Fellows) Dane, and was born in Beverly, Mass., 25 October, 1778. He was a descendant of John Dane, who emigrated from England, and settled in Ipswich, Mass., about the year 1648. Both his parents were natives of Ipswich. They died in Beverly, where they lived : the father, 5 March, 1829, in his eightieth year ; and the mother, April, 1827, aged 76 years. Mr. Dane was fitted for college at Phillips Academy, Andover, and graduated with the second honors of his class. After leaving college, he pursued his legal studies in the office and under the instruction of his uncle, Hon. Nathan Dane, of Beverly (H.C. 1778) ; and, having completed his term of study, he was admitted to the bar in Essex county in July, 1802. He was thoroughly prepared for usefulness and distinction in the honorable profession he had chosen. Besides the advantages to be derived from the large experience, exact and varied learning, and practical good sense, of his immediate instructor, he could not fail to be benefited by the intimate association of the latter with Prescott, Jackson, Putnam, and Story, who were then beginning to be distinguished for professional excellence, and became the ornaments of the bar and the bench. After his admission to the bar, Mr. Dane immediately began the practice of law in Kennebunk, at that time a part of the town of Wells ; where he soon became distinguished as an able lawyer, an upright and safe counsellor. He continued in active practice in the profession until 1837, when he retired. As a practitioner, he was courteous, faithful, and honest; and sought, by the influence of his own example, to elevate the character of the profession for integrity and moral excellence. "He concerned himself with the beginnings of controversies, not to inflame, but to extinguish them. He felt that he owed a duty to the community in which he lived, and whose peace he was bound to preserve. He was eminently a peacemaker, a composer of dissensions, and constantly aimed to prevent the mischiefs which follow in the train of litigation." To him may very justly be applied the language used in regard to another: "That he cast honor upon his honorable profession, and sought dignity, not from the ermine or the mace, but from a straight path and a spotless life."

He was the last survivor of those who were members of the bar of York when he began practice; among whom were the honored names of Mellen, King, Holmes, Hubbard, and Wallingford. He was often selected by his fellow-citizens for places of trust and responsibility. In 1816, he was chosen one of the delegates from the town of Wells to the Brunswick convention for forming a constitution for Maine, which then failed to accomplish its object; the popular majority required to authorize it not having been obtained. In 1818, he was elected by the legislature of Massachusetts one of the executive-council; but declined to accept the office, on account of professional engagements. In 1819, he was a member of the convention which framed the constitution of Maine, and took an active part in its proceedings and deliberations; and was one of the committee which draughted the constitution, Mr. Holmes being chairman. Associated with him in this important committee, among others, were Chief-Justice Whitman, Generals Wingate and Chandler, Judges Bridge, Dana, and Parris. On the admission of Maine into the Union in 1820, he was elected a member of the sixteenth Congress, from the first district, to complete the unexpired term made vacant by the election of Mr. Holmes to the Senate, and also a member of the seventeenth Congress. Subsequently he was in the state legislature, as a member of the House, in the years 1824, 1825, 1832, 1833, 1839, and 1840; and was a member of the Senate in 1829. In 1841, he was elected a member of the executive-council of Maine, but declined to accept the office. He fulfilled the duties of the various and important public trusts confided to him with acknowledged ability, great singleness of purpose, and with an earnest, patriotic desire to advance the public interest. After his retirement from the bar and from public duties, he always interested himself deeply in whatever was calculated to promote the welfare of the community. Few men have lived so long, and enjoyed so largely and uniformly the confidence, respect, and esteem of their fellow-citizens.

He married, October, 1808, Mary Clark, daughter of Hon. Jonas Clark, of Kennebunk, and grand-daughter of the Rev. Jonas Clark, of Lexington, Mass. (H.C. 1752); a lady of great excellence of character, who survived him. He had three children, two sons and a daughter. The sons survived him, prominent citizens of the county of York, — Hon. Nathan Dane, of Alfred; and Joseph Dane, jun., of Kennebunk. He was happy in his domestic and social relations; kind, affectionate, and benevolent. His death was deeply lamented by his neighbors and friends, who grieved most of all that they should see his face no more. He had usually enjoyed good health, the "ripe fruit of temperance, self-control, and a virtuous life," until seized by the malady which terminated his earthly existence. He sustained the suffering of his long and painful illness with characteristic cheerfulness and equanimity, and with Christian resignation; and at last calmly and serenely yielded up his life in the exercise of a reasonable religious faith and a Christian hope.

1800. — Dr. Samuel Weed died in Portland, Me., 24 November, 1857, aged 83. He was born in Amesbury, Mass., 10 June, 1774. His father, Ephraim Weed, was a respectable farmer. He worked on his father's farm until he was 17 years old; when he was sent to Exeter Academy, where he remained nearly a year. The next four years he spent alternately keeping school in Amesbury and Bradford in winter, and working on the farm in summer. Being now desirous of obtaining a liberal education, he went to Atkinson Academy, then under the charge of Stephen Peabody (H.C. 1769), and prepared himself for college. He entered college in 1796, the oldest member of his class. A distinguished literary gentleman, who was long intimately acquainted with him, gives the following particulars of his subsequent life: "It was one of the college customs of that day, for the freshmen, on the entry of every class, to be initiated into their new life by a wrestling-match. The sophomores challenged the new-comers to a trial of strength in this ancient and classical exercise. The senior class was the umpire, and the victors were treated to a supper on their invitation. In the contest in 1796, after a hard and manly struggle, the freshmen came off victorious, leaving three of their champions ready to continue the contest: of these, Weed was one. The Monday after, the juniors, not easy under this defeat, challenged the freshmen to a new contest with them. This was accepted, and Weed was the first to enter the list: he threw successively six of the juniors, the first of whom was the late Judge Fay, of Cambridge. Reeking with perspiration, and nearly exhausted, he was required to renew the struggle with a fresh competitor: in this struggle he was unfortunately overcome; the victor being Ebenezer Thatcher, then of Cambridge, but whose manhood and age were spent in Maine, in the discharge of many important offices, and who died in 1841. After leaving college, Mr. Weed took charge of the academy at Framingham, where he continued four years; when he was invited to unite with his classmate, Rufus Hosmer, in conducting a high-school in Medford. In this occupation he remained three years. He then began in earnest the study of his profession under the wise and paternal direction of Dr. John Brooks, afterwards governor of the commonwealth; the brave and gallant soldier, the skilful physician, the prudent statesman, and the accomplished gentleman. Here he saw the best practice, and improved his admirable opportunities to acquire an accurate knowledge of his profession. At the same time, he had the rare privilege of seeing and enjoying the company of many of the most distinguished men of the old commonwealth, as Gore, Dexter, Bigelow, &c.; and of meeting the old physicians, Danforth, Dexter, Lloyd, Rand, the elder Warren, &c., who came to Dr. Brooks for consultation or as friendly visitors. Here, too, he met the eccentric and gifted Dr. Osgood, pastor of the church in Medford, then in the vigor of his intellect and of his peculiarities. From these rich and varied stores of instruction, his mind was imbued with useful knowledge, and pleasant and instructive anecdote, which his memory laid up for the entertainment of his friends and companions through the long period of his remaining life. Dr. Weed went to Portland, and entered on the practice of his profession, in 1810. The principal physicians then there were Dr. Coffin, who had been forty-four years in the practice, and stood at the head of the profession, both in medicine and surgery; Drs. Erving, Thomas, Cummings, Harding, Kittridge, and Morrill. A very healthy town, with a population of only seven thousand, and pre-occupied with such a number of the faculty, did not afford a very cheering prospect to a new aspirant, especially when the charge for a medical visit, including medicine, was only fifty cents. At that time, it was the custom for physicians to prepare the medicines which they prescribed: patients were unwilling to go to the apothecary; and articles obtained there were not always to be relied on. It happened, fortunately for Dr. Weed, that Dr. Erving, that good Samaritan, and a most excellent man, soon after this moved to Boston. Two years before Dr. Weed came, Dr. Kinsman, one of the most learned and skilful practitioners who had ever pursued his vocation in Portland, had died; so that Dr. Weed was enabled early to enter upon a remunerating practice. He was quite successful in securing a goodly number of first-class patients, which he ever retained, and their families after them, by a calm judgment, a good knowledge of his profession, and a uniform gentlemanly deportment. Never was a physician further removed than he from cant and quackery, to which ignorant practitioners often resort to gain business and popularity. He gained the confidence of his patients, and secured their affection, by a safe and judicious application of remedies, by courteous deportment, and strict attention to the wants of the sick-chamber. His great caution sometimes gave him the appearance of doubt and hesitation: but he thought it better to be slow than to be wrong; that it was better to assist nature, than to prostrate it by hasty and violent applications. The estimation in which he was held by his numerous friends, many of whom were children of parents who had enjoyed the benefit of his earlier services, was manifested in a manner most gratifying to both parties. In December, 1852, Dr. Weed fell upon the ice, and broke his hip-joint; a severe misfortune, which disabled him from future practice. His friends, believing that, deprived of his usual resources, he must be straitened in his means of support, came cheerfully forward, and contributed to procure for him an annuity of five hundred dollars a year during his life. This at once relieved his anxiety, and made him comfortable for the remainder of his days. In 1816, Dr. Weed married Maria Condy, of Medford, an amiable and accomplished lady, whose death in 1835 was a deep and lasting sorrow, depriving him of a wise counsellor, an admirable companion, and an unfailing friend. Her grandfather, Rev. Jeremiah Condy (H.C. 1726), was a Baptist clergyman in Boston; predecessor, in the First Baptist Church, of the eloquent Stillman. By her he had three sons; of whom the only survivor is Edward Condy, of Boston. From his earliest life, Dr. Weed was an example of a true philosophical and religious moderation. His whole conduct was regulated by strict principle. He was never known to deviate from the paths of rectitude and honor: he knew no guile, and was never guilty of detraction. He had entire control over himself, and so was able to apply to useful purposes the whole vigor of his powers. As a physician, he was not rapid in his perceptions, nor fertile in expedients; but by great caution, sound judgment, and natural experience, he arrived at just conclusions in the diagnosis of disease. By a course so uniform and so worthy, he conferred dignity on his honorable profession, and grace and beauty on his daily life."

1802. — Charles Winston Greene died in East Greenwich, R.I., 24 December, 1857, aged 74. He was son of David Greene (H.C. 1768), and was born in Norwich, Conn., 3 July, 1783; but, when quite young, removed with his father's family to Boston, where he passed a great portion of his life. His mother's name was Rebecca Rose; and his father married her in the island of Antigua, of which she was a native. She died at the age of forty, leaving eight children. Mr. Greene was fitted for college at the Boston Latin School, where he won a Franklin medal for his superior scholarship. On leaving college, he entered his father's counting-room for the purpose of preparing himself for the mercantile profession, in which his father had long held a prominent rank. In 1805 or 1806, he went to England, where he remained a few months, when he returned; and on the 7th of December, 1806, he was married to Esther Ward Bowen, daughter of Hon. Pardon Bowen, of Providence, R.I., and settled in New York. She died in March, 1808, leaving no children. Mr. Greene shortly afterwards sailed for Europe; visited many ports in the Mediterranean, and went as far as Odessa, in the Black Sea, in the ship "Calumet," which was the first American vessel that visited that port, and, it is believed, was the first that ever entered the Black Sea. He remained in Europe five years; during which time he acquired a thorough knowledge of the French language, which he spoke as fluently as he did his native tongue. He returned in 1813; and, on the 27th of September of that year, he was married to Frances Bowen, a sister of his former wife. He then established himself in Boston as a merchant; but, meeting with reverses, he relinquished the mercantile profession, and engaged in the business of teaching, for which he was by nature peculiarly fitted. He opened a private school at Jamaica Plain (now West Roxbury), Mass., which he continued for more than thirty years with eminent success. In 1849, he removed to East Greenwich, R.I., where he continued his school until the 13th of February, 1856; when he was seized with a slight paralytic affection, which compelled him to relinquish his labors. During the time he was engaged in teaching, more than seven hundred youth went forth from his school, many of whom now fill high places, and have achieved deserved eminence. Among those who gratefully testify to the good influences exerted upon them, while at his school, may be mentioned George W. Curtis, the "Howadji;" J. Lothrop Motley, the historian; Frank B. Goodrich, author of the "Court of Napoléon;" Charles G. Leland, and Fletcher and Edward Webster. The great feature of this school consisted not so much in its educational advantages, though these were undoubted, as in the excellent influences which were brought to bear upon the characters of the pupils. The boys were trained to be courteous and gentlemanly, with a modest but manly bearing, and a noble scorn of all that was mean or ungenerous. Himself a gentleman of the old school, Mr. Greene labored earnestly and successfully to train up his pupils in all the virtues which belong to that type. It was to this moral training that Mr. Greene chiefly confined himself. Though admirably qualified, it was his custom to devolve upon assistants the main burden of instruction, under his general supervision. Those who have had familiar opportunities to observe how admirably he understood the nature of boys, and how wisely and well he managed them — smoothing down their rough angularities, and instilling into them gentlemanly courtesy, mutual forbearance, and a manly deference for their superiors in age and acquirements — during his thirty-nine years' experience, will be tempted to compare him, not out of empty compliment, but with full conviction, to the celebrated Dr. Arnold, the model teacher of England. It may not be out of place to chronicle an illustration of the high integrity which actuated Mr. Greene in his dealings with his fellow-men. At the close of his mercantile life, he failed to the amount of thirty thousand dollars, — a sum which, legally, he was not bound to pay; but, with a sense of obligation wholly independent of legal enactments, he discharged the entire debt out of the subsequent profits of his school. It was many years before he could accomplish it; but he steadfastly persevered until every dollar was paid. Mr. Greene employed himself for some time in writing a history of the country around the Black Sea, an account of his own voyage and observations while there and at Constantinople, with the intention of publishing them; but, on being applied to by Gen. Henry A. S. Dearborn for information on those subjects, finding the latter was preparing a work on the "Commerce of the Black Sea," he handed him his manuscripts, desiring him to make what use of them he might wish, and then gave up all thoughts of publishing any thing himself.

Mr. Greene's second wife survived him, but had no children.

1803. — Rev. Asa Eaton died in Boston, 24 March, 1858, aged 79. He was born in Plaistow, N.H., 25 July, 1778; was fitted for college by Rev. Giles Merrill, of Haverhill, Mass. (H.C. 1759). After a brief preparatory course of theological studies, he was instituted rector of Christ Church in Boston, 23 October, 1805, where he labored diligently and faithfully until May, 1829, when he resigned his rectorship; and, for eight years subsequently, was employed as a city-missionary, — laboring among the destitute in Boston, and preaching to the poor in a hall where the seats were free. From 1837 to 1841, he was connected with a literary institution in New Jersey. For a short time previous to his death, he was attached to the Church of the Advent in Boston. He was a distinguished member of the Masonic Fraternity, and at one time held the office of deputy grand-master of the Grand Lodge of Massachusetts. He was widely known throughout the county, from his long connection with the Episcopal church, his blameless life, and his entire consecration to the work of the Christian ministry. His tall and commanding figure, with locks of snowy whiteness, attracted attention wherever he went; and his memory is revered as a beloved and faithful expounder of divine truth. He married, 9 October, 1813, Susannah Storer, youngest daughter of Ebenezer Storer, of Boston (H.C. 1747), and had six children, — three sons and three daughters; of whom two sons and one daughter survived him. His wife died 26 November, 1853, aged 71 years.

1804. — Benjamin Guild died in Boston, 30 March, 1858, aged 72. He was son of Benjamin (H.C. 1769) and Eliza (Quincy) Guild, and was born in Boston, 8 May, 1785. His father was born in Wrentham, Mass., 28 April, 1749; was a tutor in Harvard College from 1776 to 1780; and was a member of the American Academy of Arts and Sciences. He was for some time a preacher; but subsequently opened a book-store in Cornhill (now Washington Street), Boston, which he kept for some years. He died in October, 1792, aged 43 years. The subject of this notice was fitted for college at Hingham Academy. He studied law with Hon. William Prescott (H.C. 1783). On his admission to the bar, he opened an office in Boston, and afterwards became a law-partner with Mr. Prescott. He was subsequently associated in the practice of his profession with Benjamin Rand, of Boston (H.C. 1808). He married, 31 March, 1817, Eliza Eliot, daughter of Samuel Eliot, a distinguished and wealthy merchant of Boston; and had five children, — three sons and two daughters, — who, with his widow, survived him. All his sons have graduated at Harvard College; viz., Samuel Eliot in 1839, Charles Eliot in 1840, and Edward Chipman in 1853. Mr. Guild was, for more than thirty years, an active and efficient member of the Massachusetts Society for the Promotion of Agriculture; was for some time its recording-secretary; and was the writer of many of its annual reports. He was a gentleman of polished manners, of an exceedingly affable and sociable disposition, and was highly respected and beloved by a large circle of acquaintance.

1805. — Ephraim Hinds died in West Boylston, Mass., 18 June, 1858, aged 77. He was son of Benjamin and Tabitha (Holland) Hinds, and was born in that part of Shrewsbury which is now within the limits of West Boylston, 7 November, 1780. His father was a farmer, and one of the earliest settlers of the town. His mother was a native of Boylston. He was fitted for college partly at Leicester Academy, and partly by Rev. William Nash, of West Boylston (Y.C. 1791). After leaving college, he taught school in Boston, Watertown, Sterling, Lancaster, Mass., and several places in Vermont. After some years spent in teaching, he entered upon the study of law under the instruction of Eleazer James, of Barre, Mass. (H.C. 1778). On his admission to the bar, he began the practice of his profession in Barre, where he resided a short time;

when he removed to Athol. From this town he went to Harvard, where he remained about thirteen years; afterwards he lived in Marlborough from 1833 to 1841; in South Brookfield from May, 1841, to May, 1845; in South Orange from May to November, 1845; in Deerfield from November, 1845, to May, 1847; and in West Boylston from May, 1847, until his death. He married, 28 April, 1823, Maria, daughter of Hutchins Hapgood, of Petersham. He was greatly respected at the bar as a man of strict veracity, of unbending integrity, sound judgment, and practical wisdom. He had been unable to walk for more than a year before his death, in consequence of a severe rheumatic affection; but was uniformly cheerful, and entirely submissive to the Divine Will. He was remarkable for his habits of punctuality, systematic arrangement of secular affairs, and rigid economy. His memory was wonderful. A few days before his death, his pastor, sitting by his bedside, quoted a passage from the xc. Psalm: "The days of our years are threescore years and ten; and if by reason of strength they be fourscore years, yet is their strength labor and sorrow; for it is soon cut off, and we fly away;" and added, "I suppose your experience, Mr. Hinds, confirms the truth of the Psalmist's declaration, that it is laborious and sorrowful work to live."—"Yes," said he, "even to breathe." He then added, "That is a brief but exact description of old age, and reminds me of a passage in Virgil."—"Can you repeat it?" asked his pastor. "Yes," he replied; and did so, as follows:—

> "Optima quæque dies miseris mortalibus ævi
> Prima fugit: subeunt morbi, tristisque senectus:
> Et labor et duræ rapit inclementia mortis."
>
> *Georg.*, lib. iii. 66–8.

> "From wretched mortals each best day of life
> First takes its flight. Diseases follow next,
> Old age disconsolate, and weary toil;
> And death, relentless, snatching them away."
>
> *Kennedy's Translation.*

At the time of his funeral, an old friend, who was his contemporary at college, and who had been associated with him, more or less, for nearly seventy years, rose, and said with deep emotion, "I have intimately known the deceased from early boyhood, and have distinct and pleasant recollections of him for more than half a century. I can truly say, that as a companion in youthful days, as a fellow-student in the school, the academy, and the college, as an associate at the bar and in the various relations of life, I have never known a man of stricter integrity, purer life and manners, or more unblemished moral character, than Ephraim Hinds." It was a beautiful and affecting tribute of respect and affection, spontaneously given with tears and a broken utterance.

Mr. Hinds left three sons and one daughter; she being the youngest child, and about twenty-one years of age. He also left an ample estate, the fruit of his industry and prudence.

1806. — Hon. WILLIAM PITT PREBLE died in Portland, Me., 11 October, 1857, aged 73. He was born in York, Me., 27 November, 1783; was fitted for college by Rev. Rosewell Messinger, of York (H.C. 1797), and graduated with high honors. He was distinguished, when in college, for his skill in mathematics, and his powers of argumentation. On leaving college, he read law, first with Hon. Benjamin Hasey (H.C. 1790), and then with Hon. Benjamin Orr, of Topsham, Me. (D.C. 1798). In 1809, he was appointed tutor in Harvard College, where he continued two years; and, while tutor, he married a Miss Tucker, of York, daughter of the collector of that port. On resigning his tutorship, he began the practice of law in his native town, and rapidly rose to the front rank in his profession. He soon removed to Alfred, Me., where he remained in practice until 1813; when, having been appointed United-States district-attorney for Maine District, he removed to Saco, and thence, in 1818, to Portland. The following sketch of his life is principally derived from an able article published in the "Portland State of Maine" soon after his death. He took an active interest in politics from early life; was at first an ardent federalist, but subsequently acted with the democratic party, became a leading advocate for the separation of Maine from Massachusetts, and wrote a pamphlet in its favor. He was a member of the constitutional convention of

Maine in 1819, and wrote its address to the people of the state. In 1820, he was appointed a justice of the Supreme Court of Maine, — associate with Hon. Prentiss Mellen (H.C. 1784), chief-justice. This office he resigned in 1829, on being appointed, with Mr. Gallatin, an agent to prepare the case of the United-States Government before the King of the Netherlands; and was finally appointed, by Gen. Jackson, minister-plenipotentiary to the Hague. His career as a public man, for which he was most distinguished, was in connection with the north-eastern-boundary question. His ability in exposing the absurdity of the decision of the Dutch king was undoubtedly chiefly instrumental in causing its defeat in the United-States Senate. He was one of the commissioners of Maine in 1832 with the Hon. Ruel Williams and the Hon. Nicholas Emery, and advised a compromise by taking lands in Michigan in exchange for lands north of the St. John; but the legislature of Maine declined the offer to this effect by the general government. At the close of his foreign mission, he returned to the practice of law in Portland. He was elected by the legislature as a commissioner with Gov. Kent and others, in 1842, to arrange the Treaty of Washington; and finally gave his sanction, though reluctantly, to the mode of settlement carried out by the Webster-and-Ashburton Treaty. This was the last political office which he held. In 1844, he was called to what he regarded as the most important duty that had ever engaged his attention, — the connecting by railway of the waters of the St. Lawrence with those of the Atlantic. He was slow to engage in that work, and his natural caution made him at first fearful of any connection with that enterprise; but, after mature reflection, he engaged in it with all the enthusiasm of youth, and all the vigor of early manhood. When his concurrence in the scheme was known, it gave to it the confidence of the public; and a large share of credit is due to him for its success. He was the first president of the corporation, and continued to hold the office until 1848; when he declined a re-election, and retired from public labors. He lived to see the work accomplished, but not to lose his interest in its prosperity. The last article, probably, which he prepared for the press, was upon the White-Mountain scenery along the route, and which was published in the "Portland Argus" a short time before his death. All his public writings display the most marked exhibition of labor, and care of preparation. He never allowed any thing from his pen to appear, without subjecting it to the most elaborate preparation. But little, however, remains that will serve as an enduring record of his labors. His reported opinions as a judge do not give any adequate idea of his power as a lawyer. He had a reputation for intellectual power far beyond any measure of success that he obtained; and those who knew him best were aware of his peculiarities of temperament and of temper, that were a drawback to popular favor. He appeared to the best advantage in the oral argument of legal questions. He stated legal propositions with a clearness and force that were rarely equalled. When all his faculties were raised into activity by the excitement of a great occasion, the pressure of a crowd, or the responsibilities of a great cause, his mind worked with the greatest ease; and he was capable, on such occasions, of bringing out an argument, that by its strength of reasoning, force of illustration, and effective eloquence, gave him the mastery over others. In 1829, the honorary degree of doctor of laws was conferred upon him by Bowdoin College.

1807.—Hon. John Glen King died in Salem, Mass., 26 July, 1857, aged 70. He was the second son of James King, Esq.; and was born in Salem, 19 March, 1787. He was fitted for college at Phillips Academy in Andover, Mass. He did not graduate with his class, but, like many others of his own and the succeeding class, left college in May, 1807, the period of what is known as "the Grand Commons-Rebellion." His degree was conferred upon him in 1818. He pursued the study of law under the instruction of Hon. William Prescott (H.C. 1783) and Hon. Joseph Story (H.C. 1798); was admitted a member of the Essex bar; began the practice of his profession in Salem, where he continued during the remainder of his life. He attained an eminent rank, and for many years was one of the leading members of the bar in

Essex county. He was repeatedly elected to offices of honor and trust. He was chosen a representative from Salem to the state legislature in 1816 and 1821; and was a member of the senate from Essex District in 1822, 1823, and 1826. He was also the first president of the common-council of Salem, under the city charter. Among his important legislative duties may be mentioned his share in the great Prescott impeachment case, in 1821. He, being at that time a member of the house of representatives, was appointed to make the impeachment at the bar of the senate, in the name of the house of representatives and of the people of Massachusetts; and afterwards was ap-appointed first of the seven managers on the part of the house to conduct the impeachment before the senate, sitting as a court; the other six being Levi Lincoln (afterwards governor), William Baylies, Warren Dutton, Samuel P. P. Fay (afterwards judge), Lemuel Shaw (afterwards chief-justice of the Supreme Judicial Court), and Sherman Leland (afterwards judge). Horatio G. Newcomb and Francis C. Gray, in the course of the proceedings, were substituted for Messrs. Lincoln and Baylies. Mr. King, although younger than several of the gentlemen comprising this eminent array of legal talent, bore a distinguished part in the conduct of the laborious and novel case. He made the opening argument; and, at the close of the proceedings, demanded judgment upon the articles on which the respondent was found guilty. The following eminent legal gentlemen were the respondent's counsel: William Prescott, George Blake, Daniel Webster, Samuel Hoar, Samuel Hubbard, and Augustus Peabody. Mr. King was, for many years, commissioner-of-insolvency, and held that office at the time of his death. He was also a member of the Massachusetts Historical Society. He was a wise and learned counsellor, whose honor and integrity were without the suspicion of a stain; whose counsel in the distribution of estates was sought from far and near; and whose association in any deed of trust gave confidence to all who were interested in its being honestly and judiciously administered. His mind was singularly acute and critical; his spirit, of that justly balanced cast, which, while wisely conservative in all its tendencies and judgments, was keenly alive to every moral and social wrong, and resolute in the maintenance of the right and the true, in the face of any weight of precedent or example on the other side. His love of literature and of books almost amounted to a passion. His precious and well-selected library was his solace through many a year of suffering; and the sight of it, around his bed of mortal sickness, cheered and enlivened the last days of his declining life. He was a scholar, and a ripe and good one. The ancient classics were his mental food and drink. He nourished his spirit, too, on the old English master-pieces, especially of the theologians, for whose range of subjects his mind had a natural affinity; but in every stage of English literature he was at home, and his fine and cultivated taste appreciated all that was truly worthy. Mr. King married Susan, daughter of Major Frederick Gilman, of Gloucester. He had six children, of whom two died in infancy: the others, with his widow, survived him. One son, John Gallison King, graduated at Harvard College in 1838.

1807. — JARED WEED died in Petersham, Mass., 6 August, 1857, aged 74. He was son of Elnathan and Lydia (Bouton) Weed, and was born in North Stamford, Conn., 5 April, 1783. He was fitted for college in North Salem, N.Y., under the instruction of a Scotch pedagogue, whom he used to speak of as "Old Johnny McNess." He had certain peculiarities of expression which he undoubtedly contracted under this Scotchman's teaching. He studied law with Hon. William Stedman, of Lancaster, Mass. (H.C. 1784), and Judge Nathaniel Paine, of Worcester (H.C. 1775). With Judge Paine he acquired a thorough knowledge of probate business, which he was said to transact remarkably well, and which he continued to practise until his death. He was admitted to the bar in Worcester, and in 1813 established himself in the practice of law in Petersham, where he resided during the remainder of his life. He made his first entries in the Court of Common Pleas in Worcester County at the November term in 1812, and continued after that to make entries at each term. He was admitted an attorney of the Supreme Judicial Court at the September term in

1816, and a counsellor of the same court at the September term in 1818. He attained a very respectable standing in his profession; was a magistrate in whom the people had confidence, an honest politician, and a most worthy and excellent man. He was, for several years, chairman of the board of county-commissioners; and filled other offices of honor and trust which were bestowed upon him by his fellow-townsmen and the citizens of his county, with credit to himself, and satisfaction to his constituents. He married, 30 April, 1821, Eliza Prentiss, of Petersham, daughter of Nathan and Lydia Prentiss (singular coincidence with the names of his parents). He had three daughters, — Elizabeth Otis, born 1822; Lydia Pennoyer, born 1823; and Mary Jane, born 1827, — the eldest of whom only survived him: the others died within six years of the death of their father. His widow survived him. He was a kind and indulgent husband and father, thoughtful for others, and exhibited wonderful patience during the last five weary years of his life while suffering from a severe attack of paralysis. His mother always said, "Jared was a good boy at home, — her best child;" and she had a large family. He was too forgetful of his own interests for his worldly prosperity; but his generous, kind heart is remembered by his friends.

Mr. Weed was descended, on the mother's side, from a family by the name of Pennoyer; one of whom, William Pennoyer, many years ago, left a legacy to Harvard College on condition of the awarding of certain benefits to such of his descendants as should be educated there, of which Mr. Weed had a share. William Pennoyer never came to this country, but lived and died in England. It is his brother Robert's descendants who have lived in the United States.

1811. — Rev. SAMUEL GILMAN, of Charleston, S.C., died at the residence of his son-in-law, Rev. Charles J. Bowen, in Kingston, Mass., 9 February, 1858, aged 66. He was son of Frederick and Abigail H. (Somes) Gilman, and was born in Gloucester, Mass., 16 February, 1791. His father had been a very successful merchant in Gloucester, but died insolvent more than sixty years ago; his insolvency having been caused by the capture of several of his vessels by the French in the war of 1798. He left a youthful widow and four male children; and, when Samuel was about seven years old, his mother took him to Atkinson, N.H., to be educated in the academy there, under the charge of Rev. Stephen Peabody (H.C. 1769), whose quaint, primitive ways are described with inimitable humor in a biographical sketch by Dr. Gilman, published in the "Christian Examiner" in 1847. Not long subsequently, the family removed to Salem, Mass.; and Samuel was for some time employed as a clerk in the old Essex Bank. He graduated with high honors in a class remarkable for eminent talent. A poem, which he delivered on his graduation, "On the Pleasures and Pains of a Student," was replete with humor, and elicited rapturous applause from a crowded audience. This poem he repeated on the evening of commencement-day, in 1852, at the residence of Hon. Edward Everett, in Boston, whither the class had been invited to celebrate the forty-first anniversary of their graduation; and added a sequel, in which he gave a retrospect of the time from their graduation to that period, paying a brief and beautiful tribute to the memory of those of the class who had deceased. The poem concluded with the following fine compliment to their host, the Hon. Mr. Everett: —

"Stay yet, dear friends! the minstrel bids you toast,
In pure, bright water, our accomplished host;
Who gives, one need not say, our class its name,
Tinged with the lustre of his well-earned fame.
Health for his labors, for his cares relief,
To him, our first and last unenvied chief!"

These two poems were printed immediately afterwards for distribution to the surviving members of the class.

Among the various pursuits which offered themselves to Dr. Gilman's choice, was that to which, by character and endowments, he was best adapted; and it was the profession which was the choice of his heart. He soon began the study of theology under the supervision of Drs. Ware and Kirkland, who then constituted the theological faculty. Fortunately for him, he was not hurried, like most young Americans, immediately and prematurely into professional life. He lingered long under the roof of his Alma Mater, maturing his mind, extending his knowledge, and laying up those intellectual and literary treasures which his future isolation rendered so important. In 1817, he was appointed tutor in mathematics at Harvard College; which office he held two years. Early in 1819, he went to Charleston, S.C., where he received a pastoral call as successor to the Rev. Anthony M. Foster; and, after a few months of probationary service, he was ordained, 1 December, 1819, as pastor of the Unitarian or Second Independent church in that city. The ordination-sermon was preached by Rev. Joseph Tuckerman, D.D., of Chelsea, Mass. (H.C. 1798). Here he labored faithfully and acceptably until his last sickness. He was universally respected by the people of the city of his residence, and his influence extended far beyond the limits of the religious denomination with which he was connected. He was the life and soul of the New-England society of South Carolina, and was always hospitable to all visitors from the North. During his residence in Cambridge, he was a frequent contributor to the "North-American Review," in which periodical his papers are marked by their polished elegance of diction, the grace and felicity of their illustrations, and their racy humor. Among his contributions were a series of able papers on the philosophical lectures of Dr. Thomas Brown, and translations of several of the satires of Boileau. One of his most noted essays was on "The Influence of One National Literature upon Another." He also wrote a fine paper on "The Writings of Edward Everett," his classmate and warm personal friend. After his removal to Charleston, he continued to write for different periodicals; his contributions embracing a wide range of subjects, from profound philosophical discussions to sparkling satirical essays. A selection of these was published in a volume a few years since, under the title of "Contributions to American Literature, descriptive, critical, humorous, brigraphical, philosophical, and poetical." Among his productions, the "Recollections of a New-England Village Choir" has, perhaps, become the most generally popular. For apt local description, a keen sense of the ludicrous, and a happy intuition of characteristic peculiarities, it has seldom been matched in the humorous literature of this country. Dr. Gilman possessed the gift of poetry, which he cultivated with no inconsiderable success. He had a luxuriant fancy, an excellent command of natural imagery, and great fluency of expression. As a pulpit-orator, he was affectionate and persuasive; equally removed from languor and vehemence; never boisterous, but always in earnest; loving the sphere of universal ethics rather than the subtleties of sectarian doctrine; and commending the great lessons he taught by the shining and noble example of his private life.

Dr. Gilman married, 14 October, 1819, Miss Caroline Howard, daughter of Samuel Howard, a shipwright of Boston; a lady of remarkable talents and acquirements. She is the author of several excellent books: viz., "Oracles from the Poets;" "Recollections of a New-England Housekeeper;" "New-England Bride, and Southern Matron;" "Poetry of Travelling in the United States;" "Tales and Ballads;" and others.

Dr. Gilman had four daughters, who survived him: viz., Abby Louisa, wife of Francis J. Porcher, merchant, of Charleston; Caroline H., widow of William Glover, planter, of South Carolina; Eliza W., wife of Pickering Dodge, Esq., of Salem; Anna, wife of Rev. Charles J. Bowen, of Kingston, Mass. He had also a son, who died young. His widow survives him. His occasioned visits to the home of his youth kept his ancient intimacies unbroken; old associations were preserved amid the excitement of novel scenes and fresh interests; and, now that he has passed away, his memory will be tenderly cherished, both by those to whom he devoted the maturity of his strength, and those among whom he has found a grave.

1812. — Hon. FRANKLIN DEXTER died in Beverly, Mass., 14 August, 1857, aged 63. He was son of Hon. Samuel (H.C. 1781) and Catharine (Gordon) Dexter, and was born in Charlestown, Mass., 5 November, 1793. He held a high rank in college, and graduated with distinction. He studied law under the instruction of Hon. Samuel Hubbard (Y.C.

1802), and was admitted in regular course to practice in Suffolk County. He established himself in Boston, where he soon rose to distinction at the bar, which could boast, during his connection with it, the names of Otis, Jackson, Prescott, Webster, Mason, and Hubbard. Among such rivals, he took rank as a leader. Several of his competitors, undoubtedly, were more successful; that is, they had more cases on their dockets, and much larger incomes by their profession: but he was one of the first to be sought in important cases, or when great legal points were to be discussed, or large interests disposed of. This position he held, with continually increasing reputation, until his retirement from practice in 1845. He was for some years a partner of Hon. Charles Greely Loring (H.C. 1812); afterwards of Hon. William Prescott (H.C. 1783); and, still later, of William Howard Gardiner (H.C. 1816) and George William Phillips (H.C. 1829). He was employed as counsel for the Knapps, in their trial for the murder of Capt. White, at Salem, in 1830; and exhibited great skill and logical acuteness in their defence against the gigantic powers of Daniel Webster, who was employed in behalf of the government. He was afterwards engaged in the defence of Mrs. Kinney, who was acquitted on a charge of poisoning her husband in Lowell. He held many public stations, which he filled with honor to himself, and advantage to the community. On the 4th of July, 1819, by appointment of the authorities of the town of Boston, he delivered the oration on the anniversary of the Declaration of Independence. He was elected a representative from Boston to the state legislature in 1825, 1826, and 1840; in 1835, he was chosen senator from Suffolk District; and in 1836, as one of the select committee, he rendered valuable and important service in shaping and improving the Revised Statutes. He was a member of the city-council in 1825. He took much interest in military affairs, and was for some time commander of the New-England Guards. He had a rare taste for the fine arts, and was a warm friend and admirer of Washington Allston. His beautiful criticism on landscape-painting, in an extended article in the "North-American Review," attests his information on this subject. "In political life," says his classmate, the Hon. Charles G. Loring, "Mr. Dexter exhibited the same love of truth, and contempt of artifice, the same gentlemanly bearing, and marked ability for debate, which distinguished him at the bar. Eminently faithful to his convictions of duty to his country, he never sacrificed or compromised them at the behest of a party, or under the more insidious and dangerous influences of private friendship or social influence. An enlightened and fervent lover of her institutions, he was not lost in blind or extravagant admiration to their peculiar weaknesses and dangers; and contemned the appeals to that infatuation, so generally characteristic of popular addresses, and so often the cloak of basely selfish hypocrisy. It was perhaps in this sphere of duty, more than in any other, that his resolution and intrepidity were displayed. In the great struggle of 1850, his convictions upon the great questions which divided the country impelled him into painful opposition to the principles avowed, and measures advocated, by the great champion of the party with which he had hitherto united himself and his associates, which drew upon him, not merely the reproaches and suspicions of the zealous partisans, and many of the public prints of the day, which he could patiently and calmly endure, but alienated many whom he had been accustomed to look upon as personal friends, who turned from him in coldness, or indulged in censure of his course; thus adding another victim to that lamentable intolerance in public opinion, by which our community has been too long and unhappily distinguished, and which seems in strange contrast with its claims to intellectual position and advancement. But no desertion of friends, no blandishment or persecution, could damp his courage, or shake his consistency. He never ceased to maintain, and press upon the public mind, the views he entertained; and happily lived long enough at last to enjoy the satisfaction of seeing them become those of the great mass of his fellow-citizens, though his sensitive mind never recovered from the wounds thus ungenerously inflicted, which, to use his own expressive language, were 'blows upon the heart.'" In 1841, Mr. Dexter accepted from President Harrison the office of district-attorney of the United States for the district of Massachusetts. To his conduct in office, his friend, who presides over the court in which his practice necessarily lay, bore ample and just testimony. Judge Sprague said, "His official duties lay mostly in the court in which I presided; and I can bear witness that they were performed with consummate ability, fidelity, and discretion. Vigilant and firm in the detection and punishment of crime, it was always with that considerate calmness which became the representative of a mild and paternal government. While he effectually repelled and exposed every effort, however bold or artful, to turn aside the course of justice, no amount of opposition in a trial, whatever its force or character, could convert it, on his part, into a contest for victory, or an occasion of self-exhibition. He had the most exact appreciation of the duties of his station, and every qualification for their performance. Indeed, no man could come nearer to the ideal of a perfect public-prosecutor." Mr. Dexter married, 28 September, 1819, Catherine Elizabeth Prescott, daughter of Hon. William Prescott. He had five children. One died in infancy: the others, with his widow, survived him. For a few years before his death, he resided permanently in Beverly. In 1857, the honorary degree of Doctor of Laws was conferred upon him by Harvard College.

1818. — JAMES BARBOUR died in Barboursville, Orange County, Va., 7 November, 1857, aged 58. He was the eldest son of the late Governor James Barbour, of Virginia, from whom he inherited talents that would have distinguished him in any walk of public life, but for a constitutional modesty, which kept him in retirement. He was born in Orange county, Va., 22 December, 1798. He graduated with distinction in a class which exceeded in numbers any previous one which had ever left the walls of Harvard. With strong literary tastes, and a mind enlarged and improved by foreign travel, he pursued the cultivation of polite learning in the intervals of leisure afforded him in the management of a large plantation; and there were few men of wider information or sounder scholarship in the state. In 1828, he accompanied his father to England, where the late Gov. Barbour was sent as minister to that country; and served as secretary-of-legation to the court of George IV. Old enough to have seen some of the greatest men in Virginia, in the unreserve of social intercourse, around his father's fireside, his conversation was rich in reminiscences of political and literary celebrities on both sides of the Atlantic, and embraced personal anecdotes of Mr. Jefferson, Mr. Madison, Mr. Monroe, Lafayette, Sir Walter Scott, and others: but he never talked for effect; and so little pretension was there in his manner, that a careless observer might have passed him by as a person of ordinary powers. But, as soon as he engaged with zest in the conversation of the moment, it was impossible not to perceive that he was a very uncommon man. A volume of his recollections would have been a great addition to the department of literature which embraces the *ana* of distinguished people.

1821. — Dr. Oliver Hunter Blood died in Worcester, Mass., 8 April, 1858, aged 57. He was son of Thomas Howard and Polly (Sawyer) Blood, and was born in Sterling, Mass., 31 May, 1800. He was fitted for college by Rev. Lemuel Capen, of Sterling (H.C. 1810). On leaving college, he determined to become a physician, and pursued his professional studies under the instruction of Dr. John Green, of Worcester (B.U. 1804). Having received his degree of M.D. in 1826, he began the practice of his profession in Brookfield, Mass., where he remained two years. He then removed to Worcester, where he resided during the remainder of his life. He married Ellen Blake, daughter of Hon. Francis Blake, of Worcester (H.C. 1789), and had eight children, — four sons and four daughters. One son died at the age of four years: his other children, with his widow, survived him. He was a man of small stature, but of great physical strength; and, on this account, when in college he became the possessor of the huge herculean club, which bore the significant name of the "Thundering Bolus;" a weapon of formidable size, which, for many years, was transmitted from class to class to the strongest member in each. Dr. Blood was a man of social and genial disposition. With a fund of ready wit always at command, he was ever a welcome guest at the festive board. His name, originally, was Oliver Blood: but, a short time before he entered college, he, with some juvenile companions, went on a hunting expedition, which was attended with but indifferent success; and on their return, merely out of sport, he assumed the name of Hunter, — *quasi lucus a non lucendo*, — which he ever after retained. Possessed of the kindest feelings, and of a most obliging disposition, he was greatly beloved, not only by his family, but by the community among whom he had so long lived.

1821. — WILLIAM FOSTER OTIS, of Boston, died in Versailles, France, 29 May, 1858, aged 56. His disease was "syncope of the heart." His death was very sudden, he having been in perfect health until about fifteen minutes before he breathed his last. He left Boston on the 17th of June, 1857, for Liverpool, and had been travelling in England and on the Continent. The last winter he spent in Paris, and had been about two weeks in Versailles at the time of his death. He was the third son of Hon. Harrison Gray (H.C. 1783) and Sally (Foster) Otis; and was born in Boston, 1 December, 1801. He was fitted for college at the Public Latin School in Boston. Having chosen the profession of law, he pursued his legal studies with his eldest brother, Harrison Gray Otis, jun. (H.C. 1811), and Augustus Peabody (D.C. 1803), of Boston. On his admission to the bar, he established himself in the practice of his profession in Boston. In early life he took an active part in political and military affairs. He was an officer in the New-England Guards; was a member of the Ancient and Honorable Artillery Company in 1828; and was commissioned as a major in the Boston regiment. He was elected a representative to the legislature in 1830, and was re-elected the two following years. On the 4th of July, 1831, he delivered an oration before the young men of Boston, which excited much attention from the spirit of "Young America" which he displayed in it; and which at that time, among the older class, was deemed to be too much in advance of the age.

He early retired from public life and from the practice of his profession, preferring the quiet of private life to political strifes and forensic contests. He was a gentleman of polished manners, affable in his deportment, and of unblemished moral character. He was, for several years, president of the Young Men's Temperance Society; was an active member of the Church of the Advent in Boston, was a liberal contributor to its support, and, at the time he left for Europe, was its senior warden. He married, 18 May, 1831, Emily, daughter of Josiah Marshall, Esq., a merchant of Boston. She was a lady of remarkable personal beauty and accomplishments, which were exceeded only by the goodness of her heart and the loveliness of her life. She died, 17 August, 1836, at the early age of 29. Her death was a severe affliction to her husband, from which he seemed never to recover. He left two daughters. His only son died 24 October, 1848, at the age of 12 years.

1828. — FREDERIC DABNEY died in Fayal, Azores, 29 December, 1857, aged 48. He was son of John Bass and Roxa (Lewis) Dabney, and was born in Fayal (where his father resided as United-States consul for many years), 2 August, 1809. He was fitted for college, partly by Rev. Henry Colman (D.C. 1805) at Brookline, and partly by Jacob Newman Knapp (H.C. 1802) at Jamaica Plain, Mass. He was one of the youngest in his class, and one of the most juvenile in appearance; he had however, a manly deportment, which won from his associates the love given to a younger brother, and the respect paid to an equal. He entered with great earnestness into the athletic sports of the gymnasium (which were introduced during his collegiate course); and was one of the most graceful and skilful performers, especially in those exercises which require agility rather than strength. He was not ambitious of college distinctions, but was faithful in the discharge of his duties; held a respectable rank in every department of study, and enjoyed the confidence and esteem of his teachers. Immediately after leaving college, he returned to Fayal, and engaged in the mercantile business as a partner in the firm of which his father was the senior member. There was his permanent residence; and he led an active, useful, and happy life. He visited Boston a few times, and spent some time in Europe, seeking the restoration of impaired health. In 1835, while in England, he married Roxana Stackpole, of Boston. His business, the duties of a wide hospitality, his books, and his family, filled up his time pleasantly and profitably. His classmates, at their periodical meetings, occasionally received an affectionate letter from him, in which tenderness of feeling that comes with growing years was in touching contrast with the boyish light-heartedness of his college-life. He was greatly esteemed and valued in the community in which he dwelt; and the general sense of the loss sustained by his death was expressed in the most emphatic manner, alike by native and foreign residents, by Catholics and Protestants. He died of disease of the lungs. He had long been in failing health, and was watched with much anxiety by his family and friends; but his summons was at last sudden. He took part in the Christmas festivities of his household, and even dined with his family the day before his death; but, in his enfeebled condition, a few hours of suffering sufficed to release his spirit. He had ten children; five of whom, with his widow, survived him.

1828. — Hon. JOHN JAMES GILCHRIST, of Charlestown, N.H., died in Washington, D.C., 29 April, 1858, aged 49. He was the eldest son of Capt. James and Susan (Wyman) Gilchrist, and was born in Medford, Mass., 16 February, 1809. His father was an active and enterprising shipmaster, sailing for many years from the ports of Boston and Salem, in the China and East-India trade; until, having acquired an ample competence, he retired from a seafaring life, and removed with his family from Medford, in February, 1822, to Charlestown, N.H., where he had purchased a farm; and devoted himself to agriculture until his death, which occurred 15 June, 1826. The subject of this notice began his preparatory studies for college under the instruction of Rev. Jaazaniah Crosby, D.D., of Charlestown (H.C. 1804). He was afterwards sent to Medford, and placed in the private academy of Mr. John Angier (H.C. 1821), where he made such rapid progress, that, although not intending, when he went there, to enter to an advanced standing, he was enabled to pass a satisfactory examination, and was admitted in 1825 to the sophomore class. His conduct, while in college, was exemplary, and his character unblemished. He was not ambitious for distinction, and his course of studies was rather general than confined to the requirements of a collegiate course; and therefore his rank in his class, although always respectable, was not so high as he might have attained. After leaving college, he began the study of the law under the instruction of the late William Briggs, of Charlestown (D.C. 1799), and completed his legal studies at the Law School in Cambridge. On his admission to the bar, he began the practice of his profession in Charlestown. He rapidly rose to distinction, and soon formed a business connection with the late Gov. Henry Hubbard (D.C. 1803). He took a prominent part in politics, and was early elected to offices of trust and importance. He repeatedly represented Charlestown in the legislature of New Hampshire, and was also elected solicitor of Sullivan county. In March, 1840, at the early age of thirty-one, he was appointed an associate-justice of the Supreme Court of New Hampshire. The ability with which he discharged the duties of this high station developed the eminent qualifications he possessed for the post to which he had been elevated; and when, on the retirement of the Hon. Joel Parker (D.C. 1811) from the office of chief-justice, in June, 1848, he was at once appointed his successor. This office he held until March, 1855; when he resigned it to accept that of judge of the United-States Court of Claims, to which he had been appointed by President Pierce, and which he held at the time of his death.

Judge Gilchrist was a man of ample and varied learning; a clear and good reasoner; and, as a judge, quick, attentive, and courteous. Apart from his judicial sphere, he was a great lover of literature, and was thoroughly versed in the standard works of England and his own country. In private life, he was possessed of a genial, social, and cordial disposition, seasoned with a fine sense of humor, and a keen perception of the ludicrous, which rendered him an agreeable and entertaining companion. He married, 25 August, 1836, Sarah Dean Hubbard, daughter of the late Gov. Hubbard, by whom he had two children, — a son and a daughter, — who, with their mother, survived him; his son being then a student of Harvard College.

In his domestic relations, as a son, husband, father, and brother, he was all that could be wished. His house was the home of hospitality; and his many friends who have been welcomed at his board will recall with pleasure the many happy hours passed in his society, with a melancholy regret "that they shall see his face no more."

1832. — Hon. ALBERT HOBART NELSON, of Woburn, died at the McLean Asylum in Somerville, Mass., 27 June, 1858, aged 46. He was son of Dr. John and Lucinda (Parkhurst) Nelson, and was born in Milford, Mass., 12 March, 1812. He was fitted for college at Concord Academy. After leaving college, he entered his name as a law-student in the office of the Hon. Samuel Hoar, of Concord, Mass. (H.C. 1802); but soon afterwards entered the Law School at Cambridge, where he completed his studies, and was admitted to the degree of Bachelor of Laws in 1837. On his admission to the bar, he began the practice of law in Concord, where he remained until 1841; when he removed to Woburn, which was his subsequent home, although he had an office in Boston. He was a well-read lawyer, a fine speaker, and a most pleasing, persuasive, and successful advocate before a jury. He was much in public life. For several years, he held the office of district-attorney for the counties of Middlesex and Essex. He was elected as a whig senator, from Middlesex District, to the legislature in 1848 and 1849; and in 1855 he was appointed one of the executive-council, which station he resigned a few months afterwards, having received the appointment of chief-justice of the Superior Court. He continued his seat on the bench until the 6th of March, 1858; when he was compelled to resign it in consequence of ill health. Mental alienation ensued, which increased to such a degree, that it became necessary to place him in the asylum for the insane, at Somerville, where he remained until his death. In the discharge of his duties as prosecuting-attorney, he was candid and courteous. His elevation to the bench was entirely satisfactory to the bar of Suffolk county; and the manner in which he discharged the duties of the station evinced the judicious decision of the executive in making the appointment. His ample experience at the bar had made him familiar with the rules of evidence and practice; and his instinctive legal perceptions and quickness of mind enabled him to decide promptly, and generally correctly, the questions that came before him.

To the town of Woburn the death of Judge Nelson was especially a loss. He had done much for its interests, and with an enthusiasm which showed that it came from the heart. Many of the public measures of the town for the last fifteen years bear the impress of his mind and hand. It was by his efforts, more than by those of any other individual, that the High School — an institution that reflects the greatest lustre on the town, its intelligence and generosity — was established; and his memory was appropriately honored at his funeral by the pupils of the school, who came forth with sorrowful countenances to pay a last sad tribute to the worth of their thoughtful benefactor.

Judge Nelson married, September, 1840, Elizabeth B. Phinney, daughter of the late Elias Phinney, of Lexington (H.C. 1801), clerk of the courts in Middlesex. His widow and one daughter survived him. He had one other child, a son, who died in infancy.

1836. — George Minot died at his residence in Reading, Mass., 16 April, 1858, aged 41. He was son of Hon. Stephen (H.C. 1801) and Rebecca (Trask) Minot, and was born in Haverhill, Mass., 5 January, 1817. His father was son of Capt. Jonas Minot, of Concord, Mass., where he was born 28 September, 1776, and has been a lawyer in Haverhill. He was appointed a judge of the Circuit Court of Common Pleas, and held the office until 1820, when the law which created that court was repealed. In 1824, he was appointed county-attorney for Essex; which office he resigned in 1830. He died 6 April, 1861. Mr. Minot's mother was a daughter of Samuel

Trask, of Bradford, Mass., and deceased several years since. He began to fit for college at Haverhill Academy, and concluded his preparatory studies at Phillips Academy in Exeter, N.H. Immediately after graduating, he entered the Law School in Cambridge, where he remained two years; when he left, and completed his legal studies in the office of the Hon. Rufus Choate (D.C. 1819). He was admitted to the Suffolk bar in April, 1839; and immediately opened an office in Boston. He rose rapidly to distinction, and soon attained an eminent rank in his profession. Possessing a mind remarkably clear and logical, his counsel was sought in cases, which, from their intricacy, required great acumen, keen discernment, and a nice discrimination. But he was more widely known by his editorial labors. He was the careful and accurate editor of the "United-States Statutes at Large," during the last ten years. He also rendered valuable assistance to the late Mr. Peters in the preparation of the first eight volumes of the statutes published in 1848, the full and complete general-index of which was the exclusive result of his labors. His name is also familiar to the legal profession as associate-reporter of the decisions of the late Judge Levi Woodbury in the first Circuit Court; and his edition of the nine volumes of "English Admiralty Reports," republished by Little, Brown, and Co., in 1854, bears evidence of his industry and learning in this branch of his profession. In 1844, he edited the work which has made his name familiar to every Massachusetts lawyer, — "The Digest of the Decisions of the Supreme Court of this State," — to which he added a supplement in 1852; and, until compelled by the state of his health to lay aside his labors, he was intending to recast the entire work, and, including the later reports, to make it more completely useful to the profession, more just to his own reputation, and to that of the court, whose learning and ability it would illustrate.

Mr. Minot was for many years solicitor of the Boston and Maine Railroad Corporation. As such, he was called on to advise in many very delicate and difficult controversies and deliberations; and in all he was remarkable at once for honesty of purpose, firmness, and discretion. Beyond his profession, he read and speculated more variously and more independently than most men of any profession. Elegant general literature; music, of which, in its science and practice, he was a lover and master; politics; theology, in its relations to a religion revealed in the Bible, and to that philosophy which performs its main achievement in conciliating faith with reason, — were his recreations. To sacred music and poetry he devoted himself with fervor. He loved especially the standard hymns and tunes of the church in which the congregation united in public worship. While in college, he was the organist of the chapel; and, during most of his maturer years, he himself conducted the sacred music of the religious society with which he worshipped. In his religious belief, while he did not receive, as a whole, the creed of any sect, he was sincere, earnest, catholic. He made the Bible his constant study; he read and explained it in his house; and his heart embraced, as his reason had acknowledged, its truths.

He married, first, in 1844, Mrs. Emily P. Ogle, widow of Dr. Richard Ogle, of Demarara, an Englishman by birth. She was the daughter of Dr. Gallup, formerly of Woodstock, Vt., but who resided many years at the Hague, Netherlands, where he married Susan Maria Eversdyk, a Dutch lady, and where this daughter was born. She died in Boston, 21 November, 1853; and Mr. Minot married, second, 12 December, 1854, Elizabeth Dawes, daughter of Thomas Dawes (H.C. 1801), a lawyer in Boston, and grand-daughter of Hon. Thomas Dawes (H.C. 1777), who is well remembered by the elder portion of the community as the learned judge successively of the Probate, the Municipal, and the Supreme courts. He left two children, — a son by his first wife, and a daughter by his second wife.

As a citizen, many will bear testimony to his private virtues and his excellence in all the social relations. As a son, he was all that could be desired, — attentive, respectful, and affectionate. He was a loving and considerate husband, and the fondest father. Yet he was judicious in the training of his son; and, with all his numerous engagements, he never neglected giving him lessons of wisdom and Christian counsel. His domestics and neighbors loved as well as respected him; for he was kind to all. He had important trusts reposed in him by friends and relations, who knew their confidence in his ability and integrity could never be shaken, or their hope in him disappointed, except by death. Fidelity to the dictates of conscience was his ruling principle of action. His faith in religion was firm, and attended him through life, and shone forth in the perfect resignation with which he bowed to the appointments of Heaven. He had all that man could desire to render life attractive. Placed in circumstances to warrant their liberal indulgence, he was happy in the exercise of his benevolent sympathies and a generous hospitality. He had numerous beloved and loving relatives and friends, a strong and vigorous intellect, and a heart disposed to employ it in the service of his fellow-man and his heavenly Father. Yet when the announcement was made, which was very sudden and unexpected to him, a few days previous to his death, that his life on earth was near its close, he was enabled to say, "God's will be done!" He besought his sorrowing friends around his bed to "trust in God, and all would be well."

The funeral services of the deceased were conducted in the church by three clergymen of different denominations: namely, the Rev. William Barrows, his pastor, Trinitarian; the Rev. Thomas Dawes, of South Boston, Unitarian; and the Rev. Thomas Worcester, D.D., of Boston, of the New-Jerusalem church. The organ at which he had so often presided was richly draped in mourning in token of respect to his memory, and the choir executed an appropriate chant as a parting requiem.

1839.—Rev. AUGUSTUS RUSSELL POPE died in Somerville, Mass., 24 May, 1858, aged 39. He was son of Lemuel and Sally Belknap (Russell) Pope, and was born in Boston, 25 January, 1819. His father was for many years president of the Boston Insurance Company, and died in Roxbury in 1851. Mr. Pope pursued his preparatory studies for admission into college, partly under the instruction of Mr. Daniel Greenleaf

Ingraham (H.C. 1809), and partly at the Boston Latin School. Immediately after graduating, he entered the Divinity School in Cambridge, where he pursued his theological studies. He was ordained pastor of the Unitarian church in Kingston, Mass., 19 April, 1843, where he faithfully discharged his ministerial duties until June, 1849; when he resigned his pastoral charge, and his resignation was accepted on the 12th of July following. On the 25th of November in the same year, he was installed over the Unitarian church in Somerville. Here he continued to labor with great acceptance to the people of his charge until his death, with the exception of a few months, about two years since, during which period he acted as state agent and lecturer for the Massachusetts Board of Education. He was a man of great energy and industry. He possessed talents well adapted to the profession he had chosen. His personal character was adorned with Christian virtues, which made him eminently useful as a minister, and beloved and respected as a man by a large circle of acquaintances. He delivered many lectures before conventions of teachers, for the Board of Education, in which he displayed much ingenuity: one particularly, on telegraphs, was highly commended. He was well versed in physics, and had great talent for mechanics. He invented the electrical apparatus to alarm the inmates of a house against burglars. He edited or prepared the first "Educational Year Book," and wrote many articles for the "Massachusetts Teacher." His published works were, — 1. Christian Union: a Discourse preached before the First Congregational Society in Kingston, 22 November, 1846. 2. Discourse commemorative of the Life and Ministry of Rev. Zephaniah Willis, delivered before the First Congregational Society in Kingston, 14 March, 1847. 3. Address at the Laying of the Corner-stone of the Free High-school House, Somerville, 17 September, 1851. 4. An Address delivered at the Laying of the Corner-stone of a House of Worship for the Allen-street Congregational Society in the City of Cambridge, 25 September, 1851 (of which there were two editions). 5. A Sermon before the First Congregational Society in Somerville, 4 July, 1852. 6. A Sermon on the

Burning of the First Church in Somerville, preached 25 July, 1852. 7. Agricultural Head-work: an Address delivered before the Middlesex Agricultural Society, 30 September, 1856.

Mr. Pope married, 2 June, 1843, Lucy Ann, daughter of Col. George and Mary Meacham, of Cambridge; by whom he had four children, two sons and two daughters, who, with their mother, survived him. An aged mother, of whose declining years he was a dutiful supporter, also survived him.

1844. — FRANCIS LOWELL BATCHELDER, of Cambridge, Mass., died at Hibernia, Fleming's Island, Fla. (whither he had gone for the benefit of his health), 9 February, 1858, aged 32. He was son of Samuel and Mary (Montgomery) Batchelder, and was born in that part of Chelmsford which is now within the limits of the city of Lowell, 2 April, 1825. He was fitted for college at Thornton Academy in Saco, Me., where his father's family resided for several years. On leaving college, he entered the Law School at Cambridge, where he pursued his legal studies, and received his degree of bachelor of laws in 1848. He opened an office in Boston, and there practised his profession during the remainder of his life, having his residence in Cambridge. Of a modest and retiring disposition, he had no ambition to gain distinction by forensic eloquence; but devoted his attention to the business of conveyancing, a branch in which he attained an honorable reputation; and no man could say that he had not well done the part of a faithful servant. Without pretension, without affectation or disguise, his numerous and constantly increasing circle of friends were witnesses of his simple and well-spent Christian life. Enemies he had none. His tastes were refined and cultivated; and an ardent love of music, in which he was a well-skilled amateur, always afforded an agreeable relaxation to the routine of daily toil. He was a zealous and faithful officer of the church to which he belonged, and took a deep interest in all its concerns. He took no active part in politics, but faithfully served in the common-council of Cambridge in 1853 and 1854. He married, 2 December, 1851, Susan Cabot Foster, of Cambridge, and had two children, a son and a daughter, who, with his widow, survived him.

1846. — Dr. EDWARD MULLIKEN died in Montpelier, Vt., 24 July, 1857, aged 30. He was son of Dr. Isaac Walter and Alicia (Shepard) Mulliken, and was born in Stowe, Mass., 21 January, 1827, where he resided until he was seven years of age, when he removed with his father's family to Lowell. He resided in Lowell two years, when he removed to Waltham, where he passed the remainder of the time until he entered college, excepting one year when at school at Concord. He was fitted for college at the school of Rev. Samuel Ripley, of Waltham (H.C. 1804). He began the study of medicine with Dr. Daniel Adams, of Keene, N.H. (D.C. 1797), with whom, and at Dartmouth, he remained one year. The subsequent two years he studied at the University of New York, where, in 1850, he received his degree of M.D. He was for some time the resident physician at the Bellevue Hospital in New-York City. After leaving New York, he practised his profession about two years in Milford, Mass., when he removed to Waterbury, Vt., and afterwards to Montpelier. At Waterbury, he formed an acquaintance with Miss Elizabeth Robbins, an adopted daughter of Gen. Robbins, to whom he was married a few months before his death. Having enjoyed advantages equal to any the country afforded, he improved them to the best advantage; was thoroughly qualified for practice; and, had he lived, bid fair to have attained to an eminent rank in his profession. He was a well-read scholar in general literature; of fine taste, and gentlemanly in his habits and manners. He had won for himself the respect of all who knew him, and his early death was deeply regretted by his friends and the community.

1850. — JOHN DAVID JONES died in New Orleans, La., 30 November, 1857, aged 27. He was son of Jesse Rouble and Rebecca (Ragan) Jones, and was born in Covington, La., 21 April, 1830. His father was born on a plantation near Richmond, Va., in October, 1787. An ancestor, the original emigrant to this country, came from Wales. His mother, who was daughter of John and Susanna (Battelle) Ragan, was born near Milledgeville, Ga., September, 1804. John Ragan was of Irish origin, and the name was formerly written O'Ragan.

The first of the name settled in North Carolina. The subject of this notice began to fit for college at home; and completed his preparatory studies at an academy in Mandeville, La., under Felix Macmanus. On leaving college, he entered the law department of the University of Louisiana, where he graduated in 1852, and, the same year, began the practice of law in the Eighth Judicial District of the State of Louisiana, which he continued with success until his death. His disease was yellow jaundice. He was unmarried. He was a young gentleman of upright character and generous disposition, with a promise of a useful and honorable life. The information of his early death was received with surprise and sorrow by his numerous friends in this part of the country.

1854.—FREDERICK WHEELER died in Framingham, Mass., 23 December, 1857, aged 25. He was the only son of Increase Sumner (H.C. 1826) and Elizabeth A. M. Wheeler; was born in Framingham, 20 April, 1832; and was fitted for college at Phillips Exeter Academy. On leaving college, he began the study of law with Hon. Charles Russell Train (B.U. 1837), with whom he remained one year. He then entered the Law School at Cambridge, and received his degree of bachelor of laws at Commencement in 1857. While engaged in his legal studies, his health became impaired, and in February, 1857, he sailed for Port au Prince; but, being wrecked on one of the Bahama Islands, he abandoned the voyage, and returned in March. A writer in the "Christian Register" thus beautifully sketches his subsequent life to the closing scene: "Disease rapidly developed, and assumed, finally, one of the several forms of consumption. Every means which medical skill or maternal love could devise to alleviate his pains was adopted; and seldom has there been a more patient, uncomplaining sufferer. It was while waiting to pass for ever away that the strength and beauty of his character were fully manifested. In his native town, at Exeter, at Cambridge, everywhere, he had won the confidence of the persons with whom he mingled; and those who knew him best loved him most. His air of manliness (as manhood came), his outspoken sincerity, and his regard for truth, have commanded the respect of persons even whose opinions were unlike his own. Friends, who had carefully noted his moral and intellectual development, had seen that his sense of honor and views of honesty were those of a Christian gentleman; that he gave promise of becoming a dignified and eloquent advocate; that he would have borne to the bar fertility of resource, keen insight, quick discrimination, surpassing faithfulness to the interests of clients, and a judgment uncommonly mature; and that his ambition to achieve distinction in politics was founded on a knowledge of the constitutional and political history of his country: but all this was for life. Mortal sickness and the torture of mortal pains came upon him. Those who ministered to his wants, saw him for death. His preparation to depart! — who of those that witnessed it will forget the spirit in which, amid intense bodily suffering, it was finished? If the scenes of the last weeks of his life may not be related here, it is still to be written, that, from the hour his pastor at his request gave him the bread and wine of the communion-supper until the silver cord of mortality was gently loosed and its golden bowl was tenderly broken, his conversation was on heaven and on the concerns of the soul. He did indeed say of the body, 'Let me sleep,' — such are his exact words, — 'let me sleep in my own native town, amid the scenes of my childhood and riper years, within the sound of the music of the bells which have so often summoned me to school and to church. Let my last resting-place be in some quiet spot in that beautiful grove which has so often been filled with my joyous shout. There, perhaps some friend who cherishes my memory will drop a flower on my grave.' On the 26th of December, in the first thick-falling snow of winter, classmates laid his body in the 'quiet spot' he had asked; and, as the sabbath sun arose, women who loved him went to the whitened mound, and placed upon it a cross and crowns and wreaths of evergreen. And, ere that sun went down, there was still another offering; for woman, too, had dropped the expected 'flower.'"

1858-59.

1787. — Rev. ABIEL ABBOT died in West Cambridge, Mass., 31 January, 1859, aged 93. He had been for several years the only survivor of his class; and, at the time of his death, was the oldest surviving graduate of Harvard College. He was the son of Deacon Abiel and Dorcas (Abbot) Abbot, and was born in Wilton, N.H., 14 December, 1765. He was a descendant of the sixth generation of George Abbot, the first of the name who settled in this country. His father was a highly respectable man, was a zealous patriot, and major of a regiment during the Revolution; and, though originally a cooper by trade, he was chiefly occupied in farming. He was remarkable for industry, equanimity, integrity, public spirit, and benevolence. Mr. Abbot was the eldest of twelve children, two of whom died in infancy. Three of the sons graduated at Harvard College, — Abiel, the subject of this sketch: Jacob, born 7 January, 1768; graduated in 1792; was ordained at Hampton Falls, N.H., 15 August, 1798; resigned in 1827; afterwards removed to Windham, N.H., where he was drowned in a pond, 2 November, 1834, while returning from divine service: Samuel, born 3 March, 1786; graduated in 1808; studied law; practised for several years in Dunstable, N.H., and Ipswich, Mass.; retired from the bar in 1818; removed to Wilton, and engaged with his brother in the manufacture of potato-starch on a large scale; and on the 2d of January, 1839, was burnt to death in a starch-mill, which he had been instrumental in establishing, in Jaffray, N.H.

Mr. Abbot's advantages of education in his earliest years were very small; being taught chiefly by untaught teachers. When he was fourteen years old, he began to study Latin under the instruction of Rev. Abel Fiske, of Wilton (H.C. 1774). In November, 1780, he was admitted to Phillips Academy, in Andover, under the preceptorship of Mr. (afterwards Rev.) Eliphalet Pearson (H.C. 1773), where he remained until July, 1783, when he entered college. A few months after graduating, he was appointed assistant of Mr. Ebenezer Pemberton (N.J. 1765), the principal of Phillips Academy; where he remained until July, 1789, on a salary of sixteen shillings per week. Immediately on leaving the academy, he began the study of theology. He remained at Andover, and prosecuted his studies chiefly by himself, with the aid of books from the library of the Rev. Jonathan French (H.C. 1771), and also from the town library. In June, 1790, he was approbated by the Andover Association as a candidate for the ministry, and preached for the first time at Amesbury, Mass. After preaching successively at Kensington, N.H., Gardner, Mass., and Cambridge, he was employed, in June, 1791, as a missionary in the district of Maine, in connection with Rev. Daniel Little, known as "the Apostle of the East," under the patronage of the Society for Propagating the Gospel. He continued in missionary labor for five months; and, notwithstanding the privations and sacrifices incident to that kind of work, his time generally passed very pleasantly. After completing his missionary tour, he preached, in 1792, in several places, as in Nelson, Greenfield, and Peterborough, N.H.; but in none of them were the people prepared for a settlement. In February, 1793, he preached at Middleton, Mass. In April, went to Penobscot, and preached there and at Castine until November. He was invited to settle in Castine, but declined the invitation. In December, he preached for a few Sundays in West Newbury, after the removal of Rev. David Tappan (H.C. 1771) to be Professor of Divinity in Harvard College. In January, 1794, he was appointed tutor in Greek at Cambridge, where he remained one year, preaching occasionally for the neighboring clergy, and also supplying the pulpit in Newbury and Malden. In January, 1795, he went to Coventry, Conn., on an invitation to preach there as a candidate. He officiated eight Sundays, and was requested to return, but declined, as he concluded that the prevailing theological views were much more Calvinistic than his own, and that he should probably find little sympathy if he were to become associated with them. In May, 1795, he preached for several Sundays in Milford, N.H. In June, at the urgent request of the people of Coventry, he returned to that place to preach as a candidate. In August, he received an unanimous call of the church and society to become their pastor. After considerable hesitation, from an apprehension that his views were not sufficiently in accordance with those of his brethren around to warrant the expectation of so peaceable a ministry as he desired, he accepted the invitation, and was ordained 28 October, 1795. There he labored faithfully, and with a good degree of acceptance, until about 1806, when some suspicions in regard to his Orthodoxy began to be excited, and several members felt themselves called upon to interrogate him directly upon the subject. The result was, that their suspicions were confirmed, and things were forthwith put in train for his ultimate separation from his charge; but no effective measures were taken until 1809, when a meeting of the church was called, at which Mr. Abbot was invited to be present, for the purpose of ascertaining his peculiar views, and the points of difference between them. But it resulted in nothing that was satisfactory. In June, 1810, there was another similar meeting, and the result was alike unsatisfactory. Finally, on the 16th of April, 1811, a convocation of his old neighbors and friends (the pastors and messengers of Tolland county) assembled, and, with great unanimity, solemnly decreed that he had forfeited both his parish and office; and that he was severed from his people, and deposed from the ministry. He had committed the old Protestant sin of regarding the Scriptures as the only standard of faith, and refusing to express his religious sentiments in the manner prescribed by men. Being subjected to scrutiny, he was found upon certain difficult points to differ in opinion from a portion of his society, including chiefly the church, as distinct from the congregation. He would not take the words set down for him. He would not stretch to the full length of the procrustean bed on which he was laid. Neither

Mr. Abbot nor the parish acknowledged the validity of the sentence, or the jurisdiction of the court; and accordingly he continued to occupy the pulpit as usual, though he and they soon afterwards joined in calling another council from Massachusetts, which assembled on the 6th of June following, reviewed the whole case, and declared Mr. Abbot's relation to his people unaffected by the decision of the consociation: nevertheless, in view of the peculiar circumstances, they concluded that his interests, and the interests of the parish, required that his pastoral relation should be dissolved. In August following, Mr. Abbot published a statement of his difficulties at Coventry, which was subsequently replied to by the Association of Tolland county, in a pamphlet said to have been written by Dr. Bassett, of Hebron. The General Association of Connecticut, which assembled in June, took notice of the matter, by request of the Tolland Association, and made a report on the subject, of considerable length.

About the 1st of September, Mr. Abbot left Coventry, went to Byfield, Mass., and took charge of Dummer Academy. Here he continued seven years and a half. In April, 1819, removed to North Andover, and settled on a farm, which he superintended for some time. In May, 1824, he removed to Chelmsford, where he and his daughter Sarah had a school. After remaining there two years and a half, he left in the autumn of 1826, and removed to Wilton. During his residence at Byfield, Andover, and Chelmsford, he often supplied for the neighboring ministers, and occupied the pulpit of North Andover for several months in succession. While at Wilton he lived on his farm, and superintended it. In March, 1827, he went to preach at Peterborough, in the pulpit rendered vacant by the recent dismission of the Rev. Elijah Dunbar (H.C. 1794). About the first of May he received a call, which he accepted, and was installed 27 June. Here he continued to discharge regularly the duties of his office until March, 1839; when, on account of a bronchial affection, he found it necessary to retire from the active duties of the ministry. He, however, retained a nominal relation as pastor until September, 1848; when, on the settlement of a new pastor, he thought best, from considerations of delicacy, not to retain any longer even a nominal pastoral relation. For some years after he ceased to preach regularly, he occasionally supplied pulpits in the neighborhood, though for several of the last years he did not undertake any public service. About four years before his death, he left Peterborough, and resided with his grandson, Rev. Samuel Abbot Smith (H.C. 1849), in West Cambridge.

He married, 19 May, 1796, Elizabeth Abbot, daughter of Capt. John and Abigail Abbot, of Andover, by whom he had three children, all daughters: 1. Elizabeth, born 22 May, 1798; married, 1822, Rev. John Abbot Douglass, of Waterford, Me. (Bowd. C. 1814); died 12 October, 1823. 2. Abigail, born 17 October, 1799, who survived her father. 3. Sarah Dorcas, born 22 June, 1801; married, 1828, Samuel G. Smith, of Peterborough, who died 9 September, 1842, aged 43. She died 11 June, 1831. Dr. Abbot's wife died 6 April, 1853.

Dr. Abbot was a man gifted with fine talents, was an able writer, and a very popular preacher. In 1838, the honorary degree of doctor of divinity was conferred upon him by Harvard College. His domestic life was most happy and affectionate, and he pursued the even tenor of his way in all modesty, gentleness, and meekness. But the noble and heroic elements were also largely developed in his character. He lived a life of unsullied integrity, extended far beyond the usual period allotted to man; and at last departed to receive the reward of a good and faithful servant.

The following is a list of Dr. Abbot's publications: 1. A Sermon at North Chelmsford, 4 July, 1825; 2. Right Hand of Fellowship at Canterbury; 3. Statement of the Coventry Case; 4. Address before the Essex Agricultural Society; 5. History of Andover; 6. Genealogy of the Abbot Family.

1788. — Dr. William Sawyer died in Boston, 18 April, 1859, aged 88. He was the last survivor of his class, and after the death of Rev. Abiel Abbot, D.D., mentioned above, was the oldest surviving graduate of the college. He was son of Dr. Micajah (H.C. 1756) and Sybil (Farnham) Sawyer, and was born in Newburyport, Mass., 1 February, 1771. His father, who was an eminent physician, was born in Newbury, 15 July, 1737; and died 29 September, 1815, at the age of 78 years. His mother was daughter of Daniel Farnham, Esq. (H.C. 1739), a highly respectable lawyer in Newburyport, who was a native of York, Me., and died May, 1776, aged 56. Dr. Sawyer was fitted for college at Dummer Academy, in Newbury. After graduating, he studied medicine with his father, and practised for a few years; but, finding the profession not suited to his taste, he relinquished it; and near the close of the last century he removed to Boston, where he engaged in mercantile business, having formed a copartnership with the late Thomas Wigglesworth (H.C. 1793), under the firm of Sawyer and Wigglesworth, at No. 69, Long Wharf. This partnership was dissolved about six years afterwards. Dr. Sawyer continued in business by himself at the same place a short time, and then went to Europe, where he resided several years. He returned to Boston about 1817, and resumed business. He was very successful, and acquired an ample fortune. He retired from active business about twenty-five years before his death, and passed the last years of his life almost constantly in reading: and the kind of reading that occupied him was really surprising; that is to say, it was hard reading, for an invalid. He especially delighted in works on astronomy; and he talked more on that than on almost any other subject. Newton's Life, Sir John Herschel's and Prof. Nicol's Works, were on his table; and Hume's too, which he was reading through. But, in alluding to Hume's, he said, "When I came to the part on miracles, I passed it over, thinking I had no more faith than I wanted." A friend carried to him Evelyn's Diary, as an amusing book for an invalid. The next time this friend saw him, he said, "Is it not remarkable that Evelyn should not have said a word about Sir Isaac Newton, living at the same time?" And then he talked at length of Newton, and ended with saying, what he often said, "He was the greatest man that has ever lived since Jesus Christ." Dr. Sawyer was a man of great modesty, of a sensitive delicacy of nature, and, from these causes, very reserved. But his tenderness and disinterestedness in more intimate relations were well known to those nearest him. Yet he shrank from any praise or expressions of gratitude which were offered to him; saying, "Let that matter rest." He was never married.

1794. — Rev. Isaac Braman died in Georgetown, Mass., 26 December, 1858, aged 88. He was son of Sylvanus and Experience (Blanchard) Braman, and was born in Norton, Mass., 5 July, 1770. He was fitted for college by Dr. Samuel Morey, of Norton (Y.C. 1777), and Mr. Stephen Palmer (H.C. 1789), afterwards minister of Needham, Mass. He graduated with high honors; and, for several years before his death, he was the only survivor of his class. After leaving college, he studied for the ministry with Rev. Jason Haven, of Dedham, Mass. (H.C. 1754), and Rev. Pitt Clark, of Norton (H.C. 1790). He was ordained, 7 June, 1797, pastor of the Second Parish in Rowley, then called New Rowley, and since incorporated into a town by the name of Georgetown. He was successor of Rev. James Chandler (H.C. 1728), who died 19 April, 1789, at the age of 83 years, and in the 58th year of his ministry. The parish was without a settled minister for nine years, and Mr. Braman was the last of sixty-four candidates who preached there on probation. He continued pastor of this society until his death, — a period of more than sixty-one years, — discharging the duties of his profession with great fidelity, and to the entire acceptance of his people, until 1842; when, on account of the infirmities of age, it was deemed necessary that he should be relieved from a portion of his labors; and, in December of that year, the Rev. Enoch Pond (Bowd. C. 1838) was ordained as colleague-pastor with him. Mr. Pond died in 1846; and in February, 1847, Rev. John Moore Prince (Bowd. C. 1841) was ordained as his successor, and continued until November, 1857, when he resigned. His last colleague and successor is Rev. Charles Beecher (Bowd. C. 1834).

Mr. Braman was a man of great originality of mind, and his sermons evinced deep thought and profound reflection. He married, August, 1797, Hannah Palmer (born 12 June, 1773), youngest daughter of Rev. Joseph Palmer, of Norton (H.C. 1747). They had five children: viz., 1. Harriet, born 17 July, 1798; married Rev. John Boardman (D.C. 1817), minister in Douglass, Mass. 2. Milton Palmer, born 6 August, 1799 (H.C. 1819); now minister of the First Church in Danvers, Mass. 3. James Chandler, born 29 September, 1801; died at sea (on his passage from Calcutta for Salem, seventy-five days out), 5 December, 1820. 4. Adeline, born 10 July, 1805; died 10 September, 1830. 5. Isaac Gordon, born 12 March, 1813; is a physician in Brighton, Mass. Mr. Braman's wife died 14 August, 1835, aged 62; and he married for his second wife, in 1837, Sarah Balch, daughter of John Balch, Esq., of Newburyport. She survived him.

1795. — FRANCIS JOHONNOT OLIVER died in Middletown, Conn., 21 August, 1858, aged 80 years. He was son of Ebenezer and Susannah (Johonnot) Oliver, and was born in Boston, 10 October, 1777. His father was a merchant in Boston, was for many years a selectman, and was warden of King's Chapel. He died 14 December, 1826, aged 74. His mother died 24 August, 1839, aged 84. Mr. Oliver was fitted for college at the public Latin School in Boston. After leaving college, he entered as an apprentice the counting-room of Joseph Coolidge, Esq., for the purpose of qualifying himself for the mercantile profession. In 1798, when a war was threatened between this country and France, he was among the young men of Boston who addressed the elder Adams, offering their services. He read the president's response in Faneuil Hall, and was the first to follow the injunctions of the president: "To arms, then, my young friends; to arms!" About the same time, the Boston Light-Infantry Company was organized, in which he took a prominent part, and was elected the first ensign. He began business in Boston as a merchant in 1805, and established himself at No. 45, Long Wharf. In 1813, he entered into copartnership with Cornelius Coolidge (H.C. 1798), under the style of Cornelius Coolidge and Co. This partnership was dissolved four years afterwards. On the 13th of June, 1818, the American Insurance Company, in Boston, was incorporated, and Mr.

Oliver was elected its first president. This office he continued to hold until the autumn of 1835, when he resigned it, and was elected president of the City Bank, where he continued by successive re-elections until 1840; when he removed to Middletown, and there passed the remainder of his life. He was elected a representative to the legislature in 1822 and 1823; and was a member of the Boston common-council in 1823, 1824, 1825, and 1828, and was its president in 1824 and 1825. In all these stations, he discharged their various duties with the strictest fidelity and integrity. In his political principles, he was an ardent federalist; and being a gentleman of fine personal appearance, great suavity of manner, and fluency of speech, he was often called upon to preside at public meetings and political caucuses.

He married (first) Mary Caroline, daughter of Richard Alsop, of Middletown; and had issue: Mary Caroline, who died in infancy; Francis Eben, who entered Harvard College, but left in his senior year on account of his health, and died in London, May, 1850, in his 37th year; Mary Alsop, who married Joseph W. Alsop, merchant of New York; Richard Alsop, who died in infancy; and Susan Heard. His wife died 29 August, 1819, aged 28; and he married (second) Mary Charlotte, daughter of Ebenezer Jackson, of Middletown (formerly of Newton, Mass.), by whom he had Caroline Alsop and George Stuart Johonnot: the latter graduated at Harvard College in 1851.

Mr. Oliver was a gentleman of unblemished moral character, and was for many years a warden of King's Chapel in Boston.

1796.—Rev. JAMES KENDALL died in Plymouth, Mass., 17 March, 1859, aged 89. He was the youngest son of Major James and Elizabeth (Mason) Kendall, and was born in Sterling, Mass., 3 November, 1769. His mother was a native of Lexington, Mass. In some reminiscences of his own life, written at the age of 84, he describes her as "a sensible and pious woman, of a strong mind, and a kind and generous heart; discreet and faithful in the discharge of all the relative duties of life:" and adds, that "her children were greatly indebted to her for their youthful training, and their early religious impressions." He pursued his preparatory studies under the instruction of Rev. Reuben Holcomb (Y.C. 1774), of Sterling; and was nearly fitted to enter college at the age of 14: but an affection of his eyes, caused by a too close application to the study of Greek in the evening, obliged him, for several years, to give up the hope of obtaining a liberal education. From that time until the age of 21, he worked upon his father's farm in the summer; and, when old enough, taught school in the winter. During that period, in which he was accumulating a capital of physical health to secure a life of such remarkable vigor, even to his ninetieth year, his eyes recovered their strength; and, gladly returning to his studies, he was prepared to enter college in 1792. In his collegiate course, he defrayed a large portion of his expenses by his own exertions, by teaching school in vacation, and by other services in term-time. In his reminiscences, he says, "It is some satisfaction to me, in looking back to this period of my life as an undergraduate, to remember that I had no mark for delinquency in college exercises, unnecessary absences, or any misdemeanor." He held a high rank as a scholar, and graduated with the second honors of his class; the late Dr. Leonard Woods, of Andover, having the first. Immediately after leaving college, he was appointed assistant teacher in Phillips Academy at Andover, of which Mr. Mark Newman (D. C. 1793) was then the principal. Here he passed two years; at the same time pursuing his theological studies under the direction of Rev. David Tappan, D.D. (H. C. 1771), then Professor of Divinity in Harvard College, and Rev. Jonathan French (H.C. 1771), minister of the Second Church in Andover. He was approbated to preach by the Andover Association in 1798. In that year, he was appointed tutor in Greek in the college, and removed to Cambridge, where he still continued his theological studies with the advice and aid of Dr. Tappan. He resigned his tutorship in 1799. During his residence in Andover, he had occasionally preached there and in the vicinity. While he lived in Cambridge, he preached more frequently; and for a short time supplied the pulpit of the First Church in Boston, and the First

Church in Quincy. He first preached at Plymouth on the second Sunday in October, 1799; and, having preached for four Sundays, on the 4th of November, 1799, he was invited to become the minister of that ancient parish. His answer of acceptance was given on Thanksgiving-Day of that year; and he was ordained 1 January, 1800. He was the sole pastor of the society for thirty-eight years. On the 3d of January, 1838, the infirmities of age having begun to come upon him, the Rev. George Ware Briggs (B.U. 1825) was ordained as his colleague; where he continued until 15 December, 1852. Rev. Henry Lewis Myrick was his colleague from 21 September, 1853, to 21 September, 1854; and Rev. George S. Ball from 8 April, 1855, to 8 April, 1857. On the 5th of January, 1859, Rev. Edward Henry Hall (H.C. 1851) was ordained as his colleague, and is now sole pastor of the society. After the settlement of a colleague, Dr. Kendall preached frequently, for a number of years, in his own pupit; in the pulpits of those with whom he was accustomed to exchange; and in comparatively distant places, during several journeys into various parts of the country. He preached his semi-centennial sermon, 3 January, 1850. He never took a formal leave of the pulpit, and never wished to bid it farewell. He preached for the last time on Thanksgiving-Day, November, 1857. One of his last public services was at the ordination of his associate minister on the 5th of January, 1859. He stood in his pulpit again to offer a fervent prayer at the close of the first services of the same pastor on Sunday, 9 January; and yet once more to take the same part at the close of service, Sunday, 17 January; and then his public ministry was ended. He was connected with his parish nearly twenty years longer than any of his predecessors. He was a man of peace, order, integrity, faith, and devotion. It is one of the strongest proofs of his true piety, that during a period of more than fifty years, when children have been born around him to grow up to mature age, and in their turn to be surrounded by children and grandchildren, amongst them all, no one was known to have breathed a word derogatory to him as a Christian or a man. Genial and cheerful, he enjoyed every bright hour: humble and trustful toward his God, he met submissively the discipline of sorrows. His experiences were the varied ones of the lot of humanity; and he accepted and used them with the conscientious purpose to be obedient to the truth, and loyal to duty. Many have seen him in his hospitable home; many have seen him in the street, moving with the steady step of a true man; many have seen him at their firesides, as the visitor, the adviser, and consoler; many have seen him in the church, and listened to his honest discourse, and his prayers of singular richness and fervor: and, of all these, many will hold him in remembrance as one they trusted, and affectionately revered. In 1825, the honorary degree of doctor of divinity was conferred upon him by Harvard College. He married, first, June, 1800, Sarah Poor, daughter of Deacon Daniel Poor, of Andover, by whom he had six children; of whom one died at birth, another at the age of thirteen days, and another at three years of age: the remaining three survived him. She died 13 February, 1809, in the thirty-third year of her age. He married, second, 17 June, 1810, Sally Kendall, daughter of Deacon Paul Kendall, of Templeton, Mass., who also was the mother of six children, five of whom survived him: the other died at Madison, Wis., 9 March, 1853, in the thirty-fifth year of his age. She died 5 February, 1845, at the age of 65. She was a very intelligent person, — of great strength and loveliness of character. In his reminiscences, Dr. Kendall says, "I have been singularly favored in my domestic relationships. Although not exempt from the trials and changes to which every man of my age, and at the head of a large family, is destined in an earthly life, I cannot be sufficiently thankful to the Father of an infinite mercy for the comfort, satisfaction, and consolation I have enjoyed during the whole period of my connection with a family." His first wife he describes as "a person of an amiable disposition, faithful and affectionate as a wife, and tender and devoted as a mother." Of his last wife he says, "She was a person of great discretion, sound judgment, and of a pure and pious mind. Like her Divine Master, she was made perfect through suffering." The following is a list of Dr. Kendall's publications, with the dates of their delivery: 1. Discourse upon the Character of Washington, delivered at the request of the Town of Plymouth, 22 February, 1800. 2. Sermon on the Death of Mrs. Jane Robbins, 21 September, 1800. 3. Sermon on the Death of Col. George Watson, 14 December, 1800. 4. Sermon on the Death of Rev. David Tappan, D.D., 4 September, 1803. 5. Sermon at the Ordination of Rev. Caleb Holmes, at Dennis, 2 January, 1805. 6. Sermon before the Ancient and Honorable Artillery Company, 2 June, 1806. 7. Sermon before the Society for propagating the Gospel among the Indians, 7 November, 1811. 8. Sermon before the Humane Society, 8 June, 1813. 9. Sermon at the Ordination of Rev. Oliver Haywood at Barnstable, 8 November, 1815. 10. Sermon in the "Liberal Preacher" for March, 1828, on Man's Accountableness to his Creator, and a Future Retribution. 11. Sermon at the Ordination of Rev. Hersey B. Goodwin, at Concord, Mass., 17 February, 1830. 12. Sermon at the Ordination of his Son, Rev. James A. Kendall, at Medfield, Mass., 10 November, 1830. 13. Charge at the Ordination of Rev. Chandler Robbins as Minister of the Second Church, Boston, 4 December, 1833. 14. Sermon on the Wreck of the Brig "Regulator," 14 February, 1836. 15. Semicentennial Sermon, 1 January, 1850.

1799. — Parker Cleaveland died in Brunswick, Me., 15 October, 1858, aged 78. He was son of Dr. Parker and Elizabeth (Jackman) Cleaveland, and was born in Rowley (Byfield Parish), Mass., 15 January, 1780. His father was son of Rev. John Cleaveland, and was born in Chebacco, parish of Ipswich, which is now the town of Essex, Mass. Rev. John Cleaveland entered Yale College; and, when in his senior year, he was, with another, expelled for embracing the doctrine of the "New Lights." Prof. Cleaveland's father was fitted for college; but the war broke out, and he relinquished his intention of obtaining a collegiate education, studied medicine, became a surgeon in the revolutionary army, and was stationed at Cambridge. Prof. Cleaveland was fitted for college at Dummer

Academy, in Newbury, Mass., under Rev. Isaac Smith (H.C. 1767). He taught school in Boxford, Mass., in his sophomore year, and in Burlington or Wilmington, Mass., in his junior year. Immediately after his graduation, he entered, as a law student, the office of Ichabod Tucker, of Haverhill, Mass. (H.C. 1791), where he remained one year. In the middle of the year 1800, he began teaching a school at York, Me.; and, at the same time, was clerk in the office of Daniel Sewall, Esq., the clerk of the Supreme Court; was with him at the courts, and continued the study of law. Here he remained until the autumn of 1803; when he was appointed tutor in mathematics at Harvard College, which office he held until Commencement in 1805, when he resigned it in consequence of having received an invitation to fill a professorship in Bowdoin College, which he accepted; and he was installed, 23 October, 1805, as professor of mathematics and natural philosophy; the college then having been in operation but a single year. The duties of this professorship, together with those of lecturer on chemistry and mineralogy, he discharged with distinguished ability until 1828, when it was deemed expedient to separate the departments of mathematics and natural philosophy, and establish a distinct professorship of chemistry and mineralogy. Mr. William Smyth, the distinguished professor of mathematics, was raised to that department, and Mr. Cleaveland was installed in the new professorship of chemistry, mineralogy, and natural philosophy. This position he occupied until his death, having acquired a world-wide reputation, and a success seldom attained by a scientific instructor. He was thus connected with the college for a period of fifty-three years, during which he devoted the whole powers of his mind and the energy of his body to the advancement of his favorite studies; and no man in the country has done more to inspire a passion and create an interest and knowledge of the details of the sciences which he taught. He spent six hours a day in his laboratory, recitation and lecture room, and was frequently engaged for sixteen of the twenty-four hours. The college never bought any minerals. James Bowdoin gave about five hundred specimens: the rest have been collected either by Prof. Cleaveland's personal labor, or by the exchange of specimens which he obtained, and they now amount to upwards of seven thousand. He became widely known in the United States, in Great Britain, and on the continent of Europe, by his great work on mineralogy and geology, which he published in 1816, in one volume, and in 1822, a second edition, in two volumes. He had contemplated publishing a third edition; but his eyesight, which had failed by incessant application, deprived him of the honor, and the world of the benefit, of his increased learning and experience from the proposed work. His high reputation as a lecturer is spread all over the country by a succession of graduates of the college, who will transmit the praise of his learning and eloquence, and will rise up with one accord, and bless his name and memory.

On the 9th of August, 1809, Mr. Cleaveland was elected a member of the American Academy of Arts and Sciences; on the 9th of September, 1814, a corresponding member of the Academy of National Sciences at Philadelphia; on the 17th of April, 1818, a member of the American Philosophical Society at Philadelphia; on the 10th of November, the same year, an honorary member of the Literary and Philosophical Society of Newcastle-upon-Tyne; on the 30th of January, 1819, an honoary member of the Mineralogical Society at Jena; on the 4th of October, the same year, an honorary member of the Mineralogical Society of Dresden; on the 26th of April, 1823, a member of the Society of Natural Science at Halle, in Germany; on the 16th of December of the same year, a member of the Mineralogical Society of St. Petersburg; on the 11th of June, 1834, an honorary member of the Literary and Historical Society at Quebec. He was also a fellow of the Wernerian Society at Edinburgh, and the Geological Society of London; and was for many years the corresponding secretary of the Maine Historical Society. In 1824, the honorary degree of doctor of laws was conferred upon him by Bowdoin College.

Mr. Cleaveland married, 9 September, 1806, Martha, daughter of Levi and Martha (Ball) Bush, of Boston, she being then but nineteen years old; and they had issue: First, Moses Parker, born 6 July, 1807 (Bowd. C. 1827); married, 21 October, 1834, Martha Richardson, of Duxbury, Mass., and settled as a physician in Natick, Mass., where he died 7 October, 1840. Second, James Bowdoin, born 17 January, 1809 (Bowd. C. 1828); settled as a lawyer at Passadumkeag, Me.; married, 13 March, 1834, Lucinda P. McKinney, of Gray, Me.; and died in 1854. Third, George, born 22 September, 1810; and died 11 May, 1811. Fourth, Martha Ann Bush, born 16 July, 1812; married, 30 November, 1837, Hon. Peleg Whitman Chandler, of Boston (Bowd. C. 1834). Fifth, Elizabeth Abigail, born 4 September, 1814; married, 16 November, 1847, George W. Woodhouse, of Dover, N.H. Sixth, Mary Ackley, born 27 September, 1816. Seventh, John Appleton, born 29 March, 1819 (Bowd. C. 1840); married, 31 December, 1844, Catharine Alexander, of Brunswick. Eighth, Nathan Smith (Bowd. C. 1840), is a druggist in Brunswick.

In private life, Professor Cleaveland was universally respected for his unblemished moral character, his genial and affable disposition as a husband, a father, and a friend, and as a public-spirited and generous citizen. His wife died about 1852.

1802. — Solomon Kidder Livermore died in Milford, N.H., 10 July, 1859, aged 80. He was the youngest son of Rev. Jonathan (H.C. 1760) and Elizabeth (Kidder) Livermore, and was born in Wilton, N.H., 2 March, 1779. His father was born in Northborough, Mass., 7 December, 1739; was ordained at Wilton, 14 December, 1768; resigned his pastoral relation, February, 1777; and died in Wilton, 20 July, 1809, aged 69. His mother was a native of Billerica, Mass. Mr. Livermore was fitted for college at Mr. Pemberton's academy in Billerica, and entered the sophomore class in 1799. He graduated with a high reputation for scholarship in a class famed for eminent talent. After leaving college, he taught the grammar-school in Cambridge for one season. Having chosen the profession of law, he pursued his preparatory studies in the office of Oliver Crosby, Esq., of Dover, N.H. (H.C. 1795). On his admission to the bar, he opened an office in Dover, where he practised for a short time; but, in 1807, he removed to Milford, where he resided during the remainder of his life, pursuing the practice of the profession until he attained the age of 70 years, when he relinquished it, although he continued to transact business relating to the settlement of estates for his neighbors until near the end of his life. He was held in high estimation by the citizens of the town where he passed so large a portion of his life, who all regarded him as an honest man, and a sincere, devoted Christian, whom no temptation, no motives of self-interest, could turn from the straightforward path of duty. In the whole course of his long life, not a stain dimmed the pure lustre of his character for integrity. Having no ambition for political office or power, his extensive attainments did not achieve so wide a reputation as they might have won. Except when the merited confidence of his townsmen selected him to represent them in the state legislature, he uniformly declined to become a candidate for office; and yet no man was more strongly sensible of the grave duties of an American citizen than he. He was a devoted student of the Bible; and its pure precepts seemed to have stamped their own beauty upon his life, his thoughts, and his conduct. Far more anxious to promote the good of others than his own interest, he always endeavored to bring to an amicable adjustment the controversies among his neighbors. No one had a more generous heart or a more open home than he; and neither his benevolence nor his public spirit was ever appealed to in vain. His death was in harmony with his life. In the calm, still beauty of a bright summer's Sunday, in the quiet of his home, with its familiar and beloved objects and associations, the hymn of divine praise scarcely cold upon his aged lips, his life gently ebbed away, and his soul went forth to meet its Maker.

He married, 6 July, 1810, Abigail Adkins, youngest daughter of Nathaniel Jarvis, of Cambridge. She survived him. The offspring of this union were four sons and four daughters; of whom two — the eldest son and daughter — died early, two — the next oldest son and youngest daughter — died after attaining maturity, and four survived their father.

1802. — Rev. ICHABOD NICHOLS died in Cambridge, Mass., 2 January, 1859, aged 74. He was the fourth son of Capt. Ichabod and Lydia (Ropes) Nichols, of Salem, Mass., and was born in Portsmouth, N.H., during the temporary residence of the family at that place, 5 July, 1784; but removed with his parents to Salem when he was but five or six years old. He was fitted for college at the Salem High School; and graduated, at the age of eighteen, with the highest honors of his class, — a class remarkable for eminent talent. Immediately after leaving college, he began the study of theology with his pastor, Rev. Thomas Barnard, D.D. (H.C. 1766). In 1805, he was appointed tutor in mathematics in Harvard College; a position he held until 1809, pursuing in the mean time his theological studies. Here his opportunities for a higher cultivation were greatly enlarged; and his strong and acute intellectual powers could not fail to be richly improved in the society of Rev. Henry Ware, John Quincy Adams, Levi Frisbie, John Farrar, and Ashur Ware, who were all associated with him in the instruction of the college. In January, 1809, he preached his first sermon to the First Congregational Church and Society in Portland, Me.; and continued to preach for the three following Sundays. On the 27th of February, the parish concurred unanimously with the church in giving him a call, and voting him a salary of twelve hundred dollars; which was much larger than any minister received in the town or state (then a district), and which was not changed during his whole ministry. The venerable Deacon Freeman, then the leading man in the parish and the town, speaking of the occasion, exultingly said, "The meeting of the parish was full and respectable; and it is a pleasing circumstance, that there was not a hand raised nor a word spoken against the subject of either vote." The invitation he accepted 20 March, and he was ordained as colleague with the Rev. Samuel Deane, D.D. (H.C. 1760), 7 January, 1809, the third pastor of that ancient church, organized in 1727, the first in the state east of Kennebunk. The Rev. Thomas Smith (H.C. 1720), the first pastor, was born in Boston, 10 March, 1702; was ordained, and the church formed, 8 March, 1727; and he continued in the pastoral office until his death, 23 May, 1795, at the age of 93, and in the sixty-ninth year of his pastorate. Rev. Samuel Deane, born in Dedham, Mass., 30 August, 1733, was ordained as his colleague, 17 October, 1764; and this was the only religious society in Portland until 1788, when the Second Parish was established. Dr. Deane's pastorate continued fifty years; and was closed only by his death, 12 November, 1814, at the age of 81 years. With him Dr. Nichols was associated five years and five months; and his connection with the society, which was terminated by his death, extended to more than forty-nine years. He was sole pastor from the decease of Dr. Deane, diligently and faithfully doing his Master's work, until 31 January, 1855; when the present pastor, Rev. Horatio Stebbins (H.C. 1848), was settled as his colleague. Dr. Nichols was then desirous of withdrawing entirely from his official station, on account of the infirm state of his health: he wished entire repose from the cares of office. But the parish was unwilling to dissolve a connection which had existed so long and so harmoniously; and he consented to retain his official relation, relieved from all duty and responsibility connected with it. On his retirement, a few members of his society tendered to him an annuity of five hundred and fifty dollars for the remainder of his life; but this tribute to his services and worth, so justly deserved and so freely offered, he declined, from that innate sense of delicacy which governed all his conduct. At the time he relinquished his duties he removed from Portland to Cambridge, which was subsequently his place of residence. This brief review of the history of the First Parish in Portland exhibits the striking fact, of an uninterrupted ministration in the parochial office for a period of more than a hundred and thirty-one years, not an hour without a pastor; that its three deceased ministers entered young upon their ministry, and died in office; and that each has labored with a colleague. Such a history, in connection with the protracted pastorates, the three averaging fifty-six years each, cannot, we think, be paralleled in the annals of the church.

"Dr. Nichols," says an eminent writer who knew him long and intimately, "not only discharged the duties peculiar to his station with fidelity, — and in which, with advancing years, he grew more earnest and spiritual, both in his discourses and devotional exercises, — but he took an active part in the philanthropic and reformatory movements of the day. He was one of the earliest and most devoted friends of the temperance cause, of the Bible society, the Sunday school, and of benevolent institutions. He did not permit his mind to grow rusty amidst the various and every-day duties of parochial life, but devoted all his leisure hours to study. He published, in 1830, a work on natural theology, which is considered as classical authority in the theological schools. He kept up not only with the theological progress of the age, but also with the wonderful advance in scientific attainment, which, in the last half-century, has almost created a new world. Nothing in the way of discovery escaped his vigilant observation, from the theories broached by visionary enthusiasts to the profound problems of La Place, Cuvier, Bowditch, and Peirce. In his latter days, after leaving his parochial duties, he had the highest gratification in a free intercourse with Agassiz upon his wonderful developments in the animal kingdom. From this new source of knowledge, his mind received a fresh impulse; and he was able to add to his great work (now in press, and to be published in a few weeks, entitled "Hours with the Evangelists," on the connection of the old and new dispensations) new proofs and illustrations of the being and attributes of God. He was equally familiar with the writings of German and English scholars, and penetrated with a clear discrimination and an unswerving love of truth into the prevailing fallacies of the philosophies of the day; and was able rightly to divine the word of truth. It is impossible that a mind naturally keen and comprehensive, and which was so thoroughly furnished by education and reflection, should not be full and instructive on all the topics which come under discussion among scholars and in the social circle. This copiousness of general knowledge gave him great power and interest in conversation, which few have surpassed. No one could be in his society, for even a brief time, without being deeply impressed with the largeness and variety of his knowledge, and his ease and felicity in the communication of it. Yet, with these rare powers, he was perfectly simple, unaffected, and unpretending. No man was farther from conceit and unpretending display. He loved to talk, not for the sake of talking, but to communicate instruction; to impart from his accumulated stores to the pleasure and benefit of others. These qualities made his society to be sought, and, wherever he was known, to be valued as a ripe and good scholar, an able and sound theologian, and a most instructive companion. We may apply to him, with great appropriateness, a truth happily expressed by Lord Coke, who said, 'When a great and learned man dyeth, much learning dyeth with him.' Though he has left a valuable legacy in his last great work, which he fondly called the rounding-off of his life, and is the complement of his learning and best thought, yet there was that in his mind and heart, as in every wise man, which cannot be stamped on the printed page: it dies with the possessor. The beautiful expression, the mild and gentle demeanor, the sensitive appreciation and communication of the good and true, the noble example of a virtuous and devoted life, — these all pass on, and leave but their subtle fragrance in the memory of surviving friends."

Dr. Nichols was early elected a member of the American Academy of Arts and Sciences, of which he held the office of vice-president. In 1821, he received from Bowdoin College the honorary degree of doctor of divinity, and the same from Harvard in 1831. It is worthy of note, that the year 1821 was the beginning of the academical honors at Bowdoin; and a wise as well as liberal beginning it was. The clerical distinction was given (and to them confined) to the two distinguished lights of the Portland pulpit, — Ichabod Nichols and Edward Payson; regarded, no doubt, throughout the state as the representative heads of the two opposing sections of its congregational body.

Dr. Nichols married first, probably in the spring of 1811, Dorothea F. Gilman, daughter of Gov. John Taylor Gilman, of Portsmouth, N.H. They had four children, all sons, of whom two survived him; viz., 1. John Taylor Gilman, who died within about a year of his birth. 2. George Henry, born

26 August, 1814 (H.C. 1833); a physician in Standish, Me. 3. John Taylor Gilman, born 24 April, 1817 (H.C. 1836); settled as a clergyman in Saco, Me. 4. Charles, born 12 April, 1819, and died the same year. Dr. Nichols's wife died 17 April, 1831; and he married for his second wife, 3 May, 1832, Martha Salisbury Higginson, daughter of Stephen Higginson, Esq., of Cambridge. She survived him.

1803. — William Draper, of Pontiac, Mich., died at the Island of Mackinaw, 9 August, 1858, aged 78. He was son of James and Lois (Battle) Draper, and was born in that part of Dedham which is now within the limits of Dover, Mass., 12 February, 1780. He was fitted for college partly by Rev. Nathaniel Emmons, D.D. (Y.C. 1767), of Franklin, Mass., and partly by Rev. Thomas Thacher (H.C. 1775), of Dedham. On leaving college, he went to Concord, Mass., and entered as a student-at-law in the office of John Leighton Tuttle (H.C. 1796). Having completed his legal studies and been admitted to the bar, he opened an office in Marlborough, Mass., where he acquired an extensive practice, and was quite successful as a lawyer. For ten years he was president of the Middlesex bar. In 1832, he removed to Nashua, N.H., where he remained until the spring of 1833; when he went to Michigan, established himself in Pontiac, and was a citizen of that place during the remainder of his life. He occupied a prominent and distinguished position in the legal profession; but was no politician, and held but very few offices during his life. At the time Congress passed the enabling act for the admission of Michigan into the Union, a convention was called under that act, that the people might determine whether they would accede to the proposition of Congress or not. Mr. Draper was the president of the convention. This was the first one, which rejected the dishonorable proposition of a democratic congress; and Mr. Draper always looked with great satifaction on the part he took in that body of men. That was an honorable post, and right honorable was the decision.

Mr. Draper was president of the bar of Oakland county, Mich., for twenty years, and held the office at the time of his decease. While few of the high earthly honors were bestowed upon him, he had, what was far better, the deserved esteem and respect of every one who knew him. He was a Christian gentleman, scrupulously upright, and for twenty-five years was an exemplary member of the Congregational church in Pontiac. He retained his mental faculties to an extraordinary degree. About two years before his death, there was a case pending in the Circuit Court of Michigan, in which he had a personal interest. He wrote out, and read to the court, a brief and an argument of marked power and great research; and was successful at last.

Mr. Draper was famed for his love of field sports; and it was his delight, in the last years of his life, to hunt and fish in and around the beautiful lakes that are so numerous in the vicinity of his late residence; and the principal reason of his visit to Mackinac, where he died, was his desire to gratify his taste in this respect. He went with several acquaintances; and had been there only a few days, when he was taken sick; and, before any of his family could reach there after hearing of his illness, his spirit had departed to another and better world.

A writer in Porter's "New-York Spirit of the Times," in announcing the death of Mr. Draper, says, "He was ever active and assiduous through his early life, and until he had acquired a competence in the practice of his arduous profession; but was never so thoroughly absorbed in it, nor in the acquisition of wealth, as to neglect his gun and his rod. To these he gave a liberal share of his time, with a keenness of relish which evinced that the love of sport was natural and inborn. He was not an indiscriminate sportsman; for he cared but little for the rifle or the hound, and looked upon the deer-chase with no favorable eye. His first loves were the fowling-piece and the well-trained pointer and spaniel; his chosen sphere of enjoyment the rich summer corn-field, or the brown hill-side covers of autumn. *Scolopax* was the bird of his choice; and, more than half a century ago, the echoes of his gun, and the cheerful call to his well-trained dogs, were wont to ring through the valleys of the old Bay State. The love of sport was a marked feature in the life of the deceased, from which his highest earthly enjoyments were derived; so marked and influential indeed, that when, after a time, mercenary pot-hunters had depopulated the region about his house, that circumstance influenced him in no slight degree in making choice of a home where the woodcock, snipe, plover, partridge, quail, and prairie-hen were more abundant, and less sought after for gain. How fresh in the mind of the writer of this notice, now in middle life, is the recollection, when a mere boy, of the exploits of the deceased over the backs of poor old Sport and Sancho, and the almost boundless admiration with which we saw him bring down thirty-eight woodcocks in succession on the Southborough meadow, without missing a bird; killing more than once with both barrels! In his earlier days, while he yet made Massachusetts his home, his associates, drawn to him by similar tastes, were to be found among the liberal and prominent men throughout that state. Of such were Hon. S. P. P. Fay, some years deceased, and long judge of probate for the county of Middlesex; his son, Hon. Richard S. Fay; Hon. Franklin Dexter, late of Boston; and very many others, whose names, once familiar, have now escaped the writer. Having changed his residence to Michigan, Mr. Draper continued the same keen and indefatigable sportsman, with little change; except that, game being more plenty and in greater variety, his days in the field were more frequent. He found fewer woodcocks, which, at the time of his arrival, had just begun to frequent the bottom-lands of the rivers, and the old French farms of Wayne and Macomb; but in their places he found the prairie-hen, the wild-turkey, the partridge and snipe, more abundant. He brought with him his small but excellent and well-chosen armament of guns, his choice stock of ammunition, and his favorite and reliable old dogs, which, in a short time, made themselves at home in their new sphere. The rod divided the sway with the gun in the sport-life of the deceased, and he was alike skilful and successful in both. If the day was bad for shooting, it was pretty sure to be good for fishing; or, if the companions who offered happened not to be devotees of old Izaak, the game-bag and the long tramp were all the same to him. Sport-love with the deceased did not arise from a mere spirit of adventure, combined with the exuberance of wealth and of animal spirits: it was a principle of his being, which grew, rather than failed, with advancing age; and yielded to no infirmity of body short of absolute sickness. Indeed, he may be said to have almost died in harness; for his last trip was undertaken by him that he might enjoy the choice sport of trout-fishing around the picturesque and beautiful Island of Mackinaw, at a time when declining years and failing strength had long since warned him that the hours upon the earth for him were short and few. Thus, with the life of a thorough sportsman, ended that of an honorable, useful man, and a sincere and exemplary Christian."

Mr. Draper married, in 1810, Harriet Eliza Payne, a daughter of Major Phineas Payne, of Concord, Mass., of revolutionary memory. They had six children, — four sons and two daughters; namely, William, Charles, Albert F., James, Eliza C., and Ann M.: all survived their father except James, who was the youngest child. Charles graduated at Harvard College in 1833, and became a lawyer in Pontiac.

1805. — Rev. EBENEZER HUBBARD died near Nashville, Tenn., 2 September, 1858, aged 74. He was son of Rev. Ebenezer (H.C. 1777) and Abigail (Glover) Hubbard, and was born in Marblehead, Mass., 12 November, 1783. His father was born in Concord, Mass., 22 May, 1758; was ordained at Marblehead, 1 January, 1783; and died 15 December, 1800, aged 42. His mother was daughter of Col. Jonathan Glover, of Marblehead. Mr. Hubbard was fitted for college at the public classical school or academy in Marblehead. After leaving college, he studied divinity with Rev. Timothy Flint, of Lunenburg, Mass. (H.C. 1800), who married his sister Abigail. He was ordained pastor of the Second Church in Newbury, Mass., 11 May, 1809. This pastoral relation was dissolved 16 October, 1810; and he was installed over the church in Middleton, Mass., 27 November, 1816; resigned his charge, 29 April, 1828; was installed at Lunenburg, 10 December, 1828. He was always a Trinitarian, as he declared, and, as he called himself, a moderate Calvinist; but was very liberal in his feelings towards Unitarians, and would not infrequently exchange with clergymen of that denomination. In consequence of this, a most unrighteous attempt was made, by some of the more rigid Orthodox, to prevent his settlement at Lunenburg, by circulating reports injurious to his moral character. They did not, however, succeed in their plot. The following extract from an article in the "Christian Examiner" for March, 1831, gives a history of this affair: —

"Rev. Mr. Hubbard, a minister of acknowledged Orthodox sentiments, and late pastor of the church in Middleton, was invited to a re-settlement in Lunenburg. It was generally known to his ministerial brethren, that he was in the practice of exchanging with Unitarians. This circumstance alone induced some Orthodox preachers in the vicinity of Lunenburg to make great exertions to prevent his installation. They went to Andover, and earnestly solicited from the Orthodox ministers in the neighborhood of Middleton some information derogatory to the character of Mr. Hubbard. False and slanderous reports were invented by an individual in Middleton, and communicated to an Orthodox minister in Danvers, and conveyed by him to the principal agent in this unrighteous work. Rev. Mr. Payson, of Leominster, having obtained the desired misrepresentations, went into Lunenburg, communicated them to an influential family, and requested them to put them in circulation, and conceal the name of the informer. He affirmed that Mr. Hubbard was a bad man, brought up his children to swear, and would prove a curse to the society if they retained him as their pastor. Such reports threw the parish into consternation, and reached the ears of the pastor elect. He proceeded immediately to the source of the evil, and eventually dragged to light the individuals concerned. By the terrors of the civil law, he compelled them to confess their wickedness, and agency in the base understanding."

Mr. Hubbard continued pastor of the church in Lunenburg until 20 November, 1833, when his connection with the society was dissolved. He studied medicine, but never practised regularly, except, perhaps, in Boxford, or rather in Lunenburg, while he was a pastor there. In June, 1838, he removed to the West, and taught school for a while in Trenton, Tenn.; and afterwards in Paris, Tenn. In 1843 or 1844, he removed to Fulton county, Ky., and settled on a farm in Hickman, which a son, dying, left him, and which he called "Clergyman's Retreat." For some years he pursued the farming business, overseeing it, and attending to his garden: while in his leisure hours he read books and wrote sermons; preaching sometimes, but having no charge. He liked the investigation of literary and scientific subjects. He gradually, for three or four years before his death, became irritable and maniacal under a disease of the brain (probably softening), until, in the spring of 1858, his mind was completely gone, so that he did not know his own wife and children; and, becoming very furious, his sons took him, in June, 1858, to the state asylum for the insane, six miles out of Nashville, Tenn., — a fine institution; where he died, not having had, during his stay there, one lucid moment.

Mr. Hubbard married, 10 June, 1808, Charlotte, daughter of Major Joseph Swazey, of Ipswich, Mass. They had nine children, six sons and three daughters, of whom three sons and two daughters are living. His wife died 30 October, 1858, in the seventy-fifth year of her age, having survived her husband not quite two months. The remains of Mr. Hubbard were conveyed to Hickman, and deposited in the family cemetery with his wife's, at "Clergyman's Retreat," owned by his son Charles.

1807. — Joshua Prescott died in Reading, Mass., 1 January, 1859, aged 78. He was son of Deacon John and Martha (Abbot) Prescott; was born in Westford, Mass., 15 November, 1780; and was the last surviving member of their family, which consisted of six sons and one daughter, who lived to mature age. Three of the sons graduated at Harvard College, — Samuel in 1799, Aaron in 1814, and the subject of this notice. He was fitted for college at Westford Academy. After graduating, he taught school in Saco, Me. He studied law with Judge James Prescott, of Groton, Mass. (H.C. 1788).

He was admitted to the bar in the spring of 1811, and immediately opened an office in Reading. He afterwards removed to Lynn, Mass., where he remained a few months; then returned to Reading, where he continued actively engaged in the practice of his profession until a few years before his decease. In 1824, he compiled a digest of the probate-laws of Massachusetts, which was considered a valuable work, and had an extensive circulation. In 1827 and 1828, he was chosen representative to the state legislature. Being much interested in agricultural pursuits, he superintended and cultivated successfully his farm, on which he resided for many years. As a citizen, and in all the social relations of life, he was kind, generous, hospitable; an honest man, and one who commanded the universal respect of the people. He never sought public office. As a lawyer, he was possessed of a sound and discriminating mind; always carefully and thoroughly examining the matter presented before he came to a conclusion. His judgment and opinion were received with great respect and confidence. He never suffered himself to sacrifice his principles of honor and integrity for pecuniary advantages; always maintaining, that a lawyer should govern himself professionally as he would as a citizen, and be guided by the rule, to do unto others as you wish or expect them to do unto you. His faith as a Christian in the unbounded love and goodness of God was firm and unwavering, and he awaited his departure with calmness and resignation. He married, in 1813, Abigail Eaton, only daughter and only surviving child of Lieut. Thomas Eaton, of Reading. He had five children. One daughter died in early infancy. Two sons and two daughters are now living. His wife is also living.

1807.—Rev. Seth Freeman Swift died in Oswego, N.Y., 12 October, 1858, aged 71. He was son of Joseph and Anna (Freeman) Swift, and was born in Sandwich, Mass., 25 April, 1787. He was fitted for college at Sandwich Academy. After leaving college, he went through a course of theological studies under the instruction of Rev. John Simpkins, of Brewster, Mass. (H.C. 1786). In the spring of 1809, he went to

Nantucket, where, for a short time, he taught a school of a high order. The Unitarians of that island, having in view the promotion of their liberal religious principles, erected the present South Congregational Church, and invited Mr. Swift to take the pastoral charge of the new society. The house was dedicated in November, 1809; and Mr. Swift, having accepted the call, was ordained 25 April, 1810. Here he labored with great fidelity for more than twenty-three years. Many of his parishioners passed away before him; but many still survive who remember him as one whose ministrations were always acceptable, because always appropriate to the various circumstances of human life. The young of his society would often, at his invitation, assemble at his house, where he would entertain them, and make them feel at home: always cheerful; welcoming them with a genial smile; taking a deep interest in their well-doing; sharing their joys and sorrows; offering counsel, that, if followed, he was certain would result in the formation of high and noble characters, as many to whom it was addressed are left to testify. He always said the right word; and it came from a warm, sympathetic heart. No one tied the nuptial knot with more grace than he. His beaming countenance brightened the joy of the occasion. In sadder hours, his apt words brought consolation to the mourner; and, in the ordinary course of life, he was a genial friend. In the autumn of 1833, he resigned his pastoral charge; and, the following winter, he was a representative from Nantucket, in the legislature. In the spring of 1834, he removed to Oswego, N.Y., and was principal of an academy at that place for two years. For the last eight years of his life he was incapacitated from any employment, in consequence of having become blind. After his removal from Nantucket, he ever retained a lively interest for the place. A few months before his death, he received a letter from a friend there, reverting to the past, calling up early memories, and speaking of his friends; and, when he found he was not forgotten, he wept like a child, showing how deeply his affections were rooted in his early home.

He married, 20 March, 1810, Valina Rawson, daughter of

Abel and Lydia (Briggs) Rawson, of New York. He had four children, — Caroline, who married Philo Stevens, of Oswego, N.Y.; Edward, Joseph, and Charles. His daughter and two sons survived him; as did also his widow. His last sickness was of short duration, but of great suffering, which he bore without a murmur. His disease was cancerous tumor in the bowels. At the time of his death he resided with his daughter, whose unceasing devotions to him were indicative of the purest affection. His son Edward too, who is well settled in Savannah, Ga., was permitted to be with him to administer to his comfort even in his last moments.

1808. — Hon. NATHANIEL WRIGHT died in Lowell, Mass., 5 November, 1858, aged 73. He was the oldest son of Hon. Thomas and Eunice (Osgood) Wright, and was born in Sterling, Mass., 13 February, 1785. He was fitted for college by Rev. Reuben Holcomb, of Sterling (Y.C. 1774). He held a very respectable rank in his class, and graduated with distinction. He pursued the study of the law in the office of Hon. Asahel Stearns, of Chelmsford, Mass. (H.C. 1797); was admitted to the bar in 1814, and opened an office in Dracut, Mass. In 1816, Mr. Stearns was elected University Professor of Law in Harvard College, and removed to Cambridge the following year. Mr. Wright succeeded to Mr. Stearns's office, and to much of his professional business; and subsequently purchased his (Mr. Stearns's) residence, which he occupied during the remainder of his life. He attained to a high rank in his profession as an able and well-read lawyer. For forensic display he had little taste, and made no pretension; but when an emergency required a sound, reliable, and disinterested opinion, he was the dependence of his community for many years. Singularly simple and almost blunt in his manners, and sparing of words, there was an honesty and independence about him which won confidence and secured respect. On the organization of the town of Lowell, Mr. Wright's judgment, counsel, and legal knowledge were under great and constant requisition. He performed an important part in the preliminary purchase of land by the founders of the town; and, in setting it off from Chelms-

ford, he was an efficient agent. When Lowell was incorporated as a town, in 1826, he was elected its first representative in the legislature, and was re-elected the two following years. He was also chosen chairman of the first board of selectmen. In 1834, he was elected to the state senate from Middlesex district. In 1836, Lowell was incorporated as a city; and Mr. Wright was elected its mayor in 1841 and 1842. He was chosen the first year as an independent candidate, and the second as the regular whig nominee. On the organization of the Lowell Bank, in 1828, he was elected, on the second of June in that year, its president; an office which he held uninterruptedly for more than thirty years, resigning it only on the 22d of October, 1858, just two weeks before his death: his failing health and strength admonishing him that his work on earth was done; a fact to which he resigned himself with calmness and cheerfulness. In all the positions which he filled, he gave entire satisfaction to those whose interests were intrusted to his care. He married, 5 March, 1820, Laura Hoar. They had five children, four sons and one daughter; viz., Nathaniel, Thomas, William Henry Prentice, Emery, and Laura Grace. Two of his sons, Nathaniel and Thomas, graduated at Harvard College, in 1838 and 1842 respectively. Nathaniel was a lawyer in Lowell, and died 18 September, 1847, aged 27. The others survived him. Thomas is a lawyer in Lawrence, Mass. Mr. Wright's wife died 21 January, 1857, aged 62.

1810.—Rev. LEMUEL CAPEN died in South Boston, 28 August, 1858, aged 69. He was son of John and Patience (Davis) Capen, and was born in Dorchester, Mass., 25 November, 1789. His father was a substantial farmer: and, early discovering in this son a taste for study, he determined to give him a liberal education; for which purpose he placed him under the charge of Rev. Peter Whitney, of Quincy (H.C. 1801), where he pursued his preparatory studies. At college he was exemplary in his conduct, was a diligent student, and graduated with a respectable rank. On completing his collegiate course, he determined to study for the ministry, and remained at Cambridge as a resident-graduate, going through his

course of theological study under the instruction of Prof. Henry Ware, D.D. (H.C. 1785), and Andrews Norton (H.C. 1804). He was ordained pastor of the church in Sterling, Mass., 22 March, 1815. He early espoused the side of Liberal Christianity, and was one of the first to preach these sentiments in the county of Worcester. In 1813, he wrote a pamphlet, which was published anonymously, entitled "Memorial of the Proprietors of the New South Meeting-house in Dorchester to the Ministers of the Boston Association;" a document which even the "Panoplist" acknowledged to be "written with more than ordinary care and ability." His pastoral relation with the church in Sterling was not of long duration. He resigned his charge, 21 June, 1819, not on account of any disaffection, but because his salary was inadequate to his frugal wants, and it could not be increased without endangering the harmony of the society. His farewell sermon, which has been twice printed, was full of the kindest interest in the people who were to be no longer under his professional charge. He then returned to his native place, Dorchester; and, from 1819 to 1822, he taught in the Stoughton School in that town. At the close of 1822, he resumed his ministerial duties, at the same time taking the part of instructor in the Hawes School in South Boston. He was installed pastor of the Hawes-Place Church, 31 October, 1827. During the interval from 1822 to 1827, he received no pecuniary compensation for his clerical services. He depended upon his salary as a teacher, which was only about five hundred dollars a year, for the support of himself and his family. All this while, and for several years afterwards, the public worship was held in one of the humblest of meeting-houses. The building was ten feet high, about a hundred feet long, and less than thirty in breadth. Under that lowly roof, he labored, in the preaching of the Word, faithfully, earnestly, and with good acceptance, for about twelve years. In 1832, he was called to part with his venerable friend, Mr. John Hawes, the founder of the religious society to which he ministered; and set forth, on the Sunday after his funeral, a discriminating account of his character and benefactions. This discourse was published, with an

"Appendix containing Historical Notices of the Hawes-Place Church and Society." That sturdy and trusty Christian man, who has left his name so favorably impressed upon the religious and educational institutions of South Boston, invariably treated Mr. Capen with the utmost confidence and regard, and consulted him often to the day of his death. Soon after his departure, and by the help of the funds which he bequeathed, a new meeting-house was built; but with the enlargement of the borders of the sanctuary, and the beautifying of its walls, and the increased comeliness of its appointments, there seems to have been no corresponding increase of the holy dispositions for which sanctuaries are built. It is often the case, that moneyed endowments lead to neither prosperty nor peace; and, in the present instance, they encouraged jealousies, expectations more ambitious than pure or considerate, and growing troubles. Mr. Capen again resigned his pastorate, with less of his own will in the surrender than before, and not with the same consciousness of perfect favor, though he carried a better consciousness in the testimony of his own breast. He delivered his farewell sermon, 23 June, 1839. It was written in his usual direct, dispassionate, and faithful manner. He never afterwards entered the settled ministry, though his heart was always in that work; and he continued, to the end of his days, preaching occasionally where his services were requested. During his whole residence at South Boston, the scantiness of his income compelled him to till his grounds with his own hands; and this he did stoutly and cheerfully. His vigorous health, which never gave way, nor showed sign of giving way, till it broke up wholly and at every point at last, enabled him to perform this kind of toil; and, moreover, he had a taste for it, and skill in it. He knew how to do the work of a farmer well, and to write about its experiences. His opinions on agricultural topics, in his contributions to the "New-England Farmer," are said to have been valued by the readers of that journal. In the midst of his pecuniary straits, no one ever knew him to be penurious or exacting or cringing or shuffling or mean. Some of the pleasantest associations of his whole existence he declared to be connected with school-keeping; and there were many to appreciate the influence of his conscientious instructions. He was often called to serve on school-committees, where he gave the best of his diligence. He was elected a representative to the state legislature in 1836, and again in 1847. When he was nearly sixty years of age, the old zeal for both his vocations, teaching and preaching, burned afresh in him. At an invitation from Baltimore to succeed Rev. Charles H. A. Dall (H.C. 1837) as a missionary to the poor, he at once left his home, — to no one dearer, — and assumed that laborious service in that southern city. A printed copy of his first quarterly report, dated 31 January, 1846, is marked with the deepest feeling of engagedness in his trying office. The singleness of his mind, and the tenderness of his heart, were likely to distinguish themselves in such a mingled work of instruction and charity; and the trustees of the Baltimore Ministry at Large bear ample testimony, in the same document, to the efficiency with which his hard duties were discharged. Besides his publications which have been mentioned, there is in the "Liberal Preacher" a sermon of his on "The Religious Education of Children," printed in June, 1831; and there is an elaborate article in the "Christian Examiner" for September, 1855, on "Dr. Codman and the Second Church in Dorchester." He was also the writer of several biographical notices of ministers and of old residents in South Boston, which have been read with interest, and even republished.

He married, 11 October, 1815, Mary Ann Hunting, daughter of Asa and Abigail (Blaney) Hunting, of Roxbury. They had nine children, six sons and three daughters, of whom five sons and one daughter with their mother survived him. His children were Francis Lemuel, born in Sterling, 17 March, 1817; John, born 8 September, 1818; Mary Ann, born in Dorchester, 19 February, 1820, — died 7 November, 1844; Edward, born 20 October, 1821; Charles James, born in South Boston, 5 April, 1823; Sarah Hawes, born 22 October, 1824, — died 5 December, 1825; Barnard, born 31 October, 1826; Jane, born 5 November, 1828; Eliphalet Porter, born 14 November, 1831,—died 19 November, 1835. Four of his sons have graduated at Harvard College; namely, Francis Lemuel in 1839, John in 1840, Edward in 1842, and Charles James in 1844.

1811.—Hon. THOMAS GREAVES CARY, of Boston, died at his summer residence in Nahant, Mass., 3 July, 1859, aged 67. He was son of Samuel and Sarah (Gray) Cary, and was born in Chelsea, Mass., 7 September, 1791. After finishing his college course, he studied law in the office of Hon. Peter Oxenbridge Thacher (H.C. 1796), of Boston. He was admitted to the Suffolk bar in 1814, and began the practice of his profession in Boston. He married, 30 May, 1820, Mary Ann C. Perkins, daughter of Hon. Thomas Handasyd Perkins, of Boston. They had seven children, two sons and five daughters, all of whom, with their mother, survived him. A short time before his marriage, he removed to Brattleborough, Vt., where he continued the practice of his profession until 1821, when he removed to New York, and engaged in the Canton trade as the senior partner in the house of T. G. and W. F. Cary. After eight or nine years, he returned to Boston, and joined the house of J. and T. H. Perkins and Co. After the dissolution of this firm, Mr. Cary became the treasurer of the Hamilton and Appleton manufacturing companies at Lowell, the affairs of which he managed, with great ability and success, to the day of his death. In 1838, he became a special partner in the house of Fay and Farwells, of Boston. This partnership continued until the dissolution of the firm in 1851. He was often solicited to allow himself to be a candidate for political honors; but he generally declined. He, however, served as a senator for the Suffolk district in the state legislature in 1846, 1847, 1852, and 1853. In his political opinions and action he was wholly free from a blind partisan spirit. Though conservative in his tendencies, he was a consistent and able advocate of real progress. He took a great interest in all questions of education and social reform, and carried through the legislature several of the most important acts on those subjects now on the statute-book; as, for example, the law relating to state scholarships. He was for many years a director of the Hamilton Bank, and president of the Boston

Athenæum. He was also a trustee of the Institution for the Blind; and took an active interest in many other charitable establishments, giving to their affairs both pecuniary support and much valuable time. He was a member of the American Academy of Arts and Sciences, and of the Massachusetts Historical Society. He frequently contributed able essays to the newspapers and the periodical publications. Hunt's "Merchants' Magazine," the "North-American Review," and several of the daily journals, were enriched by his elegant and well-considered writings. In 1847, he delivered before the city authorities of Boston the Fourth-of-July oration, which was published, and which showed the refined taste, high moral tone, and purity of style, that were peculiarly characteristic of him. He published, in 1844, "A Letter to a Lady in France on National and State Repudiation;" in 1845, "A Letter on Profits on Manufactures in Lowell," and "An Address on the Fine Arts, delivered before the Mercantile-Library Association." In the same year he delivered a lecture on banking, in which the subject was explained with great perspicuity and beauty. In 1856, besides a "Lecture on the Gold of California, and its Effects on Prices," he published the most elaborate of his works, entitled "A Memoir of Thomas Handasyd Perkins, containing Extracts from his Diaries and Letters," in 8vo; a volume of great biographical interest, presenting a masterly delineation of the life and character of that great merchant. In February, 1857, he embarked with his family for Europe; and having travelled through England, France, Italy, and Switzerland, returned, in October of the same year, to resume his various occupations at home. His health, which had not been vigorous for some years, began to give way a few months before his death. He gradually grew feebler; and, during the last week or two of his life, his decline was rapid, and he breathed his last as gently as a child falls asleep. Mr. Cary was a gentleman in the truest and best sense of the word. His manners were at once unaffected, and marked by a chivalrous high breeding, recognizing the rights of the lowest as well as those of the highest to the courtesies which sweeten the intercourse of life. In thought, word, and deed, his daily intercourse was characterized by Christian purity. Into the transactions of business, public and private, as well as into the intercourse of society and the domestic relations, he carried the principles of Christianity, as the rule of conversation, the guide of conduct, and the assurance of happiness here and hereafter.

1814. — JONATHAN PORTER died in Medford, Mass., 11 June, 1859, aged 67. He had been confined to his sick-room for more than a quarter of a century. A disease, which no skill could remove, embarrassed and afflicted him for a time, while struggling to continue his active labors; and at length compelled him, in the midst of his days, to abandon his pursuits, and shut himself up as an invalid for the rest of his life. His expectations were thus disappointed, his plans broken up, and his work left unfinished. The story of his life, though brief, is not without interest. He was son of Jonathan and Phebe (Abbot) Porter, and was born in Medford, 13 November, 1791. His father was a merchant in Medford: his mother was a native of Andover, Mass. He married, 22 July, 1823, Catharine Gray, daughter of Samuel Gray, of Medford. They had three children, one son and two daughters. One daughter died in his lifetime. His wife and the other two children survived him. Until he reached the age of about sixteen or seventeen, he was employed, as far as he had any employment, as a clerk in his father's store. It was found that he had no taste for mercantile pursuits; but from an early age he had discovered a fondness for books and study, and desired to obtain an education. When about seventeen years old, having up to that time enjoyed only the ordinary advantages of common schools, he began to prepare for college under the instruction of Dr. John Hosmer, who was the principal of a private school or academy in Medford. He prosecuted his studies at this school for about a year; and then entered Harvard College at Commencement in 1810. His class was large for that time; and is now distinguished by the eminent abilities, high position, and great fame, of some whose names stand upon its catalogue. That it possessed a large range and amount of talent, is evident from the number of its members who have obtained an honorable rank in their several callings and pursuits. In this class, and with these associates, Mr. Porter, as a scholar, stood among the first, and graduated with the highest honors. He was earnest and assiduous in the prosecution of his studies, faithful in the performance of all his duties, and exemplary in all his habits. His generous and manly bearing in the severe contests of the literary arena won for him the esteem and friendship of his classmates, which continued to the close of his life, and cheered the many long years of his feebleness and confinement. He cherished good-will toward all; rejoiced at their success, and bore with meekness his own. When he reached the end of his college term, and looked forward to the future, the prospect was bright and hopeful. His college honors seemed an earnest of other and higher, to be won on a wider field. He chose the law for a profession; and pursued his preparatory studies a part of the time in the office of the Hon. Luther Lawrence (H.C. 1801), of Groton, and a part in the office of the Hon. Asahel Stearns (H.C. 1797), of Chelmsford. They were both able and eminent lawyers, and stood high in public estimation. They were also gentlemen of high moral character, upright in all their dealings, and honorable in all their practice. Mr. Porter was a worthy pupil of such teachers, and in these schools acquired all which could be expected to be acquired in the time, — an accurate knowledge of the general principles of law, and sound professional ethics. He was admitted to the bar in the county of Middlesex in the fall of 1817, and opened an office, at first in Medford, and about a year afterwards in Boston. His intellectual endowments were well suited to the study of the law as a science. His mind was acute, discriminating, and logical; and his memory was retentive and ready. A patient, persevering, and critical investigation was to him an agreeable exercise; and he was unwilling to relinquish a subject, once taken in hand, until it was mastered and exhausted. He took pleasure in working out, with steady, patient thought, and thorough, laborious research, perplexed and difficult questions of law. He read much; and his legal learning was accurate and entensive. There can be no doubt that he was capable of reaching a high rank as a lawyer. But the practice of the law, as a business, was not so well suited to his tastes and habits. He was a scholar, fond of books and study and retirement, but had no fondness for the turmoil and strife, the "pert dispute" and "babbling hall," of professional practice. Still he had considerable business, which was always well and faithfully managed. He argued some questions of law before the Supreme Court with decided ability. He was patient, laborious, and conscientiously scrupulous and exact in the performance of all his duties. In his professional as in his private life, he was just and upright, and incapable of any unworthy artifice or trick. His principles and practice were pure, elevated, and honorable. He did not, upon coming to the bar, as is too often the case with men of the law, relinquish all attention to liberal studies. The classics still continued to be his companions. So far as he could command the time, he continued his application to general literature, and was a diligent student of metaphysics, mathematics, and the exact sciences. In 1822, he delivered the oration before the Phi Beta Kappa at Cambridge. At that time, he was in feeble health. His infirmity was such, that he thought, from time to time, that he should be obliged to relinquish the task he had undertaken; but he struggled on to the fulfilment of his engagement. Of the literary merit of his performance we have not been informed, and have no knowledge; but are apprised of the fact, that the oration was prepared and delivered under much bodily weakness and suffering. In 1830, the complaint which clung to him ever afterwards made its presence known. In the summer of that year, he made a voyage to Europe, in the hope of improving his health. In the spring of 1831, he returned with his health apparently somewhat improved. But, soon after resuming his business, the disease gained strength, and became more alarming. Now succeeded a period of much anxiety and suffering. He still hoped that recovery to health was possible, and was earnest and persevering in the use of means to that end. At times he would seem to be improved, and be encouraged; he would then become worse, and fall into despondency. So he continued on, hoping and desponding, until at length he was compelled to settle down in the conviction, that there was no prospect of his restoration to health, and that his professional and all other active pursuits must be finally and for ever relinquished. Then began a distinct and peculiar period of his life. His complaint was supposed to be a spinal affection, the precise character and extent of which was never fully ascertained. The disease gradually increased, until it deprived him of the power of moving about; and he was obliged to remain constantly in a lying or sitting posture. In this condition he remained to the end of life. Until within a year or two of his decease, he was, from time to time, subject to much pain and suffering. All the alleviation which the most affectionate and untiring attention and efforts of his family could afford he had. When all hope of recovery or amendment was extinguished, he became perfectly resigned to his condition. There was never the slightest murmuring or discontent or impatience or dejection. He was calm and cheerful, and grateful for the many mercies he enjoyed. His chamber was not shrouded in gloom, but lighted up with the mild and cheering rays of contentment and peace. He felt that the best place, the happiest place, the most honorable place, for him, was his own place, the place which Providence had assigned him. In that place he was willing and happy to remain until removed to another state of existence. Though his body was feeble, his mind retained its activity and vigor. Though confined within the narrow limits of his own room, his life was not an idle one, or without significance. For some years, he was constantly occupied in the education of his children; an employment which he greatly enjoyed, and for which he was admirably qualified. The daughters were wholly and thoroughly educated by him. He was himself, at all times, a diligent student, and never unoccupied. He was particularly fond of Greek literature, and took much interest in reading the Greek poets and historians. He was also a good English scholar; read extensively moral and religious works, and kept along with the current literature of the day. He enjoyed the visits of his friends, and took an interest in whatever interested them or the public. He saw with pleasure, and without repining, his classmates successful in the world, and winning the prizes of life. For himself, he was entirely content with his own little spot, as the theatre of his action. Thus year after year wore away, and the time of his departure drew on. There was no suffering, no new complaint, no apparent increase of the old one. His strength gradually failed; he was confined to his bed; he lost the power of speech, though evidently conscious of what was passing around him; his pulse stopped, but he still breathed: at length his lungs ceased to heave, and he ceased to live.

Mr. Porter gave ample evidence of a high order of intellectual endowments. He had a calm, well-balanced, active, and vigorous mind, an ardent desire of knowledge, and firm and unwavering moral and religious principles. Thus qualified, he might well be expected to achieve much in any field of intellectual labor. But he was suddenly stopped in his course, and his work remains incomplete. His manners were simple, unassuming, and courteous; and his feelings were liberal, social, and obliging. He was a steadfast and true-hearted friend. He loved his friends, and secured their enduring affection. His friendships ended only with his life. His large attainments as a scholar, and his pure principles, made his conversation always interesting and improving. He had no idle or frivolous talk, no gossip, no slander, no censoriousness. He was kind and charitable from principle and feeling, and gave liberally to charitable and other objects which he thought deserving. The respect in which he was held by all who knew him bore evidence to his sterling worth. Of Mr. Porter in the privacy of his domestic life this is not the fitting occasion particularly to speak. But it was in his own home where the sympathies, affections, and amenities of his daily life best exhibited the excellence of his true character. "A man's religion is the chief fact in regard to him." Mr. Porter was a religious man. He had deep religious feelings and principles. He was connected with the church under the pastoral charge of the Rev. Andrew Bigelow (H.C.

1814) in Medford, and afterwards united with the Episcopal Church by the rite of confirmation. He reverenced Christianity, and had a firm belief in the Christian Scriptures as a divine revelation. He was a constant, earnest, humble student of the Bible. His patience, resignation, and cheerfulness, during the long period of his confinement and suffering, were the triumph of his Christian faith. In the remembrance of what he was, and how he lived, his family have found consolation in their bereavement. The many years during which he was shut out from the world were not lost. This life is not the end of our being. The fruit of cultivated intellect, of chastened, purified, elevated, Christian affections, will be gathered, either in this life or a life hereafter.

1814. — WILLIAM HICKLING PRESCOTT died in Boston, 28 January, 1859, aged 62. He was son of Hon. William (H.C. 1783) and Catharine Greene (Hickling) Prescott, and was born in Salem, Mass., 4 May, 1796. His father was born in Pepperell, Mass., 19 August, 1762; was an eminent lawyer and judge; and was distinguished for his social qualities, which won for him troops of friends. He was admitted to the bar in 1787, and began the practice of his profession in Beverly. He soon afterwards removed to Salem, where he practised extensively and successfully for nineteen years, when he removed to Boston, his son being at that time twelve years of age; and there he continued his professional business until 1828, when his health obliged him to relinquish it. He twice had the offer of a seat on the bench of the Supreme Judicial Court, but in both instances declined it. He was afterwards induced to accept the office of judge of the Court of Common Pleas in Boston; but having filled it about a year, and finding its duties irksome, he resigned it. He died 8 December, 1844, aged 82. Mr. Prescott's mother was one of the noblest women that ever lived. She was the daughter of Thomas Hickling, Esq., who for nearly half a century was the American consul at the Island of St. Michael's. His grandfather, Col. William Prescott, as is well known, commanded the American forces at the battle of Bunker Hill. He died 13 October, 1795, at the age of 69.

Soon after the removal of the family to Boston, Mr. Prescott was placed under the charge of the Rev. John S. J. Gardiner, D.D., of Trinity Church, where he pursued his preparatory studies, and entered the sophomore class in 1811. He immediately gained a high rank of scholarship, and graduated with distinction. He had intended to devote himself to the profession of law; but in his junior year he lost the sight of one of his eyes, from an accidental blow; and the other, sympathizing with it, soon became enfeebled: his general health failed, and he was obliged for a time to relinquish all studies. Happily his father's circumstances were such that he was not necessitated to toil for his bread. He early determined to devote himself to a life of literature. Soon after leaving college, being advised to travel, he went to Europe, where he passed two years in an extended journey through England, France, and Italy, and vainly sought aid from the most eminent foreign oculists. He returned home restored in health, but with his sight permanently impaired. He was never able to use his own eyes for more than a short time in the day; but was constantly obliged to use the eyes of others for his studies and researches, as well as for recording the results of them. His quiet perseverance and continuous industry enabled him to triumph over this difficulty, and to achieve an amount of literary labor which is not only most honorable to his intellectual powers, but conveys a noble moral lesson to all who may be afflicted in a similar manner. His earliest literary efforts were contributions to the "North-American Review." These show the tendencies of his mind and his favorite studies. In October, 1824, he contributed a paper on "Italian Narrative Poetry," which called out some strictures from an Italian teacher in New York; to which a reply was made in the "North-American" for July, 1825. A paper on "Scottish Song" appeared in July, 1826; one on "Molière" in October, 1828; one on Irving's "Conquest of Granada" in October, 1829. The titles and dates of his other contributions are as follows: "Instruction of the Blind," July, 1830; "Poetry and Romance of the Italians," July, 1831; "Cervantes," July, 1837; "Sir Walter Scott," April, 1838;

Chateaubriand's "English Literature," October, 1839; Bancroft's "United States," January, 1841; Madame Calderon's "Life in Mexico," January, 1843; Ticknor's "History of Spanish Literature," January, 1850. These essays, except the last, were printed in one volume, in London and Boston, in 1845; and several editions have since been called for. The memoir of Charles Brockden Brown, the novelist, published in Sparks's "American Biography" in 1834, was written by Mr. Prescott. But he had long cherished a hope of being able to write a history; and, as he prosecuted his researches into Spanish literature and annals, his design assumed form. The friendly offices of the late Hon. Alexander H. Everett, then United-States minister at Madrid, were of great service in enabling him to obtain a rich and extensive body of materials for his work. These valuable books, manuscripts, and copies of official documents, reached him at a time when most men, under like circumstances, would have abandoned all hope of executing the task he undertook. An extract from the preface of his "History of Peru," dated April, 1847, will best explain what these were, and most authentically describe that peculiarity of his literary history which is so remarkable in itself, and so valuable and encouraging to others who may suffer under any physical infirmity. He says, —

"While at the university, I received an injury in one of my eyes, which deprived me of the sight of it. The other, soon after, was attacked by inflammation so severely, that for some time I lost the sight of that also; and, though it was subsequently restored, the organ was so much disordered as to remain permanently debilitated; while, twice in my life since, I have been deprived of the use of it, for all purposes of reading or writing, for several years together. It was during one of these periods that I received from Madrid the materials for my "History of Ferdinand and Isabella;" and in my disabled conditon, with my transatlantic treasures lying around me, I was like one pining with hunger in the midst of abundance. In this state I resolved to make the ear, if possible, do the work of the eye. I procured the services of a secretary, who read to me the various authorities; and, in time, I became so familiar with the sounds of the different foreign languages (to some of which, indeed, I had been previously accustomed by a residence abroad), that I could comprehend his reading without much difficulty. As the reader proceeded, I dictated copious notes; and, when these had swelled to a considerable amount, they were read to me repeatedly, till I had mastered their contents sufficiently for the purpose of composition."

After some deliberation and hesitation, he selected the reign of Ferdinand and Isabella as the subject of an extended historical work; and to this the assiduous labor of many years was cheerfully and patiently given. The work was published in 1838, in three volumes, and was received with the utmost enthusiasm both in Europe and America. Scholars and philosophers admired its depth of research, while general readers were charmed by the limpid ease and natural grace of its style, his brilliant descriptions and animated pictures. It was soon translated into French, Spanish, and German. Its author was immediately elected a member of the Royal Academy of Madrid. The popularity which it gained upon its first publication it has since steadily maintained. The seventh revised edition of the work appeared in 1854; and it is one of the established classics in the language. Mr. Prescott's literary industry was not checked by the success of his first work. He did not, for a moment, repose under his laurels. He immediately devoted himself to the investigation of another brilliant period in the history of Spain, the fruits of which appeared in 1843, in a work in three volumes, entitled the "History of the Conquest of Mexico, with a Preliminary View of the Ancient Mexican Civilization, and the Life of the Conqueror Hernando Cortez." This work was received with no less favor than that which had greeted the "History of Ferdinand and Isabella." The literary world recognized in it the same careful research, the same accuracy of statement, the same persuasive sweetness and magic beauty of style. In 1847, was published, in two volumes, the "History of the Conquest of Peru, with a Preliminary View of the Civilization of the Incas;" a work of kindred and commensurate excellence to that of the "History of the Conquest of Mexico."

Mr. Prescott now devoted himself with unabated ardor to the preparation of a work of wider range and a broader scope, — a work which he was not permitted to finish, — the "History of the Reign of Philip the Second." This was a theme requiring a larger and more comprehensive treatment than his previous works. He had now become one of the great literary names of the age, and found everywhere persons who were ready to give him assistance. Everywhere, both public and private collections and private archives were thrown open to him. It was while preparing for this work that he indulged himself with a brief excursion to England, where he was received with the utmost enthusiasm by persons of the highest distinction in literature and social life, and where the favorable impression created by his works was confirmed by his prepossessing appearance and delightful manners. He took ample time for the task which he destined to be the crowning work of his life. In the latter part of 1855 appeared the first two volumes of this work, under the title of the "History of the Reign of Philip the Second, King of Spain." The highest expectations of the public were gratified by it.

In 1856, he published an edition of Robertson's "History of the Reign of Charles the Fifth," with notes and a valuable supplement, containing an account of the emperor's life after his abdication.

But a few weeks before his death, the third volume of his "History of Philip the Second" appeared; and the public journals and reviews on both sides of the Atlantic were speaking its praises, as a work worthy the fame of its distinguished author, when the news of his decease was received.

No native author has shed more lustre on American literature than Mr. Prescott. The highest acknowledgments of literary distinction were liberally showered upon him. The University of Oxford, in 1850, conferred upon him the degree of doctor of laws. He received the same degree from Columbia College, N.Y., in 1840; from South Carolina College in 1841; and from Harvard College in 1843. He was elected a corresponding member of the Royal Society of Northern Antiquaries, Copenhagen, in July, 1837; of the Royal Academy of History, Madrid, May, 1839; of the Royal Academy of Sciences, Naples, September, 1839; of the Herculanean Academy, Naples, May, 1841; of the Institute of France, Paris, under the division of moral and political science, and in the section of general history succeeding Navarete, the Spanish historian, without the previous knowledge or solicitation of himself or friends, being the highest of all distinctions of its class, — an honor said never before to have been conferred on any native of New England, except Dr. Franklin, — 1 February, 1845; of the Prussian Imperial Academy of Berlin, February, 1845. He was an honorary-member of the Royal Society of Literature, London; of the Royal Irish Academy; of the Literary and Historical Society, Quebec; of the Mexican Society of Geography and Statistics: and was elected, in 1850, an honorary-fellow of the Society of Antiquaries, London. He was also a member of the American Academy of Arts and Sciences, the American Philosophical Society, and the Massachusetts Historical Society. In private life, he was a most entertaining and genial companion. He was as rich in the love of his friends as in the admiration of the literary world. His character was thus beautifully and eloquently described, a few days after his death, by his former pastor: "The man was more than his books. His character was loftier than all his reputation. So simple-minded, and so great-minded; so keen in his perceptions, but so kind in his judgments; so resolute, but so unpretending; so considerate of every one, and so tasking of himself; so full of the truest and warmest affections; so merry in his temper, without overleaping a single due bound; such spirit, but such equanimity; so much thoughtfulness, without the least cast of sickliness; doing good as by the instinct of spontaneous activity, and doing labor without a wrinkle or a strain; unswerving in his integrity, and with the nicest sense of honor; whom no disadvantage could dishearten, no prosperity corrupt, no honors and plaudits elate or alter one whit; modest as if he had never done any thing; retaining through life all the artlessness of the highest wisdom; with a liberal heart and open hand; the ingenuousness of youth flashing to the last from his frank face; walking in sympathy with his fellows, and humbly before God."

Mr. Prescott married, 4 May, 1820, Susannah, daughter of Thomas C. and Hannah R. Amory, of Boston. They had three children, two sons and a daughter, who with their mother survived him.

1815. — Hon. GEORGE EUSTIS died in New Orleans, 22 December, 1858, aged 62. He was the oldest son of Jacob and Elizabeth (Gray) Eustis; and was born in Boston, 20 October, 1796. He was fitted for college at the Boston Latin School. Soon after his graduation, he went abroad in the capacity of private secretary to his uncle, Gov. William Eustis (H.C. 1772), then minister to the Hague; the secretary of the legation being Hon. Alexander Hill Everett (H.C. 1806), so well known for his varied attainments, with whom he formed a friendship that was life-long. At the Hague he began his legal studies, and drew, from the clear fountains of the civil law of Holland, France, and Germany, those elementary principles and stores of learning, which, at a later period, he was destined to exhibit to such advantage in his career at the bar and on the bench. On his return from Europe, he went to New Orleans, where he completed his professional studies with Abner L. Duncan of that city, and where, on his admission to the bar about the year 1822, he established himself in the practice of law. He soon began to attract notice as an able jurist, a keen logician, and a speaker and writer of great pith and terseness. The bar of New Orleans then embraced some of the ablest juridical minds in the country. The learned, laborious, and eloquent Livingston; the vigorous, ponderous, and sarcastic Mazureau; the fluent, graphic, and sensible Grymes; the well-read, sagacious, and vigilant Hennen; and a host of other younger attorneys, — many of whom have since reached the highest places in the profession, — were the formidable rivals among whom young Eustis was thrown to struggle and contend for the prizes of professional distinction. He was not unequal to the contest. Discarding the arts of the advocate, the strategy of the mere attorney, he based his claims to consideration as a lawyer upon his logical power, his thorough knowledge of the science of law, his fine analytical talent, and his clear, perspicuous, laconic style. Oratory, or eloquence, he held in little esteem; and quibbling technicalities were his special disgust. The reason of the law, its equity and philosophy, were the objects of his constant study and search; and, in the pursuit of these, he deemed it necessary to render himself perfectly familiar with the history of jurisprudence. He was a thorough civilian, — one of the most accomplished in the United States.

He was several times elected a member of the state legislature; was secretary-of-state of Louisiana; and was for several years the leading commissioner of the Board of Currency, an institution which has been eminently serviceable in guarding and regulating the banking system. He possessed a thorough knowledge of the system of banking, and was the author of many of those reforms which have given so much stability and such a high character to the currency of the state of Louisiana. He was also attorney-general and assistant-justice of the Supreme Court of the state; which last position he resigned to enter on a somewhat lengthened tour in Europe. He was a leading member, as a conservative democrat, of the convention for amending the state constitution, in 1845; and became the chief-justice of the Supreme Court as it was remodelled by that instrument. During his term of office he performed much mental labor, with great success. He was indefatigable, and possessed an admirable method, and great command of his resources. His judicial decisions were marked by a clearness of style and logic, and a thorough acquaintance with law, which made them compare favorably with the best to be found in the English or American reports. After the adoption, in 1852, of the present constitution of the state, which provides for popular election of the judiciary, he retired from public life — being utterly opposed to the election of judges by the people — to resume his practice at the bar; which he did under flattering circumstances.

To his great professional learning he united an extensive

acquaintance with English, French, and Spanish literature; and was esteemed by his large circle of friends as a most entertaining and instructive companion; and, if his conversation was occasionally dashed with sarcasm, it was often replete with genuine humor and racy wit. He was incorruptibly honest, a high-minded gentleman, a virtuous citizen, and an excellent man. He was naturally of a vigorous, mental, and physical constitution, maintained by habits of out-door exercise. In 1849, the honorary degree of doctor of laws was conferred upon him by Harvard College.

He married, in 1825, Clarissa Allain, of Louisiana, by whom he had six children, — four sons and two daughters; one of whom, the Hon. George Eustis, jun., was for several years the representative in Congress from the First Congressional District of Louisiana. His wife survives him.

1816. — WILLIAM JOHN ALDEN BRADFORD died at sea, of Chagres fever, on the passage from Central America to New York, 28 November, 1858, aged 61 years. He was the oldest son of Hon. Alden (H.C. 1786) and Margaret (Stevenson) Bradford, and was born in Wiscasset, Me., 19 November, 1797. His father was born in Duxbury, Mass., 19 May, 1765; was ordained minister of Pownalborough (now Wiscasset), Me., 14 November, 1793; was dismissed 21 September, 1801; relinquished the ministry, removed to Boston, and was clerk of the Supreme Court. He afterwards engaged in the book-trade as a partner of the firm of Bradford and Read. Leaving trade for politics, he was secretary of state from 1812 to 1824. He published a history of Massachusetts from 1760 to 1820, and several other valuable works. He died 26 October, 1843, aged 78 years. The mother of this notice was daughter of Thomas and Isabel Stevenson, of Boston. He was fitted for college principally at Exeter (N.H.) Academy, but completed his preparatory studies at the public Latin School in Boston. After leaving college, he studied law under the instruction of Hon. James Savage, of Boston, (H.C. 1803), and practised his profession in Essex and New Bedford. He subsequently went to Iowa, and practised in Dubuque some ten or twelve years, where he was for some time district-attorney. He afterwards returned to Massachusetts; was a clerk in the United-States Branch Bank in Boston; but, finding that the confinement was injurious to his health, he resigned his situation, resumed the practice of the law, and acted as a justice in Charlestown, Mass., two or three years. He then went to Central America, intending, if he liked the country, to settle there: but, it not meeting his expectations, he concluded to return to the United States; and on the voyage home he was seized with the fever which proved fatal, and he was buried at sea. He was never married.

1816. — AUGUSTUS THORNDIKE died in Boston, 25 November, 1858, aged 61. He was son of Hon. Israel and Anna (Dodge) Thorndike, and was born in Beverly, Mass., 8 July, 1797. His father was a man of great ability and energy. It has been justly remarked, that "few individuals, endowed with such mental powers, appear in a generation; and when their influence is united, as was his, with high moral powers, and exerted during a long life on the side of virtue, and in promoting the best interests of society, it is enduring, and serves to give a character to the age in which they live." *

At an early age, Augustus manifested a quickness of apprehension, and much aptitude for learning; and Col. Thorndike was very desirous that his son should receive the best possible education. With this object in view, he sent him, when about eleven years of age, to Edinburgh, and placed him under the care of the Rev. David Irving, D.D., a very distinguished classical scholar, in whose family he resided during all the time he remained in Scotland. After some preparation, under the instruction of Dr. Irving, Augustus entered that well-known seminary called the High School of Edinburgh. There he pursued his studies with diligence, and made very satisfactory proficiency, until about August, 1813, when his father directed him to return home, for the purpose of having him enter college at Cambridge. As war existed at that time between England and the United States, some delay occurred before a suitable ship could be obtained in which he might cross the Atlantic. On the 28th

* History of Harvard College, by Josiah Quincy, vol. ii. p. 413.

of September, he left Liverpool in what was denominated a cartel, together with forty-one other Americans; and arrived at Boston on the 4th of November.

It may be proper here to state that Augustus conducted himself well while he lived in Edinburgh, and was held in good estimation by his instructors and acquaintances. The late Earl of Buchan, the friend of Washington, took much interest in him, familiarly calling him little Thorndike; and he, as well as the celebrated Francis Jeffrey, the late Lord-Advocate of Scotland, showed Augustus much attention and kindness. At the High School, at that time, there were several pupils who were sons of noblemen; and, when Augustus entered the school, these pupils manifested a disposition to be rude to this young American. One of the boys, who was son of an illustrious duke, often took the liberty to run upon and hector young Thorndike; and he seemed to be encouraged in this practice by some of his comrades. This was borne with a good degree of patience for a time; but at length it became intolerable; and Augustus, having consulted with his old friend, the Earl of Buchan, took a favorable opportunity, when he was grossly assailed by the young duke, as he was commonly called, to redress his grievances. Whereupon these two champions had a furious set-to and fight. A ring was formed, and a large majority of the boys insisted upon fair play. Augustus, who was very athletic, and was expert in boxing, gave the young duke such a severe drubbing, that he cried for quarter, and at length surrendered at discretion. The young American was cheered, and proclaimed the victor. Thenceforth he was in the ascendant, and was treated with great deference and civility by all the boys in the school.

On the return of Augustus, in November, 1813, he reviewed his studies, and made some additional preparation under the instruction of Mr. George Morey (H.C. 1811), who was then a student-at-law in Boston. On the 9th of February, 1814, Mr. Morey offered him for admission into Harvard College. He bore a very satisfactory examination, and was admitted into the sophomore class by the unanimous voice of his several examiners. Augustus went to Cambridge under circumstances not likely to insure to him a satisfactory progress through college. He entered at an advanced standing, and became at the outset a member of the sophomore class. At the High School in Edinburgh he had been thoroughly drilled in Latin and Greek, and his manner of pronouncing Greek and reciting in these studies was peculiar and striking. His advent at Cambridge produced quite a sensation among the students. His dress and manners attracted much notice. Certain members of his class, and also of the two upper classes, whose companionship was not calculated to be particularly beneficial to him, sought his acquaintance. They were disposed to express surprise at his acquirements, and at all times they courted and flattered him. He frequently spoke of the feats and exploits perpetrated at the High School in Edinburgh, and often gathered a crowd around him while he narrated what he had seen and done. He often expressed much admiration of the arrangements at the school he had just left; and, finding the rules to which he was now subject very different from those he had been accustomed to, he was not slow to manifest his dissatisfaction and disgust with the regulations at Cambridge. This state of feeling led him not unfrequently to disregard and disobey them, and he was encouraged to do so by his associates. In consequence of this, he was several times called to account by the officers of the college; and, when arraigned, he was not inclined to manifest a proper respect or deference to those who administered admonition to him. At length, on the 6th of November, 1814, having become involved in a complication of ordinary college difficulties, his relations with the university were, by a vote of the faculty, wholly suspended. He then left Cambridge, and went to Groton, Mass.; and there pursued his studies under the direction of his former instructor, Mr. Morey, who had entered his name as a student-at-law in the office of the Hon. Luther Lawrence (H.C. 1801). He remained at Groton about six months, where his conduct was unexceptionable; and he fully kept up with his class in their studies. On the 29th of May, 1815, he was again offered by Mr. Morey for admission; and, having borne a very good examination, he was again restored to his former standing in college.

At the commencement in 1816, he took his degree; but, as might well have been expected, he had no share in the special honors of the day.

After leaving college, he went to Göttingen, and there took up his residence, in company with Mr. Joseph G. Cogswell (H.C. 1806). After remaining a considerable time at Göttingen, he, with Mr. Cogswell, made an extensive tour, and visited various parts of Europe. In due time he returned to the United States. He married, about the year 1824, Henrietta Steuart, daughter of Dr. James Steuart, formerly of Annapolis, Md., and afterwards of Baltimore. The children of this marriage are four, — two sons and two daughters. Their names are Rebecca (now the wife of Lieut. H. C. Marin, of the navy), James Steuart, Charles, and Henrietta Augusta. James Steuart graduated at Harvard College in 1848, and Charles in 1854.

In the year 1836, Mr. Thorndike left Boston, with his family, for the purpose of proceeding to Scotland, and taking up his residence there for an indefinite length of time. On his arrival in Scotland, he took a lease, for a term of years, of an estate situated not far from Edinburgh, with a preserve attached thereunto, well stocked with game. On this estate he resided several years, amusing himself by shooting game in the season, and by fishing in the Tweed and the various waters in Scotland. He was as enthusiastic an angler as Izaak Walton. He visited the coast of Norway with a friend from Boston, and spent several days in fishing on the coast of that country. He invented a fly, which he used for the purpose of catching fish. It was called the Thorndike fly, and became very famous throughout Scotland. Such was his success with this artificial fly, that he was invited to go to Arundel, in England, and use it for the purpose of catching mullet in the river Arun. This was a favorite fish with Heliogabalus and other Roman emperors. They often paid for it at the rate of a sestertium ($40) for a pound. The Duke of Norfolk, through whose estate this stream runs, has a regulation forbidding the taking of mullet by the seine, net, or spear; and as this wary fish cannot be caught by a hook used in the ordinary mode, which fact his sagacious lordship well knew, the above regulation amounted to an entire prohibition. But Mr. Thorndike declined going to Arundel for the purpose suggested, until the consent of the noble duke should be first obtained. He remarked that it should not be said that an American gentleman had attempted to practise any circumvention upon the Earl-Marshal of England.

After Mr. Thorndike had resided several years in Europe, he returned, with his family, to the United States. He became owner of a beautiful estate in Newport, R.I., which he occupied a considerable period, until the marriage of his eldest daughter with Lieut. Marin. After this event, he sold his estate, broke up his establishment at Newport, and went, with his family, to Europe. He came to Boston in 1856, and remained here several months. He, at this time, took an active part in the management of his property. He built a block of stores on the site of the old Commercial Coffee-house, and to some extent superintended the work himself. He went back to Europe, and spent most of his time in Paris; and again, in the month of June, 1858, he returned to Boston, for the purpose of purchasing a mansion-house in this city, to be occupied by himself and his wife during their remaining days. At the time of his return, and for some months afterwards, he appeared to be in excellent health. In the course of the summer, he set about making that long will, which has been published, has attracted much attention, and has been pointedly commented on in divers newspapers. It was completed and executed 24 September, 1858; and was deposited, by order of the testator, in the office of the Probate Court for the county of Suffolk; to which tribunal he, without doubt, expected and intended it should, upon his decease, be presented for allowance and approval. This will bears, in a peculiar manner, the impress of Mr. Thorndike's mind. It is obviously the result of much reflection and consideration; and is, in a great measure, his own handiwork. Undoubtedly he received assistance on the occasion from one or more friends learned in the law. The circumstance that it is all in his own handwriting, furnishes, to those who knew him well, pregnant evidence that he took a deep interest in the matter, and devoted particular attention to the preparation of this elaborate instrument. This is not the place to discuss the character of this important document, or the merits of some of its provisions, the nature of which resulted from a certain family-difficulty. What the precise character of this difficulty may have been, no one can fully know and comprehend but the parties themselves: while there is no doubt, that, if he had consulted any of his judicious friends as to what sort of a will he should make, a very different instrument, in one important particular at least, would have been the result of such consultation: but the testator, in this case, chose to make and publish his own will, and not that of a friend. The will actually executed is emphatically Mr. Thorndike's own will. He alone is responsible for all its provisions, and he expected to be so responsible. It is just such a will as those who best knew Augustus Thorndike would have expected him to make, under the circumstances stated by him in the instrument.

Mr. Thorndike possessed much intellectual power and vigor. His mind was highly cultivated. He was a good classical scholar. He was a great reader of ancient and modern history. He had visited the most interesting portions of Europe. He had seen much, and had an excellent opportunity to make discriminating observations upon men and manners. He possessed a large fund of accurate information in relation to European society, and was familiar with its prevailing manners, customs, and usages. He possessed colloquial powers of a high order. He could make his conversation exceedingly pleasant and interesting. His bearing was that of a gentleman. His manners indicated good breeding, and a perfect knowledge of the forms and civilities belonging to the best society. In his opinions and feelings, he was always conservative. He was early taught to respect and venerate the principles of Theophilus Parsons, Nathan Dane, George Cabot, and other Essex statesmen. He was, during the greater part of his life, on terms of intimacy and friendship with many distinguished noblemen in England and Scotland.

He was averse to labor, especially of an ordinary kind; but he was capable of great physical exertion, and would not shrink from long, vigorous, and continued effort in any thing about which he felt a particular interest. Pride was not a stranger to his bosom. He was always desirous of having reason to be proud of every member of his family, and of whatever possession belonged to him. Any disappointment, therefore, in this respect, was to him a sore grievance and mortification. He was ever anxious to give all his children a perfect education. On some occasions, there were indications of his being actuated by a spirit of jealousy. He manifested much sensibility when he suspected that some wrong or fraud was intended to be practised upon him. Nothing provoked him so much as to discover that he had been deceived, or imposed upon. He was slow to forget or forgive a supposed injury of this kind, especially when he thought it had been accomplished by concealment or management. He had an iron will; and, whenever he had given formal notice of a particular purpose, he was very certain to fulfil it. When he had made a decision or resolve, the thing was fixed, and a change in his determination could hardly be expected. If, like the Israelitish captain, he made a vow, like him he was sure to perform it. He never harbored, for any length of time, those ordinary resentments which many persons persistently cherish. He uniformly entertained much respect for those who had been his tutors and instructors, and always expressed kind feelings towards them. Those who had been strict and severe in their discipline formed no exception to this rule. Notwithstanding he received some rebuffs during his residence at Cambridge, he manifested much affection for the university. He sent his two sons to Harvard College, where they graduated in due course; and in his last will, which has been so much criticised, he remembered his Alma Mater, and gave a legacy of twenty thousand dollars to establish a professorship of music at the college, to be managed, as far as practicable, according to the statutes of the University of Oxford. His provision respecting the management of the professorship is perfectly characteristic of the testator.

No one could question his veracity or honesty. Whatever he stated might always be implicitly relied upon; and whatever debt he owed he was certain to pay promptly, and to the uttermost farthing. Every promise he made, or contract he entered into, he never failed to perform, in the spirit and to the letter. While he exacted strict and perfect justice of others, such justice he was at all times ready to do on his part. This was with him a constant maxim and fixed principle of conduct. He was conscious of having committed errors during his career. This, notwithstanding his pride, he on several occasions confessed to some of his most intimate and confidential friends. He often regretted that he had not studied a profession, or engaged in some business, which would have required constant attention, and given him regular employment. One circumstance should not be forgotten in this connection. He eschewed the great mistakes often committed by the sons of rich men. He not only did not waste or impair the large property derived from his father's will, but greatly increased it by his prudence and good management. For this, his family certainly have much reason to express feelings of pride and thankfulness. Every member thereof may well be particularly grateful, that, by the provisions Mr. Thorndike has made for his worthy and excellent wife, he has given her the means, in her own judicious way, to make amends, in a great degree, for the most objectionable feature of her husband's will; and it is hoped that it will not be deemed impertinent to suggest, in conclusion, that her quiet and prudent management will be vastly more likely to promote justice and equity, the peace of the family, and the good of all concerned, than a long and protracted course of litigation.

1820. — Charles Butterfield died in Tyngsborough, Mass., 26 July, 1858, aged 62. He was son of Capt. Asa and Abiah (Colburn) Butterfield, and was born in Tyngsborough, 21 December, 1795. He was fitted for college at Westford Academy. Having chosen the profession of law, he pursued his legal studies under the tuition of Hon. Daniel Richardson, of Tyngsborough. On the completion of his professional studies, and having been admitted to the bar, he opened an office in his native town; but relinquished the profession a few years afterwards, and devoted himself to agriculture.

34

He was never married. He was a man of a most amiable and genial disposition, with a fund of wit ever at command. He was one of the four, of the class of 1820, who established in 1818, in college, the renowned "Med. Fac. Society." The other three were James Ferdinand Deering, of Portland, Me.; David Priestley Hall, of Pomfret, Conn. (now of New-York City); and the writer of this notice.

Mr. Butterfield was universally esteemed by the inhabitants of his native town. He represented the town in the state legislature in 1834 and 1835. Possessed of the most kind and philanthropic feelings, he was always ready to afford his services to benefit his fellow-beings. At the bedside of the sick, he was unwearied in his watchings; to the afflicted, he was a comforter; to those who needed counsel in worldly matters, his services were always freely given; and, being a well-read lawyer, he had great influence in preventing litigation.

In 1857, he was appointed librarian of the Middlesex Mechanic Association in Lowell, and took up his residence in that city. It was a quiet place among books; and, with the changes contemplated, was just the situation where he hoped to pass, in a manner suited to his tastes, among pleasant companions, many long years of a healthy and vigorous old age. He was in perfect health, was careful of himself, and was of a long-lived race; his father having lived, in robust health, to the age of 94 years. But it was decreed otherwise. In the midst of the happiness he enjoyed in his new position, and the pleasure which his friends took in having him there, he was suddenly, in February, 1858, attacked with a disease of the heart, which satisfied him at once that his plans for the future were soon to come to an end. He remarked, that, amid all the death-scenes he had witnessed, he had always hoped for a sudden exit for himself, and was happy that the nature of his disease promised this. But in this he was not gratified. He went home to die, contentedly and patiently; but for weeks he lingered with great suffering, though with perfect submission to his fate. He was greatly beloved and respected by the people among whom he passed nearly the whole of his life; and who, in his death, mourn the loss of a worthy, good man.

1822. — Rev. Benjamin Clark Cutler Parker died in New-York City, 28 January, 1859, aged 62. He was the sixth son of Rev. Samuel (H.C. 1764) and Anna (Cutler) Parker, and was born in Boston, 6 June, 1796. His father was rector of Trinity Church, Boston, and bishop of the Protestant Episcopal Church in Massachusetts. Deprived of the directing care of his father before he had completed his eighth year, he enjoyed the careful tutelage of a Christian mother, whose fidelity and consistency were a lantern in his path. He entered the Boston Latin School in the year 1808; and, having successfully pursued a literary course in that institution for three years, he left, and went into the counting-house of Blodget, Power, and Wheeler, where he remained until the dissolution of that firm, when he was transferred to the counting-house of the late James Carter, on Central Wharf. Soon after the breaking-out of the war, he, being of the age at which military duty was required, was draughted from the militia to serve on the defenceless forts in Boston harbor; but a substitute was obtained by his employer, with whom he remained a year or two longer, when, by one of those little incidents directed by the guiding Spirit, he was led to the determination to devote himself to the Christian ministry. One Sunday, after attending the services of the church, he was thoughtlessly induced to enter one of those places of refreshment which the vigilant eye of the law often overlooks or ignores; and, on coming out of that place, his thoughts became ill at ease, at what, from maternal instruction, he was convinced was a violation of the sanctity of the Lord's day. He at first thought of the pain it would give to a Christian mother, should she know where he had been; and this reflection was followed by a consideration of the reasons why she would disapprove of such a resort on such a day. Stung by the reflection, his walk homeward was prolonged, he knew not whither, until he reached the open air and sunshine of the country. There was a quietness around him not in unison with his feelings within; and it became evident to him that he was the object of an internal struggle between the world above and that below. By the grace of God, the world below was vanquished; nor did he rest until he had resolved to give himself heart and soul to the service of God. This was the beginning of a new life. From that time, he determined to relinquish the flattering prospects of mercantile advancement before him, and to renew his studies under the direction of that rare and ripe classical scholar, the late Rev. Dr. John S. J. Gardiner, of Trinity Church, the assistant and successor of his father, with the view of preparation for the ministry. He was soon prepared for college, and entered in 1818. In his freshman year, he obtained a Bowdoin prize for an essay on the Life and Character of Dr. Johnson.* He graduated with high rank. His religious sympathies received fostering encouragement under the faithful ministry of the Rev. Dr. Asa Eaton (H.C. 1803), of Christ Church, of which he became a communicant in 1816, two years before his entrance into college. While preparing for the ministry, he opened a private school in the vestry of St. Paul's Church, in his native city; and, as a remarkable instance of his perseverance, it may be mentioned, that for nearly four months he here labored with only three pupils. His persevering fidelity, however, was soon rewarded; and he was compelled to limit his numbers, and deny many applications for admission. He was ordained a deacon by Bishop Griswold, in Trinity Church, Boston; and was admitted to priest's orders at St. Michael's Church, in Bristol, R.I., 17 May, 1826. Soon after his ordination, he gave up his school, then in the full tide of successful experiment, for the beloved object of his heart, — the work of the Christian ministry. His first labors were in the church in Gardiner, Me.; but, by the persuasion of his bishop, he was induced to visit Lenox, in Massachusetts, to attempt to resuscitate a church then almost extinct in that place. Becoming interested in this new field of labor, he remained six years in that beautiful but retired village, instead of a few months as he expected. From Lenox he removed to Woodstock, Vt., where he labored for a similar period. He afterwards labored in Plainfield and other places for three years; uniting, as it were, the labors of a pious missionary with those of a faith-

* This production will be found entire in the "Aids to English Composition," a work prepared by his brother, Richard Greene Parker (H.C. 1817), p. 380.

ful parish-priest. In 1842, he removed to the city of New York, and supplied the Church of the Ascension during the absence of its rector, the present Bishop of Massachusetts. He subsequently took charge of a church in Flushing, L.I., for six months; when he was invited to the scene of his last labors, the "Floating Chapel for Seamen," where for more than fifteen years he labored with singular ability and fidelity. This was a field of labor entirely congenial to his taste, and for which he possessed signal qualifications. The hardy mariners, they who go down to the sea in ships, and behold the wonders of the Lord on the deep, were met with a sympathy, which, like a key, opened the secrets of their souls; and thousands of volumes — Bibles, prayer-books, tracts, religious stories — were sent on their missionary labors in the ships' forecastles; and many a foot, that came to the chapel to scoff, "remained to pray." His labors were brought to a sudden close. He died, after an illness of six days, of congestion of the lungs. His physical sufferings during this period were intense; but his mind was clear, tranquil, and composed. He was fully aware of his situation; but his soul, in perfect peace, reposed in Christ. Disdaining all dependence on his own merits, he trusted solely to the atoning sacrifice of his Saviour for his acceptance at the mercy-seat; and, with simple, childlike faith, he resigned himself wholly — to use his own words — "to the adorable, lovely, blessed will of God;" and, in this delightful frame of mind, he passed at last, without a struggle or a groan, to a blissful immortality.

He married, 7 February, 1833, Frances, daughter of the late Dr. Shirley Erving, — a descendant of the celebrated Gov. Shirley, — a lady whose religious sympathies had long been in unison with his own, and with whom he enjoyed a life of matrimonial harmony, extending over a period of more than a quarter of a century. She survived him. They had no children.

1825. — Dr. Clifford Dorr, of Boston, died in the McLean Asylum, Somerville, Mass., 19 August, 1858, aged 52. He was son of John and Esther (Goldthwait) Dorr, and was born in Boston, 2 November, 1805. He was fitted for college at the public Latin School in Boston. After graduating, he studied medicine under the instruction of Dr. George Hayward, of Boston (H.C. 1809); and received the degree of M.D. in 1829. He practised his profession in Braintree and Quincy, Mass., and, for a short time, in Matagorda, Tex. On the 6th of September, 1840, he sailed from New York, as a passenger, in the ship "Coriolanus," Francis A. Bertody (his brother-in-law), master, to Sydney, New South Wales; and returned home by way of Calcutta and St. Helena; arriving at New York in January, 1842. In March, 1855, he was seized with a severe paralysis of the brain; from which, however, he partially recovered the following year, and his convalescence continued for five months: but in December, 1856, he experienced a second attack, which so affected his mental faculties, that it became necessary to remove him to the Hospital for the Insane, in Somerville, where he remained until death closed the scene. He was never married.

1826.—Dr. Samuel Sawyer died in Cambridge, Mass., 5 January, 1859, aged 54. He was son of Samuel Flagg and Patience (Learned) Sawyer, and was born in Cambridge, 20 March, 1804. His father was a mason in Cambridge, and was born in Sterling, Mass. His mother was a native of Watertown, Mass., and survived him. After leaving college, he was for some time employed as a teacher in Chelmsford, Mass. He then began the study of medicine; and after going through a regular course, and receiving the degree of M.D., he settled as a physician in Fairhaven, Mass., where he practised with good success for several years. Soon after the discovery of gold in California, about the year 1849, he was applied to by a company to go to that place; which application he accepted, and went round Cape Horn. On his arrival there, he resumed the practice of his profession, and also kept an apothecary's-shop. After remaining there about four years, he returned, and settled in Cambridge, where he passed the remainder of his life. He was a very successful agent, for a year or two, among the poor in Cambridge, during which time he published one or two reports. He was also a member of the city-council; and, in 1857 and 1858, was one of the school-committee. He was highly esteemed as a physician and a citizen. He married, 23 November, 1833, Miss Lucy Tufts, of Charlestown, Mass., by whom he had six children, — all daughters, — who, with their mother, survive him.

1830. — HORATIO SPRAGUE EUSTIS died at his plantation in Issaquena County, Miss., 5 September, 1858, aged 46. He was son of Gen. Abraham (H.C. 1804) and Rebecca (Sprague) Eustis, and was born at Fort Adams, Newport, R.I., 25 December, 1811. He was fitted for college at Round-Hill School, Northampton, Mass., under the superintendence of Joseph Green Cogswell (H.C. 1806) and George Bancroft (H.C. 1817). After leaving college, he studied law; went to the West; and finally settled, as a lawyer, in Natchez, where he continued in the practice of his profession, with the exception of an interval of a year or two, until his death. He married, 10 May, 1838, Catharine, daughter of Henry Chotard, a planter. He left a widow and ten children, seven sons and three daughters.

1830. — Rev. BARZILLAI FROST died in Concord, Mass., 8 December, 1858, aged 54. He was born in Effingham, N.H., 18 June, 1804. He was fitted for college at Exeter (N.H.) Academy, under the charge of Benjamin Abbot, LL.D. (H.C. 1788), and graduated at that institution with the highest honors. He then entered the sophomore class at Harvard. While in college, he held a high rank in his class, and graduated with distinction. On leaving college, he was appointed preceptor of Framingham Academy, which situation he held two years. In 1832, he entered the Divinity School at Cambridge, where he completed his theological studies. During this period, he was appointed instructor in mathematics to the senior class in the college, in place of Prof. Farrar, who visited Europe for the benefit of his health. This situation he filled two years, pursuing his theological studies at the same time. On leaving the Divinity School, he began to preach; and in January, 1836, received an invitation to settle as pastor of the Unitarian Church and Society in Barnstable, Mass.; and, in September of the same year, he received a call to settle in Northfield, Mass.: both of which invitations he declined. On the 1st of February, 1837, he was ordained as colleague with Rev. Ezra Ripley, D.D. (H.C. 1776), over the Unitarian Church and Society in Concord. Dr. Ripley died 21 September, 1841, at the age of 90 years; and Mr. Frost continued in the uninterrupted, active, and successful discharge of his duties as pastor until the autumn of 1855, when, in consequence of a severe cold, his lungs became seriously affected, and he was obliged to relinquish his pastoral duties. In February, 1856, he sailed for St. Thomas; and, after spending nearly three months on that island, and on the islands of Jamaica, Cuba, and St. Croix, he returned to the United States. He came home by way of Charleston, S.C.; and reached Concord the last of May. His health continuing feeble, he sailed on the 24th of November for St. Croix, where he passed about five months; and, on his return, he visited the Island of Bermuda, where he remained several weeks. He arrived home the latter part of June, 1857. His health being still in a very precarious state, he was obliged, on the 13th of September, 1857, to ask a dismission, which was granted with great reluctance; his parishioners unanimously expressing on the occasion their great regret that the interesting relation which had so long existed between them and their beloved pastor should be terminated, and manifesting in various ways their strong and affectionate regard for him. His pastoral relation closed on the 3d of October, 1857.

A few weeks before the termination of his connection with the church and society, he suffered a severe affliction in the departure from this life of his distinguished and excellent parishioner, the Hon. Samuel Hoar (H.C. 1802). One of the last, and probably the very last sermon which he wrote, was that which he preached on the Sunday after the interment of his lamented and faithful friend. Though written by Mr. Frost while in a feeble state of health, it was a full and just tribute to the memory of a great and good man. For a period of about twenty years, Mr. Frost performed all the duties of an active, zealous, and faithful minister. Every good cause found in him an earnest and efficient friend and advocate. His ministry was a very useful and successful one. A satisfactory evidence of this is, that, during the whole course of his labors at Concord, he secured the entire respect, and enjoyed the uninterrupted confidence and friendship, of Samuel Hoar.

On the 24th of November, 1857, Mr. Frost, accompanied by his faithful and excellent wife, and his youngest son, a very interesting boy of about ten years of age, sailed from Boston for Fayal, one of the Azores, in the hope that it might restore him to health. After remaining at the island about eight months, he returned to his native shore. He arrived at Boston on the 17th of August, 1858. His visit to Fayal was a most unfortunate movement. It happened that the weather was, for a considerable time, cold and chilly: so inclement a season was never before known at that island. Mr. Frost suffered very much on account of the cold and dampness; and it became manifest that there was little or no chance of his recovery. In the midst of his suffering, a most distressing affliction befell him, in the loss of the child who accompanied him. On the 31st of May, the lovely boy went up a mountain near the residence of his parents, in company with a party of friends; and, on their return, he deviated from the path usually taken, and fell over a precipice into a ravine about seventy feet deep: by the fall his spine was broken. After lingering about two days, he expired in the arms of his distressed mother. Great sympathy was manifested on the occasion by the members of the several very respectable families of Fayal; and great kindness was shown to Mr. Frost and his family by all the people, during their residence on the island.

On the arrival of Mr. Frost at Boston, he was in a very prostrate condition; and was borne from the ship to the residence of a friend in the city, where he remained about a week. He was then carried to Concord, and was there received into the house of his kind and faithful friend and physician, Dr. Josiah Bartlett (H.C. 1816). Finding himself in so comfortable a mansion, among a host of his friends, consisting of his former parishioners and other esteemed acquaintances, his spirits revived, and his strength seemed to be considerably improved. He rode out a few times, and had the satisfaction of taking a parting look at the places endeared to him as having been the scenes of the cares and pleasures with which he was conversant during his Christian ministry. He took great comfort in being able to see and converse with his dear friends once more. At length, he began to grow weaker; and, about the 1st of November, the symptoms of a speedy dissolution were manifested: but he still lingered until the 8th of December, when, in the presence of his wife and son, and his faithful physician and other dear friends, his spirit took its flight to another and a better world.

Mr. Frost married, 1 June, 1837, Elmira Stone, youngest daughter of Daniel and Sally (Buckminster) Stone, of Framingham. They had four children, two of whom died in infancy. Another died in Fayal, under the circumstances above mentioned. The surviving son graduated at Harvard College in 1858; and became a student-at-law in the office of Hon. Ebenezer Rockwood Hoar, in Boston (H.C. 1835). This son stood by the bedside to smooth the pillow and administer to the wants of his languishing parent. The faithful and affectionate wife devoted herself, with unremitting care and watchfulness, to the beloved husband through all the stages of his disease, until the last moment came, when she closed his eyes, and witnessed with what faith and hope a Christian could die.

1834. — Eugene Fuller was drowned from on board the steamship "Empire City," 21 June, 1859, on the passage from New Orleans to New York *viâ* Havana. He was forty-four years old. He was the eldest son of Hon. Timothy (H.C. 1801) and Margaret (Crane) Fuller, and was born in Cambridge, Mass., 14 May, 1815. After leaving college, he studied law, partly at the Law School in Cambridge, and partly in the office of George Frederick Farley, Esq., of Groton, Mass. (H.C. 1816). After his admission to the bar, he practised his profession two years in Charlestown, Mass. He afterwards went to New Orleans, and was connected with the public press of that city. He spent several summers there; and, some two or three years ago, was affected by a sun-stroke, which resulted in a softening of the brain, and ultimately in a brain-fever, which came very near proving fatal, and left him in a shattered condition. His friends hoping that medical treatment at the North might benefit him, he embarked with an attendant on board the "Empire City," for New York. When one day out, his attendant being prostrated with sea-sickness, Mr. Fuller was left alone, and was not afterwards seen. He must have been lost overboard. The "New-Orleans Picayune" of the 30th June, with which he was some time connected, says, "His industry, reliability, and intelligence were equalled only by his invariably mild, correct, and gentlemanly demeanor; and he was liked and respected by all who knew him."

Mr. Fuller married Mrs. Rotter, a widow lady of New Orleans, originally of Philadelphia. They had five children, — three sons and two daughters.

1835. — Dr. AARON LARKIN LELAND died in Detroit, Mich., 14 November, 1858, aged 45. He was son of Joseph P. and Tryphena (Richardson) Leland, and was born in Sherburne, Mass., 21 August, 1813. His mother was daughter of Dr. Abijah Richardson, of Medway, Mass., a surgeon in the Revolutionary war. He was fitted for college by Mr. Nathan Ball (B.U. 1826), and Rev. Amos Clarke (H.C. 1804), of Sherburne. After leaving college, he pursued his medical studies with Drs. Charles Harrison Stedman and Jerome Van Crowninshield Smith, of Boston. During his pupilage, he spent much of his time in various hospitals in the vicinity of Boston: viz., at the Marine Hospital in Chelsea, of which Dr. Stedman was then the physician; at Rainsford Island, of which Dr. Smith was superintendent, and where Dr. Leland remained, and took much of the charge during a season when the small-pox was very prevalent; and also at the Lying-in Hospital on Boston Neck. In July, 1839, he removed to Pontiac, Oakland County, Mich.; and settled there in the practice of his profession, in connection with Dr. Isaac Paddack, an old and esteemed practitioner of that place. In 1847, he removed to Detroit, where he continued in successful practice until his death. He was a thorough and scientific practitioner; having brought to the aid of discriminating qualities of a high order, and a judgment of great soundness, minute and extensive reading and a wide practice. He deservedly ranked among the first medical men of the day. In his personal attributes, he was eminently prudent, thoughtful, reflecting, and sagacious; correct in every principle; of scrupulous uprightness; prompt and diligent in his profession; trustworthy and punctilious in every transaction. He won the esteem of all who knew him, by his urbane manners, his integrity of character, and his humane disposition. He married, 17 June, 1856, Sarah Elizabeth Livermore, daughter of Hon. Isaac Livermore, of Cambridge, Mass. He had two children, — a son and a daughter. The former died in infancy: the latter, with her mother, survived him.

1836. — Edward Augustus Crowninshield died in Boston, 20 February, 1859, aged 41. He was the fourth son of Hon. Benjamin William and Mary (Boardman) Crowninshield, and was born in Salem, Mass., 25 February, 1817. He was fitted for college at Round-Hill School in Northampton, Mass., under the charge of Joseph Green Cogswell (H.C. 1806) and George Bancroft (H.C. 1817). After leaving college, he went through a course of legal studies in the office of Franklin Dexter (H.C. 1812) and William Howard Gardiner (H.C. 1816), and was admitted to the bar, but never practised; his pecuniary circumstances being such as not to require him to toil for his daily bread. About the first of December, 1859, in company with some friends, he went on a pleasure-excursion to Europe, and returned the next year. In 1856, he again went to Europe, with the hope that the voyage would be the means of restoring his health, which had been for some time previously in a delicate state. He spent the winter of 1856–7 at Pau, in the south of France; thence he went to Madeira, where he passed the winter of 1857–8; and returned the following June, without having experienced any permanent relief. He was a gentleman of exceedingly pleasing manners and prepossessing appearance. Of an equable temperament, he had no ambition for public honors or political prominence; but was a great lover of literature, and was passionately fond of books. He had one of the rarest and choicest private libraries in this part of the country. His taste in bibliography was exquisite. He wanted not only the best books, but the best editions. His library was particularly rich in early American history and biography. He had a copy of the "Bay Psalm Book," the first book that was printed in New England. Among other rarities, he had an original copy of Cushman's "Plymouth Sermon;" "Purchas his Pilgrimes;" Smith's "History of Virginia and New England" (an original copy); "Hypocrisie Unmasked," by Edward Winslow; Hakluyt's Voyages, published in 1582; an original copy of "The Christian Commonwealth," by John Eliot; and a similar copy of "Bradford and Winslow's Relation," published in London; "The Schoolmaster," by Roger Ascham; "Coryat's Crudities" of 1611, from the library of the Duke of Sussex; "The Whole Book of Psalms," by Sternhold and Hopkins; a book on angling, by Bernes, bearing date of 1486; the "Nuremburg Chronicle" of 1493; King James's Works; Dibdin's bibliographical works; and "Samuel Gorton's Answer to Morton's Memorial," in manuscript.

Mr. Crowninshield read the books he bought, with discrimination and profit. His mind, manners, and language indicated refinement and scholarship. His whole life was regulated by good sense, good taste, and good feeling. He secured the esteem, the confidence, the affection, of all who were sufficiently acquainted with him to know his true character. He was for some time a trustee of the Boston Athenæum, and took a deep interest in the art-exhibitions of that institution. He was elected, 11 November, 1858, a member of the Massachusetts Historical Society; an honor to which his scholarly acquirements and literary taste justly entitled him. He married, 15 January, 1840, Caroline Maria Welch, daughter of Francis Welch, Esq., of Boston. They had three children, all sons; the eldest of whom graduated at Harvard College in 1861.

1838. — Dr. William Augustus Briggs, of Boston, died in Baltimore, Md., 19 May, 1859, aged 39. He was the only child of William and Mary (Clark) Briggs, and was born in Boston, 12 July, 1819. His father, who was a native of Little Compton, R. I, was a merchant in Boston, and died of consumption in Matanzas, Cuba (whither he had gone for the benefit of his health), 14 May, 1828, aged 37. His remains were brought back to Boston, and conveyed to Watertown, Mass., for interment. His mother was a daughter of John Clark, Esq., of Watertown, where she was born March, 1796: she died in Boston, 19 January, 1854, aged 57. Young Briggs began his preparatory studies for admission into college at Woburn Academy, under the instruction of Alfred Washington Pike (D.C. 1815). Thence he went to Framingham Academy, under Barzillai Frost (H.C. 1830). At these institutions he remained four years; and he completed his studies under Rev. Theodore Parker, of Watertown, afterwards of Boston, with whom he remained one year. After leaving college, he studied medicine at the Tremont Medical School in Boston, under the charge of Drs. Jacob Bigelow (H.C. 1806), Edward Reynolds (H. C. 1811), David Humphreys Storer (Bowd. C. 1822), and Oliver Wendell Holmes (H.C. 1829). On completing his medical studies, he began the practice of his profession in Boston; but, being left with an ample competence, it was not necessary for him to depend upon his profession as a means of support. Still, however, he was very successful; and, until his health failed, was rapidly rising to distinction. He was of a most amiable disposition, and led a blameless and exemplary life. The death of his mother was a sad affliction to him, from which he seemed never to recover. The incipient symptoms of consumption not long afterwards began to develop themselves, and he endured a long and painful sickness. But, notwithstanding all his sufferings, not a word of complaint ever passed his lips. In order to escape the rigors of a northern climate, he passed the last two winters of his life with a relative in Baltimore, where he received every attention and comfort which kind affection and endearment could procure, and where he calmly and peacefully passed away. He was never married. His remains were brought to the North, and interred at Mount Auburn.

1838.—Asa Hammond Whitney died in Vicksburg, Miss., 8 October, 1858, aged 39. He was son of Asa and Mary (Hammond) Whitney, and was born in Boston, 17 June, 1819. After leaving college, he made a voyage to the Mediterranean for his health, and subsequently went to Rio Janeiro as supercargo. On his return, he embarked in business as a junior partner in the house of Henshaw and Whitney, wholesale druggists, in Boston; but for several years resided in Cambridge, where he built and occupied the house now owned by Charles Russell Lowell, Esq. He subsequently removed to Norfolk, Va., where he managed the financial affairs of the Seaboard and Roanoke Railroad Company for many years with marked ability; and, at the time of his decease, was filling an important trust in Mississippi. He was a man of great energy and earnestness of character, of warm and cordial feelings, and most courteous and winning manners; of an ardent temperament and a strong will; a most genial companion, and a steadfast friend. He married, 3 October, 1842, Miss Laura Leffingwell Henshaw, of Alabama, niece and adopted daughter of the late David Henshaw, of Leicester, Mass. He had five children,—viz., Laura Leffingwell, Anna Henshaw, Catharine Virginia, Hammond, and Emily,—who, with their mother, survived him.

1843.—Joseph Hurd Walker, of West Townsend, Mass., died at the residence of his father, in Boston, 16 October, 1858, aged 36. He was son of Dr. William Johnson Walker (H.C. 1810) and Eliza (Hurd) Walker, and was born in Charlestown, Mass., 19 September, 1822. He was fitted for college in Exeter, N.H. He held a very respectable rank in his class, and graduated with distinction. He was particularly distinguished for talents in mathematics. After leaving college, he prepared himself for the profession of a civil-engineer, in which business he became quite distinguished. He made the surveys and superintended the construction of the Peterborough and Shirley Railroad, which he completed to the entire satisfaction of the stockholders, and at much less than the estimated cost. A few years afterwards he relinquished the business of engineering, purchased a farm in West Townsend, and devoted the remainder of his days to agriculture. He married, in 1845, Anna M. Babbit, of Charlestown. They had six children, of whom five survived him: one died in 1855. His widow also survived him.

1844. — JOSEPH BROWN SMITH died in Louisville, Ky., 6 May, 1859, aged 36. He was born in Dover, N. H., 14 March, 1823. At birth, his sight was perfect; but, ere a week had passed, a disease fastened upon his eyes, which resulted in total, incurable blindness. When three years of age, he lost his father. His mother then removed to Portsmouth, N.H., where he passed eight years. The following sketch of his life is compiled from a funeral discourse on his life and character, delivered by Rev. John H. Heywood, of Louisville (H.C. 1836). He was endowed with a mind active and vigorous, a memory very retentive and capacious. From early childhood, he was marked for his love, his yearning, for knowledge. Sent to school when but four years old, he was so fortunate as to have for his teacher a lady who had a just view of education, and whose schoolroom was pervaded by the affectionateness which makes the charm of a home. When nine years of age, he was placed in the Institution for the Blind in Boston, under the charge of Dr. Samuel Gridley Howe, who saw what was in the boy, and determined that it should be fully brought out. Under his instruction, he prosecuted his studies, until, at the age of seventeen, he was prepared to enter college. He passed through his collegiate course with credit to himself, and received, at its expiration, his diploma; being the first totally blind man who ever graduated at any college in this country. He was a good scholar in Latin, Greek, and mathematics. He was a proficient in French and German, both of which languages he understood well, and spoke fluently; and had an extensive and thorough acquaintance with the best English literature. He had a remarkable talent for music, in which, by his attainments, he became pre-eminent. At eighteen months, he could sing three tunes. When nine years of age, he composed a march. So fond of musical thought and expression was he, that, when a mere child, he was often overheard composing in his sleep. Sometimes, when between the ages of eight and ten, strains and tunes taught him by his instructor would escape him; and he would try in vain, before going to bed, to recall them. In his sleep they would come, as if conscious, that, having once been given him, they had no right to leave him long; and then he would rise, go to the piano, and, like a true poet or sculptor, embody them, not in words or marble, but in harmony. Not far from the time when he entered college, he composed an overture, which was performed by the Boston Academy of Music, and which was deeply interesting, not only as a manifestation of his rare susceptibility and extraordinary capacity, but also of the wonderful knowledge he even then possessed of the deep, intricate science of music.

In September, 1844, he went to Louisville, Ky., having been appointed professor of music in the Asylum for the Blind in that city; and there he resided until his death. With so fine a susceptibility to the influence of music, with so thorough a knowledge of its principles, he was eminently fitted to appreciate and enjoy music of the highest order. In that he revelled. His soul responded to the songs and choral symphonies in which the great masters gave expression to thoughts and emotions too vast for words, too deep for tears. Such were the rare musical powers and attainments of this gifted man; and how kindly and faithfully he employed them, there are many to testify. The private pupils whom he patiently instructed—all connected with that home for the blind to which he consecrated fourteen of the best years of his life, and for whose benefit he labored with the fidelity of an earnest, conscientious Christian teacher—can never forget him. He was a sincere, hearty Christian. He loved the Bible dearly. Eight years before his death, he connected himself with the church. In an earnest, humble, and devout spirit, he made the Christian profession, and sought to live in harmony with it. His resignation to the will of God was perfect, for life and for death, for time and eternity.

He married, first, 9 August, 1846, Elizabeth Jane Cone, who died 14 June, 1851; and second, 26 July, 1853, Sarah J. Nash. He left two sons: the elder, the child of the first marriage, bearing the name of the great composer, Joseph

Haydn; the younger, named for an intimate friend, Bryce Patten.

1848. — Enoch Lincoln Cummings died in Portland, Me., 21 January, 1859, aged 31. He was son of Col. Simeon and Mary (Cushman) Cummings; and was born in Paris, Me., 23 May, 1827. His father, who was son of Jesse and Nancy Cummings, was born in Bridgewater, or Sutton, Mass. His mother was a native of Paris. He pursued his preparatory studies mostly at North Yarmouth, Me.; and entered Waterville College in 1843, where he remained one year and two terms. He then left; went to Cambridge, where he continued his studies privately, and entered the sophomore class at Harvard in 1845. After graduating, he studied law a little more than a year with his brother, Benjamin C. Cummings, in Paris; and then entered the office of William Willis (H.C. 1813), and William Pitt Fessenden (Bowd. C. 1823), in Portland, where he completed his legal studies; and was admitted to practice in Cumberland county, in October, 1850. He immediately opened an office in Portland, and devoted himself entirely to business. His brother, with whom he studied in Paris, moved to Portland a few years after, where he died in 1857 or 1858. Their mother (a woman of great energy and good sense) and one brother survived him, both living in Paris. Their father has deceased. Had Mr. Cummings's life been spared, and an opportunity been given for the full development of his powers, his habits of industry and perseverance were such, that he would have attained a high rank in his profession. But, dear as was the tie which bound him to his associates in life, there was a closer and more endearing fellowship to which his surviving friends turned in the hour of their bereavement. The last year of his life was one of Christian activity and usefulness, which makes up his brightest record. Having, about a year before his death, united with the church of which the Rev. Dr. Chickering was pastor, he entered at once heartily into the new service to which he committed himself; and carried into it the same elements of activity and devotion which had characterized him as a business-man. A meeting of the members of the Cumberland bar was held immediately after his death, at which appropriate resolutions were passed, expressive of their profound regret and sincere sorrow at the loss of their associate, and tendering to his wife and family their deepest sympathy and heartfelt sorrow for their bereavement. Mr. Cummings married, 28 July, 1852, Annie N. Clifford, only daughter of Hon. Nathan Clifford, of Portland, an associate-justice of the Supreme Court of the United States, formerly a member of Congress from Maine, attorney-general of the United States, and minister to Mexico. They had three children, all of whom survive. Judge Clifford began practice in Newfield, a small town in York county, Me.; and removed to Portland about the year 1849.

1851. — Rev. GEORGE BRADFORD died in Watertown, Mass., 17 February, 1859, aged 30. He was son of Ephraim and Lucy (Peterson) Bradford, and was born in Duxbury, Mass., 3 June, 1828. He was a lineal descendant of Gov. Bradford of Plymouth Colony. He was fitted for college at Partridge Academy in Duxbury. While in college, he held a high rank as a scholar; was elected by his classmates to deliver the class-oration at the close of the senior year, and graduated with distinguished honors. He returned to Duxbury at the end of his collegiate course, and was for two years preceptor of the academy at which he had pursued his preparatory studies. In August, 1852, he became a member of the Unitarian church in Duxbury; and, about that time, he decided to enter the gospel-ministry, — a choice of profession of which his friends soon acknowledged the wisdom. He entered the Divinity School at Cambridge in 1853; and, after finishing the regular course of study, was ordained as pastor of the Unitarian church in Watertown, 6 November, 1856. He had only time to fairly enter upon his career of professional and social usefulness, when the symptoms of consumption, of long standing, perhaps, but hitherto scarcely observed, manifested themselves; and, after an illness of a few months, he gave way, and, sinking at the last rapidly, but peacefully died, surrounded by his friends and relatives, without pain and without regret.

"It is hard to leave the world when one has but just begun his work here," he said, on the last day of his life, to a near friend; "but death of itself has no terrors." All those who knew him intimately could well understand, that in that calm and steadfast mind, trained to early maturity by a life of Christian virtue, and imbued with the deepest Christian faith, there was no regret, except for those whom he left behind him. He was a devoted pastor, who brought to his work a mind of no ordinary depth and compass, a judgment singularly correct, and a devotion to duty which is rarely seen. His generous friendship never failed, while his exterior reserve covered a nature of wondrous geniality, and of genuine enthusiasm; and his calm, upright, and resolute walk in life seemed the characteristics inherited from the Puritan governor from whom he was descended. He married, 18 February, 1857, Ruth Ann Ford, of Duxbury, who survives him. They had no children.

1851.—Francis Oliver Dabney, of Boston, died in Beirut, Syria, 26 December, 1858, aged 28. He was son of Charles William and Frances Alsop (Pomeroy) Dabney, and was born in Fayal, Azores (where his father resided as American consul), 17 March, 1830. His mother was formerly of Brighton, Mass. He was fitted for college mostly under tutors in Fayal, and the last year under the instruction of Eben Smith Brooks, of Cincinnati (H.C. 1835). Immediately after graduating, he entered the counting-room of Messrs. Dabney and Cunningham, of Boston, for the purpose of preparing himself for the mercantile profession. He was subsequently admitted as a partner in that house, where he remained until his death. He was unmarried. On the 15th of September, 1858, he left New York, in the steamship "Africa," for Liverpool, on business of the house with which he was connected; expecting to be absent about a year. Immediately after his arrival at Liverpool, he proceeded east as far as Beirut, in which place and vicinity he intended to remain until his return home. He was in perfect health until near the middle of December; when he was seized with an alarming illness, which, in two weeks, terminated fatally. Although he died in a distant land, he was surrounded by kind and sympathizing friends; and all that love and skill could do was done to rescue him from death. The last three months of his life, he was the honored guest of a wealthy and influential Arab gentleman, who evinced a devotion and regard for him, in his last illness, that could not have been surpassed by the dearest relative. During the last days of Mr. Dabney's life, this gentleman never left his bedside; and he saw the grave close over the object of his solicitude with a grief that did honor to his heart, and that told most eloquently, to all who witnessed it, what must have been the character of one who could inspire such affection. His mortal remains were laid in the beautifully-situated cemetery of the American mission. Mr. Dabney had not gone far enough in life's journey to be known to many beyond the circle of his friends; but his energy and upright manliness struck all who came near him. Seldom are so much firmness and integrity, and such a chivalrous sense of honor, shown by one so young. For these noble qualities, he might well be esteemed by all who knew him.

1851. — WILLIAM PAISLEY FIELD, of Randolph, Mass., died at the residence of his father, in Newton Lower Falls, Mass., 5 May, 1859, aged 31. He was the youngest son of Justin and Harriet (Power) Field, and was born in Northfield, Mass., 27 December, 1827. His father, now living in Newton, and doing business in Boston as a lawyer, was the son of Samuel Field, and was born in Northfield. His mother was born in Boston. The family removed to Boston when the subject of this notice was one year old. He entered the Boston Latin School in August, 1836; and left in the spring of 1841, on account of ill health. He remained at home a year or two; after which he entered, as an apprentice, the flour-store of Messrs. Earle and Brown, No. 9, Lewis Wharf; where he remained about four years. He then suddenly determined to go to college; left the store on the 1st of May, 1847, reviewed his studies by himself, and entered the freshman class the same year. He attained a high rank in his class, and graduated with distinguished honors. In his junior year, he gained a second prize for a dissertation. In his senior year, he taught school for a short time in Harvard, Mass. He possessed great musical talent; was organist at the Episcopal church in Cambridge, when in college; and had constantly played the organ in church from the age of fourteen years. Two of his brothers — Thomas Power and Justin — graduated at Amherst College in 1834 and 1835 respectively. On leaving college, he went to Philadelphia; where he taught one year in the Protestant Episcopal Seminary. He then returned, and spent the following year in teaching private pupils in Cambridge. He entered the Law School in Cambridge, at the second term in 1853–4; and took his degree of LL.B. in July, 1855. In March, 1857, he began the practice of his profession in Randolph, Mass.; where he continued during the remainder of his life. He was unmarried. He was of an amiable disposition, and led a life of unblemished integrity.

1853. — William Henry Rowe died in Boston, 22 July, 1858, aged 27. He was son of Samuel and Lydia Ann (Fletcher) Rowe, and was born in Boston, 6 October, 1830. His father was a native of Kensington, N.H.; was a carpenter; and died in Boston, 28 August, 1843, aged 43. His mother was probably born in Newburyport, Mass. She died in Boston, 13 October, 1830, aged 23. The subject of this notice, when five years of age, was accidentally hit on the left knee by a stone, which lamed him for life. He was fitted for college at the Boston Latin School, where a Franklin medal was awarded to him for his superior scholarship. While in college, he taught school during the winter vacations, in his freshman year, in Middleton, Mass; in his sophomore year, in Deerfield, N.H.; in his junior year, in Braintree, Mass; in his senior year, in Taunton, Mass. He was a diligent student, his conduct was unexceptionable, and he graduated with high honors. Immediately after leaving college, he entered as a student the office of Fisher Allen Kingsbury, Esq., in Weymouth, Mass.; under whose tuition he pursued the study of the law two years. While in this place, he was instrumental in establishing a debating society, of which he was the leading spirit, and which was highly successful. Meeting accidentally, in Boston, some gentlemen from the West, he was induced,. by the flattering prospects held out for young lawyers in that part of the country, to go to Davenport, Io.; where he entered the office of Hon. John P. Cook, who was at that time a representative in Congress from Iowa. Here he finished his legal studies; and in March, 1856, he was admitted to the bar in Davenport. He immediately began practice, still continuing in the office of Mr. Cook. His success was very great; and he was soon in full practice, with a brilliant prospect before him. He was a man of great energy; and a too-constant attention to business probably affected his health.

Early in the year 1858, he experienced a change of heart, which induced him to resolve upon a different course of life. In a letter, dated 9 March, 1858, to a friend in Boston, he writes: "I humbly trust that I have become a Christian; that God, in his infinite mercy, has pardoned me, through the atoning merits of Christ. I feel that I am weak indeed; far, very far, from being established as a disciple of Christ: but I also feel that I have obtained something that I never had before; that my life, slowly and waveringly indeed, is inclining up to God and Christ, and away from the world and death." He further adds: "I shall probably give up the profession of law, and study for the ministry; and I earnestly pray to God that he will accept and prepare me for the holy work. With God's permission, I expect to enter the seminary at Andover at the commencement of the next term, viz., September next; and shall probably therefore return to the East in the course of a few months: when, I don't exactly know."

But upon this new profession he was not permitted to enter. In March, the incipient symptoms of that fell disease, consumption, began to be developed, and rapidly increased; and it soon became manifest that death had marked him for its victim. His illness was not known to his friends here until some time afterwards; but, when the sad news reached them, they took measures for his return to his native city. He reached Boston the 1st of July, in a state of extreme debility; and after three weeks' great bodily suffering, but in a very happy state of mind, he expired, with a full confidence of a joyful immortality. He was greatly beloved by his acquaintances and relatives, who, from his blameless life and brilliant prospects, had anticipated for him a long career of success and usefulness. He was unmarried.

1853. — John Henry Sullivan was drowned in Lake Michigan, 27 August, 1858, aged 25. On the afternoon of that day, he and Mr. R. P. Jennings went out from Milwaukie for a sail on the lake, in the "Galatea," a four-oared boat belonging to the Galatea Boat-club, of which Mr. Sullivan was a member. Both the gentlemen were skilful and experienced in the management of a boat: but a gale came on at nightfall, causing a heavy sea; and they did not return. The members of the boat-club took a tug-boat, and went in search of their friends. In the mean time the tidings reached Chicago, where Mr. Sullivan had resided for nearly two years previously to settling in Milwaukie; and a party of his friends started immediately for Milwaukie, and joined in the anxious search for the missing ones. Fragments of the "Galatea" were found scattered along the shore for a distance of six or seven miles. She was a new and beautiful boat, and the fragments were easily identified by her owners and builder. Day after day the search was renewed, and rewards were offered to enlist the services of the shore fishermen; but each day weakened the slender hope that the young men had been saved. The body of Mr. Jennings was at length found, half-buried in the sand; but Mr. Sullivan's has never been recovered. He was unmarried. He was the only son of John Whiting and Marion (Dix) Sullivan, of Boston, and was born in Dorchester, Mass. (where his parents were then temporarily residing), 30 October, 1832. He entered the Boston Latin School when only nine years old, but completed his preparatory studies at Phillips Academy in Andover, Mass. While in college he bore an unblemished character, and was much beloved by his class. In Plymouth, Mass., where he spent several of his vacations, he had many true friends, who will long remember him as a most genial companion, a kindly and pure-minded boy. After graduating, he studied law for two years in the office of Baker and Peabody, in Concord, N.H. He then entered the Law School at Cambridge, where he completed his legal studies, and soon afterwards emigrated to the West. He settled first in Clinton, Io.; but soon removed to Chicago, where he was induced to abandon the practice of his profession, and enter the commercial-agency office of B. Douglass and Co. Here he remained until the spring of 1858, when he went to superintend the Milwaukie branch of the agency. He was also connected, from time to time, with various newspapers in New England and the West, as correspondent, contributor, and literary-critic. Wherever he went, he made warm and appreciating friends, both among his business acquaintance and in general society. Not only was he highly educated, thoroughly well read, possessed of business ability and decided literary and musical talent, a most sprightly wit and lively fancy, but he had a truly kind and pure heart. He never spoke slightingly of any one, was peculiarly generous and noble in his disposition, and invariably courteous to old and young, to rich and poor alike.

When all hope of his safety was given up, the Galatea Boat-club met, and passed the following resolutions in regard to their lost brother: "Whereas we may no longer indulge the hope but that a sudden and grievous dispensation of Providence has severed the links of our brief association in the transition from this earth of a gifted and highly esteemed fellow-member, the going-out of whose life, in the full vigor of manhood and usefulness, has filled our hearts with the profoundest sorrow; and whereas, after long and patient endeavor, the poor consolation of recovering, and consigning to a fitting resting-place, all that remains to earth of our departed friend has thus far been denied us: therefore be it *Resolved*, That we deeply and sincerely deplore the removal from this life of our late friend and fellow-club-man, John H. Sullivan, whose refined and scholarly attainments, blameless life, and generous impulses, endeared him by ties of no ordinary regard to each and every member of our association. *Resolved*, That to those, who, from ties of kindred or long and happy association, were nearer and dearer to our lost companion, unto whose hearts this great affliction shall bring the tenderest sorrow, — to such, and to all who are compelled with us to taste of this bitter cup, we extend our kindliest sympathy and condolence." The Wisconsin bar also passed a series of resolutions in expression of their kind feeling and respect for him.

1854. — David Henry Mordecai, of Charleston, S.C., died in Nice, Italy, 22 January, 1859, aged 25. He was the eldest son of Hon. Moses Cohen and Isabel (Lyons) Mordecai, and was born in Charleston, 13 November, 1833. Both his parents were of Jewish origin. His father, who is a merchant, was born in Charleston in February, 1805; and is the son of Moses Cohen Mordecai, who was born in England. His mother, who is the daughter of Isaac and Rachel Lyons, was born in Philadelphia, during a temporary residence of her parents in that city, in March, 1805. Mr. Mordecai was fitted for college at home; entered the junior class in South-Carolina College in December, 1851; and remained there until December, 1852, when, with several others, he received an honorary dismissal (the college refusing to abolish the system of bursary commons), and entered Harvard the second term of the junior year. Here he immediately took a very high rank, and was one of the most brilliant scholars in his class. He remained until the 14th of April of the following year, when he was obliged to leave on account of the delicate state of his health; but the college faculty conferred upon him his degree with the rest of his class. He afterwards read law in the office of the Hon. James Lewis Petigru, of Charleston; and then went to Europe to finish his studies and improve his health. But death, with its relentless hand, — who knows no distinction between man and man, between virtue and vice, genius and imbecility, — struck him down in his promising manhood, at the very threshold of the goal at which the hopes of his family and friends would have been realized. He was, in point of talents and attainments, perhaps the first man of his age in his native state. A brilliant sphere was opened before him: his future was a perspective of the brightest auguries. Possessing a mind among the quickest in conception, a memory that appropriated without effort the treasures of learning, a judgment ripe for his years, he united with these endowments that patient perseverance, without which natural gifts are the foliage without the fruit of intellectual culture. Alas that a life so rich in promise should be so soon ended; that the associations which so intimately blended social with intellectual merit should be so suddenly severed; that the memories of friendship, the anticipations of future eminence, the images of parental hope, the visions that cluster round one with faculties so gifted, and a life so radiant in its prospects, should have been so prematurely obliterated!

1854. — Alfred Hampton Preston, of Columbia, S.C., died in Rome, Italy, 16 January, 1859, aged 24. He was the eldest son of Hon. John S. and Caroline Martha (Hampton) Preston, and was born in Abingdon, Washington county, Va., 3 June, 1834. His father, a sugar-planter, was son of Gen. Francis Preston, whose wife, Sarah Campbell, was daughter of Gen. William Campbell, of King's-Mountain celebrity (where he was commander), and niece of Patrick Henry. His mother was daughter of Gen. Wade Hampton, and was born at The Woodlands, Richmond District, S.C. Gen. Hampton's second wife, Mary Cantey, of St. Matthew's Parish, S.C., was a niece of Gen. Sumter. Mr. Preston's father had established himself in Columbia, Richland District, S.C., where he married; and he travelled to and from Virginia each season. His interest was in Louisiana, but his citizenship was in South Carolina; and he was twice in the South-Carolina Legislature. Mr. Preston travelled much in the United States. He studied with a private tutor several years; came to Cambridge 15 July, 1852; and in six weeks, under James Coolidge Carter (H.C. 1850), was prepared, and entered the junior class, 1 September, 1852. After graduating, he went to Germany to continue his studies, which were cut short by a fever, which settled upon his lungs. The slow and insidious decline which followed, resisting all that human kindness could effect, served but to show in bright characters the beautiful confidence of the young Christian in his progress to the rich inheritance, through his Redeemer, of eternal life. In his later moments, his gentleness and meek submission to the will of God were only exceeded by his cheerful enjoyment of that "peace which passeth understanding," and which divested his dying bed of any fear of the destroyer. Cut down as he was in the brightest promise of early usefulness, his bereaved parents and sorrowing friends would not recall him from that bliss which is the attainment of the righteous. He was a high-toned gentleman, an affectionate and devoted son and brother, and a true friend.

1859-60.

1796. — William Wells died in Cambridge, Mass., 21 April, 1860, aged 87 years lacking six days. He was son of Rev. William and Jane (Hancox) Wells, and was born in Bromsgrove, Worcestershire, England, 27 April, 1773. His father was a Unitarian clergyman, an intimate friend of Dr. Priestley. During the occurrence of the riots which drove that eminent theologian from his congregation and his home, Mr. Wells's chapel at Bromsgrove, fifteen miles from Birmingham, was threatened with destruction by the mob. In consequence of such a prospect, and the gloomy and distracted state of that part of the kingdom, he determined to emigrate with his family to America; and arrived in Boston in June, 1793. From Boston he went to Brattleborough, Vt., where he preached "the faith that was in him," but was not settled as pastor of any society. In 1818, the honorary degree of doctor of divinity was conferred upon him by Harvard College. He died in Brattleborough, 9 December, 1827, aged 83. Mr. Wells's mother was daughter of Rev. James Hancox, of Dudley, in Worcestershire, England. Before coming to this country, Mr. Wells, jun., had gone through a course of studies at the college in Hackney, England; having been fitted by the celebrated classical scholar, Gilbert Wakefield. After he came to America, and before going to college, he taught school in Wethersfield, Conn. He entered college in the last term of the junior year in 1795, and at once took a high rank in his class. He was particularly distinguished for his attainments in the Latin and Greek classics. In 1798, he was appointed Latin tutor in the college; an office which he held two years. He intended to study for the ministry; but as his health was delicate, his lungs being somewhat affected, he relinquished his purpose. In 1800, he visited England. In 1802, he was appointed usher in the Boston Latin School, where he remained until August, 1804. He then engaged in business as a bookseller, in Court Street, Boston; which he conducted alone until about 1815, when he formed a partnership with Robert Lilly, under the firm of Wells and Lilly. While in this business, he taught a private classical school in Boston. He retired from his partnership with Mr. Lilly about the year 1830, and removed to Cambridge; where he opened a classical school for boys, which he continued for many years with much success, until the infirmities of age compelled him to relinquish it. He was highly respected as a man of extensive literary acquirements, as well as a good and useful citizen of unblemished moral character. He had been for many years a member of the American Academy of Arts and Sciences.

He married, 3 May, 1808, Frances Boott, daughter of Kirk Boott, Esq., of Boston. The issue of this marriage was seven children, — three sons and four daughters. One of the sons deceased. The other children, with their mother, survived him. One of the daughters — Frances Boott — is the wife of Rev. William Newell, D.D., of Cambridge.

1800. — William Sawyer died in Wakefield, N.H., 5 July, 1860, aged 85. He was son of Nathaniel and Jerusha (Flint) Sawyer, and was born in Westminister, Mass., 26 October, 1774. His parents were both natives of Reading, Mass., and removed to Westminster soon after their marriage. His father died 26 July, 1797. While laboring in the field, he suddenly fell, and instantly expired. His mother died 20 February, 1821. Young Sawyer was fitted for college at Westford Academy, under Amos Crosby (H.C. 1786). While in college, he taught school, in vacation, one winter in that part of Chelmsford which is now Lowell, and two winters in his native town. He studied law with Henry Mellen, of Dover, N.H. (H.C. 1784); and, having been admitted to the bar, he, in August, 1803, established himself as a lawyer in Wakefield, where he passed the remainder of his life. He was quite successful in the practice of his profession. He was several times elected a representative to the New-Hampshire legislature; and, after the division of the county of Strafford, he was chosen president of the Carroll-county bar. He retired from professional practice many years ago, having acquired a competence; and devoted himself to agriculture and the improvement of the farming interest in his vicinity. He sustained through life an unblemished moral character.

He married, in 1804, Mary Yeaton, of Portsmouth, N.H. The issue of this marriage was five children, — three sons and two daughters. William, the eldest son, settled as a trader in Wakefield. George Yeaton, the second son (Bowd. C. 1826), studied law with his father, and settled in practice in Nashua, N.H. He became an associate-judge of the Supreme Court of New Hampshire. Charles Haven, the third son, settled on his father's farm. All the sons married. The eldest daughter married Dr. Thomas Lindsey, a physician in Lincoln, Me. The second daughter, Augusta Mehitabel, married Joseph Pike, and lived in Brookfield, N.H., a town adjoining Wakefield.

1800. — JOHN WADSWORTH died in Hiram, Me., 22 January, 1860, aged 78. He was son of Hon. Peleg (H.C. 1769) and Elizabeth (Bartlett) Wadsworth, and was born in Plymouth, Mass., 1 September, 1781. His father, who was son of Deacon Peleg Wadsworth, was born in Duxbury, Mass., 6 May, 1748. He was an officer in the revolutionary war. He joined the army as captain of a company of minute-men at Roxbury, in the beginning of the war; and, by his skill and courage, rose to the rank of brigadier-general. He was chosen representative to Congress in 1792, and was successively re-elected until 1806, when he declined a further nomination. He died in Hiram, 18 November, 1829, aged 81. His mother was born in Plymouth, 9 August, 1753. She was sister of Joseph Bartlett (H.C. 1782), the eccentric poet and humorist. Mr. Wadsworth was fitted for college at Fryeburg Academy. He was remarkably comely and graceful: his manners and carriage were polished and courtly in the highest degree. He possessed superior talents, and ranked very high as a scholar in his class.

Towards the close of his collegiate course, his health failed; and he left in the latter part of his senior year, but received his degree with his class. He soon afterwards made a voyage to Liverpool for the benefit of his health, but returned in the same vessel in which he went out. He went to the South as a teacher, and spent several years in the southern and middle states. He taught in Natchez, Miss.; was a private teacher in the Berrien family in Georgia, and also in that of Governeur Morris in New York. He then studied law with Hon. Isaac Parker (H.C. 1786), and opened an office in Vassalborough, Me., but soon abandoned the profession. While his father was a member of Congress, he passed a considerable time at Washington, much to the detriment of his business-habits. He retired to his father's residence in Hiram; and, his health being in a somewhat precarious state, he did not pursue any regular business.

He married, in 1836 or 1837, Ellen George, of Concord, N.H., or vicinity, but had no children. His wife survives him.

1802.—JAMES DAVENPORT died in Boylston, Mass., 27 April, 1860, aged 81. He was son of Matthew and Patience (Goodnow) Davenport, and was born in Sterling, Mass. (where his parents resided a few months), 24 January, 1779. His name, originally, was Matthew Davenport, which he changed about 1835, taking the name of James for a son who died in St. Louis in 1833, and because James was an ancient family name, and the name of the first Davenport who came from England to New Haven, and settled in 1656 on the present Davenport place,—situated partly in Boylston and partly in West Boylston, and a considerable part of which has continued in the family ever since. Mr. Davenport was fitted for college at Leicester Academy. After leaving college, he studied law two years with Hon. Edward Bangs, of Worcester (H.C. 1777), and one year with Hon. Tristram Burgess, of Providence, R.I. (B.U. 1796). Having been admitted to the bar, he settled in Cumberland, R.I., where he practised his profession from March, 1804, to April, 1815; when he removed to his homestead in

Boylston; where he resided during the remainder of his life, being occupied in the business of farming, although he continued to be a member of the bar and a justice of the peace. He was universally respected, and was frequently consulted, as well as called upon to act, as a trial-justice. Three or four years before his death, his mental faculties became impaired, and at times his once-strong mind seemed but a mere wreck of what it had been. It was thought that the deaths of several of his children, and the loss of his property, with other trials, seriously affected his mind. He had been failing in health the whole of the last year, in consequence of a cancer on his lip; but the immediate cause of his death was influenza, which induced inflammation of the lungs. Three days before his last, one side became paralyzed, which deprived him of the power of speech; but previously he appeared conscious of his near dissolution, and spoke of his faith and trust in God.

He married, 27 May, 1804, Sallie Andrews, daughter of Deacon Daniel Andrews, of Boylston, a most excellent man, and father of an equally excellent family. The issue of this marriage was twelve children, — six sons and six daughters; of whom six survived him, — four sons and two daughters. One son died at ten years of age, and one daughter at the age of seven months. All the others lived to maturity. Their mother survived her husband, retaining much of her youthful vigor.

1803. — Rev. David Tenney Kimball died in Ipswich, Mass., 3 February, 1860, aged 77. He was son of Lieut. Daniel and Elizabeth (Tenney) Kimball, and was born in Bradford, Mass., 23 November, 1782. When a boy, he exhibited a great passion for learning; but so industrious was he in the business of agriculture, that his father used to say that he should not know how to spare him, and send him to college, if he had health to pursue the labors of the field. He began the study of Virgil, in the district school, under the instruction of Moses Dow, of Atkinson, N.H., afterwards Rev. Moses Dow, of Beverly, Mass. (D.C. 1796). He became a student, 3 May, 1798, in Atkinson Academy, under Hon. John Vose (D.C. 1795) as preceptor. That thorough scholar, judicious teacher, and upright man always spoke of him as one of the most exemplary and amiable young men, and one of the best scholars under his instruction; and, when he was requested to name a Fourth-of-July speaker from among his students, he selected young Kimball for the purpose, who delivered an oration which was well received. Leaving the academy 14 August, 1799, he entered college. He sustained a very respectable standing in his class, attended diligently to every branch of study, but excelled in belles-lettres, almost invariably receiving distinguished marks of approbation on his themes from that accomplished scholar and accurate writer, Dr. Eliphalet Pearson. Immediately after leaving college, he was appointed instructor in Phillips Academy, Andover, where he remained one year. He then began his theological studies with Rev. Jonathan French, of Andover (H.C. 1771); having, as fellow-students, Samuel Walker (D.C. 1802), afterwards Rev. Mr. Walker, of Danvers, Mass.; Samuel Gile (D.C. 1804), afterwards Rev. Dr. Gile, of Milton; Samuel Greele (H.C. 1802), now Deacon Greele, of Boston; and John Farrar (H.C. 1803), his classmate, afterwards professor of mathematics in Harvard College. His first pulpit-performances on a Sunday were 17 March, 1805. He preached for the first time in Ipswich, 22 September, 1805. From that time until his ordination, with the exception of thirteen Sundays, he supplied the pulpit in Ipswich. On the 17th of June, 1806, the church unanimously invited him to become their pastor, and the parish concurred with only one dissenting vote. He was ordained 8 October, 1806; and there he labored, with great diligence and faithfulness, for nearly forty years before he was relieved from a portion of his duties by the assistance of a colleague. For ten or twelve years, he instructed the children of his society at the meeting-house, and at his own dwelling-house, in the Assembly's Catechism. The number of children present varied from 120 to 200. When the Sunday-school was established, 20 June, 1818, with 145 scholars, he acted as superintendent, and took part in its immediate instruction. Few men took a deeper interest in the intellectual, moral, and religious welfare of the community than he. In December,

1818, he instructed the young ladies of his society, at his house, in Wilbur's Catechism, and continued it a long time; and also, during the same time, he instructed the young of both sexes in sacred history. He preached more than a hundred sermons exclusively to the young. Fourteen evenings in one winter were occupied in a course of fourteen lectures to young men, on the text, "Is the young man Absalom safe?" in which he aimed, as far as possible, to bring before them those principles and practices which tend to the moral ruin of the young. He was one of the original signers of the Massachusetts Society for the Suppression of Intemperance, constituted in May, 1813. He was also secretary of the Education Society of Essex County and Essex North, from the establishment of the former, in 1816, to the time of his death; and, what is remarkable, never failed, it is said, in an appointment, and never went to the annual meeting unprepared with a report carefully made out. He was a man of great modesty and humility, a faithful servant in his Master's vineyard, and one of the worthiest members of the community. For many years he kept a journal, in which were recorded interesting incidents of his life. In this journal, under date of 12 October, 1806, is a prayer which he offered the Sunday after his ordination, of which the following is a part: "Teach me how to pray for this people. May they always be near my heart, especially when I address the throne of grace! While I have breath to pray, may I not cease making mention of them in my prayers!" This petition was literally answered; for the last audible prayer he uttered was "for my people."

He married, 20 October, 1807, Dolly Varnum Coburn, daughter of Capt. Peter and Mrs. Elizabeth Coburn, of Dracut, Mass., and grand-daughter of Deacon David Poor, of Andover. This union was replete with happiness. They had seven children, — five sons and two daughters; of whom two sons died before their father. The other children, with their mother, are living.

He never lost his interest in the languages. He read almost daily a portion of the Old Testament in Hebrew, and of the

New Testament in Greek. He enjoyed greatly a good recitation in Latin, and also in mathematics. He wrote in his diary, 18 November, 1859, "In the afternoon, I attended the examination of the Ipswich High School. I took the direction of a Latin class, and made a short address to the school, in which I spoke of the great interest I felt in this and all our schools, and mentioned the fact, that it is my constant practice, every evening, to seek the greatest blessing from the highest source on all the young people in this town. I then spoke of the immense amount of moral power concentrating in the scholars belonging to this school, and urged them to do all in their power for the general good.

"November 23. This is my birthday. I am now seventy-seven years old. My day of probation is almost ended. The question which I have often put to others is a solemn one to me, — Are you ready for its close? I surely ought to have my lamp trimmed and burning.

"December 11. My wife having observed that few of those who have died in our society during the time of my ministry, according to the record, were as old as we are, my thoughts, after retiring to bed, ran very much on our nearness to our eternal home; and when I awoke in the morning, as well as a number of times during the night, I found myself praying that an abundant entrance might be administered to her, and to us both, into the everlasting kingdom of our Lord and Saviour."

His mind and body were so vigorous, that he was likely, in the estimation of his family and friends, to live to a very advanced age. Though his call was sudden, and his sufferings, owing to his disease (lung fever, attacking both his lungs), extrême, not a murmur escaped his lips. It was a privilege never to be forgotten, to stand by his bedside, and witness his transition from earth to heaven. At the moment of his soul's departure from the body, there came to his lips a smile of ineffable beauty.

His attachments were very strong. He enjoyed Commencement at Cambridge exceedingly. These seasons of re-union with his beloved classmates and very many literary friends gave him heartfelt pleasure; although, as he expressed himself not long before his death, "it was sad to miss so many who have gone to their graves, with whom I have trodden the paths of literature in company."

1803. — Rev. SAMUEL WILLARD died in Deerfield, Mass., 8 October, 1859, aged 83. He was son of William and Catherine (Wilder) Willard, and was born in Petersham, Mass., 18 April, 1776. He was fitted for college principally by Rev. Nathaniel Thayer, D.D., of Lancaster, Mass. (H.C. 1789). At the close of his collegiate studies, he determined upon the gospel-ministry as his future vocation; but, immediately after graduating, he went to Exeter as assistant-preceptor in the academy at that place, where he continued until August, 1804, and employed most of his leisure time in the studies of his chosen profession, under Rev. Jesse Appleton, D.D., of Hampton, N.H. (D.C. 1792), afterwards president of Bowdoin College. His continuance with Mr. Appleton was of short duration; for early in October, the same year, he was appointed tutor in Bowdoin College; which appointment he accepted. There, too, he employed his leisure time in preparations for the ministry, under the instruction of Rev. Joseph McKeen, D.D. (D.C. 1774), president of the college. In September, 1805, he returned to Cambridge to finish the course of theological study he had begun under Dr. Appleton, and continued under Dr. McKeen. After a few weeks, he was licensed by the Cambridge Association to preach. He preached his first sermon in Deerfield, 15 March, 1807. In June, he received an invitation to settle there, and accepted it. The 12th of August was the day first appointed for his ordination; and the council assembled, composed principally of the Calvinistic persuasion. It was about this time that the first indications were made apparent that this denomination were preparing to separate themselves from the Arminian and liberal churches. The council, after a two-days' session and a rigid examination of the candidate, refused to ordain him; not deeming the principles he avowed to come up to their standard of faith. Another council was called, and he was ordained 23 September, 1807. From that time, he became a pioneer in the cause of liberal Christianity. He labored faithfully and acceptably among the people who had called him to be their spiritual guide. He early took a deep interest in public schools, and wrote a series of schoolbooks, which were long and successfully used. He was a scientific musician; and was the author of the "Deerfield Collection of Sacred Music," which deservedly held a high rank. "It aimed to secure, by the simplest and most practicable means, an invariable coincidence between the poetic and the musical emphases, and thus to combine the two powers for the high purpose of religious impression." Many of the hymns in his collection were of his own composition; and, after its publication, he committed to memory every hymn in the volume. In 1819, his sight became so dim that he could neither read nor write; and then his devoted and affectionate wife cheerfully supplied all his needs, as far as human help could do it, aided by their children and friends. In September, 1829, he resigned his pastoral charge, but continued to officiate to his people occasionally until near the close of his life. His loss of sight induced him to make attempts to strengthen his memory, which he did to a wonderful degree; and he accordingly accustomed himself to commit to memory daily something of value. His wife would read passages over and over, until he attained them; and, in his hours of solitude, he would keep repeating them. The amount thus committed became prodigious. Many books of the New Testament, and the Psalms and Prophets of the Old, he could repeat with an accuracy which was unerring. The severe affliction of blindness he submitted to with meek submission to the will of the Sovereign Disposer. For forty years, he was not able to look upon the beauties of the earth, or the glories of heaven. He had not seen the face of his beloved wife, of his virtuous children, or his troops of friends; yet not a word of complaint, not a whisper of uneasiness, nor a tear of sorrow. He was a modest but large benefactor to society, and his parish loved and respected him without cessation. If there was a truly Christian household in the state, that family circle was his; and many loved to sit, and sun themselves in the light that was ever pouring from his rich and healthy mind. He was a member of the American Academy of Arts and Sciences; and, in 1826, the honorary degree of doctor of divinity was conferred upon him by Harvard College.

He married, 30 May, 1808, Susan Barker, daughter of Dr. Joshua Barker, of Hingham, Mass. (H.C. 1772). They had three children, — two daughters and one son, — who survive him. The son inherited his father's sad infirmity of blindness. His wife died 24 August, 1857, aged 74 years.

1804. — Dr. JOHN MAITLAND BREWER died in Beverly, N.J., 5 November, 1859, aged 78. He was son of David and Comfort (Wheeler) Brewer, and was born in Framingham, Mass., 10 April, 1781. His name, originally, was John Brewer, but many years since he took the intermediate name of Maitland. He was fitted for college at Framingham Academy. He entered Brown University in 1800, where he remained two years; when he left, and entered the junior class at Harvard College, 14 October, 1802. Immediately after graduating, he was appointed perceptor of the same academy in which he had pursued his preparatory studies for college, where he continued two years. He then studied divinity with his pastor, Rev. David Kellogg, D.D. (D.C. 1775), of Framingham. After preaching a short time to good acceptance, he received a call to take the pastoral charge of the church in Dover, Mass., but declined the invitation on account of the inadequacy of the salary offered. He soon afterwards relinquished preaching, and took charge of an academy in New Bedford, Mass., where he remained several years. He then removed to Germantown, Penn., where he continued the occupation of teaching with much success as an instructor, and with pecuniary profit to himself. He afterwards went to Philadelphia, where he studied medicine. In 1837, he received the degree of M.D. from the University of Pennsylvania, in Philadelphia, and practised medicine in that city until 1850; when, having become wealthy, he removed to Beverly, N.J., where he owned real estate to a considerable amount, and where he built several houses, one of which he occupied himself, and there passed the remainder of his days. He was an expert financier, and the latter years of his life were devoted almost exclusively to "increasing his store," in which he took great satisfaction, and was highly successful. He was never married.

1808. — CHARLES FLANDERS died in Plainfield, N.H., 15 April, 1860, aged 72. He was son of Nehemiah and Sarah (French) Flanders, and was born in Newburyport, Mass., 11 February, 1788. He was fitted for college by Michael Walsh, of Newburyport. After leaving college, having chosen law for a profession, he pursued his studies partly under the instruction of Samuel Lorenzo Knapp (D.C. 1804), and partly with Little and Banister, of Newburyport (D.C. 1797). Having been admitted to the bar, he established himself in the practice of his profession in Plainfield. Possessing a clear, discerning, and logical mind, by untiring industry and devoted attention to the interests of his clients, he soon rose to distinction, and acquired an extensive and lucrative practice. For nearly fifty years, he was distinguished as an honored member of the New-Hampshire bar, an able lawyer, a safe counsellor, and an honest man. Nor were his talents and usefulness without appreciation by the people among whom he so long resided. He several times represented Plainfield in the New-Hampshire legislature: not so often as he would have done, had his political views been different. He was of the old Federal National-Republican school, to which he adhered consistently and strenuously. He was, at one time, solicitor for Sullivan county. In 1847, the honorary degree of master of arts was conferred upon him by Dartmouth College. About the year 1848, he removed to Manchester, N.H., where he resided several years; but returned to Plainfield some four or five years before his death. He was a kind husband and father, a worthy and respected citizen; fulfilling all the relations of life with conscientious and scrupulous integrity and fidelity.

He married, 20 August, 1815, Lucretia Kingsbury, of Keene, N.H. The issue of this marriage was four sons and one daughter, — Charles, George M., William M., Henry, and Ellen.

Charles was a merchant in New York, and died a few years since. George M., a lawyer, and William M., a merchant, both resided in Boston. Henry became a distinguished lawyer and writer in Philadelphia. He is the author of "Lives and Times of the Chief-Justices of the United States," in two parts: the first containing the lives of John Jay and John Rutledge, published in 1855; and the other those of William Cushing Oliver, Oliver Ellsworth, and John Marshall, in 1858. The work is written in a beautiful style, the biographies being interspersed with many stirring incidents of the times, rendering it an exceedingly fascinating book. He has also written two other works, which are esteemed high authority by the legal profession, — "A Treatise on Maritime Law," published in 1853; and "A Treatise on the Law of Shipping," published in 1858. Ellen became the wife of Dr. Norman Curtis Stevens, a much-esteemed physician in Boston.

1808. — Rev. RALPH SANGER died in Cambridge, Mass., 6 May, 1860, aged 73. He was the fourth son of Rev. Zedekiah (H.C. 1771) and Irene (Freeman) Sanger, and was born in Duxbury, Mass., 22 June, 1786. His father, who was son of Richard and Deborah (Rider) Sanger, was born in Sherborn, Mass., 4 October, 1748; was ordained at Duxbury, Mass., 3 July, 1776; dismissed, at his own request, 10 April, 1786; was installed at Bridgewater as colleague with Rev. John Shaw (H.C. 1729), 17 December, 1788. Mr. Shaw died 29 April, 1791, aged 84; and, from that time, Mr. Sanger discharged the laborious duties of pastor alone until his death, which took place 17 November, 1820, at the age of 72. In addition to his pastoral duties, he instructed a classical school. He was highly esteemed for genius and learning, reverenced as a minister, and sought for as a counsellor. He was a member of the American Academy of Arts and Sciences; and, in 1807, the honorary degree of Doctor of Divinity was conferred upon him by Brown University. The subject of this notice was fitted for college by his father, and graduated with the highest honors of his class. After leaving college, he studied divinity with his father. In 1811, he was appointed tutor at Cambridge, where he remained one year. He was ordained pastor of the church in Dover, Mass., 16 September, 1812, as successor of Rev. Benjamin Caryl (H.C. 1761), who died 13 November, 1811, at the age of 79 years. Here he labored with great fidelity, and in perfect harmony with the people of his charge, until his death, a period of forty-seven years and seven months. He was sole pastor until about a year before his decease, when the Rev. Edward G. Barker was ordained as colleague with him. Mr. Caryl was ordained 10 November, 1762; and it is worthy of note that the pastorates of these two clergymen comprised, with an interval of only ten months, a period of ninety-seven years and six months. About four years before his death, his house was set on fire by an incendiary, and destroyed. He soon afterwards removed to Cambridge, to the house of his son-in-law, Mr. William W. Gannett, where he resided during the remainder of his life, although he continued his pastoral labors over his society in Dover, as before. He was elected a representative in the state legislature from Dover in 1837, 1845, 1847, 1851, and 1854. In 1858, the honorary degree of doctor of divinity was conferred upon him by Harvard College.

Dr. Sanger was extensively known, and universally respected for his mild, amiable disposition, and spotless integrity. As a Christian minister, his wisdom, prudence, fidelity, and usefulness won for him a name that will be sacredly cherished in the church, and in many homes where his influence was felt and his labors were known. For the promotion of agriculture, of temperance, and of social elevation and improvement in every way, his labors were modestly yet earnestly employed. He was a man of scholarly and liberal attainments, of a frank and cheerful temperament, distinguished for his sterling virtues and his modest worth. In his death, a worthy man and a sincere Christian has gone to his rest.

He married, in July, 1817, Charlotte Kingman, of East Bridgewater, who was born 5 July, 1792. The issue of this marriage was six children, — four sons and two daughters.

1808. — Hon. Samuel Emerson Smith died in Wiscasset, Me., 3 March, 1860, aged 71. His death was very sudden. He retired, about eleven o'clock, in his usual health, — having just completed the solution of a difficult mathematical problem upon which he had been engaged during the evening, — and soon afterwards breathed his last. He was the seventh child and third son of Manasseh (H.C. 1773) and Hannah (Emerson) Smith, and was born in Hollis, N.H., 12 March, 1788. His parents removed to Wiscasset the year of his birth. His father, who was the son of Abijah Smith, was born in Leominster, Mass., 25 December, 1749. He was a lawyer in Leominster, in Holliston, and in Wiscasset; and was clerk of the Supreme Court. He died 21 May, 1823, aged 73. The subject of this notice was fitted for college, partly at Wiscasset, and partly at Groton (Mass.) Academy. He attained to a distinguished rank in his class, and graduated with high honors. After leaving college, he studied law, for a time, with Hon. Samuel Dana, of Groton; afterwards with his brothers Manasseh Smith (H.C. 1800), of Warren, Me., and Joseph Emerson Smith (H.C. 1804), of Boston. He was admited to the bar in Boston, 25 February, 1812, and established himself in the practice of his profession in Wiscasset. In 1819, he was elected to represent Wiscasset in the general court in Boston, and was elected to the legislature of Maine in 1820, after the separation of that state from Masssachusetts. He was appointed chief-justice of the Court of Common Pleas in 1821, and a justice of the state Court of Common Pleas in 1822; which situation he retained until 1830, when he was elected governor of Maine. He was re-elected governor for the political years 1831–32 and 1832–33, and was re-appointed justice of the Court of Common Pleas early in 1835; which office he resigned in 1837. In October, 1837, he was appointed one of the commissioners to revise the public laws of Maine. On his election to the gubernatorial chair, he removed to Augusta, where he resided until July, 1836, when he returned to Wiscasset. He was unostentatious in his intercourse with his fellow-citizens, honest in all his dealings, exemplary in his habits of life, beloved and respected by all who knew him.

He married, 12 September, 1832, Louisa Sophia, daughter of Hon. Henry Weld Fuller (D.C. 1801), of Augusta; and had five children, — all sons. His wife and children survived him.

1810. — Dr. JOSEPH EATON died at Fort Hamilton, N.Y., 17 March, 1860, aged 75. He was son of Edmund and Sally (Brown) Eaton, and was born in Reading, Mass., 24 July, 1784. His mother was a descendant of Nicholas Brown, one of the first settlers of Reading. She was also a relation of Gen. Benjamin Brown, of Reading, who was a colonel in the Revolution, and a general in the militia. The subject of this notice was fitted for college at Phillips Academy, in Andover, Mass. He was much assisted, in acquiring his education, by his relative, Rev. Oliver Brown (H.C. 1804), of Charlestown, Mass., then chaplain of the state-prison. After leaving college, he chose the medical profession; and, having pursued his studies for some time, he entered the army of the United States, 14 April, 1812, as surgeon's-mate. This position he resigned, 12 December, 1813. He was appointed hospital-surgeon's mate, 15 April, 1814; and, having completed his medical studies, he received his degree of M.D. that year. He was commissioned as assistant-surgeon with the rank of captain, 1 June, 1821; which post he retained during the remainder of his life; and, at his death, he was the senior surgeon in the service. He was an intelligent gentleman, and a faithful public servant. He married Sally Smith, of Salem, Mass. The issue of this marriage was six children, — one son and five daughters. The son, whose name is Joseph, entered the army; and, during the Mexican war, was aide to Gen. Taylor. He had the reputation of being a brave officer. The daughters have resided in the vicinity of Fort Hamilton. Their mother died about nineteen years since.

1810. — ISAAC REDINGTON HOWE died in Haverhill, Mass., 15 January, 1860, aged 67. He was son of David and Elizabeth (Redington) Howe, and was born in Haverhill, 13 March, 1791. He was prepared for college at Phillips Academy, Andover. After graduating, he began the study of law, under the instruction of Hon. George Bliss, of Springfield, Mass. (Y.C. 1784); and completed his studies with Hon. William Prescott, of Boston (H.C. 1783). After his admission to the bar, he opened an office in his native town, where he resided during the remainder of his life. He was, for many years, active in his profession, in which he acquired a highly respectable rank; but he gave up his business some sixteen years before his death, alleging, as it is said, that he did not regard it as an honest profession. In this, probably, his peace principles, which were well known, actuated him. He wrote much for the press, and was at one time associated in conducting the "Haverhill Gazette." He was a great advocate of all that related to mechanics and the arts; and, in these matters, his mind was far in advance of the age. He was never selfish or partisan in his character. He aimed at truth and independence, and never committed his conduct or opinions to the dictation of party. He was a gentleman of great kindness and gentleness of disposition. For several years before his death, he was in ill health, and was but little known away from his own fireside, being but seldom abroad. Possessed of unusual amiability, he had no enemies. He was particularly upright and honorable in all his business transactions, and left a character above reproach.

Mr. Howe married, 16 June, 1816, Sarah, daughter of Dr. Nathaniel Saltonstall, of Haverhill (H.C. 1766), and sister of Hon. Leverett Saltonstall, of Salem (H.C. 1802). They had eight children, — four sons and four daughters, — of whom three sons and one daughter, with their mother, survived their father. The children are as follows: 1. Nathaniel Saltonstall, born 24 April, 1817 (Y.C. 1835); lawyer in Haverhill, and judge of probate; has been member of the state senate. 2. Mary Cooke, born 25 March, 1819; married, 30 September, 1851, James H. Carleton, a merchant in Haverhill. 3. Caroline Matilda, born 27 September, 1821; died 9 August, 1844. 4. Ann Elizabeth, born 14 November, 1823; died 7 July, 1845. 5. William Garland, born 28 June; died 26 August, 1826. 6. Frances Garland, born 8 October, 1827; died 5 September, 1828. 7. William Garland, born 1 August, 1829; broker in Boston. 8. Francis Saltonstall, born 8 November, 1831 (H.C. 1852); lawyer in Chicago.

1810. — Rev. Cyrus Peirce died in West Newton, Mass.,

5 April, 1860, aged 69. He was the youngest of twelve children — five sons and seven daughters — of Isaac and Hannah (Mason) Peirce; and was born in Waltham, Mass., 15 August, 1790. He began his preparatory studies for college at Framingham Academy, and completed them under the instruction of Rev. Charles Stearns, D.D. (H.C. 1773), of Lincoln, Mass. While in college, he maintained the reputation of a pure, upright young man; a faithful and indefatigable student; an accurate, though not a brilliant, scholar. During his sophomore year, in the winter of 1807-8, he began his labors as a schoolteacher in the village of West Newton, — in the same town, and not far from the very spot, where he closed his life, upwards of fifty-three years afterwards. Immediately after leaving college, he accepted an invitation to take charge of a private school in Nantucket. Here he taught, two years, with great fidelity and success. During that time, he determined to study for the ministry; and, in 1812, he returned to Cambridge to pursue his theological studies. After three years spent there, he was persuaded to return to Nantucket, and resume his work as a teacher, where he remained three years. In 1818, he left, and began preaching. He was ordained pastor of a church in North Reading, Mass., 18 May, 1819. Here he remained a most faithful and discreet preacher of the gospel for eight years; but, having come to the conclusion that he was not called to preach so much as to teach, he resigned his pastoral charge, 19 May, 1827, and returned to school-keeping, as that which should thenceforth be the business of his life. In company with a relative, Mr. Simeon Putnam (H.C. 1811), he took charge of a school in North Andover, Mass. Here he remained four years; when at the earnest solicitation of his former friends, in 1831, he returned to Nantucket. His return was most cordially welcomed; and he immediately found himself at the head of a large and lucrative school. This school he continued to teach six years, during which time he was occasionally blessed with able assistants; and among them was Miss Maria Mitchell, who had been his pupil, and who has since obtained a world-wide fame as an astronomer. In 1837, he relinquished his private school, and

became the principal of Nantucket High School. This school he kept two years. In 1839, when the first normal-school on this continent was established at Lexington, Mass., he was, at the earnest solicitation of the late Horace Mann, induced to take charge of it; and entered upon his labors, 3 July, 1839. He began with only three scholars. The contrast between the full and flourishing establishment he had just left at Nantucket, and the "beggarly account of empty boxes" which was daily before him for the first three months, was very disheartening. However, he had put his hand to the plough, and of course the furrow must be driven through, ay, and the whole field be turned over, before he would relinquish his effort. He set about his work as one determined to "do with his might what his hand found to do." He soon made his three pupils conscious that there was more to be known about even the primary branches of education than they had dreamed; and better methods of teaching reading, spelling, grammar, and geography, than were practised in the schools. Their reports of the searching thoroughness and other excellent peculiarities of the normal-teacher attracted others to him. The number of his pupils steadily increased from term to term, until, at the expiration of his first three years' service, there were forty-two; at which time he was obliged to resign in consequence of failing health, and he returned to Nantucket: but, at the end of two years, he was so far recruited as to be able to resume the charge of the school, to which he was unanimously elected in 1844; it having been removed to West Newton. He continued in charge of the school until 1849, when he was again compelled to resign on account of his health. He retired with the highest recommendation of the Board of Education and others for his fidelity and success.

A purse containing five hundred dollars was contributed by his pupils and other friends, and was presented to him, to enable him to go to Europe as a delegate to the Peace Congress, then to be held shortly in Paris. This was almost the only recreation he had allowed himself to take after leaving college in 1810. He spent several months in travelling in England and on the Continent. Soon after his return, he became an associate with

Mr. Nathaniel T. Allen, a young and ardent successful teacher, in the management of an academy in West Newton. Here he labored with all the zeal of his younger days, until his health again compelled him to retire, although he nominally remained an associate until his death. He passed away calmly and serenely, with the love and respect of all who knew him.

He married, about the year 1816, Harriet Coffin, of Nantucket, but had no children.

1811.—Clarke Gayton Pickman died in Boston, 11 May, 1860, aged 68. He was the second son of Col. Benjamin (H.C. 1784) and Anstis (Derby) Pickman, and was born in Salem, Mass., 22 November, 1791. His father was born in Salem, 30 September, 1763. He was a gentleman of fortune; was a member of both branches of the state legislature and of the executive-council; a delegate in 1820 to the convention for revising the constitution of Massachusetts; and a representative in Congress, from Essex South District, from 1809 to 1811. He died 11 August, 1843, aged 79. His mother was a daughter of Elias Hasket Derby, an eminent and wealthy merchant of Salem. He was fitted for college by Jacob Newman Knapp (H.C. 1802), who for several years kept a classical school in Salem. He was taken ill in his sophomore year, and did not again reside in college; but received a degree with his class. He then turned his attention to theological studies, intending to take orders in the Episcopal church, but not under the direction of any clergyman. He was ordained a deacon, and read the service a few times; but did not afterwards pursue the profession. He was long subject to undue nervous excitement, which occasionally resulted in temporary alienation of mind to such a degree, that it was necessary, more than once, to place him in an asylum for the insane, for short periods. He possessed a benevolent disposition, which he manifested by educating several meritorious children who were left orphans in straitened circumstances. He delivered an address before the East-Cambridge Temperance Society, 22 December, 1835, and another before the Ladies' Benevolent Society at East Cambridge, 18 December, 1836; both of which were published. In the following extract from the latter, he evidently alludes to himself: —

"It has pleased God to create men with different degrees of talent; and, of course, their pursuits must be attended with different degrees of success. In the complicated concerns of human life, it must also happen, that to equal talent there cannot, at all times, be given equal opportunities of exertion. Hence it is, that, while one man is able to succeed in his object of desire, another is kept back, sometimes by weakness, sometimes by his crimes, often by a course of events which he cannot control, and for the influences of which no cause can be assigned but the good pleasure of our Creator."

For many years, he had no permanent place of abode. He resided in Charlestown, East Cambridge, Boston, and other places in this vicinity. He was never married.

1814. — BENJAMIN APTHORP GOULD died in Boston, 24 October, 1859, aged 72. He was son of Capt. Benjamin and Grizzel (Apthorp) Gould, and was born in Lancaster, Mass., 15 June, 1787; but removed, when quite young, with his father's family, to Newburyport, Mass., where most of his youthful days were passed. He was fitted for college at Dummer Academy in Newbury, Mass. While in college, he attained a high rank in scholarship, and was particularly distinguished for his attainments in the Latin and Greek classics. In April of his senior year, an offer was made to him to take charge of the public Latin School in Boston; which had become greatly reduced, both in regard to the number of its scholars, and the want of a proper discipline. Whereupon he made application to the government for leave of absence for the remainder of his collegiate course; which, in consideration of his diligence as a student, his exemplary deportment, and the urgency of the Boston school-committee to obtain his valuable services, was granted, with the further privilege, that he should receive his degree with his class at the next Commencement. In the month of May following, he began his labors as principal of the school; and the highest anticipations of his friends were realized. The institution, under his vigorous and unwearied exertions, soon rose to a degree of prosperity which it had never before attained. He continued to hold the office of principal, with undiminished popularity and success, for fourteen years. In 1828, his health having become somewhat impaired by his long and arduous labors, he resigned his situation, and entered upon mercantile business, in which he continued the remainder of his life. He became a large ship-owner, and was extensively engaged in the Calcutta trade, which he pursued with good judgment and with much success; but he always retained an interest for the school of which he was so long the head. When the Latin-School Association was formed, he was unanimously elected its president; a post which he held, by successive re-elections, until his death. He was a member of the Boston common-council in 1834, 1835, 1836, and 1837, and was for several years one of the school-committee. He was a man of extensive literary attainments, and was a member of the American Academy of Arts and Sciences. He was greatly beloved by his numerous pupils, who ever retained an affectionate regard for their faithful instructor. His moral character was without a blemish.

He married, 2 December, 1823, Lucretia Dana Goddard, daughter of Nathaniel Goddard, Esq., of Boston, — a most amiable and accomplished lady, —who survives him. They had four children, — two sons and two daughters, — all of whom are living. The elder son, Benjamin Apthorp Gould, graduated at Harvard College in 1844, and is the well-known astronomer.

1814. — Thomas Walley Phillips, of Boston, died at his summer residence in Nahant, Mass., 8 September, 1859, aged 62. He was the eldest son of Hon. John (H.C. 1788) and Sally (Walley) Phillips, and was born in Boston, 16 January, 1797. His father was born in Boston, 26 November, 1770, was an eminent lawyer, was judge of the Court of Common Pleas in Suffolk county, was for many years president of the state senate, and was the first mayor of Boston. He died 29 May, 1823, aged 52. His mother was the daughter of Thomas and Sarah Walley; was born 25 March, 1772; and died 4 November, 1845, aged 73. His brothers and sisters, all of whom survive him, are Sarah Hurd, wife of Professor Alonzo

Gray, of Brooklyn, N.Y.; Margaret, wife of Dr. Edward Reynolds, of Boston; Miriam, wife of Rev. George Washington Blagden, of Boston; Rev. John Charles Phillips (H.C. 1826), of Methuen, Mass.; George William Phillips (H.C. 1829); Wendell Phillips (H.C. 1831); and Grenville Tudor Phillips (H.C. 1836),—the last three of Boston. He was sent in early boyhood to Phillips Academy in Andover, Mass., which was founded by one of his relatives, and was there fitted for college. After graduating, he read law with Hon. Lemuel Shaw (H.C. 1800), and was admitted to the Suffolk bar in 1817. For about fourteen years, he practised law with much success in Boston, until he succeeded the late Joseph H. Pierce as clerk of the Municipal Court; the arduous duties of which office he filled with great ability, and with perfect acceptance to the public, until his decease. Although of a retiring disposition, he was at various times called from his much-loved, quiet life at home, to take part in other official duties. In 1827, he was an influential member of the common-council, under the mayoralty of the elder Quincy; and, in 1829, he performed the duties of school-committe man for the ward in which he resided. In 1834 and 1837, he served the city as a representative in the legislature. But the most important position which he occupied was that of clerk of the Municipal Court; which office he held under the appointment of Judge Peter Oxenbridge Thacher (H.C. 1796), in 1830, and which, in its various changes, he retained by successive appointments and elections. For many years, he was a worthy and conscientious member of the Masonic fraternity; having received the degrees in Mount-Lebanon Lodge, of Boston, in July, 1821. The next year, he became a member of St. Andrew's Lodge, of Boston, — one of the most ancient and respectable in the country, — in which he for many years held the office of treasurer; and was one of the members'-committee, dispensing charity with an open hand and liberal heart. In all the relations of life, he was a most worthy man; and by his genuine kindliness of heart, and amiability of character, made warm friends of all with whom he associated.

He married, 18 March, 1824, Anna Jones, daughter of

Samuel Dunn, of Boston. Two children of this marriage survived him, — John, an engineer of promise, at one time employed in the construction of railways in Chile; and Samuel Dunn (H.C. 1861), who died in the service of the Educational Commission for Freedmen, in 1862. His wife also survived him.

1814. — THOMAS WETMORE died in Boston, 30 March, 1860, aged 64. He was son of Hon. William (H.C. 1770) and Sarah (Waldo) Wetmore, and was born in Boston, 31 August, 1795. His father, who was the son of Jeremiah and Hannah (Hobbs) Wetmore, was born in Middletown, Conn., 30 October, 1749; was a lawyer by profession; practised a short time in Salem, and removed thence to Boston, where he was appointed judge of the Court of Common Pleas; an office which he held many years. He died in Boston, 18 November, 1830, aged 81. The subject of this notice was fitted for college at the public Latin School in Boston. After graduating, he studied law; and, having been admitted to the bar, he opened an office in Boston, but retired from practice many years before his death, being possessed of an ample competence of worldly estate. He was a most useful and highly respected citizen, and devoted many years of his life to the interests of the city. He was a member of the common-council from 1829 to 1832; was an alderman in 1833, 1834, 1835, 1837, 1838, 1839, 1841, 1842, 1843, 1844, and 1847. He was also for several years a member of the board of water-commissioners. He was once a candidate for the office of mayor; but there being two other candidates, and a majority of all the votes cast being necessary for a choice, there was no election; and he then withdrew from the contest. He was never married.

1818. — Rev. JOSEPH AUGUSTUS EDWIN LONG died in Hookset, N. H., 3 May, 1860, aged 65. He was son of Nathan and Mary (Blaisdell) Long, and was born in Amesbury, Mass., 8 November, 1794. His name, originally, was Joseph Long; but, in 1820, he, by authority of the legislature, took the intermediate names of Augustus Edwin. He was fitted for college at Amesbury Academy, but concluded to become a merchant; and for that purpose entered the counting-room of Zebedee Cook, on India Wharf, Boston, as a clerk, where he remained one summer: but, business being dull in consequence of the embargo which existed at that time, he relinquished his purpose of a mercantile life, went to Phillips Academy, Exeter, N.H., where he reviewed his studies under Dr. Benjamin Abbot, and entered college in 1814. Immediately after graduating, he entered the Divinity School at Cambridge as a student, where he remained one year and a half; instructing, at the same time, a select number of private pupils. He then returned to Amesbury, where he continued his theological studies with his brother-in-law, Rev. Benjamin Sawyer (D.C. 1808), now of Salisbury, Mass. He was licensed to preach by the Essex North Association, 10 October, 1820; and went immediately to Kensington, N.H., where he preached, for the first time, 29 October of the same year. He continued his labors there to good acceptance until 5 June, 1822, when he was ordained as an evangelist; the church and society not being able to settle and support a pastor. He continued to preach, and perform all the ministerial duties, until 8 April, 1823. He then went to Chelmsford, Mass., where he performed the duties of ministerial pastor six or eight months. After leaving this place, he was employed as a missionary in the state of Maine about a year and six months. He often spoke of these eighteen months as the most pleasant in his life; and the people among whom he labored spoke of him with much respect and warm affection. He then went to Hookset, where he preached most of the time until 1832; when he went to Sandown, where he preached; and at Epping, Nottingham, and Poplin (now Fremont), for three or four years. In Biddeford and Lyman, Me., he was employed, as stated supply, about two years. In the autumn of 1837, he returned to his house and home in Hookset. After this time, his health being feeble, he preached only occasionally. He was often sent for to officiate at funerals; on which occasions, he was said to be gifted in prayer, and in adapting his remarks to the bereaved mourners.

His death was very sudden. He went to Concord, N.H., the 2d of May; returned home about five o'clock, P.M., as well as he had been for some weeks; and died the next morning, exchanging this for a better world, calmly and peacefully. For some weeks previous to his death, he often said he thought he should not live but a short time; that he should die suddenly; and gave directions respecting his funeral.

He married, 9 September, 1830, Anna Matilda Milton, daughter of Rev. Charles William Milton, of Newburyport, Mass.; by whom he had a son, Joseph Samuel Head, and a daughter, Mary Jane,—both well settled in life. These, with their mother, survived him.

1819.—Hon. ROBERT CROSS died in Lawrence, Mass., 9 November, 1859, aged 60. He was son of Major William and Ruth (Stacy) Cross, and was born in Newburyport, Mass., 3 July, 1799. He was grandson of Col. Ralph Cross, of the army of the Revolution,—afterwards Gen. Cross of the militia; and was appointed, by Jefferson, collector of Newburyport. His mother was a native of Gloucester, Mass. He was fitted for college at Phillips Academy, Andover; and graduated with high honors. Immediately after leaving college, he was appointed usher in the Boston Latin School, where he remained one year. He then studied law in the office of Hon. Ebenezer Moseley, of Newburyport (Y.C. 1802); was admitted a member of the Essex bar in December, 1823; and began the practice of his profession in Newburyport, where he remained several years. He then removed to Amesbury, Mass., where he continued his profession with great industry, fidelity, and success, and enjoyed repeated marks of the public confidence. He was elected a representative to the state legislature from Newburyport in 1827. In 1832, he was chosen senator from Essex district, and again in 1842. In 1844, he removed to Marshall, in the state of Michigan, where he resided until 1849, when he returned to Massachusetts, and settled in Lawrence, where he continued in the practice of his profession until his death. He was an accomplished scholar, a sound lawyer, and, in the highest sense of the word, a gentleman,—endeared to his friends, and respected by the community.

He married, in 1828, Mary Cabot Tyng, daughter of Hon.

Dudley Atkins Tyng, of Newburyport (H.C. 1781). They had four children; viz., Robert D., Mary R. (deceased), Ralph (deceased), and Charles E. His eldest son resides in Michigan, and his youngest is a cadet at West Point. His wife died very suddenly, of cholera, in Michigan, in July, 1849.

1820. Rev. BENJAMIN KENT, of Roxbury, Mass., died in the insane-hospital at Taunton, Mass., 5 August, 1859, aged 65. He was son of Samuel and Rhoda (Hill) Kent, and was born in that part of Charlestown which is now within the limits of Somerville, Mass., 25 May, 1794. He pursued his preparatory studies under the instruction of Hon. James Russell, of West Cambridge, Mass. (H.C. 1811). He held a high rank in his class, and graduated with distinction. The part assigned to him on his graduation was a poem "On Rank and Titles;" which was replete with sparkling wit, and elicited greater applause than any other performance that day. After leaving college, he studied theology at the Divinity School in Cambridge. He was ordained, 7 June, 1826, as colleague with Rev. John Allyn, D.D. (H.C. 1785), over the Unitarian church in Duxbury, Mass. Here he labored with great fidelity, and to the entire acceptance of the society, until ill health compelled him to ask a dismission, which was with much reluctance granted 7 June, 1833. To his unwearied labors the town was much indebted for the establishment of a high-school, which, principally through his instrumentality, was begun; and by his exertions a sum sufficient for its maintenance was raised, and teachers eminently qualified for the duties of instructors were procured. It was first under the charge of Mr. George Putnam (H.C. 1826), now the Rev. Dr. Putnam, of Roxbury; who was succeeded by Mr. William Augustus Stearns (H.C. 1827), now the Rev. Dr. Stearns, president of Amherst College.

From Duxbury, Mr. Kent removed, in 1833, to Roxbury; where he taught a private academy for young ladies for several years. He was afterwards librarian of the Roxbury Athenæum until within two or three years, when the feeble state of his health compelled him to relinquish it. He was a great sufferer for many years from extremely severe headache, — so severe that it several times resulted in fits of insanity, such as to render it necessary to remove him to the hospital for the insane. He was aware when these fits were coming upon him, and would give directions for his removal when it should be necessary. But all these afflictions he endured with remarkable patience and resignation.

Mr. Kent was a great lover of antiquity. He ransacked garrets, collected many autographs and literary documents of the Pilgrims, and made several discoveries of interest. He was a man of superior intellect, great originality, keen wit, and a fine poetic taste. He delivered, several years ago, the poem before the Phi Beta Kappa Society at Cambridge. His health was broken down by hard labor. His life affords a noble example of patience, self-devotion, enthusiasm, and virtue, through a life of uncommon trials.

He married, 27 September, 1826, Eleanor Bradford, of Boston. They had four children, — all daughters, — who, with their mother, survive him.

1820. — Rev. STEPHEN SCHUYLER died in Rhinebeck, Duchess county, N.Y., 1 November, 1859, aged 58. He was son of Philip J. and Sarah (Rutsen) Schuyler, and was born in Rhinebeck, 18 April, 1801. At the age of eight years, he was sent to Medfield, Mass., to school, under the charge of Rev. Thomas Prentiss, D.D. (H.C. 1766), preparatory for entering college, where he remained three years; thence to Cambridge and Brighton three years; thence to Albany, N.Y., one year; when he entered Union College at Schenectady. There he remained two years, when he left; and in August, 1818, he entered the junior class at Harvard College. While in college, he was studious, exemplary in his deportment, attained a high rank in his class, and graduated with honors. Immediately after leaving college, he selected the profession of law, and became a student in the office of Francis Livingston, Esq., at Rhinebeck, and in that of Samuel Jones, Esq. (Y.C. 1790), who was subsequently chancellor of the state of New York, the first judge of the Superior Court of the city of New York, and finally judge of the Supreme Court of the state, by election under the new judiciary system. He received his diploma as an attorney in the Supreme Court of the state of New York in October, 1823. He then turned his attention to the study of the divine law, and became a student in the Divinity School at Cambridge for two years, from September, 1824, to August, 1826. Compelled by ill health to abandon the practice of law in the city of New York, he became, in 1830, a permanent resident of his native place, Rhinebeck. He married, 11 December, 1831, Catharine Morris. Three children were the issue of this marriage; viz., 1. Stephen R., born 23 November, 1832. 2. Sarah Catharine, born 27 April, 1840; died 8 June, 1848, aged eight years, one month, eleven days. 3. Rutsen, born 19 April, 1849; died 8 March, 1852, aged two years, ten months, eighteen days. The lady whom he married, was, by religious profession, a member of the Methodist-Episcopal church, and he became a member of the same church in 1834; was licensed as a local preacher in the same year; was ordained to the order of deacon in 1839, and to that of elder in 1844. He was a most sincere believer in the doctrine of the denomination which he had embraced, and was a faithful and efficient laborer in his Master's vineyard until his health failed. In 1851, he had a severe hemorrhage from the lungs; but, by great care, he rallied again, although he was always, after that, subject to a severe cough and occasional bleeding. For the last two years of his life, his health was very feeble. In May previous to his death, he said to his friends that he might get through the summer, but should not live through the fall. The disease gradually wasted his body away, but his mind continued calm and cheerful until the very last. He made all his arrangements for his departure to that bright world which his pure spirit was so fully prepared to enter, and he gradually passed away into that solemn darkness which mortal eye cannot pierce, but which to him, doubtless, is lighted up by the radiance of a never-ending noon. His wife survived him; and his only remaining child was a civil-engineer, residing in Mississippi.

1822.—John Frost died in Philadelphia, 28 December, 1859, aged 59. He was son of Nathaniel and Abigail

(Kimball) Frost, and was born in Kennebunk, Me., 26 January, 1800. In early life he manifested great fondness for study. He pursued his preparatory studies at the academy in Gorham, Me.; and, in 1818, he entered Bowdoin College, where he remained one year, when he left, and entered the sophomore class at Harvard College. He held an honorable rank of scholarship in his class, and graduated with high honors. In the winter immediately subsequent to leaving college, he taught school in Cambridgeport. In 1823, he was appointed principal of the Mayhew School in Boston, which position he held about four years. In 1828, he removed to Philadelphia; passing the winters of 1827–8 and 1828–9 in Cuba to recover from severe attacks of bleeding from the lungs. From 1828 to 1838, he conducted a school for young ladies; and, at the latter date, accepted the situation of professor of belles-lettres at the Central High-School in Philadelphia, which he resigned, in 1845, to devote himself entirely to literary pursuits. He was, during a great portion of his life, a book-maker, — probably the most prolific one our country has yet produced. To that pursuit he sacrificed every thing else. He made his pupils his assistants, and thus lost for his female school the patronage of some of the wealthy families. He mingled the same pursuit with his teachings in the High School, and with a similar result. The two things were incongruous, and the passion for literature triumphed. It is impossible to give a list of the numerous works he wrote and compiled. They were principally histories, many of them bearing a fictitious name on the titlepage. History was his speciality, and this exhaustless mine he worked in every way. His "Pictorial History of the United States" sold largely, upwards of fifty thousand copies having been disposed of some years ago; and it is still popular. Next to his historical works, his biographies fill the largest space. He employed writers, engravers, and designers, and had a regular workshop for the production of books. Nevertheless, his mind, which was exceedingly suggestive, was the architect of every thing. By unceasing industry in his vocation, the volumes of his compilation numbered upwards of three hundred. He was a scholar of ripe attainments, well versed in the Spanish and French languages. Although his talents and attainments were universally admitted to be of a high order, his love of study and reading never flagged. Every new publication, from which he hoped to derive fresh information, was read with attention; and his wonderfully fine memory treasured up all of interest. In 1843, the honorary degree of doctor of laws was conferred upon him by Marshall College in Pennsylvania.

He married, 4 May, 1830, Sarah Ann Burditt, daughter of James White and Mary (Rhoades) Burditt, of Boston. They had ten children, all born in Philadelphia; viz., 1. Mary Cordelia, born 28 April, 1831. 2. Caroline Augusta, born 3 July, 1833; married, 8 March, 1854, Dr. J. R. Rowand. 3. James W. Burditt, born 31 July, 1835; died 15 December, 1835. 4. Sarah Annie, born 20 May, 1837. 5. George Frederic, born 16 October, 1839. 6. Frances Emily, born 19 May, 1842; died 6 August, 1846. 7. Morton, born 6 February, 1845; died 5 February, 1847. 8. Charles William, born 10 April, 1848. 9. Arthur Burditt, born 17 January, 1851. 10. Francis Burditt, born 5 November, 1855; died 15 April, 1857.

Mr. Frost's domestic relations were those of a sincere Christian, a most loving husband, and a kind parent. A long life of incessant study and labor ended with a peaceful and happy death. Weighed down in his last years by business perplexities and troubles, his perfect trust in a protecting Providence, and his gentle loving-kindness in his family, were never disturbed by worldly difficulties. His last illness was very short, and his death fearfully sudden: yet, though often in severe bodily pain, his mind was, through all his sickness, calm, quiet, and peaceful; seeming to have laid aside all earthly cares, to wait in perfect love and hope the release from his burdens here.

1824. — Rev. GEORGE WASHINGTON BURNAP died in Baltimore, Md., 8 September, 1859, aged 56. He was son, and the youngest of thirteen children, of Rev. Jacob, D.D. (H.C. 1770) and Elizabeth (Brooks) Burnap, and was born in Merrimack, N.H., 30 November, 1802. His father was born in Reading, Mass., 2 November, 1748; was ordained pastor of the church in Merrimack, 14 October, 1772; and died 26 December, 1821, aged 73; having sustained his pastoral relationship with his people upwards of forty-nine years. His mother was the daughter of Caleb and Ruth (Albree) Brooks, of Medford, Mass., and sister of the late Gov. John Brooks. The subject of this notice was fitted for college at the academy in Thetford, Vt., and graduated with high honors. After leaving college, he studied theology at the Divinity School in Cambridge. He was ordained pastor of the First Independent (Unitarian) Church in Baltimore, 23 April, 1828, as successor of Rev. Jared Sparks (H.C. 1815), where he labored with great acceptance until his decease, a period of thirty-one years. In this outpost of the Unitarian faith, although not gifted with such an address as might be supposed to captivate a Southern audience, he soon obtained a standing in his congregation, and a reputation with the public, such as few clergymen have enjoyed; and maintained them unimpaired through his ministry. He retained to the last an earnest simplicity of character, which was his peculiar trait; and commanded universal respect for his genial disposition and high Christian aims. He was not brilliant, but was solid; and his discussions, whether social or from the pulpit, were marked by strict logic and conscientious fairness. His publications, mostly upon religious topics and moral subjects, were numerous, and of a high order of merit. His social position in Baltimore gave him a wide sphere of usefulness, independently of his labors in his pastoral relation; and he did much, by means of lectures, to elevate and refine public sentiment, and to diffuse useful knowledge. He was a member of the Maryland Historical Society; and was one of the board of trustees of the Peabody Institute in Baltimore, the building for the accommodation of which has just been erected. His thorough scholarship, and his large acquaintance with books, rendered his aid in that body most valuable, particularly in connection with the organization of the library, a subject in which he felt a deep interest. In 1849, the degree of doctor of divinity was conferred upon him by Harvard College.

He married, 18 July, 1831, Nancy Williams, daughter

of Amos A. Williams, Esq., a distinguished merchant of Baltimore. They had three children, — one son and two daughters; of whom the son and one daughter died in infancy. The other daughter and her mother are living.

He published, in 1835, a volume of "Lectures to Young Men on the Cultivation of the Mind, the Formation of Character, and the Conduct of Life;" in the same year, a volume of "Lectures on the Sphere and Duties of Woman;" in 1842, "Lectures on the History of Christianity." In 1844, he contributed to Sparks's American Biography a memoir of Leonard Calvert, first Governor of Maryland. In 1845, he published "Expository Lectures on the Principal Texts of the Bible which relate to the Doctrine of the Trinity;" a volume of "Miscellanies," and a "Biography of Henry T. Ingalls." In 1848, he published a small work entitled "Popular Objections to Unitarian Christianity Considered and Answered;" and, in 1850, twenty discourses "On the Rectitude of Human Nature." He was a contributor to the pages of the "Christian Examiner" from the year 1834.

1824. — Caleb Morton Stimson died in Newton Lower Falls, Mass., 6 July, 1860, aged 56. He was son of Samuel and Susanna (Bigelow) Stimson, and was born in Newton, 13 April, 1804. His father, who was son of Jeremiah and Sarah Stimson, was born in Boston in 1765; was brought up a merchant; travelled abroad to some extent; and finally settled in business, as a grocer, on Long Wharf, Boston, having entered into partnership with his younger brother, Caleb. He was married, 4 July, 1796, by Rev. John Thornton Kirkland, to Susanna Bigelow. They had but two children, — the subject of this notice, and one elder brother who died in infancy. When the yellow-fever broke out in Boston, his father relinquished business, removed to Newton, where he purchased a farm, on which he lived until his death, which took place in November, 1849, at the age of eighty-four years. His mother was the daughter of Thomas and Betsey (Wales) Bigelow, of Waltham, Mass. Young Stimson was fitted for college mostly by Rev. Charles Train, of Framingham, Mass. (H.C. 1805), but passed a few months in completing his preparatory studies at Milton Academy. After leaving college, he studied law in part at the Law School in Cambridge, and partly in the office of Hon. Lemuel Shaw (H.C. 1800), of Boston. He was admitted to the bar in Boston in 1827 or 1828, but did not enter into practice; for, being an only child, at his father's express desire he went to reside with him at Newton, and remained there, with the exception of some brief intervals, during the remainder of his life. Inheriting an ample competence, and his health having been for many years in a very feeble state, he pursued no regular business. Possessing a most amiable disposition, he led a blameless life, and finally passed away with calmness and composure, leaving no enemy behind him.

He married, 27 April, 1847, Charlotte Augusta Crehore, daughter of Lemuel Crehore, of Newton, but had no children. His wife survived him.

1825.—Hilary Breton Cenas died in New Orleans, 26 October, 1859, aged 53. He was son of Blaise and Catharine (Baker) Cenas, and was born in Philadelphia, 5 November, 1805. He was prepared for college by Rev. James F. Hull, rector of Christ Church, Philadelphia. On leaving college, he chose the profession of law, and pursued his studies under the instruction of William Christy and John R. Grymes, of New Orleans; and, after his admission to the bar, he opened an office in that city, where he practised for several years; but subsequently relinquished it, and established himself as a notary-public. He was a gentleman of great affability of manner, was highly esteemed for his many excellent personal qualities, and retained the confidence of a large business-acquintance in the exercise of the duties of his important profession.

He married, February, 1833, Margaret Pierce, of New Orleans, who survived him. They had thirteen children,—seven sons and six daughters,—of whom two sons and all the daughters survived him.

1830.—John White Browne, of Boston, was instantly killed in Braintree, Mass., 1 May, 1860, by accidentally falling from the platform of a railroad-car while the train was in motion.

He was fifty years of age. He was son of James and Lydia (Vincent) Browne, and was born in Salem, Mass., 29 March, 1810. His father was the eldest lineal descendant of Elder John Browne, the ruling elder of the First Church of the Massachusetts-Bay Colony at Salem, whose acceptance of the eldership the Rev. Mr. Higginson made the condition of his own settlement as pastor. His great-grandfather, for whom he was named, was John White; whose daughter, Mary White, was the wife of Elder William Browne, and mother of James Browne, the father of John White Browne. Both William and James were elders in the East Church, Salem, — Unitarian, under the pastorate of the late Dr. William Bentley (H.C. 1777), — James succeeding at the death of his father.

The subject of this notice was fitted for college at the Salem Classical School, under the charge of Theodore Ames and Henry Kemble Oliver. While in college, he was the chum of Hon. Charles Sumner. He attained a very high rank of scholarship in his class, and graduated with distinguished honors. He studied law one year at the Law School at Cambridge, one year with Hon. Rufus Choate (D.C. 1819), and one year with Hon. Leverett Saltonstall (H.C. 1802) in Salem. He practised his profession several years in Lynn, Mass.; but, about twelve years before his death, he removed to Boston, where he continued in practice, principally as a conveyancer, until his decease. In 1837, he was elected a representative to the legislature; and in 1838, during his absence from the state, he was nominated by the whig party of Essex county as a candidate for the state senate. On his return, he declined the nomination, for the reason that he was unwilling to become the candidate of any party for political office. From that time he carefully avoided political prominence (although he took a warm and constant interest in the course of public affairs), devoting himself with extreme assiduity to the business of his profession. He took an especially serviceable part in almost every effort for criminal reform, and for the improvement of prison discipline, during his long period of active professional service; and was also earnestly, though quietly, devoted to the promotion of the antislavery movement. His daily life was an exhibition of a noble, highly cultivated intellect, of the purest morality, and the gentlest kindly feelings for the welfare of the whole human race.

He married, in 1842, Martha Ann Gibbs, daughter of Capt. Barnabas Lincoln, of Hingham, Mass. They had but one child, — a daughter (Laura Lincoln Browne), — who, with her mother, survived him.

1830. — Dr. Henry Lincoln died in Lancaster, Mass., 29 February, 1860, aged 55. He was son of William and Tabitha (Kendall) Lincoln, and was born in Leominster, Mass., 11 August, 1804. His father was a farmer, and died in Leominster, 27 December, 1846. His mother was daughter of Edward Kendall, of Fitzwilliam, N.H., originally from Leominster. He was fitted for college, in part, by Hon. Joseph Gowing Kendall (H. C. 1810), of Worcester, Mass., then practising law at Leominster; and in part at Lawrence Academy in Groton. After leaving college, he went to Philadelphia, where he studied medicine under the instruction of Dr. Samuel Jackson, of that city; and received his degree of M.D. at the University of Pennsylvania in 1834. Returning to Massachusetts, he established himself in Lancaster, where he acquired an extensive practice, and was highly respected. He married, 14 February, 1838, Martha Bond; and had children, — William Henry (who died before him), Mary Catharine, Ellen Sears, Martha Bond, Francis Newhall, and Edward Hartwell. His widow survived him.

1838. — Abel Fox died of consumption, in Quincy, Ill., 14 November, 1859, aged 41 years. He was son of Oliver and Mary (Dorr) Fox, and was born in Fitchburg, Mass., 21 August, 1818. His mother was sister of the late Samuel Dorr, of Boston, for many years president of the New-England Bank. The subject of this notice was fitted for college partly at Leicester Academy, and completed his studies at Exeter (N.H.) Academy. He did not study a profession; but, soon after he graduated, removed to Quincy, Ill., and devoted himself to agriculture. He there married the widow of his brother, Henry Fox. Her maiden name was Abby Whittemore, formerly of Boston. He left no children.

1843. — Elisha Winslow Tracy died in Hampshire, Kane county, Ill., 5 February, 1860, aged 36. He was son of Elisha and Lucy C. (Huntington) Tracy, and was born in Norwich, Conn., 8 April, 1823. His name originally was Winslow Decatur Tracy, which was changed soon after he graduated. He was fitted for college at the academy in Cheshire, Conn. He pursued his professional studies at the Law School in Cambridge. Having come into possession of a considerable fortune soon after leaving college, by the death of his father, he went to Chicago, Ill. He was admitted to the bar in the fall of 1844, and at once took a high rank in his profession. The "Chicago Times" thus speaks of his abilities: "His powers of intellect were indeed remarkable. His mind possessed that comprehensive quality which beholds a subject at once in all its various aspects, and perceives their relations and bearings without the labor of study. Its habit was eminently philosophical, its tone strong and vigorous. He was no follower of other men's thoughts. His utterance, whether in a set speech or unpremeditated debate, betrayed an originality of thought, a clearness of comprehension, which are seldom found even in our most eminent men. His imagination, too, was extremely fine; and his speeches very frequently embraced figures and tropes of surprising beauty. Indeed, an elevated poetical quality, united with originality of ideas and philosophical treatment of subjects, were the distinguishing characteristics of his oratory."

Mr. Tracy never held any political office. He married, in November, 1858, Lizzie Thayer, a young and amiable lady of Chicago; and with his bride went immediately to Europe, where he spent about a year in travelling in England and on the Continent. On his return, he purchased a farm in the town of Hampshire, Kane county, with the design of abandoning the law, and engaging in agriculture. There he died, leaving a widow only twenty years of age, but no children.

1848. — James Atherton Dugan died in Brewster, Mass., 5 June, 1860, aged 33. He was son of James and Sophia (Atherton) Dugan, and was born in Boston, 4 February, 1827. He received his education wholly at the public schools in Boston, and was prepared for college at the Latin School. He was a remarkably studious, bright, and exemplary scholar when a boy; so much so, that three Franklin medals were awarded to him at three several schools which he attended; namely, at the Wells School in 1838, at the English High School in 1842, and at the Latin School in 1844. While in college, he attained a high rank in scholarship, and was a great favorite among his classmates. But in his junior year his health failed, so that he was unable to continue his studies; and he was obliged to leave. He went a voyage to Rio Janeiro, and returned with his health in a great measure restored; and his degree was conferred upon him in 1851. After his return, he taught a private school in Bedford, Mass., for some time; after which he was engaged as an assistant in the school of Mr. Epes Sargent Dixwell (H.C. 1827) in Boston. He next removed to Brewster, Mass., where he opened a private school, which he continued as long as his health would permit. He was a popular teacher, of unblemished moral character; and his early death was a sad affliction to his family and friends. His father died suddenly at Brewster, while on a visit to that place, 10 August, 1858, aged 66.

He married, 5 August, 1852, Helen, daughter of Elijah Cobb, Esq., of Brewster. They had three children, — two sons and one daughter, — who, with their mother, survived him.

1848. — Samuel Parsons died in Philadelphia, 28 October, 1859, aged 30. He was son of Samuel and Mary Brown (Allen) Parsons, and was born in Boston, 2 May, 1829. He was fitted for college at the public Latin School in Boston, where a Franklin medal was awarded to him for superior scholarship. He held a highly respectable rank in his class, and graduated with distinction. After leaving college, he pursued the study of law, partly in the office of Charles Bishop Goodrich (D.C. 1822), and partly in that of William Brigham (H.C. 1829), of Boston. Having been admitted to the bar, he opened an office in Boston; but, his health failing, he left the city, and resided for a time on his father's farm in Newton, where he in a great measure recovered, and then concluded to change his residence to Philadelphia, but did not long survive after his removal to that city. He was unmarried.

1848.—Dr. ADAMS WILEY, of Roxbury, Mass., died in Clifton, Mich., to which place he had gone for the benefit of his health, 2 April, 1860, aged 33. He was son of Thomas and Margaret (Wright) Wiley, and was born in Boston, 16 November, 1826. He was a twin,—the two graduating in the same class. As they were born the same year that the two presidents, Adams and Jefferson, died, their parents named them Adams and Jefferson respectively. The father of the subject of this notice was born in Reading, now South Reading, Mass., 7 August, 1784; and died in Roxbury, 25 May, 1860; having survived his son only seven weeks and four days. His mother was born in Boston, 23 March, 1791; and his parents were married by Rev. John Murray, 2 December, 1810. He was fitted for college at Lunenburg Academy, of which John Rodman Rollins (D.C. 1837) was principal. While in college, he was a diligent student, attained a very respectable standing in scholarship, and his deportment and moral character were without a blemish. After leaving college, he pursued his professional studies at the Tremont Medical School in Boston; and, having received his degree of M.D. in 1852, he established himself in Roxbury, where, by his judicious practice, he became quite popular, and the prospect opened to him a wide field for success and eminence in his profession. During his residence in Roxbury, he was appointed one of the physicians of the dispensary; and was also secretary of the athenæum, in which institution he took a lively interest. Amiable in his disposition and manners, cultivated in mind and tastes, genial and generous in his feelings, pure and exemplary in his whole conduct and character, he was esteemed and loved by a large circle of kindred and friends. His death came upon him somewhat unexpectedly, but it was singularly calm and beautiful; and, to quote an expression from a pencilled note written by him but the day before his decease, he was "full of faith in a God who had showed his love for sinners." He was never married.

1852.—CHARLES WENTWORTH UPHAM died in Buffalo, N.Y., 2 April, 1860, aged 29. He was the eldest son of Hon. Charles Wentworth (H.C. 1821) and Mary Ann (Holmes)

Upham, and was born in Salem, Mass., 19 August, 1830. His father, who was son of Judge Joshua Upham (H.C. 1763), of Brookfield, Mass., a refugee, was born in St. John, N.B., 4 May, 1802. His mother was daughter of Rev. Abiel (Y.C. 1783) and Sarah (Wendell) Holmes, of Cambridge, Mass.

In the summer of 1839, young Upham was sent to St. John, N.B. (where his aunt, Fanny Wendell, resided), to improve his health; where he spent nearly seven months. On his return the following year, he went to the Ropes farm in Danvers, where he passed the summer, and where he repeatedly went; his parents, on account of his health, always sending him away from school during the summer season. In the interim he attended the Salem schools, and finally there completed his preparation for college at the Latin School, under Mr. Oliver Carleton (D.C. 1824). In the summer of 1847, with Darwin Erastus Ware, of his class, and Henry Stone, who entered Harvard, but graduated at Bowdoin College, he went to Portland by steamboat. There he and his companions, dressed in pedestrian style, went on foot round the White Mountains to Andover, Me., back to Winnipiseogee, thence through Concord, N.H., home, all the way on foot, having been absent twenty-one days. In the summers of 1849 and 1851, he also made excursions to the White Mountains; and, in the vacation in his senior year, he journeyed to Brandon, Vt., to Washington, D.C., and to Providence, R.I. He was college marshal at the inauguration of President Sparks in the spring of 1849; chief-marshal at the celebration of the seventy-fifth anniversary of the battle of Bunker Hill, 17 June, 1850; chief-marshal at the railroad jubilee celebration in Boston, in September, 1851; chief-marshal at the class-day; and vice-president at the class-supper. He suggested the idea of class-daguerrotypes, first carried out in the class to which he belonged, and which has since been succeeded by photographs in later classes.

Immediately after graduating, he entered the Law School at Cambridge; and, after remaining the usual period, he received the degree of bachelor of laws; was admitted to the bar, and opened an office in Salem. In 1855, he went to Europe, where he remained about two years, enriching his mind by visiting the most interesting portions of England and the Continent, and increasing his stock of useful information; but, as he was about to leave England on his return, the first symptoms of that fell disease, consumption, appeared, which terminated his life. In the summer of 1857, he removed to Buffalo, where he established himself in the practice of his profession; having been admitted a partner with Hon. S. G. Haven and William Dorsheimer, under the firm of Haven, Dorsheimer, and Upham. The firm was originally Fillmore, Hall, and Haven. With a handsome person, fine colloquial powers, and a mind enriched by the observations and experiences of foreign travel, he was a favorite with all who knew him, and every thing seemed to promise for him a brilliant and successful career. It was, however, otherwise ordered; and he was cut down in the morning of life: but he submitted to his inevitable doom with a cheerful, Christian resignation, and with a full confidence of a blessed immortality beyond the grave.

He married, 22 June, 1859, Mary, daughter of Hon. Solomon G. Haven, of Buffalo; who survived the partner of her affections.

The members of the bar in Buffalo held a meeting on the evening of the 4th of April, at which appropriate and respectful tributes were paid to the memory of their youthful associate; and subsequently attended the funeral in a body, pursuant to a vote to that effect.

1854. — JAMES BROWN KENDALL died at the residence of his father, in Saxonville (Framingham, Mass.), 9 October, 1859, aged 25 years, lacking two days. He was the only son of Rev. James Augustus (H.C. 1823) and Maria Boyle (Brown) Kendall, and was born in Medfield, Mass., 11 October, 1834. When about two and a half years old, he removed with his parents to Saxonville; about two years later, to Stow, Mass.; and in July, 1842, to Cambridge; which place was his residence until the summer previous to his death. He was fitted for college at the Hopkins Classical School in Cambridge, under Edmund Burke Whitman (H.C. 1838), now of Kansas. He graduated with high honors. In the winter of his junior year, he taught school in Scussett (Sandwich, Mass.). After graduating, he taught with great success a private classical school in Portsmouth, N.H., for two years; in the mean time pursuing the study of law, which he subsequently continued and completed at the Law School in Cambridge. Having been admitted to the bar, he, in partnership with his classmate, Payson Elliot Tucker, opened an office in Worcester, Mass., in the summer of 1859. About two months afterwards, he was seized with typhoid-fever, of which he died after a brief illness. He was brilliant, witty, learned, of stern integrity and high moral character.

1855. — ANDREW LAMMEY YONGUE was killed on the Charlotte and South-Carolina Railroad, at Columbia, S.C., 17 November, 1859, aged 31. He was the youngest of three children (the others, a brother named Robert A., and a sister named Sarah) of William and Elizabeth (Lammey) Yongue, and was born in Buckhead, Fairfield District, S.C., 12 April, 1828. Both his parents died several years since. His father died 13 November, 1842, aged 77 years; and his mother died 19 January, 1844. He was prepared for South-Carolina College at the Mount-Zion Collegiate Institute, J. W. Hudson, principal, Winnsborough, S.C. He entered the sophomore class of the South-Carolina College, December, 1851; and left, December, 1852, with one hundred and ten others, who were compelled to leave on account of what is known as the "Biscuit Rebellion." He entered the sophomore class of Harvard College, March, 1853. It was his intention, after graduation, to prepare for the ministry: but his health became delicate from exposure during his residence at college, and passing to and fro, so that, in a measure, he had to give up study, and he settled on a farm inherited from his father; but becoming embarrassed by the deaths of his negroes, and other misfortunes, he was forced to change his business. He then taught school for eighteen months, with a view still for the ministry, if his health would permit. To raise further funds to enable him to carry out his purpose, he obtained the situation of conductor on the Charlotte and South-Carolina Railroad. About three months after entering upon his new duties, he met with the unfortunate accident which terminated his life. He attempted to step on the train while in motion: his foot slipped, and he fell under the cars; the wheels passed over both his legs. One was taken off above the knee, and the other broken above the ankle. This was on the 16th of November; and he died the next day. He bore his suffering with great patience, and not a murmur escaped his lips; believing it was the will of his heavenly Father that he should die thus, and for some good end. He died with a prayer upon his lips, "Lord Jesus, receive my spirit." He was buried at the Salem church, Fairfield District, of which he was a member. He was never married.

One calamity follows another in quick succession. Robert A. Yongue, the only brother of Andrew L., died on the 4th of February, 1860; having been left by the cars seven miles from Charleston, while warming himself at a fire by the road; and in attempting to walk over a high trestle (thirty feet), stepping on a rotten plank which gave way, he fell through the distance mentioned, on stumps, and into water four feet deep. His remains were not found until the next day. The expression of Andrew L. Yongue, that his death was for some good end, was verified: for his brother, who had been thoughtless of his latter end, was almost inconsolable at his death; from that period became a changed man; and there was good reason to believe that he was prepared for the sudden and unexpected death that awaited him. He was a graduate at the South-Carolina College some years ago. He left a widow and two children to mourn their irreparable loss.

Their sister Sarah, the only surviving member of the family, became the wife of David Milling, Esq., of Mill View, Fairfield District, S.C.; where he at one time held the office of postmaster. She was in feeble and delicate health after the melancholy deaths of her brothers, following each other in so quick succession.

1857.—EDWARD THOMAS DAMON, of Wayland, Mass., died in Cambridge, Mass., of small-pox, 30 November, 1859, aged 25. He was son of Thomas Jefferson and Rachel (Thomas) Damon, and was born in Wayland, 19 April, 1834. He began his preparatory studies for college at Lawrence Academy in Groton, Mass.; and completed them under the instruction of Mrs. Samuel Ripley, of Concord, Mass. He graduated with distinguished honors. After leaving college, he began the study of medicine, at the Medical School in Boston, under the instruction of Drs. John Ware (H.C. 1813) and Morrill and Jeffries Wyman (H.C. 1833); and, while attending the course of medical lectures, he was attacked with that loathsome disease which terminated his life. He was a great favorite wherever he was known; and his premature removal, just as a brilliant prospect for the future was opening before him, was a sad affliction to his parents and other relatives, as well as to his classmates and many friends.

1857. — GEORGE HOLLINGSWORTH died in Groton, Mass., 8 August, 1859, aged 23. He was son of John Mark and Emmeline (Cornell) Hollingsworth, and was born in Braintree, Mass., 29 July, 1836. He entered the Boston Latin School at the age of ten; and, after remaining there somewhat over two years, left, upon the removal of his parents to West Cambridge; and there he completed his preparatory studies for admission into college, under the instruction of a private tutor. He taught school during the winter of 1857–8, and subsequently was engaged in the paper-manufacturing business with his father in Groton.

1858. — AMORY POLLARD SAWYER died in Bolton, Mass., 20 May, 1860, aged 26. He was son of Nathan and Lucinda (Pollard) Sawyer, and was born in Bolton, 30 October, 1833. He was fitted for college at the high-school in Bolton. The disease by which he was so prematurely taken away was consumption, the incipient symptoms of which appeared during his junior year at college; and nearly the whole of his senior year he was absent from Cambridge, returning only to join in the festivities of Class-day. While his health permitted, he was a diligent and faithful student; of modest, unassuming deportment; winning the love of his classmates and the regard of his instructors.

1859. — HENRY HUSTON ABBOTT died in Charlestown, Mass., of typhoid-fever, after an illness of eight days, 22 July, 1859, aged 23. He was the eldest son of John Gilman and Sophia (Huston) Abbott, and was born in Charlestown, 18 July, 1836. His father was a native of Concord, N.H., and was born 27 March, 1812. His mother was born in Farmington, Me., 23 December, 1814. Young Abbott pursued his preparatory studies at the high-school in Charlestown. While in college, he was a diligent student, constant in his attendance at all recitations, modest in his demeanor, and exemplary in his conduct. He made extraordinary exertions to secure the advantages of a college education, intending afterwards to devote himself to the business of a teacher. But he was cut off in the dawning of his hopes: death marked him as the first victim in his class. His degree was conferred upon him: he was permitted, while on his death-bed, to look at his diploma; but, within forty-eight hours from his graduation, he ceased to live.

1860 – 61.

1795. — Rev. Caleb Bradley died in Westbrook, Me., 2 June, 1861, aged 89 years. He was son of Deacon Amos and Elizabeth (Page) Bradley, and was born in that part of Dracut which is now within the limits of Lowell, Mass, 12 March, 1772. His parents were natives of Haverhill, Mass. He labored on his father's farm until he was seventeen years of age; when he began the study of the Latin language, under the instruction of Rev. Solomon Aiken, of Dracut (D.C. 1784). He afterwards studied for three months with Rev. Simon Finley Williams, in Methuen (D.C. 1785). The next year, he entered Atkinson (N.H.) Academy, where he completed his preparatory studies; and in August, 1791, he entered Dartmouth College, where he remained two years; when he left, and entered the junior class in Harvard College; where he graduated, in due course, with a respectable standing. In an autobiography, he stated, that, while in college, he "was never absent from prayers, nor from any of the college exercises; was never admonished or fined." Immediately after graduating, he began the study of divinity with Rev. Henry Cumings, of Billerica, Mass. (H.C. 1760). Within a year afterwards, he was approbated by the Andover Association, and preached his first sermon in Billerica. He was ordained pastor of the church in Falmouth (now Westbrook), Me., 9 October, 1799. He continued his pastoral labors in this place, with great diligence and fidelity, until 28 April, 1828, when he resigned his charge; and, on the following day, the Rev. Henry Cushing Jewett (B.U. 1824) was ordained as his successor. The society were desirous that Mr. Bradley should remain as senior pastor, and that Mr. Jewett should be settled as his colleague; but he preferred to be relieved from the burdens and responsibilities of the pastoral charge. He did not, however, give up preaching, but continued his ministerial labors. For more than six years, he officiated as chaplain at the city poor-house in Portland, and was twice delegated by the Maine Missionary Society to act as missionary in the county of Cumberland; and he continued to preach occasionally in various places.

He married, 16 November, 1801, Sally Crocker, of Taunton, Mass. She died 27 April, 1821, leaving six children. He married for his second wife, in 1827, Mrs. Susan Partridge (widow of Nathaniel Partridge), whose maiden name was Susan Smith, originally from Wrentham, Mass. She died 3 November, 1843; and he married for his third wife, 26 December, 1844, Mrs. Abigail Codman, widow of James Codman, Esq., of Gorham, Me. She died 17 August, 1854. She was a native of Halifax, Mass.

1797. — Hon. Daniel Appleton White died in Salem, Mass., 30 March, 1861, aged 84 years. He was son of Capt. John and Elizabeth (Haynes) White, and was born in that part of Methuen which is now the city of Lawrence, 7 June, 1776. In June, 1792, he entered the academy in Atkinson, N.H., where he was fitted for college. He graduated with the highest honors of his class. With a love of sound learning and classic literature, his mind was richly imbued with the elementary course of college-life, and formed a sure foundation for future progress in intellectual culture. In 1799, he was appointed a tutor in the Latin department of the college; which post he occupied until 1803. During that time, he had entered his name as a student-of-law in the office of Francis Dana Channing, of Cambridge (H.C. 1794). He was always deeply interested in the success of the college; and as a general supervisor of all its concerns, as a temporary member of the faculty, and member of the board of overseers, he never lost sight of its interests. In September, 1803, he went to Salem for a year, and entered the law-office of Hon. Samuel Putnam (H.C. 1787), afterwards judge of the Supreme Court. In Judge Putnam's office, the late Hon. John Pickering (H.C. 1796) was a fellow-student; and, jointly with that distinguished scholar, young White prepared, for the use of the college, an editon of "Sallust," which was published by Cushing and Appleton; but the whole edition, as soon as it was ready for delivery, was destroyed by fire. In 1804, Judge White was admitted to the Essex bar, and established himself in the practice of law, in Newburyport, in the days when there were legal giants in Essex, and when his discipline and well-stored mind insured for him a successful practice. At this interesting period of our political history, his talents and discretion drew him into the arena of political life; and, from 1810 to 1814, he was a conspicuous member of the senate of Massachusetts, under the administration of Gov. Strong; and was a firm supporter of his patriotic and practical policy. In November, 1814, he was elected a member of Congress from Essex North District, and commissioned; but, before the meeting of Congress, he resigned, to accept the office of judge of probate, to which he was appointed by Gov. Strong, upon the resignation of Judge Holten, in May, 1815. In 1817, he moved to Salem, where he passed the remainder of his life; continuing to fill the office of probate-judge, with uncommon ability, until he resigned it in the summer of 1853; blessed with an old age, serene and bright to the latest moment; and enjoying, by universal consent, the distinction of being regarded as, beyond dispute, the first citizen in the community where he resided.

Judge White's vast literary resources were always at the command of his friends and the public; and he was the dispenser of a liberal hospitality, and the patron of every good enterprise — moral, æsthetic, and educational — which tended to foster the highest interests of the community. He was one of the founders and directors of the Divinity School at Cambridge; was an overseer of Harvard College from 1842 to 1853; delivered the address at the second meeting of the Association of the Alumni in 1844. He was the founder of the lyceum in Salem; was the president of the athenæum, and presided over the Essex Institute from its first establishment; was a member of the Massachusetts Historical Society; of the American Academy of Arts and Sciences; and received from Harvard College, in 1837, the degree of doctor of laws. He delivered eulogies on the decease of Dr. Nathaniel Bowditch and Hon. John Pickering. He was the author of several other addresses and memoirs of great literary merit. Early in his judicial career, he wrote a valuable book on probate jurisdiction. As an author, he was master of a singularly clear and nervous style, which was exhibited through a period of more than sixty years. But it was in the intimate relations of family and friendship that his graces and excellences as a man and a Christian were most remarkable; and these were continued literally to the the very last minute of his most consistent life, in loving recognitions, sentences of faith, and prayer, and hymns of praise.

Judge White married, first, 24 May, 1807, Mrs. Mary van Schalkwyck, daughter of the late Dr. Josiah Wilder (Y.C. 1767), of Lancaster, Mass. She died 29 June, 1811; and he married, second, in Salem, 1 August, 1819, Mrs. Eliza Wetmore, daughter of William Orne, Esq., late of Salem, merchant. She died 27 March, 1821; and he married, third, in Charlestown, 22 January, 1824, Mrs. Ruth Rogers, daughter of Joseph Hurd, Esq., late of Charlestown, merchant. He had, by his first wife, three daughters; by his second wife, one son,— William Orne White, — graduated at Harvard College in 1840, and became a Unitarian minister in Keene, N.H.; by his third wife, one son, — Henry Orne White, — who graduated at Harvard College in 1843, and became a physician in Salem; also two other sons, who died in infancy.

1798.—Isaac Fiske died in Cambridge, Mass., 11 March, 1861, aged 82 years. He was the youngest son of Jonathan and Abigail (Fiske) Fiske, and was born in Weston, Mass., 4 December, 1778. His father was son of Nathan and Mary (Fiske) Fiske, and was born in Weston, 15 December, 1739. His mother was daughter of Thomas and Mary (Pierce) Fiske, and was born in Weston, 16 August, 1739. The ancestors and brothers of Mr. Fiske were remarkable for their longevity. Three of his brothers died at the ages respectively of 75 years, 92 years and 4 months, and 93 years and 6 months; a sister died at upwards of 86 years; and a brother, now living, has arrived at the age of 87 years. Mr. Fiske was fitted for college by his brother, Rev. Thaddeus Fiske (H.C. 1785). After leaving college, he studied law with Hon. Artemas Ward, then of Weston (H.C. 1783) ; was admitted to the bar in 1801, and succeeded to the lucrative business of Mr. Ward after the removal of the latter to Charlestown. He approved himself to be an example of constancy, skill, and fidelity, in his official duties ; verifying the proverb of Solomon, that "the hand of the diligent maketh rich." He was for more than thirty years register of probate for the county of Middlesex, having been appointed by Gov. Brooks in 1817. In transacting the business of this office,—an office of great responsibility,—he was remarkable alike for accuracy and despatch, and no less for his readiness to give advice and directions, when called for, to those who were intrusted, as executors or administrators, with the settlement of the estates of the deceased. In the midst of his useful labors in this office, he was superseded in the year 1851, in consequence of a political change in the administration of the government of Massachusetts, in compliance with a usage not uncommon, by which the public good is often sacrificed to party preferences. It is believed that at the time of his death he was the oldest member of the Middlesex bar, counting from the date of admission; and, in point of age, he was the oldest, with one or two exceptions. He was elected representative to the state legislature in 1808, 1812, 1813, and 1814. In 1820, he was a member of the convention which revised the constitution of Massachusetts. He was a justice of the Court of Sessions, until that court was superseded by the appointment of county commissioners.

He married, 7 November, 1802, Susan Hobbs, daughter of Ebenezer and Eunice (Spring) Hobbs, of Weston; and the issue of this marriage was six sons and one daughter, of whom two sons only survived him. The oldest son, Augustus Henry Fiske, graduated at Harvard College in 1825, and is a distinguished lawyer in Boston. Mr. Fiske's wife died 8 January, 1831, aged 48 ; and he married, in 1832, Sophronia Hobbs, sister of his former wife, who survived him.

1800.—Rev. CHARLES LOWELL died in Cambridge, Mass., 20 January, 1861, aged 78 years. He was son of Hon. John (H.C. 1760) and Rebecca (Russell) Lowell, and was born in Boston, 15 August, 1782. His father was son of Rev. John Lowell (H.C. 1721) of Newbury, Mass., in which town he was born 17 June, 1743. He was a lawyer in Boston; was a member of the convention which framed the constitution of Massachusetts; and was one of the founders of the American Academy of Arts and Sciences. In 1789, he was appointed, by Washington, judge of the District Court of Massachusetts. He died in Roxbury, Mass., 6 May, 1802, aged 58 years.

The subject of this notice was a student at Andover Academy three or four years, under Abiel Abbot (H.C. 1787) and Mark Newman (D.C. 1793); and was afterwards placed under the instruction of Rev. Zedekiah Sawyer (H.C. 1771), in South Bridgewater, where he completed his preparatory studies, and entered the sophomore class in 1797. After leaving college, he studied law one year with his elder brother, John Lowell, jun. (H.C. 1786), when he relinquished it for the study of theology. In the autumn of 1802, he went to Scotland, and entered the divinity-school of the Edinburgh University, where, among his fellow-students, was the renowned Sir David Brewster. He took a letter of introduction from Dr. James Currie, of Liverpool, to Dugald Stewart, whose lectures he attended, and whom he considered, from the gracefulness and eloquence of his delivery, the copiousness and beauty of his illustrations (often extemporaneous), as the finest lecturer he had ever heard. He also attended the lectures of Hope and Murray in chemistry, of Brown in rhetoric, and of others. In Edinburgh, he formed an intimate acquaintance and established a correspondence with Dr. Thomas Brown, the distinguished successor, as he had been the pupil, of Dugald Stewart. He was well acquainted with Francis Jeffrey, the editor of the "Edinburgh Review." In the summer of 1803, he made a pedestrian tour through the Highlands of Scotland; and, after spending another winter in Edinburgh, he left that city for London in the spring of 1804. He took a letter of introduction from

Earl Buchan to Earl Stanhope, father of Lady Hester Stanhope. He visited Porteus (bishop of London), Mr. Wilberforce, and other distinguished persons; from all of whom he received great attentions. Wilberforce introduced him into a favorable place in the House of Commons, where he heard Pitt, Fox, Sheridan, and other distinguished men. Pitt, he said, had a sharp face and a very large nose. In his manner he was very vehement, and by no means graceful; constantly moving his body forward, and beating the air in the same direction with his right arm. Fox was more calm, and somewhat colloquial; Sheridan, graceful in his manner, and speaking as if reciting from a book. He also witnessed the performances of John P. Kemble, and his sister, Mrs. Siddons. He attended on the preaching, among others, of John Newton, and the eccentric but eloquent Rowland Hill.

From London, Dr. Lowell went to Paris at an eventful period, and had frequent opportunities of seeing Napoléon Bonaparte, who had just become emperor, and whose assumption of the imperial purple rendered him extremely unpopular. He was present at the first appearance of Napoléon after he was proclaimed emperor. He saw Talleyrand the day before he died. After a tour through Holland and Switzerland, he returned to Scotland, and spent another winter in Edinburgh. In the spring of 1805, he left Edinburgh; passed a little time with a maternal uncle at Clifton, near Bristol, Eng.; preached at Bristol and Hackney; and returned to his native country. On his return home, he studied divinity with Rev. Zedekiah Sanger, of South Bridgewater, and Rev. David Tappan (H.C. 1771), professor of divinity at Cambridge. He was ordained over the West Church in Boston, 1 January, 1806. As a preacher, he was eminently popular; and he was almost adored by his parishioners. Graceful as an orator, with a voice of uncommon sweetness, he preached with such an ardor and sincerity, that he seemed to his hearers to be almost divinely inspired. He continued sole pastor of the church for more than thirty-seven years. His health having become feeble, the Rev. Cyrus Augustus Bartol (Bowd. C. 1832) was ordained as his colleague, 1 March, 1837, where he still remains: but Dr. Lowell continued his pastoral connection with his church until his death; although he was unable to officiate, except occasionally, for several years before his decease. Soon after his colleague was ordained, he revisited Europe. In Edinburgh, he met Dr. Brewster and others of his former fellow-students. He spent a day very agreeably with Dr. Chalmers at Burnt Island, two miles beyond the Frith of Forth. He was in London the first winter of his tour, and attended the lectures of Dr. Faraday, as he had those of his predecessor, Sir Humphry Davy, many years before; attended the meetings of the Royal Society, and many other societies. He was a few months in Paris, where he saw M. Coquerel and other distinguished persons. He went to Belgium, Holland, Hamburg, Copenhagen, where he met Prof. Rafn; visited the falls of Trolhætta, which are among the most remarkable in Europe. He continued his tour to Pomerania, Berlin, Dresden, Prague, Bavaria, the Rhone, Baden Baden, Switzerland, Mont Blanc; crossed Mont Cenis to Milan and Florence, and wintered at Rome. He was presented to the pope in the winter of 1839; was present at the fooleries of the carnival, and saw the magnificent spectacle of the illumination of St. Peter's. From Rome he went to Genoa, Naples, Sicily, Switzerland, Mount Etna, Malta, and Athens, where he was admitted a member of the Archæological Society of Athens at the Parthenon. Thence he went to Smyrna and Constantinople, and was at the latter at the time of the death of Sultan Mahmoud, — which was occasioned by delirium tremens, — whose funeral procession on the water was very imposing; and was also there when his successor, Abdul Medjid, was proclaimed, whose installation was most splendid with barbaric pearl and gold, like some of the scenes in the "Arabian Nights." He visited Rhodes, Cyprus, Joppa, Jerusalem, Bethlehem, Beirut, Damascus (where there is a street called "Strait," as in the New Testament), Alexandria, Cairo, the pyramids, the ruins of Baalbec, Thebes, and the tombs of Sesostris and the Pharaohs, the Red Sea, Trieste, Corfu, Vienna,

Nîmes, and Paris, after two years' absence. He saw the Emperor Nicholas at Töplitz.

The honorary degree of doctor of divinity was conferred upon him by Harvard College in 1823. He was also a member of the Massachusetts Historical Society. He published seventeen occasional sermons, and two or three small volumes.

He married, in October, 1806, Harriet B. Spence, of Portsmouth, N.H.; left five children, — three sons and two daughters, — of whom three are well known to the literary public; viz., Prof. James Russell Lowell, Rev. Robert Traill Spence Lowell (an Episcopal clergyman in New Jersey), and Mrs. S. R. Putnam. His wife died 30 March, 1850.

In a sermon which he preached about forty years after his ordination, he says, "Is it amiss for me, in this connection, to say, that I am not conscious of having ever heard of sickness or trouble in any of your families, that I have not gone to do what became me as your minister to do; or that I have ever known any considerable accession to the sources of your happiness, that I have not rejoiced with you in your joy, and endeavored to lead you to a grateful improvement of the goodness of God to you? One thing more I may claim to say, — that my pastoral visits have never been spent in idle gossiping. I have aimed to make them useful, however much I have failed to do so. A minister of religion, I have felt that it became me to teach religion, not only 'publicly,' but 'from house to house,' to 'watch for souls.' God forgive me that I have not been more faithful, as one who must give an account!"

1800. — Hon. LEMUEL SHAW died in Boston, 30 March, 1861, aged 80 years. He was son of Rev. Oakes (H.C. 1758) and Susannah (Hayward) Shaw, and was born in Barnstable, Mass., 9 January, 1781. His father was born in Bridgewater, Mass., 10 June, 1736; was ordained over the First Church in Barnstable, 1 October, 1760; and died 11 February, 1807, aged 70. His mother was a native of Braintree, Mass. He was fitted for college principally by his father; but studied a few months with Rev. William Salisbury (H.C. 1795), of Braintree. On leaving college, in order to disencumber his beloved father of the expenses of his education, he became usher at the Franklin (now the Brimmer) School, in Boston, of which the late Dr. Asa Bullard (D.C. 1793) was the principal, where he remained one year; and was also during that time assistant-editor of the "Boston Gazette." He then studied law with David Everett (D.C. 1795), part of the time in Boston, and partly in Amherst, N.H. He was admitted to the bar in Hopkinton, N.H., in September, 1804; and afterwards in Plymouth, Mass., in November of the same year. He began the practice of law in Boston, in December, 1804, where he resided during the remainder of his life. In 1811, he delivered a discourse before the Boston Humane Society; and on the 4th of July, 1815, an oration before the town-authorities of Boston. In this oration we find an explanation of the opposition of a powerful party among us to the last war with Great Britain, and a magnanimous and prompt concession that the contest has strengthened the bonds of our political union. He says, "We rejoice in the belief that the danger which we once feared from the ascendency of French principles is for ever removed. The secret spell which seemed to bind us in willing chains to the conqueror's car is for ever broken. No sophistry can again deceive us into a belief that the cause of Bonaparte is the cause of social rights, or create a momentary sympathy between the champion of despotism and the friends of civil liberty. One of the most alarming points of view in which the sincere opponents of the late war with England regarded the measure was, that it tended to cement and perpetuate that dangerous and disgraceful connection."

In politics, Judge Shaw was a decided federalist, and was secretary of the Washington Benevolent Society. In 1811 he was elected a representative to the state legislature, was continued in that office for four succeeding years, and was again elected in 1819. In 1820 he was a member of the convention for revising the constitution of the state. In 1821 and 1822, he was a member of the senate; and again in 1828 and 1829. Before Boston became a city, he held various town offices; was a member of the board of firewards, a selectman, and one of the school-committee. In 1822, while in the senate, he was chairman of the joint-committee of the legislature on a city charter for Boston; embodied the same in the form of a report to the town, which was accepted; drafted the city charter; and wrote the act of incorporation establishing the city of Boston, granted by the state legislature, 23 February, 1822; with the exception of the fourteenth section, relative to public theatres and exhibitions, and the act establishing a police-court; which were drafted by Hon. William Sullivan, and went into operation at the same time. In 1830, his friends wished to nominate him as a candidate for representative to Congress; but he would not accept the nomination. He was an active member of the Boston-Library Society, the Humane Society, the Massachusetts Historical Society, the Massachusetts Congregational Charitable Society, the Society for Propagating the Gospel among the Indians in North America, and the American Academy of Arts and Sciences. He was an overseer of Harvard College twelve years, and one of the corporation twenty-seven years. On the 23d of August, 1830, he was appointed chief-justice of the Supreme Court, in place of Isaac Parker (H.C. 1786) deceased. He held this office until the 31st of August, 1860, when he resigned it. During the whole period of his devotion to the state judiciary, he made records of the legal transactions under his superintendence, comprising upwards of fifty volumes of several hundred pages each. He was blessed with an extraordinarily large, powerful, and vigorous frame, which alone could have sustained the pressure of the unremitted and vast exertions of his powerful intellect for eighty years. His ample and warmly-feeling heart was quite as remarkable as his intellect. A more generous and social man never lived. His fund of mirthful and racy anecdote was inexhaustible. His honor, integrity, and Christian faith were never questioned. The honorary degree of doctor of laws was conferred upon him by Harvard College in 1831, and by Brown University in 1850.

He ever felt a devoted veneration for his parents. His mother was a lady of more than ordinary powers of intellect; and of his father he thus warmly expressed himself in a speech at the centennial celebration at Barnstable, 3 September, 1839: "Almost within sight of the place where we now are, still stands a modest spire, marking the spot where a beloved father stood to minister the holy word of truth and hope and salvation to a numerous, beloved, and attached people, for almost half a century. Pious, pure, simple-hearted, devoted to and beloved by his people, never shall I cease to venerate his memory, or to love those who knew and loved him. I speak in the presence of some who knew him, and of many more, who, I doubt not, were taught to love and honor his memory as one of the earliest lessons of their childhood."

Judge Shaw married, 6 January, 1818, Elizabeth, a daughter of Josiah Knapp, a merchant of Boston; and had by her two children, — John Oakes and Elizabeth Knapp. His wife died 13 January, 1822, aged 36 years. He married for his second wife, in August, 1827, Hope, a daughter of Dr. Samuel Savage (H.C. 1766), of Barnstable; by whom he had two children, — Lemuel and Samuel Savage. The former graduated at Harvard College in 1849, and is a lawyer in Boston. His wife and all his children survive him.

1800. — BENJAMIN WELLES died in Boston, 21 July, 1860, aged 78 years. He was son of Samuel and Isabella (Pratt) Welles, and was born in Boston, 13 August, 1781. He studied for college in part at the Boston Latin School, under Master Samuel Hunt (H.C. 1765), and during one year with Rev. Thomas Prentiss, of Medfield, Mass. (H.C. 1766). On leaving college, he studied law for some time with Hon. Levi Lincoln, of Worcester, Mass. (H.C. 1772), and afterwards with Hon. Harrison Gray Otis, of Boston (H.C. 1783). In 1803, he went to England, and pursued his professional studies there. In 1804, he joined his classmate, Washington Allston, in Paris. A few months afterwards, they went together to Switzerland, and passed St. Gothard in their carriage, being the first persons who had traversed it. They went to Lombardy, and by Lake Como to Rome, passing through Bologna, where Allston examined the great paintings of the Caracci and other great masters. They next went to Florence. The plague, prevailing in Leghorn, detained them at Rome two months, during which time Allston employed himself in painting. At Rome Mr. Welles staid about two months, and Mr. Allston a year. Mr. Welles returned to Boston in 1804. In 1807, he, in company with Stephen Higginson, William Parsons, Thomas H. Perkins, and others, engaged in an iron-mining company in Vergennes, Vt. In 1812, Mr. Welles was appointed sole agent of the establishment, and took up his residence in Vergennes. He met Lieut. M'Donough at Burlington, in a small gunboat, strapping a block, and made an engagement to supply the iron and cannon-balls for the ships, which were all built at Vergennes for the lake-service; the iron-work amounting to $47,000. In 1816, he became a partner with Hon. John Welles (H.C. 1782), who was his cousin, in the auxiliary house in Boston to the banking-house of Welles and Co., of Paris. This connection continued twenty-eight years, until the death of Samuel Welles (H.C. 1796), which took place in Paris, 31 August, 1841.

He married, 1 August, 1815, Mehitable Stoddard Sumner, eldest daughter of Gov. Increase Sumner (H.C. 1767); by whom he had two daughters, Elizabeth and Georgiana, and one son, Benjamin Samuel. His wife died 31 January, 1826; and he married, for his second wife, Susan Codman, daughter of William Codman, Esq., of New York, by whom he had one daughter, Susan; who married, 14 January, 1856, Russell Sturgis, jun., of Boston.

Mr. Welles was highly respected in the community as a gentleman of the old school. He left a very large estate.

1801.—Hon. Stephen Minot died in Haverhill, Mass., 6 April, 1861, aged 84 years. He was son of Capt. Jonas and Mary (Hall) Minot, and was born in Concord, Mass., 28 September, 1776. His father was son of Dea. Samuel and Sarah (Prescott) Minot; was born in Concord, 25 April, 1735; and died in his native town, 20 March, 1813, aged 78 years. His mother was daughter of Rev. Willard Hall (H.C. 1722), of Westford, Mass. She was born 30 July, 1738, and died 3 November, 1792, aged 54 years. The subject of this notice was fitted for college at Westford Academy. He held a very respectable rank in his class at college. Having selected law as a profession, he pursued his legal studies under the instruction of Hon. Samuel Dana, of Groton, Mass. On his admission to the bar, he settled in New Gloucester, Me., in which town and the town of Minot he practised about one year. He then removed to Haverhill, where he remained until his death, with the exception of a residence of three years in Methuen, where he owned a cotton-factory. He was a learned and accurate lawyer. His mind was clear in its perception, and logical in its conclusions. He was appointed, in 1811, judge of the Circuit Court of Common Pleas, and held the office until 1820, when the law which created that court was repealed. In 1824, he was appointed county-attorney for Essex; which office he resigned in 1830. He was elected a representative to the state legislature in 1825, and would have been re-elected, but refused to be a candidate again. He was firm in purpose, exact and punctual in method and habit, of strict integrity, fearless in spirit, ever prompt to say or do whatever his judgment approved; of great regularity and temperance in his manner of life; in his private relations a true, affectionate, generous friend. His house was the abode of kindness and a generous hospitality. In conversation, he was genial, and rich in anecdote. For several years, having withdrawn from professional labors, he spent much of his time in mathematical studies, and in reading the Latin classics. He also possessed a strong mechanical talent, of which many instances remain; among them an organ of fine musical powers, wholly the work of his own hands. He was a liberal supporter of the institution of religion, the ministrations of which he attended with great regularity. To him the Unitarian faith was dear. His religious principles were firm, and sustained him in the trials of life and in the hour of death. "He set his house in order," and awaited with perfect composure the coming of the angel of death.

> "Calmly he gave his being up, and went
> To share the joys that wait a life well spent."

Mr. Minot married, 9 November, 1809, Rebecca Trask, daughter of Samuel Trask, of Bradford, Mass. She died 27

November, 1832; and he married, for his second wife, Ellen P. Gardner, daughter of Hon. Stephen Partridge Gardner, of Bolton, Mass., who survived him. He left two children,—Mrs. Pitman, of Reading, Mass.; and Charles Minot, Esq., superintendent of the Erie Railroad, New York. The late George Minot, Esq., who died 16 April, 1858,—a sound and able lawyer of Boston, author of "Minot's Digest," a work well known to the profession generally,—was his youngest son.

1806.—Dr. NATHANIEL JACOB died in Canandaigua, N.Y., 3 February, 1861, aged 78 years. He was the eldest son of Nathaniel and Lucy (Jacob) Jacob, and was born in Hanover, Mass., 16 July, 1782. His father, who was son of Dr. Joseph Jacob, was born in Hanover, 6 April, 1750; was an industrious farmer, of good natural abilities; died 22 September, 1822, aged 72 years. His mother, who was daughter of Joshua Jacob, was born in Hanover, 3 November, 1748; and died 20 March, 1812, aged 63 years. The subject of this notice was fitted for college at Bridgewater Academy, under the tuition of Rev. Zedekiah Sanger, D.D. (H. C. 1771). After leaving college, he studied medicine, under the instruction of Dr. Nathan Smith, of Hanover, N.H.; and settled in Canandaigua in 1810, where he was one of the early principals of the academy in the village, and practised as a physician. He was for some time professor of anatomy in the Fairfield Medical Institute in the state of New York.

He was one of the principal founders of St. John's Episcopal Church in Canandaigua. He was a citizen of much public spirit, and served as military surgeon on the frontier in the year 1812. At one time, he filled the office of trial-justice. He was a zealous and active member of the medical profession, but retired from practice many years before his death.

He married, 8 March, 1812, Hannah Sanborn, of Canandaigua. She was the first white inhabitant born (in 1789) in that village; her parents being one of four families who emigrated from Lyme, Conn. It took them four weeks to make the passage; going in boats up the Hudson, the Mohawk, and on from one lake to another by creeks. By his wife he had ten children, of whom only four are now living; one in Buffalo, and the others in Canandaigua. His wife survived him.

1808.—LLOYD NICHOLAS ROGERS died in Baltimore, 13 November, 1860, aged 72 years. He was born in Baltimore, 20 September, 1788. He held a very high rank of scholarship in his class, and graduated with distinguished honors. He studied law, and settled in Baltimore. He had the ability to attain distinction in his profession; but, as he inherited a very large fortune, he had no necessity to labor for a subsistence, and he virtually hid his talent in a napkin. He was not known beyond his immediate acquaintance.

1809.—HENRY BARNEY SMITH died in Boston, 1 April, 1861, aged 71 years. He was son of Barney and Ann (Otis) Smith, and was born in Boston, 26 October, 1789. He was fitted for college by Rev. Nathaniel Thayer, of Lancaster, Mass. (H.C. 1789). After leaving college, he began the study of law in Litchfield under Judge Reeve, and afterwards studied with Hon. William Sullivan, of Boston (H.C. 1792). He was admitted to the Suffolk bar; but, having inherited an ample fortune, he did not pursue his profession. He was an inveterate democrat in politics; and possessing strong mental powers, with great facility of address, he was one of the most eloquent speakers of his party at democratic caucuses in Faneuil Hall. He was for some time president of the Boston Debating Society. In 1822, he delivered an oration at a democratic celebration of the 4th of July, in Dorchester; and another, at a similar celebration at the Marlborough Hotel in Boston, in 1824. On the 4th of July, 1830, he delivered an oration before the Washington Society in Boston. It was said of him then, that "he is an uncompromising democrat, who has sketched the protean visage of aristocracy in thoughts that breathe, and words that burn."

He retired from political life many years before his death, and devoted himself to the care of his large possessions. He was never married.

1812.—GEORGE EDWARD HEAD died in Boston, 5 July, 1861, aged 68 years. He was son of Joseph and Elizabeth (Frazier) Head, and was born in Boston, 25 February, 1793.

His father (who was son of Joseph Head, who came from England in the neighborhood of Norwich) was born in Boston, 1 January, 1761; was for many years a highly respectable merchant; and was a member of the first board of aldermen, on the organization of the city-government, in 1822. He was a director in the Massachusetts Bank from the year 1810 until his death. He died 30 December, 1836, aged 76 years. His mother, who was daughter of Nathan and Elizabeth (White) Frazier, was born in Andover, Mass., 25 February, 1764; and died 2 October, 1798, aged 34 years. The subject of this notice began to fit for college at Phillips Academy in Exeter, N.H. He subsequently pursued his studies under the instruction of Rev. John S. J. Gardiner, D.D., of Boston; and completed them in the Boston Latin School, where a Franklin medal was awarded to him in 1807. After leaving college, he studied law at the law-school in Litchfield, Conn., under the instruction of Judges Reeve and Gould; and, on his admission to the bar, established himself in Boston. Born to affluence, he did not aim at eminence; but, endowed by nature with a remarkably clear intellect and refined taste, he took pleasure in the development of his mind by the pursuit of studies which were in accordance with his fancy rather than the dry routine of his profession; although, had necessity required his entire devotion to law, his talents would have enabled him to attain an eminent distinction as a barrister. That he enjoyed the confidence and respect of the community was manifested by the stations to which he was elevated. He was elected a representative to the state legislature in 1836, 1837, 1847, and 1848. He was a member of the board of aldermen of Boston in 1846, 1847, and 1848; and, in the last-named year, he was chosen a permanent-assessor; which office he held, by successive elections, until his death, with the exception of the year 1855. He was at one time urged by his friends to allow the use of his name as a candidate for the mayoralty, but declined. In private life, his ready wit and genial humor, combined with high-toned morality, endeared him to his family and his numerous acquaintances.

He married, 26 February, 1815, Hannah Catlin, daughter of Grove Catlin, of Litchfield, Conn., and great-grand-daughter of Joseph Wadsworth, who hid the charter of Connecticut in the oak. The issue of this marriage was six children; of whom four, — two sons and two daughters, — with their mother, survive. One of the sons, John Frazier Head, graduated at Yale College in 1840; and the other, George Edward Head, at Harvard College in 1852. Both became physicians. One of the daughters is the wife of Bishop Eastburn, of Boston.

1812. — Nathaniel Whitworth White died in Halifax, N.S., September, 1860, aged 67 years. He was son of Capt. Gideon and Deborah (Whitworth) White, and was born in Shelburne, N.S., 25 February, 1793. His father was a loyalist, joined the British army at the time of the Revolution, and rose to be a captain. He left the country, and settled at Shelburne, where he was appointed a judge. After the Revolution, living in that little town, and not mingling with the Americans, he retained his bitter feelings. When the war of 1812 broke out, he took his son away from college, only about two weeks before Commencement; and the son was therefore not present when his degree was conferred upon him. He also took away with him another son, who was fitting to enter. He died in Shelburne in 1833, aged 82 years. He was born in Plymouth, and was a descendant of Peregrine White. Mr. White, after leaving college, settled as a lawyer in Halifax, where he practised two-thirds of his life. He was afterwards master-in-chancery. He died of disease of the heart. He was never married.

1813. — Orville Luther Holley died in Albany, N.Y., 25 March, 1861, aged 69 years. He was son of Luther and Sarah (Dakin) Holley, and was born in Salisbury, Conn., 19 May, 1791. He was the eighth child of a family of nine, all of whom he survived. The eloquent Rev. Horace Holley, pastor of the Hollis-street church in Boston, was his brother. He was fitted for college probably at Greenfield Hill, in Fairfield, Conn. He held a high rank of scholarship in college, was particularly distinguished for his graceful oratory, and graduated with distinction. He studied law in New York, and practised his profession successively in Hudson, Canandaigua, and the city of New York. His tastes led him, at an early period of his career, to journalism; and he was successively editor of the "Anti-Masonic Magazine," published in New York, the "Troy Sentinel," the "Ontario Repository," and the "Albany Daily Advertiser." He superintended the publication of the "New-York State Register" for several years. In 1853, the New-York legislature authorized the purchase of the correspondence and other papers of George Clinton, the first governor of that state, then on deposit in the office of the secretary of state; and appropriated the sum of five hundred dollars for arranging, indexing, binding, and lettering the same. The labor of indexing and arranging these manuscripts was intrusted principally to Mr. Holley, by whom the work was very judiciously and thoroughly performed under the direction of the library-committee. The collection numbered twenty-three volumes of folio size. In January, 1838, under the first administration of Gov. Seward, Mr. Holley was chosen surveyor-general of the state of New York; and, during the last ten years of his life, he was occupied in duties connected with the department of the secretary of state: but, for the last twenty years, severe bodily infirmities compelled him to forego, to a great extent, the honors of public position. His great solace during the years of infirmity were his literary studies, by which he was most distinguished; and his "Life of Benjamin Franklin," written during a period of severe suffering, is not excelled as a chaste and comprehensive biography. His acquirements in history were equalled by few men. He was a close student of medical science. Few clergymen of eminence were so well versed in theology, while his acquaintance with English polite literature was exhaustive. His conversation, for terseness, variety, and finish, was most eminent. The range of his thoughts was wide, his mind catholic and genial, his manners full of courtesy and grace. He left the impression of one, who, through excess of sensibility or fastidiousness of taste, has never marshalled his powers to any enterprise fully worthy of them. The wonder was, that a man of such a stamp and presence, so evidently made up of every creature's best, was not a great poet, philosopher, or saint; for he looked fully capable of being either.

Mr. Holley belonged to a family which has largely contributed to enlighten our American superstition. Two of his brothers, Horace and Myron, were eminent propagandists of Liberal Christianity, but neither was superior to him in intelligence, zeal, and devotion to the work of emancipating the people from spiritual despotism. It was one of the chief desires of his later years to establish a strong liberal church in the capital city of New York. He gave himself freely to the work of organizing such a movement. His efforts, more than any thing, secured the re-establishment of the drooping church in Albany. For several years, he was clerk of the society, superintendent of the sunday-school, often conducted public worship, and, it is said, paid yearly one-eighth of his entire income into its treasury.

Mr. Holley was never married; and, during his later years, lived what would be called a lonely life; but it was the best for the peculiar cast of mind in his condition of health.

1815. — Hon. Ezra Hunt, of Bowling Green, Mo., died in Troy, Lincoln county, in that State, 19 September, 1860, aged 70 years. He was in attendance upon the Circuit Court, in session there, in his usual health. Having spoken on a case in his charge in the afternoon, and having eaten his supper after the adjournment of the court, he said he was not very well, went to a fire in a retired room at his lodgings, was conversing with a lady with apparent cheerfulness, when he suddenly appeared to be falling from his chair. He was caught, and physicians were called, who found that the vital spark had fled, and he ceased to live. He was the ninth and youngest son of Daniel and Mary (Phillips) Hunt, and was born in Milford, Mass., 7 April, 1790. He was a descendant of the sixth generation from William Hunt, one of the original settlers of Concord, Mass. He was fitted for college at Leicester Academy; of which Luther Willson (W.C. 1807), afterwards minister of Petersham, Mass., was preceptor. He was distinguished for his knowledge of mathematics and the exact sciences; and at Commencement, when he graduated, the subject assigned to him was "The Study of the Mathematics." Immediately after leaving college, he was appointed preceptor of Leicester Academy; where he remained until the autumn of 1817, when he went to Cambridge for the purpose of studying divinity. He remained there, with the exception of four months devoted to keeping school in Lincoln, Mass., until May, 1818; when he went to Pulaski, West Tenn., and took charge of an academy on a salary of seven hundred dollars per annum. He was invited to remain another year, with a salary of twelve hundred dollars, but declined. While in charge of the academy in Pulaski, he pursued the study of the law, under the direction of the late Judge William C. Carr; and, at the end of one year, obtained a license to practise in the states of Missouri and Illinois. He practised three years in the town of Louisiana, in Missouri. From this place, he removed to St. Charles in the same state.

In 1831, he removed to Bowling Green, Pike county, Mo. He was the first lawyer that ever settled in that county; and it is stated that he attended every term of the Criminal Court in the county, either as lawyer or judge, from the territorial days of 1819 until his death. He was appointed, 6 January, 1836, judge of the Circuit Court for that judicial district, with a salary of a thousand dollars per annum; and discharged the duties of the office with ability and impartiality, to the general satisfaction of the people of the circuit. He decided questions of law, but never addressed juries. When he made any communication to the jury, it was in writing. In the convention called to revise the constitution of the state of Missouri, in 1845, he was a member for Pike and Ralls counties, composing a district; and acted as chairman of the judiciary committee in that body. By a change in the constitution of Missouri, in 1849, the term of offices of the judges was limited to eight years; and, simultaneously with the limitation, new judges were appointed all over the state. Judge Hunt, who had held the office many years, was superseded by a man, who, if he had no other claim, could allege most vigorous party services. Judge Hunt was a diligent student all his life; and, having accumulated one of the largest and best private libraries in the state of Missouri, had with its use, aided by a discriminating, logical mind, made himself a learned and sound lawyer, as well as a ripe scholar in general literature; and in all the relations of his life, both public and private, he was faithful, just, and true.

In 1830, he visited Massachusetts; and, on the 18th of May in that year, he married, in Connecticut, Maria E. Pettibone, then sixteen years old, daughter of the late Rufus Pettibone (W.C. 1805), judge of the Supreme Court of Missouri. Judge Pettibone married a New-York lady, and his daughter Maria was born in New York. The issue of this marriage was seven children; of whom four, with their mother, survived him.

1815. — Hon. Gayton Pickman Osgood died in North Andover, Mass., 26 June, 1861, aged 64 years, lacking eight days. He was son of Isaac and Sally (Pickman) Osgood, and was born in Salem, Mass., 4 July, 1797; but removed with his parents in his infancy to North Andover, which was ever afterwards his place of abode. His father was for some time clerk of the courts for the county of Essex. His mother was daughter of Col. Benjamin Pickman (H.C. 1759), and sister of Col. Benjamin Pickman (H.C. 1784), of Salem. He was well fitted for college at the Franklin Academy in North Andover. He attained a high rank of scholarship in his class while in college. After graduating, he studied law with Benjamin Merrill, of Salem (H.C. 1804). He began the practice of law in Salem, but in 1819 removed to North Andover, and left the profession. Possessed of ample property, he lived a retired life. He enjoyed his library, a very valuable one, especially in classical literature, which continued to hold a primary place in his studies to the close of his life. He was formerly known as a prominent politician of the democratic school. He was the leading opponent of Caleb Cushing in his early competition for the office of representative to Congress, — a contest long to be remembered, — and was elected for one term, 1833–35. In 1844, he was a candidate for elector-at-large in Massachusetts of President of the United States; but was not elected, having been nominated by the democratic party. He was several times elected a representative to the legislature: the last time, however, he refused to take his seat, which, in consequence, remained vacant for the entire session. He sought the pleasures of home, and it was only at the earnest solicitation of friends that he allowed the use of his name as a candidate for office. His range of study and reading was very extensive; and his political and miscellaneous lectures evince much thought and great research, and abound with apt illustrations and eloquent appeals.

> "From his cradle
> He was a scholar, and a ripe and good one."

He was benevolent, sensible, and intelligent; and united modesty with merit to a degree as unusual as it is amiable.

He married, 24 March, 1859, Mary Farnham, of North Andover, but had no children. His wife survives him.

1822. — NATHANIEL INGERSOLL BOWDITCH died in Brookline, Mass., 16 April, 1861, aged 56 years. He was the eldest son of Nathaniel and Mary (Ingersoll) Bowditch, and was born in Salem, Mass., 17 January, 1805. His father, the eminent mathematician of world-wide fame, was born in Salem, 26 March, 1773; and died in Boston, 16 March, 1838, aged 65 years. The subject of this notice was fitted for college in Salem by Abiel Chandler (H.C. 1806). He graduated with high honors, although the youngest in his class. He studied law under the instruction of Hon. William Prescott (H.C. 1783) and Hon. Franklin Dexter (H.C. 1812), and was admitted to the Suffolk bar in 1825. A few years afterwards, he relinquished the practice of law, and devoted himself to business as a conveyancer and examiner of titles of real estate; in which he enjoyed a large and lucrative employment, and won the esteem of all with whom he had intercourse, by the suavity of his manners, and his noble and generous character. He married, 23 April, 1835, Elizabeth B., eldest daughter of Ebenezer Francis, well known as the wealthiest gentleman of

Boston. For some years Mr. Bowditch was in the enjoyment of a very large income, which he distributed in a thousand nameless rills of beneficence for the relief of suffering humanity. Mr. Francis died 21 September, 1858; and, soon after that event, Mr. Bowditch retired from business, and took up his residence in Brookline. Soon afterwards, he was attacked by a terrible and incurable disease, — a cancerous affection in one of his thigh-bones; and for eighteen months he was wasting away under this painful disorder, unable to move, except slightly to raise his head in the bed. But gently, patiently, nobly, was the discipline borne. To go into his sick-chamber was like going into a chapel; and such dews fell upon the heart there as fall upon the lilies of heaven. You saw the sufferer upon his couch, propped up by pillows, pale and worn; but his smile was sweet, his greeting was cordial, his interest in life was unabated. Books, the society of his family, intercourse with his friends, filled up his days. Slowly and gradually the last hour came, and now "Goodness and he fill up one monument."

His wife survives him, with four children, — one son and three daughters.

1822. — Rev. NATHANIEL GAGE died in Cambridge, Mass., 7 May, 1861, aged sixty years. He was son of Nathaniel and Betsey (Kimball) Gage, and was born in North Andover, on the line between North Andover and Boxford, Mass., 16 July, 1800. His father was a farmer; and Nathaniel worked on the farm while a boy, attending public schools until he was about sixteen years of age. His father determined that one of his sons should go to college. The younger son, Daniel, declined, and chance fell to Nathaniel; although his father regretted it, as he was so apt at farming. He began to fit for college at Bradford Academy, under Benjamin Greenleaf (D.C. 1813); and finished his preparatory studies under the instruction of Rev. Peter Eaton (H.C. 1787), of Boxford, whose meeting the family attended. Before he entered college, he taught school in Boxford, pursuing at the same time his studies with great perseverance. He entered, at the age of seventeen, without conditions. While in college, he taught school every winter, successively in Newton, Goffstown, N.H., Wayland, and Bolton. In summer vacations, he worked on the farm at home. He ranked very high in scholarship while in college. He had the oration on class-day, the salutatory oration at Commencement, and the valedictory oration when he took his second degree. After graduating, he pursued his theological studies at the Divinity School in Cambridge; during a part of the time, teaching school in Cambridgeport. In 1825, he was appointed tutor in mathematics in college, and held the office one year. He was ordained pastor of the Unitarian church in Nashua, N.H., 27 June, 1827, where he remained seven years. He was dismissed in 1834; and immediately went to Haverhill, Mass., where he was installed 2 July of the same year. There he remained seven years. Thence he went to Petersham, where he was installed 6 October, 1841, and remained there four years. From Petersham he went to Lancaster, where, for about one year, he supplied the pulpit of Rev. Edmund Hamilton Sears (U.C. 1834), who was in ill health. Then he had a call at Westborough, where he went in the spring of 1851, and remained six years without being installed. In April, 1857, he removed to Cambridge; and in the summer of that year he began to preach in Ashby, where he continued his ministrations as long as he lived, going there on Saturdays, spending two Sundays and the intervening week, then returning to his home in Cambridge. On the 18th of April, 1861, while on his way from Cambridge for Boston on foot, he was attacked with apoplexy. He was carried home, where he lingered until the 7th of May, when he died.

Mr. Gage was a man of a most genial and kindly spirit, a true and devoted friend, a conscientious and self-sacrificing Christian. Many have wondered that he had not risen to higher eminence in the church. It is surprising that he should have escaped reverses, and maintained so respectable and uniform a standing, with his guiltless nature and sensitive heart.

> "Of manners gentle, and affections mild,
> In wit a man, simplicity a child."

His heart was warm and sympathetic, joyous in prosperity, but in seasons of adversity overflowing with the tenderest sensibility. In private life, he was most interesting and genial. Possessing no small share of wit, always cheerful and buoyant, he was the life of the social circle; tender and loving, he was the idol of his home.

He published a Sermon, delivered at the installation of Rev. A. Dumont Jones over the Congregational Church in Wilton, N.H., January 1, 1834; 8vo; Nashua, N.H., 1834; pp. 32. An Address before the Essex Agricultural Society at Topsfield, September 27, 1837, at the Annual Cattle Show; 8vo; Salem, 1838; pp. 27. A Discourse delivered in Windham, N.H., 5 November, 1834, at the Interment of Rev. Jacob Abbot and Capt. John Dinsmore, who were drowned 2 November; Nashua, N.H., 1835; 8vo, pp. 24. An Address on Intemperance, pronounced at Nashua Village, N.H., April 4, 1829; published by request; 8vo. Dunstable, N.H., pp. 21. Sons and Daughters of the Times; a Sermon delivered in Haverhill, Mass., on Fast Day, April 5, 1838. Haverhill; pp. 28.

He married, 1 August, 1827, Abby Richardson, daughter of Hon. Stephen Partridge and Achsah (Moore) Gardner, of Bolton. She was the fourth of eight daughters, four of whom became widows within four years. Their children were, — 1. Ellen Gardner, born 9 July, 1828, at Nashua; married, 5 October, 1854, Rev. Charles Henry Wheeler (Bowd. C. 1847), of South Danvers. 2. Abby, born February, 1831; died 1832, aged 17 months. 3. Louisa Charlotte, born 18 October, 1833, at Nashua; married, 20 September, 1855, Franklin, son of Augustus and Harriet (Child) Perrin, born 9 August, 1830, in Boston. 4. Nathaniel, born 1835; died November, 1839. 5. Minot Gardner, born 11 September, 1841; graduated at Harvard College in 1861.

1822. — Hon. Francis Osborn Watts died in Roxbury, Mass., 28 September, 1860, aged 57 years. He was son of Francis and Mehitable (Lord) Watts, and was born in Kennebunk, Me., 9 August, 1803. He was great-grandson of Judge

Samuel Watts, of Chelsea, Mass., and grandson of Dr. Edward Watts, of Portland, Me. His father was a merchant in Kennebunk; and, on his removal to Boston, he engaged in business, as a wholesale grocer, on Long Wharf, which he continued about twelve years. In 1832, he was elected president of the Atlantic Insurance Company; which office he held until 1844, when he resigned it on account of ill health. He died 6 April, 1846. His mother was a devout Christian woman, who died when he was little more than nine years old. In 1815, at the age of twelve years, he entered Thornton Academy in Saco, Me., where, under the instruction of Mr. Ezra Haskell (Y.C. 1811), he pursued his preparatory studies until 1818, when he removed, with his father, to Boston, and completed his studies at Mr. Gideon French Thayer's school, in Chauncy Place. Immediately after leaving college, he began the study of law in the office of Mr. Augustus Peabody, in Boston (D.C. 1803); where, with the exception of a single intervening term at the law school in Northampton, under Judge Samuel Howe (W.C. 1804), he completed his legal studies; and was admitted to the Suffolk bar in October, 1825, at a little more than twenty-two years of age. But, though so young, his abilities and attainments and general character were such, that he was immediately received as a law-partner by Mr. Peabody, with whom he continued six years. A year later, he formed a partnership with Mr. William Joseph Hubbard (Y.C. 1820); and, many years afterwards, he records of both his partners, "I believe I may say I have never had an unpleasant word with either of them." Some few years before his death, he practised in connection with Owen Glendour Peabody (D.C. 1842), the son of his former partner. From 1826 until near the close of 1840, he was a worshipper, and, for most of that time, a communicant, in the Unitarian church: but in the spring of 1841, having changed his religious views, he joined the Protestant Episcopal church; to which religious faith he ever afterwards adhered. He was esteemed by his acquaintances as a singularly faultless man; commanding respect and confidence by the strength of his mind, the respectability of his attainments, the soundness of his judgment, the modesty of his self-estimation, the uprightness of his dealings, the sweetness of his temper, and the amenity of his manners. As a lawyer, he held a highly respectable rank, and was greatly esteemed by his professional associates. In 1846, he was elected a senator from the Suffolk district to the state legislature; where he distinguished himself as an able debater, and a most valuable member of the senatorial board.

He married, 1 May, 1826, Caroline Goddard, born 25 February, 1804, daughter of Thacher and Lucy Goddard, of Boston, by whom he had seven children, — three sons and four daughters; of whom two daughters only survive. His wife died 25 July, 1850, aged 44 years and 5 months. He married for his second wife, 21 January, 1854, Caroline Keith Bradbury, daughter of Charles Bradbury, of Boston, who survives him; but has had no children.

1823. — EDWARD VERNON CHILDE died in Paris, France, 23 January, 1861, aged 56 years. He was son of David Weld and Abigail (Dorr) Child, and was born in Boston, 13 March, 1804. His name was originally Ebenezer Dorr Child, and was changed, by an act of the legislature, 8 February, 1823. His father was a very respectable merchant, and died in Boston, 3 February, 1830, aged 58 years. The subject of this notice was fitted for college at the Boston public Latin School. After leaving college, he studied law in the office of Hon. Daniel Webster (D.C. 1801). He did not, however, pursue the profession. On the death of his father, he inherited an ample fortune, which was subsequently very much increased by his inheriting also the estate of a deceased brother. In 1828, he went to Europe, where he remained about two years; when he returned. About the year 1834, he again went to Europe; resided several years in Italy and Germany. He then became a permanent resident in Paris, and devoted himself to literature. He was a regular correspondent of the "London Times" for nearly eleven years. His first letter to the "Times" was dated Paris, 3 November, 1845; and the last, 7 June, 1856. He was also correspondent of the "New-York Courier and Enquirer" from 17 October, 1846, to 4 December, 1856. Both these series of letters he had printed in 1857, in a duodecimo volume making 259 pages, for private circulation.

He married, in 1831, Mildred Lee, daughter of Gen. Henry Lee, of Virginia. He left three children, — one son and two daughters: viz., Edward Lee Childe, residing in Paris; Florence, the elder daughter, married to Count Henry Soltyk, of Cracow, Austrian Poland; Mary, the younger, married Robert Gilmor Hoffman, of Baltimore, Md. His wife died in Paris, 24 June, 1856.

1823. — JOSEPH HENRY FARLEY died in Pittsfield, Mass., 4 January, 1861, aged 55 years. He was the fourth son of Eben and Lydia (Coolidge) Farley, and was born in Boston, 7 September, 1805. His father was born in Ipswich, Mass., 24 March, 1775; was a merchant in Boston, of the firm of Swett and Farley; and died 27 September, 1826, aged 51 years. His mother was born in Watertown, Mass., 18 March, 1776; and died 14 November, 1813, aged 37 years. The subject of this notice was fitted for college at Phillips Academy in Exeter, N.H. After graduating, he engaged in mercantile business, and settled in New-York city; having become a member of the firm of Felix M. Walton and Co., importers of dry goods. The house became insolvent; and Mr. Farley subsequently entered into partnership with Calvin Angier, of New York, in the sale of boots and shoes. Here he was again unfortunate. He left New York, and went to Lenox, Mass., where he resided with a younger brother; but he fell into a morbid and depressed state of mind, which the kindness of his friends could not restore, but resulted in mental alienation, during which he terminated his life by his own hand. He was never married.

1823. — Rev. JAMES TRASK WOODBURY died in Milford, Mass., 16 January, 1861, aged 57 years. He was son of Hon. Peter and Mary (Woodbury) Woodbury, and was born in Francestown, N.H., 9 May, 1803. His father was born in Beverly, Mass., in 1767, and removed to New Hampshire, where he engaged in mercantile and agricultural pursuits; was fifteen years a representative, and two years a senator, in the state legislature. He died in 1834. His mother was daughter of James Woodbury, who was born in Beverly, but removed to Mount Vernon, N.H., in 1782. He was a subaltern in Col. Robert Rogers's regiment of rangers; and was near Wolfe when he fell at the storming of Quebec. The subject of this notice was a brother of the late Hon. Levi Woodbury (D.C. 1809), who was governor of New Hampshire, senator in congress, secretary of the navy, and afterwards secretary of the treasury under President Jackson, and associate-justice of the Supreme Court of the United States. He began to fit for college at the academy in Francestown, N.H., and completed his preparatory studies at Phillips Academy, Andover, Mass. After leaving college, he studied law with his distinguished brother Levi, in Portsmouth, N.H. He was admitted to the bar of his native state in 1826, and at once opened an office for the practice of law in Bath, N.H. Having a thorough education, possessing talents of a high order, with an unblemished character, strong physical and intellectual powers, he had every prospect of becoming eminent in his profession.

But, in the midst of his bright prospects of future eminence, his ambition was suddenly checked, and his whole course of life changed. Under the preaching of Rev. David Sutherland, of Bath, where he resided, he became a sincere convert to the Christian faith, to the advocacy of which he devoted the rest of his life. After a long struggle with himself, and contrary to the advice of many friends, he relinquished his profession as a lawyer, and placed himself under the instruction of Rev. Lyman Beecher, D.D. (Y.C. 1797), of Boston, as a student of divinity. After completing his course of study, he soon had an invitation to settle as pastor of the church in Acton, Mass., and was ordained 29 August, 1829, where he continued pastor for twenty-two years. In the spring of 1852, at his own request, he was dismissed from the church; and, on the 15th of July the same year, was installed pastor of the First Church in Milford, Mass., where he continued to discharge his ministerial duties until his death. He was elected representative to the state legislature from Acton in 1851 and 1852. He was first elected with special reference to his making an appeal to the state for aid in the erection of a monument, in the town of Acton, to the memory of Capt. Isaac Davis, who fell at the old North Concord Bridge, 19 April, 1775. When the order for the appropriation came up for consideration, it found little favor : indeed, it was said that scarce five men could be found who favored its passage. On the 5th of February, 1852, he made a speech which occupied two hours in delivery. It was the only time he ever addressed a legislative assembly. Every eye was riveted upon him, as he proceeded in his peculiar graphic description of the opening scenes of the revolution, and held up in his hands the trappings that were worn by the hero on that eventful day, pierced as they were by the bullets of the invader. The excitement was intense ; the cause was gained ; the appropriation was voted by a large majority.

Mr. Woodbury possessed a genial nature, with fine social feelings, which endeared him to a large circle of friends. His visits to his people were frequent and interesting. As a preacher of the gospel, he was devoted to his work ; and the degree of success which attended his ministerial labors testifies to his faithfulness as a pastor.

He married, in 1826, Augusta Porter, a daughter of the late Jonathan Porter, of Medford, Mass. He left three children, — Augusta, married to George G. Parker, counsellor-at-law in Milford ; George Porter, married, and resides in Milford ; Charlotte Elizabeth, 18 years of age. His wife survived him.

1829. — James Dutton Russell died in Brighton (Longwood village), 10 June, 1861, aged 51 years. His name was originally James Russell Dutton ; and was changed by act of the legislature, 21 February, 1820. He was son of Hon. Warren (Y.C. 1797) and Elizabeth Cabot (Lowell) Dutton, and was born in Boston, 7 January, 1810. He was fitted for college in the Boston Latin School. Immediately after graduating, he entered the Law School in Cambridge, where he remained somewhat more than a year ; and then entered as a student the office of Hon. Franklin Dexter, of Boston (H.C. 1812). In October, 1832, he was admitted in Boston as attorney of the

Court of Common Pleas, and opened an office at No. 5, Court Street. At this time he was an ensign in the Boston Light Infantry. In 1833, he visited Europe. Possessing an ample competence, he did not pursue his profession as a means of living. About ten years before his death, he made Longwood his permanent residence.

He married, 4 November, 1835, Helen Hooper, daughter of William Hooper, Esq., of Marblehead. The issue of this marriage was four children, — two sons and two daughters, — all of whom are living. Their mother died 27 February, 1848, at the age of 31 years.

1831. — MOSES HAGAR died in Philadelphia, 18 November, 1860, aged 56 years. He was the eldest son of Elijah and Mary (Jones) Hagar, and was born in Westminster, Mass., 9 September, 1804. His father died 27 April, 1841, aged 83 years and 6 months. He pursued his studies, preparatory to entering college, at Stow, Mass., New Ipswich, N.H., Leicester and New Salem, Mass.; also with Dr. John White, in Westminster. After graduating, he began the study of law; but was not, probably, admitted to the bar. He was at one time clerk of court in Philadelphia; but, for some time previous to his death, he held an agency in one of the various railroad-offices in that city. He was never married.

1831. — JOSEPH RICKETSON WILLIAMS died in Constantine, Mich., 15 June, 1861, aged 52 years. He was the oldest son of Capt. Richard and Rebecca (Smith) Williams, and was born in Taunton, Mass., 14 November, 1808; but removed soon after his birth, with his parents, to New Bedford. His father was a highly respectable shipmaster; and, after his retirement from the sea, held for many years the office of postmaster of New Bedford. At the age of sixteen years, the subject of this notice was apprenticed in a counting-room in Boston. He remained there two years; but, disliking a mercantile life, he relinquished his place, with the intention of obtaining a collegiate education. He pursued his preparatory studies at Sandwich Academy, under the instruction of Luther Barker Lincoln (H.C. 1822). He gained a high rank of scholarship in his class, and graduated with distinguished honors. He taught school in his sophomore year in Concord, Mass., and in his senior year in Northborough, Mass. After leaving college, he studied law in the office of Hon. John Davis, of Worcester, (Y.C. 1812), was admitted to the bar, and began the practice of his profession in New Bedford. Soon afterwards, Hon. John H. Clifford, of New Bedford, offered him a partnership in a lucrative practice, which he declined on account of his health. He was always a student; and as a writer, if he had addressed himself persistently to any department of letters, would have been distinguished. He was at one period an acceptable contributor to the "North-American Review." An admirable and exhaustive article upon the whale-fishery appeared in its pages, prepared by him while he was in Mr. Clifford's office. If he had devoted himself resolutely to his profession, he would have obtained a high position in it. The precarious state of his health from the time of his admission to the bar, and the necessity which he thought it impressed upon him for a more out-of-door life, and in a different climate, only prevented him from being one of the men of mark in his native state, and returning in a larger measure to his Alma Mater the fruits of her planting. In 1835, he relinquished his profession, — having accepted the agency of an extensive New-England company for investments in Western lands, — and went to Toledo, O. The place, then small, offered few inducements, beyond the opportunity for speculation in city property, in which Mr. Williams successfully engaged. He built the American Hotel in 1836, and remained there until 1839, when he removed to Constantine, Mich. He there engaged in the milling business, built a fine mill, and was for several years very successful in this vocation. Between the years 1837 and 1853, he became identified with the political interests of the state of Michigan. He was elected a member of the constitutional convention of Michigan. He was twice a candidate for United-States senator against Gen. Cass, before the organization of the republican party, and was three times a whig candidate for Congress in the district in which he lived; and, although his party was greatly in the minority, he came within a small vote of an election. In 1853 he purchased the "Toledo-Blade" establishment, and returned to that city. Under his management, the "Blade" became, from the first, the advocate of republican principles, and did more to inaugurate the republican party in Northern Ohio than all the other papers in the state. Mr. Williams was in failing health when he assumed the management of the "Blade;" and, though eminently qualified by capacity and taste for the occupation, it was one that did not, as he anticipated, favor his disease. After an editorial career of three years, he sold the paper to its present proprietors, to occupy the position, at the hands of the Michigan legislature, of president of the Agricultural College of Michigan. This institution, located at Lansing, was but just incorporated; and, being unlike any institution in the country, it was, of course, an experiment. Mr. Williams was deemed the most suitable person to inaugurate it, by the character and ability of his writings and addresses upon the subjects of agriculture. His failing health was the impediment in the way of success; and, after a year of laborious exertion, he was obliged to abandon this position, and seek relief at Havana and Bermuda. He returned from the South in the spring of 1860, considerably improved, and was elected the following fall a member of the senate of Michigan, which body did him the honor to elect him their president; an office for which his talents eminently qualified him. By the resignation of the lieutenant-governor, Hon. James Birney, Mr. Williams became acting lieutenant-governor of the state; which office he held at the time of his death.

He married, in Buffalo, N. Y., 20 May, 1844, Sarah Rowland Langdon, daughter of John and Charlotte Langdon, and a grand-niece of Gov. John Langdon, of New Hampshire; who, with three daughters, survived him.

1832. — Dr. JOSEPH JAMES LLOYD WHITTEMORE died in Paris, France, 14 October, 1860, aged 49 years, lacking one day. He was the only child of Capt. Isaac and Betsey (Tower) Whittemore, and was born in Scituate, Mass., 15 October, 1811. His father was educated a merchant in the counting-room of Bordman and Pope, of Boston. On coming of age, he was first employed as supercargo in one of their ships then trading on the north-west coast. Afterwards he had command of several of their ships in the same trade until he died in 1818, and was buried on Madison's Island, in the Pacific Ocean. He had acquired a handsome property, the fruit of his maritime industry, which his young son inherited. His mother was daughter of Matthew Tower, of Scituate. Placed under the guardianship of the late Dr. Cushing Otis (H.C. 1789), of his native town, he was liberally provided for, and his education attended to with all wisdom, discretion, and the most paternal kindness. He was fitted for college at the Derby Academy in Hingham, Mass. His ample resources pecuniarily, and his large genial and social qualities, combined with an almost absorbing genius and taste for music, were not calculated to induce a very close and untiring application to the prescribed studies, although his talent for acquiring readily a knowledge of the languages, classic and modern, was remarkable. He needed the spur of the *res angusta domi* to make him hold high rank as a college student. Lacking this, and the other spur of literary ambition, it is almost needless to add, that he did not graduate "with all the honors." Immediately after leaving college, he began, 1 September, 1832, the study of medicine in Boston, in the Medical School under the superintendence of Dr. James Jackson (H.C. 1796), and remained there until April, 1833. He embarked, 1 April, 1833, in company with his classmate Tarbell, for Liverpool, to prosecute his studies at the medical schools of Paris, where he remained three years. In May, 1834, he was married at Dover, Eng., to Victoire Marie Anne Adelaide Bellenger, of Paris; who survived him, without children. He left Paris, 1 July, 1836, for Heidelberg, Germany, to finish his medical studies. Having passed a most creditable examination (in the French tongue as a medium of communication) before the medical department of the Heidelberg University, and obtained his diploma, he returned to Paris, 21 May, 1837. He then embarked for home, where he arrived 1 July, 1836; and 1 September, 1837, began the practice of medicine in his native town. He succeeded, with only a short interval, to the large practice of his late guardian, Dr. Otis, whose place he seemed almost providentially to have been fitted to supply. His European education and universal popularity as a fellow-townsman combined to render the claims upon his skill very numerous and constant, and his labors very arduous and unremitting, including a wide range of travel by night and by day. His wife having become dissatisfied with Scituate as a place of residence, he was persuaded to give up his practice, and remove to New-York city. But, having from his observations there concluded that dentistry would prove more lucrative to him as a stranger in that large city than the practice of his profession as a physician, he placed himself under the instruction of the late Dr. Burdell, at that time an eminent and successful practitioner of the dental art. After an itinerary practice in Vermont and Massachusetts for a few years with varying success, he was strongly urged to establish himself at Rio Janeiro as a dentist; and he accordingly embarked at Boston for that place in the fall of 1843. His genial and refined manners, his unobtrusive deportment, and undivided attention to his business, very soon won for him hosts of friends, and an overflowing patronage, until in a few years he was honored in his calling with the preference of the emperor and the royal family; thereby supplanting a jealous and unprincipled rival, and bringing to nought all the "devilish enginery" of his malice and falsehood. For the last ten years or more, up to the time of his leaving Rio, he retained his post of honor as "dentist to the royal family of Brazil."

On the 7th of April, 1860, he left Rio, *viâ* Southampton, with the intention of coming home; and on his passage was struck with paralysis, which rendered him insensible for four days. He recovered partially, landed at Southampton, remained there three weeks, and was then removed to Amiens, France. Here he hired a pleasant house and garden, as his home for the coming winter, in the hope of recovering his health and bodily activity, so as to revisit the home of his youth in the ensuing spring. But he soon afterwards left Amiens, and went to Paris, where he concluded to pass the winter. But alas for all human hopes! After breakfast, on the 14th of October, while in the act of replacing his watch, he was struck again with paralysis; and looking up to his wife with the remark, "I can't put it back," he fell into her arms, and never spoke or knew any thing afterwards. He died in the evening of that day, having very nearly completed forty-nine years of his existence. The funeral-service of the deceased was performed by a clergyman of the Protestant church. If report speaks true, the doctor had accumulated quite a large property during his residence at Rio. Some, who claim to know, placed it as high as eighty thousand dollars.

1834.—THADDEUS CLAPP died in Dorchester, Mass., 10 July, 1861, aged 50 years. He was the second son and third child of Capt. William and Elizabeth (Humphreys) Clapp, grandson of Capt. Lemuel and Rebecca (Dexter) Clapp, and a descendant in the seventh generation from Nicholas and Sarah Clapp, of Dorchester. He was born in Dorchester, 11 May, 1811. He was fitted for college at the academy of Hiram Manley (H.C. 1825), in Dorchester. In college he attained a distinguished rank, and graduated with the second honors of his class. Immediately after leaving college, he taught, for a short time, a private school in Brookline. He was superintendent of the sunday-school of the First Church and Society in Dorchester for about two years from 1836. On the 16th of February, 1837, he entered his name with Col. Loammi Baldwin, of Charlestown, Mass., as a student in engineering; but, on account of ill health, did not prosecute his studies. On taking his degree of master of arts, in 1837, the Latin valedictory oration was proffered to him by President Quincy; which, on account of feeble health, he could not accept. He was secretary of the board of school-committee in Dorchester several years, and wrote some of the annual reports; among them those for the years 1842 and 1843, which were printed. In the fall of 1838, he went to Franklin, La., where he was, for some six or seven months, a tutor in the family of William T. Palfrey, Esq., brother of Hon. John G. Palfrey, postmaster of Boston, (H.C. 1815). He returned to Dorchester in the summer of

1839. About the year 1840, he engaged in horticultural and pomological pursuits, which he continued during his life. He became quite celebrated among the fruit-growers for his theoretical and practical knowledge, and obtained many premiums for choice varieties of fine samples of fruit. He was a member of the Massachusetts Horticultural Society and the Norfolk Agricultural Society. He was of a most amiable disposition, and led a life of unspotted integrity. He married in Claremont, N.H., 11 August, 1857, Mary H. Dustin, daughter of Rev. Caleb Dustin; but had no children. His wife survived him.

1834. — Rufus Hosmer died in Lansing, Mich., 20 April, 1861, aged 45 years. He was son of Hon. Rufus (H.C. 1800) and Amelia (Paine) Hosmer, and was born in Stow, Mass., 16 July, 1816. His father was born in Concord, Mass., 18 March, 1778; and was a lawyer in Stow. He was a member of the executive-council in 1839, and died very suddenly in Boston, 19 April, 1839, aged 61 years. His grandfather, Hon. Joseph Hosmer, was born in Concord, 25 December, 1735; and was one of the most honored and distinguished citizens of the town. He took a conspicuous part in the events of the revolution. He was a representative five, and a senator twelve, years. He was appointed sheriff of the county in 1792, and filled the office fifteen years. He died 31 January, 1821, aged 85 years. His maternal grandfather, Major Phineas Paine, was a native of Randolph, and was a hero of the revolution. He served in the army three years, being at Morristown, Valley Forge, White Plains, and Monmouth. From Randolph he removed to Milton Hill, and there married Nancy Babcock. Many years afterwards, he removed to Concord, where he died.

The subject of this notice was fitted for college at the academy in Stow. After leaving college, he studied law in his father's office, and attended lectures at the Law School in Cambridge. In 1838 he went to Michigan, and soon afterwards was admitted to the bar. He began the practice of his profession in Pontiac, Oakland county; at first in partnership with his cousin, Charles Draper (H.C. 1833), and afterwards with the late George Wisner. He was very successful, and attained a high rank as a lawyer. But, after a few years, he relinquished the profession, removed to Detroit, and became editor of the "Daily Advertiser," in that city; in which position he remained about seven years; when, having been appointed state-printer, it became necessary for him to reside in the capital of the state; and he removed to Lansing, where he became part owner and editor of the "Lansing Advertiser." Here he remained about three years; and relinquished his situation, a few days before his death, to accept the appointment of consul at Frankfort-on-the-Main, which had been conferred upon him. While making preparations for his departure to his foreign post, he was prostrated by an attack of apoplexy, which terminated his life after a few days' illness. As an editor and an agreeable and finished writer, he had few superiors. But it was for his high social qualities, his keen wit, his ready repartee, and his powers of conversation, that he was best known and most admired in the various communities in which he resided.

He married, in 1840, Sarah Chamberlin, daughter of Dr. Olmsted Chamberlin, of Pontiac. His wife survived him; as did also three children, — two daughters and an infant son. A year ago, in May last, he lost his then only son, Rufus, at the age of eighteen years. The little boy, who survives him, was only ten days old when his father died; and, the day before he was taken sick, he named him Rufus, making the third generation who bore that name.

1840. — Dr. BENJAMIN HEYWOOD died in Worcester, Mass., 21 July, 1860, aged 39 years. He was the eldest son of Dr. Benjamin Franklin (D.C. 1812) and Nancy (Green) Heywood, and was born in Worcester, 16 July, 1821. He was fitted for college at the classical school in Worcester, under Charles Thurber (B.U. 1827). Immediately after leaving college, he began the study of medicine under the instruction of his father, attended his first course of medical lectures in Boston, and the two succeeding courses in Philadelphia; and, in the spring of 1843, received the degree of M.D. at the University of Pennsylvania, in Philadelphia. He then began the practice of his profession in Worcester, and continued it until the spring of 1846; when he went to Europe, for the purpose of perfecting himself in the theory and practice of surgery in the city of Paris. He returned in 1847, and resumed the practice of his profession in Worcester, and continued until almost the day of his decease: having prescribed, within three days of his death, for an old patient; and prescribing, also, mainly for himself during his long illness of more than a year. He combined, with high attainments in theoretical knowledge, rare skill in diagnosis, and discriminating judgment in the application of his remedial agents. Few men of his years in the profession were more successful practitioners, both in medicine and surgery. Descended from a line of ancestry eminently distinguished in medicine and surgery, he seemed to have acquired the art of healing almost by intuition. Apprehending readily the obscure as well as the prominent indications of disease, his remedies were adapted with rare skill and success. He was never married.

1846. — JOHN DOWNES AUSTIN, of Boston, died in White Plains, N.Y., 28 February, 1861, aged 34 years. He arrived at New-York city from Boston, on Thursday, 26 February, on a visit to some relatives. On Wednesday, he expressed apprehensions of an attack of temporary insanity, with which he had been affected on two former occasions; and, should it occur, he feared he might attempt to commit suicide. He therefore wished that his friends would keep all implements of harm out of his way. In consequence of this, a friend kept watch of him during the night, and he rested quietly. About daylight on the 28th, this watcher fell asleep. He slept about twenty minutes; and, when he awoke, he found that Mr. Austin had disappeared. Search was immediately made for him, but in vain. On Friday, 1 March, his hat was found in Bronx River, not far from Williams Bridge, and his shirt on the bank of the river near by; which led to the inference, that he had committed suicide by drowning: and a careful search of the river was made for his body, but with no success. Search was continued by his friends and the police, and a reward of one hundred dollars was offered for the discovery of his body. On Thursday, 11 April, a man was fishing from a boat in a pond at White Plains, when he observed a strange object in the bottom of the water. Assistance was procured; and the object, which proved to be the body of Mr. Austin, was drawn up. A very affecting incident connected with the matter was the sudden death of his elder brother, Mr. William Downes Austin, formerly of the United-States navy, at a village in New Jersey, on the 4th of April. He was plunged into great grief at the disappearance of his brother John, and joined in the search of the missing man. He repaired to New Jersey to view the body of a man who had been found there. He had been called to breakfast, and replied that he would be down soon; but, not appearing, a servant went to his room again, and found him lying dead upon his bed, his eyes suffused with tears.

The subject of this notice was son of William and Hepzibah (Downes) Austin, and was born in Boston, 10 February, 1827. He resided in Boston, Roxbury, Lowell, and Dedham, Mass.; at Ravenwood Plantation, La.; and Columbia, Tenn. He attended school some time at the last-named place. In 1839 and 1840, he made voyages to New Orleans. He was fitted for college at the school of Mr. Stephen Minot Weld (H.C. 1826) at Jamaica Plain. After graduating, he pursued the study of the law in the office of Bradford Sumner, of Boston (B.U. 1808); completed his studies at the Law School in Cambridge, where he received the degree of LL.B. in 1848; and was admitted to the Suffolk bar in 1849. In 1850, he removed to Taunton, Mass., where, for a short time, he practised law in company with Horatio Pratt (B.U. 1825). In 1853, he went to New York to reside; but shortly afterwards returned to Boston. In 1854, he practised law in Boston. In 1856, after the death of his father, having relinquished law, he passed one or two winters at Water Proof, La., superintending the affairs of a plantation belonging to a connection.

Mr. Austin was a person of excellent abilities and understanding, with a mind well stored with general information. The wandering life which he led, as a boy, would seem to have had some influence on his late career, and to have unfitted him for the pursuit of a profession; on which, through an inherited competency, he was not obliged to rely for a livelihood. He was never married.

1849. — Dr. Horace Walter Adams died in Boston, 17 February, 1861, aged 33 years. He was son of Charles Frederick and Caroline Hesselrigge (Walter) Adams, and was born in Boston, 8 December, 1827. He was fitted for college at the public Latin School in this city. He adopted the practice of medicine for a profession, and pursued his studies at the Tremont Medical School in Boston. He chose his native city as the field of his practice, and was early appointed a dispensary physician; and so deeply did he interest himself in this practice, that at one time he had charge of the invalid poor, under the auspices of that benevolent institution, for wards four, five, and six. His labors in this department of practice were very various, extensive, and arduous; yet he cheerfully and faithfully responded to all their requirements.

He was a sincere lover of his profession, which was adopted, not from necessity, but from a real and abiding interest in its pursuit, which induced him to devote to its practice the best energies of his life. His services were very frequently demanded at the Eye-and-Ear Infirmary in Boston, where he established a character for reliable judgment, and gentleness of treatment of those delicate organs, which made him a skilful operator at that institution. He was untiring in industry and zeal for those patients whom he attracted about him: indeed, his devotion to his profession was at times so absorbing, that he felt it due to his own health that both his body and mind should have occasional recreation. Accordingly, he was accustomed from time to time, as he felt the need thereof, to engage with one or two friends in sporting excursions, of which he was remarkably fond; and it was on an occasion of this nature that he contracted the disease which terminated his life.

On Tuesday, 5 February, 1861, he left Boston, in company with Mr. Francis Lowell Gardner, a member of the junior class at Harvard College, and two other friends, to spend a few days at Cotuit Point, a town on the South Shore. On Sunday, the 10th of February, Mr. Gardner, having contracted a very severe cold which affected his throat, died of diphtheria, most unexpectedly to his friends and associates. Dr. Adams attended Mr. Gardner most assiduously; and he was brought so immediately in contact with his friend and patient at the last hours of his life, that he unconsciously imbibed some portion of the fatal disorder into his throat and lungs, which became immediately affected on his return to Boston, where he died on the Sunday following, 17 February, of the same disorder. He was never married.

Dr. Adams was not only an accomplished physician, but his genial manners, his kindness of heart, and his own ready sympathy with the sick and suffering, so won the confidence of his indigent patients, that their affection for him often outlived their convalescence, and led them, as was repeatedly the case, to consult him and seek his judicious advice upon pecuniary matters; to which, although foreign to his profession, he always gave the most careful attention: and for his untimely departure there were very many of his patients whose hearts were made really desolate; some who wept bitter tears for the loss of their "good physician."

1854. — William Gaston Pearson died in Oakland, Marion county, Cal., 19 January, 1861, aged 26 years. He was born in North Carolina, 24 March, 1834. He was at St. James College, Maryland, five years, — three in the preparatory school, and two in the college. He entered the sophomore class in Harvard College in September, 1851; left, on account of ill health, in November, 1853; but took his degree with his class. He went to Europe, where he remained a year; then back to this country for a while; then to Cuba for a winter; and thence to San Francisco, Cal., where his disease (consumption) seemed to be arrested. He returned to the Atlantic states in 1857 or 1858, and went to farming on his family estate at Brentwood, near Washington, D.C. His health continued pretty good until the spring of 1860, when a violent pleurisy again prostrated him. He failed rapidly, and on the 1st of December he sailed again for California, in hopes of a recovery; but he was too far gone, and died 19 January, soon after his arrival.

1856. — Isaac Nelson Beals died of consumption, in Dexter, Me., 5 August, 1860, aged 29 years. He was son of Isaiah and Lucy (Bradstreet) Beals, and was born in Dexter, 12 June, 1831. He was fitted for college at small academies and high-schools in the villages of Dexter, St. Alban's, and Corinna, Me.; being governed in his choice of a school from term to term by circumstances and the abilities of the teacher. In his preparation for college, as well as during his college career, he was obliged to rely mainly upon such pecuniary resources as he could control by his own labor, principally in school-teaching. In September, 1853, he entered the sophomore class in Waterville College, Me.; having pursued the studies of the first year by himself, while teaching school, or while at home in the intervals of teaching. One who was a classmate with him at Waterville remarks, that "on entering college he at once took a high rank, which he constantly improved." At the end of the junior year, he left Waterville; and in September, 1855, he entered Harvard at the beginning of the senior year. Here he exhibited the same studious traits which appear to have characterized his course at Waterville. In the winter after he entered Harvard, he taught Westbrook Seminary, in Westbrook, Me.; and in April, 1856, having received the appointment of principal of the high-school, Quincy, Mass., the faculty of the college gave him permission to begin his school before taking his degree; and he immediately entered upon his duties there. His labors in this school were highly satisfactory to the committee; who state, in their report, that "at each visitation they witnessed proofs of thorough and faithful training, and heard recitations, which, in some respects, were wonderful." In September, 1858, he became principal of the high-school in Somerville, Mass., which appeared to have been unpopular in the town, and in a chaotic state; but in the face of much opposition, and with constant ill health, he gave to the school, in less than a year, a high intellectual character and a faultless discipline. In discipline, indeed, he appeared ever to have excelled. In the summer of 1859, he accepted an invitation to take charge of a new high-school to be opened in Newton, and located in the village of Newtonville; and entered upon his duties in September. Here he remained until ill health compelled him to resign, in April, 1860. His physical powers were by nature capable of great endurance; but excessive mental labor from his boyhood, to which he was urged by his ambition to excel, backed by his almost unconquerable will, together with constant mental anxiety while bearing the responsibilities of prominent public schools, wore him out; and when at length he was induced to give up work, which was several months after his physician began persuading him to do so, he was ill and exhausted beyond the chance of recovery. Immediately after his resignation, by the advice of his physician, he went to Philadelphia to seek the benefit of a milder climate. He returned in May, without any permanent improvement. He then went to his native place in Maine, hoping that the climate there might be beneficial; but all to no purpose. He rapidly declined until death closed the scene. A communication from an intimate friend of the deceased to Mr. William Wirt Burrage, the secretary of the class, who kindly furnished the above sketch, says, "During the last few weeks of his illness, his character presented a very pleasant phase of mildness and tenderness, strongly contrasting with his habitual temperament. He was a great sufferer, but bore his pain patiently, and never murmured a word at his lot. In the last few days, he realized, more fully than did his friends, how near death was, talked composedly of it, and was prepared to meet it bravely and manfully. He was an ardent lover of nature, and spent hours out of doors for no other purpose than to admire its beauties, seeking varied landscape views from every hill-top and mountain. He ignored religious forms, but was no stranger to religion itself."

He married, 9 August, 1859, Caroline Rowena Burgess, who had been his assistant at the high-school at Quincy. She was the daughter of Josiah and Nancy W. (Fuller) Burgess of Waltham, Mass. His younger and only brother Charles, who, like Isaac, inherited from his parents a decided character and great strength of will, died in 1857, about 25 years of age, from illness brought on a few years before by physical over-exertion, into which he had been led by his ambition. The family survivors of the deceased are his widow, who lives in Cambridge; and his father and mother, who live in Dexter, Me.

1856. — THOMAS THAXTER died in Methuen, Mass., 15 August, 1860, aged 26 years. He was son of Thomas and Ruby (Bradstreet) Thaxter, and was born in Methuen, 24 December, 1833. He was a twin. His brother Robert died when two years of age. His father, whose first known ancestor, Deacon Thomas Thaxter, was born in Machias, Me., 2 November, 1792, settled in Hingham, Mass., in 1635. He was connected with the Methuen Manufacturing Company, and died 27 January, 1842. His mother, whose first known ancestor was Gov. Simon Bradstreet, was born in Billerica, Mass., 4 July, 1800; and died in Methuen, 21 June, 1845. His parents were married 2 September, 1827. On the death of his mother, Mr. John Davis, of Methuen, was appointed guardian of the surviving children, Ruby and Thomas. Thomas lived for a short time upon a farm with Deacon Edward Carleton; and about October, 1846, began to attend a private school kept by Moses Burbank and wife, and boarded with his uncle, Mr. William Thaxter. Here he remained a year, and then entered a family boarding-school in Fairhaven, Mass., kept by Rev. William Gould, where he remained about thirteen months. In 1849, he went to Phillips Academy, Andover, to prepare for college, where he remained a year and a half. While in Andover in 1851, he joined the Congregational (Orthodox) church in Methuen. In September, 1852, he entered the freshman class in Yale College, where he remained until May, 1854, when he took up his connexions. In September, 1854, he entered the junior class at Harvard. Towards the end of the term, a weakness of his eyes obliged him to remit his studies; and in April of the following term he was compelled, from a general failure of health, to leave college. He did not return until January, 1856; from which time he remained until graduation. During the time he was able to study, he gained a very high rank in his class, and a reputation for persevering industry and ambitious scholarship. On leaving college, he intended to pursue a business career, and entered the counting-room of E. and T. Fairbanks and Co., dealers in scales, No. 24, Kilby Street, Boston, but soon left on account of his health; and, with the hope of improving it, he went, in April, 1857, to Fairbault, Minn., on a visit to his uncle, Mr. William Thaxter, where, and in the vicinity, he remained working on a farm until November of that year.

His health having apparently improved, he, in December, began to teach a public school in Stillwater, Minn., and, 1 September, 1858, became principal of the high-school; but it was soon apparent that his health was not sufficient to sustain the labor. Before the end of his first term, he entered the school-room one morning, feeling very weak; had proceeded with but few recitations, when he fainted; was obliged to dismiss his school, never to resume it. Symptoms of incipient consumption were developed, followed by hemorrhage at the lungs. But by his ambition and perseverance he rallied in a degree, and took a class of private pupils, who recited to him a few hours daily. The secretary of his class, to whom we are indebted for the foregoing particulars, concludes his record by quoting an account of the last portion of his life from one who had the best opportunity of learning the incidents: "As long as he was able to work, so long did he persist in doing so, even to within a short time of his decease. But, as daily and weekly he became sensible of a gradual decline, he began to feel a desire to be among his early friends; and in September, 1859, he returned to the East, to the house of Mr. Davis, his former guardian, where he remained until his death. For a short time after his return home, he seemed stronger. He could not rest unemployed; and, against the wishes of his friends, he began book-keeping for a firm in Lawrence, Mass., with whom he remained three months. Here it was painfully evident to his friends that his life was fast ebbing away. He would frequently say, 'Am I lazy? or am I growing weaker?' He was confined to his bed only four days, and to the last of his life manifested the same desire to wait upon himself, which had been one of the prevailing traits of his character during his long sickness. Through the many months of his last sickness, he often spoke of dying with the calmness that characterizes the Christian. When dying, his mind was calm and clear; and almost his last words were, 'I want to go to heaven: I want to begin to work there.'"

He left, as the only survivor of his immediate family, a sister, — Mrs. Ruby T. Tenny, of Methuen.

1861–62.

1796. — HENRY ABBOT died in Andover, Mass., 13 January, 1862, aged 84 years. He was the fourth child and second son of Capt. Henry and Phebe (Abbot) Abbot, and was born in Andover, 8 April, 1777. His father was son of Henry; was born in Andover, 10 January, 1725; and died 21 February, 1805, aged 80 years. His mother was daughter of Deacon Isaac Abbot, of Andover; was born 26 November, 1746; and died 29 June, 1833, aged 86 years. He was fitted for college at Phillips Academy, Andover. After leaving college, he engaged in mercantile business in Bedford, Mass. He did not, however, remain there long; but went to sea, in the capacity of captain's-clerk, with Capt. David Woodward, of Charlestown, in the ship "Catharine," of Boston, owned by Samuel Torrey, Esq.: it was a voyage around the world. Sailing from Boston, they touched at Rio Janeiro, and, doubling Cape Horn, proceeded up the west coast of South America, stopping at various places along the coast, until they reached California, whose golden treasures were then undreamed of; yet, as far as their voyage was concerned, the gains of their traffic along that coast exceeded those of many of the present day who meet with more than average success in the land of gold. Their next destination was Canton; where they arrived, after stopping on their way at the Sandwich Islands, which were then in their primitive condition of barbarism. Taking in a cargo of Canton goods, the ship returned to Boston by way of the Cape of Good Hope. At the Isle of France, on his return voyage, Mr. Abbot was greatly and agreeably surprised to meet his brother, whom he supposed to be at home; and learned from him the death of their father, who, at the age of eighty years, was in good health when he parted from him. He made one more similar voyage with the same captain, in the ship "Dromo;" which was also owned by Samuel Torrey. His attachment to Capt. Woodward was very strong. He spoke of his treatment of him as being like that of a father, and also of his kind and considerate treatment of his crew; while, at the same time, his authority over them was unimpaired. After his return from his last voyage, he engaged in trade at Andover; but soon afterwards, in partnership with his brother, went into the wholesale grocery-business in Boston. Owing to the embarrassments brought upon the trade by the embargo at that time, their business was unsuccessful; and Mr. Abbot returned to Andover. About 1814, he visited the Western country; crossing the Alleghany Mountains on foot, and, from Pittsburg, navigating the Ohio River, with a single companion, in a small boat, to the falls of the Ohio River at Louisville, Ky. There were but few inhabitants along the Ohio at that early day; and the principal places where he stopped to transact business (which are now large and flourishing cities) were at that time small settlements, composed of a few log-cabins. At Lexington, Ky., he met with Mr. Newman (afterwards Prof. Samuel P. Newman, of Bowdoin College), and returned home in company with him, performing the whole journey on horseback. He afterwards went a journey South as far as Georgia, to visit his brother. On his return home, he settled down in Andover with his mother, on the home-farm, and remained there until her death. He then removed to Chester, N.H.; and, after residing there about six years, returned to Andover, and lived there, amidst old scenes and old acquaintance, until his death.

He was a member of the Old South Church in Andover for thirty-eight years. He was unswerving and decided in his religious convictions and principles, earnest and consistent in his Christian life. In his family he was social, warm-hearted, and cheerful; and, in his intercourse with society, genial and friendly; generally lively, and often jocose, in the company of his friends. In politics, early in life, he was fully convinced of the correctness and true policy of the principles of the federalists, and honestly contended for the interests of that party. He naturally fell in with the sentiments of the whigs when that party came into existence, advocated their principles, and heartily co-operated with them. In his last years, he uniformly acted and voted with the republicans; and cast his last vote for the candidates of that party, at the last November election. He was abroad until a few weeks before his death, retained his faculties to the last, and died, not of disease, but of old age.

He married, May, 1807, Judith Follansbee, — a niece and adopted child of Dr. Abiel Pierson, of Andover. He had six children, — four daughters and two sons. Three of the daughters and one son survived him. His wife also survives him; being now eighty years of age.

1798. — Hon. RICHARD SULLIVAN died in Cambridge, 11 December, 1861, aged 82 years. He was the third son of Hon. James and Mehitable (Odiorne) Sullivan, and was born in Groton, Mass., 17 July, 1779. His father was born in Berwick, Me., 22 April, 1744. He was a lawyer by profession, and began practice in Georgetown, Me.; but soon afterwards removed to Biddeford, Me. In February, 1778, he removed to Groton, Mass.; and, in 1782, he removed from Groton to Boston. He was a judge of the Supreme Court, and attorney-general of Massachusetts. In 1807, he was chosen governor of the state; was re-elected in 1808, and died while in office, 10 December, 1808. Mr. Sullivan's mother was the daughter of William Odiorne, a ship-builder, of Durham, N.H., where she was born 26 June, 1748; and died in Boston, 26 January, 1786. Young Sullivan was fitted for college at the Boston Latin School. He was well prepared for pursuing the prescribed studies in the college course, but did not presume so far upon his acquirements as to pass superficially over the assigned tasks. As a scholar, he was among the most distinguished of his class. His character was spotless, his disposition kind and benevolent, his manners polished, without affectation or parade. After leaving college, he studied law in the office of his father, and was admitted to the Suffolk bar in 1801, but did not long pursue his profession, as he had an ample competence of worldly goods. In his early manhood, he took much interest in political affairs. He was elected a senator in the state legislature from Suffolk in 1815 and the two following years; was a member, from Brookline, of the convention for revising the constitution of the state in 1820; was a member of the governor's council in 1820 and 1821. In 1823, he was the candidate of the federal party for lieutenant-governor of the state, the Hon. Harrison Gray Otis being the candidate for governor; but the ticket was defeated. In 1821, he was elected a member of the board of overseers of Harvard College, and held that office until the board was newly constituted by an act of the legislature of Massachusetts in 1852, which was accepted by the corporation and overseers of the college. He was public-spirited and philanthropic; and the records of several of our most valuable public institutions, founded during the first thirty years of the present century, bear ample testimony to his services in their behalf. It was at a meeting of gentlemen at his house that the project of the Massachusetts General Hospital was first seriously started; and, among those who aided in rearing that beneficent establishment, the labors of few were more earnest or efficient than those of Mr. Sullivan. Removing into the country, and residing for many years in the neighboring town of Brookline, he was among the first of those, who, nearly half a century ago, gave an impulse to rural tastes and pursuits, to the advancement of agriculture, and to that culture of fruits and flowers, which, now widespread, does so much to embellish and refine life among us. Here, at his beautiful estate in the country, surrounded by his wife and daughters, he had a home, which, in the dignity and grace that presided over it, in the intellectual and moral refinement that pervaded it, in the holy love and faith that sanctified it, was the model of a Christian home; and comes up to the thoughts of all who remember it, as being as near an approach to a picture and miniature of heaven as they may ever hope to see on earth.

He married, 22 May, 1804, Sarah Russell, a daughter of the eminent and wealthy merchant, Thomas Russell, of Boston;

and shortly after, in company with her, made an extensive tour in Europe. The issue of this marriage was four sons and four daughters, of whom only two sons survived him. His wife died 8 June, 1831.

1799. — Gen. WILLIAM HYSLOP SUMNER died in West Roxbury (Jamaica Plain), Mass., 24 October, 1861, aged 81 years. He had been helpless from paralysis for four years; and, for the last two years of his life, was hardly able to utter a sentence intelligibly. He was the only son of Hon. Increase (H.C. 1767) and Elizabeth (Hyslop) Sumner, and was born in Roxbury, 4 July, 1780. His father was born in Roxbury, 27 November, 1746; was associate-judge of the Supreme Court from 1782 to 1797; was governor of Massachusetts from 1797 until his death, 7 June, 1799. His mother was the daughter of William and Mehitable Hyslop; was born in Boston, 5 August, 1757; and died 28 December, 1810, aged 53 years. William Hyslop was an eminent and prosperous merchant in Boston, but about 1781 removed to Brookline, Mass., where he died 11 August, 1796, aged 84 years. The house in which the subject of this notice was born was formerly owned by Judge Robert Auchmuty, a royalist, and was confiscated. He was first sent to school under the charge of Master Abiel Heywood (H.C. 1781), principal of the grammar-school in Roxbury; next under Rev. William Emerson (H.C. 1789), afterwards minister of the First Church in Boston, who was succeeded by Rev. Calvin Whiting (H.C. 1791), he being followed by Rev. John Pipon (H.C. 1792), afterwards minister in Taunton, Mass. About this time, Gen. Lincoln marched his troops against Shays during the rebellion. Young Sumner, then about six years old, saw the troops, under Major Spooner, march from Meeting-House Hill in Roxbury, where the church now stands in which the Rev. Eliphalet Porter then preached. From the Roxbury school he was taken away in 1789; was placed in the family of his uncle, Charles Cushing (H.C. 1755), and sent to the writing-school of Master Oliver Wellington Lane (H.C. 1772), in the westerly part of Boston. When Gen. Washington visited Boston in that year, the boys of all the schools formed the front lines of the streets through which he passed; and Sumner well remembered the dignified manner in which Washington received the plaudits of the people in the streets and houses; and that he, with the rest of the boys in the school, about seventy in number, carried long quills with the feathers on; and, when Washington passed, they paid him a salute by rolling those quills in their hands. In 1793, he was sent to Phillips Academy in Andover, where he was fitted for college. He remained there two years. During the first part of that time, he was under Ebenezer Pemberton (N.J. 1765), then under Abiel Abbot (H.C. 1787), and finally under Mark Newman (D.C. 1793). When he entered college, in 1795, the rooms in the college buildings were so full, that for three years he lived in the house of the late Prof. Wigglesworth. He held a respectable rank of scholarship in his class. In his senior year, he delivered an English oration at exhibition. The subject was, "The Spirit of Innovation." It was a creditable performance. At commencement, the part assigned to him was a colloquy with John Harris on "The Importance of a National Character to the United States;" but, on account of the death of his father a few weeks before, his performance was omitted. Immediately after graduating, he entered the office of Hon. John Davis (H.C. 1781), under whose instruction he pursued his legal studies; was admitted to the bar in 1802, and opened an office at No. 4, Tremont Street, Boston; and subsequently removed to Scollay's Building, where he occupied an office with Judge Davis, when the latter was appointed judge of the District Court as successor of Judge Lowell. He early distinguished himself by his successful defence of John Whiting, of Franklin, who was indicted for robbing himself, when he was carrying money to be exchanged in Maine for money of the Franklin Bank, of which he was an officer. He said he was assailed by robbers, and showed the holes, in the top of the chaise, made by the bullets which the pretended robbers fired at him.

Gen. Sumner was aide-de-camp to Governors Strong and Brooks, — to the former in 1806 and from 1813 to 1816, and to the latter from 1816 to 1818, when he was appointed adjutant-general by Gov. Brooks, and then relinquished the practice of the law. He held the offices of adjutant-general and quartermaster-general under Governors Brooks, Eustis, Lincoln, and Davis, until 1834; when, upon his resignation, General Dearborn was appointed his successor. In 1808, and the eleven following years, he was one of the representatives of Boston to the legislature. On the 10th of September, 1814, he was appointed by Governor Strong executive-agent to repair "to the district of Maine (which was then invaded by the enemy), and promptly to provide any practicable means for the defence of that part of the state." On the same day, the commissioners for the sea-coast defence (Hon. David Cobb, Timothy Pickering, and John Brooks) also confided to him their full power. In December, 1814, he was appointed by the board of war to borrow money of the banks to pay off the troops which had been called out in Maine; and when it was afterwards proposed to send three commissioners, two from Massachusetts and one from Maine, to the general government, to confer with it upon the measures of defence of the state in future, the members of the legislature from Maine agreed upon him as their commissioner to represent the interest of that part of the state. In 1816, he was sent, with Hon. James Lloyd, to present the Massachusetts claim to the general government for militia services. In November, 1826, he was appointed by the secretary of war a member of the board of army and militia officers, of which Gen. Scott was president, to report a plan for the organization of the militia, and a system of cavalry tactics. In December, 1831, he contracted for the purchase of Greenough's half of Noddle's Island (his sister and uncle owning the other half), and projected the settlement of it as a part of the city of Boston; and, with other gentlemen, founded and put in operation the East-Boston Company, which thus came into possession of the whole island, and under auspices of which the improvements which have given East Boston its present measure of prosperity have been carried on. Since that time, he has done much for the welfare and adornment of the place. A few years since, he gave land to the value of six thousand dollars, the income to be applied to setting out shade-trees on the island. He also gave land to the value of eighteen or twenty thousand dollars for the erection of a library-building by the library-association which bears his name, and to which he gave his own private library. He wrote a very elaborate history of East Boston, comprising eight hundred pages, with numerous engravings. He was a member of the Massachusetts Historical Society.

He married, first, 4 October, 1826, Mrs. Mary Ann Perry, daughter of Hon. James DeWolf, of Bristol, R.I., and widow of Raymond H. J. Perry, brother of Commodore O. H. Perry: she died 14 July, 1835. He married, second, 13 December, 1836, Mrs. Maria Foster Greenough, daughter of Elisha Doane, of Cohasset, and widow of David Stoddard Greenough, of Jamaica Plain: she died 14 November, 1843. He married, third, 18 April, 1848, Mary Dickinson Kemble, of New York, daughter of Peter Kemble, grand-daughter of Gen. Cadwallader, and niece of Gov. Thomas Gage. She survived him. He had no children by any of his wives.

1800. — Rev. Daniel Kimball died in Needham, Mass., 17 January, 1862, aged 83 years. He was son of Lieut. Daniel and Elizabeth (Tenney) Kimball, and was born in Bradford, Mass., 3 July, 1778. Until he was sixteen years old, he worked on his father's farm in summer, and attended the district school in winter. He was fitted for college at Atkinson Academy, N.H., under the instruction of John Vose (D.C. 1795). He held a respectable rank in his class, and graduated with honors. After leaving college, he was assistant-teacher in Sandwich Academy one year. For the next six months, he had charge of a school in his native town. He then returned to Cambridge as a theological student, under the direction of Rev. David Tappan, D.D. (H.C. 1771), Hollis Professor of Divinity; was approbated, and began preaching in the spring or summer of 1803: and, on taking his degree of master of arts that year, he pronounced the Latin valedictory oration. At the same time, he was appointed tutor for the Latin department.

This office he held two years; and, on resigning it, he returned to Bradford, where he resided more than two years, supplying vacant parishes, and giving what were termed "labors of love," pursuing theological and miscellaneous reading and study. In August, 1808, he was appointed preceptor of Derby Academy, in Hingham, Mass., where he remained until the spring of 1826. In addition to the duties of preceptor, he often preached, sometimes in neighboring pulpits in supply, or giving "labors of love." He was ordained at Hingham, as an evangelist, 17 December, 1817. In the spring of 1826, he removed to Needham, where he purchased a farm, and opened a boarding and day school for children of both sexes, which he continued until 1848, devoting himself at the same time to agricultural pursuits. His published works were, A Lecture in Poetry on Temperance; also another Address on Temperance, on the 4th of July; An Address before the Peace Society at Hingham, of which he was president; a Sermon on Unitarianism, preached at Milton, Mass., where he supplied the pulpit at intervals for a few years; a Discourse before the American Institute of Instruction, at the State House, on the Employment of Female Teachers.

He was president of the Needham Lyceum for twenty-five years, and was for nearly as many years chairman of the school-committee. He was a representative to the state legislature in 1846. In his religious principles he was a firm Unitarian. He was highly respected as a man of unblemished character, a kind friend, a hospitable neighbor, and a devoted husband and parent.

He married, 23 March, 1808, Betsey Gage, of Bradford, daughter of Peter and Mary (Webster) Gage, descended, on her father's side, from Major Benjamin Gage, an officer in the American army in the struggle for our national independence. The children of this marriage were as follows (all born in Hingham): 1. Elizabeth Tenny, born 23 March, 1810; died 2 April, 1833. 2. Harriet Webster, born 1 December, 1812 (afterwards widow of John M. Washburn). 3. Daniel, born 1 October, 1814; died 17 December, 1827 (was fitted for college at the time of his death). 4. Benjamin Gage, born 5 May, 1816 (H.C. 1837). 5. Mary Jane, born 19 October, 1817 (now wife of Hon. James Ritchie, of Roxbury) (H.C. 1835). 6. Henry Colman, born 25 February, 1820 (H.C. 1840). 7. Charles David Tenny, born 6 September, 1821; died at Hingham, 24 July, 1822. 8. Charlotte Sophia (Mrs. Hoadley), born 31 July, 1823; died at Lancaster, 12 June, 1848. 9. Clara Anna, born 7 January, 1825; died at Needham, 25 December, 1847. Mr. Kimball's wife survived him.

1801. — Henry Newman died in Boston, 28 July, 1861, aged 78 years. He was son of Henry and Deborah (Cushing) Newman, and was born in Boston, 16 May, 1783. His father was a distinguished merchant. His mother was daughter of Hon. Thomas Cushing (H.C. 1744), representative of Boston, and speaker of the house, in 1763; when he so warmly espoused the cause of his country in the disputes with Great Britain, that Dr. Johnson in his "Taxation No Tyranny," speaking of the Americans, said, "If their rights are inherent and underived, they may, by their own suffrages, encircle with a diadem the brows of Mr. Cushing." He was also lieutenant-governor of the state. The subject of this notice was fitted for college at the Boston Latin School. While in college, his father became involved in consequence of speculations in Georgia lands, and President Willard generously paid a part of young Newman's college dues. Immediately after graduating, he entered as an apprentice in a merchant's store, but soon relinquished the situation; began the study of law with Hon. Thomas Dawes (H.C. 1777), and completed his legal studies with Hon. William Prescott (H.C. 1783). Soon after his admission to the bar, he went to the South, and spent most of the time for twenty years in Washington and other southern cities; being engaged in securing the family property in the Georgia lands, and obtaining remuneration through the government at Washington. He was also agent for Joseph Blake, and several others, who had claims for lands in Virginia and other southern states. This led him to great intimacy with many eminent gentlemen at Washington, — among others, Gen. Jackson, — who treated him with great kindness. He thus obtained an exhaustless fund of information concerning those gentlemen, which rendered him a very interesting companion.

A few years ago, when a committee of the Alumni of Harvard College was appointed to raise funds for the college library, the chairman of the committee, the late Thomas G. Cary, called on Mr. Newman to ask him to take charge of the subscription in his class. He readily accepted the office; and, without any special solicitation, handed Mr. Cary his check for five hundred dollars as his own subscription, saying that he was not so well able to give as he had once been, having lost some of his property; and that he wished to contribute while he was yet able, as further losses might put it out of his power to do so: thus giving, as a reason for subscribing, what many would have considered an ample excuse for refusing to give at all. He was remarkable for his constant and unostentatious charities. He was a member of the Cincinnati Society, through his uncle, Capt. Samuel Newman, who was an officer of distinction in the revolutionary war, and was killed, under Gen. Sinclair, in a battle with the Indians. His manners were highly finished and gentle, of the old school. Never was a more kind-hearted man, a more devoted son, or affectionate brother. He was never married.

1802. — Deacon Samuel Greele, of Boston, died in Swampscott, Mass., where he went to pass the summer, 16 August, 1861, aged 78 years. He was son of Samuel and Olive (Read) Greele, and was born in Wilton, N.H., 3 July, 1783. He was fitted for college at the academy in New Ipswich, N.H. After graduating, he studied divinity with Rev. Jonathan French, of Andover, Mass. (H.C. 1771). He preached for several years, but was never ordained as a minister over any society; and he resigned the sacred profession, much against his will, on account of temporary ill health. He then became a devoted and useful teacher. He was for some time preceptor of an academy in Marblehead. He then removed to Boston, where he taught a private school from 1816 to 1822. In 1825, he entered into partnership with John Baker, under the firm of Baker and Greele, in the business of manufacturing printing-types. This firm was dissolved in 1827; and, the next year, Mr. Greele took into partnership Mr. Henry Willis; and they continued the business, under the firm of Greele and Willis, until 1832, when Mr. Greele retired from active business. He was a devoted member of various charitable and benevolent institutions. He was an officiating deacon in the Federal-street church for nearly fifty years, first under the ministry of Rev. Dr. Channing, and subsequently under Rev. Dr. Gannett. His steady and sincere adherence to the liberal faith, through all the fluctuations of time and opinion, was remarkable. He was a faithful worker in the American Unitarian Association. He was elected a representative from Boston in the state legislature in 1838, 1840, 1841, 1842, and 1843. He was a member of the board of aldermen in Boston in 1834, 1835, and 1836. He was the friend and associate of the young, his heart being always youthful; and nothing pleased him better than the society of little children. His fund of anecdote, geniality of temper, and unfailing flow of spirits, made him the most agreeable of visitors and companions. His perfectly regular habits, yearly journeyings, and equanimity of temper, no doubt contributed to his long life. He was always surrounded by the most untiring and devoted love; and he passed away in sweet patience, without a murmur.

He married, 3 May, 1812, Lydia Maria Sewall, daughter of Chief-Justice Samuel Sewall, of Marblehead (H.C. 1776). She died in Boston, 11 August, 1822, in the 32d year of her age, leaving no children. He married for his second wife, 19 October, 1823, Louisa May, daughter of Col. Joseph May, of Boston. She died 14 November, 1828, at the age of 36 years, having had two children, — a son and a daughter. The son graduated at Harvard College in 1844. He married for his third wife, 18 October, 1831, Maria Antoinette Paine, daughter of Hon. Robert Treat Paine, of Boston (H.C. 1749). She died 26 March, 1842, aged 58 years, leaving no children. He married for his fourth wife, 8 October, 1844, Sarah Follansbee Emerson, of Newburyport, who survived him.

1802.—Rev. CHARLES WELLINGTON died in Templeton, Mass., 3 August, 1861, aged 81 years. He was the sixth child and fifth son of William and Mary (Whitney) Wellington, and was born in Waltham, Mass., 20 February, 1780. His parents had eight sons and five daughters. One of these sons, Isaac, was drowned while a member of the senior class in Harvard College, 12 November, 1796. No other death took place among these children till more than fifty years afterwards. The subject of this notice was fitted for college partly at New-Salem Academy, and partly by Rev. Charles Stearns, D.D., of Lincoln, Mass. (H.C. 1773). About the time of graduation, he, with others, consulted Rev. David Tappan (H.C. 1771), Hollis Professor of Divinity, about their theological studies, and obtained from him a recommendation of a list of books for perusal for that purpose. But Dr. Tappan died 27 August, 1803; and Dr. Henry Ware (H.C. 1785) was not appointed to succeed him until May, 1805. These young men, therefore, pursued their studies alone, as resident graduates; meeting together occasionally for reading of essays, and comparison of views.

He was ordained pastor of the Unitarian church in Templeton, 25 February, 1807, as successor of Rev. Ebenezer Sparhawk (H.C. 1756), who was born in what is now Brighton, 15 June, 1738; was ordained 18 November, 1761; and died 25 November, 1805, aged 67 years. Dr. Wellington continued his ministerial relation to his society until his death, a period of more than fifty-four years. About 1839, his health began to fail, so much as to interrupt the constancy of his public services; and temporary provision was made for his aid: but he supplied the pulpit most of the time until 1843, when arrangements were made for the settlement of a colleague, and, 24 February, 1844, Rev. Norwood Damon was ordained as his assistant. Mr. Damon resigned his ministry, 1 November, 1845; and the supply of the pulpit was resumed by the senior partner. He preached most of the time until August, 1846. On the 13th of January, 1847, Rev. Edwin Goodhue Adams was ordained as his colleague; where he still continues. On the 25th June, 1857, Dr.

Wellington preached a half-century sermon from his ordination. It was printed as prepared for the anniversary-day, four months before; from which time it was postponed on account of the author's ill health. A very large concourse of parishioners and of other friends assembled on the occasion, and made most gratifying testimonials of esteem and affection in which they had held their aged pastor. In his sermon he gives a brief and very modest account of his labors. His influence as a minister was second to that of no one in the western section of Worcester county. That influence was always exerted in favor of religious and civil freedom, of Christian order, and scriptural piety. In 1854, the honorary degree of doctor of divinity was conferred upon him by Harvard College.

Dr. Wellington married, 29 June, 1807, Anna Smith, of Boston. The issue of this marriage was three sons and six daughters, of whom two sons and all the daughters survived their father. The two surviving sons graduated at Harvard College in 1838 and 1846 respectively. His wife died 24 April, 1830; and he married for his second wife, 27 July, 1831, Adelaide Russell, of Templeton, who survived him. By his second wife he had one child, a daughter, who died young.

1804. — Dr. Jonathan Wild died in Braintree, Mass., 6 December, 1862, aged 77 years. He was the oldest child of Jonathan and Deborah (Wild) Wild, and was born in South Weymouth, Mass., 3 April, 1784; but, when he was about a year old, his parents removed to Braintree, where they lived and died. His father was the son of Capt. Silas Wild, and his mother was the daughter of Micah Wild, all of Braintree. Young Wild was fitted for college under the instruction of Rev. Dr. Jonathan Strong, of Randolph (D.C. 1786). After graduating, he studied medicine with Dr. Ebenezer Alden, of West Randolph, father of the present Dr. Ebenezer Alden (H.C. 1808), of Randolph. After completing his studies, he settled in Braintree, where he continued in active and successful practice until 1844, when he retired from the profession. His personal interests were seriously affected by his too-indulgent leniency towards his patients; for, had he been more rigid in exacting his dues for his professional services, he would have become a wealthy man; but he suffered his accounts to remain uncollected, much to his pecuniary detriment.

He married, first, 12 December, 1811, Nancy Lynfield, of Randolph, by whom he had three children, — all daughters, — of whom one only survived him. His wife died 23 August, 1827. He married for his second wife, 11 February, 1830, Livia D. Thayer, of Braintree, sister of Col. Sylvanus Thayer (D.C. 1807), the distinguished engineer, an officer in the Military Academy at West Point. By his second wife he had three children, — two daughters and one son, — of whom one daughter deceased before him. The other two children, with their mother, survived him.

1806. — Rev. William Turner Torrey died in Madison, Lake county, O., 29 October, 1861, aged 75 years. He was the second son of James and Eunice (Turner) Torrey, and was born in Kingston, Mass., 5 February, 1786. His mother was the eldest daughter of Rev. Charles Turner (H.C. 1752), who was born in Scituate, Mass., 3 September, 1732; was ordained at Duxbury, Mass., 23 July, 1755; dismissed 10 April, 1775; was afterwards chaplain of Castle William, and senator in the state legislature: died in the town of Turner, Me., August, 1818, aged 86 years. A classmate of the subject of this notice has furnished some particulars of his life, from which we extract the following: "Torrey entered college in 1802. During all the term of his collegiate course his moral character was unblamable, his diligence in study exemplary, his standing in the class highly respectable. He graduated with collegiate honors. After he received his degree, he studied theology under Rev. Dr. John Reed, of West Bridgewater (Y.C. 1772). Dr. Reed was a decided Unitarian; and Torrey, at that time, was of the same sentiments. Soon after he was licensed to preach, he took charge of the only Congregational church in New Bedford, but was not ordained. It was when the Unitarian controversy, early in this century, was at its height; when the *odium theologicum* pervaded many of the religious societies of this order in Massachusetts. It may not be too strong an expression to say, that it raged at that time in New Bedford. The church and society were split between the two factions. The majority of the church — technically so called — separated from the society, and held distinct worship at another place; while the society, as a body, continued in the old place of worship, and adhered to Unitarianism.

"Torrey, a young man, undrilled and unskilled in ecclesiastic tactics, found himself, in this logomachy, in a moral, or rather immoral, atmosphere, not congenial with his natural disposition, which was full of benevolence to all. His situation became unpleasant; and he finally removed to Canandaigua, in New York, and was settled over a Unitarian society there. [He was ordained at Marlborough, Mass., in January or February, 1812, as minister of the Congregational church in Canandaigua, and resigned in the latter part of the year 1817.] He could not have been settled there long, when he experienced a change of religious feeling and of religious views, and became as orthodox in sentiment (using the term in its claimed and generally accepted sense) as before he was liberal. As was to be expected, he did not continue over the church in Canandaigua long after this. He was installed 1 January, 1818, in Plymouth, Mass., near his native town; and resigned 12 March, 1823. His heart was naturally a loving one; and his new views, if possible, increased the intensity of this love to all. Free from dogmatism, yet was he earnest and sincere. This charity, in its true sense, and his full belief in what he viewed all-important in religion, prompted him to revisit his former associates of the liberal order, and to kind efforts to convince them of their doctrinal errors; which met with but little success."

From Plymouth, Mr. Torrey went to Newport, R.I., where he ministered to the church, once under the charge of Dr. Samuel Hopkins, about three years; ending in the course of the year 1829. In 1830, he removed to Murray, Orleans county, N.Y., and settled on a farm. He was afterwards formally installed there as a pastor of a church. In November, 1853, he ministered to a parish in West Greece, N.Y., until March, 1856.

Afterward, when past the age of 70 years, he removed to Ohio, and preached for two years from January, 1858, to a church in Edinburgh, Portage county, O.

He married, 2 June, 1814, Betsey James, daughter of William James, of Scituate. They had four sons, — Charles W., Josiah J., Francis, and Samuel, — of whom only the first named is living; he being a minister, settled in Madison, O., when his father died at his house. His wife died 30 April, 1852, at East Cleveland, O., also at the residence of their only surviving son.

1808. — EDWARD FENWICK CAMPBELL died in Augusta, Ga., 27 September, 1861, aged 75 years. He was son of Macarton Campbell, a planter; and was born in Augusta, Ga., 25 January, 1786. He was fitted for college by Rev. Jonathan Homer (H.C. 1777), of Newton, Mass. He had the tastes of a gentleman of fortune from Georgia. His habits were good; he made no efforts, apparently, to obtain college honors. After graduating, he studied law, and was admitted to the bar in Georgia, but never practised. He inherited a plantation and much wealth from his father; also inherited many slaves, but never bought or sold any. His residence was in Georgia, where he occupied himself in cultivating his plantation. His character was one of singular honor, delicacy, and generosity: he was a very indulgent master.

He married, in 1814, Maria Hull, daughter of Gen. William (Y.C. 1772) and Sarah Hull, of Newton, Mass. She died in Augusta, Ga., in 1846. He never married again. His wife prepared for publication a work entitled "Revolutionary Services and Civil Life of Gen. William Hull; prepared from his Manuscripts, by his Daughter, Mrs. Maria Campbell." In an address to the reader, she says, "Gen. Hull left behind him memoirs of his revolutionary services, in manuscript, which he had written for the gratification of his children and grandchildren. These memoirs are the basis of the present work. His spirit pervades the whole; and my endeavor has been, that it should not be obscured. The facts are in substance precisely as he has related them. But, as his manuscript was not prepared for the press, it was necessary, to a certain extent, that the arrangement of the work, and sometimes the style, should be changed." To this work was added, by Rev. James Freeman Clarke, of Boston (H.C. 1829), grandson of Gen. Hull, "History of the Campaign of 1812, and Surrender of the Post of Detroit." Mr. Clarke, in his preface, alluding to the before-mentioned work, says, "This, which was written by himself (Gen. Hull), was prepared for the press by his daughter, Mrs. Maria Campbell, wife of Edward F. Campbell, Esq., of Augusta, Ga. It was a favorite and cherished object of this lady to erect this monument to the memory of her father, and her life was spared by a kind Providence just long enough to enable her to complete it. Amid painful sickness and the languor of disease, she labored diligently until it was finished. This labor of love seemed to sustain her failing strength; and when she reached its termination she could say, 'Lord, let me now depart;' and the daughter passed into the spirit-land to meet the parent whom she had so tenderly loved. But another labor yet remains to be performed. Mrs. Campbell did not attempt the history of the campaign of 1812, and surrender of Detroit; and though deeply convinced that her father deserved praise, not blame, for his share in this transaction, yet she shrank from a work which she feared might involve her in angry controversy, and prevent the simple narrative of her father's revolutionary labors from being appreciated. She left to another hand, and another time, this part of the work. This task has been committed to the present writer; who, with no qualifications except a strong conviction of the justice of the cause he advocates, founded on careful study and examination, joined with an earnest wish to be candid and conscientious, has undertaken the work. He is indeed about to defend a grandfather, and one whom he remembers with mingled feelings of affection and respect."

1815. — SAMUEL R PUTNAM died in Boston, 24 December, 1861, aged 64 years. He was the eldest son of Hon. Samuel (H.C. 1787) and Sarah (Gool) Putnam, and was born in Salem, Mass., 2 April, 1797. His father was son of Gideon Putnam, of Danvers, Mass., where he was born 13 April,

1768; was a lawyer in Salem, but afterwards removed to Boston; was judge of the Supreme Court of Massachusetts, a station which he held with dignity and honor. He died 3 July, 1853, aged 85 years. His mother was daughter of John Gool and Lois (Pickering) Gool, a sister of Hon. Timothy Pickering (H.C. 1763), of Salem. His studies, preparatory for admission to college, were conducted by Jacob Newman Knapp (H.C. 1802). His collegiate life was without reproach. On leaving college, he concluded to adopt a mercantile life; and he entered the counting-room of Pickering Dodge, Esq., of Salem, where he served his apprenticeship. He ever afterwards spoke of Mr. Dodge with great esteem and respect. He made several voyages, as supercargo, to the East Indies. For many years he was engaged in business in Europe, particularly in the city of Antwerp. Here he established a house, and had as a partner an Englishman by the name of Alfred Barrow, a most estimable gentleman, for whom Mr. Putnam named his eldest son. This son died early in life, of Asiatic cholera, while travelling in Italy. He conducted his business with skilful enterprise and success. In the course of time he returned to his native country, and still maintained his character as a merchant in Boston. His interest in the education of his children prompted him, in 1851, to return to Europe with his family; and he spent with them three years in Paris, and nearly two years in Italy and Germany. He then returned, and again made Boston his home. He was not what is considered a public man. His own position in society he was careful to adorn by integrity and honor; and whatever influence he exerted was mainly through the power of his example. A friend, who knew him intimately, in speaking of him, says, "Goodness deserves commemoration, especially in the modest merit that makes no claim. Its immediate and irresistible impression was of unpretending kindness, and an utter honesty and constitutional transparency that knew not how to deceive. That a nature so unassuming should be so noble and generous, was a perpetual charm. Our friend's humility had another delightful combination with the directness and energy of his mind. His action or speech was always forthright. Never had a soul cleaner and fuller expression of all its meaning in the manners, every look and word. Such was his unvarnished and confiding sincerity, that, after he had spoken, nothing remained for him to add or explain. He did not reflect on himself as a subject, but with unconscious beauty appeared himself for every object his reason and conscience owned as just; never involved, but in all his dealings open as the day. In his business he showed great practical ability, and a judgment in all affairs on which others associated with him could lean. What seemed unsentimental promptness or remarkable ability in the concerns of this world was united with a wonderful and womanly tenderness of heart, making the eyes often moist and tearful above the ever-firm and manly lips. His faculties were not confined to any special vocation; but he was deeply interested in his country and all mankind. He was earnest in his decisions, but never narrow. Always in a large charity was his appreciation of others. He was as broad in his intellectual culture as in his moral aims. He had a great taste for art, and enjoyment of its masterpieces abroad; and, in the latter part of his life, acquired a command of the German tongue, which few seek save in youth. But finely foremost in him were the qualities of his heart, as they who loved him and lived with him so well know. Performing his duties constantly, and bearing his trials patiently, he has followed the distinguished jurist, his father, and all his own sons."

He married, 25 April, 1832, Mary, daughter of Rev. Charles Lowell, D.D. (H.C. 1800), of Boston, by whom he had three sons and one daughter. His first and third sons died some time before him. His second, and then only surviving son, Lieut. William Lowell Putnam, fell a martyr to his country; having died in Maryland, 22 October, 1861, of a wound received the day previous in the battle of Edwards Ferry. His death will be identified with the military glory of America, as it shall be reflected from deeds of valor in the cause of freedom, earnest resolves and decisive acts in support and establishment of equal laws and righteous government. Mr. Putnam's widow and one daughter remain to cherish his memory, and illustrate his sympathies and affections.

1817. — Hon. SAMUEL ATKINS ELIOT died in Cambridge, 29 January, 1862, aged 63 years. He was son of Hon. Samuel and Catharine (Atkins) Eliot, and was born in Boston, 5 March, 1798. His father was an eminent and wealthy merchant. He was fitted for college at the Boston Latin School. He attained a high rank of scholarship in his class, and graduated with honors. After leaving college, he entered the Divinity School at Cambridge, and went through a course of theological study, but did not enter upon the clerical profession. He was a gentleman of great personal worth, and was repeatedly honored by elevation to offices of distinction. In 1834, he was elected a representative to the state legislature; and, in 1843, he was chosen a senator from Suffolk district. He was a member of the board of aldermen in 1834 and 1835; and was mayor of the city in 1837, 1838, and 1839. In 1850, he was elected a representative to the thirty-first Congress from Suffolk district, where he remained two years; but, at the close of his term, he declined to be a candidate for re-election. In 1853, he became a partner in the extensive commission house of Charles H. Mills and Co., of Boston, where he remained six years, when the copartnership was dissolved; and he soon afterwards removed to Cambridge, where he passed the remainder of his life. In 1859, he was elected president of the Boston Gas-light Company. He was treasurer of Harvard College from 1842 to 1853. He was for many years a warden of King's Chapel, in Boston. He was a gentleman of unblemished moral character, of accomplished deportment, social and affable in his intercourse with his fellow-citizens; and, in the many and important positions in which he was placed, he discharged his duties with great fidelity, with an honest conviction of what he thought to be right, and to the entire satisfaction of his constituents.

He married, 13 June, 1836, Mary Lyman, the beautiful and accomplished daughter of Hon. Theodore Lyman, of Boston. Their children were one son and four daughters, as follows: Mary L., Charles William, Elizabeth E., Catharine A., and Fannie A.; all of whom, with their mother, survived him, all but the last two being married.

1817. — Daniel Gilman Hatch, of Covington, Ky., died in Exeter, N.H., 13 March, 1862, aged 63 years. He was the oldest son of Samuel and Mary (Gilman) Hatch, and was born in Exeter, 3 August, 1798. He was fitted for college at Phillips Academy, Exeter. He left college in the last term of his senior year, before commencement; and first taught an academy in King-George county, Va., on the Upper Neck, so called, between the Potomac and Rappahannock Rivers. In consequence of the unhealthiness of the location, he went, a year afterwards, to Dinwiddie county, Va., where he remained almost twenty years, devoting himself to teaching. He carried into his profession an enthusiasm for education, and a personal regard for the welfare of his scholars, which alike insured success, and won for him the regard of the many young men who were benefited by his instruction. He was a member of the celebrated Virginia convention in 1829. About 1837, he removed to Kentucky, settling at Georgetown, where he embarked in commercial pursuits. Here his fine business capacity and stern integrity soon gave him much influence; and, though no longer a professional teacher, his knowledge of every branch of educational science rendered good fruits. He was, until the day of his death, a trustee of the college in that village; was for a time its treasurer, and held other offices in connection with it, by which he was enabled to promote its financial soundness, and add to its educational efficiency. His zeal in behalf of instruction did not confine itself to this institution. As he had done in Virginia, so, during his residence in Kentucky, he was constantly finding positions as teachers for young men and women from the East; thus giving deserving employment, and providing the means of a better education for the children of his neighbors and friends. It is stated that during his life he obtained at the West situations for over fifty persons, male and female; and such was his discrimination, that in only one or two cases did they disappoint his expectations. About ten years before his death, he was called to Harrodsburg to take the cashiership of the Commercial Bank in that place. His management was admirable. In 1856, foreseeing the approaching financial crisis, he induced the directors to call in a large proportion of its wide circulation, thus enabling the institution to ride out the gale without detriment. Soon afterwards he removed to Covington, and became a member of the firm of Buckner and Hall, of Cincinnati; but for a year or two he had withdrawn from active business. The almost simultaneous death of his venerable parents, just a year before his decease, called him temporarily to the home of his childhood. He proposed only a few months' stay, and had taken his family with him. His health had long been somewhat impaired; but there was nothing to forbid the hope for him of many years more of usefulness, until attacked with a sudden acute disease. He breathed his last beneath the roof under which he was born. He was a kind father, a sincere and devoted friend, a sterling patriot, and an earnest member of the Baptist church, and was officially connected with most of the benevolent enterprises of that denomination in the state of his residence.

He married, 30 May, 1822, in Dinwiddie county, Va., Ann Eliza Thompson; by whom he had one son and two daughters, of whom the son and one daughter survive him. The other daughter, named Mary E. Prudentia, married, 15 April, 1852, Col. B. R. Johnson, professor in the Nashville military university. She died in Nashville, 22 May, 1858, aged 32 years. His wife died 13 April, 1837. He married for his second wife, in Georgetown, Ky., 12 February, 1840, Mary R., daughter of Kinsley and Mary Hall, of Exeter, N.H.; by whom he had two sons and six daughters, of whom two daughters died before their father. The other children, with their mother, survived him.

1818.—John Prentiss died in Baltimore, Md., 31 August, 1861, aged 62 years. He rode into the city in a carriage with one of his students, from his residence at Medfield, about three miles distant; and, while crossing the Northern Central Railway near the junction of Cathedral and Biddle streets, his vehicle was run against by a train of cars: he was thrown out, and instantly killed.

Mr. Prentiss was the third son and seventh child of Rev. Thomas (H.C. 1766) and Mary (Scollay) Prentiss, and was born in Medfield, Mass., 10 August, 1799. His father was son of Rev. Joshua (H.C. 1738) and Mary (Angier) Prentiss, and was born in Holliston, Mass., 27 October, 1747; was ordained pastor of the church in Medfield, 31 October, 1770; and died 28 February, 1814, aged 66 years. His mother was daughter of Dr. John Scollay, of Boston, where he held the office of town-clerk over forty years. She died 23 September, 1841, aged 82 years. The subject of this notice pursued his preparatory studies for admission to college under the instruction of his father, until the death of the latter; and, in April of the same year, he was at placed Phillips Academy in Andover, where he completed his studies. In his sophomore year, he taught school in Wayland, then called East Sudbury; and, in his junior and senior years, in Medfield. He graduated with a fair reputation for scholarship, and with a character untainted by any of the vices of college-life, to the influences of which he had been exposed, without experience, or any knowledge of the world, and with no guide or protection but the principles of a pure religion and the precepts of a stern morality breathed from the lips and illustrated by the life of one of the best and tenderest of mothers. Notwithstanding the practice of the strictest economy throughout his college course, he found himself, at its close, not only without resources, but encumbered with debts which had been unavoidably contracted. To acquit himself of his obligations, and to furnish him with the means of prosecuting the study of theology, which he had chosen as a profession, he was induced to accept an appointment to the charge of the Female High School in Charlestown, Mass., then just instituted. Here, with one female assistant, he had intrusted to his instruction and management three hundred pupils. That he discharged the duties of this arduous office acceptably, may be inferred from the fact, that, at the close of the academic year, the engagement was renewed, and was continued, until, having accomplished the object for which he had assumed it, in the winter of 1819–20 he relinquished it to enter the Divinity School at Cambridge. His connection with the school continued until the autumn of 1822. During this time, his studies were occasionally interrupted by ill health; and for several months were partially suspended by his having the charge of the private female school of Rev. Henry Colman (D.C. 1805), in Boston, who, from severe sickness, was compelled to relinquish it for that period. During this engagement, he was a member of Mr. Colman's family; and the acquaintance thus begun ripened into an intimate friendship, which ended only with the death of this distinguished clergyman and accomplished gentleman and scholar at Islington, near London, 17 August, 1849, whilst engaged in agricultural inquiries in Europe, under the auspices of the government of Massachusetts. At the close of his theological course of study, Mr. Prentiss was compelled, from bodily indisposition, to abandon for a time, as he then supposed, the profession which he had chosen, and the preparatory studies for which he had just completed. The greater part of the year 1823 he passed at his native village, under his mother's roof, in the vain hope of recovering his health. Early in the winter of this year, he was induced, by the advice of his physician, to try the effect of a milder climate; and accepted the appointment of a tutorship in Baltimore College, Md. His health being measurably restored by his residence in a southern climate, in the spring of 1824 he took charge, as principal, of one of the state academies of Maryland at Garrison Forest, about ten miles from the city of Baltimore, in Baltimore county; where he remained until the autumn of 1825. With health re-established, and with the reputation of being a faithful and successful teacher, at the solicitation of many parents whose children had been under his instruction, he removed to Baltimore at the above date, and opened a private school for boys; in which he was eminently successful. The hazard he would run in exposing himself to the rigors of a northern climate forbade his return to New England to reside; whilst the social relations he had formed, and the reputation he had established as a teacher, induced him to make Baltimore his place of residence, and school-teaching his occupation for life. In the summer of 1833, he was elected president of the collegiate, and principal of the academic, department of Baltimore College; which situation he retained for eight years. During this period, he was most laboriously and successfully employed in the direction of this institution, having under his charge a large number of pupils, and associated with him many assistant instructors. Convinced by much reflection, and long experience and observation, that the business of instruction could and ought to be conducted without resort to corporal punishment, in entering on the duties of his office, in a public statement of the principles on which the institution would be conducted, he rejected entirely the use of the rod and all physical infliction as a means of discipline. This plan was a novel one, — one which it was believed had never been attempted in any similar institution in this country. It was regarded by most persons, at the outset, as visionary and impracticable, and the public avowal of it as, of course, impolitic. Its practicability was, however, abundantly demonstrated, and the expediency of its adoption completely vindicated, by an experiment of eight years' continuance, — the period of Mr. Prentiss's administration of the affairs of this department of the university of Maryland. In 1841, in consequence of his health being sensibly impaired by the great amount of labor inseparable from the proper discharge of the duties of the office which he held, he resigned his situation, and retired to a country-seat which he had purchased, three and a half miles from the city of Baltimore; where he continued to reside during the remainder of his life. As the occupation to which he had devoted so much of his life had become an essential part of his being, he here opened a private boarding-school for boys. By uniting several occupations and amusements with the more serious and sedentary duties of instruction, his health was completely restored. This place he named Medfield, for his native town. Here, in a family that afforded the attractions of home to his pupils, he labored modestly and diligently, for twenty years, in the formation of mental and moral character. Himself of that broad church which never separates itself, for any creed, from any soul, but finds in every soul an opportunity for Christian charity and work, without professions he silently led his scholars towards Christian faith and practice, by their expression of his own beautiful and gentle life. He had the rare faculty of being both teacher and friend; and the strong ties that bound him to his pupils through the years were seldom broken. A conversation so even and so gentle made his discipline strong; and even reproof from him lost its smart and provocation, it was uttered from so gentle lips.

That he had no sympathy with the unnatural and infamous rebellion which has been brought upon our country by ambitious, political, and unprincipled demagogues, will be plainly seen by the following extract from a letter, which he wrote a few days before his death, to a near relative in Massachusetts: "I can hardly believe that I have sunk so low in your estimation as to be suspected, for an instant, of having any participation or sympathy with this execrable Southern rebellion. There are, as you suppose, some good Union people here. I am proud to be classed as a humble member of that honorable fraternity. Moreover, I am happy to add, on most satisfactory evidence, that the Unionists constitute a decided majority in the state of Maryland, and at least a very large and most respectable minority in the monumental city, or mob-town, as you may choose to call Baltimore! God save our commonwealth, if she should ever be so forgetful of her interest or her honor as to make a league with those states which are in arms against their government! As to our city, no power, human or divine, could save it from utter desolation and ruin in that event."

Mr. Prentiss married, 22 December, 1825, Amelia F. Kennedy, of Baltimore. The issue of this marriage was nine children, — five sons and four daughters, — of whom four sons only survived him. The oldest son is a physician, and resides on his father's estate. His wife died February, 1857; and he married for his second wife, July, 1858, Sarah Watson, of Nantucket, Mass., who survives him. By his second wife he had one child, which died when a few months old.

1818. — Rev. CHARLES ROBINSON died in Groton, Mass., 9 April, 1862, aged 68 years. He was the eldest son of Caleb and Judith (Robinson) Robinson, and was born in Exeter, N.H., 25 July, 1793. His father was a native of Exeter; as were also his grandfather and great-grandfather on the paternal side, both of whom bore the Christian name of Caleb. His grandfather was a major or a lieutenant-colonel of the New-Hampshire militia, in the battle of Bunker Hill. He afterwards served as an officer in the continental army during the revolution, and died soon after his return from the war. His mother was born in Gloucester, Mass. Her father's name was John Robinson. He was an Englishman, and followed the sea as a profession. He settled in Gloucester, and married Hannah Lane. They had four children, — all daughters; and his wife died in giving birth to Robinson's mother. Her husband was then at sea; and, when he returned, the news of the death of his wife made such an impression upon him, that he sickened, and died a few days afterwards, — leaving four fatherless and motherless children, who were taken and cared for by their grandmother Lane, until the oldest was married, and removed to Exeter. Robinson's mother, at that time but a child, went with her. His father died at the age of about 32 years, leaving his wife, with four young children, without property: but she was a woman of very extraordinary physical and mental powers, — of great endurance, industry, and ingenuity, — which enabled her to bring up her family through great hardships, until they were able to help themselves; and then Robinson and two sisters devoted themselves to the attainment of an education somewhat above the humble condition of their lives. His mother lived to the age of 87 years, almost always enjoying good health.

He was fitted for college at Exeter Academy. He held a high rank of scholarship in his class, and graduated with honors. After leaving college, he went to Maryland, where he was president of Washington College for one year. He then returned, and studied theology at the Divinity School in Cambridge. He was ordained over the Unitarian church in Eastport, Me., 30 October, 1822; resigned his charge, 1 April, 1825. He was installed at Groton, 1 November, 1826; and resigned in October, 1838; installed at Medfield, 16 October, 1839; resigned 1 September, 1850; installed at Peterborough, N.H., 4 December, 1851; resigned 24 June, 1860. He then returned to Groton, where he resided until his death.

He married, for his first wife, 3 July, 1827, Jane Park, only daughter of Stewart J. Park, of Groton; and had one child, Jane,—born 17 March, 1828,—who lived only five days. His wife died 23 March, 1828.

He married, for his second wife, 1 January, 1830, Diantha Prentiss, daughter of Hon. John Prentiss, of Keene, N.H. She died at Medfield, 18 May, 1843,—no children.

He married, for his third wife, 11 September, 1844, Sally May Cotton, daughter of Rev. Ward Cotton (H.C. 1793), of Boylston, Mass., and had by her two children; viz., Sarah Jane, born 29 July, 1845,—died 8 October, 1847; and Charles Cotton, born 22 May, 1849,—who survived him. His wife died 6 June, 1849.

He married, for his fourth wife, 1 September, 1850, Elizabeth Jane Burton, daughter of Jonathan Burton, of Wilton, N.H., and had one child; viz., William Burton, born 3 April, 1854; who, with his mother, survived him.

1818.—Dr. Simon Whitney died in Framingham, Mass., 2 September, 1861, aged 62 years. He was the youngest but one of nine children of Nathaniel Ruggles and Abigail (Frothingham) Whitney, and was born in Watertown, Mass., 30 October, 1798. His father was son of Simon and Mary (Ruggles) Whitney; was born in Watertown, 19 March, 1759; was a teacher in early life, afterwards a trader and farmer: died 17 December, 1833. His mother was daughter of James Frothingham, for many years deacon of Dr. Jedediah Morse's church in Charlestown, Mass. The subject of this notice began his preparatory studies for college under the instruction of Abiel Jaques (H.C. 1807), at Newton Corner, Mass., where he remained about one year; and completed his studies under Samuel Hunt, of Watertown (H.C. 1765). Mr. Hunt was born in Watertown, 25 October, 1745; was appointed master of the Boston Latin School, 8 November, 1776, where he remained until January, 1805; when he resigned, and returned to his native place. He afterwards went to the West; and died in Lexington, Ky., 8 October, 1816, aged 71 years. After leaving college, Mr. Whitney taught school six months in

Brighton; then went to Charlestown, where he taught six months; and there he began the study of medicine, under the instruction of Dr. William Johnson Walker (H.C. 1810), where he remained until 1822, when he received his degree of M.D.; and established himself in Framingham, where he passed the remainder of his life. He soon acquired an extensive practice, and gained the confidence of the community in which he resided. His practice was in accordance with the plain principles of the science of medicine. He dealt in no occult sciences, nor patent medicines, which none but the initiated could understand. His fine powers of observation, perception, and discrimination, enabled him to gather up, in the range of his extensive practice, a large amount of experience and practical knowledge; and made him always welcome to the chamber of sickness and suffering, which his genial spirit and manners brought confidence to, and brightened with the light of faith and hope. As a citizen, he was honored and trusted; for he was always ready, with heart and hand and purse, to do any good word or work. In the Christian church, he was a strong pillar and a beautiful example, in ever treading in the footsteps of "Him who went about doing good." He was repeatedly honored by offices of honor and trust. He was surgeon of the regiment in that vicinity five years; captain of an infantry company; leader of the choir thirty years; was frequently elected selectman, and chairman of the board; was a justice of the peace for fifteen years; and was representative to the state legislature from Framingham in 1853.

He married, 6 May, 1824, Mary Walker, daughter of Timothy Walker, Esq., of Charlestown, and sister of Dr. William J. Walker, with whom he studied medicine. The issue of this marriage was eight children: viz., 1. Elizabeth Walker, born 8 April, 1825; married, 30 August, 1845, John W. Osgood, M.D., a practising physician in Saxonville, Mass., who have had three children,—two sons and one daughter. 2. Mary, born 16 August, 1826, and died the next day. 3. Allston Waldo, a graduate at the Harvard Medical School in 1852, and a practising physician in South Framingham. 4. Abby Walker, born 23 July, 1829. 5. Henry Augustus, born 11 January, 1831; was drowned while bathing, 22 July, 1840. 6. Harriet Lincoln, born 3 October, 1833. 7. Clarence, born 1 January, 1838. 8. James Bradish, born 22 August, 1843. His wife survived him.

1818. — Hon. JOHN HUBBARD WILKINS died in Boston, 5 December, 1861, aged 67 years, lacking five days. He was the youngest son of Deacon Samuel and Dorcas (Towne) Wilkins, and was born in Amherst, N.H., 10 December, 1794. He was also grandson of Rev. Daniel Wilkins (H.C. 1736), the first settled minister of his native town. It was the intention of Deacon Wilkins that his youngest son should become a merchant. He accordingly left home early in life, and was employed in the store of a Mr. Randall, in the neighboring town of Mount Vernon. After remaining there about a year, he went to Boston, and was employed in the store of Mr. David S. Eaton, on Long Wharf, where he continued until the war with England began, in 1812. He then conceived the idea of obtaining a more thorough education, and, having purchased some books, returned to his native town with the view of preparing for college. His father told him that a college education would be very expensive; that he was unable to assist him; and that, if he entered college, he would not succeed in going through the course. He replied, that he thought he would try. He was fitted for college by Rev. Humphrey Moore (H.C. 1799), of Milford, N.H. He attained a distinguished rank of scholarship in his class, and graduated with high honors. Immediately after leaving college, he was appointed preceptor of Taunton Academy, where he remained one year. He then entered the Divinity School in Cambridge, where he studied theology two years. In 1821, he came to Boston, and entered the bookstore of Hilliard, Gray, and Co., as a salesman; and, in 1826, he was admitted as a partner in that well-known publishing house, where he remained until 1832, when he withdrew. The next year he formed a copartnership with Mr. Charles Bolles, under the style of John H. Wilkins and Co., as paper-dealers, in Water Street. In 1835, Mr. Bolles withdrew. Mr. Wilkins then took in as a partner Mr. Richard B. Carter, and they continued business under the firm of Wilkins and Carter; and, in 1844, Hon. Alexander H. Rice (U.C. 1844), for two years mayor of Boston, and afterwards a representative in Congress, was admitted as a partner, under the style of Wilkins, Carter, and Co. In his business, Mr. Wilkins displayed great talent and stern integrity. He was a skilful financier, was very successful, and acquired an ample competence. In 1853, the National Bank was established in Boston. Mr. Wilkins, having been elected its president, withdrew from mercantile business, and devoted himself to the interests of that institution; which he did with rare ability. He held the office of president until October, 1861, when, at the annual meeting, he, on account of ill health, declined to be a candidate for re-election.

Mr. Wilkins was a most useful and valued citizen, and the estimation in which he was held was often manifested. He was elected a member of the Boston common-council in 1840, 1841, 1842, and 1843; was an alderman in 1844, 1848, and 1849; was elected to the senate in the state legislature in 1850 and 1851; and was a member of the state convention in 1853. He was for five years president of the Cochituate Water Board. He was once a candidate for mayor, but failed of an election by a few votes.

In 1822, he published a work entitled "Elements of Astronomy," for the use of schools and academies. This treatise met with a rapid sale. The encouragement he received induced him to correct and somewhat enlarge his work; and, in 1823, he issued a second edition. Subsequently, the book was stereotyped. In 1822, the celebrated mathematician, Warren Colburn (H.C. 1820), wrote thus to Mr. Wilkins: "I have examined your treatise on astronomy, and I think that subject is better explained, and that more matter is contained in this, than in any other book of the kind with which I am acquainted." During the discussion of the subject of introducing water into the city of Boston, Mr. Wilkins took a prominent part. He wrote several pamphlets on the question, which were printed, and contributed many valuable articles in the newspapers. At the consecration, 24 June, 1852, of Mount-Hope Cemetery, in Dorchester and West Roxbury, he acted as president of the corporation, and made some introductory remarks, which were published in the pamphlet containing the order of services. He was one of the most active and efficient members in establishing the New-Jerusalem (Swedenborgian) Church in Boston, of which his classmate, Rev. Thomas Worcester, D.D., is the pastor. The total amount of his donations to the society, it is said, were not less than fifty thousand dollars.

He married, 17 November, 1826, Mrs. Thomasine E. Minot; she being a sister of the late Professor William Cranch Bond, of Harvard College. He had no children. His wife survives him.

1819. — Rev. William Farmer died in Lunenburg, Mass., 24 June, 1862, aged 69 years. He was son of Jonas and Mary (Whitney) Farmer, and was born in Townsend, Mass., 24 February, 1793. He was fitted for college at the academies at New Ipswich, N.H., and Groton, Mass. After leaving college, he studied divinity with Rev. Thomas Beede, of Wilton, N.H. (H.C. 1798), and Rev. Eli Smith, of Hollis, N.H. (B.C. 1792); but completed his theological studies at the Divinity School at Cambridge. He was ordained over the Unitarian church in Belgrade, Me., 18 May, 1831. Here he remained about six years, when he resigned his pastoral charge. He preached afterwards, about two years, in Dresden, Me.; and, for a year or more, in various places, — in West Boylston and Lunenburg, Mass., in Fitzwilliam, N.H., and Pomfret, Vt. He had been an invalid for many years, and suffered often from pulmonary hemorrhage and other serious symptoms before he relinquished preaching. His decline was very gradual; and his bodily sufferings, which towards the last were particularly irritating, were borne with great patience. He was a true Christian, and was warmly interested in every thing that concerned his Alma Mater.

He married, 15 October, 1851, Mrs. Lovina Jackson. They had no children. His wife survived him.

1819. — Joseph Hardy Prince died in Boston, 18 November, 1861, aged 60 years. He was son of Capt. Henry and Sarah (Millet) Prince, and was born in Salem, Mass., 7 June, 1801. He was fitted for college partly by Abiel Chandler (H.C. 1806), and partly by Samuel Adams (H.C. 1806). After leaving college, he studied law in the office of Hon. John Pickering, of Salem (H.C. 1796); and began the practice of his profession in Salem. He was a representative to the state legislature from Salem, in 1825. In 1834, he was appointed an inspector in the Boston custom-house. He was private-secretary for Com. Eliot, of the frigate "Constitution," in 1835, on the voyage to France to bring home the Hon. Edward Livingston, the American minister, on account of the differences with that nation. On his return, he pursued the practice of law in Boston. In 1848, he was appointed to the surveyor's department of customs. After leaving that office, he resumed his profession, which he continued to the end of his life. He was ever tenaciously devoted to the democratic party, and was an early advocate of Andrew Jackson. He delivered an oration on the 4th of July, 1828, before the Washington Society. Afterwards, when Andrew Dunlap moved that a copy be requested for the press, Mr. Prince said, "If I have done any thing towards rekindling the fire of the old democracy, if I have contributed a pebble to the pile in the cause of principle against corruption, I shall be satisfied."

Mr. Prince married, late in life, Mary Hunt, of Salem; but had no children.

1821.—Dr. JONAS HENRY LANE died in Boston, 5 September, 1861, aged 61 years. He was son of Jonas and Eunice (Kendall) Lane, and was born in Lancaster, Mass., 28 January, 1800. His name was originally Henry Lane; but, by act of the legislature, he was allowed to prefix the name of Jonas, which he did from respect to his father. He began his preparatory studies for entering college at Groton Academy, where he remained one term; then he went to Leicester Academy; and he completed his preparatory studies at the scientific-school in Lancaster, under the instruction of Jared Sparks (H.C. 1815), afterwards president of Harvard College. He attained a distinguished rank of scholarship in his class, and graduated with high honors. He studied medicine with Dr. Silas Pearson, of Westminster, Mass. He was, while studying his profession, for some time house-physician at the Massachusetts General Hospital in Boston, and subsequently an assistant at the McLean Asylum for the Insane, at Somerville. On receiving his degree of M.D., in 1826, he began the practice of his profession in Boston, where he passed the remainder of his life; having attained a highly respectable rank in his profession, gained an extensive practice, and reaped a rich reward for his skill, fidelity to his profession, and his amiable and exemplary life. Modest in his deportment, he never entered public life, or sought any office. He held the even tenor of his way; was as faithful and diligent in his attendance on the poor to whom he was called, and who were unable to compensate him for his services, as he was to those who had abundant wealth to reward him. He was a cheerful, happy Christian; and was emphatically "the beloved physician."

He married, 6 October, 1830, Frances Ann Brown, of Norwich, Conn. The issue of this marriage was three daughters and one son; of whom the son and two of the daughters, with their mother, survived him.

1824. — John Mark Gourgas, of Quincy, died in Roxbury, Mass., 28 June, 1862, aged 58 years. He was son of John Mark and Margaret (Sampson) Gourgas, and was born at Milton Upper Mills, Mass., 25 March, 1804. He was fitted for college at Exeter (N.H.) Academy. He studied law in the office of Hon. Lemuel Shaw (H. C. 1800), and settled in Quincy. He was never married.

1825. — Isaiah Thomas was lost at sea, probably the last week in February, 1862. He was the son of Isaiah and Mary (Weld) Thomas, and was born in Worcester, Mass., 29 November, 1805. His father was the oldest son of Isaiah Thomas, the eminent printer, and author of the "History of Printing;" and was born in Boston, 5 September, 1773. His mother was daughter of Edward Weld, of Boston. The subject of this notice was fitted for college at Leicester Academy. After graduating, he went to Cincinnati, O., where he was, for a time, editor of the "American" newspaper, and afterwards was a merchant in that city; thence he removed to New York. In January, 1862, he was appointed consul to Algiers, and took passage in the ship "Milwaukie," Capt. Rhodes, from New York for Havre, with his only daughter and two of his sons, thence to proceed to Algiers. The ship sailed on the 21st of February, and was never afterwards heard from. It is supposed she foundered, on the 28th of the same month, in a gale which occurred at that time.

He married, 30 May, 1831, in Cincinnati, Mary Ann Ruder, of that city; by whom he had four sons and five daughters, — of whom four of his daughters had deceased. Two sons only survived him, — one in a mercantile house in Boston, and the other in the army. His wife died about nine years since.

1827. — Cornelius Conway Felton, of Cambridge, Mass., died in Chester, Penn., 26 February, 1862, aged 54 years. He left Cambridge about three weeks previously for Washington, D.C., and stopped at the residence of his brother, Samuel Morse Felton (H. C. 1834), where he was suddenly taken ill with a disease of the heart, of which he had several times before had attacks. He was son of Cornelius Conway and Anna (Morse) Felton, and was born in West Newbury, Mass., 6 November, 1807. His father was born in Marblehead. His mother was born in Newbury, died in 1825; and his father married for his second wife Mrs. —— Boynton, whose first husband was a farmer in Saugus, Mass. She was a Torrey, of Scituate, Mass. She died many years ago at the McLean Asylum in Somerville, Mass. In 1815, he moved with his father to the corner of Chelsea, which belonged to a parish in Saugus. His father lived in great poverty during the war of 1812, although he had a good business as a chaise-maker, to which he served his apprenticeship with Mr. Abner Greenleaf, of West Newbury. But the whole establishment was broken up by the war; and, to earn a livelihood, he became a toll-keeper at Chelsea, on the Newburyport turnpike. When he married his second wife, he took her farm, with its encumbrances, in Saugus, and carried it on several years; then he sold it, and went to Charlestown, where he was employed in the construction of the Warren bridge, of which he had the charge, and was one of the toll-keepers of it. When the Fitchburg railroad was put in operation, he was contractor for all the wood burned on the road, and at the same time bought a farm in Littleton, Mass., where he died.

From his early youth, young Felton was very fond of study; which propensity was encouraged by his mother. His father, seeing his passion for learning, thought he might afford to send him to school one quarter; and he was placed in the academy at Bradford, Mass., under Benjamin Greenleaf, and under the tutelage of the venerable Joshua Coffin. From Bradford, he returned to the town-school in Saugus. Early in the summer of 1822, his father sent him to the private school of Mr. Simeon Putnam, in North Andover (H.C. 1811). When he went there, he intended to study one quarter. Mr. Putnam was an enthusiastic scholar; a great lover of the classics; a man very austere in his manners, but gentle and kind to all who wanted to study, and awakened an extravagant enthusiasm in all his pupils. After some time, knowing Felton's father's circumstances, he called him up to him one day, and told him he wanted him to go to college, and would trust him for his tutorage until he could repay it. He therefore remained at the school one year and three months. In that period, he read Sallust four times, Cicero's Orations four times, Virgil six times, Græca Minora five or six times, and the poetry of it, until he could repeat nearly the whole by memory; the Annals and History of Tacitus, Justin, Cornelius Nepos; the Anabasis of Xenophon; four books of Robinson's Selections from the Iliad; the Greek Testament four times: besides writing a translation of one of the Gospels, and a translation of the whole of Grotius de Veritate, which he carried in manuscript to college. He also wrote a volume of about three hundred pages of Latin exercises, and one of about two hundred pages of Greek exercises. He also studied carefully all the mathematics and geography requisite to enter college. These severe studies greatly affected his health. Still, while in college, he studied a great deal of extra Greek; also modern languages — French, German, Spanish, Italian, and Portuguese — and some Hebrew. In the winter vacation of his freshman year, he was employed in the college library. In the sophomore year, he taught school in Concord; in the junior year, in Bolton; during the rest of the junior year, or six months, he taught mathematics in Round-Hill School, kept by Cogswell and Bancroft, in Northampton. He was also one of the editors of the "Harvard Register." After graduating, he was engaged for two years with his classmates, Cleveland and Sweetser, in the charge of the Livingston-county high-school at Geneseo, N.Y. He was then appointed Latin tutor in Harvard College; and the next year was appointed tutor in Greek, which office he held two years; and, in 1834, he was appointed Eliot Professor of Greek Literature. This professorship he held until the 16th of February, 1860, when he was chosen president of the college. In 1833, he published an edition of Homer, with English notes and Flaxman's illustrations, which has since passed through several editions, with revisions and emendations. In 1840, a translation by him of Menzell's work on "German Literature," in three volumes, was published among Ripley's "Specimens of Foreign Literature." In the same year, he gave to the public a "Greek Reader," containing selections in prose and verse from Greek authors, with English notes, and a vocabulary: this has since been frequently reprinted. In 1841, he published an edition of the "Clouds" of Aristophanes, with an introduction and notes; since revised, and republished in England. In 1843, he aided Prof. Sears and Prof. Edwards in the preparation of a work on classical studies, containing essays on classical subjects, mostly translated from the German. He assisted Prof. Longfellow in the preparation of the "Poets and Poetry of Europe," which appeared in 1845. In 1847, editions of the "Panegyricus" of Isocrates, and of the "Agamemnon" of Æschylus, with introductions and English notes, were published by him. A second edition of the former appeared in 1854, and of the latter in 1859. In 1849, he translated, from the French, the work of Prof. Guyot on physical geography, called "The Earth and Man;" and, in the same year, he published an edition of the "Birds" of Aristophanes, with an introduction and English notes, which was republished in England. In 1852, he edited a selection from the writings of Prof. Popkin, his predecessor in the Eliot professorship, with an introductory biographical notice. In the same year, he published a volume of selections from the Greek historians, arranged in the order of events. The period from April, 1853, to May, 1854, was spent by him in a European tour; in the course of which he visited Great Britain, France, Germany, Switzerland, Italy, and Greece; giving about five months to the last-named country, visiting its most interesting localities, and carefully studying its architectural remains. In 1855, he revised, for publication in the United States, Smith's "History of Greece," adding a preface, notes, and a continuation from the Roman conquest to the present time. In the same year, an edition of Lord Carlisle's "Diary in Turkish and Greek Waters" was prepared by him for the American press, with notes, illustrations, and a preface. In 1856, a selection by him from modern Greek writers, in prose and verse, was published. Besides the above, he compiled an elementary work on Greek and Roman metres; was the author of a life of Gen. Eaton, in Sparks's "American Biography;" of various occasional addresses; and of numerous contributions to the "North-American Review," "Christian Examiner," and other periodical publications. A series of vigorous articles on spiritualism, which appeared in the "Boston Courier" in 1857–8, were understood to have proceeded from his pen. He delivered three courses of lectures before the Lowell Institute in Boston, on subjects connected with the history and literature of Greece. In the summer of 1858, he made a second visit to Europe, partly on account of his impaired health, and partly to complete some investigations into the language, topography, and education of Greece. He was a member of the Massachusetts Board of Education, and one of the regents of the Smithsonian Institution; a member of the American Academy of Arts and Sciences, and of the Massachusetts Historical Society; and a corresponding member of the Archæological Society of Athens. The degree of doctor of laws was conferred upon him by Amherst College in 1848. He was a gentleman of genial and social habits, and was warmly loved by a large circle of friends.

He married, in the summer of 1838, Mary Whitney, daughter of Asa Whitney, a merchant of Boston. She died 12 April, 1845, leaving two daughters. He married, for his second wife, 28 September, 1846, Mary Louisa Cary, daughter of Hon. Thomas Greaves and Mary (Perkins) Cary, of Boston. By his second wife he had two sons and one daughter, who, with their mother, survived him.

1829. — JOSIAH QUINCY LORING died in Weston, Mass., 6 April, 1862, aged 51 years, lacking four days. He was the youngest son of Elijah and Abigail (Rand) Loring, and was born in Boston, 10 April, 1811. He was a pupil of the somewhat celebrated Lawson Lyon, of Boston (H.C. 1805); but subsequently entered the Boston Latin School. At this school he was fitted for college. He entered in 1825. He left college at the end of his sophomore year; but rejoined his class at the beginning of his senior year, and graduated with them. In November, 1829, he entered the Law School at Cambridge. Here he remained one year; when he relinquished the study of the law, and passed the winter of 1830–31 in Boston, pursuing some favorite mathematical studies with Rev. Tilly Brown Hayward, of Boston (H.C. 1820). In the summer of 1831, he taught a school at Jamaica Plain, Roxbury; and in the autumn following went into his father's counting-room, having at length reached the occupation he had most desired. He did not, however, long pursue mercantile business. He finally removed to Weston, where he had purchased a farm; and was engaged in agriculture the remainder of his life. He was possessed of excellent natural gifts, of a fine literary taste, and of many scholarly acquirements. He was a man of the most unbending integrity, of a high sense of honor, and of most benevolent feelings, manifesting themselves in many a generous deed. If he had faults, others were not made the sufferers, except as they sympathized with *his* suffering and pain. Intimately known to but few, those few will never forget his many kind and generous qualities.

He married, 27 December, 1849, Miss Christian W. Renton, daughter of Dr. Peter Renton, of Boston. They had four children; of whom three, with their mother, survived him.

1831. — Alexander Ramsay Bradley died in Fryeburg, Me., 16 February, 1862, aged 52 years. He was the third son of Robert and Abigail (Bailey) Bradley, and was born in Fryeburg, 5 November, 1809. His father was born in Concord, N.H., 17 June, 1772; removed to Fryeburg in 1801, where he resided until his death. His great-great-grandfather, Samuel Bradley, was killed by the Indians, near Concord, N.H., 11 August, 1746. His maternal grandfather was Col. Ward Bailey, of Lemington, Vt.; and his maternal grandmother was Mary Sargeant, sister of Hon. Nathaniel Peaslee Sargeant (H.C. 1750), formerly chief-justice of the Supreme Court of Massachusetts. The early studies of young Bradley were pursued under the instruction of Rev. Benjamin Glazier Willey (Bowd. C. 1822), of Conway, N.H.; in whose house he passed several years, preparatory to entering Phillips Academy in Exeter, N.H., where he was fitted for college. While in college, he was remarkable for his social amenity, and for his athletic characteristics. After graduating, he pursued his professional studies in the office of his uncle, Col. Samuel Ayer Bradley (D.C. 1799), who was, at that time, in partnership with John S. Barrows, Esq., of Fryeburg. He there acquired a good knowledge of law as a science, although having a distaste for the practice, as he had also for the details of business; the characteristics of his mind being rather for general literary pursuits. In 1835, on motion of Hon. Charles Stewart Daveis, he was admitted to the bar; but, for some years, was engaged in the speculations in timber-lands, in which, at that time, the fortunes of so many were embarked. More fortunate, if not wiser, than numbers who make similar ventures, he returned to the practice of law with some small capital yet remaining; and thenceforth attended to his professional duties, without much interruption, until the time of his death. His practice, though somewhat extensive, both in his own state and in New Hampshire, was never a source of much profit to himself; the chief reason of which was his neglect of keeping proper accounts, and collecting his dues. In his social and domestic relations, he was fortunately and happily situated. He married, November, 1835, Mary O. Barrows, daughter of William Barrows, Esq., of Yarmouth, Me.; by whom he had thirteen children, — ten sons and three daughters. Two sons and two daughters died at an early age. His wife died 27 December, 1861. There are eight sons and one daughter living. The first and second sons graduated in the same class at Bowdoin College in 1858; the elder of whom, Samuel Ayer Bradley, is now professor of mathematics in Western Union College, Fulton, Ill.: the second, Alexander Stuart Bradley, who has been engaged in surveying western government-lands for the last two or three years, came home in the fall of 1861 to see his sick parents; and, in consequence of their decease, remained to take care of the younger members of the family, and pursued the study of law.

The attachment of Mr. Bradley for his wife was one that years, and the care and trouble attendant upon providing for a large family, never diminished, but strengthened; and her death, which occurred after a lingering illness of consumption, entirely prostrated him. He seldom left his room after that event; and there is no doubt that the final attack of the disorder which proved fatal to him was brought on by excessive grief at her loss. A week before his death, it was evident that the faculties of his mind were giving way; and he did not regain possession of them during life; passing into total unconsciousness a few hours before he expired. All who were intimate with him bore testimony to the unusual amount of general knowledge which he possessed, which rendered him exceedingly entertaining and instructive in his social intercourse with them; and to his high character as an honorable and upright man.

1832. — Rev. CHARLES MASON died in Boston, 23 March, 1862, aged 49 years. He was son of Hon. Jeremiah (Y.C. 1788) and Mary (Means) Mason, and was born in Portsmouth, N.H., 25 July, 1812. His father, who was an eminent jurist, and one of the most brilliant members of the bar, was born in Lebanon, Conn., 27 April, 1768; and died in Boston, 14 October, 1848. The subject of this notice was fitted for college by Rev. Andrew Preston Peabody (H.C. 1826). He held a high rank of scholarship in his class, and graduated with honors. After leaving college, he began the study of theology at the seminary at Andover, and completed his course of studies at the New-York Episcopal Seminary. He was ordained as deacon, in Boston, 31 July, 1836. He was inducted rector of the Episcopal church in Salem, Mass., 31 May, 1837, where he continued a faithful and beloved teacher of the gospel until 30 May, 1847, when he resigned his pastoral charge, and removed to Boston. He was inducted rector of Grace Church, in Temple Street, Boston, in September, 1847. Being possessed of a competence, his generous nature was evinced by the fact, that he gave his entire salary back to the church. No clergyman in the city probably labored more earnestly than he to advance the cause of religion. He was of an amiable and social disposition, a kind husband and parent. The honorary degree of doctor of divinity was conferred upon him by Harvard College in 1858; and he received the like honor from Trinity College in Hartford, Conn., the same year. He was elected a member of the Massachusetts Historical Society, 10 November, 1859.

He married, 11 June, 1838, Susan Lawrence, daughter of Amos Lawrence, of Boston, by whom he had three daughters and one son. His wife died 2 December, 1844. He married for his second wife, 9 August, 1849, Anna Huntington Lyman, of Northampton, Mass.; by whom he had two daughters and one son. All his children and his second wife survived him.

1833. — THOMAS BUTLER POPE died at his residence in Appleton Place, Roxbury, near Longwood, 15 January, 1862, aged 48 years, lacking seven days. He was son of Lemuel and Sally Belknap (Russell) Pope, and was born in Boston, 22 January, 1814. His father was a very respectable citizen, and, for many years, president of the Boston Insurance Company. He died in Roxbury in 1851. His mother was sister of the late Nathaniel Pope Russell, Esq., and second cousin of Rev. Dr. Jeremy Belknap. He was fitted for college at the Boston Latin

School, and entered at the beginning of the sophomore year. His course in college was acceptable. After graduating, he entered the Law School of the University, and subsequently studied in the office of Hon. Charles Greely Loring, of Boston (H.C. 1812). In the summer of 1836, he was admitted to the Suffolk bar, and began to practise. In 1840, he formed a partnership with Charles Henry Parker (H.C. 1835), which continued until 1853, and then terminated on that gentleman becoming treasurer of the Suffolk Savings Bank.

Though beginning the practice of law under good auspices, and, in some respects, manifesting proficiency, he was tempted to enter into speculations quite foreign to his profession. In this he simply followed the example of many other lawyers: but, with him, his ventures met with disasters; and, being continued, resulted in bankruptcy of fortune, though his probity was unscathed. His affairs were so much embarrassed in 1858, the year when his class celebrated their "silver wedding," that he was with difficulty induced to attend the meeting. In 1859, he went into insolvency. His pecuniary misfortunes preyed upon him, and, it was thought, somewhat affected his mind for several of the last years of his life. The disease of which he finally died was softening of the brain, which began to come on, it was thought, about two years before his death. On the 1st of April, 1861, whilst riding from Boston, he was seized with an attack of paralysis, affecting his lower limbs. He was conveyed to his home, and never left it again. After lingering more than nine months, he died.

He married, 3 June, 1846, Gertrude, daughter of the late John Binney, Esq., of Boston, who survived him. He left also three daughters, — Gertrude Binney, born 1847; Louisa Binney, born 1855; and Mary Binney, born 1858.

1837. — Dr. John Foster Williams Lane died in Boston, 25 August, 1861, aged 44 years. He was son of Frederick and Eliza (Bonner) Lane, and was born in Boston, 14 June, 1817. He was fitted for college at the Boston Latin School, where a Franklin medal was awarded to him in 1831. He left the school at that time; and, being only thirteen years of age, his parents, thinking he was too young to enter college, sent him to Europe; and he spent two years in Italy and France, studying the modern languages. He returned in 1833, and entered the freshman class. He attained a high rank of scholarship in his class, and graduated with distinction. After leaving college, he studied medicine under the instruction of Dr. Winslow Lewis (H.C. 1819). On receiving his degree of M.D., he established himself in Boston, where he soon acquired an extensive practice. His prospects were flattering for attaining an eminent rank in his profession; but he was very suddenly cut off in the prime of life. He married, 3 June, 1849, Phebe A. Stewart, of Boston, who survives him. He had no children.

1837. — David Henry Thoreau died in Concord, Mass., 6 May, 1862, aged 44 years. He was son of John and Cynthia (Dunbar) Thoreau, and was born in Concord, 12 July, 1817. His father, who was a pencil-maker, son of John and Jeannie (Burns) Thoreau, was born in Boston. His grandfather came from St. Helier, on the Island of Jersey, and was of French origin. A Burns left property in Sterling, Scotland, to his wife, the said Jeannie Burns, and said it was worth attending to; but the papers to obtain it, though three attempts were made, never reached Scotland. This was about fifty years ago. His grandfather had a brother Philip in the Island of Jersey. He was a cooper; but business was dull; and he shipped as a sailor on board a vessel in which John Adams went to France, in the American revolution. He came to this country about 1773. After the termination of the war, he went into business at No. 45, Long Wharf, Boston, in a very small way, in company with a Mr. Phillips, under the firm of Thoreau and Phillips. He accumulated a large property, and removed to Concord, where he died of consumption about one year afterwards, in consequence of a cold caught in patrolling the streets in Boston, in a heavy rain in the night, when a Catholic riot was expected, about 1801. His first wife died not long before he did; and he married a Miss Kettle, of Concord, sometimes spelled Kettell, by whom he had no children. Mr. Thoreau's mother was daughter of Asa and Mary (Jones)

Dunbar, and was born in Keene, N.H. Her mother belonged to the Jones family of Weston. Her father, Rev. Asa Dunbar (H.C. 1767), was a minister in Salem, and afterwards a lawyer in Keene, an eminent freemason; died 22 June, 1787, aged 42 years, and was buried with masonic honors. Young Thoreau was fitted for college at Concord Academy by Phineas Allen (H.C. 1825). While in college, he kept school six weeks in Canton, and boarded with Orestes A. Brownson. They studied the German reader together very industriously, and talked philosophy till eleven o'clock, nights. Thoreau became sick, and was obliged to leave his school. This was in his junior year. After graduating, he taught the public school a few weeks; then a private school in Concord two or three years. Not long afterwards, he spent six months as a private tutor in the family of William Emerson (H.C. 1818), on Staten Island, N.Y. For two years at one time, and one year at another, he was a member of the family of Ralph Waldo Emerson (H.C. 1821) in Concord. With the exception of the six months at Staten Island, he resided constantly in Concord, leading chiefly an agricultural and literary life; supporting himself by his own hands, being a pencil-maker; often employed as a painter, surveyor, and carpenter. Nearly every year, he made an excursion on foot to the woods and mountains in Maine, New Hampshire, New York, and other places. For two years and two months continuously, he lived by himself in a small house or hut of his own building, about a mile and a half from Concord village. He was well known to the public as the author of two remarkable books, "A Week on the Concord and Merrimack Rivers," published in 1849; and "Walden, or Life in the Woods," published in 1854. These books have never had a wide circulation, but are well known to the best readers, and have exerted a powerful influence on an important class of earnest and contemplative persons. He led the life of a philosopher, subordinating all other pursuits and so-called duties to his pursuit of knowledge, and to his own estimate of duty. He was a man of firm mind and direct dealing; never disconcerted, and not to be turned, by any inducement, from his own course.

He had a penetrating insight into men with whom he conversed, and was not to be deceived or used by any party, and did not conceal his disgust at any duplicity. As he was incapable of the least dishonesty or untruth, he had nothing to hide; and kept his haughty independence to the end. He was never married.

1841. — CHARLES FREDERICK SIMMONS was lost at sea, in February or March, 1862, at the age of 41 years. He was the youngest son of Hon. William (H.C. 1804) and Lucia (Hammatt) Simmons, and was born in Boston, 27 January, 1821. His father was born in Hanover, Mass., 9 July, 1782; was a lawyer in Boston, and for many years one of the judges of the Police Court; and died 17 June, 1843, aged 61 years. His mother was a native of Plymouth. He was a school-boy at the Latin School in Boston, and nearly ready to enter college, when ill health compelled an absence for several months of country life: his preparatory studies were finished under the direction of his brother, the Rev. George Frederick Simmons (H.C. 1832); and he entered Harvard College in 1837. After the usual college course, he studied law in the office of David A. Simmons; and except as interrupted by ill health, at one time, in his early professional life, — being from this cause absent for three years from his office, — he was in general practice as a lawyer in Boston, devoting himself during the last three years chiefly to conveyancing, and to the law of real estate. At an early period of the war, he received a commission as adjutant of the Fourteenth Massachusetts Volunteers, when he gave all his energy to the formation of that regiment. The exposures and hardships of military life were cheerfully borne by him; but a long march with his regiment, in severely cold and stormy weather, proved too much for his physical strength: from the ill effects of this march he never recovered. After a long furlough, during which he hoped, in vain, quickly to regain his customary health, he resigned his commission, and, for the benefit of a sea voyage, left Boston, in the English brig "Gypsy," on the 25th of February, 1862, for St. Jago, Cuba. Violent gales swept along the Atlantic coast during the early part of March, and in these the brig must have foundered: after her departure from Boston, no tidings of the brig, her passengers, her crew, ever came; no floating spar, no fragment, was ever seen.

Mr. Simmons was a man of artistic tastes, of reserved manners, of great penetration, and much power of sarcasm. The influence of his residence at Concord, during the last year of his life, led him to embrace the soldier's life early and earnestly, and to associate the welfare of the negro race closely with the objects of the war.

1842. — George Edward Rice, of Boston, died in Roxbury, Mass., 10 August, 1861, aged 39 years. He was son of Henry and Maria (Burroughs) Rice, and was born in Boston, 10 July, 1822. He was fitted for college partly at the Latin School in Boston, and partly at the school of Mr. E. L. Cushing (H.C. 1827). After leaving college, he studied law with Charles G. Loring (H.C. 1812) and William Dehon (H.C. 1833), of Boston, and practised his profession in his native city. He was a gentleman of fine literary taste; and contributed valuable articles to the best periodicals in the country, including the "North-American Review." He also possessed much poetical talent, with keen wit. He was author of several humorous plays, which were performed at theatres, and received with great applause. He published several matters of a humorous character, and subsequently two small volumes of poems, under the titles of "Ephemera" and "Nugamenta." He was widely known as a writer of genuine sarcastic wit. He was possessed of a sensitive mind and nervous temperament, easily excited by any unusual event of joy or sorrow.

He married, 28 December, 1857, Tirzah Maria Crockett, daughter of George W. Crockett, Esq., of Boston. She died 10 January, 1859, at the age of 27 years, without issue.

1845. — George Dwight Guild died in Brookline (Longwood Village), 5 May, 1862, aged 37 years. He was son of Moses and Juliette (Ellis) Guild, and was born in Dedham, Mass., 17 March, 1825. He was fitted for college at Wrentham Academy. After graduating, he began the study of law at the Law School at Cambridge; and completed his studies in the office of Charles Mayo Ellis (H.C. 1839), of Boston. On his admission to the bar, he established himself in the practice of his profession in Boston, where he remained until his death. He devoted himself to his profession with great assiduity, and soon acquired an extensive practice. He was a safe counsellor; and his legal acquirements, had his life been spared, would probably have obtained for him judicial honors. Single-hearted integrity was the basis of his whole intellectual life. His gentleness and uncompromising uprightness commanded the esteem and insured the confidence and respect of all with whom he came in contact.

He married, 13 September, 1860, Mary M. Thomas, daughter of William Thomas, Esq., president of the Webster Bank in Boston. His wife and an infant child survive him.

1849. — Henry Middleton Rutledge Fogg, of Nashville, Tenn., was killed in the battle of Somerset, Ky., 19 January, 1862, aged 31 years. He was the second son of Francis Brinley and Mary (Rutledge) Fogg, and was born in Nashville, 16 September, 1830. His father was a son of Rev. Daniel Fogg (H.C. 1764), an Episcopal clergyman of Brooklyn, Conn.; was born in Kensington, Conn., 18 August, 1743; married Deborah Brinley, daughter of Francis Brinley, of Newport, R.I., and Alef, his wife, a daughter of Hon. Godfrey Malbone, of that city; and died in Brooklyn in 1815, aged 72 years. His mother was daughter of Hon. Edward Rutledge, of Charleston, S.C. He was a fine scholar, and graduated with high honor. After leaving college, he visited Europe; and, on his return, studied law with his father, one of the ablest lawyers and ripest scholars in the valley of the Mississippi. It may be added that the latter studied law with his relative, the Hon. William Hunter, of Newport, R.I., who received his legal education in London. On being admitted to the bar, Francis Brinley Fogg removed to Nashville, Tenn., and became the partner of the late Felix Grundy; and in their office the late President Polk acquired his legal education. Young Fogg became a promising lawyer; was talented and spirited. A little South-Carolina blood, probably, led him into the rebel army. He left his business to become an aide to Gen. Felix K. Zollicoffer; and they were both killed in the battle at Somerset. Fogg's brother, Francis Brinley Fogg, jun., was educated at the university in Nashville, Tenn.; but studied his profession at the Law School in Cambridge, graduating in 1846. He returned to Nashville, where he began to practise with marked success. He died, after a brief illness in that city, in February, 1848. Fogg's parents are now left childless, having lost their only daughter a few years ago.

1849. — Dr. John Smith Nichols died in Nevada, Cal., January, 1862, aged 35 years. He was the ninth child and third son of Ezra and Waity Gray (Smith) Nichols, and was born in Middleton, Mass., 20 June, 1826. His father was born in October, 1789; was married in Seabrook, N.H.; and died in September, 1848. The son was fitted for college at Andover. After leaving college, he studied medicine with Dr. Ezra Addison Searle Nichols, of Cambridge. He received his degree of M.D. in 1851, and established himself in the practice of his profession in Cambridge. He afterwards removed to Woonsocket, R.I.; and finally went to California.

1849. — Col. Everett Peabody died in Pittsburg, Tenn., 6 April, 1862, aged 31 years. He was killed in battle. He was the second son of Rev. William Bourne Oliver (H.C. 1816) and Eliza Amelia (White) Peabody, and was born in Springfield, Mass., 13 June, 1830. His father was son of Hon. Oliver Peabody (H.C. 1773), of Exeter, N.H., where he was born, 9 July, 1799; was ordained at Springfield, October, 1820; and died 29 May, 1847. His mother was the second daughter and eighth child of Major Moses and Elizabeth Amelia (Atlee) White, of Rutland, Mass.; and was born 24 May, 1799. The subject of this notice was fitted for college by his father, and entered the University of Vermont, at Burlington, as freshman, in 1845, where he remained one year; then left, and entered as sophomore at Harvard College in 1846. On leaving college, he concluded to adopt engineering as a profession; and he was employed on the Cochituate water-works one or two months, under Mr. Chesborough. He then went on to the Cleveland, Columbus, and Cincinnati Railroad, as a leveller. He rose rapidly in his profession. Went on to the Pacific Railroad, in Missouri, in 1851; went on to the Maysville and Lexington Railroad, Ky., in 1852; became chief of the Memphis and Ohio Railroad in 1853; became resident-engineer on the Hannibal and St. Joseph Railroad in 1855; chief-engineer of the Platte-County Railroad in 1859. When the war broke out, he raised a battalion, received a commission as major, and was busily employed in repairing and defending the railway-communications of Northern Missouri. He commanded twelve hundred men at the siege of Lexington. He was slightly wounded in the chest, and severely in the foot, which lamed him for life. He was confined to his bed for two months, and went on crutches for two more. He re-organized his regiment (the Twenty-fifth Missouri) in spite of great opposition, and was ordered to join Gen. Grant's army. Upon his joining the force under Gen. Grant, the command of a brigade under Gen. Prentiss was assigned to him, on the exposed left wing of the army nearest the enemy; and here, in the unequal conflict which that wing maintained, he was killed. He was six feet and one inch in stature, very broad and powerful; hardy and rugged, hardly knowing what sickness was; gay, and careless of the future; very chivalrous, and of dauntless courage.

1850. — Dr. Edward Brooks Everett died in Boston, 5 November, 1861, aged 31 years. He was son of Hon. Edward (H.C. 1811) and Charlotte Gray (Brooks) Everett, and was born in the house of his grandfather, Hon. Peter Chardon Brooks, at Medford, Mass., 6 May, 1830. He went with his parents to Europe in 1840 (his father having been appointed minister to the Court of St. James), and was at school successively at Paris, Florence, Paris again, and London, while his father resided in Europe, from 1840 to 1845: at London, he was at King's-College School, under Dr. Major. He returned home with his parents in 1845; and was for a short time at the Boston public Latin School, and then at the private school of Daniel Greenleaf Ingraham, of Boston (H.C. 1809), by whom he was offered for admission to college. After graduating, he studied medicine at the Tremont Medical School in Boston, and received the degree of M.D. in 1853. He had given much attention to veterinary science, under the impression that it ought to be held in much higher consideration than it is. His health, however, soon began to fail; and he never engaged in the practice of his professsion.

He married, 24 October, 1855, Helen C., daughter of Benjamin Adams, of Boston. He left a son of six and a daughter of four years of age, whose mother also survives him.

1851.—ARTHUR HERBERT POOR died in New-York city, 11 January, 1862, aged 31 years. He was son of Benjamin and Aroline Emily (Peabody) Poor, of Boston; and was born in Stow, Mass. (where his parents resided for a short time), 6 December, 1830. He was fitted for college at the Boston Latin School. In his class he held a high rank of scholarship, and graduated with honors. On leaving college, he entered the counting-room of Messrs. Read, Chadwick, and Dexter, commission-merchants, of Boston; and in January, 1855, was admitted as a partner of the firm. He exhibited great enterprise, energy, and skill in business; and soon afterwards went to New York to take charge of the branch-house of the firm in that city. In the early part of the year 1861, he had occasion to visit some of the western states, on business of the house; and while on his journey he took a severe cold, which terminated in an affection of his lungs, of which he died after a long illness. He was greatly esteemed by his relatives, as well as by the house with which he was connected in business.

He married, 10 January, 1855, Harriet Leonard, daughter of William A. F. Sproat, of Taunton, Mass., by whom he had two children,—one son and one daughter,—who, with their mother, survive him.

1851.—GEORGE DOANE PORTER died in Medford, Mass., 25 November, 1861, aged 30 years. He was son of Jonathan (H.C. 1814) and Catharine (Gray) Porter, and was born in Medford, 21 June, 1831. His father was born in Medford, 13 November, 1791; was a lawyer in that town; and died 11 June, 1859. His mother survived him. He was fitted for college chiefly by his father, and entered one year in advance. After graduating, he studied law under the instruction of William Brigham, of Boston (H.C. 1829). On his admission to the bar, he opened an office in Boston, and another in Medford; but soon afterwards confined his business solely to Medford. He was much respected in his native town for his good sense, honesty, and faithfulness. He was for several years a diligent and useful member of the school-committee.

He married, 8 August, 1860, Lucretia A. Holland, and had one son; who, with his mother, survived him.

1854. — HENRY BLATCHFORD HUBBARD, of Boston, died in Chicago, Ill., 13 February, 1862, aged 29 years. He was the third son of Hon. Samuel (Y.C. 1802) and Mary Ann (Coit) Hubbard, and was born in Boston, 8 January, 1833. His father was born in Boston, 2 June, 1785; was appointed associate-judge of the Supreme Court of Massachusetts in 1842; and died 24 December, 1847, aged 62 years. The subject of this notice entered the Boston Latin School at the age of twelve, and there pursued his preparatory studies. While in college, he resided with his brother, Gardiner Greene Hubbard (D.C. 1841), in Cambridge. At the end of his junior year, on account of ill health and an affection of his eyes, he left college, and sailed for Europe, 18 June, 1853. He returned 19 September, 1854, too late to graduate with his class. He received his degree, out of course, in 1857. He began the study of law with his brother, Gardiner Greene Hubbard; but in September, 1855, he entered the Law School in Cambridge. He left the Law School in 1856; and was clerk, engineer, and treasurer of the Cambridge water-works until the fall of 1859. His health failing, he sailed for California, 25 December following, in the ship "Andrew Jackson." While in California, he was attached to the United-States Coast Survey as magnetic and astronomic assistant. He returned in the spring of 1861, without any improvement of his health. In September following, he went to visit his brother, William Henry Hubbard (B.U. 1845), in Chicago, where he died. His remains were brought home, and interred at Mount Auburn 17 February, 1862.

He was never married.

1855.—LANGDON ERVING died in Baltimore, Md., 20 May, 1862, aged 27 years. He was son of John and Emily Sophia (Elwin) Erving, and was born at Fort Henry, Md., 20 November, 1834. His father is a colonel in the United-States army, son of John, a retired gentleman, and was born in Boston. His mother was daughter of Thomas Elwin, of England, a lawyer, who never practised his profession. His (Thomas Elwin's) wife was the only child of Gov. John Langdon, of Portsmouth, N.H. The subject of this notice, for the first ten years of his life, did not live a year in any one place. He was at North Carolina, Michigan, Georgia, South Carolina, and Philadelphia: at nine or ten years of age, he was at Fort Hamilton, in New-York harbor. He was christened, when very young, by Rev. Charles Burroughs, D.D., of Portsmouth, N.H. In September, 1845, he began to attend school at Perignot's, in New York, where he staid, with the exception of going to Cincinnati and Kentucky, until he entered college. He attained a distinguished standing of scholarship in college, ranking as the fifth in a class numbering 81. After graduating, he entered the Law School at Cambridge; and, having obtained his degree of LL.B. in 1857, he established himself in the practice of his profession in Baltimore.

He married, 18 December, 1860, Sophie C. Pennington, of Baltimore; and left one daughter, born 27 September, 1861.

1855.—GEORGE FOSTER HODGES, of Roxbury, Mass., died at Hall's Hill, near Washington, D.C., 30 January, 1862, aged 25 years. He contracted a violent cold while on a visit to Washington, which the damp exposure of camp life intensified, till it became a fever, of which he died after an illness of ten days. He was son of Almon Danforth and Martha (Comstock) Hodges, and was born in Providence, R.I., 12 January, 1837. His father was born in Norton, Mass., 25 January, 1801. He came to Boston in his youth, and served his apprenticeship in the store of Messrs. John D. Williams and Co.; and afterwards began business in Providence, R.I., under the firm of Stimpson and Hodges, as wholesale grocers, where he continued more than twenty years. In 1845, he removed to Boston, and formed a copartnership with Mr. John L. Emmons (who was a fellow-apprentice with him in the store of Messrs. Williams), under the style of Hodges and Emmons. In November, 1850, he was chosen president of the Washington Bank; which office he now holds, having retired from commercial business. Young Hodges's mother was a native of Providence. She died in Roxbury, 29 August, 1849. The subject of this notice was fitted for college by Rev. Moses Burbank (Waterv. C. 1836), at his private school in Newton, Mass., and entered the sophomore class in 1852. He was one of the youngest in his class, but attained a highly respectable rank, and graduated with honors. After leaving college, he studied law, first in the office of Peleg Whitman Chandler, of Boston (Bowd. C. 1834), and completed his studies at the Law School in Cambridge, where he received his degree of LL.D. in 1860. Immediately after he graduated, he went to the Warren-street Chapel in Boston, and asked whether he could not be of some service in carrying out the objects of that most useful institution, and pressed his desire to be employed in whatever way he could be useful. He was immediately engaged in the evening school, teaching the simplest rules of arithmetic and writing to adults, who in their youth had not enjoyed the privileges of instruction. After he had begun the practice of his profession, in the first case in which he was employed he was successful. With the reward he had earned, and of which he had so much right to be proud, he went to the treasurer of the chapel. "This," said he, "is one-half of my first fee. Take it, that it may do good to others." When the call came for the Massachusetts militia to rally for the support of their flag, in April, 1861, he sought his friend and classmate, Col. Lawrence, of the Fifth Massachusetts Regiment, and told him that his heart was in the struggle, and that he had determined to enlist with his regiment; but, there being no vacancy for him as an officer, he enlisted as a private in the Charlestown City-Guards, but was soon promoted by his classmate to the office of paymaster. At the battle of Bull Run he manifested great bravery, standing at the colonel's side, even when urged to lie down, when shot and shell were coming against them like an avalanche. Col. Lawrence publicly stated, soon after his return, that he owed his life to the chivalrous exertions of his friend. Returning to Massachusetts with his regiment, his military taste was again gratified by his appointment as adjutant of the Eighteenth. The universal testimony of his intimate friends is, that he was of a frank and generous nature, amiable and warm-hearted, and enjoyed the esteem and respect of all his classmates and friends. The noble object to which he devoted, and in the end gave up, his life, is a guaranty to the world that their confidence was not misplaced. An officer of his regiment, at his funeral, said of him, "He had a good word for everybody. He was kind and obliging to all. He gained the respect and regard of both officers and men."

He was never married.

1855. — Rev. William Ward Meriam was murdered 3 July, 1862, on his way from Constantinople to Philippopolis. He was born in Princeton, Mass., 15 September, 1830; and was therefore 31 years old at the time of his death. After the death of his father, in 1834, his mother removed with her four children to Cambridgeport, where she resided until her death in 1850. The subject of this notice was fitted for college at the high school in Cambridgeport. In 1850, he became deeply impressed with the importance of a religious life; and the next year he united with the Orthodox Congregational church in Cambridgeport. Immediately after leaving college, he entered the Andover Theological Seminary, where he graduated in 1858. Having resolved to devote his life to missionary services, he married, 1 September, 1858, Susan Dimond, of Cambridgeport; and was ordained at the same place, 29 November of that year. He sailed from Boston for his mission, with his wife and several other missionary laborers, 17 January, 1859; arrived at Smyrna 22 February, and at Adrianople 22 April. After spending some months at the latter place, studying the Turkish language, he went in October, with Mr. Clark, another missionary, to the new station Philippopolis (Western Turkey), which was subsequently the field of his labors. He had greatly endeared himself to the people in the vicinity of his residence; had just acquired a knowledge of the Turkish language, and was prepared to prosecute his work successfully. In May, 1862, he made a tour through sixty or seventy villages in the neighborhood of his residence. At the time of his death, he was on his way home from Constantinople, where he had been to attend the annual meeting of the missionaries of Western Turkey. His wife and child and one or two missionaries were with him; when the party were met by a company of five mounted brigands, by whom Mr. Meriam and one of his companions were killed. Mrs. Meriam carried the body of her husband forty-eight long and weary hours, in order that she might bury it in the home of his mission-life; but the shock to her own system was too great for her to bear, and she died of typhoid-fever on the 25th of July, — twenty-three days after the death of her husband. She was a graduate of the Cambridge High School, and for many years a most successful teacher in the public schools of the place. Three of the five brigands were afterwards arrested, were tried, convicted, and were all executed on the 8th of January, 1862.

The child of Mr. Meriam arrived at Boston, 12 May, in the bark "Smyrniote" from Smyrna, in good health; and found a new home in the family of Mr. J. N. Meriam, in Cambridge.

1858. — George Bradford Chadwick, of Boston, died in Northampton, Mass., 12 August, 1861. He was the third of four children, and only son of Dr. George (D.C. 1825) and Susan Brewster (Gilbert) Chadwick, and was born in Ipswich, Mass., 3 January, 1836. His father graduated at Dartmouth College with the second honors of his class. After leaving college, he pursued the study of medicine; and, having received the degree of M.D. in 1828, he began the practice of his profession in Ipswich, where his four children were born. Shortly after the birth of his fourth child, he relinquished the practice of medicine, removed to Chelsea, and began business as a merchant, in Milk Street, Boston, with his brother-in-law,

Samuel S. Gilbert, under the firm of Gilbert and Chadwick. His mother was daughter of Hon. Benjamin Joseph Gilbert, of Hanover, N.H. (Y.C. 1786), a lawyer by profession; and married Sally Shepard, of Boston. His great-grandfather, Joseph Gilbert, was a native of Brookfield, Mass. The father of the subject of this notice took a severe cold in the autumn of 1843, which resulted in a rapid consumption; and he died, 11 November of that year, at the house of his father-in-law, who had removed from Hanover to Boston.

Young Chadwick first entered the Adams School, in Mason Street, Boston. He was afterwards transferred to the Brimmer School, where a Franklin medal was awarded to him in 1850. He that year entered the Boston Latin School, where he remained a little more than a year; and then entered the private Latin school of Epes Sargent Dixwell (H.C. 1857), in Boylston Place, where he completed his studies for entering college, leaving the school in January, 1854. While in college, he held a respectable rank of scholarship. He had a strong partiality for architecture; and, at commencement, an essay was assigned to him: the subject was, "Architecture in the United States." After leaving college, he studied architecture for some time under the instruction of Mr. George Snell, of Boston; and intended to make that business his profession.

1858. — James Jackson Lowell was born in Cambridge, Oct. 15, 1837. He was the second son and fourth child of Charles Russell and Anna Cabot (Jackson) Lowell, and the grandson of Rev. Charles Lowell, D.D. (H.C. 1800), and of Patrick T. Jackson. He was fitted for college at the private school of Rev. Thomas Russell Sullivan, and at the Boston Latin School, where he took the first rank. Early in the freshman year, he was acknowledged to be the first scholar in his class; a place which he held without dispute through his college course. After graduation, he taught private pupils in Cambridge for a year; and then entered the Law School, while still continuing his private instruction and residing with his parents in Cambridge. At the breaking-out of the rebellion, he became an interested member of a drill-club which was formed in Cambridge, and has since furnished many excellent officers to the army. In July, 1861, he joined the Twentieth Massachusetts Regiment as first lieutenant in Capt. Schmitt's company.

On 21 October, 1861, he was wounded in the thigh at Ball's Bluff; passing several weeks at home in consequence. He rejoined his regiment as soon as he was fit, and, in the absence of the captain, took the command of his company, which he retained through the Peninsula campaign, until, during the "seven days," he was wounded mortally in the battle of Glendale, June 30. He was left in the hands of the enemy, it being the opinion of the surgeons that he could not live more than a few hours. He lingered, however, until the fourth of July, — a day most fitting to be associated thus with the memory of this patriot soldier. His whole bearing, after receiving the fatal wound, was marked by a characteristic composure and undemonstrative fortitude. He bade his men go forward without minding him. To a fellow-officer he said that his wound was similar to that of his cousin, William Lowell Putnam, at Ball's Bluff, whom he spoke of meeting shortly. The only message which he sent home was to the effect that he was doing his duty when he fell; and, after he was left in the enemy's hands, so clearly and so dispassionately did he talk of the nature of the war, and of the reasons which had led him to devote his life to it, that our surgeons, who had remained to care for the wounded, told the rebel officers to talk with him if they wished to see how a true and brave Northern soldier thought and felt.

Some weeks elapsed before certain news concerning his death reached his family; but at length the return of one of his fellow-prisoners put it beyond doubt. Few have fallen so widely lamented, or have been felt to be a greater loss to the community, as was manifested by the heartfelt tributes which were paid to his memory in very numerous letters to his parents, in a printed sermon by Rev. C. A. Bartol, D.D. (Bowd. C. 1832), and in many other ways. Nor can the loss of one whose character was so living ever cease to be freshly felt. His springing step, his cheery voice, his eye shining with a deep interior light, are intimately associated, to all who knew him, with the Cambridge streets and walks. The outward bearing marked the quality of the man. There was a charm in his whole air and manner that attracted even the chance beholder; the more because he was himself so unconscious of it. A lover of nature and natural things, he was thoroughly and entirely natural. Simple, pure, and wise, abstemious in personal tastes and habits, reticent of his judgment of others, he was severe in his judgment of himself, so that he might almost have been called ascetic, but for the fresh and hearty enjoyment which he took in all social pleasures.

He had a singular truthfulness, which sometimes put on the appearance of bluntness; nor did he conceal the quick displeasure which moved him at any deception or ungenerosity: but he was equally ready to more than repair any fault of impulse. His unobtrusive kindness was continually occupied in quiet benefits. Deliberate in decision, he was speedy in thought: his mind worked carefully and surely, as well as quickly, in its processes; although he weighed the practical results of his conclusions with the utmost care, and was slow to take an irrevocable step.

A high and delicate honor, loyalty to the principles of truth and freedom, a fine sense of justice, which was instinctive, took in him the place of a natural aptitude for war, which he had not especially. At his second college exhibition, he had spoken on "Loyalty." In a military note-book for his private use, he had written the motto, from one old French army list, "The true characteristic of a perfect warrior should be fear of God, love of country, respect for the laws, preference of honor to pleasures, and to life itself." It was the unconscious statement of the principles which led him into the service of his country. He went calmly and seriously, because he felt it to be his duty to go. He comprehended the nature and importance of the contest; and, realizing fully the personal danger also, was willing to give his life to the cause. In a letter to some classmates who had presented him with a sword, written in the spring of 1862, he said, almost prophetically, "When the class meets in years to come, . . . let the score who went to fight for their country be remembered with honor and praise; and let not those who never returned be forgotten, — those who died for the cause, not of the constitution and the laws (a superficial cause: the rebels have the same), but of civilization and law, and the self-restrained freedom which is their result."

Such a noble spirit can never be forgotten. Honorable by blood and name and nature, devotedly beloved, rarely gifted in all intellectual and moral qualities, pre-eminent among his fellows, who rejoiced in that undisputed pre-eminence, their pride and affection follow him with fresh sorrow, and yet with joy that a heroic death was permitted to round and complete a life short in years, but long in the acquisition of those gifts and graces which are among the possessions of the soul, and can never die.

1858. — NATHANIEL RUSSELL, of Plymouth, Mass., died at Drummondtown, Accomac county, Va., 25 March, 1862, aged 24 years. He was son of Nathaniel (H.C. 1820) and Catharine Elizabeth (Elliott) Russell, and was born in Plymouth, 13 June, 1837. He was fitted for college at the high-school in Plymouth, under John William Hunt (Mid. C. 1847), and afterwards under Franklin Crosby. He had a particular partiality for vessels; for any kind of navigable craft. He intended to be a merchant, and become interested in navigation. Soon after leaving college, he became attached to the United-States Coast Survey, under Capt. Harrison, of Plymouth, stationed in Eastern Virginia. His death was sudden: on the 18th of March, he was attacked with lung-fever, and died one week afterwards. He was a young man of frank, cordial manners, and was endeared to all his acquaintances. Retiring and quiet, almost self-distrustful, as he was, his unaffected simplicity and openheartedness could not fail to win him friends. Kind, affectionate, devotedly fond of his relatives and friends, an upright man and sincere Christian, he has gone early to receive the rewards of a life well spent.

1858. — FRANK HOWARD SHOREY died in Dedham, Mass., 24 January, 1862, aged 24 years. He was son of John and Cornelia (Guild) Shorey, and was born in Boston, 2 November, 1837. His father was a merchant in Boston: he died about ten years since. His mother was a native of Dedham: but, on her marriage, she removed to Boston, where she resided five or six years; after which she returned to Dedham, and has since resided there. He was fitted for college at the Dedham High School. He entered Dartmouth College, where he remained two years; then left, and entered the junior class in Harvard. He attained a high rank of scholarship in his class, and graduated with distinction. He was a very good *belles-lettres* scholar, and possessed great love for the natural sciences. Botany was to him a favorite pursuit. After leaving college, he studied law, under the instruction of Thomas Lafayette Wakefield, of Boston (D.C. 1843); and was admitted to the Suffolk bar in December, 1849. He immediately began the practice of his profession in Boston, with cheering prospects of success. Soon afterwards he became a member of the Episcopal church in Dedham, of which the Rev. Samuel Brazer Babcock (H.C. 1830), is rector. About a year before his death, the fatal signs of consumption appeared. He was patient in suffering, waiting calmly the result. His whole life was beautifully consistent, pure; and his death was serene and cheerful. He was never known to swerve from moral rectitude; and yet, with delicate sensitiveness, he discarded self-merit, and died with the Saviour's name upon his lips, as his only but perfect hope. He was never married.

1859. — Major HENRY JACKSON HOW was killed in one of the battles fought during a retreat of the army from Fair Oaks to Malverton, on James river, 30 June, 1862. He was son of Phineas and Tryphena (Wheeler) How; was born in Haverhill, Mass., 22 October, 1835; and was therefore 26 years old at the time of his death. He was fitted for college at Phillips Academy, Andover, Mass., and entered in 1854, but left in the first term, in his freshman year. He re-entered in the class of the next year. After leaving college, he was engaged most of the time in the manufacture of hats, until the breaking-out of the rebellion, when he resolved to devote himself to the cause of his country. He entered into the service with his whole soul, and proceeded at once to raise a company, which was attached to the 19th regiment. He was a fine soldier; six feet in height; of splendid personal appearance, great physical power, and indomitable courage. He received a commission as major. The regiment left for Washington on the 28th of August last, and was stationed on the Upper Potomac. Major How was engaged in much active service, and exhibited the utmost intrepidity on the battle-field, until, at last, his life was sacrificed in the cause to which he has so nobly devoted himself.

1860. — Julius Sedgwick Hood, of Lynn, Mass., died in Louisville, Ky., 21 December, 1861, aged 21 years. He was son of George and Hermione (Breed) Hood, and was born in Lynn, 7 October, 1840. His father was son of Abner and Mary (Richardson) Hood; was born in Lynn, 10 November, 1806. While young, he removed with his parents to Nahant, where he passed his youth, with the exception of a few years which he spent at school in Hanover, N.H. Having, by his own unaided exertions, accumulated a small capital, he went, in 1827, to St. Louis, Mo., where, in company with John C. Abbott, he established a boot-and-shoe business, in which he was interested until 1841. Returning to Lynn in 1835, he established himself in Boston as a commission boot, shoe, and leather merchant; in which business he continued until his death. He for some time took an active part in public life, being for several years a member of the Massachusetts legislature. He was also, in 1850, the first mayor of Lynn, and was re-elected in 1851; and a member of the Massachusetts constitutional convention in 1853. He died 27 June, 1859. His mother was born in Lynn, 18 March, 1812. She was daughter of Aaron Breed, born in 1761, a soldier in the revolutionary war, and an adjutant in the war of 1812. He was also a member of the state legislature for several years. He died in 1817. The subject of this notice was fitted for college at the Lynn High School, under Mr. Jacob Batchelder and Mr. Gordon Bartlett. In college, his attainments in scholarship were distinguished, and he graduated with the second honors of his class. On account of his feeble health, he did not enter upon the study of any profession or upon any business. A few weeks before his death, he left his home in Lynn for Lexington, where he had a brother residing; hoping, in a more congenial climate, to regain his lost strength, or, at least, to lengthen a life so dear to those who looked to him for counsel and assistance. "His death," writes one who knew him well, "was calm and beautiful: he felt more than willing to go and do the work and achieve the usefulness there which he had hoped to do here." He was a true and warm-hearted friend; a man strong in principle, and earnest in a Christian life.

1860.—WILLIAM MATTICKS ROGERS died of typhoid fever, in the army, near Richmond, June, 1862. He was the only son of Rev. William Matticks (H.C. 1827) and Adelia (Strong) Rogers, and was born in Boston, 26 October, 1838. He was fitted for college at Phillips Academy, Andover, Mass. He held a respectable rank of scholarship, and was greatly beloved by his classmates. He was one of the class-committee. Immediately after graduating, he went to Europe, and began the study of law and of the German language in Heidelberg, where he remained one year; and, when the rebellion broke out, he at once determined to devote himself to the cause of his country. He immediately returned, and enlisted as a private in Company A, of the Eighteenth Massachusetts Regiment. He was soon afterwards made a sergeant, and, subsequently, sergeant-major. Had his life been spared, he would probably soon have received a commission. But it was otherwise ordered: his life was sacrificed while contending for the preservation of the Union.

1862–63.

1791. — Dr. John Walton died in Pepperell, Mass., 21 December, 1862, aged 92 years. He was the son of John and Keziah (Viles) Walton, and was born in Cambridge, Mass., 29 October, 1770. He was fitted for college in his native place. He held a respectable rank in his class, and graduated with honors. He studied medicine under the instruction of Dr. Oliver Prescott, of Groton, Mass. (H.C. 1783), and settled in Pepperell; where he practised his profession for more than sixty years, and was much respected by the people of the town of which he was so long a resident. On the 4th of September, 1832, he was chosen a deacon of the Unitarian church in Pepperell. He never held a political office.

He married, in Newton, Mary Bullard, by whom he had seven sons and one daughter; of whom the daughter and three sons survived him. His wife died in the spring of 1848.

1801. — Rev. John Okill Stuart died in Kingston, C.W., 5 October, 1862, aged 86 years. He was son of Rev. John Stuart, and was born in the missionary-house at Fort Hunter, on the banks of the Mohawk River, N.Y., 29 June, 1776. His father was the last missionary to the Mohawk nation. In 1787, at the age of eleven years, he was placed at school in the academy in Schenectady, N.Y. (now Union College), where he received instruction preparatory to his reception into a higher seminary. In 1792, he was sent to the academy at Windsor, N.S., where he remained two years. In 1795, he was appointed teacher of a public grammar-school in Kingston, and continued in that office and employment till June, 1798; and that year he entered the sophomore class in Harvard College; but he did not remain with the class much more than a year, although he received his degree with the others of the class who had gone through the whole course. In June, 1800, he was ordained as minister of the United Church of England and Ireland by Dr. Mountain, bishop of Quebec; and, in 1801, was appointed missionary, by the Society for the Propagation of the Gospel in Foreign Parts, at York (now Toronto), C.W., at that time the seat of government. There he served his vocation and ministry from 1800 to 1812; established a congregation, and built a church; and, on the decease of his father (who was rector of St. George's in Kingston), by invitation of the congregation, and upon application to the bishop, he was appointed his successor; and, in 1812, removed from York (now Toronto) to Kingston. From 1812 to 1822, he served the congregation at Kingston as their parish minister; and, in the latter year, he was collated by the bishop to be archdeacon of York, in the diocese of Quebec. In 1839, when the diocese of Quebec was divided, and Toronto taken from it, he resigned his commission, and was collated by the bishop to be archdeacon of Kingston, in the diocese of Toronto, and continued in that office until 1862; when, on the subdivision of the diocese of Toronto into that of Ontario, he surrendered his commission of archdeacon of Kingston, and was preferred to be dean of Ontario. In 1830, he had an assistant-minister to St. George's, who continued his aid and work, he, however, continuing as rector of St. George's; and, at the time of his death, was one of the officiating clergymen in the cathedral of the diocese of Ontario, in the city of Kingston. Therefore, for more than sixty years, he resided in nearly the same place; preaching to a people to whom his whole course of life, and all his sayings and doings, were known, and retaining and enjoying their respect and esteem. He was not brilliant, nor particularly gifted, nor very learned; but he had great moral worth. In all his communications, he was perfectly sincere, wholly free from artifice, deception, guile. With an exterior somewhat grave and reserved, almost stern, he had ardent and warm attachments. In communing with him, one felt a perfect satisfaction that he was truthful in all he said. Without making professions of attachment, he was always inclined to do kind things whenever it was in his power.

He married, 2 October, 1803, Lucy Brooks, daughter of Gov. John Brooks, of Medford, with whom he became acquainted in 1798, during a residence of several months in the town, completing his studies for admission into college. She died in 1813, leaving one son, — George Okill Stuart, the only surviving male descendant of Gov. Brooks, — a counsellor-at-law of high standing, who has been mayor of Quebec. He married a second wife, Ann Ellice Stuart, who died in Kingston, 28 November, 1836, aged 70 years.

1802. — HENRY ADAMS died in Somerville, Mass., 13 November, 1862, aged 83 years. He was son of Rev. Zabdiel (H.C. 1759) and Elizabeth (Stearns) Adams; was the ninth of eleven children, ten of whom lived to adult age; and was born in Lunenburg, Mass., 13 May, 1777. His father was son of Ebenezer Adams, of Quincy, Mass., where he was born 5 November, 1739; was ordained at Lunenburg, 5 September, 1764; died 1 March, 1801, aged 61 years. His mother was daughter of Rev. David (H.C. 1728) and Ruth (Hubbard) Stearns: she was born in Lunenburg, 20 April, 1742; and died August, 1800, aged 58 years. His father was successor of her father in the church of Lunenburg. The subject of this notice was fitted for college, partly at Groton Academy, and partly by Dr. John Hosmer, of Medford. He studied law with his brother, Zabdiel Boylston Adams (H.C. 1791), in Charlestown, Mass., where he afterwards practised his profession. Subsequently he resided for about four years in Richmond, Va., where he taught a private school; then returned, and again practised his profession in Ashburnham, Mass., where he resided about four years. Thence he removed to Lexington, Mass., having relinquished his profession; and, for the last twenty years of his life, he resided in Somerville, where he devoted himself to agricultural pursuits, to which he had a great partiality.

He married, 1 January, 1806, Susan Forster, daughter of Jacob and Rebecca Forster, of Charlestown, Mass., by whom he had three children (all sons), of whom the only survivor is Edwin Forster Adams, a merchant in Boston. His wife died in Lexington, 12 January, 1834. He married for his second wife, 8 October, 1835, Sarah K. Hawkins, daughter of Col. Nathaniel Hawkins, of Somerville, then a part of Charlestown. She died without issue, in Somerville, 17 December, 1851. He married for his third wife, 4 November, 1852, Mrs. Arphia Besent, a widow, of Cambridgeport, whose former husband was a foreigner. She survives him.

1802. — ANDREW RITCHIE died in Newport, R.I., 7 August, 1862, aged 80 years. He was son of Andrew and Isabella (Montgomery) Ritchie, and was born in Boston, 18 July, 1782. He was fitted for college at Phillips Academy in Andover. He held a distinguished rank of scholarship, and graduated with the second honors of his class; but, when he took his degree of master of arts in 1805, the valedictory oration was assigned to him. He studied law in the office of Rufus Greene Amory (H.C. 1778), and practised his profession in Boston. Having inherited an ample competency, he did not aim at distinction at the bar, although his legal attainments were of the first order. On the 4th of July, 1808, he delivered the annual oration before the town authorities of Boston, in which he said, "We are not required, like young Hannibal, to approach the altar, and vow eternal hatred to a rival nation; but we will repair to the neighboring heights, at once the tombs and everlasting monuments of our heroes, and swear, that, as they did, so would we rather sacrifice our lives than our country." On the morning of the day when he delivered this oration, the Hon. Fisher Ames died in Dedham. In his address, while alluding to Bonaparte, he said, "His conduct has declared, plainer than language can express, that he will endure no neutrals; and that, too, under a persuasion that we dare not become his enemy. If we are thus summoned to take our side in this momentous contest, which will in a few years determine the political destiny of the civilized world, let the alternative be decided by the intelligence, the virtue, and patriotism of the country." He then uttered the following apostrophe on the death of Mr. Ames: "But, alas! the immortal Ames, who, like Ithuriel, was commissioned to discover the insidious foe, and point out our danger, has accomplished his embassy, and, on this morning of our independence, has ascended to heaven. Spirit of Demosthenes! couldst thou have been a silent and invisible auditor, how wouldst thou have been delighted to hear from his lips those strains of eloquence which once, from thine, enchanted the assemblies of Greece!"

Mr. Ritchie married, 27 March, 1807, Maria Cornelia Durant, daughter of Cornelius Durant, a West-India planter. Her father was an officer of the revolution; was afterwards for many years an eminent merchant of Boston, where he died 5 May, 1812, aged 80 years. In consequence of this marriage, after the death of his father-in-law, Mr. Ritchie became, by right of his wife, owner of a plantation in the Island of St. Croix. By the Danish law, he, to retain possession of the estate, was required to reside there; and for many years this was his place of residence, although he often visited Boston, and spent a great part of his time in the United States. He therefore did not long practise his profession. His wife died in Paris, France, without issue.

He married for his second wife, 9 December, 1823, Sophia Harrison Otis, daughter of Hon. Harrison Gray Otis, of Boston (H.C. 1783), by whom he had three children, — two sons and one daughter, — who, with their mother, survive him. The sons graduated at Harvard College respectively in 1845 and 1846; and the daughter is the wife of a physician in Paris, France.

1805. — Moses Gill died in Shrewsbury, Mass., 21 August, 1862, aged 81 years. He was son of Michael and Anna (Gill) Gill, and was born in Westminster, Mass., 20 December, 1780; but removed to Princeton, Mass., with his parents, when two years of age, where he passed his youthful days. His parents were cousins; his mother being daughter of John Gill, of the firm of Edes and Gill, well known as printers in Boston. He was born in Charlestown, Mass.; served a regular apprenticeship with Samuel Kneeland, and married one of Kneeland's daughters. He died 25 August, 1785. He was nephew of Hon. Moses Gill, who was lieutenant-governor of Massachusetts, and acting-governor from 7 June, 1799, to 20 May, 1800.

It being the wish of his uncle (Gov. Gill) that he should have a collegiate education, he left him, by his will, ample means for his support while in college, and during his subsequent life; but this provision was not carried into effect, for his uncle's will was destroyed at his decease. He was fitted for college partly by Rev. Joseph Russell (Y.C. 1793), of Princeton, and partly at Leicester Academy. On leaving college, he taught school for some time in Dorchester and Charlestown, Mass. He then began the study of divinity at Suffield, Conn., and finished his studies with Rev. Ebenezer Gay (Y.C. 1787), of that place. He received his license to preach, after having been thoroughly examined as to his views and qualifications, at Boylston, Mass., 29 June, 1808, by the unanimous vote of the association in that vicinity. He was a teacher in Boston, public and private, from 1812 till 1829; preaching occasionally during the time. He then, owing to ill health, removed into the country, which it was thought prolonged his life. After leaving Boston, he taught in Waltham, Chelmsford, and Acton, during the winter seasons; attending to agriculture in the summers. He also taught in Boylston, Northbridge, and Shrewsbury, until within a few years of his death, when he met with a fall which disabled him from walking, except with crutches; and had also other infirmities, which he endured patiently. He was one of the school-committee in Shrewsbury about five years; was chairman and secretary most of the time. He died suddenly; having been as comfortable as usual during the summer, until the morning of his death, when he was taken ill, and survived but a few hours, passing away without a struggle. He was of a cheerful, mild temperament, enjoying the company of his friends, kind and sympathizing, an affectionate husband and father.

He married, 2 October, 1810 (at that time teaching in Roxbury), Mary Baldwin, daughter of Capt. Henry Baldwin, of Shrewsbury, in which town she was born 2 July, 1787. The issue of this marriage was two children, — a son and a daughter, — both of whom, with their mother, survived him.

1806. — Daniel Henshaw died in Boston 9 July, 1863,

aged 81 years. He was son of Col. William and Phebe (Swan) Henshaw, and was born in Leicester, Mass., 9 May, 1782. His father was born in Boston in 1735, and removed to Leicester in 1748. He was an officer in the revolutionary army. He died February, 1820, at the age of 85 years. His mother was daughter of Dudley Wade and Beulah Swan, of Leicester, where she was born 12 January, 1758; and died 5 November, 1808, aged 55 years. The subject of this notice was fitted for college at Leicester Academy. After leaving college, he studied law in part with Nathaniel Paine Denny (H.C. 1797), of Leicester, and in part with Judge Nathaniel Paine (H.C. 1778), of Worcester. He practised his profession twenty-one years in Winchester, Mass. In 1830, he was practising in Worcester, and afterwards for several years in Lynn, where he had the management of a public newspaper, — the "Lynn Record." On becoming an editor, he gave up his professional business, and continued for fourteen years in the arduous and responsible place of leading editor of a paper; and, after that period, often contributed valuable and interesting articles, chiefly of a biographical or historical character, to sundry newspapers, which were read with interest. He had a great taste for genealogy, and a fund of wit. He read many amusing papers before the Historic-Genealogical Society, several of which were published in the Boston papers. After his connection with the paper in Lynn had terminated, he removed to Boston; where he resided — with the exception of a year or two in Wisconsin with a relative — until his death.

He married, 19 November, 1821, Deborah Starkweather, daughter of Deacon Charles Starkweather, of Worthington, Mass., where she was born 2 November, 1796. She died 6 July, 1851, leaving two daughters and one son.

1809. — Hon. William Elliott died in South Carolina, February, 1863, aged 74 years. He was son of William Elliot, and was born in Beaufort, S.C., 27 April, 1788. He entered college at the age of 18, and took a very high rank of scholarship in his class; standing as the second, Samuel Bird ranking as the first, scholar in the class. On account of ill health, however, he was obliged to return home before completing his academical career; but his degree was conferred upon him by the government in 1810, the year after his class graduated. For many years he devoted himself to the management of his estates, and served with credit in both branches of the state legislature. During the nullification-crisis in South Carolina in 1832, he held the office of senator in the state legislature, but resigned upon being instructed by his constituents to vote to nullify the tariff law. He afterwards participated less frequently in public affairs; his letters against secession, signed "Agricola," and published in 1851, being among his latest expressions of opinion on political subjects. He contributed largely to the periodical press of the South. His published works consisted of an "Address before the St. Paul's Agricultural Society" (Charleston, 1850), and "Carolina Sports by Land and Water" (1856). He was also the author of "Fiesco," a tragedy printed for the author in 1850, and of a number of occasional poems of merit; few of which, however, have been published.

1812. — Samuel William Dexter died in Dexter, Mich., 6 February, 1863, aged 70 years. He was son of Hon. Samuel (H.C. 1781) and Catharine (Gordon) Dexter, and was born in Charlestown, Mass., 18 February, 1792. He first entered college with the class which graduated in 1811, but remained only a few months; when he took up his connexions, and entered the freshman class the following year. A few years after he left college, he purchased a township of land in Michigan, which he named Dexter, and in which he resided until his death.

1812. — Benjamin Daniel Greene died in Boston, 14 October, 1862, aged 68 years. He was the eldest son of Gardiner and Elizabeth (Hubbard) Greene, and was born in Demarara, South America, — where his parents were then residing, — 29 December, 1793. His father was well known as the wealthiest citizen of Boston. His mother, whose virtues and amiable character were long remembered by her contemporaries, and who was a sister of the late John Hubbard, of Boston, died during his early childhood. Her maternal cares were assumed and fulfilled by Elizabeth Copley, a sister of Lord Lyndhurst, —

the present Mrs. Gardiner Greene, — between whom and her adopted son a cordial affection subsisted through life. The subject of this notice was fitted for college in the Boston Latin School, where a Franklin medal was awarded to him in 1807. He held a respectable rank in his class, and graduated with honors. After leaving college, he became a student-at-law in Litchfield, Conn.; and entered upon the practice of his profession, which he soon relinquished for that of medicine. Passing four years abroad, he travelled extensively in Europe, and completed his studies in the schools of Edinburgh and Paris. Attracted by scientific pursuits, he was highly appreciated as a botanist, and became the intimate friend and correspondent of Sir William Hooker, and other men of distinguished attainments. He was a liberal contributor to the Boston Society of Natural History; was its first president; and his valuable library, uncommonly rich in scientific works, was ever open to the researches of his associates. He was a member of the American Academy of Arts and Sciences.

He married, 30 May, 1826, Margaret Morton Quincy, daughter of Hon. Josiah Quincy, of Boston. She survives him. They had no children.

1812. — GEORGE WASHINGTON HEARD died in Ipswich, Mass., 21 April, 1863, aged 70 years. He was son of John and Sarah (Staniford) Heard, and was born in Ipswich, 5 February, 1793. He began to fit for college under the instruction of Rev. Asahel Huntington (D.C. 1786), of Topsfield, Mass.; and completed his preparatory studies at Phillips Academy in Andover. After leaving college, he studied medicine with Dr. John Gorham, of Boston (H.C. 1801); and received his degree of M.D. in 1815, but did not enter upon the practice of his profession. He engaged in business as a distiller in Ipswich, which had been previously his father's occupation. After pursuing this employment several years, he abandoned it, from conscientious motives, and removed to Boston, where, in 1837, he entered into partnership with James Haughton, under the firm of James Haughton and Co., dealers in dry goods. This partnership continued until 1844, when Mr. Heard withdrew. He returned to Ipswich, and engaged in agricultural pursuits, which he continued during the remainder of his life. He was much respected in his native town; was noted for his courtesy, kind feelings, and private liberality; and the families of volunteers in the war had reason to be thankful for his unostentatious donations for their relief. In 1862 he was elected a representative to the state legislature from Ipswich, but did not take his seat; having been obliged to resign it on account of ill health.

He married, 6 November, 1823, Elizabeth Ann Farley, daughter of Robert Farley, of Ipswich. The issue of this marriage was four sons and one daughter. The sons and their mother survived him.

1813.—Dr. David Osgood died in Boston, 23 February, 1863, aged 69 years. He was the only son of Rev. David (H.C. 1771) and Hannah (Breed) Osgood, and was born in Medford, Mass., 23 December, 1793. His father was born in Andover, Mass., 14 October, 1747; was ordained pastor of the first church in Medford, 14 September, 1774; and was one of the most eminent divines of his day. He died 12 December, 1822, aged 75 years. His mother died 7 January, 1818, aged 70 years. She belonged to Charlestown, Mass., and was granddaughter to Richard Foster, who was high sheriff under the old government. The subject of this notice was fitted for college by Dr. John Hosmer, of Medford. He held a respectable rank of scholarship in college, and graduated with honors. After graduating, he studied medicine with Dr. John Jeffries, of Boston (H.C. 1763); and, on receiving his degree of M.D. in 1816, began practising his profession in Boston, where he continued his duties until his death. As a member of the Massachusetts Medical Society, he was respected in his profession for his skill, promptitude, and kindness. He had a warm and generous nature, which never failed in its response to calls for assistance and advice; was always lenient and kind towards real suffering. To his poor patients he was an unfailing friend, whose patience no length of unpaid service could exhaust; one whose unobtrusive and unostentatious charity made him an always-welcome visitant. With a mind open to conviction, he was not afraid of questioning his early opinions. A signal proof of this occurred during a visit to Europe in 1839. At Paris, a friend introduced him to Dr. Hahnemann, the founder of the school of homœopathy. The German philosopher spoke with warmth of his system, and offered his visitor the loan of a copy of the "Homœopathic Novum Organum." This book, though not entirely satisfactory to Dr. Osgood, led him to further researches, and he ended in becoming a very successful practitioner on the homœopathic system. During a second journey to Europe, he visited his distinguished patient, Miss Fredrika Bremer, who was under his charge when she was in Boston, and who feels lasting gratitude for his successful treatment of her case. Her printed commendations of his skill and friendliness are the just sentiments of a discriminating mind and a feeling heart. As a friend, he was not demonstrative and impetuous, but reserved and sure. As a husband, he was all devotion to the chosen of his life; while she most promptly repaid every service, and most heartily returned every affection.

He married in November, 1821, Mary Ann Elder, of Portland, Me., who survived him. They had no children.

1813. — ROYAL TURNER died in Randolph, Mass., 31 December, 1862, aged 70 years. He was the only son of Seth and Abigail (Wales) Turner, and was born in Randolph, 6 December, 1792. He was fitted for college under the tuition of Rev. Jonathan Strong (D.C. 1786). On leaving college, he engaged in mercantile pursuits, in which he was eminently successful. He was much occupied in public business, always to the satisfaction of his employers. In early life, he was a practical surveyor, and assisted in locating the first railroad built in this country; namely, that leading from the stone-quarries in Quincy to Neponset River. In 1815, he received a lieutenant's commission, and rapidly passed through all the grades of promotion until he reached the colonelcy in 1823. He was honorably discharged in 1825. In 1818, and in several subsequent years, he was elected one of the selectmen of the town. He was also clerk and treasurer from 1823 to 1828. He was commissioned justice of the peace in 1826, and of the quorum in

1833; and continued in office until his death. He was appointed bank-commissioner from Norfolk in 1830. On the incorporation of the Randolph Bank, in 1836, he was appointed cashier, and held the office until 1842, when he was elected its president, and continued in that position until his death. During this long period, he watched over its interests with paternal solicitude, and left it in a state of prosperity rarely attained by similar institutions. He was a director in the Bridgewater and Middleborough and Fall-River railroads until their union with the Old-Colony in one corporation; and afterwards he was often consulted with regard to important measures. In all financial matters, his judgment was much respected; and, when deliberately made up, seldom needed a revision. Although his intercourse with society was necessarily restricted by a defect in his hearing, which increased as he advanced in life, yet he was social in his temperament, and took a deep interest in passing events. He was exemplary in all the vocations and duties of life, and was a regular attendant upon public worship, although for many years unable to hear a syllable uttered during the service. Symptoms of organic disease of the brain began to manifest themselves some months before his death, and continued to increase in intensity, until they terminated in partial paralysis, and ultimately in apoplectic coma, and the extinction of life. His death was felt to be a great loss, not only to his family, but also to the business circle in which he moved. Such was his integrity, energy, and promptness in executing every trust committed to him, and such his accuracy in all pecuniary transactions, as to command the confidence of his associates and of the public. Although very decided in his opinions, it was observed by the directors of the bank, after his decease, that, during the long period of his presidency, no one could call to mind any unkind word or act towards his associates in any of their deliberations or transactions.

He married, 14 September, 1818, Maria White, born 27 June, 1800, daughter of Major John White, of Weymouth. They had children; viz., 1. Maria White, born 30 October, 1819; died 31 October, 1819. 2. Seth, born 29 July, 1821;

now cashier of Randolph Bank. 3. Royal White, born 10 March, 1823. 4. Ann Maria, born 15 November, 1825; who married, in 1849, Isaac Sweetser, a merchant in Boston. 5. Abigail Wales, born 10 February, 1830.

1815. — Rev. CONVERS FRANCIS died in Cambridge, Mass., 7 April, 1863, aged 67 years.

He was the fourth child and second son of Convers and Susanna (Rand) Francis, and was born in West Cambridge, 9 November, 1795. He was fitted for college at the Medford Academy, under the charge of John Hosmer. He held a distinguished rank of scholarship in his class. After graduating, he studied theology in the Cambridge Divinity School; was approbated by the Boston Association; and preached his first sermon, 15 November, 1818, in Rev. Dr. Osgood's pulpit in Medford. He was ordained pastor of the Unitarian church in Watertown, Mass., 23 June, 1819, where he remained twenty-three years. In 1842, he was appointed "Parkman Professor of Pulpit Eloquence and the Pastoral Care" in Harvard College, which appointment he accepted; and 21 August, 1842, delivered his valedictory sermon in Watertown. He immediately entered upon the duties of his professorship, which he continued until the end of his life. He was earnest and indefatigable in his researches after sacred truth. From a principle of self-respect, he was prompted to regard as true the conclusions which his mind had established; yet he was far from being unreasonably tenacious of his opinions. His mind was enriched with the best thoughts of authors. He read with avidity, but with attention; noting with care peculiarities of opinions, and sentiments distinguished for beauty and power. He was, in an eminent sense, ambitious to know the truth through whatever medium, be that medium only authoritative. He held an important and responsible office. He was not only a Christian learner: he was also a Christian teacher. He knew full well the impression that instruction makes upon open and sensible minds; and it was commendable in him, that, in his anxiety to teach nothing but the truth, he should seek the guidance of other minds, hallowed by equally holy motives with his own, to share with him the responsibilities of his sacred vocation.

He possessed a heart alive to social affections. His friendly interest, where it found a fitting and accordant place, was sincere and ardent; and he did not suffer it to be limited to any point beyond which it could by any means be influential for good. Although no elaborate work proceeding from his pen has been given to the public, he manifested his interest in science and literature by publishing several valuable papers in our best accredited periodicals. Among his publications were "Errors of Education," a discourse at the anniversary of Derby Academy, in Hingham, 21 May, 1828; Address on the 4th of July, 1828, at Watertown; An Historical Sketch of Watertown, from the first settlement of the town to the close of the second century, in 1830; A Discourse, at Plymouth, 22 December, 1832; A Dudleian Lecture, at Cambridge, 8 May, 1833; The Life of Rev. John Eliot, the Apostle to the Indians, in the fifth volume of Sparks's American Biography, 1836; The Life of Sebastian Rale, Missionary to the Indians, in the seventh volume (new series) of Sparks's American Biography, 1845; Memoir of Rev. John Allyn, D.D., of Duxbury, 1836; Memoir of Dr. Gamaliel Bradford, 1846; Memoir of Judge Davis, 1849 (the last three were published in the Collections of the Massachusetts Historical Society); many articles in the "Christian Disciple," the "Christian Examiner," the "American Monthly Review," the "Unitarian Advocate," the "Scriptural Interpreter," the "Juvenile Miscellany;" several translations from Herder, at different times; Obituary Notice of Miss Eliza Townsend, 1854; and a large number of occasional discourses. He was a member of the Massachusetts Historical Society. In 1837, the honorary degree of doctor of divinity was conferred upon him by Harvard College.

He married, 15 May, 1822, Abby Bradford, daughter of Rev. John Allyn, D.D., of Duxbury, by whom he had two children, — one daughter and one son. The son graduated at Harvard College in 1854. His wife was born in Duxbury, 15 January, 1796: she died in Cambridge, 17 December, 1860, aged 64 years. The two children survive their parents.

1816. — Samuel Buckminster Rice died in Brookfield,

Mass., 28 May, 1863, aged 64 years. He was son of Dr. Tilly (B.U. 1777) and Eunice (Reed) Rice, and was born in Brookfield, 14 June, 1798. He was fitted for college at Leicester Academy. Immediately after graduating, he entered the counting-room of Messrs. Bordman and Pope, in Boston, for the purpose of preparing himself for business as a merchant. While in their employ, he went to the East Indies in the ship "Brilliant," belonging to them. On the passage, the ship sprang a leak; and he labored so long and so severely at the pumps, that it seriously affected his health, which he never afterwards fully recovered. At the expiration of his apprenticeship, he returned to Brookfield, but did not enter into mercantile business. He was afterwards connected with an iron-foundry and glassworks in that town, but relinquished the business some time before his death. He was never married.

1817. — Rev. Thomas Russell Sullivan died in Boston, 23 December, 1862, aged 63 years. He was son of John Langdon and Elizabeth (Russell) Sullivan, and was born in Brookline, Mass., 13 February, 1799. He was fitted for college principally at Dummer Academy in Newbury. He held a respectable rank of scholarship in his class. After leaving college, he studied theology in the Divinity School at Cambridge. He was ordained pastor of the Unitarian church in Keene, N.H., 28 December, 1825, where he faithfully and zealously performed his duties until May, 1835, when he resigned his charge. He soon afterwards removed to Boston, where he opened a private school, which he continued until his death. His beautiful Christian character is thus eloquently delineated by Rev. William Orne White (H.C. 1840), now pastor of the church in Keene, over which Mr. Sullivan was settled: "He has gone, — the man who knew how, in the apostolic sense, to magnify his office; the serious and reverend ambassador of God; the simple-hearted and guileless Christian; the friend whose heart was pierced with the sorrows of his people; the writer skilled in controversy, yet rejoicing more when he could utter affectionate and sober words of practical counsel. In a 'furnace of affliction' he has indeed been tried and proved; and at last, from sharp and mysterious visitations of chastisement, he has been permitted to rest from all earthly toil, to lay down his heavy cross, and to be led by the hand of the good Shepherd 'in green pastures by the still waters.' The scholarly mind of this true-hearted man enabled him to achieve enduring success as a wise and faithful teacher for many years after his retirement from the scenes of his ministry. From time to time, however, he delighted in the privilege of resuming, in various pulpits, his early and cherished duties. He was one whom no change of occupation could secularize; one who might have always said, in perfect sincerity, 'I will dwell in the house of the Lord for ever.' Now that, safe from every rough blast, the tears wiped from his eyes, his faith and patience accepted, he has 'sweetly fallen asleep in Jesus,' it is precious to remember that here, where he so patiently served the Church of Christ for nine and a half years, in what was then an outpost of our Zion, not a shadow rests upon his memory. 'Good and faithful servant,' we bid thee a reluctant farewell; while we rejoice that all who ever knew thee, if they value purity, honor, truth, will find words of respect and affection springing to their lips, whenever they hear the name of THOMAS RUSSELL SULLIVAN."

Mr. Sullivan married, 19 January, 1826, Charlotte C. Blake, of Worcester, by whom he had six sons and two daughters, all of whom but one son survived him. His wife died 2 July, 1863, aged 59 years.

1818.—Rev. PETER SIDNEY EATON died in Chelsea, Mass., 13 March, 1863, aged 64 years. He was son of Rev. Peter (H.C. 1787) and Sarah (Stone) Eaton, and was born in Boxford, Mass., 7 October, 1798. His father was born in Haverhill, Mass., 15 March, 1765; ordained at Boxford, 7 October, 1789; died in Andover, 14 April, 1848, aged 83 years. His mother was daughter of Rev. Eliab Stone (H.C. 1758), of Reading. Young Eaton pursued his preparatory studies under the instruction of his father. On leaving college, he was employed some time as a teacher in Phillips Academy, Andover. He subsequently studied divinity at the theological seminary in that town, and graduated there in 1822. He was ordained at Amesbury, 20 September, 1826, where he continued his pastorship about eleven years, where his labors were so arduous as to seriously affect his health; and by the advice of his friends he resigned his charge, and wholly relinquished the duties of the ministry. He spent several years afterwards as a teacher, principally in Andover. From Andover, he removed to Chelsea, where he resided the remainder of his life. His health was somewhat impaired; but he endeavored to exert an influence, by all the means he might possess, favorable to the interests of religion and good morals.

He married, 4 December, 1828, Elizabeth Ann Leman, of Charlestown, Mass., by whom he had three children: Sidney Payson, born in Amesbury, 16 September, 1829; Henry Martyn, born in Amesbury, 28 June, 1835; Elizabeth Anne, born in Worcester, 16 May, 1841. His wife and all his children survived him.

1818. — Charles Octavius Emerson died in York, Me., 22 June, 1863, aged 64 years. He was son of Edward E. and Abigail (Lyman) Emerson, and was born in York, 27 March, 1799. He was fitted for college at Phillips Exeter Academy. After graduating, he began the study of law in the office of Jeremiah Bradbury in York, where he remained one year. In October, 1819, he went into the office of Luther Lawrence (H.C. 1801) in Groton, Mass., where he continued his studies until October, 1821, when he was admitted to the bar in Concord, Mass. He then returned to his native town, where he practised his profession until his death. From 1823 to 1830, he was frequently elected to fill the office of clerk and treasurer; was representative in the legislature in 1827, 1828, and 1829. His life was happy and useful. He was an honorable, religious, and unambitious gentleman.

He married, 24 June, 1829, Harriet Jane Phillips, daughter of Deacon John Phillips, of Portland, Me. Their children were, — 1. Charles Edward, born 5 April, 1830; died 25 March, 1832. 2. Francis Philip, born 2 September, 1831. 3. Abbie Clara, born 17 March, 1833. 4. Edward Octavius, born 6 June, 1834. 5. Andrew Samuel, born 25 February, 1837. 6. Harriet Eliza, born 11 March, and died 23 September, 1840.

1818. — JOHN FLAVEL JENKINS died in White Plains, N.Y., 12 September, 1862, aged 66 years. He was son of John and Abigail (Hall) Jenkins, and was born in Gloucester, Mass., 6 February, 1796. His father, who was a celebrated writing-master, and was author of "The Art of Writing," &c., was born in Dorchester, Mass., in 1755, and died in Wilmington, Md., in 1823. His mother was daughter of Dan Hall, of Peekskill, N.Y., who was son of Caleb Hall, of Attleborough, Mass.; and was born in Peekskill, in 1765. The subject of this notice, when about six weeks old, went with his parents to New-York city; whence they soon left for Peekskill, where they resided until he was seven years old. He then went to the residence of his grandparents in Boston, which he made his home, except while pursuing his studies in the country. As he obtained his education by his own unaided exertions until he entered college, he labored on a farm at first, and afterwards taught, to defray his expenses. He was obliged to change his place of study several times, according to the state of his funds; and taught school for three winters while in college. He held an eminent rank of scholarship in college; and in the classics, in general literature, in natural sciences, and in mathematics, he manifested equal ability to excel; so that, at commencement, the salutatory oration was assigned to him. After graduating, he taught the Roxbury Grammar School one year. In 1819, he received the appointment of tutor of mathematics in Transylvania University, Lexington, Ky. In 1820, he was made professor of mathematics in place of Professor Bishop, afterwards president of Athen's College, O. In 1823, the death of his father required his presence in the East, and he resigned his professorship. In 1824, he took charge of Middletown Academy, Monmouth county, N.J., where he remained nearly eleven years, except one interval, when he taught a select school in Freehold, the adjoining town. He was there until invited to the city of New York, and appointed principal of the

Mechanics' - Society School; where he remained until 1839, when, in consequence of ill health, he resigned, and removed to the country. In January, 1840, his health being in some degree restored, he assumed the charge of North-Salem Academy, Westchester county, N.Y., where he remained until 1853; when he removed to White Plains, where he passed the remainder of his life, engaged in business as civil engineer and surveyor. He married in Lexington, Ky., 14 March, 1822, Mary Ann Thayer Pike, daughter of Job H. Pike, of Providence, R.I., who derived his descent from Sir George Pike, Bart., of the Isle of Wight. The issue of this marriage was twelve children: viz., 1. John Pike, born at Middletown, N.J., 12 April, 1827; a lawyer at White Plains. 2. Mary Abigail, born at Freehold, N.J., 28 April, 1827; married A. W. Lobdell, of North Salem, in 1860. 3. James Mason, born in Middletown, N.J., in 1831; died in infancy. 4. Emily Maria, born in Middletown, 4 February, 1832. 5. Oliver Richardson, born in Middletown, 20 November, 1833. 6. James Henry, born in New-York city, 15 December, 1835. 7. Caroline Hall, born in New York, 12 February, 1838; died at the age of six months. 8. Caroline Hall, born in North Salem, 27 March, 1840. 9. Horatio Gates, born in North Salem, 12 February, 1842. 10. Everett Lent, born in North Salem, 18 July, 1843; died in infancy. 11. Henry Clay, born in North Salem, 28 November, 1844. 12. George Mead, born in North Salem, 25 June, 1847. His wife survived him.

In a letter to one of his classmates, he says, "As I began to teach before I entered college, and taught every winter- and two summer- vacations while there, and have continued teaching in college or academy ever since, I may take rank among the oldest teachers in the country. There are comparatively few who have taught for thirty-six years continuously. During that period, I have helped to form, or rather to develop, the minds of many who were afterwards distinguished and useful. Several of my early scholars have been members of Congress. I therefore trust I have done some good in my day; and, though I have acquired no great amount of wealth or fame, I have ascertained that a good degree of happiness may exist without either."

At the time of his death, three of his sons were in the army: one a captain, and another a sergeant, in the 25th Connecticut Volunteers, under Banks; and the third, fife-major in the 17th Connecticut Volunteers, under Sigel. The eldest son had been connected with the army for the previous eighteen months, and was about to resume the practice of the law at White Plains.

1823.—CHARLES CARROLL died in Baltimore, Md., December, 1862, aged 61 years. He was son of Charles and Harriett (Chew) Carroll, and was born in Baltimore, Md., 25 July, 1801. His father was born in Annapolis, Md., and was educated in Liege, Europe. His grandfather, Charles Carroll, of Carrollton, was born in Annapolis, 20 September, 1737; died 14 November, 1832, aged 95 years; and was the last survivor of the signers of the Declaration of Independence. Each of the three was named Charles, and each was an only son. The mother of the subject of this notice was a daughter of the chief-justice of the state of Pennsylvania. After going through his preliminary studies at home, he was sent to Mount-St.-Mary's College, near Emmettsburg,—a Roman-Catholic institution in Maryland. He remained there for a year or two; when his grandfather, who superintended his studies, determined to give him the advantages of a European education. In 1817, he was sent to Paris; where, in company with his cousin, Charles Carroll Harper, he entered the college of St. Stanislaus, and remained there three years. After a short tour through Italy and Switzerland, of which he has left a very interesting diary, he returned home, and immediately proceeded to Harvard College; where, in 1821, he entered the sophomore class. [It may not be amiss to mention here, that a large portion of his class became engaged in some disturbances at college only a few weeks before commencement, and were summarily dismissed: among them was Mr. Carroll; and it was not till 1855 that his degree was forwarded to him by the faculty of the college.]

Having thus completed his course at college, he entered the law-office of his uncle, Robert Goodloe Harper (N.J.C. 1785), where he remained two years; and, in 1825, he married Mary Digges Lee, a grand-daughter of Gov. Thomas Simon Lee, of Maryland. In November, 1832, his grandfather, having died, left him his tract of land in Maryland, called Donghoregan Manor, consisting of about twelve thousand acres, together with the care of some two hundred slaves. The estate had become much impoverished; but Mr. Carroll, by devoting his life to the improvement of his property, for his own pleasure and the benefit of his family, succeeded in gathering around him one of the largest and most respectable tenantries in the state, and, by judicious management, increased many fold the productive qualities of the manor-lands.

He always took a very lively interest in the public questions of the day; but the sphere of duties which he had marked out for himself did not incline him to engage in political life. A few years since, he built up and enlarged the old Catholic chapel at the manor, ornamenting it with a marble altar made by the American artist Bartholomew in Rome, and erecting a handsome monument to the memory of his grandfather, whose remains lie there. For some years previous to his death, he had been afflicted with a very severe catarrh, or, as it is called by some, "hay fever." This trouble visited him every autumn, causing great suffering, when finally a disease of the heart became developed, which terminated in dropsy, of which he died. He left a family of six children living, and three grandchildren, representatives of a son who died a few months previous. The "home-quarters" of Donghoregan Manor he devised to his eldest son of Charles Carroll; and all the residue of his property to be divided equally among his children, share and share alike. He survived his wife only three years; she having died at the manor in December, 1859.

Mr. Carroll was greatly endeared to his friends by a remarkably kind and genial nature, which derived a peculiar attraction from the ease and refinement of his manners, and found ample illustration in the liberality with which he ministered the traditional and elegant hospitality of Donghoregan Manor; a virtue which he has transmitted with the inheritance to a most worthy successor in his eldest son, the present proprietor of the old homestead. He was, in its more exalted sense, a gentleman, —

cordial, frank, and honorable in every relation of duty, — a beloved husband and father, a most humane and considerate master of his servants, and a generous and trusty friend. Possessing, by an hereditary necessity, a large number of slaves attached to the manor, he was forced to give much attention to the questions involved in this relation; and no man in Maryland ever brought to it a more liberal and intelligent study: the result was the conclusion which he has expressed in his will, and in conformity with which his whole conduct through life was directed, — a conviction, namely, that this class of dependants was too helpless for freedom without the preliminary nurture and education that alone can make it valuable to its possessor, and that it is one of the highest and most necessary duties of the proprietor to bestow that boon upon the slave before he commits him to the hazards of self-defence. In accordance with this view, Mr. Carroll has enjoined it upon his children to give their attention to this preparation, with the further intimation of his desire that the slaves committed to them shall not pass into bondage to another generation.

1824. — Rev. WILLIAM HAZZARD WIGG BARNWELL died in Germantown, Penn., March, 1863, aged 56 years. His name was originally William Barnwell, but was altered in 1856. He was son of Col. Robert Gibbs and Elizabeth (Wigg) Barnwell, and was born in Beaufort, S.C., 27 July, 1806. He was brother of Hon. Robert Woodward Barnwell (H.C. 1821), who has been senator in Congress from South Carolina. After leaving college, he studied law in Litchfield, Conn., and South Carolina. He was admitted to the bar at Coosawhatchie in 1827. Some time in the month of September, 1831, he experienced a change of heart, relinquished the bar, united himself with the Episcopal church, and began the study of divinity. He was ordained deacon in the Episcopal church in Beaufort, S.C., 14 April, 1833; and, in 1834, was ordained by Bishop Bowen, rector of the Pendleton Church in South Carolina, where he remained six months. He was then called to Charleston, and was instituted rector of St. Peter's Church, which was built for him, and where he continued some twenty years. Then he left, and came north to Philadelphia, where he resided a few years. In 1857, he became insane, and was removed to Germantown, where he died.

He married, 26 November, 1820, his cousin, Catharine Osborn Barnwell, daughter of Edward Barnwell, of Beaufort, S.C., where she was born 27 April, 1809.

1824. — REV. ROBERT BRENT DRANE (name originally Lillbourne Brent Drane) died of yellow-fever in Wilmington, N.C., 16 October, 1862, aged 65 years. He was born in that part of Maryland which is now in the District of Columbia, 9 January, 1797. He was fitted for college at Phillips Academy in Andover, Mass. For a few years after he graduated, he kept a classical school in Salem, Mass. He was settled as an Episcopal clergyman in Hagerstown, Md., where he remained several years. In 1836, he became rector of St. James Church in Wilmington, N.C. In 1843, much to the regret of his parishioners, he took charge of a small college near Louisville, Ky.; but after a few years, at the urgent solicitation of his old parishioners, he returned to Wilmington, where he remained until his death. He was much beloved by his people, and hardly any man could be more self-sacrificing and hard-working than he was. In 1843, he published a brief history of the parish over which he was settled, and which was one of the oldest in the state. In 1844, the honorary degree of doctor of divinity was conferred upon him by South-Carolina College.

When the troubles incident to the last presidential election threatened to destroy the Union, he took firm ground to sustain it; but when these efforts proved unavailing, and the capture of Fort Sumter compelled all to decide for the South or the North, he came out fully and strongly for the former; and, for the last year, hardly a man in the town advocated the doctrine of secession with more force and energy. The most prominent members of his church had long before been ultra secessionists, which may have influenced him in his course. But this great and leading congregation is now nearly broken up: of the young men, a large part have fallen victims to the war; and subsequently the old men and females, with their pastor, fell before the pestilence, and have gone to that bourn from which no traveller returns.

• He married, May, 1828, Augusta Endicott, daughter of Captain Moses and Anna (Towne) Endicott, of Danvers, Mass., where she was born 25 July, 1803; by whom he had two sons, — Robert and Henry, — the former of whom died about three years since. His wife died in Wilmington, 7 July, 1847. He married afterwards a lady of North Carolina.

1829. — Rev. Reuben Bates died in Stowe, Mass., 1 December, 1862, aged 54 years. He was son of Caleb and Mary (Douglas) Bates, and was born in Concord, Mass., 20 May, 1808. He was fitted for college, partly at the Westford and partly at the Groton Academy. Immediately after leaving college, he entered the Divinity School in Cambridge, from which he graduated 18 July, 1832. He was faithful as a student, as he was always faithful in every thing; but his success and usefulness in active life surpassed any expectations his class had formed of him. As he proceeded in his studies in divinity, it became manifest how the heart was quickening the intellect. His first sermon in the theological school was a marked success; not, indeed, on account of any very new or brilliant thoughts; but it was so full of devotion and piety, that it moved all hearts. In him was fulfilled the saying of Scripture, — "His eye was single, and his whole body full of light." For a short time after he left Cambridge, he supplied the pulpit in Saxonville, Mass. He was ordained at New Ipswich, N.H., 1 June, 1834; where he remained until 31 March, 1835, when he was dismissed at his own request. He was installed at Ashby, 13 May, 1835. In February, 1844, he went to Havana, having suffered from an attack of bronchitis. He returned in June, his health having improved. Two months afterwards, his health again failed; and he resigned his pastorate, 31 August, 1845. During the winters of 1845 and 1846, he was representative from Ashby to the state legislature. His health having improved, he was installed in Stowe, 18 June, 1846. In the summer of 1859, his health again compelled him to give up his parish. He continued, however, to reside among his people, taking an active interest in every good work; having charge, as school-committee, of the public schools, and superintending the sunday-schools until within about three months of his decease. Both in Ashby and in Stowe, his labors were rewarded with much fruit of spiritual and moral good. Very modest and unassuming, he was independent and fearless in all his work. He did nothing to be seen of men; but he labored with all earnestness, industry, and self-devotion, and with careful thought and sound judgment, to see how he could do the most good. His people felt the power of a steady and strong influence in favor of rational, practical Christianity; wherein, by work and examples, he was faithful to the end.

He married, 11 February, 1835, Sarah Elizabeth, daughter of Jeremiah Prichard, of New Ipswich, by whom he had two children,—George Prichard, born 7 August, 1836, who is now a clerk in a mercantile house in Boston; Charles Francis, born 31 October, 1840, and died 30 April, 1842. His wife died in Ashby, 10 April, 1842, aged 33 years. He married, for his second wife, 25 November, 1842, Helen T., widow of Clinton Atwater, of Michigan, and daughter of Daniel Tuttle, of Boston; who survives him, and resides in Stowe.

1829.—FREDERICK WILLIAM CROCKER died in Barnstable, Mass., 11 June, 1863, aged 54 years. He was son of David and Rachel (Bacon) Crocker, and was born in Barnstable, 16 April, 1809. He was fitted for college, in part, at the Sandwich Academy, under the instruction of Rev. Warren Goddard (H.C. 1818), and in part at Phillips Academy, Andover. After graduating, he was for seven years in business in Barnstable. In February, 1837, he removed to Boston, and went into the navigation and commission business in company with James Huckins and Zenas D. Bassett. This connection continued two years, when it was dissolved; and he was in business alone until 1842, when he formed a partnership with Dwight Ruggles as booksellers. This continued but one year; and, in 1843, he returned to Barnstable to reside. Inheriting a good estate, he thenceforth took a deep and earnest interest in the improvement of his native town, and identified himself with its social and literary progress. At the third anniversary of the Cape-Cod Association, held in Barnstable, 2 August, 1854, he delivered a humorous and appropriate poem, subsequently printed in the "Yarmouth Register." He was, we believe, a frequent contributor of political and literary articles to the county journals. His "Song for Harvest," written for an agricultural meeting in 1858 (set to the tune of "Old Hundred"), has much of poetic beauty and merit. The annual meetings of his class have been much indebted to him for very racy and witty contributions, as well as for the remarkably kindly and genial spirit which he invariably brought with him. Few of the class possessed more striking characteristics; and very few classes or communities of men can show a more honest and truthful man than Frederick William Crocker. A hearty hater of cant and shams of every description, he knew how to appreciate every sterling and generous characteristic in man; and, to those in whom he could confide, he proved himself a warm and true friend. In 1855, he was appointed, by the Supreme Court of Massachusetts, clerk of the courts for the county of Barnstable. After the amendment of the constitution of the state, requiring election by the people to the county offices, he was elected to the same office with but a single dissenting vote, — a rare instance of almost unanimity.

He married, 6 April, 1851, Louisa G. Sawyer, of Bolton, Mass., by whom he had four children, who, with their mother, survived him.

In this class, the following members had died prior to 1851: viz., Nathaniel F. Derby, of Salem, who died 13 July, 1830; Henry B. McLellan, of Boston, who died 4 September, 1833; Andrew Ritchie, of Boston, who died at Palermo, Sicily, 10 July, 1837; Albert Locke, of Lowell, who died 26 September, 1840; William Emerson Foster, of Boston, who died 23 January, 1843; John Rogers Thurston, who died 23 November, 1843; John Parker Bullard, of Clinton, La., who died 29 January, 1845; Nicholas Devereux, of Salem, who died 2 March, 1848; Solomon Martin Jenkins, of Easton, Md., who died 15 May, 1848; John Hubbard, of South Berwick, Me., who died 3 October, 1848.

1829. — Dr. William Young died in Hingham, Mass., 1 July, 1863, aged 54 years. He was son of Alexander and Mary (Loring) Young, and was born in Boston, 12 January, 1809. He was fitted for college in the Boston Latin School, where a Franklin medal was awarded to him in 1825 for his good scholarship. While in college, he did not associate much with his classmates. After graduating, he studied medicine with Dr. George Cheyne Shattuck (D.C. 1803); and received his degree of M.D. in 1834, when he opened an office in Essex Street, Boston. After a few years, he relinquished the practice of his profession, and removed to Scituate, and subsequently to Hingham, where he remained until his death.

1833. — Col. Fletcher Webster was killed at the second battle of Bull Run, Va., 29 August, 1862, aged 49 years. He was son of Hon. Daniel (D. C. 1801) and Grace (Fletcher) Webster, and was born in Portsmouth, N.H., 23 July, 1813. He was fitted for college at the Boston Latin School. He held a respectable rank of scholarship; and such was his popularity with his associates, that he was chosen class-orator at the conclusion of their collegiate studies. After leaving college, he studied law with his father; was admitted to the Suffolk bar, and practised his profession in Boston. He was private-secretary to his father during a portion of the period when the latter held the office of secretary of state under John Tyler's administration. In 1843, he became secretary of legation under Hon. Caleb Cushing, who was then sent out as minister to China. In 1847, he was representative to the state legislature. In 1850, he was appointed surveyor of the port of Boston; an office which he held until the spring of 1861, when he was removed. Immediately afterwards, on the breaking-out of the war, he proceeded to raise a regiment; which was one of the earliest for the three-years' service. In July of that year, he proceeded to the seat of war; and from that time he was assiduously devoted to the practical duties of the field, sealing and crowning his career by his death in battle. A few weeks previously, he was granted a furlough to return home, and attend the funeral of his youngest daughter, aged thirteen years. He was also ill himself, and needed rest. He was urged to address mass-meetings to aid enlistments in Massachusetts; but his physician forbade the exertion. During the year, he had belonged to the corps of Gen. Banks, whom he highly respected and esteemed; but was subsequently transferred to the corps of Gen. McDowell. He died as the great defender of the Constitution would have been willing to see a son die, — fighting for the defence of the Union.

He married Caroline Story White, daughter of Stephen White, of Salem. The issue of this marriage was four children, — two sons and two daughters, — of whom both of the sons and one daughter, with their mother, survive.

1836. — Grenville Tudor Phillips, of Boston, died at the house of his brother, George William Phillips, in Saugus, Mass., 25 May, 1863, aged 46 years. He was the youngest son of Hon. John (H.C. 1788) and Sally (Walley) Phillips, and was born in Boston, 14 August, 1816. His father, who was son of William and Margaret (Wendell) Phillips, was born in Boston, 26 November, 1770; was an eminent lawyer; was president of the senate of Massachusetts; and was elected, in May, 1822, the first mayor of Boston. He died 29 May, 1823, just at the close of the year of his mayoralty. His mother was daughter of Thomas and Sarah (Hurd) Walley; was born 25 March, 1772; and died 4 November, 1845. He was fitted for college at the Boston Latin School. After leaving college, he studied law in the office of Hon. Peleg Sprague (H.C. 1812) and William Gray (H.C. 1829). He was admitted to the bar in 1839, and began the practice of his profession in Boston. Soon after the death of his mother, he went to Europe, where he remained a few years, and then returned home; but his parents being dead, and the family broken up, he returned to Europe, spent some time in England and in Spain, but made his permanent residence in France, and was absent fifteen years. His death was very sudden, caused by disease of the heart, of which he had previously had one attack. He was never married.

1839. — SAMUEL ELIOT GUILD, of Boston, died at his summer residence at Nahant, 16 July, 1862, aged 42 years. He was son of Benjamin (H.C. 1804) and Eliza (Eliot) Guild, and was born in Boston, 8 October, 1819. He was fitted for college at the private school of Henry Russell Cleveland (H.C. 1827) in Boston. He held a high rank of scholarship in his class, and graduated with distinction. After leaving college, he studied law for some time in the office of William Gray (H.C. 1829), afterwards with Theophilus Parsons (H.C. 1815), of Boston, and completed his studies at the Law School in Cambridge. He was admitted to the Suffolk bar in 1841, and established himself in the practice of his profession in Boston, where he resided until his decease. He was not ambitious of public life, and never held or sought office. In the practice of his profession, he pursued the course which was most congenial to his taste, — a department which, though it does not bring the practitioner conspicuously before the public, opens to him an honorable and useful career. As a chamber-counsel, conveyancer and manager of property, his good sense, his conscientious fidelity to his clients, and his quiet and uniform industry, gave him all the success which his desires coveted or anticipated. He was a gentleman of high moral instincts. He was, in early life, a communicant in the Rev. Dr. Gannett's church, and ever walked worthily of his religious profession. He was ever ready to promote the best interests of the community; kind, charitable, endowed with all the amenities of a gentleman, having a pleasant word for all with whom he might have intercourse.

He married, 9 February, 1847, Elizabeth H., daughter of Henry Gardner Rice (H.C. 1802), of Boston. The issue of this marriage was two children, — a daughter and a son, — who, with their mother, survive.

1842. — Col. WILLIAM LOGAN RODMAN was killed in the attack on Port Hudson, Miss., 27 May, 1863, at the age of 40 years. He was the only son of Benjamin and Susan (Morgan) Rodman, and was born in New Bedford, Mass., 7 March, 1823. He was fitted for college at the Friends' Academy in New Bedford. After graduating, he entered into mercantile business. He visited California during the gold fever, and returned, by way of Calcutta and the overland route, through Europe. He was absent about two years; and with this exception, and his college-life, he was always a resident of New Bedford. He was a member of the common-council of that city in 1852; and, in 1860 and in 1862, represented wards one and two of his native city in the legislature. He enlisted in the service of his country from the purest motives of patriotic duty; relinquishing the blessings of friends and home, and all the attractions which wealth could command, to assume the position of a volunteer captain. He was rapidly promoted to be major and lieutenant-colonel; and was the first officer from New Bedford who had fallen in battle. The illness of Col. Ingraham devolved upon him the command of the regiment during the assault of the 27th and the preceding six-days' fighting, wherein he bore a most gallant part. The "New-Bedford Mercury" thus spoke of this lamented officer: "It is fresh in the memory of every one in this community, with what earnestness and zeal Col. Rodman devoted himself to the successful labor of raising a company of volunteers for the war, at a time when the work of recruiting moved heavily here. His rapid promotion from the captaincy of this company to the position, first of major, and then of lieutenant-colonel, of the regiment, has been justified by the testimony of his superior officers, who have warmly commended the care taken of his men, and, most of all, by his gallant conduct in action, where he proved himself — as his friends knew he would, in the hour of danger — faithful to his duty, a brave soldier. There will be many to mourn for him; remembering how he possessed the fine qualities which mark the gentleman, the generous nature which made him a true friend, and that amiable disposition which endeared him to his family and kindred."

Col. Rodman was never married.

1843. — Rev. Arthur Buckminster Fuller was killed in the battle at Fredericksburg, Va., 12 December, 1862, aged 40 years. He was the third son of Hon. Timothy (H.C. 1801) and Margaret (Crane) Fuller, and was born in Cambridge,

Mass., 10 August, 1822. At the age of twelve, he spent one year at Leicester Academy. He was fitted for college by his sister Margaret (who afterwards married Count Ossoli), at Groton, and Mrs. Ripley, wife of Rev. Samuel Ripley, at Waltham. During his college course, he united with the church connected with the university. Immediately after graduation, he purchased Belvidere Academy, in Belvidere, Boone county, Ill., in which, assisted by a competent corps of instructors, he taught for the two succeeding years. During this time he occasionally preached, as a missionary, in Belvidere and destitute places. He was a member of the Illinois conference of Christian and Unitarian ministers, and by them licensed to preach. His first sermon was preached October, 1843, in Chicago, to the Unitarian church then under the charge of Rev. Joseph Harrington (H.C. 1833). In 1845, he returned to New England; entered, one year in advance, the Cambridge Theological School, where he graduated in 1847. After preaching three months at West Newton, he accepted a call to the pastorate of the Unitarian society in Manchester, N.H., over which he was ordained 29 March, 1848, and remained there a little more than five years, when he resigned his charge, and was installed over the New North Church in Boston, 1 June, 1853. Failing health induced him to resign his city pastorate, and close his labors there, 31 July, 1859. He accepted, however, a call for six months to the charge over the Unitarian church in Watertown, Mass., which was afterwards renewed for an indefinite time. In 1854, he was chaplain of the house of representatives in the legislature; and, in 1850, he was chaplain of the senate. In 1855, he was selected to deliver a bi-centennial oration, by the citizens of Groton, Mass., on the two-hundredth anniversary of the settlement of that town; which he did on the 31st of October of that year. After the war broke out, he determined to devote himself to the cause of his country. He was appointed chaplain in the army, 11 August, 1861; and he then resigned his charge of his society in Watertown. He proceeded to the seat of war, where he continued until his death. At the battle of Fredericksburg, he reported himself to Capt. Dunn, of Company D, Nineteenth

Regiment, whose company was deployed as skirmishers in the principal street, and said he wanted to do something for his country. He took a musket, and in five minutes fell dead, pierced by a rebel ball.

Mr. Fuller was a gentleman of great enthusiasm, an energetic preacher, untiring in the pursuit of the objects at which he arrived; and, in his patriotic zeal in behalf of his country, he sacrificed his life.

He married, 18 September, 1850, Elizabeth G. Davenport, daughter of Joseph G. and Mary H. Davenport, of Andover, Mass. She died 4 March, 1856. He married, for his second wife, 28 September, 1859, Emma Lucilla Reeves, who survives him. He left three children.

1843. — Seth Webb died in Scituate, Mass., 31 August, 1862, aged 39 years. He was son of Seth and Eliza (Dunbar) Webb, and was born in Scituate, 14 February, 1823. He was prepared for college, partly at a private school in Hingham, Mass.; partly at the academy in Bridgewater; and from May, 1837, to August, 1839, at Phillips Academy in Exeter, N.H. He held a distinguished rank of scholarship in his class. After leaving college, he passed the time from November, 1843, to June, 1844, in travelling; having gone to New Orleans, Jamaica, and Cuba, back to New Orleans, up the river to Cincinnati, and through the country home. He then pursued the study of the law in the office of Hon. George Tyler Bigelow (H.C. 1829) and Manlius Stimson Clarke (H.C. 1837), and afterwards with Hon. Charles Greely Loring (H.C. 1812). He was admitted to the Suffolk bar in Boston, at the July term of the Court of Common Pleas; and 1 October, 1845, went into practice with O. Z. Chapman, Esq., the partnership continuing until 1848. From January, 1847, to the autumn of 1848, he kept a law-office also in Brighton, Mass., where he resided most of the time. In the fall of 1848, he gave up his Brighton office and his connection with Mr. Chapman. He then opened an office in Boston, which he continued until 1 May, 1851, when he went into partnership in Boston with Charles Gideon Davis (H.C. 1840), under the firm of Davis and Webb.

In 1858, he removed to New York, where he was admitted to the bar, and practised there during that and the following year. He then returned, and practised a short time in his native place (Scituate), until he gave up his profession on account of ill health. In July, 1861, he was appointed United-States commercial agent at Port-au-Prince, in Hayti; whither he repaired, and remained, until, on account of serious illness, he got leave of absence, and returned to his native place, where he died, after a long illness, of consumption.

He married, in Boston, 18 November, 1852, Helen Gibbons, daughter of George M. and Mary D. (Billings) Gibbons (having been changed from Gibbens, which was the original name). They had no children. His wife died very suddenly, 16 June, 1858.

1847. — George Andrews died in Salem, Mass., 26 August, 1862, aged 38 years. He was son of John Hancock and Nancy (Page) Andrews, and was born in Salem, 13 March, 1824. His father was a merchant of Salem, and died some years since. His mother was daughter of Samuel Page, of Danvers, and Rebecca (Putnam) Page, of Sterling, and was a direct descendant of Gen. Israel Putnam. He was fitted for college at the Salem public Latin School, under the instruction of Oliver Carlton (D.C. 1824). After leaving college, he studied law in the office of Hon. Asahel Huntington, of Salem (Y.C. 1819); and was admitted to the Essex bar in due course. He practised his profession in Salem during his life. He was a representative from Salem to the legislature in 1858; was for many years a member of the school-committee, a justice of the peace and quorum, a special-justice of the Salem Police Court, a member of the Essex Institute, a trustee of the Salem Athenæum, a trustee, secretary, and treasurer of the Plummer Farm School, and vice-president of the Salem Lyceum. In his death, his native city lost a conscientious, faithful, upright man. By his will, in addition to several private legacies, he bequeathed to the city of Salem $1,500, the income of which is to be given to the high-school scholars most distinguished, not for scholarship only, but for faithful and correct deportment. If this disposition of the fund is refused by the school-committee, it is then to be appropriated to furnish fuel for poor and destitute families; $300 to the Salem Marine Society; $500 to the Seaman's Widow and Orphan Association; $500 to the Seaman's Orphan and Children's Friend Society; $500 to the Essex Institute; $100 to the Fraternity of Odd Fellows.

He was never married.

1848.—John Franklin Goodrich died of brain-fever, in the rear of Vicksburg, Miss., 4 June, 1863, aged 36 years. He was son of Allen and Mary (Emerson) Goodrich, and was born in Mount Vernon, N.H., 13 August, 1826. He was fitted for college by the wife of Rev. Samuel Ripley, of Waltham, Mass. After graduating, he was employed as a clerk, one year, in one of the manufacturing companies in Waltham. He then went to California, where he remained five years; and on his return settled in Epworth, Dubuque county, Io. When the rebellion broke out, he felt it his duty to enlist; and went into camp in Iowa, 15 September, as a private in the Twenty-first Regiment, for three years. He was always in the advance in every engagement, and was the first to enter the rifle-pits in the charge of Black River; and was in the thickest of the fight in the attempt to carry Vicksburg by storm, in which his company lost thirty-three men in killed, wounded, and missing. He was in ill health when he went into this, his last battle; and, though he came out unharmed, he was immediately taken with a fever, which, together with the previous severe marching and fighting, terminated fatally. Among his classmates, he was always considered as modest, unpretending, intimate with but few of them, leading a religious life; and at a meeting of his class, several years after he left college, he was duly remembered, with a wish that he might become as rich as he was good.

He married, 12 September, 1857, Marion Pratt, of Iowa, whose parents were originally from Connecticut. The issue of this marriage was three children,—two sons and one daughter,—who, with their mother, survive him.

1848.—Col. William Oliver Stevens died from injuries received in the battle near Chancellorsville, Va., 5 May,

1863, aged 36 years. He was son of William (H.C. 1819) and Eliza Leach (Watson) Stevens, and was born in Belfast, Me., 3 February, 1828. His father was born in Andover, Mass., 21 January, 1799; was a lawyer in Andover, but removed to Lawrence, where he now resides; and is judge of the Police Court in that city. His paternal grandfather was a soldier in the revolutionary war, and was in the battle of Bunker Hill. His mother was born in Boston, 22 March, 1802; was daughter of George and Eliza Watson, and grand-daughter of John Watson, of Clark's Island, Plymouth, formerly president of the Pilgrim Society. The subject of this notice was fitted for college at Phillips Academy, Andover. After graduating, he studied law, during a year and a half, with his father, and, for a year and a half afterwards, with Hon. Thomas Wright (H.C. 1842), of Lawrence. He practised his profession, with much success, at Newmansville, Fla., for ten months, but was obliged to leave on account of the debilitating influence of the climate. He was summoned on one occasion, at midnight, to the prison grates, as counsel for a man who had just been committed on a charge of murder. A hideous countenance met his glance through the grates; and, upon his asking the name of his client, the answer was, "William Stevens!" In 1852, he went into the practice of his profession in Dunkirk, N.Y. In 1859, he was elected, by a very flattering vote, district attorney of Chatauque county, in which Dunkirk is situated; filled the office for two years, to the great acceptance of the bench, the bar, and the whole people; and resigned the unexpired term of three years for the military service of his country, in the spring of 1861. He married, 23 May, 1855, Virginia I. Grosvenor, daughter of Hon. Godfrey Grosvenor, of Geneva, N.Y. By this marriage he had two sons, — George Watson, seven years of age at the time of his father's death, and William Grosvenor, twenty months; and one daughter, who died in infancy.

Col. Stevens joined the Excelsior Brigade, at Staten Island, N.Y., as captain of a company raised in Dunkirk; was elected major before leaving Staten Island; took a conspicuous part in the battles of Williamsburg, — where he was slightly wounded, and where his regiment lost over two hundred men, — of Fair Oaks, of White-oak Swamp, and Malvern Hill; losing in the last-named battle sixty-one out of three hundred men. He was commissioned colonel of the Third Excelsior Regiment on the 10th of October, 1862; his commission dating from 6 September. His regiment was attached to the Third Army Corps, under Gen. Sickles. He led it at the bloody battle of Chancellorsville, on Sunday, the 3d of May, 1863. The battle began at daylight. His horse was shot under him at about six o'clock; after which he headed his regiment on foot. At about half-past seven he received a mortal wound, from a minie ball, through his chest. A captain and two privates of his regiment were in the act of raising him to carry him from the field, when the officer was shot. A private received his sword, with the injunction, "Carry it to my wife; remember me to my boy." He was conveyed to a hospital within the rebel lines, about a mile from the Chancellor House, where he was kindly cared for by our own surgeons and by the enemy, bearing his sufferings without a murmur or a groan; during most of the time speaking with cheerfulness and hopefulness; and, during his moments of delirium, speaking as to his command, "Forward, men! steady!" He died, without a struggle, at eight o'clock on Tuesday evening, 5 May. Immediately after the fall of Col. Stevens, a flag of truce was sent into the enemy's lines to recover him; but Gen. Lee would not receive it. The general in immediate command of the Excelsior Brigade on that day, in writing to a friend in Boston, said, "The Excelsior did splendidly, and lost heavily; but no one is to be so much regretted as Col. Stevens, who was killed in my sight. He was truly a splendid officer, and magnificently brave; in fact, too good a man to be a soldier, and food for powder: for he was a fine lawyer, and has left an interesting wife and boys. It was the most terrific fight I have ever passed through."

Dr. Butler, a surgeon in the rebel army, told the father of Col. Stevens, who went within their lines to recover his son's body, and who remained there ten hours, that the appearance and bearing of Col. Stevens were so attractive and soldierly, that he called several officers of the confederate army to his room, to witness his manly beauty and demeanor. Rev. George Patterson, chaplain of the Third North-Carolina Volunteers (rebel), finding him in a room with fourteen other wounded men, was attracted to his person, procured for him a bed and a private room: for thirty-six hours he watched over him as his own father, washed his body, bathed his temples, gave him medicine and nourishment; spoke with him of his wife, his boys, his parents, and his friends, and commended him in prayer to God; closed his eyes in death; caused him, after death, to be dressed in his own uniform; took from his neck the locket of his wife; his money, bills, and change from his pocket, with all his private papers; folded them in an envelope, and caused them to be sent to his wife. This chaplain said to our informant, "I was born in Boston. My father was a Greek: my mother, if alive, resides in Raynham, Mass. Go and see her; tell her of her son; for she does not know that I am alive."

Soon after he was carried into the hospital, Col. Stevens was asked by the surgeon in attendance, "What regiment do you belong to?" The reply was, "The Excelsior."—"Does that regiment belong to the Eleventh Corps?"—"No, sir," was the emphatic reply: "my corps never runs from the enemy!"

Upon the death of Col. Stevens, resolutions, in the highest degree honorable to his fame as a soldier, a lawyer, a citizen, as a man, were adopted by the officers of the Excelsior Brigade, by the Supreme Court of New York in Chatauque county, by the members of the bar, and by the citizens of Dunkirk.

1849.—JOHN PEGRAM MAY was killed in the second battle of Bull Run, Va., 29 August, 1862, aged 31 years. He was son of David May, of Petersburg, Va., and Maria W. Pegram, of Booneville, Va.; and was born in Petersburg, 18 November, 1829, the oldest of five boys and two girls. He was married, 15 May, 1850, in the First Presbyterian Church in Petersburg, by Rev. A. B. Van Zandt, to Mary Dandridge, daughter of the late Nathaniel Hanna, M.D. He was killed while in the rebel service.

1850. — Henry Edson Hersey died in Hingham, Mass., 24 February, 1863, aged 32 years. He was son of Capt. Stephen and Maria (Lincoln) Hersey, and was born in Hingham, 28 May, 1830. His father, who was son of Jonathan and Ruth (Nichols) Hersey, was born in Hingham, 3 September, 1797. He was a shipmaster, and was lost at sea, having sailed on a voyage several years ago, and the vessel never being heard of afterwards. His mother was daughter of Welcome and Susanna (Gill) Lincoln, and was born in Hingham, 16 September, 1806, where she still resides. The subject of this notice early manifested a scholarly taste; and, after going through the customary course of instruction provided by the public schools of his native town, he was fitted for college at Derby Academy in Hingham, under the tuition of Luther Barker Lincoln (H.C. 1822). He entered the sophomore class in 1847, in which he at once took a high rank, and won the esteem of his associates, both by his attainments as a scholar, and his demeanor as a gentleman. At commencement, the salutatory oration was assigned to him. After leaving college, he was employed as a private teacher in Charlestown, N.H.; studying law, at the same time, in the office of Hon. Edmund Lambert Cushing (H.C. 1827). He afterwards continued his professional studies in Boston in the office of Hon. Peleg Whitman Chandler (Bowd. C. 1834), and then completed his preparatory course in the office of Judge John Phelps Putnam (Y.C. 1837). He was admitted to the Suffolk bar in September, 1854, and entered upon the practice of his profession in Boston; opening an office also in his native town, which he made his place of residence. Soon after establishing himself in business, he began to be honored with important and responsible trusts by his townspeople. He was repeatedly chosen a member of the school-committee, in which capacity he rendered much efficient and valuable service. He was one of the trustees of Derby Academy, and in that office his fine scholarship and his zeal in promoting the work of sound and liberal culture were exerted in a way that was creditable to himself, acceptable to his colleagues, and satisfactory to the public. For several years he was superintendent of the First-Parish Sunday School. By a diligent use of his talents, and faithful attention to business, he had put himself in a way to obtain a successful practice. The future was looking fair and promising, when his health began to fail, and, sadly to his disappointment, in the fall of 1861, he was obliged to relinquish the duties of his profession; and he made a voyage across the Atlantic, accompanied by his wife, and passed some months in Spain and the south of France. Soon after his return, in the summer of 1862, it became evident his health was not materially improved; and, after remaining a short time in Hingham, he sought the relief which he hoped the climate of New Hampshire might afford. There he remained a few months, when his vital energies had become so exhausted, that he once more returned to the quiet repose and loving care of home. Here the slow wasting of consumption terminated in his decease at his mother's residence.

He married, 20 March, 1856, Catharine, only daughter of Col. H. H. Sylvester, of Charlestown, N.H.

1851. — WILLIAM NYE DAVIS, of Boston, died in Nice, France, 24 February, 1863, aged 32 years. He was son of John Watson (H.C. 1810) and Susan Holden (Tallman) Davis, and was born in Boston, 2 December, 1830. He began his preparatory studies for college at the Boston Latin School, where he remained nearly five years, leaving in the spring of 1847, when he became a pupil of Shattuck Hartwell (H.C. 1844), who was at that time a tutor in college, with whom he continued until he entered the freshman class at the beginning of the second term, February, 1848. After graduating, he began the study of law in the Law School in Cambridge, and completed his studies under the instruction of William Howard Gardiner (H.C. 1816), of Boston. On his admission to the Suffolk bar, he established himself in the practice of his profession in Boston.

He married, 24 March, 1856, Mary C., daughter of William Howard Gardiner, of Boston. They had no children. In 1860, on account of pulmonary affection, he went to France, accompanied by his wife, for the benefit of his health. While residing in Nice, he met with a most heartrending affliction, on the 8th or 9th of February, 1863, by the sudden death of his wife, caused by her clothes accidentally taking fire. This sad event completely overcame him. He was soon afterwards attacked twice by severe hemorrhage from the lungs, and survived his wife only about two weeks.

1851.—Major WILLIAM DWIGHT SEDGWICK died at Keedysville, Md., 30 September, 1862, of wounds received at the battle of Antietam, 17th of the same month, aged 31 years. He was the only son of Charles and Elizabeth (Dwight) Sedgwick, and was born in Lenox, Mass., 27 June, 1831. At the age of fourteen years, his father sent him to Illinois, where he spent a summer with a farmer, who was a relative, and who then lived in a log-house; where he learned and performed every kind of farm-work of which a boy of that age is capable. His father believed, that, without some personal knowledge and expeperience of labor, he could not have a proper sympathy with laboring men. He spent one year at a French school in New York, and one in a boys' school taught by Rev. Samuel P. Parker (H.C. 1824) in Stockbridge, Mass.; and pursued the studies preparatory to admission into college under the instruction of his mother, and at the academy in Lenox. After leaving college, he spent a winter in a law-office; then went abroad, and studied a portion of his professsion, first in the University of Göttingen, and then in that of Breslau. He was abroad about seventeen months. Soon after his return, he entered the Cambridge Law School, where he remained a year, and then established himself as a lawyer in St. Louis, Mo. After the breaking-out of the war, he forsook his profession, and was commissioned as a lieutenant in the Second Massachusetts Regiment. He went into the service with the regiment; was made ordnance-officer of Gen. Banks's corps; and was soon promoted to the rank of major on the staff of his kinsman, Gen. Sedgwick, with many and weighty duties faithfully discharged. All through the fearful battles before Richmond, he went with little food, almost without sleep, for days, worn down with fatigue and exhaustion, fighting at every step, and winning the praise of his chief. In the great battle of Antietam, while attempting to rally and re-form a regiment in some disorder, he received a fatal wound. Seven hours and a half — from half-past eight in the morning until half-past three in the afternoon — he lay on the hard ploughed ground; while the shells, the cannon-balls, and the bullets of the foe were showering over and around him. As he was lying there, his body from his waist to his feet paralyzed, and unable to move, he felt for his diary, and wrote in it a few modest, manly words, "Say that he tried to do his duty;" and making some suggestions in behalf of his family. At the close of a long letter, in which he gave his share of the dreadful news and sufferings of the retreat from before Richmond, he said, "My country is welcome to every drop of my blood." He was fully persuaded that the war would be fruitless, comparatively, unless slavery were completely eradicated; and said, "I love my wife and children as well as any man; but I would engage never to see them again, if thereby I could secure the eradication of slavery."

He married in 1857, at Hanover, Germany, Louisa Frederica Tellkampf, daughter of Professor Adolf Tellkampf, of that place. He left three little girls, the youngest of whom he never saw. She was born in July, 1861, after he had enlisted in the army, and bidden what proved to be his last farewell.

1851. — Rev. THEODORE TEBBETS died in New-York city, 29 January, 1863, aged 31 years. He was son of Hon. Noah (Bowd. C. 1822) and Mary Esther (Woodman) Tebbets, and was born in Parsonsfield, Me., 1 April, 1831. His father, the son of James (a blacksmith) and Mary (Nutter) Tebbets, was born in Rochester, N.H., 26 December, 1802; was a lawyer and circuit-judge of the Court of Common Pleas of New Hampshire; and moved from Parsonsfield to Rochester, in November, 1834 or 1835, where he died 9 September, 1844. His mother was daughter of Jeremiah Hall (D.C. 1794), a lawyer of Portsmouth, N.H., and Sarah (Chase) Woodman; was born in Portsmouth, 12 January, 1808; and was grand-daughter of Stephen Chase (H.C. 1764), a merchant of Portsmouth. In May, 1845, the subject of this notice went to Parsonsfield to live on a farm; and in the following August left, and entered

Phillips Academy in Exeter, N.H. In August, 1847, he entered Bowdoin College, but returned to Exeter to fit for admission, a year in advance, at Harvard, as all his friends went to Cambridge. He procured a dismission from Bowdoin, and entered the sophomore class of Harvard, in August, 1848. Being entirely without property, he was supported by his own exertions, and by the funds for assisting poor students at Exeter and Cambridge. He taught school, in the winter of 1847–8, in Rochester, N.H. He attained a high rank of scholarship in college. He took the first Bowdoin prize for English composition, in the senior year, for a dissertation on "The Characteristics of a Philosophical History;" also the prize for Latin prose composition, for a dissertation, "De Sepulchris Etruscis;" and, at commencement, the fifth English oration was assigned to him. After graduating, he entered the Divinity School at Cambridge, where he remained till February, 1852. From March, 1852, to July, 1853, he was teacher of the ancient languages in Exeter Academy; and from October, 1854, to July, 1855, was proctor in college. He was ordained as pastor of the Smith Unitarian Church in Lowell, as successor of Rev. Henry A. Miles (B.U. 1829), 19 September, 1857. He preached two Sundays, and was taken with a typhoid-fever, from which he did not recover entirely for a year. He resigned his pastorate in May, 1856, and spent the summer at the Isle of Shoals. In January, 1857, he received a call from the First Parish in Medford, as successor of Rev. John Pierpont; and was installed 15 April, 1857. In the autumn of 1858, he was attacked with symptoms of pulmonary disease, which resulted in a slight hemorrhage in February, 1859: he had preached in the mean while, with the exception of one Sunday. He left New York for the South, 14 February, 1859, and spent the winter in Savannah and Florida; but returned in the spring, and resumed preaching. He preached three half-days, and then was attacked with a severe hemorrhage from the lungs; went to the Isle of Shoals, 1 August, where he remained till 18 November, gaining health and strength. He went to Savannah again, 14 January, 1860; and thence to Florida, where he remained till 3 May; thence to Savannah, and returned to Medford. Finding the life of a minister was out of the question, he sent in a peremptory resignation ; preached for the last time, 12 July ; and his resignation was accepted 1 August, 1859.

He afterwards went into business as a coal-dealer in Boston, and opened an office at No. 3, Merchants' Exchange ; but was soon afterwards obliged to relinquish it on account of his health. The closing years of his life tested and testified to the strength of his religious faith. With unsurpassed patience, a patience that veiled itself with cheerfulness, asking neither for sympathy nor pity, he submitted to the loss of all his most cherished pursuits. Not only the profession he so loved, but all study and continuous effort, must be relinquished ; and yet no one ever heard him refer to baffled hopes, or indicate that he was peculiarly unfortunate. His faith in the all-wise Father was the pillar of fire through the darkness.

His printed works were several articles in the "Monthly Religious Magazine ;" also a sermon in the same magazine for May, 1858, on "The Revival ;" "A Memoir of the late Judge Tebbets, of New Hampshire ;" "A Memoir of William Gibbons."

He married, 3 June, 1857, Ellen Sever, daughter of Col. John and Anna Dana Sever, of Kingston, Mass. They had one son, John Sever, born 4 July, 1858.

1852.—Dr. Samuel Foster Haven was killed at the battle of Fredericksburg, 13 December, 1862, aged 30 years. He was the only son of Samuel Foster (H.C. 1826) and Lydia Gibbon (Sears) Haven, and was born at the house of his grandfather, Hon. Samuel Haven (H.C. 1789), in Dedham, Mass., 20 May, 1831. In August of the same year, he went with his parents to live in Dracut, Mass., where they resided a little more than one year. They then removed to Lowell, where his father practised law. After living there three years, he spent the winter of 1835-6 in Dedham. In April, 1836, he was sent to Salem to live with a private family. About a year afterwards, he returned to Dedham ; and soon afterwards went to a boarding-school in Needham, where he remained three years.

In 1839, he went to live in Worcester with his father, who had removed thither in 1837, where he now resides, and holds the office of librarian of the Antiquarian Society. The subject of this notice was fitted for college at the Worcester High School.

In January, 1853, he began his medical studies in the office of Dr. Henry Sargent, of Worcester; and was next in the Medical School at Boston. The last year of his studies, he had the appointment of house pupil at the Massachusetts General Hospital. He graduated at the Medical College, 7 March, 1855; and, the same year, he was admitted a member of the Massachusetts Medical Society. In the summer of the same year, he went abroad for professional improvement, with particular reference to the department of ophthalmology. He spent a winter in Paris, and passed the following year partly at Vienna and partly at Berlin. On his return to Boston, he took an office in Asylum Street; but, in the spring of 1858, he removed to Worcester, where he proposed to attend chiefly to diseases of the eye. At the beginning of the war, he immediately offered to enter the service; and, when the Fifteenth Massachusetts Regiment was organized, he joined it as assistant-surgeon. The illness and absence of the senior-surgeon left him alone in the medical care of the regiment for many months; and, on the ultimate retirement of that officer, he was commissioned in his place. During the whole of his service, he devoted all his energies to the discharge of his duties, and never left his post for rest or recreation. Believing it to be his duty to be where he could render instant aid to the wounded, he always accompanied his regiment into battle, entirely regardless of personal exposure. When his regiment went into the engagement at Fredericksburg, where he lost his life, he was remonstrated with by the medical director of the division for wanting to go with them, and ordered to report himself at the hospital; but his desire to be with the men was so urgent, that he was permitted to accompany them: and he was killed by a shell, while marching by the side of the color-bearer, 13 December, 1862.

He had neither the faculty nor disposition for slighting any part of his duty; and, whatever he undertook to do, his nature required him to do earnestly and thoroughly. By his presence in the midst of the conflicts, he is said, by an officer, to have saved lives that must otherwise have been lost for want of immediate attention; and the consciousness of such a possibility, in his judgment, not only justified, but demanded, the personal exposure of the surgeon to the same risks that were encountered by the men. He was a careful student, and fond of literary and scientific research. Two of his essays were printed; one on "Intestinal Obstructions," and one on "Cysterci within the Eye." When he entered the army, he had nearly ready for the press a chronological catalogue of books and pamphlets printed in this country from its settlement to the period of the revolution, with an introductory chapter. This was a continuation and extension of a list which was begun by Isaiah Thomas, the author of the "History of Printing in America," but never completed, or arranged from the materials he had gathered. He was in the battles of Ball's Bluff, Yorktown, Fair Oaks, Savage's Station, the seven-days' fighting on the retreat to Harrison's Landing, Antietam (where his regiment was very badly cut to pieces), and the first battle of Fredericksburg.

1852. — Capt. William Duncan McKim was killed in the rebel service in the battle of Chancellorsville, 3 May, 1863, aged 30 years. He was son of William and Margaret D. (Hollins) McKim, and was born in Baltimore, Md., 27 June, 1832. His father was son of William Duncan and Susan (Haslett, of the Eastern Shore of Maryland) McKim, and was born 21 December, 1808; is a banker in Baltimore; one of their most esteemed citizens and straight-out union-men. His mother was daughter of John Smith and Rebecca (Dugan) Hollins, and was born in Baltimore, April, 1810. The subject of this notice always lived in Baltimore; was fitted for college by Michael R. McNally, and entered at the beginning of the second term of the sophomore year.

1852. — Col. Paul Joseph Revere died of wounds received in the battle of Gettysburg, Penn., 4 July, 1863, aged 30 years. He was son of Joseph Warren and Mary (Robbins) Revere, and was born in Boston, 10 September, 1832. His father was son of Paul Revere of revolutionary history, who changed his name from Revoir. Paul's father's name was Apollos; was born in France; went to the Isle of Guernsey when young; and his father, Simeon, was obliged to leave the country at the revocation of the edict of Nantes. The mother of the subject of this notice was a daughter of Judge Edward Hutchinson Robbins (H.C. 1775), of Milton. In 1839, young Revere went to Milton Academy, where he remained four years under Mr. Marsh; then went about a year and a half to the Boston Latin School; then about a year to Rev. Samuel Ripley (H.C. 1804), of Waltham; then about a year to Mr. William Hathorne Brooks (H.C. 1827), of Boston; then to Dr. W. A. Davis, of Dorchester, previously of Roxbury; then, about six months before entering the sophomore class, was with John Brooks Felton (H.C. 1847), in Cambridge. He did not study any profession after leaving college. When the war broke out, he volunteered his services in behalf of his country. He was commissioned major in the Twentieth Regiment of Volunteers; was in the battle of Ball's Bluff, where he was taken prisoner, carried to Richmond, and kept in close confinement for several months; being one of the officers held by the rebels as hostages for the rebel privateersmen. After his exchange, he was promoted to be colonel of the Twentieth Regiment.

He married, 17 March, 1859, Lucretia Watson, daughter of Rev. William Parsons Lunt (H.C. 1823), of Quincy. The issue of this marriage was two children, — one son and one daughter, — who, with their mother, survive him.

1852. — Dr. Robert Ware died in Washington, N.C., 10 April, 1863, aged 29 years. He was son of Dr. John (H.C. 1813) and Helen (Lincoln) Ware, and was born in Boston, 2 September, 1833. He was fitted for college at the Boston Latin School. On leaving college, he determined to enter the medical profession. He began his studies under the instruction of his father, with whom he continued until May, 1854; when he went to Europe, where he remained until September, 1855, spending about six months of the time in Paris, studying in the French hospitals. On his return, he continued his studies with his father, and graduated at the Medical School in 1856, when he began the practice of his profession in Boston. In July, 1857, he was appointed one of the district physicians of the Boston Dispensary. He was remarkably successful in his practice; which increased rapidly, as his father was intending to relinquish the profession to his son. On the breaking-out of the war, he was one of the first physicians to enter the service of the Sanitary Commission, and continued in its service until the close of the Peninsula campaign in Virginia. He was subsequently appointed surgeon of the Forty-fourth Massachusetts Regiment, with which he left for the seat of war. On his arrival in North Carolina, his arduous labors and exposures to the unhealthy climate brought on a fever, of which he died, after a few days' illness. Such is the brief record of a life of stainless virtue, and of modest, wise, and effective devotion to the public service. His manly, thoughtful, earnest simplicity indicated all the ancestral virtues that were shining in his character. Few gave such promise of eminence in his profession. But one so wise, so virtuous, was well prepared to sacrifice his life in the service of his country.

He was never married.

1852. — Major Sidney Willard was killed in the battle of Fredericksburg, Va., 14 December, 1862, aged 31 years. He was son of Joseph (H.C. 1816) and Susannah Hicklin (Lewis) Willard, and was born in Lancaster, Mass., 3 February, 1831. In 1831, he, with his parents, removed to Boston, which was his subsequent residence. He was fitted for college at the Boston Latin School. While an undergraduate, he was a diligent student, and held a respectable rank in his class. In his junior year, he taught school, during the winter vacation, in Deerfield, Mass. He was distinguished for his athletic powers and his invincible courage. After graduating, he entered the Harvard Law School, and remained there a little more than one term. From April, 1853, to May, 1854, he was teaching in Charlestown, N.H., and at the same time studying law in the office of Judges Cushing and Gilchrist. In June, 1854, he entered the office of Hon. Charles Greely Loring (H.C. 1812), of Boston.

He was admitted to the bar, 19 April, 1856. In July, 1856, he went to the West, and returned to Boston, after an absence of about three months. In October, 1856, he opened an office in Court Street, where he remained until he left for the seat of war. His moral character was irreproachable. From moral conviction, he was strongly antislavery in his principles. From 1854, besides being occupied by his profession, he was more or less engaged in giving instruction to private pupils. He wrote an article entitled "A Night in a Wherry," which was published in the "Atlantic Monthly" for October, strongly indicative of his insensibility to fear. In the summer of 1862, he determined to devote himself to the service of his country; and, having a taste for the military art, was commissioned as a major of the Thirty-fifth Regiment of the Massachusetts troops. He was employed for some time before his departure in drilling soldiers, at which he was very expert.

He married, 21 August, 1862, Sarah Ripley, daughter of Augustus Henry Fiske (H.C. 1825), of Boston; and left the next day, with his regiment, for the seat of war; bidding, sad to say, a last farewell to his newly married wife.

1853.—Lieut.-Col. Wilder Dwight died in a hospital, near Boonesborough, Md., 19 September, 1862, of wounds received in the battle of Antietam. He was son of William (H.C. 1825) and Elizabeth Amelia (White) Dwight, and was born in Springfield, Mass., 23 April, 1833. His father was son of Hon. Jonathan Dwight (H.C. 1793); was born in Springfield, 5 April, 1805; and was a lawyer in that place; but subsequently removed to Boston, where he engaged in manufactures, residing in Brookline. His mother was a daughter of the late Hon. Daniel Appleton White (H.C. 1797), and was born in Salem, Mass., 4 August, 1809.

He was fitted for college at Phillips Academy in Exeter, N.H. He attained a distinguished rank of scholarship in his class, and graduated with high honors. Immediately after graduating, he entered the Law School at Cambridge, where he gained the first prize in 1855. He then visited Europe, where he spent fifteen months, travelling through Spain, in company with Hon. Millard Fillmore. On his return, he pursued his law-studies in the office of Hon. Caleb Cushing (H.C. 1817), the attorney-general of the United States; and in that of Hon. Ebenezer Rockwood Hoar (H.C. 1835), and Horace Gray, jun., Esq. (H.C. 1845). He was admited to the bar in 1856, and began practice in Boston in 1858, where he soon gave promise of future eminence in his profession; and no man of his age had a higher position at the bar when he left the profession for the field. He had studied law with great assiduity; and his knowledge of the sciences was not only extensive and exact, but also systematic and practical. He frequently, during the four years he was in practice, appeared before the Supreme Court; and many of his arguments there displayed learning, research, and vigorous practical logic, which promised to make him leader of the profession.

When the war broke out, he left his profession to serve his country; and, with Col. Gordon, organized the Second Massachusetts Regiment; one of the first two regiments which entered the field under the President's original call for three-years' men. In the summer of 1861, he was commissioned as major, and served through the laborious campaign on the Potomac. The Second Massachusetts, under Col. Gordon, covered the disastrous retreat of Gen. Banks down the Shenandoah. At Winchester, after a display of individual courage and admirable presence of mind, he was taken prisoner, but was immediately paroled. When Col. Gordon, for his distinguished services, was promoted to the rank of brigadier-general, Major Dwight became lieutenant-colonel of the regiment. After his exchange, he returned to active service; and in the battle of Antietam, 16 September, 1862, received his mortal wound. He was distinguished for singular independence of character. His thought was clear and well defined, his statements lucid, his convictions strong. The same rare traits adorned his short professional career; and, seconded by other shining qualities, enabled him to achieve a reputation, as a military officer, beyond that of most civilians. His clearness of insight, his promptness of execution, his decision of character, his insensibility to fear, and his dignified familiarity, won the confidence, the admiration, and the love of his command.

1854. — Capt. Richard Chapman Goodwin was killed in the battle at Cedar Mountain, Va., 9 August, 1862, at the age of 28 years. He was the oldest son of Ozias and Lucy N. (Chapman) Goodwin, and was born in Boston, 11 October, 1833. He went to a private school in Boston until 1845, and then entered the Latin school, where he was fitted for college. After graduating, he determined to pursue the mercantile profession; and in August, 1854, he entered the counting-room of William Story Bullard, of Boston; but soon afterwards went abroad, where he spent several years in foreign travel, and returned in 1858. In 1861, immediately after the breaking-out of the rebellion, he raised a company of Massachusetts volunteers, of which he was appointed captain; and was attached, as Company K, to the Second Regiment, under Col. George H. Gordon.

1854. — Edmund Rhett died in Spartansburg, S.C., 15 February, 1863, aged 29 years. He was son of Hon. Robert Barnwell and Elizabeth (Burnet) Rhett, and was born in Charleston, S.C., 19 November, 1833. His time, before entering college, was passed between Washington, Charleston, and his father's plantation on the Ashepoo River. He returned from Washington in 1848; when his father resigned the seat he had held in the lower house for about thirteen years. He entered the sophomore class of the South-Carolina College in 1850; took an honorable dismission, with one hundred and ten others, in December, 1852, on account of certain differences which arose between the students and the college-government; and entered, in March, 1853, the junior class, half advanced, at Harvard. In alluding to himself, he said, when in college, "As my first appearance in this world of jests was amidst the disturbances of nullification in South Carolina, so probably will my life continue through a series of political struggles and commotions only; but the last act which it shall witness will be more effective, and more finally decisive for the maintenance of the integrity of my state, than the first."

He afterwards studied law in Charleston, and intended to practise in California; but he afterwards became assistant-editor of the "Charleston Mercury," of which paper his father was proprietor.

1854. — Lieut.-Col. JAMES SAVAGE died in the hospital in Charlottesville, Va., 22 September, 1862, of wounds received in the battle at Cedar Mountain on the 9th of August, aged 30 years. He was the only son of Hon. James (H.C. 1803) and Elizabeth Otis (Stillman) Savage, and was born in Boston, 21 April, 1832. He was fitted for college at the Boston Latin School, and held a respectable, but not distinguished, rank in his class.

The love of excellence, rather than the ambition to excel, was always a controlling motive in his life and conduct. He secured the respect of his teachers by the correctness and purity of his course, and was much beloved by his classmates for the rare truth and nobleness of his character. He early showed a great love for music; and this, with the study of horticulture, equally an object of his regard, filled all his leisure hours. Soon after leaving college, he went to Europe, where he remained two years, profiting by the instructions of Professor Liebig and others, at Munich and Berlin, in agricultural chemistry, and other departments; visiting, with a student's appreciation, the galleries of art, and cultivating his taste for music. Upon his return, he was undetermined as to the path in life he should take, having no decided taste for either of the so-called learned professions, and having found, by six months' reading of law, that the confinement incident to them was incompatible with his health. With more than common muscular strength and activity, a person manly and vigorous, and presenting all the external aspects of health, his constitution was such as to make sedentary employments pernicious, and much exercise in the open air necessary. Fond of rural employments, of which he had acquired no small knowledge from his studies and observations at home and abroad, and enjoying nature with a poetical enthusiasm, he determined to make agriculture his profession; and, with that view, purchased a small farm in the town of Ashland, where, for two years, he spent most of his time in the practical labors of the husbandman. In the midst of these occupations, he became interested in the great questions of the day, and gave his heartiest sympathy to the cause of human freedom. The strong love of justice inherited from his father, showing itself in indignation against wrong and oppression in every form, was confirmed at this time by his reading and reflection, and prepared him to take an active part in the defence of free principles whenever they were assailed. Following these convictions, as well as his interest in the occasion itself, he attended the meetings in connection with the death of John Brown, held in December, 1860, where he remained through the day, despite the insults of a vulgar and excited mob, and showed then, and on subsequent occasions, his determination, at all personal risks, to protect freedom of discussion, and, as he said, "to give fair play." With these characteristics, it need hardly be said that he responded to the first call of his country for defenders in the field with a deep and earnest enthusiasm. Already, in anticipation of such a call, he had been devoting himself to the practice and study of military tactics as a member of a drill-club, and had shown his superior fitness for the duties of a soldier. With his friends Dwight and Curtis, he worked zealously in organizing the Second Regiment of Massachusetts Volunteers, since so distinguished for its discipline, valor, and sacrifices; and, with his friend and lieutenant, Henry Higginson, recruited the company placed under his command. His regiment left Boston on the 8th of July, 1861. Its subsequent career is part of the history of the country. In all its fortunes, whether successful or adverse, Capt. Savage bore a distinguished part. During fourteen months of his laborious service, he never asked a furlough; nor was he ever absent from his post, except when suffering from a fever contracted on picket-duty on the Potomac. The men under his command were noted for their orderly conduct, as well as for their endurance and unflinching courage in all the trials of camp and march and battle-field. With a heart as tender as it was brave, his profession served to bring out more distinctly the gentle and generous qualities, which, in times of peace, had made him so dear to his kindred and friends. This union of gentleness with the sterner traits of character is illustrated by the incident, that in the Shenandoah campaign, while pursuing a squad of rebel cavalry who had fired on our pickets, he snatched from the ground the first flower of spring, a humble hepatica, as it attracted his attention in the dry oak-leaves, not relaxing for an instant his eager chase. Of his tender thoughtfulness, what more touching evidence could be given than his offering of roses to the dying German bugler of the New-York Eighth, at Winchester, accompanied by kind words in the language that recalled his fatherland?

The following tribute to Col. Savage's worth as a patriot and soldier is copied from the "Boston Daily Advertiser," to which it was contributed by Col. Samuel M. Quincy, soon after the news of Col. Savage's death: —

"Of Col. Savage's life previous to the war, of the services of the regiment to which he belonged, and the manner of his death, others have written. It is my desire simply to bear witness to the estimation in which his character was held, and the appreciation which it received among his fellow-officers. He was universally acknowledged to have entered the service simply and entirely from his sense of duty, and conviction of right. With others, although patriotism was, beyond doubt, the underlying motive, still each man was conscious of a variety of inducements and reasons which influenced his final decision. Not so with Savage: the cause of freedom and right was to be fought for; and, beyond that, he never thought of looking. For his character, as it was developed and brought to our notice by the varied duties and experiences of the campaign, the feeling of admiration was universal. To an almost feminine gentleness and amiability he joined the indomitable energy and resolution which became the man. When, before the regiment had yet been in action, officers around their camp- or picket- fires at night would discuss its probable behavior, there was one universal sentiment; viz., that 'Jim Savage,' at least, would fight, as it was once expressed, 'like Mr. Valiant-for-Truth, until his sword clove to his hand:' and this prediction he well fulfilled at Newtown, Winchester, and Cedar Mountain; on which last disastrous field he fell, struck by two bullets. As he lay on the field, he was found by Capt. Russell, whom he earnestly requested not to remain, but to save himself; which request, it is needless to say, that officer disregarded, though at the expense of his own safety. Col. Savage was taken to Charlottesville, where it is gratifying to think that he found friends, and where, on the 22d of October, 1862, his mortal frame had no longer strength to retain the soul of one of the bravest Christian gentlemen that ever drew sword for the right since the world began. He was the only man ever known to the writer who seemed fully to observe the title given to the model of French knighthood, — *Chevalier sans peur et sans reproche.*"

1856. — Lieut. Stephen George Perkins was killed in the battle at Cedar Mountain, Va., 9 August, 1862, at the age of 26 years. He was son of Stephen H. and Sarah S. (Sullivan) Perkins, and was born in Boston, 18 September, 1835. He was fitted for college partly by Thomas Gamaliel Bradford (H.C. 1822), and partly by William Parsons Atkinson (H.C. 1838). After graduation he travelled in Europe, and returned in October, 1857. He joined the Law School in Cambridge at the March term in 1858; and joined the Scientific School in September, 1859, as a student in mathematics; where he remained until he resolved to devote his services to aid in the preservation of the Union. He received a commission as second-lieutenant in Company H, of the Second Regiment, under Col. George H. Gordon; where he remained, discharging his duty with great ardor, until his life was sacrificed in defending the flag which was so dear to him.

1857. — Capt. Howard Dwight was killed by guerillas 7 May, 1863, at Courtableau, on the Mississippi River, while bearing despatches from his brother, Gen. Dwight, — to whose staff he was attached, — to Gen. Banks. He was son of William (H.C. 1825) and Elizabeth Amelia (White) Dwight, and was born in Springfield, Mass., 29 October, 1837. He was fitted for college at Phillips Academy, Exeter, N.H. After graduating, he went to the West, where he was engaged in business when the war broke out. He immediately enlisted, and devoted what proved to be the remainder of his life to the service of his country. The manner of his death is thus described in a New-Orleans paper: "He left the headquarters of his brother on the morning of the 4th; and, proceeding rapidly along the road from Alexandria to Franklin, on reaching Courtableau, he was hailed by three rebel guerillas. He stopped, and asked them who they were; when they presented their revolvers, and asked him to dismount. As there were three to one, and the captain was unarmed, he was forced to comply; remarking, 'I cannot help myself, and therefore surrender.' But the heartless representatives of the chivalry retorted, 'We don't want a prisoner:' and they immediately fired two shots at him, one of which took effect in his leg; but the other, which proved mortal, passed through his head. The guerillas then left him lying on the road; but the body was watched over by a small boy who had witnessed the cold-blooded transaction, and who afterwards related the circumstances to some of Gen. Dwight's cavalry which happened to pass that way soon after, and found the body."

His genial social qualities, his unflinching bravery, and his sterling character, had endeared him to his fellow-officers; and his death and the manner of it will not be quickly forgotten.

A meeting of the members of his class in college was held on the 20th of May, and a series of resolutions passed expressive of their sense of his merits as a genial companion, a beloved classmate; and "that the atrocious circumstances of his death make it peculiarly a martyrdom; and that his cherished memory shall give a new earnestness to our loyalty to the great cause in the defence of which he fell."

1857.—Samuel Breck Parkman was killed in the battle of Antietam, Md., 17 September, 1862, aged 26 years. He was born in Savannah, Ga., 1 November, 1836. He was in the rebel army, first-lieutenant of Reed's Battery, from Georgia; and was major upon Gen. Longstreet's staff when he was killed. He was left an orphan at an early age, by the loss of both parents in the steamer "Pulaski," which was destroyed by fire, when off the coast of North Carolina, on her passage from Charleston for Baltimore, 14 June, 1838. Among the names of those lost were Mr. S. B. Parkman, Master Parkman, Miss A. Parkman, Miss C. Parkman, Miss T. Parkman. In a paragraph in the account of the burning of the steamer, it is stated that "the persons by the name of Parkman were the family of S. B. Parkman, of Savannah, and formerly of Westborough, Mass." They were probably descendants of Rev. Ebenezer Parkman (H.C. 1721), who was born in Boston, 5 September, 1703; was ordained pastor of the church of Westborough, 28 October, 1724; and died 9 December, 1782, aged 80 years. The subject of this notice was cared for by an aunt, who supplied the place of a mother to him. He had two sisters. He passed some time at the military-school in Sing-Sing, N.Y., before entering college. After graduating, he read law in Savannah, and was admitted to practice in due time; became a member of the Georgia Historical Society; and finally joined the Savannah troop of cavalry. In the summer of 1860, he travelled in Europe; returned in the fall, and visited Boston.

He married, in December, 1860, Nannie Bierne, of Virginia, a very wealthy lady.

1857. — George Whittemore was killed in the battle of Antietam, Md., 17 September, 1862, at the age of 25 years. He was the son of George and Anna (Mansfield) Whittemore, and was born in Boston, 19 December, 1836. He was educated at the public schools in Boston; and was prepared for admission to college at the public Latin School, where a Franklin medal was awarded to him in 1853. His parents removed from Boston to Gloucester, Mass., during his last year at the Latin school; and this town was his home during his college-course. Soon after entering upon his college-course, he attained a high rank among the best scholars in his class, and graduated with honors. During three of the winters while in college, he taught school in Gloucester and Northampton. After graduating, he was for a time an assistant in the private latin-school of Mr. Epes Sargent Dixwell (H.C. 1827) in Boston. He then studied law in the office of John Jones Clark (H.C. 1823) and Lemuel Shaw (H.C. 1849) in Boston. He was of an amiable disposition, modest and unassuming in his man-

64

ners. His tastes were naturally quiet and scholarly; yet he had a spirit of adventure and a fondness for manly sports, which led him, after three years teaching, and reading law, to join a party for travel and exploration to the South-west. His arrangements, however, were not carried out, and he returned after a brief absence. In August, 1861, he enlisted for three years in Capt. Saunders's company of sharpshooters, determined to devote himself to the service of his country. On the morning of his departure for the seat of war, he, after an examination, was admitted to the Suffolk bar. He was an excellent marksman; and, from his first fight in a skirmish at Edwards's Creek to the day of his last battle, he did his duty with his corps as a true soldier of the flag.

1858. — PAUL MITCHELL ELIOT died in the city of New York, 26 November, 1862, aged 25 years. He was son of Hon. Thomas Dawes and Frances Lincoln (Brock) Eliot, and was born in New Bedford, Mass., 13 September, 1837. His father was son of William Greenleaf Eliot, and was born in Boston, 20 March 1808. He graduated at Columbian College, Washington, D.C., in 1825, his parents having resided many years in Washington; is a lawyer in New Bedford, and is now a representative in Congress from the First Congressional District of Massachusetts. The mother of young Eliot was a native of Nantucket. He was a student at the Friends' Academy in New Bedford, under the instruction of Mr. Abner Jones Phipps (D.C. 1838), from 1847 to 1850, when he entered the Bristol Academy in Taunton, Mass., under Mr. Henry Blatchford Wheelwright (H.C. 1844), where he completed his preparatory studies for entering college. After graduating, he determined to engage in mercantile business. In October, 1858, he went to St. Louis, and, 1 January, 1859, entered the counting-room of the Atlantic-Mills Co. in that city, where he remained one year, and, 1 January, 1860, entered the store of F. B. Chamberlain and Co.; and while there, having been engaged one very hot day in marking goods in the sun, he was affected by a sun-stroke, from which he never recovered. In November of that year, he left St. Louis on account of ill health, and spent the winter in Washington, where his father was attending Congress; and in March, 1861, returned to New Bedford. His brain having been affected, the disease produced mental imbecility. His father took him to New York, and placed him in a private hospital under the charge of a distinguished physician, but without any benefit. He remained there more than a year, when death ended the scene.

1858. — Dr. Henry Augustus Richardson died of consumption, in Cambridge, 1 July, 1863, aged 26 years. He was born in Boston, 25 November, 1836, the son of George C. and Susan Gore (Moore) Richardson. His father, now a merchant in Boston, was the son of a physician in Royalston, from whom Henry probably derived a fondness for the study of medicine, and a power of accurate observation, that led him to the same profession. When he was very young, his family removed to their present residence in Cambridge, where he prepared for college at the Hopkins Classical School, and at the High School. In 1853–4, he completed his studies at Exeter Academy, entering the freshman class in 1854.

He early developed a taste for chemistry; and, in college, he added a keen interest in anatomy and other branches of medical science, and, with a set of congenial minds, turned his attention to personal investigations. For six months before graduation, he attended lectures at the Harvard Medical School, and in October, 1858, became a pupil of Dr. C. A. Davis, at the Marine Hospital in Chelsea, where he remained three years. During this period, he followed certain courses at the school; in 1860–1, attended regularly all the lectures; and received his degree in July, 1861. His classmates, Drs. Francis and Cobb, were associated with him at the hospital in the latter part of his residence. In May, 1861, he became assistant-physician in the hospital. In August, he passed examination in Boston; was commissioned acting assistant-surgeon, and appointed to the steamer "Cambridge," Capt. Parker, of the North-Atlantic blockading squadron. In this duty he remained nearly a year; the steamer being constantly employed in the blockade of Beaufort and Wilmington, N.C. In his exposure to cold and wet, and restraint from exercise, while upon this service, the development of the disease commenced, which had been fatal to his mother and older brother.

In July, 1862, he was forced by his ill health to resign his commission; and spent the following months, till November, in the southern part of New Hampshire. As a last expedient, to stay the disease by residence in a dryer climate, he went to Minnesota, and spent the winter and spring at St. Paul. But the winter was extraordinarily open; and the melting snow filled the air with moisture, so that he derived no benefit from the change. In March, he was joined by his brother, and seemed to gain strength till his return home in the last of May. From this time he rapidly failed, but remained constantly cheerful and social, though perfectly aware of the nature of his decline. On class-day, being unable to witness the festivities on the college-grounds, he invited several classmates to a quiet party in his own room. One of his last acts was to send for the photographs of his class, that he might recall their memories, and enjoy the pleasure of their silent society.

Dr. Richardson lacked the brilliant gifts that have made others distinguished. He was not ready of speech, or skilful in gathering the learning of books, but was conscious that his peculiar talent would be discovered in studies requiring a power of exact and complete observation. In this he remarkably excelled, and he wisely guided himself by it in the choice of a profession. He was sincere, courteous, and frank, though reserved, generous, and devoted in his friendships to a remarkable degree; signally free from vanity; devoid of envy or malice; sympathizing, cheerful, full of animal spirit and the zest for nature, and gifted with a quick sense of humor. His firmness and self-reliance fitted him peculiarly for his profession, while his personal traits made him a favorite in every professional and social relation.

1858. — Lieut. THOMAS JEFFERSON SPURR died in Hagerstown, Md., 27 September, 1862, of wounds received in the battle of Antietam, on the 17th of the same month, at the age of twenty-four years. He was son of Samuel D. and Mary A.

(Lamb) Spurr, and was born in Worcester, Mass., 2 February, 1838. He was fitted for college at the Worcester High School, under the instruction of Mr. George Capron (B.U. 1847). At the outset of his college career, he took rank with the foremost; but, in the second term of his junior year, an affection of the eyes came upon him, compelling him to withdraw from his studies for a while. He made a voyage to Fayal, returned with improved health, and resumed his connection with his class; but was compelled to employ the aid of a "reader." He was honored by his classmates with an election to the Phi-Beta-Kappa Society, as a token of the rank which he would have held but for his affliction. After graduating, he studied law in the office of his brother-in-law, George Frisbie Hoar (H.C. 1846); and in September, 1859, he entered the Law School at Cambridge, and continued his studies until the first of April, 1861, when he sailed for Russia, in the bark "Ethan Allen," for a pleasure-trip, to return through England in the autumn. Hearing of the rebellion, he hastened home to offer his services to his country. He was commissioned as first-lieutenant in Company G, in the Fifteenth Regiment of Massachusetts Volunteers, and held his commission until his death. At the battle of Antietam, he fell while forming his company in line. He was removed by a rebel officer to the shade of a haystack, where he lay four days. On the 21st, he was found by his friends, and removed to a better shelter; and, on the 22d, was moved to Hagerstown, eight miles, where his mother, his family-physician, and other friends, met him on the 24th; and on Saturday, the 27th, he tranquilly passed away. He expressed no regret at his fate, saying that he knew that many must fall, and he would claim no exemption. His character exhibited a combination of womanly gentleness with manly strength: he was "pure in heart," and a true Christian.

The following letter from Lieut.-Col. Kimball, of the Fifteenth Regiment, is indicative of the estimation in which he was held by his associates in arms: —

"WARRENTON, VA., Nov. 18, 1862.

"The death of Lieut. Spurr was a sad blow to the regiment. His place cannot be filled. He came among us a stranger to us all; but by his manly traits of character, his kind, noble, and generous nature, he won the esteem of all, — officers and men. He was ever faithful to his trust; and his courage and bearing were undoubted. His memory will be most dearly cherished by his comrades; and they will always point with pride to his private virtues and his military career, which were such as it would be alike honorable and manly to follow. His noble bearing on the battle-field of Antietam, where he refused to be carried to the rear when mortally wounded, was worthy of the man, the hero, he was; and won the praise of all his companions."

1859. — Capt. GEORGE WELLINGTON BATCHELDER was killed in the battle of Antietam, 17 September, 1862, aged 23 years. He was son of Jacob (D.C. 1830) and Mary W. (Wellington) Batchelder, and was born in Lynn, Mass., 20 December, 1838. His mother was daughter of the late Rev. Charles Wellington, D.D., of Templeton, Mass. (H.C. 1802). He was fitted for college at the Lynn High School under the instruction of his father. He held a respectable rank of scholarship in his class, and graduated with honors. After leaving college, he studied law about a year and a half in the office of Perry and Endicott, of Salem. At his country's call in April, 1861, he was one of the first to enlist in the ranks; and, two days after his return with the three-months' troops, he enlisted for three years. He was commissioned as first lieutenant in Company C of the Nineteenth Regiment, and was afterwards promoted to the captaincy of the same company. On the evening previous to the eventful 17th of September, he gave to his lieutenant, the late lamented Newcomb, special directions to be followed if it should be his lot to fall on the next day; and, in the hottest of the battle of the 17th, called him again to his side, repeated his injunctions, and informed him where he would find a record of his wishes. Among these occurs the following sentence, written with a pencil, though unsigned by him: "I wish my books to go to my father and mother, and, after their decease, to be given to Harvard College." His sisters, who alone are interested in the final disposition of his books, will be ready at the appointed time to execute the sacred trust.

A letter from Lieut. Hill, of the Nineteenth Regiment, says, "While rallying his company, George received two wounds, — one from a fragment of a shell, and one from a bullet. His health impaired by disease from which he had not recovered, and the loss of blood, rendered the wound fatal. He died in the afternoon of the same day, passing from sleep to death quietly and without a struggle, — his last words, 'Mother, O my mother!'" Lieut. Hill continues: "We all feel, that, in losing him, we have met with an irreparable loss. How can we feel otherwise, when, by his kind and cheerful disposition, his upright and honorable dealings with all, his brave and unflinching courage, he has bound himself so closely to us all?" He well deserved the compliment I once heard paid him by a fellow-officer, who said of him, "He was the most honorable man I ever knew." With a well-stored mind, and a communicative disposition, it was impossible to be long in his society without learning something. As an officer, he had no superior. Firm, yet gentle, he secured the love and respect, as well as the cheerful and ready obedience, of his inferiors. Sharing with his men, without complaint, the dangers and hardships of the campaign, he secured their confidence, and, in battle, urged them on to deeds of valor by his own noble example. He died in a noble and just cause, — the cause he espoused, and for which he endured so many hardships and privations to sacrifice his life for his country. Another fellow-officer says, with impressive beauty of expression, "We had pictured for him a glorious future: shall it be less bright because not wrought out in our presence?" Another, a clergyman and a classmate, after a visit to the old college-rooms, writes, "I could not restrain a sharp pain at his early death; but there followed a soothing satisfaction at the thought of his generous self-sacrifice for his country's sake, and I felt the stimulus of his brave example. The spirit that hath such power to quicken and strengthen our spirits cannot die."

1859. — HENRY WELD FULLER died in Roxbury, Mass., 3 May, 1863, aged 23 years. He was son of Henry Weld (Bowd. C. 1828) and Mary Storer (Goddard) Fuller, and was born in Augusta, Me., 7 December, 1839. His father was son of Henry Weld Fuller (D.C. 1801), of Augusta. His mother was daughter of Nathaniel and Lucretia (Dana) Goddard, of Boston. He was fitted for college at the Roxbury Latin School under the instruction of Mr. Augustus Howe Buck. During his collegiate course, he met with a severe accident in the streets of Boston; having been knocked down by a runaway horse, whereby his spine was injured, and from which he never fully recovered. In consequence of this, he was interrupted in his studies in college for a considerable time, and was thus prevented from gaining such a standing of scholarship as his talents would have enabled him to take. Immediately after graduating, he entered the Law School at Cambridge, where he remained until his impaired health obliged him to leave; and his bright prospects of entering upon the active duties of life were thus early extinguished to enter into the brighter scenes of another existence. The great charm of his genial nature was his kindness of heart and perfect disinterestedness. The sunny cheerfulness of his character sustained him through the weary days and sleepless nights of his long illness, and seemed to triumph over the insidious malady to which he finally succumbed. His tastes were simple and pure; and they reflected the character of his mind, which was allied to every thing noble, generous, and true, and were strikingly exemplified in his fondness for whatever was most refined and elevated in literature and art.

1859. — FRANCIS CURTIS HOPKINSON died in Stanley Hospital, in Newbern, N.C., 13 February, 1863, aged 24 years. He was the eldest son of Hon. Thomas (H.C. 1830) and Corinna Aldrich (Prentiss) Hopkinson, and was born in Keene, N.H., 11 June, 1838. He was fitted for college in the Boston Latin School, where he was distinguished for his acquirements in the classics. During his college-course, he was distinguished for his facility in English composition and Latin versification, for which he took a Bowdoin prize. He also contributed several humorous articles for the "Harvard Magazine." After graduating, he was employed for some time in writing critical notices for the "Boston Daily Advertiser," and was soon afterwards engaged for a similar service for the "Atlantic Monthly." He was at this time a student-at-law in the office of Horace Gray, jun. (H.C. 1845), and the late Wilder Dwight (H.C. 1853); and was completing his studies at the Law School in Cambridge, when the call came for the nine-months' men. He then felt that the war was a matter of self-defence and of honor to the North. He enlisted, in August, 1862, from Cambridge, in Company F, Massachusetts Forty-fourth, as a private. He was in both of Gen. Foster's expeditions, and was warmly engaged at the battle of Whitehall, near Goldsborough, N.C. In that battle he fought with Company A, his own company not being engaged; and he was highly praised by his officers. He caught a fever while on picket on the 18th of January; and, during his entire illness, he was delirious, with very brief intervals. From the time he enlisted, he seemed to have a strong presentiment that he should not return; and he remarked to a friend, that he hoped he should not die in a hospital. It seemed, however, to Infinite Wisdom, that his wish in this respect should not be granted. Esteemed by his officers, his wit, vivacity, cheerfulness, and good nature were the traits which endeared him to his companions of the barrack. By them he was elected to preside at the dinner given by the company upon Thanksgiving day, when his few touching remarks showed how dearly he loved the home which he had sacrificed so readily to what he deemed his duty.

1859. — Capt. NATHANIEL BRADSTREET SHURTLEFF fell at the battle of Cedar Mountain, near Culpepper, in Virginia, 9 August, 1862, at the age of twenty-four years. He was born in Boston, 16 March, 1838, and was the first-born child of his parents, Nathaniel Bradstreet (H.C. 1831) and Sarah Eliza (Smith) Shurtleff, both of whom are now living in Boston, their native city. His grandparents, on his father's side, were Dr. Benjamin (B.U. 1796) and Sally (Shaw) Shurtleff, who took up their abode in Boston on marriage, about the commencement of the century, leaving the county of Plymouth, where their ancestors had dwelt since the first settlement of the Old Colony, nearly all of the most remote of them having come to New England in either the "May Flower," "Fortune," or "Ann," the three earliest vessels that conveyed the Pilgrim forefathers to these shores. On his maternal side, his grandparents were Hiram and Sarah Remington (Beal) Smith, also of Boston.

The subject of this notice received his early school-training in the Boston public schools, and took a Franklin medal in 1850 at the Adams School, then kept in Mason Street; and another in 1855 at the public Latin School, where he was fitted for college under the pupilage of that eminent scholar and teacher, Francis Gardner (H.C. 1831), and from which he immediately entered the university, chumming the first year with his schoolmate and classmate, Clinton A. Cilley, and rooming alone the remainder of the college course. On leaving college, he entered active life with all those high hopes which naturally belong to youth, ambition, cultivation, and brilliant talents. Even in his college and in his schoolboy days, the determined character and firm-set principles which marked him as a man shone forth. The eldest son of a family possessing an unusually large share of the Puritan blood of the first settlers of New England, and long identified with Protestantism, he became a Roman Catholic while at school, and for the remainder of his life was a devoted adherent of that communion, humbling himself to his new faith, and gathering around him large numbers of the young and neglected, to whom he gave instruction, and over whom he watched with the strictest vigilance and almost parental care. Immediately after leaving college, he entered the novitiate of the order of Jesuits, at Frederick City, in Maryland, and there continued until the following February, when, failing in health, in consequence of the strict personal discipline, hard study, enfeebling deprivations, and self-sacrificing labors, he was obliged to undergo, he set aside, for a while, his great purpose of life; and thereupon entered the law office of William Brigham (H.C. 1829) in

Boston, where he was making good progress in his studies when the present unnatural rebellion broke out.

Having an ardent temperament, and being an enthusiast for the unsullied preservation of the constitution, and for the union of the states, which he warmly advocated by his public acts and speeches, he, on the 20th of April, 1861 (the day after the brutal assault upon the Sixth Regiment of Massachusetts Volunteers by a mob in Baltimore), determined to devote himself to the cause of his country, and tendered his services to Fletcher Webster (H.C. 1833), to assist in enlisting the Twelfth Regiment for the three-years' service; and, on the following Monday morning, opened papers in the Merchants' Exchange, in Boston, for that purpose. So great was the success of this effort, that, in less than three days from the opening of these papers on the 22d of April, the regiment was filled and the lists closed, men enough for sixteen full companies having offered for the service; and the organization of the regiment was completed in the short space of sixteen days; for, on the 7th of May following, the Webster Regiment (for by this name it will ever be remembered) was uniformed, armed, officered, and in camp at Fort Warren, in Boston harbor. Mr. Shurtleff, who had served as a private in the Independent Company of Cadets of Boston, was elected by Company D, which he joined, as captain; and the company, in consequence of being adopted by the Latin School, took for name "The Latin-School Guard." Nearly three long and dull months to the soldiers, who were anxious for service, were spent by this regiment at Fort Warren; and, although it was sooner mustered into the United-States service, it was not until the 23d of July, 1861, that this magnificent regiment, whose excellence for drill and discipline had become famous, left Fort Warren for the seat of war. A short time before leaving the fort, the Latin-School boys presented their adopted company with a classic standard, constructed after the ancient form of that borne by the Roman maniple. The following extract from Capt. Shurtleff's almost prophetic speech of acceptance will clearly exhibit his feelings, and the truly heroic and noble sentiments which governed every action of his life. He spoke in behalf of his company, as follows: —

"I hardly know in what way best to return to you, my fellow-schoolmates, on behalf of the Latin-School Guard, our sincere and heartfelt thanks. I thank you for your sympathy for me, and more especially my command. Our thanks for the standard which you have presented us, much as we shall prize it as an emblem of the esteem in which we are held by the members of the Latin School, are as nothing in comparison with the gratitude we feel toward you for the innumerable favors you have shown us in a way in which we are much more likely to be neglected. Presentations of banners and swords, where a grand display is to be made and speeches exchanged, are very pleasant things; while the more substantial favors, such as we have received from you, are too apt to be overlooked and neglected." After referring to the causes of the delays which the regiment had suffered in getting into the field for active service, he continued, referring to the standard: "But, sir, our eagle, upon which the sun smiles now so auspiciously, differs in one marked respect from the old Roman eagle. That was the signal for carnage. Wherever that eagle was seen to float, chains and slavery were sure to follow. Ours is our own noble American eagle, which raises its talons to strike those only who destroy the holy Temple of Freedom. Yes, we will 'strike till the last armed foe expires.' Our eagle will strike his beak into the brain of every man who shall be found with arms in his hands, lifted against the Constitution of the country; but, unlike the Roman eagle, when victory has crowned our banners, when our flag waves proudly once more, then his thirst for blood will be satiated, his talons will sink into their place, and he will return to you, no longer the fierce bird of war, but the emblem of the victory of truth and freedom over error and oppression. Although I can never hope to meet my schoolmates again with my ranks as full as they are to-day (for we are liable to the chances of war; and it may be that I, who now address you, will lay my bones beneath some Southern soil), it may be that these, my children, for whom I would lay down my life, — not one of them will ever return; but, should that be our fate, it will be, at least, a glorious one. We ask only, that, if it be our lot to fall in the cause of liberty and justice, it may be remembered by you all, that for liberty we fought, and for liberty we fell; and that our eagle shall be returned to you; and that upon the walls of your beautiful hall, where many an ancient Roman relic hangs, you may place this eagle; and when some visitor shall look upon it, all grimed with smoke and blood, — not blood of Gaul or Allobrogian, but of our own citizens who fought and bled for freedom, — and ask its history, some future master of the school may say, 'In the year 1861, a son of the great expounder of the Constitution went forth to fight the battles of his country, and under his command went a company representing the Latin School. They fought, triumphed, and died; and that eagle was their standard.'"

From the time Capt. Shurtleff left Massachusetts, until his decease, he was constantly engaged in the service, except a few weeks in the subsequent September, when he was brought home, reduced nearly to death by the malarious fever so prevalent in western Maryland. From 26 January to 24 February, 1862, the last month that the Webster Regiment formed part of the division under Major-Gen. Banks, Capt. Shurtleff was detailed from his command to act as divisionary judge-advocate, — a duty which he performed to the highest satisfaction of his commanding general and those under him. The regiment was not put under fire until August, 1862; and it was then, on the 9th of that month, at the battle of Cedar Mountain, that Capt. Shurtleff — his company having been placed in an advanced position — was slain, the first to fall, as he was the first to enlist in its number. The regiment, having fallen into an ambush, had been ordered to lie down to avoid the fire of the enemy; and his solicitude for the safety of his men cost him his life. He raised himself upon his elbow to see if they were protected, received a ball in his breast, had only time to utter, "I am shot! — Mary! — pardon!" and was dead before he could be carried from the field. His dying expressions were those of a true man, who, in the solemn moment when he felt that he had given his earthly all for the cause he served, humbly and touchingly reposed in spirit with the God he worshipped. His body was conveyed by a trusty servant to Washington, where it was embalmed, and afterwards transported to Boston; where, on the 16th of August, in accordance with his own request, the funeral services were performed in the Church of the Immaculate Conception, in the imposing manner of the Jesuits, by a high-mass requiem. The remains were attended to Mount Auburn by the Cadets and a large concourse of citizens and official persons. And there they repose, his last resting-place being marked by the emblem of the cross to which in early life he had consecrated himself.

This notice cannot be better closed than with the following appropriate tribute to his pure and noble life, from the pen of a young friend who knew him well: —

"And so was laid to rest all that remained here of Nathaniel B. Shurtleff, jun., in the first morn of life, well educated, brilliant, enthusiastic, and courageous. Early in college-life, he took a religious stand that marked him there — of all places — as singular indeed; but he never swerved from his position and belief to the day of his death. He was fixed in his opinions, and never hesitated to avow them.

"Brought up a Protestant, at an early age he became a Catholic, and unhesitatingly placed himself at the service of the church. For whatever labor he was needed, he was ready. He worked energetically and faithfully among the poor of his city; he, with the reputation of being the best writer and most eloquent speaker of his class at Harvard, devotedly toiled in the Sunday school, teaching the poor and ignorant; he rallied men around him as he drew his sword; he offered his life to his country, and his country has accepted and received the sacrifice. His last words were, not of home or earthly endearments, but of spiritual yearnings.

"He who, being a Protestant, condemns, in voice or heart, Nathaniel B. Shurtleff, let him lead a more devoted life, possess a more obedient spirit, live more earnestly, die more heroically; let his last words show that his daily thoughts have been on heaven and with heavenly persons, and then let him leave the judgment with his Maker. For my own part, if I do not believe his creed as he did, yet do I consider his example as truly noble, manly, and pious. We may be happy to leave behind us as pleasant memories, — memories that will only brighten when the radiance of eternal sunlight shall be poured upon the acts of each man's life."

1860. — Capt. Edward Gardiner Abbott was killed in the battle at Cedar Mountain, Va., 9 August, 1862, at the age of 21 years. He was the oldest son of Hon. Josiah Gardiner (H.C. 1832) and Caroline (Livermore) Abbott, and was born in Lowell, Mass., 29 September, 1840. He was fitted for college at the Lowell High School. After leaving college, he began the study of law in the office of Samuel A. Brown, Esq., of Lowell. As soon as the rebellion broke out, he was one of the first to offer himself for the defence of his country. He raised the first company in the Second Regiment, under Col. George H. Gordon, of which he was appointed captain; was the first captain who was sworn into the service in this state, and devoted himself with characteristic energy to the duties of his new profession. At the time of Gen. Banks's retreat, in the spring of 1862, he commanded two companies with a gallantry and coolness which elicited warm commendation from the officers on the field. His nature was manly and brave, and his affections were strong. In a postscript to a letter to his father, dated 2 August, — perhaps the last letter he ever wrote, — he says, "I wish to tell you how deeply affected I feel by your kindness in this and all other matters; and I promise you, that, with God's help, I will never do any thing to cause you to be sorry for it, or ashamed of me." His father, in a letter to the mayor of Lowell, tendering his thanks to the people of that city for their deep sympathy with him and his family in their bereavement, and in which he speaks of his son, who fell so gallantly doing his duty, says, "I have no certain information of the facts immediately connected with my son's death, except, generally, from the fact of his position as senior captain, his company was much exposed. His general writes me that he saw my son fall; that his countenance in death was as 'proud and defiant, though placid,' as when he marched to the fight. His colonel, among other things, said his voice, in giving his command to his men, in the thickest of the fight, was as cheerful and calm as if on parade. In a pencilled note from my other son, in the same regiment, he says, 'Ned fell while cheering on his men.' I think I can add that he has repaid the many kindnesses he and his command have received from Lowell, by so acting that his native city can point to nothing in his life to be ashamed of."

1860. — Lieut. Edgar Marshall Newcomb died at Falmouth, Va., 20 December, 1862, from wounds received in the battle of Fredericksburg on the 13th of the same month, aged 22 years. He was son of John J. and Mary S. Newcomb, and was born in Troy, N.Y., 2 October, 1840; but his parents removed to Boston when he was a few months old, where his life was passed. He was fitted for college, partly at Chauncy-Hall School, and partly at the Latin School, in Boston. He held a respectable rank of scholarship in his class; but, before his collegiate course was completed, his health became so much impaired, that he left in his senior year, before commencement, and went to Europe in the summer of 1860. He spent the autumn in travelling on foot through England and France, with the hope of improving his physical condition. It had long been his purpose to become a minister of the gospel; but on his return from Europe, his health being still delicate, he entered his father's counting-room, and engaged in active business for a while. When the war broke out, with a generous disregard of his pecuniary interests, and of a home surrounded by all the attractions that make life pleasing, he came forward to volunteer as a soldier in the ranks, to defend the government of his fathers, and assert its rightful supremacy. He enlisted as a private in the Nineteenth Massachusetts Regiment when it was first formed, shared its fortunes, and contributed to its glory. Earning his promotion, step by step, he became sergeant-major, second- and finally first- lieutenant. That he did his duty as a faithful and brave officer, was fully shown by those who were with him in the hour of peril. Capt. Chadwick, in whose company he served, in alluding to his death, wrote as follows: "He was wounded in the legs in the fight of 13 December, before the batteries and rifle-pits on the enemy's left. The ball struck the brass band of his sword, passed through the left leg, and grazed the right. He was wounded while holding the American flag high above his head, having just given up the state-colors. Both color-sergeants had been shot down," — seven in succession. Other accounts say, "And Edgar sprang forward, and picked up both flags, holding one in each hand, and called upon the men to stand by their colors. No braver officer or man ever stood upon the battle-field than Lieut. Edgar M. Newcomb; and I am the more proud to say so, from the fact of the association existing between us. He was loved and respected before; but that love and respect was more than doubled by his daring bravery and unflinching courage." His letters to his friends at home illustrated his enthusiastic devotion to the cause of his country. He had passed with his regiment through fourteen battles and skirmishes, unscathed. He frequently officiated as chaplain of his regiment; preaching to the men, and holding prayer-meetings. Yet his modesty and reserve were such that he never mentioned the fact in his letters, and it was only learned by his friends after his decease. To his brother, who was with him in his dying hours, he remarked, "You have a work to perform in this life, and I will be with you. I feel that I shall be nearer to my friends after death than ever." Retaining his senses perfectly until his death, he called the men and his fellow-soldiers to his side, and gave to each a dying message, — to meet him in heaven. Dying there, in the sound of battle, he devised his property equally to the societies for home and foreign missions.

1860. — Lieut.-Col. Charles Redington Mudge was killed in the battle of Gettysburg, 2 July, 1863, aged 23 years. He was son of Edward Redington and Caroline A. (Patten) Mudge, and was born in New-York city, 22 October, 1839. He was fitted for college at the private school of Thomas Gamaliel Bradford (H.C. 1822) in Boston. With the exception of a few months passed in preparing to enter business with his father, he was in the service of his country, having joined the Second Massachusetts Infantry, — the first three-years' regiment raised for the war. He went into the service with his whole soul. He was commissioned as first-lieutenant; was promoted to be captain, 8 July, 1862; and was subsequently made lieutenant-colonel. While encamped at Brook Farm, he slept on the bare ground to prepare himself for the life which he was to lead. His regiment was spoken of as a model for its admirable drill. When they covered the rear of Gen. Banks's retreat, Col. Mudge was with them in their dangerous path; and in the battle of South Mountain he received his first wound. The officers of his regiment never failed to express their opinion of his military qualities and abilities in the highest terms. But there are other traits in his character which will be remembered with the warmest affection by his young contemporaries. In his college-course, his popularity was universal; and he was a favorite in every clique, and in the most dissimilar sets. Every one was his friend in need; and no one would have hesitated a moment to have asked his services, with the certainty of a kind reception.

1861. — Lieut. PARDON ALMY was killed in the battle at Bull Run, Va., 30 August, 1862, at the age of 26 years. He was son of Pardon and Mary (Cook) Almy, and was born in Little Compton, R.I., 4 July, 1836. His father was son of Sanford and Lydia (Gray) Almy, and his mother was daughter of Samuel and Hannah (Little) Cook. All his ancestors have been residents of Rhode Island for some generations back.

The subject of this notice was fitted for college at Pierce Academy in Middleborough, Mass. He held a very respectable rank of scholarship in his class. Immediately after graduating, President Felton gave him a letter to Gov. Andrew; and the governor authorized him to recruit a company in New Bedford, for three years or the war: but as the military enthusiasm had not been kindled there, the accomplishment of his purpose appearing too uncertain, and feeling that his duties were in the service of his country in the army, he accepted a lieutenant's commission in the Eighteenth Regiment of Massachusetts Volunteers, Col. James Barnes, where he served until his death. Some idea of his reputation and standing in the service may be inferred from the following extract of a letter to his brother from Major Joseph Hayes, who was in command of the regiment when he fell. He says, "I can only express to you my sincere sympathy in your great bereavement, and add my testimonial to the high character of Lieut. Almy as a soldier and a man. His conduct in the engagement in which he fell is mentioned in the highest praise by all the officers who were engaged with him. He fell in the very front, while bravely cheering on his men under a most galling fire, and displayed to the last a spirit of intrepidity and gallantry surpassed by no one. He was always prompt, faithful, zealous, and cheerful too, in the performance of his duty as a soldier; and I do not know a single blemish in his character as a man, but could enumerate many, very many, virtues that he possessed. You have lost, sir, a noble brother, and the country a gallant soldier."

A meeting of his classmates was held in Boston on the 16th of September, when they passed a series of resolutions bearing testimony to his virtues.

He was highly esteemed by his friends and relatives for his many good qualities of head and heart, for his sterling principles and uniformly correct conduct; and they confidently looked forward to a long life to him of usefulness to his fellow-citizens, and of honor to himself: but his career was abruptly terminated, and the hopes of his friends were blighted.

1861. — Capt. HENRY JONAS DOOLITTLE died in Racine, Wis., 10 August, 1862, aged 23 years. He was the eldest son of Hon. James R. and Mary Lovina (Cutting) Doolittle, and was born in Rochester, N.Y., 4 March, 1839. In 1851, he removed with his parents to Racine, and soon afterwards became a pupil in Racine College. Two years later, he became personally interested in the truths of the gospel, and soon after united with the First Baptist Church in Racine. In his class, he held a respectable rank of scholarship. At the time of his graduation, the rebellion had just begun to exhibit its gigantic proportions. With his fellow-students in college, he received a military drill; and was employed with them, by order of the governor, in guarding for a time the Massachusetts arsenal at Cambridge. After spending a few months with his father (who was a senator in Congress) in Washington, he returned to Racine, and was engaged in drilling Capt. Lyon's company in that city, and a company at Darlington, and had the promise of the post of major in one of the Wisconsin regiments; which post, however, he failed to obtain. Early in the following spring, he accepted a position, with the rank of captain, upon the staff of Gen. C. S. Hamilton, with whom he served on the Peninsula; then for a short time at Harper's Ferry; and subsequently near Corinth. In July, he applied for a ten-days' furlough, in order to complete the family-circle gathered in commemoration of the twenty-fifth anniversary of his parents' marriage. Ere he received his furlough, he was attacked with typhoid-fever, and went home to die. In the delirium of fever, after his return, he imagined himself still on his journey, and piteously entreated that he might be taken home; and God took him home, — a home which war shall never invade, and sorrow shall never mar, and death shall never enter. Strong in body, sound in mind, of rare energy, he sacredly devoted himself to his country's cause, and for his country he fell a martyr. His friends have this consolation, — that he was a Christian patriot, a kind brother, and a faithful son; and it is a comfort that he breathed his last, not amid the horrors of battle, but under the paternal roof.

1861. — Capt. WILLIAM YATES GHOLSON was killed in the battle of Hartsville, Tenn., 7 December, 1862, aged 20 years. He was son of Hon. William Yates (N.J.C. 1825) and Elvira (Wright) Gholson, and was born in Pontotoc, Miss., 11 March, 1842, but removed with his parents to Cincinnati in 1845. His mother belonged to a Virginia family, which had removed to Mississippi, where Mr. Gholson married her. He began to fit for college with Mr. Joseph Vernon, of Cincinnati, and completed his preparatory studies in the private school of Eben Smith Brooks (H.C. 1835) in the same city. After graduating, he began the study of the law with his father; but, when the President made a call for three hundred thousand men, he determined to engage in the cause of his country. In September, 1862, he was commissioned as captain in the One-hundred-and-sixth Regiment of Ohio Volunteers. In October following, he was appointed provost-marshal of South Frankfort, Tenn. On the 8th of November, he was acting-assistant-adjutant-general of the Thirty-ninth Brigade, Fourteenth Army Corps, on the staff of Col. Moore. He fell while rallying his men. He was pierced with three bullets, — one near the heart, one in the forehead, and one in the temple. His intelligent patriotism demanded a country worthy of a sacrifice; and if, at last, he did not find it, it will hasten into being sooner because he fell evoking it. He was by nature ardent and aspiring; of independent thought and active conscience, generous and affectionate. In his death, he bequeathed a conspicuous example of courage in the midst of general incapacity and cowardice; and left no room for his many friends to grieve, except for their own loss.

1861. — Samuel Dunn Phillips, of Boston, died at St. Helena Island, Beaufort, S.C., 5 December, 1862, aged 23 years. He was son of Thomas Walley (H.C. 1814) and Anna Jones (Dunn) Phillips, and was born in Boston, 12 December, 1838. He began to fit for college under the instruction of Mr. Thompson Kidder, of Boston; but, from 1852 to 1857, he was studying in the Boston Latin School. After graduating, he began the study of medicine, under the instruction of Dr. Edward Reynolds, of Boston (H.C. 1811). In January, 1862, he was teaching a school in Tewksbury, Mass. In March following, he turned his attention to the unfriended blacks at Port Royal, S.C.; and, on presenting himself before the Educational Commission, he was approved, and sent out among the first. His deep religious convictions and eminent conscientiousness, joined with an ever-active benevolence and constant cheerfulness, gave him a near approach to the hearts of his people, and caused him to rank among the most useful of the superintendents. He made a visit to his home on account of indisposition, and returned much sooner than the precarious state of his health warranted; and thereby his life was sacrificed to his devotedness to his mission.

1861. — Thomas Rodman Robeson died in Gettysburg, Penn., 6 July, 1863, of a wound received in battle, 3 July, aged 22 years. He was son of Thomas Rodman and Sibyl (Washburn) Robeson, and was born in New Bedford, 7 November, 1840. His father died 13 August, 1848; and his mother removed subsequently to Brookline, and afterwards to Cambridge, where she now resides. He was fitted for college in Brookline, by William P. Atkinson (H.C. 1838). He left his class in April, 1861, to drill at Fort Independence; and, on the formation of the Second Regiment Massachusetts Volunteers, he enlisted in it, and was commissioned, 28 May, 1861, as second-lieutenant:

30 November, 1862, he was promoted to be first lieutenant, and soon afterwards detached for duty in the signal-corps. In this service, he was present at the battles of Roanoke Island and Newbern, in February and March, 1862. In the following spring, his eyes becoming inflamed, he returned to his regiment, and took part with it in all its many battles and hardships to the time of his death. He was wounded, 9 August, 1862, in the right fore-arm, at the battle of Cedar Mountain, Va. He was promoted, 10 August, 1862, to be captain; and was, at the time of his death, the senior captain of his regiment. In the battle of Gettysburg of the morning of Friday, 3 July, he was making a charge with his regiment, when he was mortally wounded by a minie-ball in the upper part of his right thigh. He was a brave and efficient officer, cool in action, always manly and dignified, and much esteemed by his men and his fellow-officers.

1862. — Lieut. HENRY ROPES was killed in the battle of Gettysburg, Penn., 3 July, 1863, aged 24 years. He was son of William and Mary Ann (Codman) Ropes, and was born near London, Eng., where his parents were temporarily residing, 16 May, 1839. His father is a native of Salem, and an eminent merchant of Boston. His mother was a daughter of Hon. John Codman, of Boston. He was fitted for college by Sidney Willard (H.C. 1852), late major of the Thirty-fifth Massachusetts Regiment, killed at Fredericksburg, 14 December, 1862. He was commissioned as second-lieutenant of the Twentieth Massachusetts Regiment, 25 November, 1861, and as first-lieutenant, 2 October, 1862; was with the regiment until his death, going through the Peninsula campaign, — siege of Yorktown, Fair Oaks, seven-days' battles, Antietam; storming of the city of Fredericksburg, 11 December, 1863; and was never wounded until he met his death at the battle of Gettysburg. When in college, he took great interest in boating and other manly exercises, and was selected to be one of six men who composed the crew of the "Harvard," and was in this representative boat of the college during some of her proudest triumphs. He was well fitted by his physical strength to assume the hardships of a campaign, but was cut down in the flower of his youth in the struggle with the enemy. His last march, the longest ever accomplished in one day by the Army of the Potomac, was borne with the utmost cheerfulness. He was the life of all about him, encouraging the weary, inspiring and enlivening the men of his command, whose testimony has been given to the beautiful spirit and kindly temper with which the fatigues of the day were endured by him. The last act of his life, of which there is any record, is touchingly characteristic. The battle of the day before had been severe, and many wounded were left upon the field. With noble self-forgetfulness, he went out at night with his cup of cold water to soothe and relieve those who were fainting and dying from wounds and thirst. Few instances of rarer patriotic impulse have been seen. Six weeks before his death, he visited his friends after the battle of Chancellorsville, and said, in reply to the hope they expressed that he would not return to the army, that no position of influence or wealth which could be offered to him, would, for an instant, tempt him to leave his regiment until the war was closed. War had no fascination for him; he longed for a righteous and honorable peace: but, until that was proclaimed, he would never sheathe his sword.

1862. — JOHN HENRY TUCKER was killed in the attack on Port Hudson, Miss., 27 May, 1863, at the age of 28 years. He was son of Ebenezer and Eliza Bradlee (Foster) Tucker, and was born in Cambridge, Mass., 19 February, 1835. He studied at the public schools in Cambridge until April, 1851, when his father thought it best that he should learn a trade. He was accordingly apprenticed to his brother, who was a carriage-painter. Although the drudgery which fell to his lot as a young apprentice was not at all to his taste, he persevered until he acquired such a proficiency in his trade, that, when his time expired, his master offered him high wages to remain as journeyman. In the winter of 1855, he joined the Mechanic Apprentices' Library Association, where the literary exercise proved very attractive to him; and the library afforded him information which was eagerly collected. Such was his success in this institution, that, on the occasion of the thirty-sixth anniversary of its foundation, he was chosen orator, and delivered an oration on the "Position of the Mechanic in Society," at the Meionian, 22 February, 1856. This oration has been printed. The future of literature thus opened to him proved so attractive, that he endeavored to advance yet further; and, as a means, determined to enter college, if possible. In December, 1856, he entered the Cambridge High School; and in July, 1858, was admitted to Harvard College. During his college-course, he won the respect of all his classmates by his unassuming modesty and his high religious principle. Naturally quiet and retiring, he passed to and from recitations almost unknown by many of his class; but those who knew him well valued him perhaps more for the very qualities which restrained him from active participation in class-matters. Devoting himself to the study of theology, and the ministry of the Baptist church, which he joined in 1850, he felt that his country needed him in a service in every way opposed to his tastes, but in one where he might do good. He joined the Thirty-eighth Regiment. Among the first, he fell at the attack on Port Hudson.

INDEX OF ALUMNI;

WITH THE YEARS OF GRADUATION AND DECEASE.

INDEX OF CLASSES.

ERRATA.

Page 4, 8th line from bottom, for "E." read "E".
" 12, 14th line from bottom, for "BARTLETT" read "BARTLET."
" 15, 12th line from bottom, for "S." read "S".
" 21, 11th line from bottom, for "CLARK" read "CLARKE."
" 60, 9th line from top, for "1815" read "1812."
" 103, 3d line from bottom, for "EDMOND" read "EDWARD."
" 114, 17th line from top, for "ARTEMUS" read "ARTEMAS."
" 145, 15th line from bottom, after "lawyer" read "son of Benjamin and Patience (Carver) Coombs, born in Middleborough in 1810."
" 145, 3d line from bottom, for "1814" read "5 October, 1813."
" 148, 12th line from bottom, for "GALES SEATON" read "JOSEPH GALES SEATON."